T0305812

Globalization, Firms, and Workers

World Scientific Studies in International Economics
(ISSN: 1793-3641)

World Scientific Studies in International Economics includes works dealing with the theory, empirical analysis, and evaluation of international economic policies and institutions, with topics covering international macroeconomics and finance, international trade theory and policy, as well as international legal and political economy. Monographs and edited volumes will comprise the core of the publications.

The complete list of the published volumes in the series can be found at
https://www.worldscientific.com/series/wssie

81 World Scientific
Studies in
International
Economics

Globalization, Firms, and Workers

Ann E Harrison
University of California, Berkeley, USA

Keith E Maskus
University of Colorado Boulder, USA

World Scientific

NEW JERSEY · LONDON · SINGAPORE · BEIJING · SHANGHAI · HONG KONG · TAIPEI · CHENNAI · TOKYO

Published by

World Scientific Publishing Co. Pte. Ltd.

5 Toh Tuck Link, Singapore 596224

USA office: 27 Warren Street, Suite 401-402, Hackensack, NJ 07601

UK office: 57 Shelton Street, Covent Garden, London WC2H 9HE

Library of Congress Control Number: 2021941353

British Library Cataloguing-in-Publication Data
A catalogue record for this book is available from the British Library.

World Scientific Studies in International Economics — Vol. 81
GLOBALIZATION, FIRMS, AND WORKERS

Copyright © 2022 by World Scientific Publishing Co. Pte. Ltd.

For photocopying of material in this volume, please pay a copying fee through the Copyright Clearance Center, Inc., 222 Rosewood Drive, Danvers, MA 01923, USA. In this case permission to photocopy is not required from the publisher.

ISBN 978-981-123-946-5 (hardcover)
ISBN 978-981-123-947-2 (ebook for institutions)
ISBN 978-981-123-948-9 (ebook for individuals)

For any available supplementary material, please visit
https://www.worldscientific.com/worldscibooks/10.1142/12346#t=suppl

Desk Editors: Priyanka Murugan/Sylvia Koh

Typeset by Stallion Press
Email: enquiries@stallionpress.com

Printed in Singapore

About the Editors

 **Ann E. Harrison** is Dean of the Haas School of Business at the University of California, Berkeley. Previously, she was the William Worster Professor of Multinational Management at the University of Pennsylvania's Wharton School and served as the Director of Development Policy at the World Bank. She was also a professor in Berkeley's Department of Agricultural and Resource Economics from 2001 to 2011. Harrison has also held positions at Columbia, Harvard, and the University of Paris. Harrison has dedicated her career to research and policymaking in development economics, international trade, and global labor markets. She is one of the most highly cited scholars on foreign investment and multinational firms. She is the author of dozens of journal articles and the editor of three books, including *Globalization and Poverty*. Harrison earned her Ph.D. in economics from Princeton University. Born in France, she is a dual citizen of the U.S. and France.

Keith E. Maskus is Arts and Sciences Professor of Distinction in Economics at the University of Colorado, Boulder. He was Chief Economist of the US State Department from 2016 to 2017 and a Lead Economist at the World Bank in 2002. He also served as a Research Fellow at the Peterson Institute for International Economics and a consultant for the World Bank and the World Intellectual Property Organization. Maskus received his Ph.D. from the University of Michigan. He has written extensively about various aspects of global intellectual property rights, international trade and investment, and technology transfer. His most recent book is *Private Rights and Public Problems: The Global Economics of Intellectual Property in the 21st Century.*

Acknowledgments

We would like to thank the following publishers and journals for granting their permissions to reproduce the articles:

Publishers
American Economic Association
Elsevier
John Wiley & Sons
Open Knowledge Repository
SAGE Publications
The MIT Press
University of Chicago Press Publishers

Journals
American Economic Review
American Economic Journal: Macroeconomics
Industrial and Labor Relations Review
Industrial Relations
Journal of Development Economics
Journal of International Economics
Journal of Labor Economics
Review of Economics and Statistics
World Development
World Bank Economic Review

Contents

Chapter 1

Introduction

Keith E. Maskus and Jed Silver

Ann Harrison has devoted her career to path-breaking empirical research that explores the intersection of international trade, foreign direct investment (FDI), and the consequences for workers and firms. Many of her studies focus on emerging markets, such as India and China. She is particularly concerned about the impact of opening up economies on worker welfare. Does a trade reform leave workers better off? Does it reduce or increase inequality? Are multinational firms benevolent agents who raise wages in host economies? Or, do they exploit loopholes in regulations to drive a global race to the bottom? One interviewer characterized her work as giving a voice to the voiceless, especially workers in sweatshop industries or multinational firms who were not the focus of academic studies in the past.

Another characteristic aspect of this deep research is its painstaking attention to data collection, econometric specification, and robust analysis, all of which mark her studies as illuminating and convincing. Harrison believes deeply in letting the data speak for itself. She also believes that academic work should have relevance for the important policy questions of our day, such as whether or not globalization is good for the poor, or whether US firms that offshore their manufacturing activities help or hurt the local workforce. Her work poses important questions, ranging from how trade liberalization affects wages in developing countries to the influence of firms engaged in

1

international activities on factor markets and productivity. During the early years of her career, which began at the World Bank, Harrison traveled around the world finding detailed, firm-level data in developing and emerging countries, a task that now is in the toolkit of most trade and development economists.

These characteristics are evident in the chapters to follow, which are briefly outlined in this introductory chapter. In selecting them, Harrison suggested that we highlight several key thematic areas. Topics were chosen for their ability to constitute a comprehensive and coherent volume that permits the reader to explore the breadth of empirical trade and FDI research. For example, if a developing economy liberalized its trade barriers and became more open to foreign investment, would it experience more productivity through technology transfer and learning or greater distress from a weak ability of domestic firms to compete? Either outcome is plausible, and an important part of Harrison's work is devoted to the question, without preconditions or bias. For another, does offshoring of jobs by multinational firms generate net job losses in the source country or a shift of employment from low-skilled to high-skilled positions? Has globalization contributed to a fall in the return to labor globally, as critics suggest? Does industrial policy enhance or diminish innovation, and how does the answer depend on beneficial market competition? Such themes should interest all economists and they form the backbone of the contributions here.

Ann Harrison's career stands out in another way. While accumulating this deep body of research in her scholarly life, she found the time, rather uniquely among international economists, to engage in important policy work. For example, she served as Director of Development Policy at the World Bank from 2009 to 2011, a time in which emerging and developing countries were trying to escape the global financial crisis. Most recently, she was appointed Dean of the Haas School of Business at the University of California at Berkeley. Harrison believes that the increasing separation between so-called academic study and policy has undermined the ability of world leaders to make good economic decisions for the benefit of all groups in society. In particular, she believes that insufficient attention was paid

by economists to supporting the losers from globalization, which as
a result has undermined support for further trade and investment
reforms. The academic profession seems to feel that one cannot be
both a public intellectual and a serious scholar. Such a perception has
greatly undermined the quality of public dialogue and has relegated
too much excellent research to obscurity.

The balance of this introduction offers a roadmap of the contributions reprinted in this volume. They are selected to demonstrate
the breadth of analytical approaches and questions encompassed in
Harrison's research. They also illuminate the value of carefully specified empirical approaches and data collection for answering novel
and important research questions. Readers will gain a clearer understanding of how trade reform, FDI, technology transfer, factor prices,
and employment fit together and how they inform current policy
debates. Together, the chapters highlight the range of contributions
Ann Harrison has made to linking trade and development in a sound
analytical framework.

Part 1: Trade, Investment, and Factor Incomes

One of the central questions in international economics is how opening to trade and investment changes wages and capital incomes. It is
a central element of standard trade theory, with the canonical predictions that relatively abundant factors of production should benefit
and relatively scarce factors should suffer from open trade, or that
fixed factors in declining industries will be made worse off while those
in expanding sectors will gain. More recent theory based on heterogeneous firms, learning, and innovation adds considerable nuance
to that basis. Ultimately, such impacts depend on the structure of
markets, institutions, and regulations, meaning that straightforward
predictions based on aggregate factors are unlikely to play out in
actual practice.

Despite such foundations, relatively little was known about the
effects of specific trade reforms on factor incomes in developing
economies, particularly using microeconomic data, before Janet Currie and Ann Harrison pioneered such work in a 1997 study of Morocco

(Chapter 2). The chapter begins by pointing out the many dimensions along which wages, employment, and profits could adjust to trade reforms. Morocco was a strong test case: it reduced its trade and investment barriers considerably in the 1980s after a significant economic crisis. Using detailed enterprise data to trace such adjustments over time, they find almost no effect on employment and wages for the average firm. However, major exporters and firms in the sectors most affected by the tariffs and quotas do significantly reduce employment, while parastatals surprisingly increase employment. This puzzle led to another question: was this limited responsiveness due to labor market regulations, imperfect competition among firms, or other factors? They estimate a dynamic model of labor demand and find that the speed of labor adjustment in private firms is comparable to that of industrial countries, which is incompatible with the sluggish response to trade reform. On the contrary, they find that monopolistic Moroccan firms, protected by high trade barriers, reacted to the tariff cuts by absorbing lower profit margins and raising productivity. In this case, workers are insulated from the adjustment to trade reforms but do not benefit from increased productivity. However, firms in the most affected industries and major exporters both cut margins and reduce employment. To reach such detailed conclusions, Currie and Harrison develop a theoretical model and estimate a corresponding framework that permitted firm-level strategic decisions. In some ways, this model anticipated later theorizing about heterogeneous firms. This was an early example of how to elicit important conclusions from micro data that would not have been detected with more aggregated information.

The Morocco paper was followed in 1999 by a paper written with Gordon Hanson, studying how wage inequality was affected by trade liberalization in Mexico (Chapter 3). Again, this analysis uses microeconomic, firm-level data to assess how trade reforms affected various types of firms and, therefore, workers of different skill classes. A simplistic reading of standard Heckscher–Ohlin trade models would suggest that inequality in a country like Mexico should fall when it opens up to trade, as global markets allow the country to export its low-skilled labor-intensive goods, raising the demand for such workers. Harrison and Hanson find that Mexico's major trade liberalization in 1985 had its largest negative impact on the real wages of relatively unskilled labor, an outcome opposite to what would be predicted by standard trade theory. The essential reason is that the tariff cuts invited more competition through imports from even lower-wage developing economies, a channel not often considered in the trade literature. The medium-term outcome was a sharp rise in the wage gap between skilled and unskilled workers in Mexico following the policy change. This paper was one of the earliest to show that trade and inequality have complex relationships that depend on local circumstances, a lesson that later analysts have taken to heart.

Similarly, a 1996 paper with Brian Aitken and Robert Lipsey (Chapter 4) shows that higher levels of FDI are associated with higher wages in the United States, Mexico, and Venezuela. The key theoretical insight is that foreign firms may possess intangible productive assets (e.g. knowledge) that are more easily transferred to foreign subsidiaries than licensed at arm's length to local firms. This puts upward pressure on wages, to the extent that these assets raise the marginal productivity of labor. Such effects may spill over to domestically owned firms, as discussed at length in Part 2. The authors use manufacturing surveys to show that after controlling for industry, region, and year dummies, a higher share of labor employed by foreign firms is associated with significantly higher wages in all three countries. The relationship holds despite selection into higher-wage locations by foreign firms and differential firm size and capital intensity. However, when only considering domestic firms' wages, a similar positive relationship only holds in the United States: there is no discernible relationship between FDI presence and wages in Mexico and a significant negative relationship in Venezuela. They argue that the results in Mexico and Venezuela are consistent with productivity differentials being internalized by foreign-owned firms, with few opportunities for spillovers.

Chapter 5 presents a previously unpublished paper demonstrating that globalization is associated with a decline in the share of income going to labor in poor countries and an increase in rich countries. Harrison argues that globalization reduces the costs of capital mobility, which increases firms' bargaining power relative to workers. The paper presents stylized facts showing heterogeneous trends in labor shares across countries, in conflict with the common assumption of constant factor shares. Harrison then derives an estimating equation to test the prediction of changing labor–income shares in response to changes in trade openness, capital account restrictions, and capital flows. She finds that while the changes in different factor shares are primarily related to changes in factor intensity, measures of globalization also play a role. The results suggest that capital controls are associated with higher proportions of labor income and that trade exposures are associated with lower labor shares. The focus on income shares rather than levels also presents different criteria for policy evaluation than much of the trade literature, and speaks more directly to the rising focus on inequality in the context of globalization.

Part 2. Spillover Impacts of Foreign Direct Investment

The previous paper is a natural transition to Ann's work on spillovers from foreign direct investment. This has been a central question in the trade and industrial organization literatures, especially in developing-country contexts. On the one hand, the entry of foreign firms may hurt domestic firms through competition when foreign firms are more productive (i.e. have lower marginal costs) and by raising factor prices. On the other hand, there may be positive externalities from knowledge and technology transfer to domestic firms, as well as increased demand due to input–output linkages.

Prior to Ann and Brian Aitken's 1999 AER paper on spillovers in Venezuela (Chapter 6), the literature on spillovers mostly consisted of case studies of spillovers due to technology transfer from multinationals. Aitken and Harrison (1999) use national panel data, which they demonstrate are important for addressing possible upward bias due to selection of FDI into higher-wage, more productive areas. As in Aitken, Harrison, and Lipsey (1996) above, they find that individual plants that receive foreign equity do increase their total factor productivity (TFP), which is the proportion of output growth not attributable to specific production inputs such as capital and labor. This productivity is the main driver of income growth in neoclassical models. However, this finding pertains to cross-sectional specifications and the effect disappears when controlling for plant fixed effects. In contrast, increasing foreign ownership in the sector is associated with significantly lower TFP for firms with no foreign ownership. This may be termed the market-stealing effect, which afflicts smaller domestic firms by more because they cannot compete as effectively with foreign entrants. Put differently, lower TFP is consistent with smaller firms becoming less able to cover their fixed costs, thereby losing market share and being pushed higher up their average cost curves.

One potential mechanism that illustrates the theoretically ambiguous impact of foreign firm entry on domestic firms is its effects on access to credit. While FDI may bring scarce capital into developing countries, if foreign firms borrow from domestic credit institutions, local firms may be crowded out. Intuitively, in a country like Cote D'Ivoire, where many banks had French roots and many of the multinationals were from France, bankers may have been more willing to lend to multinationals rather than local businesses. Chapter 7 presents the 2003 paper by Harrison and Margaret McMillan, finding evidence of such crowding out in Cote D'Ivoire.

In contrast, Chapter 8 presents the 2004 paper by Harrison, Inessa Love, and McMillan using a cross-country panel showing that FDI relaxes credit constraints on average. The paper extends the Fazzari, Hubbard, and Peterson (1988) methodology using correlations between investment and cash flow to test for credit constraints. Intuitively, if there were no credit constraints, then a firm's level of investment should be solely determined by its expected future profitability and not its financial structure. The analysis in both Chapters 7 and 8 augments firm-level Euler equations to include a borrowing constraint. This constraint has a shadow value they proxy with the debt-to-assets ratio (DAR) and interest–coverage ratio (COV) in the paper on Cote d'Ivoire and with cash on hand in the cross-country article. These measures should be correlated with investment only if information asymmetries restrict borrowing. Thus, if borrowing by foreign firms exacerbates local firms' credit constraints, then the interaction between DAR and COV and the level of foreign borrowing should be positive.

Harrison and McMillan (2003) find this to be the case for domestic but not foreign firms in Cote D'Ivoire, implying that the sectoral level of FDI is associated with significantly greater sensitivity of investment to credit constraints. However, Harrison, Love, and McMillan (2004) find the opposite result using cross-country data. They also find that restrictions on capital transactions are associated with more credit constraints for domestic firms. This is intuitive, given that the ability to access finance from abroad would reduce firms' reliance on local credit sources. Harrison and McMillan (2003) note that interest rate regulations led the Ivorian banking sector to be heavily rationed, perhaps explaining its divergence from the more general results in the later paper.

Ann's 2014 paper with Luosha Du and Gary Jefferson (Chapter 9) shows that China's 2001 accession to the World Trade Organization (WTO) and the tax holidays it offered to foreign investors are associated with higher TFP for domestic firms. Using variations in sectoral FDI, the paper finds robust positive effects of these variables on the TFP performance of domestic firms with forward or backward (vertical) linkages to multinational corporations (MNCs). However, only foreign firms appear to benefit from horizontal linkages to other foreign firms. Presumably, smaller domestic firms in the same sectors as MNCs are less able to capture the productivity impacts of FDI. The authors then turn to the effect of WTO entry, finding that it was associated with significantly higher TFP for Chinese enterprises that supply inputs to foreign firms. Similarly, much of the effects of tax holidays were centered among firms with such linkages, but this is only robust for firms exposed to subsidized FDI. Notably, the effects on suppliers of foreign firms come despite the fact that WTO entry obliged China to reduce local content requirements. This reflects the book's general lesson about the importance of competition for promoting positive externalities.

Part 3: Foreign Direct Investment and Offshoring

The next set of chapters focos on how offshoring affects source-country workers. Ann and her frequent coauthor Margaret McMillan wrote a series of papers using firm-level data from the US Bureau of Economic Analysis (BEA) to document patterns of offshoring by US-based MNCs. This research measures the impact of offshoring production on American workers.

The first in this series of papers is with McMillan and Clair Null (Chapter 10). They introduce the BEA data and present some stylized facts about offshoring at the firm level. On average, changes in employment at US parent locations and foreign affiliates are positively correlated, suggesting that US and foreign labor are complements. However, for firms with affiliates in low-income countries, domestic employment falls as foreign employment rises, indicating they are substitutes. Moreover, the contraction in US jobs outweighs the expansion of jobs in developing countries, suggesting that domestic labor is also displaced by the substitution of capital in addition to labor in affiliates in developing countries. They then aggregate employment to the industry level to account for both between-firm substitution and within-firm substitution. At the industry level, there is broad complementarity in home and foreign employment for many sectors, but domestic displacement due to substitution via developing-country workers in a few highly visible industries. This result highlights one source of the divergence in opinions between economists and the general public about offshoring.

Harrison and McMillan (2011) extend these stylized facts with a more formal econometric analysis (Chapter 11). They find that a fall in wages in low-income destinations is associated with lower US parent employment, but there is no significant effect of high-income wages in destinations on US jobs. They then control for different measures of vertical integration within firms and find that for firms who export to low-income affiliates for further processing, domestic and foreign workers are complements. In contrast, US and foreign workers are substitutes for firms that export to high-income affiliates for further processing. This sheds light on the importance of distinguishing between different types of offshoring.

A related 2014 paper with Avraham Ebenstein, McMillan, and Shannon Philips (Chapter 12) links industry-level data on trade and offshoring to worker-level data on wages and occupations. This allows them to use a similar identification strategy to analyze wage changes due to workers exiting manufacturing and experiencing occupational downgrading. They find no significant effects of industry-level exposure to trade and offshoring on wages, but large negative effects of occupational exposure for workers performing routine tasks. However, for routine workers in export-intensive industries, wages are positively linked to export growth. Using their measure of occupational exposure, they find that workers who switched occupations due to trade experienced substantial declines in real wages. This result underscores the importance of distributional outcomes from trade and offshoring.

Chapter 13 returns to the effects of FDI in destination labor markets. It is Ann's 2010 AER paper with Jason Scorse on the impacts of anti-sweatshop activism in Indonesia. They use a difference-in-difference strategy comparing textile, footwear, and apparel (TFA) plants to the rest of manufacturing and comparing TFA plants in districts with contractors for major apparel companies to those elsewhere. They find significantly higher real wage changes, both in the TFA sector as a whole and, even more, in districts with contractors, on top of those induced by higher minimum wages. The authors also address whether these wage increases were associated with lower employment. There is no evidence of negative employment effects from exposure to anti-sweatshop campaigns, but they find that higher minimum wage laws do significantly reduce employment. They also found that the campaigns decreased profits, slowed productivity growth, and increased the probability of closures for small plants. The results can be interpreted as a form of rent-sharing, in which the pressure from activists and regulations forces firms to redistribute profits to workers in the form of higher wages.

Part 4: Industrial Transformation in Developing Countries

The final two chapters turn to trade policy's implications for industrial transformation in developing countries. The so-called "new-new" trade literature predicts that trade liberalization can lead to productivity growth by reallocating market share to more productive firms (Melitz 2003). In contrast, older trade papers focused on aggregate productivity effects through firm learning. In Chapter 14, Ann, Leslie Martin, and Shanthi Nataraj examine Indian trade, FDI, and licensing reforms and find evidence of "learning" in the sense of improved average firm productivity. In contrast, they only find evidence of "market stealing" in the period immediately following the reforms. They then use special techniques to identify the effects of individual liberalization measures on productivity growth. By far the largest share of growth can be attributed to lower input tariffs. This evidence on productivity growth from the Indian manufacturing sector will be increasingly important as other countries continue to industrialize and open up to trade.

In the final chapter, Harrison, along with Philippe Aghion, Jing Cai, Mathias Dewatripont, Luosha Du, and Patrick Legros, uses a comprehensive dataset of medium and large firms in China to evaluate the merits of industrial policy. They show that industrial policy is associated with greater innovation when it encourages more competition. The critical insight is that industrial policy alone is neither always good nor bad: the critical distinction is how it is designed. The paper emphasizes the distinction between industrial policies that prevent competition (such as picking winners or protecting failing firms from closure) and those that promote competition (such as encouraging entry into concentrated sectors).

The paper starts with a simple model, which predicts that subsidies targeted to more productive sectors can increase competition within those sectors, thereby spurring innovation. Further, the benefits of these policies increase in the *ex-ante* degree of competitiveness. Essentially, rather than picking winners, government policy should pick firms with incentives to use support for innovation rather than capturing rents. They find evidence that Chinese subsidies and tax holidays targeted to sectors with higher Lerner indices (which measure the degree of competitiveness) have larger positive impacts on productivity and productivity growth. These policies appear to be more effective when they are more dispersed across firms. Of course, explicitly targeting policies toward sectors that appear to be more competitive can create perverse incentives for rent-seeking activities in other industries. Thus, successes may be difficult to replicate in other contexts. Nevertheless, this paper makes an important argument for the potential benefits of targeted industrial policy.

Taken as a whole, Harrison's work marries the neoclassical trade literature's focus on gains from trade in the aggregate with real-word policy concerns about the distributional effects of trade. Harrison sees herself as "giving voices to the voiceless". When trade theory collides with the real world, practical outcomes are not always as rosy as those predicted by standard theory. While the simple Heckscher-Ohlin trade theory has always acknowledged that the gains from trade often create both winners and losers in each country, Harrison's work provides tangible insight on identifying the losers, quantifying their costs, and compensating them. This provides relevant and specific insights for policy makers looking to take advantage of opportunities for growth offered by globalization while doing so as equitably as possible. Similarly, international economists often argue that multinational firms bring in much-needed technology and generally lead to positive spillovers for host-country firms. Yet, if capital markets are imperfect, capital is more mobile than labor, or firms have market power, outcomes may be quite different. Ann Harrison believes that a more clear-eyed view of the pros and cons of globalization in a capitalist world would do much to help spread its benefits to all.

PART 1

Trade, Investment, and Factor Incomes

Chapter 2

Sharing the Costs: The Impact of Trade Reform on Capital and Labor in Morocco*

Janet Currie, *University of California, Los Angeles, and National Bureau of Economic Research*

Ann Harrison, *Columbia University and National Bureau of Economic Research*

We examine the impact of recent trade reforms. Although employment in the average private sector manufacturing firm was unaffected, there were significant employment losses to exporters and highly affected firms. Parastatals increased employment by hiring low-paid temporary workers. Many firms did not adjust wages or employment. We examine two possible explanations. First, barriers to labor market mobility could have impeded adjustment. Second, we develop a model of labor demand which allows for imperfect competition and endogenous technological change. Our results suggest that although labor markets were flexible, many firms cut profit margins and raised productivity rather than reducing employment.

I. Introduction

There is a considerable gap in our knowledge about exactly how wages and employment in developing countries adjusted to the trade reforms

This article was prepared under funding from the research project, "Labor Markets in Developing Countries," RPO 678-10. We would like to thank Simon Commander, Richard Freeman, Edward Leamer, Duncan Thomas, and seminar participants at UCLA, UC Davis, the NBER, and the World Bank for helpful comments.

S44

*This article originally appeared in *Journal of Labor Economics*, **15** S44–S71

15

of the 1970s and 1980s. On the one hand, reforms may have led to a downward shift in the demand for labor—particularly in import-competing sectors. On the other hand, adjustment may have occurred through changes in real wages. Yet another possibility is that labor markets were unaffected and firms adjusted to greater competition through reductions in profit margins. What in fact occurred? Who paid the price?

Although the most radical trade reforms in the last 2 decades have occurred in developing countries, recent efforts to examine labor market adjustments to global competition have focused on industrial country experience. In part, this focus reflects lack of data: until recently, few developing country micro-level data sets covering the period coinciding with trade reforms were available.

This article begins to fill this gap by examining the impact of a broad-based trade reform initiated in Morocco during the 1980s. As a result of pressure due to a payments crisis in 1983, Morocco virtually eliminated quantitative restrictions on imports and reduced the maximum tariff from 165% to 45% over a 6-year period. These reductions are enormous compared to those typically negotiated by industrial countries. The Canada–United States Free Trade Agreement, for example, resulted in an overall reduction in Canadian tariffs of 2.5% between 1988 and 1991, and the maximum tariff reduction was under 9% (Gaston and Trefler 1994). Hence, the sheer magnitude of the changes in Morocco suggest that if trade reform has a significant adverse impact on wages or employment, it should be apparent in these data.

This article contributes to the debate on trade and employment linkages in two other respects.[1] First, using a new data source—micro-level detail on individual enterprises—we are able to trace the relationship between changes in trade policies and manufacturing employment at the firm level. Although trade reforms are generally implemented at the sector level, we show that within a sector their effects vary significantly across firm characteristics such as ownership (public vs. private) and degree of export orientation. In fact, firm characteristics have a decisive impact on the response to trade reform: although the reforms in Morocco had almost no impact on aggregate wages and employment, publicly owned firms and export-oriented firms were strongly affected. By using firm-level data we are also able to directly apply a model derived from the firm's labor demand decision and to control for unobserved, constant firm-level determinants of labor demand using firm fixed effects.

---

[1] In an earlier version of the article, we also compared estimates of the effects of tariffs and quotas to those obtained using measures of import penetration. Arguably, the latter measures both the policies in effect, and the effect of those policies, whereas the former is a purer measure of policy. We found that the two types of measures were highly correlated and that the estimates obtained were very similar.

Second, our use of micro data allows us to answer a question that has puzzled labor economists in both industrial and industrializing countries. Several of the (industry level) studies that measure the impact of trade reform on wages and employment find almost no impact on wages and small effects on employment. In this article, we analyze two possible reasons for the sluggish response. We begin by exploring the most popular explanation for the lack of an employment response: labor regulations in developing countries inhibit both the reallocation of labor and wage flexibility. Feliciano (1994) finds no impact of the Mexican trade reform on employment, attributing her results to the difficulties of firing workers under Mexican labor law. Anecdotal evidence for Venezuela suggests that employment reallocation following the trade reform in 1989 was inhibited by restrictions on layoffs in the formal sector.

We show that despite the existence of formal barriers to worker dismissals and minimum wage laws, labor market regulations cannot explain the sluggish labor market response to trade reforms in Morocco. In part, this is due to poor compliance with existing regulations. Despite the existence of a stringent minimum wage, half of all workers in the formal sector are paid below the minimum. And although firing a permanent worker in Morocco is a difficult and time-consuming process, temporary workers can be easily dismissed. It is technically illegal to hire workers on repeated temporary contracts, but it appears that firms have responded to hiring and firing laws by (illegally) switching to "permanent" temporary workers.

Instead, the lack of an employment response for many of the firms in our sample can be explained in the context of imperfect competition. As Harrison (1994) emphasizes, many developing country markets are characterized by few players and high barriers to entry. In such a context, firms may choose to adjust to trade reform by reducing profit margins and raising productivity. These points are developed in the context of a formal model below.

We begin with a discussion of necessary background information including a review of previous work on trade reform, and trade reform in Morocco. Section III discusses the model, and Section IV presents the data. Section V presents the empirical results, and Section VI discusses why some firms may not have adjusted wages or employment to trade reform. Section VII discusses some general equilibrium considerations. Conclusions and suggestions for future research appear in Section VIII.

II. Background

A. Previous Work on Trade Reform

One of the first attempts to measure the partial equilibrium effects of import competition is Grossman (1986, 1987). Grossman analyzed the impact of tariff protection on the U.S. steel industry and nine other import-competing industries, finding that wages are fairly unresponsive to (tariff-inclusive) import prices but that employment responses in some sectors have been quite significant. Grossman concludes from the low wage elasticities and higher employment elasticities that there is fairly high intersectoral labor mobility within the United States. Other cross-industry studies of the United States include Freeman and Katz (1991), Revenga (1992), and Gaston and Trefler (1994). These studies also find significant effects of changes in import competition on employment, but smaller effects on wages. In the United States and Canada, it appears that trade policy changes lead to employment reallocation across industries, with very little effects on wages.

Evidence on trade and employment linkages is much weaker for developing countries. Krueger (1983) describes a project sponsored by the National Bureau of Economic Research (NBER) to analyze the linkages between trade policies and employment in 10 industrializing countries. The NBER studies focused on (1) measuring the relative labor intensity of exportables versus import-substituting production and (2) measuring the extent to which greater protection encourages a shift toward more capital-intensive means of production. Krueger and her colleagues found that moving toward a more neutral trade regime led to greater labor intensity in production. However, none of the case studies directly measured the actual impact of trade reforms on wages or employment.

Rama (1994) adopts a partial equilibrium approach similar in spirit to Revenga (1992) and Freeman and Katz (1991) to examine the relationship between tariffs, employment, and wages in Uruguay. Using four-digit industry-level data over a 6-year period, Rama finds no impact of the reform on wages, but a negative impact on employment. A reduction in the tariff-inclusive price of imports by 1% led to an employment drop of between .4 and .5 percentage points.

The only study that has analyzed the impact of trade reform on employment and wages using micro data is Feliciano (1994). Feliciano uses repeated cross-sections of household surveys in selected cities to examine the impact of the Mexican trade reforms on wage levels and wage dispersion. She does not find any significant impact of tariff changes on wages but does document an increase in wage dispersion over the period of the reform. She finds no impact on aggregate industrial employment, but her sample is better suited for examining wage effects than employment effects.

B. Trade Reform in Morocco

Following independence in 1956, Morocco's economic development strategy was primarily based on import-substituting industrialization and agricultural self-sufficiency in a highly protected domestic market. For more than 2 decades, trade and industrial policies were based on high tariffs and on quantitative restrictions in imports. Furthermore, during the 1970s, the Moroccan government expanded growth through high levels of public spending, financed through foreign borrowing and rising receipts from phosphate exports. These policies culminated in a first balance of payments crisis in 1978, forcing authorities to implement a stabilization program with the support of the International Monetary Fund (IMF).

A second payment crisis erupted in 1983, forcing authorities to take emergency measures. All imports were subject to licensing. In consultation with the World Bank and with the support of a Trade and Industrial Policy Loan (ITPAI), the government introduced structural adjustment measures designed to eliminate the bias against export activities, liberalize the import regime, and enhance the allocative role of the financial sector (United Nations Development Program–World Bank 1990).

The trade reform introduced in 1983 called for the eventual elimination of the Special Import Tariff (SIT), a uniform tariff levied on the cost, insurance, freight value of imports, the lowering of the maximum customs duty from 400% to 45%, and a reduction in quantitative restrictions. Changes in the industrial code were also undertaken to promote exports, and the exchange rate was devalued. Quantitative restrictions, the principal instrument of protection for domestic goods until 1984, were progressively dismantled. Most goods were gradually transferred from List B (imports requiring prior authorization for import) to List A (imports requiring no prior authorization) beginning in 1983. List C, which included all prohibited import items, was formally abolished in 1986.[2]

Tables 1 and 2 document the reductions in tariff and quota coverage between 1984 and 1990. The major accomplishment of the trade reform was to substantially reduce the coverage of import licenses (quotas), from 41% of all imports in 1984 to only 11% of all imports in 1990. Progress in reducing tariffs was less significant, in part due to the conversion of existing quotas to tariffs. The major accomplishment of the tariff reform was to reduce the dispersion in tariff protection within the manufacturing sector. Although average tariffs declined only slightly, from 32.5% in 1984 to 28.6% in 1990, the maximum tariff fell from 165% to 45% during the period. Average import penetration increased only slightly, in part due to domestic contraction combined with the devaluation.

Small changes in tariffs and import competition mask significant movements across manufacturing subsectors. The averages in table 2 show that

---

[2] Nevertheless, Morocco is still far from an open economy. The tariff structure remains complicated despite the lowering of the maximum tariff, and the dispersion of the tariff rates remains high, although significantly reduced in recent years. Morocco's tariff structure is such that tariffs rise with the stage of processing, resulting in effective rates of protection that are considerably higher than nominal rates. This effect is reinforced by the prevalence of quantitative restrictions (List B) on products at a high stage of processing.

Table 1
Trade Reform in Morocco, 1984–90

	1984	1985	1986	1987	1988	1989	1990
Average tariff (%)	32.5	32.7	32.5	30.2	28.0	28.5	28.6
Maximum tariff (%)	158.2	165.0	165.6	106.1	45.0	45.0	45.0
Coverage of import licenses (%)	41.0	36.1	29.3	25.7	23.0	17.0	11.3
Import penetration (%)*	37.6	37.4	36.4	36.7	36.5	38.6	39.0
	(36.3)	(35.0)	(34.0)	(33.8)	(33.5)	(34.8)	(35.1)

* Import penetration defined as imports/(imports + sales − exports). Number in parentheses gives alternative definition of import penetration as imports/(imports + sales).

trade reforms in some sectors were quite dramatic. In textiles, clothing, leather products, and beverages and tobacco, significant reductions in both tariff and quota coverage led to very large increases in import penetration. These significant changes in policy allow us to use the relatively short time series available to analyze the impact of trade reform on manufacturing employment.

III. The Model

We assume that a firm-specific production function can be described as

$$q = AL^{B1}I^{B2}, \tag{1}$$

Table 2
Trade Reform by Manufacturing Subsector

	Tariffs		Quota Coverage		Import Penetration*			
	1984	1990	1984	1990	1984	1984	1990	1990
10 Food products	23.0	32.8	35.9	24.6	5.0	(5.0)	6.3	(6.2)
11 Other food products	49.7	32.3	68.0	33.9	36.4	(35.7)	30.5	(27.3)
12 Beverages and tobacco	90.6	36.6	73.3	20.1	3.5	(3.5)	21.8	(21.8)
13 Textiles	52.9	35.6	75.6	55.7	27.0	(25.7)	37.1	(30.7)
14 Clothing	70.5	44.7	93.3	26.0	3.6	(2.3)	10.1	(3.5)
15 Leather and shoes	43.0	31.7	69.7	32.8	22.6	(20.3)	39.3	(21.9)
16 Wood products	26.6	25.8	54.5	0	20.2	(19.1)	20.8	(18.6)
17 Paper and printing	17.4	25.6	70.1	0	24.4	(24.4)	20.6	(18.9)
18 Mineral products	23.9	29.1	28.3	0	11.3	(11.0)	13.9	(13.5)
19 Basic metals	9.3	13.1	17.4	0	68.7	(59.4)	68.3	(55.8)
20 Metallic products	31.7	32.6	37.2	0	22.5	(22.3)	25.8	(25.2)
21 Machinery and equipment	11.5	16.3	22.0	2.8	73.6	(73.5)	69.8	(69.7)
22 Transport materials	15.9	22.8	27.8	4.6	66.5	(65.2)	62.0	(57.6)
23 Electronics	21.6	27.5	18.7	1.0	56.7	(53.0)	57.0	(46.3)
24 Precision equipment	22.9	26.3	6.7	0	85.6	(81.0)	81.8	(81.3)
25 Chemical products	21.3	20.8	22.6	6.5	31.2	(30.5)	35.2	(29.3)
26 Rubber and plastics	33.0	36.3	48.8	2.1	29.1	(29.0)	35.2	(33.9)
27 Other industrial	55.3	39.0	27.6	0	80.9	(80.5)	78.3	(75.6)

* See note in table 1.

where real output q is a function of labor inputs L and other inputs I. The input parameters $B1$ and $B2$ are assumed to be each less than unity, but their sum may exceed one, indicating increasing returns to scale. The "Hicks neutral" technology parameter, A, varies over time and across plants. We assume that firms are imperfectly competitive Cournot firms. Total domestic output is given by Q, while import volumes are denoted by M. Domestic prices are denoted by P, foreign prices are given by P^*, and the exchange rate is E. Firms maximize profits subject to an industry-level quota constraint δ:[3]

$$\max P(Q)q - wL - rI$$
$$\text{subject to } MP^*E/[MP^*E + QP(Q)] \leq \delta. \tag{2}$$

We assume that the international price and import volumes are exogenous with respect to the individual domestic firm. The wage rate is w, and the prices of other inputs are denoted by r. Domestic and imported goods are imperfect substitutes. In the spirit of Grossman (1986, 1987) we define the aggregate demand function as

$$Q = D^{\pi L}\{EP^*(1 + \text{TAR})/P\}^\varepsilon, \tag{3}$$

where TAR are ad valorem tariffs and π is the rate of secular demand shift.

We assume that the firm's wage depends on both the alternative wage available to its employees, defined as the average wage for all other firms in the same sector, as well as its employment:

$$w = (\text{ALTWAGE})^{B3} L^{B4}, \tag{4}$$

where the alternative wage (ALTWAGE) is deflated by a general price index (CPI).[4]

---

[3] An alternative way to model the impact of quotas and tariffs would be directly through product demand. In this alternative approach, trade policy could affect mark-ups through its impact on the elasticity of demand. This alternative framework yields an estimating framework which is very similar to the one presented here.

[4] The wage depends on the alternative wage but is not expected to be exactly equal to the alternative wage: for example, in a contracting model, the own wage will be higher than the worker's next best alternative if there is any rent to be divided between workers and firms. Note that the worker's next best alternative wage will be some function of our ALTWAGE measure and the probability that a worker who lost his or her job would be reemployed in the same industry. Estimation of reduced form employment equations that omit the alternative wage produce very similar estimates of the effects of trade policy.

The assumption that individual firms face upward-sloping labor supply curves allows for the possibility of market power in the labor market (cf. Currie 1991). This assumption is not critical for either the model or the estimation of employment. However, this more general specification is useful for estimating the wage equations which are discussed later in the article.

From (2), the first-order conditions with respect to L are given by

$$P\partial q / \partial L(1 + \lambda_1\delta) = w(1 + B_4)\theta, \qquad (2')$$

where

$$\theta = \frac{1}{1 - 1/\varepsilon[s + \lambda_1\delta(1 - s)/(1 + \lambda_1\delta)]}.$$

The term λ_1 is the shadow value of the quota constraint. The mark-up term, θ, is a positive function of an individual firm's market share s and quota coverage, but is negatively related to the elasticity of demand, ε. Quotas also affect wages directly, with the quota premium given by the term $(1 + \lambda_1\delta)$. Under the presence of quotas, wages are set above the value of their marginal product.

If we take logs, and combine (1), (2), (3), and (4), we can derive the following reduced form for employment:

$$\begin{aligned}
\log L = C + &\alpha_0 t + \alpha_1 \log I + \alpha_2 \log A - \alpha_3 \log \text{ALTWAGE} \\
&+ \alpha_4 \log EP^* + \alpha_5 \log(1 + \text{TAR}) \qquad (5) \\
&- \alpha_6 \log \theta + \alpha_7 \log(1 + \lambda_1\delta).
\end{aligned}$$

To arrive at (5), we assume that domestic firms are symmetric, which allows us to derive a firm-specific product demand function from (3) by dividing both sides by the number of firms, n, which is allowed to vary over time. In the estimation which follows, we will use actual quota coverage ratios (QRCOV) to measure δ. The QRCOV measures the share of total domestic demand that is subject to quota restrictions. To simplify the analysis, we will also assume that $\log(1 + \text{TAR})$ can be approximated by TAR and that the $\log(1 + \text{QRCOV})$ can be approximated by QRCOV.

If the elasticity of demand, ε, is greater than one, then it is possible to sign the coefficients in (5): the model suggests that the coefficients on inputs (I), productivity (A), the foreign price level (EP^*), tariffs (TAR), and quotas will all be positive; the coefficients on the alternative wage and margins (θ) are expected to be less than zero. Given that the model incorporates some market power, an elastic elasticity of demand is plausible.

We could simply estimate (5), which suggests that protection should unambiguously raise labor demand. Yet reduced form estimation of L must also take into account the fact that the level of technology (A) and the extent of market power (θ) are both in turn affected by competition from imports. Our model suggests that mark-ups should be positively related to quota coverage; for estimation, we adopt a more general speci-fication.[5] We hypothesize the following relationship between market power and trade policies:

$$\log \theta = \eta_0 + \eta_1 TAR + \eta_2 QRCOV, \quad \text{where } \eta_1, \eta_2 > 0. \quad (6)$$

Later in the article, when we estimate the relationship between margins and trade policies directly, we will be able to test the restriction that only quotas (and not tariffs) should affect mark-ups.

We would expect productivity to be affected by a number of factors. In particular, the age and type of the capital stock, and the degree of public ownership would be likely to affect productivity. We might also expect protection to exert a negative impact on productivity. We will capture such factors as age and location with a plant specific fixed effect, f_i. Hence:

$$\log A = \gamma_0 - \gamma_1 TAR - \gamma_2 QRCOV + f_i, \quad \text{where } \gamma_1, \gamma_2 > 0. \quad (7)$$

Combining (5), (6), and (7) yields the following reduced form equa-tion for estimation:

$$\begin{aligned}
\log L = {} & \alpha_0 t + \alpha_1 \log I - \alpha_3 \log ALTWAGE + \alpha_4 \log EP^* \\
& + (\alpha_5 - \alpha_2\gamma_1 - \alpha_6\eta_1)TAR \\
& + (\alpha_7 - \alpha_2\gamma_2 - \alpha_6\eta_2)QRCOV + f_i.
\end{aligned} \quad (8)$$

In a reduced form specification such as (8), employment is a positive function of other inputs and the international price P^*, and a negative function of the alternative wage, ALTWAGE. However, it is not possible to sign the effects of trade policy. Changes in trade policy, as captured

---

[5] In our model, the nonequivalence of quotas and tariffs is due to a different reason than in Bhagwati (1965). In Bhagwati's original article, the nonequivalence of quotas and tariffs arises from the fact that for a domestic monopolist, a tariff on imports rotates the demand curve while a quota shifts the curve downward. In our formulation, only quotas affect market power due to the constant elasticity of demand specification. However, the empirical specification is general enough to allow both tariffs and quotas to affect market power.

Morocco   S53

by tariffs (TAR) and quotas (QRCOV), have three offsetting effects on labor demand. First, increased competition from imports leads to falling output prices and a downward shift in labor demand. Second, if reducing trade barriers raises productivity, this could actually lead to an increase in labor demand. Third, lowering trade barriers reduces market power, which causes firms to expand production and increase labor demand. Intuitively, in an imperfectly competitive world, firms have several options when faced with greater international competition. They could cut output and reduce their labor force. Alternatively, they could respond by increasing productivity or cutting profit margins. To the extent that some rents were captured by workers in the form of higher wages, firms could also respond by cutting wages (by substituting temporary workers for permanent workers for example). In the remainder of the article, we will attempt to disentangle these different responses by Moroccan firms to the trade reform.

A. Public Sector Enterprises

It is possible that public sector enterprises are significantly more constrained in their ability to fire workers than private firms. Restrictions on laying off workers can be incorporated into the model by allowing public sector firms to maximize profits subject to a constraint that L must be greater than or equal to some level V. If we allow for a labor constraint, it is easy to show that under the revised first-order conditions, public sector firms set wages above the value of their marginal product:

$$P\partial q/\partial L(1 + \lambda_1\delta) = (w - \lambda_2)(1 + B_4)\theta, \qquad (2'')$$

where λ_2 is the shadow value of the constraint. If V is binding, it is also easy to see that any factor which would normally lead to a reduction in labor demand, such as a decline in price or a reduction in quotas or tariffs, will have a reduced effect. In fact, public sector firms could possibly be asked to expand while other firms are contracting, acting as a social safety net for the rest of the economy. Under these circumstances, we could even see perverse (positive) effects of a reduction in tariffs or quota coverage on employment for public sector firms.

B. Exporters

Consider two possible types of exporters. On the one hand, there are exporters who sell substantially the same product in domestic and foreign markets. For these firms, output is determined by the world price, although trade restrictions may enable them to sell their product in the domestic market at a higher price. Trade reform will reduce profit margins without affecting output or employment.

On the other hand, exporters may sell substantially different products in the domestic and foreign markets. Suppose, for example, that a textile manufacturer produces both a labor-intensive native product and a highly mechanized product for sale on the export market. Trade reform will reduce the price of the domestic good, causing the manufacturer to shift resources from the domestic product to production of goods for the foreign market. In this case, employment will fall and productivity will rise for the exporter, and the extent of the shift will be greatest among firms that have the greatest access, experience, and expertise in foreign markets. These predictions are tested below.

IV. The Database

The data for this article are taken from the Moroccan Census of Manufacturing, which annually surveys all manufacturing firms with at least 10 employees or with sales revenue exceeding 100,000 dirhams (approximately U.S.$11,000 at the average 1984–89 official exchange rate). The number of firms in the survey averages between 4,007 (1985) and 5,200 (1989) firms a year. A survey of the informal (manufacturing) sector in 1988 suggests that the formal sector firms in the census probably account for only 10% of all enterprises in manufacturing but for 87% of total production and 74% of total employment (World Bank 1993). The firm's activity is described by a four-digit Moroccan nomenclature of economic activities (Nomenclature Marocaine des Activities Economiques or NMAE). An aggregation to two-digit codes leads to the 18 industrial sectors listed in table 2.

The annual surveys collect firm-level information about sales revenue, output, exports, labor cost, the number of employees, and materials costs. Our model specifies that our inputs (I) should be included in the reduced form for labor demand. Data on capital stock are highly imperfect and missing in about half the cases. Hence, we rely on the firm fixed effects to absorb at least the effect of mean capital stock over the period.[6] However, we do include material inputs, which are calculated as the difference between (real) output and (real) value added. Plants report both the number of permanent employees and the number of days worked by temporary workers. To compute a total employment measure, the number of days worked by temporary labor was divided by 225 and added to the number of permanent employees. We estimate that the permanent (formal sector) workforce works only 225 days per year, after accounting for a 5-day work week, holidays, and vacations.

The primary focus of this article is on the employment effects of the trade reform, due to the imperfect nature of the information on wages. Moroccan firms report total expenditure on personnel (*frais de personnel*)

---

[6] Similarly, the amount and type of capital at the start of the sample period will be captured by the fixed effect.

that include both wages and social security costs. Labor costs for temporary and permanent employees are combined, making it difficult to compare the wages of the two types of workers. A firm-specific average wage
was calculated by dividing the total labor bill by the total number of
(permanent and temporary) employees. This wage measure reflects both
changes in worker remuneration and changes in the composition of the
labor force. Wages were divided by the consumer price index (CPI) to
arrive at a real wage measure.

Since no measure of the international prices faced by Moroccan consumers was available, we were forced to use the U.S. export price index
series calculated by the Division of International Prices at the U.S. Bureau
of Labor Statistics. This series is compiled from interviews with individual
exporters. A concordance between the U.S. export price series, which is
classified SITC revision 3, and the Moroccan classification was created.
The price index was then adjusted by multiplying it by a U.S.-Dirham
exchange rate index based in the same year. Consequently, our price index
takes into account both changes in international prices as well as exchange
rate changes, such as the devaluation of the Moroccan currency.

Table 3 provides an overview of the firms in our data set. The original
sample included 32,280 observations, but 7,917 observations were excluded for various reasons. We excluded 1,885 observations with missing
values on tariffs and quotas, as well as 3,490 observations that failed a
number of cleaning checks. These included firms without employees,
firms where production rose by more than 50% in 1 year but the labor
force fell by more than 50%, firms in which average wages increased by
more than 75%, firms with average wages in excess of 500,000 dirhams,
and firms where the share foreign-owned exceeded 100%. We also excluded firms with fewer than three nonmissing observations over the 7-
year period, which reduced the sample size by 2,542 observations.[7]

The first column of table 3 shows the mean characteristics of all firms
in the sample, while columns 2 through 7 illustrate the differences between
various groups of firms. Panel A shows levels, while Panel B shows the
difference between the mean value over the 1984–86 period and the 1988–
90 average value.

Column 2 shows means for firms with some public ownership. Overall,
only 3% of firms have any public ownership—the mean public share is
only .01. Those firms that did have public ownership, however, tended
to have a sizable equity share controlled by the government: among firms
with any public ownership, the mean share was 50%. Although parastatals
account for only a small fraction of formal sector firms, they account for
a significant fraction of employment and output. In 1990, parastatals

---

[7] We first determined that most of these firms were not missing data because
they were new entrants.

Table 3
Variable Means

	All	Parastatals	Private High Impact	Private Exports <.25	Private Exports >.25
A. Levels:					
Employment	75.26	470.70	97.50	41.01	155.41
	(1.26)	(26.47)	(2.23)	(.78)	(3.77)
Share temporary	.08	.21	.06	.07	.16
	(.001)	(.01)	(.002)	(.001)	(.004)
Share skilled workers	.04	.05	.03	.05	.02
	(.004)	(.02)	(.02)	(.001)	(.001)
Average firm wage	15.95	32.13	11.97	15.98	12.68
	(.08)	(.67)	(.11)	(.09)	(.16)
Output price index	116.40	115.51	110.85	117.27	111.93
	(.12)	(.74)	(.17)	(.13)	(.21)
Tariffs	.35	.30	.48	.33	.48
	(.002)	(.01)	(.003)	(.001)	(.003)
Quota coverage	.32	.33	.54	.29	.49
	(.002)	(.01)	(.01)	(.002)	(.01)
Export share in sector	.20	.19	.56	.11	.65
	(.002)	(.01)	(.004)	(.002)	(.004)
Import share in sector	.55	.63	.20	.56	.48
	(.02)	(.12)	(.01)	(.02)	(.07)
Public share	.01	.51	...	...	...
	(.001)	(.02)			
Firm age	16.10	24.04	14.19	16.24	13.82
	(.08)	(.57)	(.14)	(.09)	(.19)
Revenue (thousands)	19.36	244.60	9.85	9.37	13.80
	(.76)	(23.01)	(.26)	(.26)	(.37)
Materials inputs (thousands)	11.46	135.14	7.15	7.34	10.23
	(.52)	(16.59)	(.21)	(.20)	(.29)
No. of observations	26,249	769	6,832	21,445	4,134
B. Difference 1988–90 average and 1984–86 average:					
Total employment	14.36	78.74	20.98	5.54	52.74
	(1.85)	(31.29)	(1.40)	(.44)	(3.40)
Share temporary	.03	.07	.02	.02	.04
	(.002)	(.07)	(.002)	(.001)	(.003)
Share skilled workers	.16	.04	.02	.03	.01
	(.003)	(.01)	(.001)	(.001)	(.001)
Average firm wage	1.42	1.66	1.65	1.50	1.24
	(.13)	(1.03)	(.06)	(.05)	(.19)
Output price index	27.68	29.95	23.46	29.02	.96
	(.23)	(1.60)	(.11)	(.10)	(.03)
Tariffs	−.04	−.07	−.20	−.02	−.22
	(.003)	(.02)	(.005)	(.001)	(.005)
Quota coverage	−.17	−.16	−.26	−.02	−.27
	(.004)	(.02)	(.005)	(.001)	(.01)
Export share in sector	.04	.04	.12	.03	.12
	(.002)	(.01)	(.002)	(.001)	(.002)
Import share in sector	−.15	.01	.07	−.13	−.29
	(.05)	(.05)	(.01)	(.02)	(.14)
Public share	.001	.02	...	...	...
	(.03)	(.001)			
Revenue (thousands)	7.65	95.59	1.55	1.19	3.56
	(.87)	(25.76)	(.12)	(.88)	(.23)

NOTE.—"High impact" refers to firms most affected by the changes in tariffs and quotas. Standard errors are in parentheses.

accounted for 26% of output, 11% of employment, and 30% of exports. Publicly owned firms dominate the phosphates and chemicals (including fertilizers), iron and steel, and beverages and tobacco sectors. The large role played by publicly owned firms warrants the special attention we pay to these types of plants.

A comparisons of columns 1 and 2 indicates that publicly owned firms are much larger than the average firm and have both a higher share of temporary workers and a slightly higher share of skilled workers in the total labor force.[8] (Skill levels are only available for permanent workers, and only in 1986 and 1990.) These firms also grew faster than other firms, and more of this growth was in the form of additional temporary workers. In addition, publicly held firms were older, had higher revenues, and paid higher wages. The positive wage differential between parastatals and other plants is remarkable and only partly accounted for by the higher share of skilled employees.

The means comparing public firms with the rest of the manufacturing sector are striking for two reasons. First, they appear to refute the stylized "fact" that public sector employees in developing countries are underpaid (Lindauer, Meesok, and Suebsaeng 1988), although this result must be confirmed using individual-level data from labor force surveys in which worker characteristics can be controlled for. Second, it is evident that the public sector is not unusually restricted in its ability to hire temporary workers. In fact, the share of temporary workers in publicly held firms is almost three times as high as in private firms. The high and growing share of temporary workers provides some a priori evidence against the view that parastatals are more firmly bound by labor market regulations that could impede adjustment. More evidence on the relative speeds of adjustment of publicly and privately held plants will be presented below.

The third column breaks out privately held firms in the four industry sectors that were most affected by trade reform, in the sense that they had the largest changes in import penetration ratios (sectors 12–15 in table 2). Firms in these "high impact" sectors account for about one-quarter of all private sector firms. They are larger but had somewhat lower sales and paid lower wages than other firms. However, surprisingly, both wages and employment grew faster than in the average firm. These firms also showed strong increases in *both* import shares and export shares, relative to the average firm, which suggests that many of these high impact firms were export-oriented and that much of the growth in employment was export led.

Trade reforms may have increased exports by reducing tariffs on imported inputs. They also coincided with an exchange rate depreciation,

---

[8] There is no occupational breakdown available for temporary workers. In our analysis, we assume that temporary workers are mostly unskilled.

as described above. These factors suggest that export-oriented firms may have been net beneficiaries of the whole package of new policies. In order to investigate this hypothesis, private sector firms were broken into those with mean export shares less than .25 or greater than or equal to .25, where the means were taken over the whole sample period. More than four-fifths of private sector firms had export shares smaller than .25. Export-oriented firms tend to be larger, to have more temporary workers, and to have lower wages than other firms. Panel B shows that they were also the fastest growing, although wages lagged behind those of other firms. Perhaps more surprising is the fact that despite large reductions in tariffs and quotas, the sector import share fell most for the most export-oriented firms. These figures show that if we wish to isolate the effects of tariffs and quotas, it is necessary to control for other policy changes such as exchange rate devaluations that occurred contemporaneously and, hence, provide a justification for the inclusion of year effects in our empirical model.

Finally, it is worth noting one trend that affected all firms—the share of the labor force classified as "skilled" increased over time. Although it is not shown in table 3, we also find that the share of skilled workers in the permanent workforce rose. Coupled with the increase in the share of temporary workers, this pattern suggests that in many cases, the least skilled permanent workers were replaced with temporary workers.

V. Results

Table 4 shows regressions of the log of total employment on tariffs and quotas that are based on equation (8). Since this is the first study that we know of that makes use of direct measures of trade policy, we present estimates of the impact of these two measures of trade policy separately.[9] For the majority of plants, the trade reform had essentially no impact on employment. Estimates based on data aggregated up to the four-digit level are shown in the first column, for the sake of comparability with previous studies. However, for the estimation using aggregate data, we exclude the alternative wage, which is not exogenous at the industry level. These sectoral estimates suggest that trade policy had little impact on employment. The coefficients on both tariffs and quotas are statistically insignificant, with point estimates close to zero.

Estimates based on firm level data, which include controls for firm-specific fixed effects, are shown in column 2. These figures are consistent

[9] In principle, one could combine tariffs and quotas into a single index of protection. However, there is no agreement in the trade literature about how this should be done. Alternatively, one could estimate models (as we did in a previous version of this article) that include tariffs, quotas, and the interaction between them. These models are considerably less transparent than those presented here and do not yield additional insights into the effects of trade policy.

Table 4
Effects of Trade on Employment

	All-Industry Level	All-Firm Level	Parastatals	Private High Impact	Private Exports <25%	Private Exports >25%
A. Tariffs:						
Tariff	.002	.002	−.255	.165	.069	.233
	(.143)	(.03)	(.121)	(.055)	(.037)	(.081)
International price	.119	.223	.031	.010	.235	−.065
	(.432)	(.051)	(.242)	(.127)	(.056)	(.152)
Log alternative wage	...	−.066	−.055	−.031	−.040	−.164
		(.019)	(.103)	(.048)	(.020)	(.060)
Log materials	.759	.133	.097	.174	.122	.198
	(.011)	(.004)	(.028)	(.009)	(.004)	(.013)
R^2	...	.96	.96	.95	.95	.92
B. Quotas:						
Quota coverage	.057	.010	−.003	−.048	.044	−.049
	(.088)	(.017)	(.098)	(.034)	(.019)	(.048)
International price	.057	.220	.083	.003	.237	−.057
	(.431)	(.051)	(.243)	(.128)	(.056)	(.158)
Log alternative wage	...	−.066	−.084	.008	−.042	−.137
		(.019)	(.104)	(.046)	(.020)	(.060)
Log materials	.759	.133	.088	.173	.122	.120
	(.011)	(.004)	(.028)	(.009)	(.004)	(.013)
R^2	.85	.96	.96	.95	.95	.92
No of observations	1,172	21,098	612	4,834	17,363	3,123
No. of firms	...	4,475	116	1,118	3,622	735

NOTE.—Standard errors are in parentheses. All equations include time dummies.

with those obtained at the sector level and suggest that for the average firm, trade policy measured using tariffs or quotas has no effect on employment. The point estimates on tariffs and quotas are both small in magnitude and statistically insignificant. In contrast, the coefficients are statistically significant and positive for the international price and material inputs, as well as significant negative for the alternative wage, as predicted by our model.

In columns 3–6, we measure the effects of trade policy on employment for different types of firms. The results suggest that firm characteristics significantly affect both the sign and the magnitude of employment responses to trade policy. Column 3 shows estimates for parastatal firms, those with some degree of public ownership. The results for employment suggest that decreases in tariffs were associated with significant increases in employment. This response is consistent with the idea that parastatal employment acts as a social safety net, absorbing employees displaced from other sectors.

Column 4 measures the impact of tariffs and quotas on firms in the most highly affected sectors. The results suggest that tariff reductions had a significant impact on employment. The coefficient on tariffs, .165, implies that a reduction in tariffs of 10 percentage points would lead to a decline in employment of 1.65%. The impact of quotas, however, is not statistically significant.

The last two columns of table 4 compare the responses of private sector firms with small mean export shares (an average of less than 25% of sales over the entire period) and those with larger mean export shares. It appears that the decrease in employment due to a reduction in tariff protection is higher for export-oriented firms. In terms of our model, this result suggests that firms with export sales are likely to have lower profit margins than firms oriented primarily toward the domestic market. It appears that exporters adjusted to a contraction of the domestic market by cutting employment, while nonexporters used other means of adjustment. This hypothesis will be tested further below, when we explicitly examine the effects of the trade reform on profit margins.

Although the focus of our analysis is primarily on employment, we also extended the analysis to examine the relationship between wage determination and trade policy. An analogous reduced form equation for wages can be derived from combining (4) and (8). The sign of the coefficients should be the same as for labor demand, with the exception of the sign on ALTWAGE (which should now be positive). We report estimates of the wage equations in table 5, parts A and B.

Once again, we first report the results for the sample aggregated to the

Table 5
Effects of Trade on Wages

	All-Industry Level	All-Firm Level	Parastatals	Private High Impact	Private Exports <25%	Private Exports >25%
A. Tariffs:						
Tariff	−.003	.033	.259	−.035	−.049	−.118
	(.001)	(.019)	(.100)	(.053)	(.038)	(.077)
International price	.004	−.011	.003	.109	.002	−.013
	(.290)	(.051)	(.200)	(.123)	(.057)	(.144)
Log alternative wage	...	.033	.237	.006	.002	.155
		(.019)	(.085)	(.047)	(.021)	(.057)
Log materials	.098	.044	.021	.042	.043	.052
	(.007)	(.004)	(.023)	(.008)	(.004)	(.0112)
R^2	.35	.83	.86	.79	.83	.75
B. Quotas:						
Quota coverage	.012	.019	.006	−.006	.002	.068
	(.059)	(.017)	(.081)	(.033)	(.019)	(.045)
International price	.093	−.016	−.051	.118	−.005	−.056
	(.292)	(.051)	(.202)	(.123)	(.057)	(.149)
Log alternative wage	...	.032	.264	−.002	.003	.139
		(.019)	(.087)	(.045)	(.021)	(.057)
Log materials	.099	.044	.031	.042	.043	.051
	(.007)	(.004)	(.023)	(.008)	(.004)	(.012)
R^2	.34	.83	.86	.79	.83	.75
No of observations	1,172	21,098	612	4,834	17,363	3,123
No. of firms	...	4,475	116	1,118	3,622	735

NOTE.—Standard errors are in parentheses. All equations include time dummies.

four-digit level. The coefficients on tariffs and quotas are small in magnitude and statistically insignificant. The results are unchanged in column 2, where we estimate a wage equation at the plant level for all plants in the sample. In contrast to our earlier results, however, taking into account firm characteristics generally does not alter the results in columns 1 and 2. The coefficient on tariffs and quotas is statistically insignificant except in the public sector.

Unlike private sector enterprises, parastatals show a large and significant association between tariff protection and wages. The coefficient on tariffs, .259, suggests that a 10 percentage point decline in tariffs would lower public sector wages by 2.6%. In conjunction with our employment results, it appears that the public sector responded to tariff reductions by actually expanding its labor force and reducing wages. In part, the public sector responded by adding temporary workers, who are paid significantly less than permanent employees.

The results in table 4 indicate that cross-sectoral changes in tariffs and quotas had little discernible impact on wages (with the exception of the public sector), which suggests that the labor market is fairly fluid for private firms. The results on employment also suggested that only a minority of firms actually adjusted their labor force to changes in tariffs and quotas: in particular, publicly owned firms, firms in highly affected sectors, and exporters. The lack of a labor market response for the majority of firms appears puzzling in light of the large tariff changes and quota reductions described earlier in the article. In the next section, we explore alternative explanations for a sluggish response by some firms.

VI. Alternative Explanations for Different Labor Market Responses to Trade Reform

One of the more popular explanations for the lack of a labor market response in developing countries is imperfections in the labor market. Minimum wages may impede wage adjustment, while hiring and firing laws may affect labor mobility. We discuss these possibilities below and then turn to an alternative explanation: market power in the product market.

A. Labor Market Explanations

In Morocco, anecdotal evidence suggests that despite the existence of formal barriers to dismissals and stringent minimum wages, the labor market is actually quite fluid. In principle, private firms must first obtain permission from government bodies to fire permanent employees and must then pay a severance payment to dismissed employees ranging from 5 weeks (for 5 years of service) up to 38 weeks (for 15 years of service). Yet in practice, restrictions on dismissals apply only to the largest, formal sector enterprises. In addition, many enterprises have responded to restrictions on firing permanent workers by hiring temporary employees, who can be easily dismissed. The share of temporary workers in manufacturing rose steadily between 1984 and 1990.

Another possible impediment to labor market adjustment is minimum wage laws. To the extent that minimum wages are binding, they could act as a barrier to downward wage adjustment, explaining the lack of any wage response to tariff and quota changes. In Morocco, the real value of the minimum wage rose by 4.4% annually during the 1980s, which suggests that it could have played an important role in the adjustment process.

In practice, however, the evidence suggests that the minimum wage did not prevent wage adjustment in Morocco. Harrison and Islam (1993) present evidence of widespread noncompliance with the minimum wage. Using data for 1986, they find that average wages at the plant level were below the minimum for at least half of the firms in their sample. In addition, discussions with labor inspectors suggested that they are significantly understaffed and likely to address only the most serious labor code violations. To test for the possibility that a binding minimum wage could account for sluggish wage adjustment, we reestimated models similar to those reported here, dividing the sample into firms with average wages close to the minimum and other firms. Firms with wages close to the minimum were defined as having average wages (after subtracting out mandated payroll taxes of 12%) within 10% of the legislated minimum. The results were generally unaffected (and consequently are not reported here), although there is some evidence that firms with average wages close to the minimum actually experienced greater wage adjustment in response to the reforms.

One way to test whether a sluggish adjustment of the labor force could explain the low elasticities of employment response to trade form is to estimate a dynamic model of labor demand, in which employment today depends on past employment and on determinants of current desired employment. This would allow us to examine whether a firm's response to trade shocks is related to the speed with which it adjusts to changes in desired employment levels more generally. Unfortunately, we are not able to estimate dynamic models using the whole sample of firms, because only large, well-established firms have enough observations to allow us to identify both the effect of lagged employment and the firm-specific fixed effects.

Dynamic models of labor demand are presented in table 6. Since it is well known that the coefficient on lagged employment will be biased toward zero in the presence of fixed effects, we use a Generalized Method of Moments (GMM) procedure suggested by Arellano and Bond (1991).[10] Our models include one lag of employment. We report Sargan

---

[10] Arellano and Bond show that their procedure is more efficient than the usual solution of instrumenting lagged employment with second lags of the dependent variable.

Table 6
GMM Estimates (All Variables in First Differences) of Log Employment with Adjustment Costs

	All-Firm Level	Parastatals	Private High Impact	Private Exports <25%	Private Exports >25%
A. Measuring trade policy with tariffs:					
Lag (ln employment)	.157	.310	.074	.197	.070
	(.045)	(.084)	(.118)	(.043)	(.132)
Tariff	−.057	−.222	.087	.041	.053
	(.060)	(.135)	(.096)	(.069)	(.169)
International price	.039	.167	−.068	.014	−.084
	(.086)	(.254)	(.195)	(.092)	(.249)
Log alternative wage	.009	−.099	.077	.027	−.054
	(.033)	(.112)	(.072)	(.036)	(.108)
Log materials	.067	.064	.084	.061	.127
	(.009)	(.019)	(.021)	(.009)	(.027)
Sargan test	31.1	8.0	11.3	18.7	10.7
A-B test	−.84	−.91	.91	−.09	−.69
B. Measuring trade policy with quotas:					
Lag (ln employment)	.159	.303	.074	.200	.068
	(.045)	(.085)	(.012)	(.043)	(.132)
Quota coverage	−.054	.085	−.175	−.033	−.098
	(.032)	(.087)	(.076)	(.035)	(.100)
International price	.036	.160	−.038	.009	−.021
	(.086)	(.263)	(.196)	(.092)	(.255)
Log alternative wage	.004	−.104	.082	.025	−.061
	(.033)	(.115)	(.071)	(.036)	(.106)
Log materials	.067	.064	.084	.061	.126
	(.009)	(.019)	(.021)	(.009)	(.027)
Sargan test	31.9	8.8	12.2	18.5	10.7
A-B test	−.82	−.92	.96	−.07	−.75
No. of observations	7,668	296	1,348	6,612	760
No. of firms	1,917	74	337	1,253	190

NOTE.—Standard errors are in parentheses. All regressions include five time dummies. The Sargan test is an overidentification test distributed as a chi-square with 14 degrees of freedom. The critical value is 23.68 at the 95% confidence level. The A-B test is a test of second-order serial correlation, which is distributed as a standard normal. It is described in more detail in Arellano and Bond (1991).

tests of the implied overidentifying restrictions and a test of serial correlation based on the GMM residuals.[11] These tests indicate that it is not necessary to include additional lags of employment. The results of the Sargan test show a further advantage of disaggregating the data—although the overidentifying restrictions are violated in the sample as a whole, they are not rejected when coefficients are allowed to vary with firm type.

With the exception of parastatals, all the firms have coefficients on lagged employment of 0.2 or less, indicating that employment adjustment takes place within the year. Hence, these estimates are in the same range as most of the industrial country estimates surveyed by Hamermesh

[11] For further details, see Arellano and Bond (1988, 1991).

(1993).[12] However, it is interesting to note that in terms of speed of adjustment, private sector firms in Morocco appear to be more similar to North American firms than to European firms—the latter typically adjust employment more slowly. The coefficient on lagged employment of 0.31 for parastatals implies that they adjust much more slowly—these firms have carried only two-thirds of the eventual adjustment they will make within 1 year. These results suggest that the small impact of the reform cannot be attributed to an inflexible labor market, since even firms that show little adjustment to the trade reforms appear to adjust quickly to changes in desired labor demand more generally.

B. Adjusting Productivity and Profit Margins

Our results suggest significant heterogeneity in the way firms respond to trade reform. Parastatals show perverse employment responses, while domestically oriented firms and firms outside of highly affected sectors show very little employment response at all. If our model is correct, then we expect firms with small or perverse employment responses to adjust by cutting profit margins and raising productivity.

To identify the differential impact of the trade reform on margins and productivity, we borrow the framework outlined in Harrison (1994). Returning to our earlier framework, we would like to be able to estimate the structural equations (6) and (7). We could, for example, try to derive a measure of A, which is alternatively referred to as Hicks neutral technology or total factor productivity (TFP). Although a number of studies have in fact derived a measure of A in levels or changes and regressed it on trade policy, Harrison (1994) shows that such an approach is incorrect if there is imperfect competition. Instead, we estimate a production function that allows trade policy to affect both margins and productivity.

If we begin with the production function from equation (1), totally differentiate, and divide through by q, this yields

$$dq/q = (\partial q/\partial L)(dL/q) + (\partial q/\partial I)(dI/q) + dA/A. \quad (9)$$

If we combine (9) with (3) and the first-order conditions for other inputs, we have the following:

$$dq/q = \theta[(wL/Pq)(dL/L) + (rI/Pq)(dI/I)] + dA/A. \quad (10)$$

The value of wL/Pq and rI/Pq is simply the share of each factor in total output. We will allow for one other input, materials, in the estimation. We will denote the share of labor and materials α_l and α_m. If we allow

---

[12] See Hamermesh (1993), chap. 7, table 7.1.

trade policy to affect both margins and productivity, we can estimate the
following for a firm I at time t:

$$dy_{it} = B_0 + B_1 dx_{it} + B_2[dx*\text{TAR}]_{it} + B_3[dx*\text{QRCOV}]$$
$$+ B_4\text{TAR}_t + B_5\text{QRCOV} + df_{it}/f_{it} + u_{it} \quad (11)$$
$$\text{where } dx = [\alpha_l dl + \alpha_m dm]_{it}, dy_{it} = dq/q, B_1 = \theta,$$
$$\text{and } B_4\text{TAR}_t + B_5\text{QRCOV} + df_{it}/f_{it} = dA/A.$$

Lower-case variables y, l, and m are equal to lnq, lnL, and lnM; q, L,
and M, are firm-specific output, labor, and other inputs. The extent to
which the coefficient B_1 exceeds unity is a measure of market power. The
term df_{it}/f_{it} is a firm-specific effect in the growth rate. If productivity
increased during the reform, the coefficients on tariffs and quota coverage
B_4 and B_5 should be negative. If tariffs and quotas allow firms to exercise
greater market power, then the coefficients B_2 and B_3 should be positive.
Our estimation results for (11) are presented in table 7. The coefficient
on B_1 is significantly above one for all subsets of firms, indicating that
Moroccan firms do exercise some market power. Margins are highest for
public sector firms and lowest for exporting firms.

Table 7
Impact of Tariffs and Quotas on Margins and Productivity

	All-Firm Level	Parastatals	Private High Impact	Private Exports <25%	Private Exports >25%
A. Tariffs					
B_1 (measure of mark-ups)	1.097	1.159	1.071	1.090	1.049
	(.004)	(.023)	(.009)	(.005)	(.013)
B_2 (impact of tariffs on market power)	.000	.078	.040	.012	.053
	(.009)	(.071)	(.016)	(.012)	(.021)
B_4 (impact of tariffs on productivity)	−.044	−.002	−.039	−.040	−.146
	(.022)	(.146)	(.034)	(.027)	(.047)
R^2	.96	.96	.97	.97	.96
No. of observations	18,509	575	5,580	15,187	2,747
B. Quotas:					
B_1 (measure of mark-ups)	1.089	1.152	1.042	1.084	1.061
	(.003)	(.019)	(.010)	(.003)	(.011)
B_3 (impact of quotas on market power)	.021	.087	.071	.028	.028
	(.006)	(.040)	(.012)	(.006)	(.014)
B_5 (impact of quotas on productivity)	−.038	−.211	−.040	−.034	−.029
	(.012)	(.109)	(.022)	(.014)	(.027)
R^2	.96	.96	.97	.97	.96
No. of observations	18,508	615	5,580	15,186	2,746

NOTE.—Standard errors are in parentheses. All equations include time dummies and firm fixed effects.

The positive and statistically significant coefficient for B_3 provides strong support for the hypothesis that quota protection led to greater market power and that reductions in quota coverage also led to a reduction in margins. As suggested by the model, quotas were more likely than tariffs to have a significant impact on our measure of market power.

As expected, the trade reform was associated with significant increases in productivity, as indicated by the negative coefficients on B_4 and B_5. However, not all firms responded by raising productivity. In particular, firms in highly affected sectors failed to significantly increase productivity, in contrast to other enterprises. Surprisingly, public sector enterprises showed the greatest increases in productivity in response to reductions in quota coverage.

These results, in combination with the results presented earlier, suggest two broad approaches to the trade reform. Nonexporting, private sector firms outside of the most affected industries responded primarily by raising productivity and cutting profit margins. Firms in highly affected industries reacted primarily by cutting margins and employment, with no significant increases in productivity. Exporters reacted in every possible dimension: they cut margins, reduced employment, and raised productivity. Public sector enterprises, who increased employment in response to the reforms, nevertheless did adjust by raising productivity and lowering wages.

VII. Some General Equilibrium Considerations

Anne Krueger's (1983) book on trade and employment in developing countries argues that trade reforms should have expansionary effects on the labor market in cases where a nation's comparative advantage lies in labor-intensive goods. Krueger argues that industrializing countries typically protect their capital-intensive sectors, which implies that trade reforms would increase the relative price of labor-intensive goods and expand employment in those sectors. Although this article is primarily partial equilibrium in nature, it is interesting to speculate on whether Krueger's argument is valid for Morocco.

We begin the analysis with an examination of the firm-level data. If the trade reform did restore the comparative advantage to labor-intensive goods, then we would expect a reallocation of output toward labor-intensive firms. As a result, we would expect capital-intensive firms to make greater labor force adjustments. The first row of table 8 confirms that this is indeed the case. If we exclude public sector firms and split the sample into two equal groups, we see that employment reallocation was only significant for firms with higher capital-labor ratios. In fact, the negative coefficients on tariffs and quotas in the first two columns of table 8 suggest that declines in tariffs and quotas corresponded with increases in employment for labor-intensive firms, although these effects are not statistically significant. Estimates of the effects of tariffs and quotas

Table 8
The Role of Capital Intensity in Adjustment to Trade Reform

Impact of Trade Policy on	Low Capital Labor/ Ratio		High Capital/Labor Ratio	
	Tariffs	Quotas	Tariffs	Quotas
Employment	−.048	−.040	.097	.110
	(.048)	(.026)	(.060)	(.030)
Wages	.054	−.026	−.065	.027
	(.049)	(.027)	(.060)	(.030)
Mark-ups	.000	.038	.015	.019
	(.014)	(.009)	(.017)	(.009)
Productivity	.014	−.014	−.110	−.057
	(.034)	(.018)	(.042)	(.021)

NOTE.—Standard errors are in parentheses. The table shows coefficients on tariffs/quotas only. Underlying specifications are similar to those in tables 4, 5, and 7 above.

on mark-ups and productivity (corresponding to those shown in table 7) suggest that more capital-intensive firms reduced margins somewhat less than more labor-intensive firms but exhibited much greater increases in productivity in response to the reforms. Thus, this firm-level analysis is broadly consistent with the Krueger hypothesis.

However, most recent efforts to analyze the general equilibrium effects of trade reform on the relative returns to skilled and unskilled labor have focused not on within-industry variation but on differences across industries. The evidence in table 9, although not conclusive, suggests that the cross-industry variation in the pattern of protection and trade reform is not consistent with the Krueger hypothesis. Although labor-intensive sectors do account for most of the labor force growth during the second half of the 1980s, these were also the most protected sectors before liberalization, and they experienced the largest declines in tariffs and quotas. Morocco is not the only developing country to protect precisely those sectors where it has the greatest comparative advantage: Hanson and Harrison (1995) report a similar phenomenon for Mexico.

As indicated in table 9, employment grew fastest during the second half of the 1980s in the clothing sector (sector 14), which is also the most labor-intensive sector in Morocco. Between 1985 and 1990, the clothing sector increased its share of the manufacturing labor force from 3% to 22%. However, table 9 also shows that clothing was one of the two most protected sectors in Morocco prior to the trade reform and also experienced the largest declines in tariff and quota protection. How was the sector able to grow so fast and yet experience such sharp declines in tariff and quota protection?[13] The explanation seems to lie in the exchange

_____
[13] It is possible that the largest reductions in tariffs and quotas were made in sectors where they were expected to have the smallest adverse impact (perhaps

rate devaluations and institutional reforms which made it increasingly attractive to produce for the export market. Together, the trends at the industry-level and our firm-level analyses suggest that the clothing industry would have grown even faster in Morocco in the absence of trade reform and that, within this sector, it was the relatively capital-intensive firms that were most affected by reform.

VIII. Conclusions and Suggestions for Future Research

This article examined the impact of recent trade reforms in Morocco on employment and wages. Although employment in the average firm was unaffected by the tariff reductions and the elimination of quotas, there was a significant employment response in exporting firms and in the firms most highly affected by the reforms. The 21-point decline in tariff protection experienced by firms in most affected sectors—textiles, beverages, and apparel—was associated with a 3.5% decline in employment. Among exporting firms a 24-point decline in tariff protection was associated with nearly a 6% decline in employment.

Our results indicate that parastatals behaved quite differently than privately held firms. They actually increased employment in response to tariff reductions, mostly by hiring low-paid temporary workers. As a result, wages fell. Productivity in these firms also increased as quota coverage fell.

A significant fraction of manufacturing firms did not adjust either wages or employment in response to the trade reforms. We examine two possible explanations for this puzzle. First, we explore the possibility that barriers to labor market mobility, such as hiring and firing laws, could impede adjustment to reform. Our estimates of adjustment costs suggest that Morocco's formal sector labor force is in fact quite flexible, especially relative to European countries. However, as Hamermesh (1993) points out, it would be desirable to estimate dynamic models using quarterly or even monthly data because of aggregation biases. Ideally, one would also like to incorporate information about bottlenecks in other factors of production that might impede the adjustment of employment.

Second, we develop a model of labor demand which allows for imperfect competition and endogenous technological change. Our results suggests that many firms, including those that failed to adjust employment, responded to the reforms by cutting profit margins and raising productivity. This suggests another, less painful mode of adjustment:

---

because those sectors were growing rapidly in any case). In this case, the estimated effects of tariffs and quotas will be biased toward zero.

Table 9
The Evolution of Employment, K/L Ratios, Tariffs, and Quotas by Sector

Sector	1985 % of Employment	1990 % of Employment	Labor Force Growth, 1985–90	K/L Ratio in 1985	Tariff Rate in 1985	Quotas in 1985	Change in Tariffs, 1985–90	Change in Quotas, 1985–90
10	.11	.07	24.60	152.65	.47	.49	−.10	−.21
11	.13	.14	64.38	48.16	.45	.76	−.09	−.41
12	.03	.02	16.49	153.88	.88	.99	−.44	−.58
13	.21	.17	34.64	49.56	.55	.80	−.15	−.13
14	.03	.22	249.66	7.00	.74	.96	−.29	−.83
15	.03	.02	27.02	69.69	.59	.69	−.23	−.18
16	.04	.03	33.87	23.87	.29	.81	−.01	−.81
17	.05	.04	29.65	100.85	.29	.05	.05	−.05
18	.07	.06	45.14	186.01	.22	.24	.07	−.24
19	.01	.00	−11.91	458.19	.06	.13	.04	−.13
20	.08	.05	13.09	28.69	.29	.30	.03	−.30
21	.02	.02	49.12	28.41	.11	.05	.07	−.04
22	.03	.03	53.74	60.50	.18	.37	.06	−.28
23	.04	.03	27.80	42.12	.19	.15	.07	−.14
24	.00	.00	98.07	53.19	.18	.02	.03	−.02
25	.08	.07	43.67	295.57	.30	.22	−.06	−.17
26	.03	.03	42.55	56.33	.48	.13	−.05	−.09
27	.00	.00	81.60	4.92	.53	.46	−.16	−.46

firms with excess profits could absorb the shock, leaving the labor force unaffected.

Many questions remain unanswered. Unlike industrialized countries, developing countries have big informal sectors. Before we can draw firm conclusions about the distributional impact of reform, we need to look at the effects on these workers—perhaps using other measures of living standards besides wages (cf. Thomas, Lavy, and Strauss 1996). More disaggregated wage measures—which would allow us to examine the impact of the reforms on inequality within the formal sector—would also be desirable. Finally, although we have emphasized several advantages of using firm-level panel data, there are also limitations—the most notable being that we analyze a sample of continuing firms and do not consider the effects of entry and exit. If the factors that cause existing firms to grow (shrink) also encourage entry (exit), then the total effect of the trade reforms could be larger than the effects shown above.

References

Arellano, Manuel, and Bond, Steven. "Dynamic Panel Data Estimation Using DPD—a Guide for Users." Working Paper 88/15. London: Institute for Fiscal Studies, 1988.

———. "Some Tests of Specification for Panel Data: Monte Carlo Evidence and an Application to Employment Equations." *Review of Economic Studies* 58, no. 2 (April 1991): 277–97.

Bhagwati, Jagdish. "On the Equivalence of Tariffs and Quotas." In *Trade, Growth, and the Balance of Payments,* edited by Richard Caves, Harry Johnson, and Peter Kenen. Chicago: Rand McNally, 1965.

Currie, Janet. "Employment Determination in a Unionized, Public-Sector Labor Market: The Case of Ontario's School Teachers." *Journal of Labor Economics* 9, no. 1 (1991): 45–66.

Feliciano, Zadia M. "Workers and Trade Liberalization: The Impact of Trade Reforms in Mexico on Wages and Employment." Photocopy. Cambridge, MA: Harvard University, 1994.

Freeman, Richard. "Labor Market Institutions and Policies: Help or Hindrance to Economic Development?" Paper prepared for the World Bank's Annual Conference on Development Economics, Washington DC, World Bank, April 1992.

Freeman, Richard, and Katz, Lawrence. "Industrial Wage and Employment Determination in an Open Economy." *Immigration, Trade, and the Labor Market,* edited by John M. Abowd and Richard B. Freeman. Chicago: University of Chicago Press, 1991.

Gaston, Noel, and Trefler, Daniel. "The Role of International Trade and Trade Policy in the Labour Markets of Canada and the United States." *World Economy* 47, no. 4 (January 1994): 45–62.

Grossman, Gene. "Imports as a Cause of Injury: The Case of the U.S. Steel Industry." *Journal of International Economics* 20 (1986): 201–23.

———. "The Employment and Wage Effects on Import Competition in the United States." *Journal of International Economic Integration* 2 (1987): 1–23.

Hamermesh, Daniel. *Labor Demand.* Princeton, NJ: Princeton University Press, 1993.

Hanson, Gordon A., and Ann E. Harrison. "Trade, Technology, and Wage Inequality in Mexico." Working Paper no. 5110. Cambridge, MA: National Bureau of Economic Research, May 1995.

Harrison, Ann E. "Productivity, Imperfect Competition and Trade Reform: Theory and Evidence." *Journal of International Economics* 36, nos. 1–2 (February 1994): 53–73.

Harrison, Ann E., and Islam, Roumeen. "Morocco Private Sector Assessment: The Labor Market." Photocopy. Washington, DC: World Bank, 1993.

Krueger, Anne O. *Trade and Employment in Developing Countries.* Chicago: University of Chicago Press, 1983.

Lindauer, David; Meesok, O. A.; and Suebsaeng, P. "Government Wage Policy in Africa: Some Findings and Policy Issues." *World Bank Research Observer* 3 (January 1988): 1–25.

Rama, Martin. "The Labor Market and Trade Reform in Manufacturing." In *The Effects of Protectionism on a Small Country,* edited by Michael Connolly and Jaime de Melo. Washington, DC: World Bank Regional and Sectoral Studies, 1994.

Revenga, Anna. "Exporting Jobs? The Impact of Import Competition on Employment and Wages in U.S. Manufacturing." *Quarterly Journal of Economics* 107, no. 1 (February 1992): 255–84.

Thomas, Duncan; Lavy, Victor; and Strauss, John. "Public Policy and Anthropometric Outcomes in Cote d'Ivoire." *Journal of Public Economics* 61, no. 2 (August 1996): 155–92.

United Nations Development Program–World Bank Trade Expansion Program. *Morocco 2000: An Open and Competitive Economy.* Country Report 7. Washington, DC: World Bank, November 1990.

World Bank. "The Kingdom of Morocco: Developing Private Industry in Morocco." Report No. 11557-MOR. Washington, DC: World Bank, January 1993.

Chapter 3

TRADE LIBERALIZATION AND
WAGE INEQUALITY IN MEXICO[†]

GORDON H. HANSON and ANN HARRISON*

During the 1980s in Mexico the wage gap between skilled and unskilled workers widened. The authors assess the extent to which this
increased wage inequality was associated with Mexico's sweeping trade
reform in 1985. Examining data on 2,354 Mexican manufacturing
plants for 1984–90 and Mexican *Industrial Census* data for 1965–88, they
find that the reduction in tariff protection in 1985 disproportionately
affected low-skilled industries. Goods from that sector, the authors
suggest, may have fallen in price because of increased competition from
economies with reserves of cheap unskilled labor larger than Mexico's.
The consequent increase in the relative price of skill-intensive goods
could explain the increase in wage inequality.

D uring the 1980s, Mexico experienced
a dramatic increase in wage inequality. The wages of more-educated, more-
experienced workers rose relative to those
of less-educated, less-experienced workers.
While such events are interesting in their
own right, what makes the change in
Mexico's wage structure particularly note-
worthy is that it coincided with a sweeping

liberalization of trade. In 1985, Mexico
announced that it was joining the General
Agreement on Trade and Tariffs (GATT),
bringing an end to four decades of import-
substitution industrialization. The government proceeded to drastically reduce most
trade barriers in the following three years.
It was in 1985 that wage inequality in Mexico
began to rise.

In this paper, we analyze data on 2,354
Mexican manufacturing plants for 1984–90
together with Mexican *Industrial Census* data
for 1965–88 to assess the extent to which
the increase in the skilled-unskilled wage
gap in Mexico was associated with the opening of the Mexican economy. The motivation for studying the Mexican case is to
understand the apparent global trend toward greater wage inequality. Since the
1970s, the wages of skilled workers have
increased relative to those of unskilled workers in the United States and in Great Brit-

*Gordon H. Hanson is Associate Professor, De-
partment of Economics and School of Business Administration, University of Michigan, and Faculty
Research Fellow at the National Bureau of Economic
Research. Ann Harrison is Assistant Professor, Graduate School of Business, Columbia University, and
Faculty Research Fellow, NBER. This research was
sponsored by the World Development Report 1995
and World Bank research project 678-29, "Technology Spillovers, Agglomeration, and Direct Foreign
Investment." Hanson acknowledges financial support from the Center for the Study of Western Hemi-
spheric Trade at the University of Texas.

271

[†]This article originally appeared in *Industrial and Labor Relations Review*, **52** 271–288

ain.[1] Several recent studies link the rise in wage inequality to the increased openness of the U.S. economy, arguing that competition from low-wage countries has reduced the relative demand for unskilled workers and caused their wages to fall relative to those of skilled workers (Leamer 1993, 1998; Wood 1994; Feenstra and Hanson 1996a). Other studies instead associate rising wage inequality with technological change (Davis and Haltiwanger 1991; Bound and Johnson 1992; Lawrence and Slaughter 1993; Berman, Bound, and Griliches 1994). The reasoning is that the advent of computer technology has made skilled workers increasingly important in the workplace.

The focus of the literature has so far been on developed economies. Wage changes in middle- and low-income countries have received little attention.[2] This is unfortunate. If trade is contributing to wage changes in developed countries, then we should observe the opposite wage movements in developing-country relative wages. If global skill-biased technical change is the cause of relative-wage changes, then we should observe similar relative wage movements in high-wage and low-wage countries. Given Mexico's proximity to the United States and its recent opening to trade, the country is an ideal candidate in which to look for such changes.

The Stolper-Samuelson Theorem

The link that standard trade theory identifies between trade and wages is embodied in the Stolper-Samuelson (1941) theorem

and its generalizations (Ethier 1984). The Stolper-Samuelson logic is that trade affects relative factor rewards by changing relative prices. To explain wage changes in Mexico with this logic, we would need a succession of events such as the following. Trade liberalization causes the prices of skill-intensive goods to rise relative to those of non–skill-intensive goods. The price changes reduce the demand for labor in non–skill-intensive industries and increase the demand for labor in skill-intensive industries. The resulting shift in employment toward skill-intensive industries contributes to an increase in the relative demand for skilled workers, which causes their wages to increase relative to those of unskilled workers.

This story is consistent with either of two hypotheses. The first is that Mexico has a wealth of skilled labor and a dearth of unskilled labor relative to the rest of the world. In its reserves of skilled labor, Mexico is far behind the United States, of course, but it may have a decisive edge over low-income countries, such as China. The second hypothesis is that under import substitution Mexico extended trade protection preferentially to industries that make relatively intensive use of unskilled labor. Trade liberalization would then have a disproportionately large impact on non–skill-intensive sectors. Although such a policy would seem at odds with Mexico's presumed comparative advantage in low-skill activities, political considerations may have led the government to protect these industries. In either case, the Stolper-Samuelson explanation for the observed wage changes implies that (1) the relative prices of skill-intensive goods have increased, and (2) there has been a shift in employment toward skill-intensive sectors.

Recent literature on Mexican labor markets provides important insights into changes in the country's wage structure, but has yet to fully identify the channels through which trade affects wage inequality. Feliciano (1993) and Cragg and Epelbaum (1996), both using household-level data, found that the return to schooling increased in Mexico during the late

---

[1]On wage dispersion in the United States, see Davis and Haltiwanger (1991), Bound and Johnson (1992), and Katz and Murphy (1992); for international evidence, see Davis (1992).

[2]One notable exception is Robbins (1995), who found mixed evidence that trade contributes to increased wage inequality in developing countries. In Chile, Colombia, Costa Rica, and the Philippines, the relative wage of skilled workers rose following trade liberalization, while in Argentina and Malaysia wage inequality was stable or declining during periods of increased openness to trade.

1980s. Revenga (1997), using plant-level data, found that blue-collar wages and employment were more responsive to changes in trade protection than those of white-collar workers, which she attributed to the fact that blue-collar workers were relatively concentrated in industries that underwent the largest reduction in protection levels. Feenstra and Hanson (1997) found that the Mexican regions in which the relative demand for skilled labor rose most in the 1980s were those in which foreign investment was most concentrated, suggesting that foreign capital inflows may have contributed to rising wage inequality. Finally, Bell (1997) studied the impact of minimum wages on employment in Mexican manufacturing plants over the period 1984–90. Though real minimum wages fell substantially over the sample period, she found that minimum wages had no impact on manufacturing labor demand, which she attributed to the fact that the minimum wage was not binding for most manufacturing plants during the sample period. In 1984 minimum wages were 42% of the average blue-collar Mexican manufacturing wage; in 1990 the figure was 31%.[3] Bell's results are important, for they suggest that the decline in Mexican minimum wages during the late 1980s cannot account for the increase in wage inequality.

Relative Wages and Employment in Mexico

Data are available from two sources. We have annual data on 2,354 Mexican manu-

facturing plants for the period 1984–90 from the Secretariat of Trade and Industrial Promotion (SECOFI). The SECOFI sample is the only plant-level data source available in Mexico. It is fortunate for our purposes that the sample period spans the implementation of trade reform.

One cause for concern is that by design the SECOFI sample covers only medium and large plants.[4] In 1986, there was an average of 321 workers per establishment in the SECOFI sample, compared to 67 across all manufacturing establishments. To ensure that the empirical regularities we identify in the SECOFI sample are representative of Mexican industry as a whole, we also use data on manufacturing establishments from the Mexico *Industrial Census*. We have *Census* data on employment, number of establishments, and total payroll by state and two-digit (ISIC) manufacturing industry for the period 1965–88, at roughly five-year intervals. To a first approximation, the SECOFI sample is representative of the overall mix of industrial activity in Mexico. Unreported results show that the distribution of employment across two-digit (ISIC) industries in the SECOFI sample and in the *Industrial Census* are nearly identical.

A final issue we need to address before turning to the data is how to measure wages. To identify the effect of trade on relative wages, we must be able to distinguish workers by skill level. The SECOFI sample and

---

[3]The evidence on manufacturing wages does not imply that the minimum wage was nonbinding in all sectors, as manufacturing workers tend to be relatively highly paid. Using household-level earnings data for 1988, Bell found that a substantial number of individuals, most of whom were women working in the informal sector (outside of manufacturing), earned less than the legal minimum wage, which suggests that there is a high degree of non-compliance with minimum wage law in Mexico. Widespread non-compliance is an additional reason that the fall in real minimum wages may not have had substantial labor market consequences.

[4]In 1989, the SECOFI plants accounted for 29% of total manufacturing employment, as measured by the Mexico *Industrial Census*. One additional problem with the SECOFI sample of plants is that it contains a balanced panel—we do not observe entry or exit. This is unfortunate, for it means that we cannot explore the relationship between plant mortality and the relative employment of skilled workers.

While the SECOFI sample is representative of Mexican manufacturing overall, there is one important sector that is missing in the data. The sample by design excludes off-shore assembly plants, the so-called *maquiladoras*. Maquiladoras import from abroad virtually all of the inputs they use to assemble final goods. The plants in the SECOFI sample, in contrast, are more vertically integrated establishments.

Table 1. Average Tariffs and Import-License
Requirements by Two-Digit Industry, 1984–90 (Percent).

Industry		1984	1985	1986	1987	1988	1989	1990
31—Food Products	t	42.9	45.4	32.1	22.9	14.8	15.8	16.2
	q	100.0	80.1	62.2	33.3	20.8	20.6	16.8
32—Textiles, Apparel	t	38.6	43.2	40.4	26.6	16.8	16.6	16.7
	q	92.9	66.8	38.0	31.1	2.8	1.1	1.0
33—Wood Products	t	47.3	48.5	44.9	29.9	17.7	17.6	17.8
	q	100.0	75.6	25.7	0.0	0.0	0.0	0.0
34—Paper, Printing	t	33.7	36.5	34.8	23.7	7.7	10.1	9.9
	q	96.7	54.1	11.2	9.5	3.4	4.1	0.0
35—Chemicals	t	29.1	29.9	27.0	20.5	13.4	14.3	14.4
	q	85.7	54.0	21.1	4.8	0.0	0.0	0.0
36—Stone, Clay, Glass	t	37.1	38.5	33.8	22.4	13.8	14.3	14.3
	q	99.0	53.1	5.2	0.0	0.0	0.0	0.0
37—Basic Metals	t	13.6	16.7	18.4	13.8	7.9	11.0	11.0
	q	93.3	47.4	0.0	0.0	0.0	0.0	0.0
38—Metal Products	t	43.1	46.3	30.0	20.8	14.1	15.9	16.1
	q	90.7	74.8	54.7	51.4	42.7	44.1	44.1
39—Other Industries	t	40.9	42.9	40.5	27.5	17.1	18.1	18.4
	q	100.0	50.0	0.0	0.0	0.0	0.0	0.0

Notes: t = Production-weighted average tariff rate; q = weighted-average share of production subject to import-license requirements.

Source: Authors' calculations, SECOFI sample data.

the *Industrial Census* classify workers in two categories: *obreros,* who are equivalent to blue-collar workers, and *empleados,* who are equivalent to white-collar workers. The activities of blue-collar workers include machine operation, production supervision, repair, maintenance, and cleaning; those of white-collar workers include management, product development, administration, and general office tasks. We identify white-collar workers as skilled labor and blue-collar workers as unskilled labor. We measure earnings as the average annual salary or average hourly wage for each type of worker in a given plant. The white-collar–blue-collar distinction has obvious limitations, but the substantial wage differences between the two types of workers suggest that the division is a useful one.[5]

There are no data for Mexico that provide a more detailed plant-level breakdown of employment by type and by industry.[6]

The Liberalization of Trade

To frame the discussion, we begin by considering the dimensions of trade reform in Mexico. Mexico's economy was largely closed to trade from the 1950s until the mid-1980s. The government initiated a conscious policy of trade protection in the late 1940s, when it raised tariffs and insti-

[5]Berman, Bound, and Griliches (1994) and Schmitt and Mishel (1996) provided evidence for the United States suggesting that the white-collar–blue-collar classification is a reasonable division of the labor force by skill.

[6]A second problem with the blue-collar–white-collar classification is that neither data source breaks down non-wage compensation by worker type. Our measure of earnings excludes non-wage payments. This omission does not appear to be egregious, as wages account for the majority of payments to workers. In the SECOFI sample, the wage share of total compensation was 0.71 in 1984 and 0.69 in 1990; in the *Industrial Census,* the wage share of total compensation was 0.73 in both 1985 and 1988.

TRADE LIBERALIZATION AND WAGE INEQUALITY IN MEXICO   275

Table 2. Average Annual Real Wages in Manufacturing, 1984–1990.
(Values in 1980 Pesos)

Year	White-Collar		Blue-Collar		White-Collar/Blue-Collar	
	Annual Earnings	Hourly Wages	Annual Earnings	Hourly Wages	Annual Earnings	Hourly Wages
1984	138,793	62.127	72,528	32.191	1.914	1.930
1985	143,692	63.856	74,952	32.783	1.917	1.948
1986	137,444	60.641	68,525	29.929	2.006	2.027
1987	134,474	59.014	67,559	29.243	1.991	2.018
1988	122,241	53.557	57,781	24.729	2.116	2.166
1989	145,487	64.278	62,755	26.809	2.318	2.398
1990	160,502	70.460	64,935	27.691	2.472	2.545

Source: Authors' calculations based on SECOFI sample data.

tuted a system of import licenses. Successive administrations expanded trade barriers, mainly by increasing the range of goods covered by import licenses. These licenses effectively gave the government the discretion to impose import quotas at will. The government also used export controls to direct production toward the domestic market.

The government decided to open the economy to trade in 1985. It moved swiftly, drastically lowering most trade barriers within three years. In mid-1985, the national average tariff was 23.5%, and import-license requirements covered 92.2% of national production. By December 1987, import-license coverage had been reduced to 25.4% of national production and the average tariff had been reduced to 11.8%, with a maximum rate of 20%. Concurrent with reform, the government abolished export controls and devalued the nominal exchange rate.

Table 1 shows annual production-weighted-average tariffs and import-license coverage by two-digit (ISIC) industry for the period 1984–90.[7] In 1984, the average

tariff ranged from 13.6% in basic metals to 47.3% in wood products; import licenses were required for over 85% of products in all two-digit industries. The government first cut import-license requirements, reducing average import-license coverage to below 4% by 1988 in all industries except food products and metal products. It then proceeded to reduce tariffs; by 1990, the maximum tariff rate in any industry group was 18.4%, for "other industries." The only industry that continued to enjoy relatively high levels of protection was metal products, due to import restrictions on automobiles.

Concomitant with trade reform, the Mexican government removed many barriers to foreign investment, including limits on the foreign share of equity ownership in a Mexican firm and requirements that foreign firms obtain government approval for technology transfer from abroad and other activities (Feenstra and Hanson 1997). In 1983, following the onset of the Mexican debt crisis, there was a de facto relaxation of restrictions on foreign investment. These changes were codified into law in 1989.

In the mid-1980s, the Mexican government also launched a program to privatize state-owned firms (Lopez-de-Silanes 1997). Within manufacturing, two sectors, basic metals (iron and steel) and petroleum products, were subject to wide-scale state ownership. Privatization affected a far larger share of production in these industries than in other two-digit manufacturing indus-

---

[7]The tariff and import-license data we use are from unpublished records of SECOFI, available on request from the authors. These data are discussed extensively in Ten Kate (1992) and Ten Kate and de Mateo V. (1989).

Figure 1. Ratio of White-Collar to Blue-Collar Average Wages in Mexico, 1965–1988.

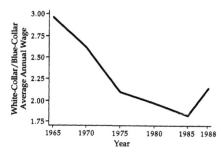

Source: *Industrial Census.*

and 1990, the ratio of average hourly white-collar and blue-collar wages increased from 1.93 to 2.55; the ratio of average annual white-collar and blue-collar earnings show a similar change, increasing from 1.91 to 2.47. The rise in the skilled-unskilled wage differential was due to a combination of real-wage increases for white-collar workers and real-wage decreases for blue-collar workers. Between 1984 and 1990, average real hourly wages for white-collar workers increased by 13.4%, while those for blue-collar workers decreased by 14%.[11]

The *Industrial Census* shows similar movements in the white-collar–blue-collar wage gap. Figure 1 plots the ratio of average annual white-collar wages to average annual blue-collar wages in Mexican manufacturing for the period 1965–88. Between 1985 and 1988, the white-collar–blue-collar wage ratio rose from 1.84 to 2.16, which matches the movements in the SECOFI sample over the same time period. Of greater significance, the rise in the wage gap after 1985 appears to have halted a two-decade trend toward decreasing wage inequality.

The wages we report are average levels and do not control for changes in the composition of the labor force or for changes in the distribution of skill. In general, one should exercise caution in speculating about individual-level wage changes based on average wage changes. Nevertheless, the changes in relative wages in Table 2 are so large and occur over such a short period of time that it is extremely unlikely that they could be accounted for by compositional changes. The wage changes we report are consistent with household-level data on wage changes in Mexico over the

tries.[8] Further, in iron and steel, conflicts between unions and new owners over the interpretation of pre-existing (that is, government-negotiated) collective bargaining agreements led to the virtual collapse of production in several large plants. To distinguish the effects of trade reform from those of privatization, we present some of our results excluding petroleum products, iron, and steel from the sample of manufacturing industries.[9]

Wages and Employment

Since 1984, there has been a dramatic increase in white-collar–blue-collar wage inequality among manufacturing workers in Mexico. Table 2 shows average real wages and average relative wages for the SECOFI sample of plants.[10] Between 1984

---

[8]The Mexican constitution places myriad restrictions on the ownership of subsoil resources. These restrictions prevented petroleum refineries from being privatized, but some petrochemical firms were transferred to private hands.

[9]Currie and Harrison (1997) suggested that parastatal firms behave quite differently from private firms.

[10]Real wages are calculated as nominal annual remuneration per worker or per hour worked, deflated by the June consumer price index in a given year.

---

[11]The total change for the period masks large real-wage swings that occurred within the period. Real white-collar wages declined by 16.1% between 1985 and 1988 and then increased sharply, surpassing their 1985 levels by 1989. What the real-wage swings may reflect is unanticipated inflation in 1986 and 1987. While unexpected inflation can perhaps account for a temporary decline in wages for both types of workers, it cannot account for the increase in the white-collar–blue-collar wage gap over the period.

TRADE LIBERALIZATION AND WAGE INEQUALITY IN MEXICO   277

Table 3. Relative Employment, All Manufacturing, 1984–1990.

Year	Number of Workers			Thousands of Hours Worked		
	White-Collar	Blue-Collar	Ratio	White-Collar	Blue-Collar	Ratio
1984	234,851	545,477	0.431	524,666	1,229,016	0.427
1985	239,847	560,738	0.428	539,713	1,282,056	0.421
1986	242,189	550,963	0.440	548,925	1,261,465	0.435
1987	241,528	545,937	0.442	550,368	1,261,272	0.436
1988	243,741	549,839	0.443	556,327	1,284,741	0.433
1989	248,840	566,737	0.439	563,229	1,326,644	0.425
1990	250,066	577,405	0.433	569,629	1,353,991	0.421
Log Change, 1984–90	0.063	0.057		0.082	0.097	

Source: Authors' calculations based on SECOFI sample data.

same period reported in Feliciano (1993), Cragg and Epelbaum (1996), and Bell (1997).

One source of relative-wage changes is shifts in the demand for different skill categories. An increase in the relative demand for skilled labor would cause an increase in both the wages and employment levels of skilled workers relative to those of unskilled workers.[12] Table 3 shows the ratio of white-collar to blue-collar employment for the SECOFI sample. Between 1984 and 1990, there was virtually no aggregate change in relative employment. The ratio of white-collar to blue-collar employment increased from 0.431 to 0.433; the ratio of white-collar to blue-collar hours worked decreased from 0.427 to 0.421. Industry-level data also fail to indicate substantial changes in relative employment. Unreported figures show that four (of nine) two-digit industries experienced an increase in the relative employment of white-collar labor, while five two-digit industries experienced a decline. No industry showed large changes in either direction.[13]

The *Industrial Census* shows somewhat larger changes in relative employment. Figure 2 plots the ratio of white-collar employment to blue-collar employment for the period 1965–88. The ratio fell from 0.346 in 1985 to 0.328 in 1988. The relative-employment movements after 1985 arrested a two-decade trend toward greater relative employment of white-collar workers. We also calculate relative employment by two-digit industry for the *Industrial Census* in 1985 and 1988 (not shown). Seven (of nine) industries show a decline in relative white-collar employment, while two show an increase.

One possible explanation for the rising skill premium and the declining use of skilled labor is that the supply of skilled labor shifted to other sectors or migrated abroad. This could account for both a reduction in the share of skilled employment and an increase in the skilled wage. There is no evidence suggesting that the composition of Mexican emigrants changed over the 1980s. Borjas (1994) found that the average education level of Mexican immigrants in the United States arriving between 1980 and 1990 was the same as that

---

[12]There is considerable evidence that rising wage inequality in the United States is due to an increase in the relative demand for skilled labor (Bound and Johnson 1992; Katz and Murphy 1992).

[13]One explanation for the lack of relative employment changes is that the supply of skilled labor is inelastic in the short to medium run. While this idea is plausible, it would require a high degree of immo-

bility between manufacturing and other sectors on the part of skilled labor. The secular increase in relative white-collar employment from 1965 to 1985, which is evident in Figure 2, suggests that skilled labor is relatively mobile.

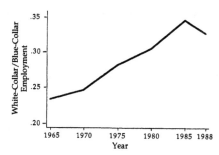

Figure 2. Ratio of White-Collar to Blue-Collar Employment in Mexico, 1965–1988.

Source: Industrial Census.

of pre–1980 arrivals. The average educational level of Mexican immigrants to the United States is lower than that of immigrants from any other major source country. Borjas also found that during the 1980s the wages of Mexican immigrants in the United States declined relative to those of ethnically similar U.S. natives. This suggests that, if anything, there was an increase in the relative emigration of *unskilled* workers from Mexico during the 1980s. There is also little evidence of a shift of employment out of manufacturing into other sectors. The manufacturing share of the total labor force increased during the 1980s, rising from 16.7% in 1980 to 19.9% in 1988.

The Heckscher-Ohlin Model: Prices, Industry Composition, and Wages

The data show a substantial increase in the skilled-unskilled wage gap in Mexico following the liberalization of trade, but little change in the relative employment of skilled labor. One explanation for this pattern, consistent with the Stolper-Samuelson theorem, would be that trade increased the relative price of skill-intensive products. In this section, we search for evidence of Stolper-Samuelson effects.

Relative prices and skill intensity. To determine if relative price changes correspond to the observed relative-wage changes, we consider the correlation between relative-price changes and relative skill intensity. In a many-good, many-factor world, there is no general definition of relative factor intensity. The crude measure of skill intensity that we use is the log ratio of white-collar to blue-collar employment. If relative price increases in skill-intensive sectors account for increasing returns to skill, then we should see a positive relationship between skill-intensity and price increases in the 1980s.

Table 4 reports regressions of the log change in output prices on the log ratio of white-collar to blue-collar employment over the 1984–90 period. The unit of observation is the four-digit manufacturing industry.[14] We measure employment as the average annual number of workers by skill type. Since we are looking at discrete, rather than infinitesimal, price changes, we average log relative white-collar employment over the first and last period. We use two measures of prices: gross output prices, measured using a four-digit producer price index, and value-added prices, calculated using the output price index, input price indices, and input cost shares.[15] We also

---

[14]The four-digit industry classification code we use is that in the SECOFI data, which is based on Mexico's *Industrial Census.* It is similar to the SIC code used in the United States.

[15]We can write the log change in the industry gross output price between 1984 and 1990 as

$$\Delta \log PPI = vashare * \Delta \log PVA + matshare * \Delta \log PMAT + energyshare * \Delta \log PENERGY,$$

where PPI is the industry producer price index, PVA is the price of value-added, PMAT is the price index for material inputs, PENERGY is the price index for energy, and Δ indicates the change over 1984–90. The shares of value-added, materials, and energy in total costs are given by *vashare, matshare,* and *energyshare,* where the shares are averaged over the first and last period. Given this equation, we can calculate the log change in the value-added price as

$$\Delta \log PVA = (1 / vashare)(\Delta \log PPI - matshare * \Delta \log PMAT - energyshare * \Delta \log PENERGY).$$

Table 4. Relative Price Changes and Skill Intensity. (Dependent Variable: Change in Log Price, 1984–1990)

Prices	Log Ratio of White-Collar Employment to Blue-Collar Employment	N	R-Square
All Sectors			
Gross-Output Prices	0.039 (0.76)	125	0.006
Value-Added Prices	−0.003 (−0.02)	125	0.000
Excluding Petroleum Products, Iron, and Steel			
Gross-Output Prices	−0.011 (−0.25)	119	0.001
Value-Added Prices	−0.129 (−0.99)	119	0.010

Notes: Observations are all four-digit Mexican manufacturing industries in the SECOFI sample. All regressions are weighted by the average industry share of total manufacturing output in 1984 and 1990. T-statistics, based on heteroskedasticity-consistent standard errors, are reported in parentheses. Log relative white-collar employment is the average for 1984 and 1990. Coefficient estimates for constant terms are not shown.

Table 5. Trade Protection and Skill Intensity.

Trade Law	Log Ratio of White-Collar to Blue-Collar Employment	
	All Industries	Excluding Petroleum Products, Iron, and Steel
Tariff 1984	−0.136	−0.184**
Import License 1984	−0.006	−0.003
Tariff Change, 1984–90	0.150*	0.195**
Import License Change, 1984–90	−0.076	−0.087

Notes: The table shows raw correlations of the log ratio of white-collar to blue-collar employment averaged in 1984 and 1990, the average industry import-license coverage rate in 1984, the change in industry tariff from 1984 to 1990, and the change in industry import-license coverage rate from 1984 to 1990. Observations are for either the 125 four-digit Mexican manufacturing industries or the 119 industries excluding petroleum products, iron, and steel. Correlations are weighted by the average industry share of total manufacturing output in 1984 and 1990.
*Statistically significant at the .10 level; **at the .05 level.

redo the analysis excluding petroleum products, iron, and steel industries, where state-owned firms initially played a large role and where substantial privatization occurred. To be consistent with the four-digit definitions of output prices, tariffs, and import-license coverage rates (all of which the Mexican government constructs by applying output weights to more disaggregated data), we weight all regressions by the industry share of total manufacturing output; results using employment weights are similar.

We find no significant correlation, positive or negative, between price changes and relative white-collar employment using either gross output prices or value-added prices. Excluding petroleum products, iron, and steel leaves the results unaffected.

Although the findings do not support Stolper-Samuelson effects, there are several possible explanations. One problem is

that changes in product prices reflect many changes in the economy in addition to trade reform, such as privatization and deregulation. Industry-wide price changes may thus be a poor measure of changes in trade policy. A more serious problem is that industry price changes may be a poor measure of actual price changes. Price indices capture changes in the prices of goods firms actually produce, rather than price changes for a fixed set of goods. If trade causes firms to alter the mix of goods they manufacture (Feenstra and Hanson 1996b), then our measure of product price changes will confound pure price changes with compositional effects. One indication of problems in using product price data is that correlations between price changes and skill intensity for the United States are sensitive to changes in either the time period or the sample of industries (Lawrence and Slaughter 1993; Krueger 1995; Schmitt and Mishel 1996).

An alternative price-based measure of changes in trade policy is tariffs. Indeed, for a small open economy, which is a reasonable description of post–trade reform Mexico, changes in tariffs fully capture trade policy–induced changes in product prices. We examine whether the pattern of tariffs and import licenses varied across industries according to the skill intensity of production. Table 5 presents raw correlations of industry tariffs and import-license coverage rates in 1984, changes in these variables over the 1984–90 period, and the log ratio of white-collar to blue-collar employment for four-digit manufacturing industries.

In light of the wide range of trade protection measures used in the literature, it is worth describing our measures in detail. The tariff for a four-digit industry is the production-weighted average administrative ad valorem tariff across all products within the industry. The import-license coverage rate for a four-digit industry is the fraction of output within the industry that is subject to import-license requirements. Both tariffs and coverage rates are thus percentage values. We calculate changes in these variables as the time difference over the 1984–90 period. Import-license coverage rates are somewhat difficult to interpret, as they are an indirect indication of quantity restrictions on trade. While import licenses give the government the discretion to impose quotas, we have no information on where quotas were actually binding.

Pre–trade reform tariff levels appear to have been lower in skill-intensive industries than in non–skill-intensive industries. Relative white-collar employment is negatively correlated with 1984 tariffs. This correlation is not statistically significant for all manufacturing industries, but it is significant once petroleum products, iron, and steel are excluded. More important, it also appears that tariff reductions were smaller in skill-intensive industries. There is a positive correlation between relative white-collar employment and the change in tariffs over 1984–90. This correlation is statistically significant at the 10% level for all industries and significant at the 5% level

when we exclude petroleum products, iron, and steel.[16] In both samples of industries, relative white-collar employment is negatively correlated with import-license coverage rates in 1984 and with the change in coverage rates over 1984–90, but neither correlation is statistically significant.

The correlations between tariffs and skill intensity in Mexico are supportive of Stolper-Samuelson effects. Skill-intensive sectors were less protected and consequently had smaller reductions in tariff levels. Why Mexico protected low-skill industries is a puzzle, given the country's presumed comparative advantage in these sectors. Similar patterns of protection have been reported for other developing countries. Currie and Harrison (1997) found that in Morocco protection was significantly higher in sectors with a higher share of unskilled workers, such as textiles and clothing. They also found these sectors to be the most export-intensive. Paradoxically, the Moroccan government gave greater protection to the sectors in which it had the highest comparative advantage, if comparative advantage can be measured by export orientation. For Mexico, Revenga (1994, 1995) also found that the pattern of protection was skewed toward export-intensive sectors. The evidence suggests that developing countries often protect sectors in which they are likely to have a comparative advantage, such as the sectors with a high share of unskilled workers. In this light, it is not surprising that increasing wage inequality is observed in developing countries undergoing trade reforms.

The results presented in Tables 4 and 5 suggest that while changes in trade policy are consistent with Stolper-Samuelson effects, changes in product prices are not. Since Mexico historically protected sectors with more unskilled workers, tariffs fell less in sectors with more skilled workers. In a

---

[16]At the plant level, we also find a positive and statistically significant correlation between relative white-collar employment and either the initial tariff level or the change in tariffs.

Stolper-Samuelson framework, this translates into an increase in the relative wage of skilled workers. Below, we explore the extent to which price changes and commercial policy were correlated during the 1980s.

Correlations between price changes and trade policy changes. We present correlations between product price changes and commercial policy in Table 6. We again use two measures of product prices, gross output prices and value added prices. We include an interaction term between tariffs and import-license coverage rates to account for the fact that the application of tariffs and quotas may be correlated across industries. Since the interaction term makes it difficult to evaluate the impact of an individual policy using the reported coefficient estimates, we report the net impact of tariffs and import licenses on product price changes at sample means for tariffs and licenses. To control for possible nonlinearities in how import licenses translate into trade protection, we include two additional indicator variables. In regressions using initial protection levels as regressors, we include a dummy variable for whether import licenses covered 100% of goods produced in the industry, which may indicate cases in which binding quotas were more likely. In regressions using the change in protection levels as regressors, we include a dummy variable for whether import licenses were completely eliminated in the industry, which may indicate cases in which the reduction in quotas was most significant.

First, consider the correlation between price changes and initial levels of trade protection. For either measure of prices and for either sample of industries, the coefficients on tariffs and import-license coverage rates are negative and statistically significant, while the coefficient on the interaction term between tariffs and import licenses is positive and statistically significant. The net impact of policy changes shows that for gross-output prices (column 1) the impact of initial tariffs on price changes is negative, suggesting that prices fell more in sectors with higher initial tariffs. We obtain a similar result excluding

petroleum products, iron, and steel (column 5). When we use value-added prices instead of gross-output prices (columns 3 and 7), the net impact of initial tariffs is reversed. Price changes appear to be higher in industries with higher initial tariffs. It is important to note, however, that in all cases the net impact of initial tariffs on price changes is very small relative to mean price changes for the sample period.

For import licenses, the findings are more consistent. For either price measure, the net impact of initial import licenses on price changes is positive (columns 1, 3, 5, 7), suggesting that relative price changes were higher in sectors with higher initial license coverage. As with tariffs, the net impact of import licenses is very small relative to mean price changes for the period. Despite the statistical significance of the coefficients, initial levels of trade protection appear to say little about the magnitude of price changes over the sample period.

Next, consider the correlation between price changes and changes in protection (columns 2, 4, 6, 8). In all regressions, price changes are positively correlated with the change in tariffs and the change in import-license coverage rates but negatively correlated with the interaction between tariffs and import licenses. These correlations, however, are statistically significant at the 10% level only for gross-output prices, excluding petroleum products, iron, and steel (column 6). Despite the lack of statistical significance, it is worth considering the net impact of changes in trade policy on product price changes. In all regressions, the net impact of either the change in tariffs or the change in import licenses on price changes is positive, providing weak evidence that relative prices rose in sectors that experienced the smallest reductions in trade protection.[17] It is again the case that the net impact of changes in trade policy

---

[17]Somewhat in contrast to these results, relative prices appear to have increased in sectors that completely eliminated import licenses.

Table 6. *Relative* Price Changes and Trade Policy.
(Dependent Variable: Change in Log Prices, 1984–90)

Independent Variable	All Industries				Excluding Petroleum Products, Iron, and Steel			
	Dependent Variable: Gross-Output Prices (mean = 2.85)		Dependent Variable: Value-Added Prices (mean = 2.69)		Dependent Variable: Gross-Output Prices (mean = 2.85)		Dependent Variable: Value-Added Prices (mean = 2.70)	
Tariffs	−0.030 (−2.90)	—	−0.085 (−2.40)	—	−0.030 (−3.14)	—	−0.085 (−2.46)	—
Import Licenses	−0.010 (−2.27)	—	−0.032 (−2.25)	—	−0.009 (−2.27)	—	−0.030 (−2.22)	—
Tariffs*Licenses	0.0003 (2.86)	—	0.001 (2.46)	—	0.0003 (3.10)	—	0.001 (2.51)	—
Complete License Coverage	0.043 (0.48)	—	0.080 (0.36)	—	−0.042 (−0.58)	—	−0.066 (−0.32)	—
Change in Tariffs	—	0.009 (1.58)	—	0.021 (1.34)	—	0.009 (1.65)	—	0.021 (1.39)
Change in Licenses	—	0.002 (1.48)	—	0.006 (1.09)	—	0.002 (1.77)	—	0.006 (1.17)
Change in Tariffs* Licenses	—	0.0001 (−1.56)	—	0.0002 (−1.53)	—	−0.0001 (−1.61)	—	−0.0002 (−1.52)
Eliminated Licenses	—	0.157 (2.89)	—	0.581 (1.79)	—	0.165 (2.94)	—	0.598 (1.85)
Net Impact of Policy:								
Tariffs	−0.002	0.017	0.009	0.037	−0.002	0.017	0.008	0.037
Licenses	0.001	0.004	0.004	0.010	0.003	0.004	0.009	0.011
N	125	125	125	125	119	119	119	119
R^2	0.040	0.047	0.050	0.085	0.090	0.075	0.069	0.101

Notes: Observations are four-digit Mexican manufacturing industries. All regressions are weighted by the average industry share of total manufacturing output in 1984 and 1990. T-statistics, based on heteroskedasticity-consistent standard errors, are reported in parentheses. See text for description of tariffs and import-license coverage rates. Complete License Coverage is a dummy variable equal to one if 100% of goods in the industry were subject to import-license requirements in 1984. Eliminated Licenses is a dummy variable equal to one if the industry eliminated all import-license requirements between 1984 and 1990. The Net Impact of Policy is calculated at mean values for tariffs and import-license coverage rates, whether in levels or changes. Coefficient estimates for constant terms are not shown.

on product prices is very small relative to mean values for price changes over the 1984–90 period.

Regressions of product price changes on tariffs and import licenses provide weak support for the Stolper-Samuelson theorem. We do find that relative price increases were higher in sectors with smaller reductions in trade barriers, which, coupled with our finding that skill-intensive sectors had the lowest reductions in tariffs, would be consistent with Stolper-Samuelson, but this correlation is neither statistically significant nor economically significant. The weak correlation between price changes

and changes in trade policy again suggests that aggregate price indices may be poor measures of actual product price changes.

Reallocation of employment and skill intensity. Strictly speaking, Stolper-Samuelson does not require that trade reallocate labor across industries. Relative price changes alone may generate changes in relative factor awards. Nevertheless, if the relative prices of skill-intensive goods rose, we would expect reallocation of labor toward those sectors.

Despite the magnitude of trade reform, there was little employment reallocation across industries. In unreported results, we

TRADE LIBERALIZATION AND WAGE INEQUALITY IN MEXICO   283

Figure 3. Relationship between White-Collar Employment Growth and Skill Intensity in Mexico, 1984–1990.

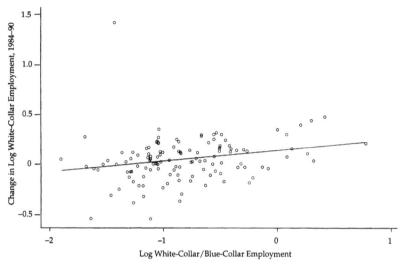

Source: SECOFI.

construct industry shares of national employment by type of worker for 1984 and 1990. The largest relative-employment declines occurred in textiles and apparel (ISIC 32), whose share of total manufacturing employment fell from 0.128 to 0.112, and iron and steel (ISIC 37), whose employment share fell from 0.075 to 0.061; these two industries also experienced a decline in absolute employment over the period. The largest relative employment increases occurred in food products (ISIC 31), whose employment share increased from 0.195 to 0.214, and metal products (ISIC 38), whose employment share increased from 0.266 to 0.280; these two industries experienced absolute employment growth over the period. The changes in industry employment shares resulted almost entirely from changes in relative blue-collar employment; the distribution of

white-collar employment across industries stayed nearly constant over the period.

Even though changes in industrial composition following trade reform were small, we want to know if the industries that experienced the most employment growth are those that are relatively intensive in the use of skilled labor. To see if there was a shift in employment toward skill-intensive sectors, we ask whether employment growth was higher in sectors that employed a relatively high share of white-collar workers. Figure 3 plots the change in log employment of white-collar workers between 1984 and 1990 against the average log ratio of white-collar to blue-collar employment in 1984 and 1990 by four-digit industry. The relationship between skill intensity and employment growth is positive and statistically significant, suggesting employment growth was higher in skill-intensive sectors.

56   *Globalization, Firms, and Workers*

284   INDUSTRIAL AND LABOR RELATIONS REVIEW

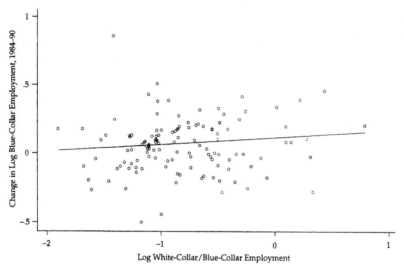

Figure 4. Relationship between Blue Collar Employment Growth and Skill Intensity in Mexico, 1984–1990.

Source: SECOFI.

Figure 4 shows that there is also a positive, though weaker, correlation between blue-collar employment growth and skill intensity. Hence, there is evidence that employment growth was relatively high in skill-intensive sectors.

The role of foreign direct investment. We have found that skill-intensive sectors were less protected than non–skill-intensive sectors and thus had smaller reductions in trade barriers (Table 5), which suggests that trade reform may have contributed to an increase in the white-collar–blue-collar wage gap. While there is weak evidence linking changes in trade protection to changes in product prices (Table 6), there is no direct evidence linking relative price increases to skill-intensive sectors (Table 4). One possibility is that changes in commercial policy are a more precise measure of how trade reform affected product prices in Mexico than are changes in aggregate price indices.

A second possibility is that changes in trade policy are correlated with other changes in the Mexican economy, which affected skill-intensive sectors positively. Feenstra and Hanson (1997) suggested one such possibility. They examined whether foreign outsourcing influences the demand for skilled and unskilled labor in Mexico. Outsourcing by U.S. firms to Mexico increased dramatically during the 1980s, following Mexico's relaxation of restrictions on foreign direct investment. At the level of regional manufacturing industries, they found that the relative demand for skilled labor was positively correlated with the change in the number of foreign off-shore assembly plants, which suggests that foreign direct investment may have contributed to increasing wage inequality in Mexico.

TRADE LIBERALIZATION AND WAGE INEQUALITY IN MEXICO 285

Table 7. Foreign Direct Investment, Skill Intensity, and Trade Policy.
(Dependent Variable: Change in the Log Stock of Foreign Capital, 1984–90)

Independent Variable	All Industries		Excluding Petroleum Products, Iron, and Steel	
	(1)	*(2)*	*(3)*	*(4)*
Log Ratio of White-Collar to Blue-Collar Employment	0.052 (1.28)	0.065 (1.75)	0.027 (0.75)	0.048 (1.22)
Tariffs	0.010 (0.56)	—	0.010 (0.56)	—
Import Licenses	0.006 (0.95)	—	0.008 (1.39)	—
Tariffs*Licenses	−.0001 (−0.53)	—	−0.0001 (−0.58)	—
Complete License Coverage	0.101 (0.85)	—	−0.023 (−0.37)	—
Change in Tariffs	—	0.008 (0.98)	—	0.006 (0.74)
Change in Licenses	—	0.001 (0.39)	—	0.0002 (0.11)
Change in Tariffs*Licenses	—	−0.0001 (−1.08)	—	0.0001 (−0.75)
Eliminated Licenses	—	−0.280 (−4.83)	—	−0.249 (−4.06)
N	115	115	109	109
R^2	0.149	0.216	0.140	0.198

Notes: Observations are four-digit Mexican manufacturing industries. All regressions are weighted by the average industry share of total manufacturing output in 1984 and 1990. T-statistics, based on heteroskedasticity-consistent standard errors, are reported in parentheses. See text for description of tariffs, import-license coverage rates, and the measure of foreign capital. See notes to Tables 5 and 6 for other variable definitions. Coefficient estimates for constant terms are not shown.

To pursue this issue, we examine whether the correlation that we find between trade policy and skill intensity could be proxying for the correlation between foreign investment and skill intensity. In Table 7, we report regressions of the change in the stock of foreign capital on relative white-collar employment and either the level of or change in trade protection in Mexico.

There are no published data on the aggregate stock of foreign capital by industry in Mexico. We use the SECOFI data to generate such a measure. For each plant, the data indicate the share of equity ownership by foreign agents, as well as the value of fixed capital at year-end replacement cost. For a given four-digit industry, we measure the change in the stock of foreign capital as the change in the value of fixed capital in plants that have a foreign equity ownership share of at least 5%.[18]

One problem with this measure is that the share of foreign equity ownership is only available in 1990, while the value of fixed capital is available in all sample years. Our measure is thus the change in the capital stock over 1984–90 in plants that were at least 5% foreign-owned in 1990.[19]

---

[18]In 1990, 24.8% of the plants had a foreign equity ownership share of at least 5%. Aitken, Hanson, and Harrison (1997) showed that most foreign investment in Mexico is from the United States.

[19]Feenstra and Hanson (1997) measured the change in the foreign capital stock as the change in the number of off-shore assembly plants, which are the agents of foreign outsourcing in Mexico, at the region (and not industry) level. The SECOFI sample

Since foreign investment in Mexican manufacturing increased over the sample period, our measure likely over-estimates the industry change in the foreign capital stock (since more plants were foreign-owned at the end of the period than at the beginning). To examine whether upward bias in the change in the foreign capital stock contaminates the regression results, we tried alternative minimum foreign equity ownership shares (10%, 20%, 30%, 50%) to calculate the change in the foreign capital stock. Results using these alternative measures are very similar to those reported in Table 7.

It does not appear that foreign investment can account for the observed correlation between skill intensity and trade protection. In Table 7, the correlation between the change in the log foreign capital stock and log relative white-collar employment, while positive in all cases, is statistically significant at the 10% level in only one regression. There is also no statistically significant correlation between changes in the foreign capital stock and either the initial level of or the change in tariffs or import-license coverage rates. The only statistically significant correlation between foreign investment and trade protection is a negative relationship between growth in foreign capital stock and the complete elimination of import licenses in a sector (columns 2 and 4). This provides support for tariff-jumping explanations of foreign investment. Foreign firms seem to have avoided sectors from which all quota protection was removed.

There is some contrast between our results and those in Feenstra and Hanson (1997), but this may be attributable to the different definitions of foreign capital used in the two papers. Feenstra and Hanson

measured changes in the foreign capital stock by the change in the number of foreign off-shore assembly plants, which follows from their emphasis on foreign outsourcing. The SECOFI sample, however, excludes these plants by design (see notes 4 and 19). Thus, we find a weak positive correlation between foreign investment and skill intensity, excluding plants that are dedicated exclusively to foreign outsourcing.

To summarize our findings, over the period 1984–90 Mexico experienced an increase in the white-collar–blue-collar wage gap; little change in the ratio of white-collar to blue-collar employment; a fall in trade barriers, with evidence that initial tariff levels and reductions in tariffs were lower in skill-intensive sectors than in non-skill-intensive sectors; higher employment growth in skill-intensive sectors; and higher foreign investment in sectors that maintained import quotas than in sectors that dropped them. We do not find that relative prices rose in skill-intensive sectors, although industry price indices may be noisy measures of product-price changes.

Conclusion

We have examined changes in the relative wages and relative employment of skilled and unskilled workers in Mexico that followed the country's 1985 trade reform. Since the enactment of trade reform, there has been a dramatic increase in the skilled-unskilled wage gap. The relative-wage changes have occurred without large changes in relative employment. One of our primary concerns has been to search for the effects of trade reform on relative prices and the sectoral distribution of labor that could explain the relative-wage changes.

While we do not find a positive correlation between skill intensity and relative product price changes during the 1980s, we do find that Mexico offered relatively high trade protection to low-skill industries. The reduction in trade barriers was most dramatic in these sectors, which suggests that trade reform affected unskilled

---

of plants that we use excludes off-shore assembly plants by design (see note 4). Thus, we measure the change in the foreign capital stock using a non-overlapping sample of plants (and we measure foreign capital at the industry rather than region level).

TRADE LIBERALIZATION AND WAGE INEQUALITY IN MEXICO   287

labor disproportionately. This finding is consistent with a world in which Mexico has an intermediate abundance of skilled labor. The exposure of Mexico to competition from China and other countries that have abundant unskilled labor appears to have contributed to a decrease in the relative wages of unskilled workers.

REFERENCES

Aitken, B., Gordon Hanson, and Ann Harrison. 1997. "Spillovers, Foreign Investment, and Export Behavior." *Journal of International Economics,* Vol. 43, No. 1/2, pp. 103–32.

Bell, Linda A. 1997. "The Impact of Minimum Wages in Mexico and Columbia." *Journal of Labor Economics,* Vol. 15, No. 3, pp. S102–S126.

Berman, Eli, John Bound, and Zvi Griliches. 1994. "Changes in the Demand for Skilled Labor within U.S. Manufacturing: Evidence from the Annual Survey of Manufacturers." *Quarterly Journal of Economics,* Vol. 109, No. 2, pp. 367–98.

Borjas, George J. 1994. "The Economics of Immigration." *Journal of Economic Literature,* Vol. 32, No. 4, pp. 1667–1717.

Bound, John, and George Johnson. 1992. "Changes in the Structure of Wages in the 1980s: An Evaluation of Alternative Explanations." *American Economic Review,* Vol. 82, No. 3 (June), pp. 371–92.

Cragg, Michael I., and Mario Epelbaum. 1996. "Why Has Wage Dispersion Grown in Mexico? Is It the Incidence of Reforms or the Growing Demand for Skills?" *Journal of Development Economics,* Vol. 51, No. 1, pp. 99–117.

Currie, Janet, and Ann Harrison. 1997. "Sharing the Costs: The Impact of Trade Reform on Capital and Labor in Morocco." *Journal of Labor Economics,* Vol. 15, No. 3, pp. S44–S72.

Davis, Stephen J. 1992. "Cross-Country Patterns of Change in Relative Wages." In Olivier Blanchard and Stanley Fischer, eds., *NBER Macroeconomics Annual 1992.* Cambridge, Mass.: MIT Press.

Davis, Stephen J., and John Haltiwanger. 1991. "Wage Dispersion between and within U.S. Manufacturing Plants, 1963–86." *Brookings Papers on Economic Activity: Microeconomics 1991.* Washington, D.C.

Ethier, Wilfred J. 1984. "Higher Dimensional Issues in Trade Theory." In Ronald W. Jones and Peter B. Kenen, eds., *Handbook of International Economics.* Amsterdam: North-Holland.

Feliciano, Zadia. 1993. "Workers and Trade Liberalization: The Impact of Trade Reforms in Mexico on Wages and Employment." Mimeo, Harvard University.

Feenstra, Robert C., and Gordon H. Hanson. 1996a. "Globalization, Outsourcing, and Wage Inequality." *American Economic Review Papers and Proceedings,* Vol. 86, No. 2, pp. 240–45.

———. 1996b. "Foreign Investment, Outsourcing, and Relative Wages." In Robert C. Feenstra, Gene M.

Grossman, and Douglas A. Irwin, eds., *Political Economy of Trade Policy: Essays in Honor of Jagdish Bhagwati.* Cambridge: MIT Press, pp. 89–127.

———. 1997. "Foreign Direct Investment and Relative Wages: Evidence from Mexico's Maquiladoras." *Journal of International Economics,* Vol. 42, No. 3/4, pp. 371–94.

Katz, Lawrence, and Kevin M. Murphy. 1992. "Changes in Relative Wages, 1963–1987: Supply and Demand Factors." *Quarterly Journal of Economics,* Vol. 107, No. 1 (February), pp. 35–78.

Krueger, Alan B. 1995. "Labor Market Shifts and the Price Puzzle Revisited." Mimeo, Princeton University.

Lawrence, Robert Z., and Mathew J. Slaughter. 1993. "Trade and U.S. Wages: Great Sucking Sound or Small Hiccup?" *Brookings Papers on Economic Activity,* Vol. 2, pp. 161–227.

Leamer, Edward. 1993. "Wage Effects of a U.S.–Mexico Free Trade Agreement." In Peter M. Garber, ed., *The Mexico–U.S. Free Trade Agreement.* Cambridge, Mass.: MIT Press.

Leamer, Edward E. 1998. "In Search of Stolper-Samuelson Linkages between International Trade and Lower Wages." In Sharon M. Collins, ed., *Imports, Exports, and the American Worker.* Washington, D.C.: Brookings Institution Press, pp. 141–203.

Lopez-de-Silanes, Florencio. 1997. "Determinants of Privatization Prices." *Quarterly Journal of Economics,* Vol. 112, No. 4, pp. 965–1026.

Revenga, Ana. 1997. "Employment and Wage Effects of Trade Liberalization: The Case of Mexican Manufacturing." *Journal of Labor Economics,* Vol. 15, No. 3, pp. S20–S43.

———. 1995. "North American Integration and Factor Price Equalization: Is There Evidence of Wage Convergence between Mexico and the United States?" Mimeo, World Bank.

Robbins, Donald. 1995. "Trade, Trade Liberalization, and Inequality in Latin America and East Asia: Synthesis of Seven Country Studies." Mimeo, HIID.

Schmitt, John, and Lawrence Mishel. 1996. "Did Trade Lower Less-Skilled Wages during the 1980s? Standard Trade Theory and Evidence." Mimeo, Economic Policy Institute.

Stolper, Wolfgang, and Paul A. Samuelson. 1941. "Protection and Real Wages." *Review of Economic Studies,* Vol. 9, No. 1 (November), pp. 51–68.

Ten Kate, Adrian. 1992. "Trade Liberalization and Economic Stabilization in Mexico: Lessons of Experience." *World Development,* Vol. 20, No. 5 (May), pp.

659–72.

Ten Kate, Adrian, and Fernando de Mateo Venturini. 1989. "Aperatura Comercial y Estructura de la Protección en Mexico: Un Analisis de la Relación entre Ambas." *Comercio Exterior*, Vol. 39, No. 6 (June), pp. 31–43.

Wood, Adrian. 1994. *North-South Trade, Employment, and Inequality*. Oxford: Clarendon.

Chapter 4

Wages and foreign ownership
A comparative study of Mexico, Venezuela, and the United States[†]

Brian Aitken[a], Ann Harrison[b,c], Robert E. Lipsey[c,d,e]

[a]International Monetary Fund, .., USA
[b]Columbia University, .., USA
[c]NBER, 50 East 42nd Street, 17th Floor, New York, NY 10017-5405, USA
[d]Queens College, .., USA
[e]Graduate Center, CUNY, .., USA

Revised 1 October 1995

Abstract

This paper explores the relationship between wages and foreign investment in Mexico, Venezuela, and the United States. Despite very different economic conditions and levels of development, we find one fact that is robust across all three countries: higher levels of foreign investment are associated with higher wages. However, in Mexico and Venezuela, foreign investment is associated with higher wages only for foreign-owned firms – there is no evidence of wage spillovers leading to higher wages for domestic firms. The lack of spillovers in Mexico and Venezuela is consistent with significant wage differentials between foreign and domestic enterprises. In the United States, where the evidence suggests some wage spillovers from foreign to domestic enterprises, wage differentials are smaller.

---

1. Introduction

Recent developments in growth theory emphasize the important role played by human capital formation. Although human capital is acquired through formal schooling, research and development, or even international trade, Lucas (1993) argues that on-the-job training is by far the most important avenue. In particular, he shows that on-the-job training is associated with rapid growth when the labor force moves quickly into more and more productive activities. This is the so-called 'quality ladder', described in Grossman and Helpman (1991a, 1991b).

[†]This article originally appeared in *Journal of International Economics*, **40** 345–371

346   *B. Aitken et al. / Journal of International Economics 40 (1996) 345–371*

Apart from scattered case studies (see, example, the steep learning curves in Liberty Ship production described in Lucas, 1993), empirical evidence on the linkages between human capital formation, on-the-job training, and economic growth is limited. In this respect, micro-level evidence on multinational enterprises could be quite useful. Since foreign direct investment presumably represents a transfer of technology or ideas to the host country, it provides an opportunity to identify empirically the linkages between human capital formation, on-the-job training, and productivity growth. Entry by foreign multinationals provides the host country with access to knowledge. This access is enhanced if the foreign investor's knowledge is absorbed by domestic workers, increasing the domestic stock of human capital and making the local labor force permanently more productive. Moreover, foreign direct investment can facilitate the spread of knowledge to domestically owned firms, either directly through, for example, the training of suppliers, or indirectly through imitation and labor mobility.

Beyond its contribution to human capital through on-the-job training, foreign direct investment can play an important role by facilitating the flow of ideas across national borders. Indeed, Romer (1993) refers to the 'idea gap' to describe differences in the utilization of productive knowledge across countries, as opposed to the differences in physical capital and levels of education, or the 'object gap'. Romer argues that cross-country data and other evidence support the claim that a country's growth performance has as much to do with its utilization of ideas embodied in foreign direct investment as with the accumulation of capital or the extent of secondary-school enrollment. While Romer emphasizes the spread of knowledge from developed to developing countries, this does not preclude idea gaps from existing in certain industries between countries of equal development. The relevant question is whether foreign direct investment contributes to growth by filling idea gaps that exist between countries, whether developing or developed.

Evidence that multinational firms play a significant role in 'catch up' can be examined by measuring the impact of foreign direct investment (FDI) on domestic wages. If multinationals bring ideas to the host country, foreign investors should put upward pressure on wages as the marginal productivity of workers in those plants rises. If this productivity advantage is significant, equilibrium wages should rise in response to increases in FDI. If, however, FDI affects labor demand in the same way as domestic investment, the role of foreign direct investors in transmitting productive knowledge is limited.

This paper measures the impact of foreign direct investment on wages in the United States, Mexico, and Venezuela, drawing implications for the role of foreign investors in the transmission of knowledge and the formation of human capital. We find in Section 2 that, in all three countries, wages are higher where foreign-owned production is greater. However, in the case of Mexico and Venezuela, the higher overall wage is due to higher wages only in foreign-owned firms – there are no positive wage spillovers to domestic enterprises. Section 3 examines the evidence on wage differentials between foreign and domestic firms.

B. Aitken et al. / Journal of International Economics 40 (1996) 345–371   347

2. Testing for wage spillovers

2.1. Foreign direct investment and the spread of intangible assets

Foreign direct investors in a country presumably have access to productive knowledge not available to host-country domestic producers. The 'industrial organization' approach to foreign direct investment suggests that multinational firms can compete locally with domestic firms only because multinational firms possess intangible productive assets such as technological know-how, marketing and managing skills, export contacts, coordinated relationships with suppliers and customers, and reputation.[1] Often the intangibility of these assets makes them much less costly to transfer to subsidiaries in a host economy than to license at arm's length to host country firms. Direct investment is the manner in which the multinational firm overcomes the market imperfections related to the sale of intangible productive assets.

Data restrictions make it difficult to test directly whether in fact foreign ownership carries any productive advantage. While it is usually the case that foreign firms exhibit higher labor productivity than domestic firms, they also tend to congregate in capital intensive industries and, particularly in developing countries, in regions with more advanced infrastructure. In one of the few statistical tests of the issue, Aitken and Harrison (1993) find that for Venezuelan manufacturing plants, after controlling for capital stock and factors affecting productivity such as size, industry and location, higher foreign equity participation is strongly correlated with higher plant total factor productivity.

Even if foreign investors bring their productive advantage to the host economy, it is far from evident that foreign firms play a quantitatively significant role in the spread of productive knowledge to domestic firms. There is no doubt that foreign investors often can facilitate the spread of productive knowledge; numerous case studies illustrate the channels through which foreign investors have improved the performance of domestic firms, including improved access to technology, management and marketing practices, and buyer–seller linkages in foreign markets.[2] In addition, foreign firms typically show a stronger commitment to technical and managerial training, particularly for skilled workers.[3]

However, the empirical evidence on the overall impact of foreign firms in the diffusion of knowledge remains mixed. In support of an important role for foreign firms as export catalysts, Aitken et al. (1994) find that Mexican manufacturing firms were significantly more likely to export when foreign firms were located nearby. Caves (1974) and Globerman (1979) find that domestic firms in sectors with greater foreign ownership were more productive. This result was confirmed in

---

[1] See Caves (1982) and Helleiner (1989) for surveys on technology and foreign direct investment.
[2] See Rhee and Belot (1989), Mody et al. (1991), for recent case studies.
[3] See Reuber (1973, p.202), Goncalves (1986).

348   *B. Aitken et al. / Journal of International Economics 40 (1996) 345–371*

the case of Mexico in a series of studies summarized in Blomström (1989). Aitken and Harrison (1993) however, find that this relationship disappeared in Venezuela after controlling for the fact that foreign investment is concentrated in more productive industries; while foreign investment raises productivity overall, the gains are internalized or captured by other foreign firms, with productivity in domestic firms actually declining. This result is consistent with a 1970s OECD study of 65 subsidiaries in twelve developing countries, which found little evidence of spillovers to domestic firms. The study attributed this finding to a number of factors, including limited hiring of higher-level domestic employees, very little labor mobility between foreign and domestic firms, limited domestic subcontracting, and few incentives for multinationals to diffuse knowledge to local competitors (Germidis, 1977).

2.2. Modeling framework

The impact of multinational firms' wages can be interpreted in a standard supply and demand framework for labor. Given the local supply of labor, the demand schedule will be represented by the marginal product of labor derived from the aggregate production function for all firms – domestically- and foreign-owned – producing in the local labor market. If foreign-owned firms have a productive advantage over their domestically owned counterparts, an increase in foreign presence in the labor market – all else equal – will raise productivity, thereby raising labor demand for a given set of factors. Provided the labor supply curve in the local labor market is upward sloping, the result will be an increase in the equilibrium wage.

More explicitly, we start with a production function for a given location and industry given by

$$Y = A(DFI)f(X,L), \tag{1}$$

where *DFI* is the share of labor in the market employed by foreign firms and serves as a proxy for foreign presence in the industry and region, *L* is the labor employed by the industry, and *X* includes all other factors of production. Equilibrium in this labor market is achieved when

$$W = PRICE*MP_L = PRICE*[A(DFI)f_1(X,L(W))], \tag{2}$$

where *W* is the wage, and *L(W)* denotes the labor supply curve.

The hypothesis that we test is that foreign-owned firms raise the overall marginal productivity of labor. To test this, we regress wages in a given location and industry on foreign presence, controlling for other factors that affect wages or overall labor demand. Log-linearizing Eq. (2) yields

$$\log W = C + \alpha_1 DFI + \alpha_2 \log PRICE + \alpha_3 \log X - \alpha_4(v \log W), \tag{3}$$

B. Aitken et al. / Journal of International Economics 40 (1996) 345–371   349

where v is the elasticity of labor supply. In a Cobb–Douglas specification for production, where the only other input X is capital, α_3 and α_4 would be equal to the output shares of capital and labor. We estimate the reduced form of Eq. (3), which becomes

$$\log W = 1/[(1 + \alpha_4 v)(C + \alpha_1 DFI + \alpha_2 \log PRICE + \alpha_3 \log X)] \qquad (4)$$

or

$$\log W = C' + [\alpha_1/(1 + \alpha_4 v)]DFI + [\alpha_2/(1 + \alpha_4 v)] \log PRICE$$
$$+ [\alpha_3/(1 + \alpha_4 v)] \log X. \qquad (5)$$

If foreign investors bring with them knowledge that raises average productivity, then α_1 will be greater than zero. Since Eq. (5) is a reduced form for wages and not a labor demand equation, however, we do not directly observe α_1. Instead, we estimate $\alpha_1/(1 + \alpha_4 v)$. Since the value of $\alpha_4 v$ is positive, as long as labor supply is not perfectly elastic ($v =$ infinity), wages will increase with foreign investment when α_1 is positive. If labor mobility between industries and regions is significant, resulting in a more elastic labor supply, the estimated coefficient on DFI will understate the true impact of foreign enterprises on domestic wages.

Since the effects of foreign ownership may vary across worker characteristics, we estimate separate wage equations for skilled (sk) and unskilled (usk) workers. The X variables include capital stock (KSTOCK) and royalty payments (ROYAL-TY), which proxy for industry-specific acquisition of technology. We also include an industry dummy (SIC), and a region dummy (LOC) that captures various location specific factors such as the human capital of the labor force, agglomeration, and infrastructure. DFI is measured as the share of labor employed by foreign-owned firms in the industry (SIC) and region, while e is a random shock. This yields the two estimating equations:

$$\log W_{sk} = \alpha_0 + a_1 DFI + \alpha_2 \log PRICE + \alpha_3 ROYALTY + \alpha_4 KSTOCK$$
$$+ LOC + SIC + e, \qquad (6)$$

$$\log W_{usk} = B_0 + B_1 DFI + B_2 \log PRICE + B_3 ROYALTY + B_4 KSTOCK$$
$$+ LOC + SIC + e. \qquad (7)$$

If the coefficient on foreign share, α_1 or B_1, is positive, then a greater foreign presence increase wages in the region. Since the capital stock measure, KSTOCK, includes both domestic and foreign capital, Eq. (6) and Eq. (7) control for the increases in capital stock that could accompany the foreign investment and independently lead to wage increases. In other words, the coefficient on capital captures the 'direct' impact of DFI on wages (via labor demand), whereas the coefficient on DFI measures the 'indirect' impact via technology.

If foreign firms 'steal' the best domestic workers or only invest in the most productive or highest paying domestic firms, increases in *DFI* should be uncorrelated with log *W*, since the overall pool of labor has not changed, and α_1 and B_1 should be zero. If foreign firms only invest in regions or industries that pay higher wages, then α_1, and B_1 would be zero since *SIC* and *LOC* are included in the regression.

2.3. Data issues

The data for Venezuela, Mexico, and the United States to estimate Eq. (6) and Eq. (7) were all taken from manufacturing surveys. For Mexico, data are drawn from a sample of 2113 Mexican manufacturing plants surveyed by the Secretariat of Trade and Industrial Promotion (Secofi). The variables include factor usage, domestic and foreign sales, equity ownership positions by country of origin, price indices on inputs and outputs, four-digit industry classification, and the state in which the plant is located. For Venezuela, the data are taken from the Venezuelan industrial survey (*Enquesta Industrial*), which is conducted annually by the National Statistical Bureau. The survey covers all plants in the formal sector with more than 50 workers, as well as a large sample of smaller plants. The data contain information on foreign ownership, assets, employment, detailed cost information, location, and product destination.

Individual plant data for Venezuela and Mexico were aggregated up to a four-digit industry level, while industry level data by state were used for the United States. The plant-level databases for Venezuela and Mexico were aggregated up to the detailed industry level to capture the fact that wages are determined at a broader level than at the individual firm.

However, estimating Eq. (6) and Eq. (7) using the data at the plant level (see Table 3) yielded very similar results.

Wages are defined as the log of average wages for each four-digit industry, region, and year. As with all plant data, wages must be defined as the total wage bill for each skill category at the plant level (including basic wages and overtime but excluding benefits) divided by the number of employees in that skill category. In Mexico and the United States, location is defined by state, while in Venezuela, plants are identified at the state and district level. Capital stock is in log form, defined as the reported capital stock at the firm level, adjusted for inflation and aggregated up to the industry and district/state level for each year. To avoid endogeneity problems, *KSTOCK* is lagged one period. Price effects are captured by the log of the four-digit producer price. If available, a regional CPI is also included.

The definition of foreign owned in the US data was ownership of 10% or more of equity in the enterprise owning an establishment by a foreign resident, and all employees of such establishments were classified as employed by foreign-owned firms. The definition of foreign owned in the Venezuelan and Mexican data was ownership of any equity in the enterprise by foreign residents, but workers in each

B. Aitken et al. / Journal of International Economics 40 (1996) 345–371 351

establishment were then allocated between foreign and domestic ownership according to the shares in equity. In addition, the United States data did not begin to become available until 1987, and are therefore used here only in cross-sectional form, while the data for Venezuela cover the period 1977 through 1989, and those for Mexico 1984 through 1990, thus providing variation over time as well as geographically within each country.

2.4. Empirical results

The estimation results for Venezuela and Mexico are reported in Table 1. The first four columns of Table 1 report the impact of foreign investment in Venezuela, where foreign investment is measured as the share of employment in enterprises with foreign equity investment at the region–district level. The first two columns report the impact of foreign investment on aggregate wages for foreign and domestic enterprises combined. For both skilled and unskilled workers, a higher share of foreign employment raises overall wages. The impact is similar across both skill groups. The coefficient, which varies from 0.22 (for unskilled workers) to 0.29 (for skilled workers), suggests that a 10% increase in the share of foreign investment in overall employment in a region and industry would raise wages by 2.2 to 2.9%. The results also suggest that payments for royalties, which proxies for acquisition of technology, are highly correlated with wages. An increase in the share of royalty payments in sales from 0 to 1% would increase wages between 0.7 and 2.1%.

The next two columns of Table 1 report the relationship between foreign investment and wages for domestic enterprises only – enterprises with no foreign equity share. The results suggest that in Venezuela there are no positive wages spillovers from foreign investment to domestically owned enterprises. In fact, the wage effects appear to be negative. The negative impact is likely to be due to a combination of two factors. First, to the extent that foreign enterprises poach on domestic competitors, selecting the best workers, this could account for the observed negative coefficient on *DFI*. Second, as we show in Aitken and Harrison (1993), increasing foreign competition has been associated in the short run with declining productivity of domestically owned plants in Venezuela, which is reflected here in lower wages. Although the net impact of more foreign investment is positive, as shown in the first two columns, all the benefits are concentrated in firms with foreign equity. These results are consistent across skilled and unskilled workers.

The results using the same specification for Mexico are reported in the last four columns of Table 1. For Mexico, only the output price is included in the estimation, since a regional price deflator was not available. The first two columns for Mexico, which report the impact of foreign investment on overall wages, are generally consistent with the Venezuelan results. A 10% higher share of foreign firm employment would be associated with skilled wages 2.2% higher. However,

352   B. Aitken et al. / Journal of International Economics 40 (1996) 345–371

Table 1
The relationship between foreign direct investment and manufacturing industry wages in Mexico and Venezuela (dependent variable: log wage (W))

	Venezuela				Mexico			
	All enterprises		Domestic only		All enterprises		Domestic only	
	Sk wages	Usk wages	Sk wages	Usk wages	Sk wages	Usk wages	Sk wages	Usk wages
DFI	0.2870 (5.8)	0.220 (6.4)	-0.166 (3.2)	-0.142 (4.0)	0.215 (10.3)	0.033 (2.1)	-0.055 (1.4)	0.024 (0.8)
KSTOCK	0.111 (40.0)	0.069 (39.9)	0.109 (38.5)	0.069 (38.9)	0.080 (23.8)	0.060 (23.4)	0.079 (19.1)	0.053 (17.5)
ROYALTY	2.117 (5.6)	0.682 (2.6)	1.340 (3.5)	0.554 (2.0)	1.894 (5.0)	1.455 (5.2)	2.129 (3.3)	1.522 (3.5)
OUTPUT PRICE	0.019 (0.7)	-0.019 (1.0)	0.037 (1.3)	-0.013 (0.7)	0.115 (2.4)	0.112 (3.1)	0.070 (1.2)	0.084 (2.0)
REGION PRICE	0.065 (0.6)	-0.275 (3.7)	0.0658 (0.6)	-0.254 (3.4)	–	–	–	–
Industry dummies	Yes	Yes	Yes	Yes	Yes	Yes	Yes	Yes
Region dummies	Yes	Yes	Yes	Yes	Yes	Yes	Yes	Yes
Year dummies	Yes	Yes	Yes	Yes	Yes	Yes	Yes	Yes
N	10870	12322	10793	12263	4717	4726	3650	3664
R-square	0.47	0.44	0.44	0.41	0.50	0.56	0.46	0.53

Note: t-statistics in parentheses.

B. Aitken et al. / Journal of International Economics 40 (1996) 345–371   353

the positive impact of foreign investment is significantly lower for unskilled workers than for skilled employees.

The last two columns report the impact of foreign investment in Mexico on wages for domestic enterprises only. The results suggest that foreign investment had either no impact or a slightly negative (but statistically insignificant) impact on skilled and unskilled wages in domestically owned Mexican establishments. The results are consistent with those for Venezuela in pointing to no spillovers from foreign investment to wages in domestic enterprises.

Could the negative or zero impact of foreign investment on wages in domestic enterprises reflect 'poaching' by foreign enterprises? If foreign enterprises simply steal away the best workers from domestic enterprises, more foreign investment will be associated with higher wages in joint ventures and lower wages in domestic enterprises. Yet if foreign investment simply led to a reallocation of labor towards firms with foreign equity and had no impact on labor productivity, then the impact of DFI on aggregate wages would be zero. It is clear from Table 1, however, that higher foreign investment is associated with higher wages for the labor force as a whole.

The impact of foreign investment on US wages is presented in Table 2. As mentioned above, the results in Table 2 exploit only the geographical and industry variation in foreign investment and wages. State and industry effects on wage levels are represented not by dummy variables, as for Venezuela and Mexico, but by quantitative variables. For state effects, these are averages across detailed industries of state wages relative to national wages. For industry effects, they are averages across states of industry wages relative to state wages. The average wage in an industry in a state was regressed on DFI and the two control variables for industry and state wage levels. As in Venezuela and Mexico, the higher the share of employment in foreign-owned firms, the higher the average wage, after taking account of state and industry wage effects. A very different picture emerges, however, for wages in domestically owned plants. In the United States, a larger share of foreign firms in employment is associated with both higher average wages and higher wages in domestic establishments. Thus, in the United States, the

Table 2
The relation between foreign direct investment and wages in the United States 1987: cross-state regressions (dependent variable: average wage, by industry and state)

DFI^a	Wages in all establishments 37.192 (11.1)	Wages in domestic establishments 34.368 (10.3)
State wage level[b]	3.564 (2.4)	3.457 (1.4)
Industry wage level[b]	9.379 (2.3)	9.547 (4.2)
N	1091	1091
R-square	0.12	0.11

Note: t-statistics in parentheses.
[a]Employment in foreign-owned establishments as per cent of total employment in that industry in that state.
[b]For definition, see text.

evidence is consistent with positive spillovers from foreign investment to domestic wages. These results provide a direct contrast to the lack of spillovers in Venezuela and Mexico, where it appears that all the positive wage effects of foreign investment are concentrated in foreign enterprises.

2.4.1. Venezuela and Mexico: robustness

We also explored the robustness of the results in Table 1 by altering the basic specification in four different directions. First, we re-estimated the results using plant-level instead of industry-level data. Second, we incorporated the impact of plant age on wages. Third, we took into account the impact of plant size, since foreign investors tend to be concentrated in larger plants – where wages are typically higher. Finally, we addressed the issue of endogeneity of foreign investment and wages. None of these alternative specifications affected the results reported in Table 1.

The results in Table 1 were derived by aggregating up plant-level information to industry-level aggregates. In Table 3, we tested whether the wage effects reported in Table 1 are robust across both plant-level and industry-level samples. The impact of foreign investment at this disaggregated level can be decomposed into two effects: the direct impact of ownership at the plant level, and the spillovers from a foreign investment presence in the industry and region. If the results in Table 1 for Venezuela and Mexico are correct, then we would expect that all the beneficial effects of foreign investment would be internalized within the plant.

The results in Table 3 also take into account the role of vintage in wage determination. One alternative explanation for the higher wages observed in foreign-owned enterprises is that new investment is associated with higher worker productivity. If foreign investors are disproportionately represented among new investors, the positive correlation between foreign participation and wages could represent a 'vintage' effect. Two obvious proxies for vintage effects are the age of a plant and the extent of new investment. Since plant age is available only for Venezuela, vintage effects are captured by adding plant age for Venezuela and current real investment for Mexico.

As indicated is in the first four columns of Table 3, the impact of ownership on wages is robust to the inclusion of an age variable. Plant-level foreign investment is associated with significant increases in wages, with the coefficients very close in magnitude to those reported in Table 1. Consistent with the earlier results, the positive effects of foreign investment are completely internalized within each plant, with negative or insignificant spillovers as indicated by the coefficient on regional *DFI*. The coefficient on the age variable is positive and statistically significant, indicating that wages are higher in older plants. This result is at odds with the hypothesis that newer plants are likely to have more productive workers. One explanation for the result is that older plants may also be larger, a possibility that we explore below.

B. Aitken et al. / Journal of International Economics 40 (1996) 345–371   355

Table 3
Testing for vintage effects in Mexico and Venezuela (dependent variable: log wage (W))

| | Venezuela | | | | Mexico | | | |
| | All enterprises | | Domestic only | | All enterprises | | Domestic only | |
	Sk wages	Usk wages	Sk wages	Usk wages	Sk wages	Usk wages	Sk wages	Usk wages
DFI (plant level)	0.354 (12.8)	0.239 (12.2)	–	–	–	–	–	–
DFI (region)	-0.059 (1.7)	-0.030 (1.2)	-0.061 (1.5)	-0.067 (2.4)	0.211 (10.1)	0.037 (2.2)	-0.014 (0.4)	0.039 (1.3)
Age of plant	0.005 (16.2)	0.002 (12.7)	0.005 (16.0)	0.002 (12.2)	–	–	–	–
Investment	–	–	–	–	–	–	–	–
KSTOCK	0.084 (49.8)	0.049 (46.4)	0.085 (47.4)	0.048 (44.0)	0.024 (6.0)	0.012 (3.8)	0.032 (6.5)	0.013 (3.7)
ROYALTY	0.332 (1.5)	-0.060 (1.2)	0.231 (1.0)	-0.050 (1.0)	0.054 (11.6)	0.052 (14.2)	0.053 (9.5)	0.045 (10.8)
Output price	0.034 (1.5)	0.013 (1.0)	0.037 (1.6)	0.012 (0.8)	3.259 (6.2)	2.037 (5.2)	1.880 (2.9)	-.060 (1.1)
Region price	0.153 (1.8)	-0.164 (3.1)	0.186 (2.1)	-0.150 (2.8)	0.097 (2.1)	0.118 (3.2)	0.050 (0.9)	0.013 (1.0)
Industry dummies	Yes	Yes	Yes	Yes	Yes	Yes	Yes	Yes
Region dummies	Yes	Yes	Yes	Yes	Yes	Yes	Yes	Yes
Year dummies	Yes	Yes	Yes	Yes	Yes	Yes	Yes	Yes
N	31232	41898	29033	39624	4093	4268	3650	3234
R-square	0.35	0.29	0.44	0.33	0.53	0.57	0.47	0.54

72   *Globalization, Firms, and Workers*

356   B. Aitken et al. / Journal of International Economics 40 (1996) 345–371

For Mexico, vintage effects are captured using the value of current real investment. Current real investment is defined as the sum of the current year's investment excluding purchases of land, with each component of investment (such as machinery, transport equipment, and construction) deflated by an appropriate price deflator. Since the estimation for Mexico is conducted at the industry level, plant-level investment was aggregated to the industry level for each region and year. As indicated in the last four columns of Table 3, our earlier results for Mexico linking higher wages to foreign ownership are robust to the inclusion of current investment. Although the coefficient on investment is positive and significant, indicating the new investment does contribute to higher wages, the point estimates on the foreign investment variable remain unaffected.

In Venezuela, we find that younger plants actually pay lower, not higher, wages. One reason may be that older plants also tend to be much larger. In Table 4, we add a control for plant size, measured as plant sales relative to average sales within that four-digit industry and year. Although the coefficient on relative plant size is highly significant, indicating that larger plants do indeed pay higher wages, again the positive impact of foreign investment is unaffected. The positive association between foreign ownership and wages is apparently not due to either the larger size or the relative newness of multinational firms' plants.

It is conceivable that the wage differences could reflect worker heterogeneity across firms. Controlling for differences between workers is difficult in plant-level data, which typically have limited information on worker characteristics. One possible solution, however, is to focus on the same enterprise over time, the recalled fixed effects model. If heterogeneity of the labor force is likely to be a bigger issue across plants, while the same plant keeps a relatively similar labor

Table 4
Further tests of plant heterogeneity for Venezuela, adding plant size and first differences (dependent variable: log wage (W))

	Adding plant size (levels)		Adding plant size (first differences)	
	Skilled wages	Unskilled wages	Skilled wages	Unskilled wages
DFI (plant level)	0.257 (9.4)	0.172 (8.8)	0.142 (3.0)	0.093 (2.8)
DFI (region)	−0.041 (1.2)	−0.020 (0.8)	0.081 (1.6)	0.096 (2.7)
Age of plant	0.004 (13.2)	0.002 (9.9)	–	–
Plant size	0.039 (34.7)	0.026 (32.4)	0.060 (23.6)	0.049 (26.7)
KSTOCK	0.062 (34.9)	0.036 (32.9)	0.006 (2.2)	0.000 (0.2)
ROYALTY	0.351 (1.7)	−0.063 (1.2)	−0.261 (−0.9)	−0.024 (0.4)
Output price	0.041 (1.9)	0.018 (1.3)	−0.028 (1.0)	−0.125 (7.5)
Region price	0.141 (1.7)	−0.170 (3.3)	−0.038 (12.0)	−0.129 (6.3)
Industry dummies	Yes	Yes	No	No
Region dummies	Yes	Yes	No	No
Year dummies	Yes	Yes	No	No
N	31232	41898	20361	29791
R-square	0.37	0.31	0.05	0.04

B. Aitken et al. / Journal of International Economics 40 (1996) 345–371   357

force from one year to the next, then focusing on changes within a plant can address the issue. We present the fixed effects specification, where all the variables in Eq. (6) and Eq. (7) are transformed into first differences, in the last two columns of Table 4. Variables that do not change from year to year, such as industry and region dummies, are excluded from this specification.

The explanatory power of the first differences specification is much weaker, but the coefficient on *DFI* at the plant level, while somewhat reduced in magnitude, is still highly statistically significant. Within a plant over time, an increasing foreign ownership share is associated with rising wages for both skilled and unskilled workers.

To the extent that foreign investment is attracted to sectors or regions where wages are higher (or lower) or rising (or falling), we could be over (or under) estimating the impact of foreign investment on wages. Table 5 reports two-stage least squares (2SLS) estimates for Venezuela and Mexico. In addition to the other exogenous right-hand side variables in Eq. (6) and Eq. (7), we added two sets of instruments for foreign investment. The first set was drawn from the NBER manufacturing database, which reports average wages by sector over time. We included both the average (real) wage by sector and year, as well as the labor share in both value added and output as instruments. The rationale for using these instruments is that one major motivation for foreign investment – particularly into Mexico – is to escape high labor costs at home. Since the United States is the major source of foreign investment in both Mexico and Venezuela, wages for the US would appear to be good instruments for foreign investment in those countries.

The results from the first set of instrumental variables regressions are reported in the first two columns of Table 5. In the last two columns, three additional

Table 5

The relationship between foreign direct investment and manufacturing industry wages in Venezuela and Mexico: two-stage least squares estimates (dependent variable: log wage (W))

| | Coefficient on foreign investment | | | |
| | 2SLS (1)[a] | | 2SLS (2)[b] | |
	Skilledwages	Unskilledwages	Skilledwages	Unskilledwages
Venezuela				
All enterprises	6.829 (6.0)	2.949 (4.5)	4.077 (5.5)	1.982 (4.1)
Domestic only	−2.964 (1.5)	−0.266 (0.3)	−0.553 (.5)	.726 (0.8)
Mexico				
All enterprises	0.197 (8.7)	0.016 (0.9)	0.182 (7.9)	0.013 (0.7)
Domestic only	−0.060 (1.4)	0.027 (0.9)	−0.057 (1.4)	0.024 (0.8)

Note: *t*-statistics in parentheses.

[a] Instruments for *DFI* include US wages by SIC industry, the US labor share in value added (by SIC) and the US labor share in output.

[b] Instruments for *DFI* include all those described in (1), plus the distribution of foreign investment in Mexico (for Venezuela), the distribution of foreign investment in Venezuela (for Mexico), import penetration, and the share of foreign investment in the region for all other manufacturing sectors.

instruments are also included. The first instrument is the distribution of foreign investment in Mexico (for Venezuela), or the distribution in Venezuela (for Mexico). Although the sectoral distribution of foreign investment in Venezuela should be uncorrelated with wages in Mexico, it is likely to be correlated with the pattern of foreign investment in Mexico. The two other instruments include (1) import penetration, which is positively correlated with foreign investment in both countries, and (2) the concentration of foreign investment in the region, defined as the sales-weighted share of foreign equity for all other industries within the region. This last instrument captures the fact that foreign investors are often drawn to regions where there is already a significant foreign presence.

The results in Table 5 are comparable to the ordinary least squares (OLS) results reported earlier, particularly for Mexico where the point estimates change only slightly. For Venezuela, the pattern is also the same, with a negative impact of foreign investment on wages for domestically owned enterprises, but an overall positive impact when both domestic and foreign enterprises are included. The only major difference is that the 2SLS point estimates for the impact of foreign investment in Venezuela are much higher than for the OLS estimation. The results suggest that a 10% increase in the share of foreign investment would lead (for all enterprises) to 30 and 70% increases in wages for unskilled and skilled workers respectively. These magnitudes seem quite large, suggesting that the OLS results are more plausible than the 2SLS estimates.

2.4.2. Interpreting wage spillovers

The results above show that in Mexico and Venezuela, higher or increasing foreign investment is associated with higher wages for both skilled and unskilled workers. These wage increases are consistent with studies showing that foreign firms have a productive advantage, suggesting that their presence shifts the labor demand curve. However, the higher wages associated with foreign investment in Mexico and Venezuela are not associated with higher wages paid by domestic firms. One possibility is that foreign and domestic firms simply operate in different labor markets. If foreign firms incur higher search costs than domestic enterprises which are familiar with the local labor market, foreign enterprises may discourage turnover once a worker joins the firm. One way to inhibit turnover is to pay higher wages. Foreign firms may also invest more in worker training, which would also lead them to pay high wages as a means of inhibiting turnover. Another possibility is that foreign enterprises in developing countries operate in a different labor market because of institutional factors. Foreign enterprises typically have less bargaining power vis-à-vis labor unions than domestic firms, and are more likely to adhere to legislation mandating minimum wages, overtime pay and other benefits.

Another explanation for lack of spillovers is that the ability to absorb new technology is more limited in Mexico and Venezuela than in the United States. Firms in Venezuela and Mexico may find it more difficult to absorb new

B. Aitken et al. / Journal of International Economics 40 (1996) 345–371 359

technology than US firms due to a lower level of managerial and technical skills. For example, Eaton and Kortum (1994) emphasize the ability to absorb technology as an important factor in explaining patenting, while Kokko (1994) points to a greater probability of technology spillovers from foreign firms in more advanced domestic sectors.

While there is little evidence that higher wages in foreign firms spill over to domestic firms in Mexico and Venezuela, the data appear to support spillovers in the United States. Whether these spillovers are the result of human capital accumulation or simply higher productivity in foreign-owned firms is unclear. A greater foreign presence in the US market could lead to higher wages for workers in domestic firms if foreign firms cause an overall shift in the aggregate demand curve – leading to upward pressure on wages faced by both sets of firms. Wage spillovers from multinational firms to domestic US workers could in principle occur even without any increase in the human capital of workers in domestically owned enterprises. This 'pecuniary' spillover is likely to be extremely difficult to disentangle from a spillover due to increases in human capital. However, one way to distinguish the two types of spillovers would be to test whether higher wages in domestic firms are also accompanied by higher productivity – which would suggest a human capital spillover, not merely a wage effect due to upward pressure on wages exerted by the foreign entrants. As we discuss below, the evidence across all three countries suggests that wage spillovers are generally associated with higher productivity in domestic plants, while the absence of wage spillovers appears to accompany persistent productivity differentials.

2.4.3. Productivity differentials and wages

Evidence on productivity differences between foreign and domestic enterprises in developing countries is reported in Aitken and Harrison (1993) for Venezuela, in Haddad and Harrison (1993) for Morocco, in Harrison (1993) for Côte d'Ivoire, and in Luttmer and Oks (1993) for Mexico. All these studies find that foreign enterprises have higher levels of labor and total factor productivity, although the evidence on growth rates of productivity is more mixed. In addition, Harrison (1993) reports wage and labor productivity comparisons across foreign and domestic enterprises by sector for the Ivory Coast, Morocco, and Venezuela. For all three countries, the cross-sector correlation between higher productivity and higher wage differentials between domestic and foreign enterprises is striking. This suggests that the positive relationship between foreign ownership and wages involves some increase in human capital.

The results in Table 1 pointed to a positive relationship between wages and the foreign share of employment for all establishments, but a negative relationship between foreign investment and wages in domestically owned establishments, at least for Venezuela and possibly (to a lesser extent) for Mexico. If the observed wage differentials between foreign and domestic enterprises can be explained by productivity differentials, the positive wage impact of foreign investment on remuneration in joint ventures and the negative impact on remuneration in domestic competitors should translate into a productivity impact that is positive for joint ventures and negative for domestic competitors. This is exactly what both Aitken and Harrison (1993) find for Venezuela and Luttmer and Oks (1993) find for Mexico. Foreign investment is associated with higher productivity for those enterprises that receive the foreign investment, but with lower productivity in other firms. This suggests that the observed wage differentials are entirely consistent with the productivity story. It appears that in Mexico and Venezuela the gains from foreign investment – higher productivity and higher wages – were internalized by the foreign-owned firms.

For the United States, data comparing foreign and domestic firms at the establishment level have only recently become available.[4] A simple comparison of productivity, defined by value added per employee, between foreign-owned and domestically owned establishments shows a margin of roughly 10% in favor of foreign-owned establishments (Lipsey, 1995, table 27).[5] A comparison for 1987 of shipments per employee, weighting observations by total employment in each industry in each state, shows that for this measure, at least (value added is not available), the inclusion of the geographical control almost doubles the difference between foreign-owned and domestically owned establishments in manufacturing industries, (Lipsey, 1995, table 26). The effect of the geographic control was smaller for non-manufacturing industries.

The differences in value added per employee are smaller than those in shipments per employee. If they incorporate the same bias from ignoring state differences they could reflect substantial productivity margins in favor of the foreign-owned establishments, but even if there were no bias, the data indicate a labor productivity differential of almost 10%. This productivity differential is surprisingly similar to the wage differentials between foreign and domestic enterprises for the United States reported in Section 3.

One explanation for higher value added per worker in foreign-owned plants might be that the capital input per worker is higher. We do not have capital stock data but if we are willing to take non-wage value added as a proxy for payments to

---

[4]Ideally, we would like to use the same breakdown of data as for the analysis of wage rates to ask whether the presence or growth of foreign-owned establishments affects labor productivity or changes in productivity. Unfortunately, the data relating to productivity that are divided between foreign-owned and domestically-owned establishments are more limited than those relating to wages. Data on value added per employee, which we use as a proxy for productivity, are not available for 1987, and those for later years are confined to manufacturing and do not incorporate a geographical breakdown. Furthermore, they are subject to manipulation for minimization of taxes, and while there are undoubtedly some such valuation problems within domestically-owned firms, the opportunities for tax saving may be greater when intrafirm transactions cross national borders. We also lack an adequate time span over which to observe changes in productivity, and we lack information on capital input that might help to explain levels of and changes in labor productivity.

[5]Computed for 1988, 1990 and 1991. The productivity comparison across all industries is weighted by total employment in each industry.

B. Aitken et al. / Journal of International Economics 40 (1996) 345–371   361

owners of capital, we can make a comparison. It shows that non-wage value added per worker was, on average, 14% higher in foreign-owned establishments than in domestically owned establishments within industries. Thus, the higher labor productivity suggested by the higher value added per worker seems to be associated with higher capital intensity in foreign-owned establishments. That relationship is confirmed by the fact that, across the 105 industries, the ratio of value added per worker in foreign-owned establishments to that in domestically owned establishments (which we have used as a proxy for relative labor productivity) is almost completely explained by the relative non-wage value added per worker (which we have thought of as a proxy for capital intensity).[6]

That relationship is not surprising in view of the larger size of the foreign plants, but it could also represent other factors, especially since non-wage value added is about half of total value added and is the part of value added that would be affected by these factors. Foreign-owned plants might be earning higher profits from exploiting their firm-specific technology or other assets, or because they have received concessions from state and local governments, or they may be exaggerating their profits to transfer them to these plants by undervaluing inputs purchased from parents or other affiliated entities. The last of these possibilities does not seem particularly plausible in view of the widespread suspicion that foreign firms are artificially minimizing, rather than maximizing, the share of their profits they report earning in the United States.

Across 105 three-digit US manufacturing industries in 1990 we can analyze the relation between labor productivity, as proxied by value added per employee, and the extent of foreign ownership, along the lines of the studies for Mexico and Venezuela. Eq. (8) and Eq. (9) describe this relationship when no control for capital intensity is included, for all establishments:

$$VAE = \quad 49.61 + \quad 236.40FES \qquad \bar{R}^2 = 0.251$$
$$\qquad\qquad (7.48) \qquad (6.01) \tag{8}$$

and domestically owned establishments:

$$VAE = \quad 49.27 + \quad 232.63FES \qquad \bar{R}^2 = 0.225$$
$$\qquad\qquad (7.05) \qquad (41.47) \tag{9}$$

where VAE = value added per employee ($1000s), FES = share of employment in foreign-owned establishments; t-statistics in parentheses.

---

[6]This statement is based on the results of the following regression:

$$VAE(F/D) = \quad 0.383 + \quad 0.628NWVAE(F/D) \quad \bar{R}^2 = 0.970$$
$$\qquad\qquad (26.8) \qquad\qquad (57.9)$$

where $VAE(F/D)$ = value added per worker, foreign-owned / domestically-owned, and $NWVAE(F/D)$ = non-wage value added per worker, foreign-owned / domestically-owned.

Since value added per employee is closely related to capital intensity, we add non-wage value added per employee as a proxy for capital intensity in Eq. (10) and Eq. (11), for all establishments:

$$VAE = \underset{(22.63)}{20.07} + \underset{(2.33)}{12.84FES} + \underset{(82.69)}{1.086NWVAE} \qquad \bar{R}^2 = 0.989 \tag{10}$$

and domestically owned establishments:

$$VAE = \underset{(22.59)}{20.21} + \underset{(2.40)}{13.30FES} + \underset{(85.56)}{1.080NWVAE} \qquad \bar{R}^2 = 0.989. \tag{11}$$

As in Mexico and Venezuela, a higher foreign presence in an industry is associated with higher productivity for the industry as a whole. In contrast to the relationship in those two countries, higher foreign presence in an industry in the United States is associated with higher productivity in domestic establishments, a relationship that is consistent with the fact that higher foreign presence in a US industry is also associated with higher wages in domestically owned establishments. Thus, the productivity data and the wage data for the United States suggest spillovers from foreign-owned to domestically owned establishments that are not visible in Mexico and Venezuela.

Another hint of a productivity effect of foreign ownership can be drawn from an examination of changes in 1991 for US affiliates newly acquired by foreign firms in 1990. If these are compared with existing affiliates, by industry, sales per employee in the newly acquired affiliates increased relative to those in the existing affiliates. That increase in the sales per employee involved a reduction in employment by the new affiliates in most, though not all, industries, while existing affiliates in most industries increased employment (Lipsey, 1995, tables 21 and 22).

2.4.4. Implications for wage differentials

The evidence on productivity presented above, combined with the results in Tables 1–5, suggests that foreign investment is associated with both productivity and wage increases. Increased foreign investment raises productivity, and the resulting benefits to the firm are shared with its employees in the form of higher wages. However, those productivity and wage increases are diffused to domestic enterprises only in the case of the United States. One implication is that wage differentials between foreign and domestic enterprises should exist in both Mexico and Venezuela, but should be dissipating over time in the United States. With rapid turnover, workers in foreign enterprises should have transmitted their human capital to other enterprises, resulting in an aggregate increase in wages across both domestic and foreign enterprises. Below, we explore the extent of wage differentials between foreign and domestic enterprises in Mexico, Venezuela, and the United States.

B. Aitken et al. / Journal of International Economics 40 (1996) 345–371   363

3. Comparing wages in domestic and foreign enterprises

With high turnover or rapid rates of technological diffusion between foreign and domestic enterprises, wage differentials between foreign and domestic enterprises should become (over time) quite small. From this perspective, high wage differentials could reflect the lack of spillovers between foreign and domestic enterprises. Other possibilities, consistent with observed wage differentials, are that higher foreign wages are due to characteristics other than foreignness per se – such as plant size, location, type of industry, or skill mix. We explore these possibilities below. Even after controlling for these characteristics, wage differentials between foreign and domestic enterprises persist in Mexico and Venezuela, but become quite small in the United States. These results are consistent with evidence on wage spillovers from foreign investment in the United States but a lack of wage spillovers in the two developing countries.

3.1. Cross-section comparisons

We begin with a cross-section comparison of wages in domestic and foreign-owned enterprises in the three countries since time series data are not available for the United States. Since the most detailed data for the United States are available only for 1987, we have chosen similar years for Venezuela (1987) and Mexico (1990). In our wage comparisons, we hope to understand the extent to which differences across foreign and domestic firms are due to differences in industry composition, geographic location, and skill levels of employees.

In the US case, establishments are defined as foreign owned if the foreign equity share is 10% or more. To enable us to make comparisons across countries, in this section we adopt the same definition of foreign-owned establishments for Mexico and Venezuela.

Table 6 compares wages across domestic and foreign establishments. In all three countries, wages in foreign-owned manufacturing establishments are higher than in domestically owned establishments by a factor of 30%. If we compare total compensation, which includes benefits, the ratios are somewhat similar (total compensation was not available for the US). For Mexico and Venezuela, we also examine wage differentials for skilled and unskilled workers. The foreign wage premium is fairly consistent for both skilled and unskilled workers, which suggests that higher wages paid by foreign firms in those two countries are largely not explainable by a different skill mix of workers in foreign-owned firms. Table 6 also shows that the compensation differential stays almost the same if we use total compensation instead of wages to compare foreign and domestic firms. Since total compensation is not available for the US in 1987, in the remainder of this section we focus only on wage differentials (excluding benefits) between foreign and domestic firms.

Table 6
Comparing wages in domestic and foreign establishments: Mexico, Venezuela, and the United States

	Wages	Wages and benefits		
Mexico (1990)				
Manufacturing (all)			1.32	1.38
Skilled labor	1.32	1.38		
Unskilled labor	1.30	–		
Venezuela (1987)				
Manufacturing (all)			1.31	1.31
Skilled labor	1.21	1.21		
Unskilled labor	1.25	1.25		
United States (1987)				
Manufacturing			1.29	–
Non-manufacturing	1.12	–		
Total industry	1.29	–		

3.2. Impact of industry composition

We can ask how much of these differences is 'explained' by differences in the industry composition of foreign and domestically owned plants. How much difference would remain if foreign-owned plants were in the same industries as domestically owned plants (domestic weights) or domestically owned plants were distributed in the same way as foreign-owned plants (foreign weights), with no changes in the wage levels? We can answer this question by computing relative wages (foreign/domestic) at the sector level, then calculating a weighted average wage across sectors. The weighted average is computed two ways: using the foreign and the domestic distribution of employment across sectors. If foreign and domestic wages are equal within sectors, and differences between foreign and domestic wages are due only to different industry mix among domestic and foreign firms, our weighted mean ratio of foreign to domestic wages should be close to unity.

The results are reported in Table 7. Since the wage differential for all three countries remains far from zero, industry mix cannot provide the whole explana-

Table 7
Wages per worker, foreign/domestic ratio with industries weighted identically

Host country	Industry	Weights	
		Foreign	Domestic
Mexico (1990)	Manufacturing	1.30	1.12
Venezuela (1987)	Manufacturing	1.22	1.19
United States (1987)	Manufacturing	1.04	1.05
	Non-manufacturing	1.12	1.18
	All industries	1.10	1.14

B. Aitken et al. / Journal of International Economics 40 (1996) 345–371   365

tion for the wage differential. In the US, about half of the aggregate difference in manufacturing compensation per worker, but a smaller share outside of manufacturing, can be accounted for by industry distribution. In Mexico, over two thirds of the wage differential can be explained by industry distribution, while in Venezuela only one third of the wage difference is explained by industry composition.

The impact of industry mix on aggregate wage differentials can also be explored by asking how average wages would compare in foreign and domestic plants if the same wages were paid within each industry but differed only in industry composition. We recalculated average domestic wages by sector, and then derived a weighted foreign and domestic wage using foreign and domestic weights respectively. The resulting ratio of foreign to domestic wages captures pure differences in industry composition across both sets of firms, since within the same industry we assume that both sets of firms pay the same wages.

The impact of industry composition is given in another way in Table 8. In the US, the industry composition of employment led to higher pay in foreign-owned plants, by margins of about 7% in both manufacturing and non-manufacturing. However, foreign affiliates were much more concentrated in the relatively high-wage manufacturing sector than were domestically owned firms (41% against 21%). That difference added another 7% or so to the aggregate wage differential. This suggests that, in the United States, half of the industry-mix effect reflected differences in compensation within manufacturing and non-manufacturing, while half reflected the greater concentration of foreign affiliates in manufacturing, a fairly high-wage sector.

The results for Mexico and Venezuela for manufacturing alone are quite different from those for the United States. For these two countries, differences in industry composition for foreign and domestic firms account for higher wage margins of 5.8% (Mexico) and 13.6% (Venezuela). This suggests that only 20 to 30% of the aggregate wage differential can be explained by a different composition of foreign and domestic firms. Although Table 8 does indicate that foreign firms are located in higher wage sectors, it also shows that this is only a small part of the explanation. To the extent that foreign investment also affects domestic wages positively, the results in Table 8 are also likely to overstate the importance of industry composition. What could appear to be the attraction of foreign

Table 8
Impact of industry composition on wage per worker in foreign and domestically owned establishments

Host Country	Industry	Foreign/domestic wages
Mexico	Manufacturing	1.06
Venezuela	Manufacturing	1.14
United States	Manufacturing	1.07
	Non-manufacturing	1.07
	All industries	1.14

investors for high-wage sectors could in fact be an outcome of high levels of foreign investment.

3.3. Location of foreign affiliates

Another possible explanation for differences in wages between foreign-owned and domestically owned establishments could be the geographic location of foreign-owned affiliates. If, for example, foreign firms were more likely to be located in high-wage states or regions within any given industry, they might pay higher wages in each industry on average even if within each state they paid exactly the same amount as domestically owned firms and therefore were presumably hiring an equally skilled labor force. Or location in high-wage states might offset and obscure a tendency to hire less skilled workers. Thus, ignoring the location of foreign affiliates might mislead an observer into mistaking location effects for differences in average skills employed by foreign affiliates, or in the prices they pay for any given skills. This would not be an issue with completely integrated and perfectly competitive labor markets across states and regions, but that would be a strong assumption to make.

To remove possible location effects, we have calculated ratios of affiliate to domestic firm wages per worker at the two-digit (US) and four-digit (Mexico, Venezuela) level in each state, and then weighted these ratios by the state–industry composition of affiliate employment and domestic firm employment. That procedure can be interpreted as assuming, in effect, that each state is a competitive labor market. The weighted ratios are given in Table 9.

In the US case, geographic location cannot account for the observed wage differential between foreign and domestic enterprises. Foreign firms pay 6 or 7% more than domestic fires in manufacturing, as compared with the 4 or 5% reported in Table 7, where location is ignored. The difference is even greater in non-manufacturing industries where foreign firms pay 12 to 15% more. The lower differential in Table 7 than in Table 9 for manufacturing suggests that in the United States, foreign enterprises tend to locate in low-wage states within each

Table 9
Impact of geographic location on wage per worker in foreign and domestically owned establishments

Host country	Industry	Weights	
		Foreign	Domestic
Mexico (1990)	Manufacturing	1.260	1.160
Venezuela (1987)	Manufacturing	1.140	1.122
United States (1987)	Manufacturing	1.071	1.062
	Non-manufacturing	1.149	1.117
	All industries	1.120	1.103

B. Aitken et al. / Journal of International Economics 40 (1996) 345–371 367

industry. Ignoring location may result in some understatement of the degree to which foreign affiliates pay higher compensation to workers than domestic firms.

In Mexico, location appears to explain less than 50% of the observed wage differential, but unlike the US case, it does appear that foreign enterprises are more likely to locate in higher wage regions. This tendency is even stronger in Venezuela: the fact that foreign enterprises tend to operate in high-wage regions accounts for as much as two thirds of the observed wage differential between foreign and domestic enterprises.

3.4. Impact of establishment size in manufacturing

Foreign-owned manufacturing plants are typically much larger than domestic enterprises, both in the United States and abroad (see, for example, Howenstine and Zeile, 1994, on the US; Lipsey and Swedenborg, 1981, on Sweden; and Blomström, 1989, on Mexico). Since larger firms also tend to pay higher wages, the foreign–domestic wage differential could be related to the larger size of foreign-owned enterprises. For the United States, there appears to be no difference between foreign and domestic wages after controlling for the size of the plant, in a regression across industries with observations for both foreign and domestic plants. The results are reported in Table 10. Independent variables included physical capital intensity (defined as the non-employee compensation share of value added), plant size or scale (defined as average value added per establishment), and a dummy variable for foreign ownership.

In Mexico, however, differences between foreign and domestic wages persist after controlling for both size (plant scale) and capital intensity. Higher wages in foreign establishments are most significant for skilled workers, although the difference in wages remains (barely) significant for unskilled workers as well.

Whether one considers size of establishment as an explanation for wage differences depends partly on the purpose of the analysis. If one wishes to know whether production functions or technology differ between foreign-owned and

Table 10

Impact of plant size on wages in foreign-owned and domestically owned manufacturing establishments (dependent variable: wage per worker)

Independent variables	US[a]	Mexico		
	All	Skilled	Unskilled	All
Plant size	0.07 (11.35)	0.04 (6.42)	0.01 (5.62)	0.02 (5.05)
Capital intensity	0.59 (0.90)	1.56 (0.70)	−0.42 (0.47)	0.95 (2.64)
Foreign dummy	−0.09 (−0.43)	3.78 (3.78)	0.56 (1.43)	2.03 (3.07)
N	624	239	239	239
R-square	0.21	0.24	0.13	0.17

Note: *t*-values in parentheses.

[a]Results for the United States taken from Howenstine and Zeile (1994).

domestically owned establishments, size of output is clearly an essential variable. For a judgment about labor market impacts of foreign investment, the relevance of size is not as clear, partly because the reason for the correlation between size of establishment and wage rates is not obvious. If a host country wishes to decide about the desirability of inward foreign direct investment, and if such investments are typically associated with large size relative to domestic establishments, it should not matter to the host country whether any benefits stem from foreignness or from size.

3.5. Time-series comparisons (Venezuela only)

One shortcoming of the cross-section comparisons above is that we cannot control jointly for differences in industry composition, size, and capital intensity. Controlling for all these effects concurrently would require a time series, which we only have for Venezuela and Mexico. In Table 11, we report the wage differentials between foreign and domestic establishments for Venezuela, after controlling for industry effects, size, and capital intensity. The dependent variable is the log wage of skilled workers, with all data estimated at the plant level. We begin with no controls, then add a series of controls to estimate whether the relationship between foreign ownership and higher wages disappears. These results allow us to compare wages across firms within the same industry, plant size, and capital–labor ratio.

The results show that wage differentials between foreign-owned and domestic plants persist after controlling for all these factors. However, the wage differential falls from a 50% premium paid to workers in foreign firms when no controls are added to between 16 and 18% after including controls for industry, size, and capital–labor ratio. The wage differential seems to remain whether the foreign affiliate has majority or minority foreign ownership.

Table 11

Time series comparisons of wages paid by foreign and domestic manufacturing establishments in Venezuela (coefficient on foreign ownership dummy) – dependent variable: log wage of skilled workers ($N = 41121$)

	Foreign share $\geq 50\%$	Foreign share $<50\%$	R-square
No controls	0.489 (23.2)	0.513 (34.3)	0.09
Controlling for 2-digit SIC	0.465 (22.5)	0.474 (32.3)	0.14
Controlling for 4-digit SIC	0.377 (18.7)	0.387 (26.8)	0.19
Controlling for size and 4-digit SIC	0.179 (9.8)	0.158 (11.6)	0.35
Controlling for size, capital/labor ratio, and 4-digit SIC	0.179 (9.8)	0.157 (11.7)	0.35

Notes: *t*-statistics in parentheses. All regressions include annual time dummies.

B. *Aitken et al. / Journal of International Economics 40 (1996) 345–371* 369

4. Concluding remarks

This paper explores the relationship between wages and foreign investment in Mexico, Venezuela, and the United States. Despite very different economic conditions and levels of development, we find one fact which is robust across all three countries: higher levels of foreign investment are associated with higher wages. However, in Mexico and Venezuela, foreign investment was associated with higher wages only for foreign-owned firms – there is no evidence of wage spillovers leading to higher wages for domestic firms. In the United States the evidence is much stronger in favor of wage spillovers.

The lack of spillovers in Mexico and Venezuela is consistent with significant wage differentials between foreign and domestic enterprises. These wage differentials persist after controlling for size, geographic location, skill mix, and capital intensity. These wage differences, together with productivity differences, are consistent with greater human capital formation in foreign firms and lower turnover. In the United States, where the evidence suggests wage spillovers from foreign to domestic enterprises, wage differentials are smaller. In fact, a large part of the wage differential seems to disappear after accounting for the fact that foreign-owned enterprises are larger and more capital intensive than their domestic counterparts. The smallness of the wage differential, combined with wage spillovers from foreign to domestic enterprises, is consistent with knowledge spillovers from foreign to domestic enterprises in the United States.

5. Unlinked references

US Department of Commerce, 1993; US Bureau of the Census, 1990, 1992; US Department of Commerce, 1992, 1994a,b

Acknowledgments

We would like to thank Mukul Kumar and Sherry Zhang for excellent research assistance. We would also like to thank Robert Baldwin, Phil Swagel, and participants at the ISIT NBER October 1994 meeting for helpful comments and suggestions.

References

Aitken, B. and A. Harrison, 1993, Does proximity to foreign firms induce technology spillovers?, PRD Working Paper (World Bank).

370   B. Aitken et al. / Journal of International Economics 40 (1996) 345–371

Aitken, B., A. Harrison, and G. Hanson, 1994, Spillovers: Foreign investment, and export behavior, Working Paper 4967 (NBER).

Blomström, M., 1989, Foreign investment and spillovers (Routledge, London).

Caves, R., 1974, Multinational firms, competition and productivity in host-country markets, Economica.

Caves, R., 1982, Multinational enterprise and economic analysis (Cambridge University Press, Cambridge).

Eaton, J. and S. Kortum, 1994, The Internationalization of US Patenting, NBER–CEPR International Seminar on International Trade (ISIT), October 1994.

Germidis, D., 1977, Transfer of technology by multinational corporations (Development Center of the OECD, Paris).

Globerman, S., 1979, Foreign direct investment and 'spillover' efficiency benefits in Canadian manufacturing industries, Canadian Journal of Economics, February.

Goncalves, R., 1986, Technological spillovers and manpower training: A comparative analysis of multinational and national enterprises in Brazilian manufacturing, Journal of Development Economics 11, July.

Grossman, G. and E. Helpman, 1991a, Quality ladders and product cycles, Quarterly Journal of Economics 106, 557–586.

Grossman, G. and E. Helpman, 1991b, Innovation and growth in the global economy (MIT Press, Cambridge).

Haddad, M., and A. Harrison, 1993, Are there positive spillovers from direct foreign investment? Evidence from panel data for Morocco, Journal of Development Economics, October.

Harrison, A., 1993, Foreign investment in three developing countries: Determinants and consequences, in M. Roberts and J. Tybout, forthcoming.

Helleiner, G.K., 1989, Transnational corporations and foreign direct investment, in H. Chenery and T.N. Srinivasan, Handbook of development economics, Vol. 2, C. 27.

Howenstine, N.G. and W.J. Zeile, 1994, Characteristics of foreign-owned US manufacturing establishments, Survey of Current Business 74, 34–59.

Kokko, A., 1994, Technology, market characteristics, and spillovers, Journal of Development Economics 43, April.

Lipsey, R.E., 1995, Foreign-owned firms and US wages, Report to the US Department of Labor.

Lipsey, R.E. and B. Swedenborg, 1981, Foreign takeovers of Swedish firms, Working Paper 641 (NBER).

Lucas, R., 1993, Making a miracle, Econometrica 61, 251–272.

Luttmer, E. and D. Oks, 1993, Productivity in Mexican manufacturing industries (World Bank).

Mody, A., J. Sanders, R. Suri, C. Rao, F. Contreras, 1991, International competition in the bicycle industry (World Bank).

Reuber, G.L., 1973, Private foreign investment in development (Clarendon Press, Oxford).

Rhee, Y.W. and T. Belot, 1989, Export catalysts in low-income countries, Discussion Paper 72 (World Bank).

Romer, P., 1993, Idea gaps and object gaps in economic development, Journal of Monetary Economics 32, 543–573.

US Bureau of the Census, 1990, 1988 annual survey of manufactures (US Government Printing Office, Washington D.C.).

US Bureau of the Census, 1992, 1990 annual survey of manufactures (US Government Printing Office, Washington, D.C.).

US Department of Commerce, 1992, Foreign direct investment in the United States: Establishment data for 1987 (Bureau of Economic Analysis and Bureau of the Census, Washington, D.C.).

US Department of Commerce, 1993, Foreign direct investment in the United States: Establishment data for manufacturing, 1990 (Bureau of Economic Analysis and Bureau of the Census, Washington, D.C.).

US Department of Commerce, 1994a, Foreign direct investment in the United States: Establishment data for manufacturing, 1988 (Bureau of Economic Analysis and Bureau of the Census, Washington, D.C.).

US Department of Commerce, 1994b, Foreign direct investment in the United States: Establishment data for manufacturing, 1991 (Bureau of Economic Analysis and Bureau of the Census, Washington, D.C.).

Chapter 5

Has Globalization Eroded Labor's Share? Some Cross-Country Evidence

Ann Harrison

Department of Agricultural and Resource Economics,
329 Giannini Hall, University of California,
Berkeley, CA 94720
National Bureau of Economic Research (NBER),
Cambridge, MA 02138, USA

Abstract

In recent years, economists and other social scientists have devoted extensive research efforts to understanding the widening wage gap between high-skill and low-skill workers. This paper focuses on a slightly different question: how has globalization affected the relative share of income going to capital and labor? Using a panel of over one hundred countries, this paper analyses trends in labor shares and examines the relationship between shares and measures of globalization. Contrary to recent literature, the evidence suggests that labor shares are not constant over time. Over the 1960 to 2000 period, labor shares in poor countries fell, while shares in rich countries rose. These changes in labor shares are driven by changes in factor endowments and government spending, as well as by traditional measures of globalization, such as trade shares, exchange rate crises, movements in foreign investment, and capital controls. In particular, the results suggest that rising trade shares and exchange rate crises reduce labor's share, while increasing capital intensity, capital controls and government spending increase labor's share.

"The widening of inequalities of income distribution in the 1990's is without precedent in the post-World War II history of the U.S. economy. The share of national income going to the owners of capital through corporate profits is surging. The share going to compensation is falling. This is not the way a democracy is supposed to work. ..."

Stephen Roach of Morgan Stanley, as interviewed in
The New York Times, February 4, 1996

"Although advanced countries were exporting capital-intensive goods and importing labor-intensive goods, as of the early 1990s there had been virtually no change in the distribution of income between capital and labor; the share of compensation (wages plus benefits) in U.S. national income was the same in 1993 as it had been in 1973. So at most the trade story could apply to a shift in the distribution of income between skilled and unskilled workers, rather than between workers and capital."

Krugman and Obstfeld,
International Economics: Theory and Policy, 2003

I. Introduction

In recent years, economists and other social scientists have devoted extensive research efforts to understanding the widening wage gap between high-skill and low-skill workers. The increasing wage gap between the "haves" and the "have-nots" has been well-documented not only in the United States but also in many other developed and developing countries. Much of this research effort has focused on trying to identify the importance of factors such as immigration, the supply of different kinds of workers, skill-biased technical change, and globalization. Globalization has been broadly defined to include everything from falling prices for goods which use low skill labor (such as garments) to increasing outsourcing by multinationals.

This paper focuses on a slightly different question: how has globalization affected the relative share of income going to capital and labor? Numerous reports in the popular press describe a struggle between capital and labor, with owners of capital winning at the expense of labor. These accounts typically present owners of capital as having greater bargaining power compared to labor, ostensibly because capital is footloose and can quickly relocate to wherever it can find the highest returns. Rodrik (1997), in his book *Has Globalization Gone Too Far*, describes a similar type of bargaining game between capital and labor. Despite these claims, however, there have been almost no efforts to test the relationship between globalization and labor's share.

This paper begins by examining long run changes in the distribution of income between owners of capital and labor. Several macroeconomists have reported that the share of GDP accounted by capital income (profits) has increased, while labor's share of GDP (wages) has declined. Blanchard (1996) documents these changes for a number of European countries, while Poterba (1997) examines trends in the United States. In Europe, the change is enormous: labor's share of aggregate income has declined as much as ten percentage points of GDP. In the United States, the trend is still discernable but much smaller: labor's share in national income has declined by several percentage points in GDP. Anthony Atkinson, reviewing the evidence presented by Poterba and others, concludes that in the majority of the G-7 countries there has been a shift toward nonlabor income since 1980 (Atkinson, 1997).

The macro-economists who have examined this trend have explored in some detail the role of labor supply and labor demand shifts, the role of technological change, and other factors, but have not focused on international competition as a potential explanation. But a number of trade economists, such as Rodrik (1997), Slaughter (1996), and Richardson and Khripounova (1996) have argued that globalization is affecting labor by increasing the elasticity of labor demand. Slaughter (1996) presents convincing evidence that the elasticity of demand for labor is rising, and relates it to measures of globalization. Although he finds that labor demand within US

manufacturing is becoming more elastic, there is no strong relationship between changes in labor elasticity and globalization. In another
study, Budd and Slaughter (2000) show that union wage determination in Canada is affected by changing profits in both Canada and
the United States. Their work suggests that globalization does affect
union wages, although they do not test the impact on labor shares.
Diwan (1999) shows that financial crises have systemically led to a
decline in labor's share relative to capital, but does not address the
role of globalization directly.

    This paper begins by outlining a framework which shows how
globalization could account for changes in the share of labor income
in GDP. In this imperfectly competitive framework, firms and workers bargain over excess profits, and whoever has the stronger bargaining position receives a larger share of the profits. Bargaining
strength depends on a number of factors, including the fixed costs
of relocating and the alternative return available elsewhere. To the
extent that the fixed costs of relocating are much larger for workers
than for capital, this could lead capital's share of national income to
rise relative to labor.

    The empirical section of the paper begins by examining the styl-
ized facts on labor shares in the United States and in other countries.
The dataset, constructed using United Nations national account
data, provides information on the share of labor compensation in
national income or GDP across 100 countries and over 40 years. The
results show that labor and capital shares have fluctuated significantly in the last 30 years, contrary to the assumptions of constant
factor shares embedded in any models which use a Cobb-Douglas
production technology. Across poor and middle income countries,
the share of GDP going to wages and benefits is declining. However,
the global trend masks major differences across countries. In the
United States, capital and labor shares have remained fairly constant over the last 35 years, while in Japan labor's share in GDP has
consistently increased. The perception of falling labor shares in high
income countries is driven primarily by the European experience. In
Europe, many countries exhibit a dramatic fall in labor shares. Overall, the results suggest that labor's share is rising in rich countries,

and falling in poor countries. As pointed out by Gollin (2002), however, fluctuations in labor's share are significantly reduced if labor's
share is expanded to include self-employment income. In this paper,
we show that this conclusion continues to hold in the time-series data
as well. Nevertheless, even if we include self-employment income in
our definition of labor's share, this new dataset still shows significant
variation across countries and over time. While Gollin focused on
cross-country data for a smaller set of countries at one point in time,
this paper focuses on time series variation across a broader sample
of countries.

The remaining part of the paper explores the relationship between
labor shares and its determinants. The results suggest that changing
labor shares are driven by changes in factor endowments, as well as
by traditional measures of globalization, such as movements in trade
shares, exchange rate crises, movements in foreign investment, and
capital controls. In particular, rising trade shares and exchange rate
crises reduce labor's share, while capital controls and government
spending increase labor's share. Section II outlines the theoretical
framework for estimation. Section III discusses estimation issues,
while Section IV discusses the empirical results. Section V concludes.

II.   Theoretical Framework for Estimation

This framework combines the approach used by general equilibrium
researchers in international trade to test for Stolper Samuelson effects
(see, for example, Balaban and Harrigan (1997)), with the more
partial equilibrium approach used by labor economists to test for
rentsharing. Tests of general equilibrium trade theory typically transform equations for determining the quantity of a firm's revenue into
an equation where labor's share in revenues is a function of both
final goods prices and changing factor inputs. Harrigan (1997) and
others assume that product and factor markets are perfectly competitive. We relax that assumption, introducing the possibility that firms
make excess profits. We then allow the rents to be divided between
firms and employees on the basis of bargaining strength, which in
turn is a function of the firm's expanding affiliate presence abroad.

This approach differs from previous work by Borjas and Ramey (1995), who examine the link between rising wage inequality and falling industry rents. They assume that the fraction of rents allocated between workers and owners is constant; what changes is the extent of rents as global conditions become more competitive. Borjas and Ramey (1995) and Abowd and Lemieux (1993) also assume that bargaining power is fixed; in this proposal, bargaining power varies with the ease of relocation abroad. Unlike previous work, we include capital in the production function, which allows us to model rent-sharing as a function of both worker bargaining power and capital's bargaining power. The framework is complementary to, but differs from, Rodrik (1997) and Slaughter (1996), who argue that rising labor demand elasticities could shift the incidence of nonwage costs, costs associated with the implementation of labor standards, and government taxes towards labor.

Output and Factor Markets

Firms and workers first choose the profit maximizing level of output, and then bargain over the rents. This approach was pioneered by Brown and Ashenfelter (1986) and in the bargaining literature, has come to be known as the efficient bargaining model. An alternative approach would have been to allow employment to be chosen taking into account the negotiated wage, the so-called right to manage model. Like Blanchard and Giavazzi (2001), we propose an efficient bargaining model because we want to capture the possibility that the actual wage may be different from the marginal revenue product of labor. In this framework, the share of rents going to workers depends on the relative bargaining strengths of labor and capital. A natural extension of this work is to explore the consequences of relaxing the assumption of efficient bargaining.

We assume there are only two factors of production, labor and capital. The representative firm uses a vector $\mathbf{v}$ of inputs, with ν_L units of labor and ν_K units of capital. The competitive return to factors is given by the vector $\boldsymbol{w_0} = (w_{L0}w_{K0})$. The wage under perfect competition would be w_{L0}, and the return to capital would be w_{K0}. Total returns are denoted by the vector $\mathbf{w} = (w_L w_K)$ with excess returns given by the difference between the two vectors. The utility functions for labor and capital are denoted by:

$$U_L = (w_L - w_{L0})\nu_L \tag{1a}$$

$$U_k = (w_K - w_{K0})\nu_K \tag{1b}$$

The revenue function is denoted by $G(\mathbf{P}, \mathbf{v})$. The price vector $\mathbf{P}$, in turn, can be written as a function of the production function $\mathbf{Y}(\mathbf{v})$, so we have $\mathbf{P}(\mathbf{Y}(\mathbf{v}))$. Under imperfect competition, excess profits are equal to:

$$G(\mathbf{P}(\mathbf{Y}(\mathbf{v})), \mathbf{v}) - \mathbf{w_0}\mathbf{v} \tag{2}$$

Maximizing (2) with respect to $\mathbf{v}$ yields the following first order condition:

$$\left[\frac{\delta \mathbf{Y}}{\delta \mathbf{v}}\right] \mathbf{P} = \mu \mathbf{w_0} \text{ where } \mu = \left(\frac{1}{\varepsilon} + 1\right)^{-1} \tag{3}$$

The elasticity of demand is given by ε. We can implicitly define the optimal choice of $\mathbf{v}$ as:

$$\mathbf{v}^* = \mathbf{R}(\mathbf{P}, \mu, \mathbf{w_0})$$

The excess rents given by (2) can be written as:

$$\text{Rents} = G(\mathbf{R}) - \mathbf{w_0}\mathbf{R} \tag{4}$$

Thus, total revenue, $G(\mathbf{R})$, factor demands, $\mathbf{v}^*$, and *total* rents are determined by equations (1) through (4) and are independent of labor and capital's bargaining power.

Bargaining Over Rents

Labor and capital bargain to determine their share of the rents. The outcome of bargaining, if we assume Nash bargaining, can be derived from finding the solution to maximizing — over w_L and w_K — the following:

$$[(w_L\nu_L - U_{L0})(w_K\nu_K - U_{K0})]$$

Before we can solve for $\mathbf{w}$, we need to define the threat points. We assume that if bargaining breaks down, capital or labor has the option to leave the firm, incur a fixed cost F_L or F_K, and receive alternative returns w_L^* or w_K^*. These alternative returns are not necessarily equal to the competitive return. For example, if there is significant unemployment and labor is not very mobile, labor's alternative return might be unemployment benefits which may be less than the competitive return. Alternatively, capital's alternative return may exceed the competitive return if capital can relocate to countries in which capital is relatively scarce. Nor have we defined whether the alternative return is set locally or abroad. However, since labor's fixed costs of relocating to a foreign country are likely to be extremely high while capital's costs are much lower, in the empirical section which follows we will define the alternative wage based on the local labor market and the alternative return to capital based on returns abroad. We will assume that fixed costs are proportional to the quantity of the factor employed, so that we can write $F_i = f_i \nu_i$. Consequently, we can write the threat points as:

$$U_{L0} = w_L^* \nu_L - f_L \nu_L \qquad (5a)$$

$$U_{K0} = w_K^* \nu_K - f_K \nu_K \qquad (5b)$$

So our maximization problem becomes:

Maximize $\quad \{w_L \nu_L - w_L^* \nu_L + f_L \nu_L\}\{w_K \nu_K - w_K^* \nu_K + f_K \nu_K\}$

over w_L and w_L and subject to $w_L \nu_L + w_K \nu_K = G(R)$ $\qquad (6)$

The first-order conditions with respect to w_L and w_K are (where λ is the multiplier on the constraint):

$$\nu_L(w_K v_K - w_K^* v_K + f_K v_K) = \lambda \qquad (7)$$

$$\nu_K(w_L v_L - w_L^* v_L + f_L v_L) = \lambda \qquad (8)$$

Combining these first-order conditions yields the following expression for the wage:

$$w_L = \frac{1}{2}\left[\frac{G(R)}{\nu_L} + w_L^* + (f_K - w_K^*)\frac{\nu_K}{\nu_L} - f_L\right] \qquad (9)$$

The expression for the return on capital is analogous to (9). With bargaining, wages depend positively on labor productivity, but now they also depend positively on the alternative returns to labor and the fixed cost to capital of relocating and negatively on the alternative return to capital and the fixed cost to labor of relocating.

Multiplying both sides of (9) by v_L and dividing both sides of (9) by $G(R)$ yields the following expression for the labor share S_L:

$$\frac{w_L \nu_L}{G(R)} = S_L = \frac{1}{2} + \frac{1}{2}\left[\frac{w_L^* \nu_L}{G(R)} - \frac{f_L \nu_L}{G(R)} - \frac{w_K^* \nu_L}{G(R)} + \frac{f_K \nu_K}{G(R)}\right] \quad (10)$$

The expression for capital's share is analogous to (10). Recognizing that the alternative returns equal the competitive return plus some premium, we can show that if both parties have equal bargaining strengths, factor shares depend only on $\frac{1}{2}\left[\frac{w_{0L}\nu_L - w_{0K}\nu_K}{G(R)}\right] + \frac{1}{2}$. In this case, the factors each receive their competitive share $w_{0i}\nu_i$ for $i = L$, K and then divide equally the excess profits between themselves. If, however, fixed costs of relocating or alternative returns to the factors differ, then excess profits will not be split equally across factors. In particular, labor's share will rise if: (1) alternative returns to labor rise (2) alternative returns to capital fall (3) fixed costs to capital of relocating rise or (4) fixed costs to labor of relocating fall.

Using what appears to be a very different approach, which incorporates monopolistic competition, unemployment and Dixit-Stiglitz utility functions in a general equilibrium framework, Blanchard and Giavazzi (2001) also derive an expression for labor's share which is remarkably similar to equation (10). One major difference is that they *assume* that worker rents are a function of labor market institutions, while we *derive* the share of rents going to workers as a function of global market factors. Under perfect competition, labor's share will be equal to $w_{L0}v_0/\mathrm{G}(R)$, where $\mathrm{G}(R)$ is equal to **PY** and **P** is equal to marginal costs. In Blanchard and Giavazzi (2001), labor's share is equal to the competitive share, multiplied by $(1+\mu\beta)/(1+\mu)$. Labor's share rises with an increase in bargaining power, which is proxied by β. They do not model the determinants of bargaining power, stating only that they are a function of labor market institutions. In our framework, labor's share is also equal to the competitive share plus a fraction of the excess rents as determined by worker bargaining power. However, bargaining power is determined by global market factors, which are explicitly incorporated into the bargaining framework.

III. Estimation Issues

To transform (10) into an estimating equation, we begin by rewriting w_i^* as equal to what the factor would have received under perfect competition, plus a premium above or below the competitive return derived from relocating: $w_i^* = w_{i0} + \emptyset_i$. Next, we note that $\frac{w_{0L}\nu_L}{G(R)}$ and $\frac{w_{0K}\nu_K}{G(R)}$, which are simply $\frac{w_{0L}\nu_L}{\mathbf{PY}(\mathbf{v}^*)}$ and $\frac{w_{0K}\nu_K}{\mathbf{PY}(\mathbf{v}^*)}$ and can be rewritten as $\frac{(d\ln Y/d\ln \nu_L)}{\mu}$ and $\frac{(d\ln Y/d\ln \nu_K)}{\mu}$, using the first order conditions. To simplify the analysis, we will begin by assuming only one price. We will relax this assumption later, to allow relative prices of labor- and capital-intensive goods to vary. The final estimating equation will depend on which functional form we choose to approximate the production function, Y. We assume that Y can be approximated by a translog function:

$$\ln Y = a_{00} + \sum_i b_{0i} \ln \nu_i + \frac{1}{2} \sum_i \sum_m b_{im} \ln \nu_i \ln \nu_m \qquad (11)$$

Differentiating (11) with respect to each $\ln \nu_i$ yields the following:

$$\frac{w_{0L}\nu_L}{PY(v^*)} = b_{0L} + \sum_{m=2} b_{Lm} \ln\left(\frac{\nu_{Lm}}{\nu_{lm}}\right) \qquad (12a)$$

$$\frac{w_{0K}\nu_K}{PY(v^*)} = b_{0K} + \sum_{m=2} b_{Km} \ln\left(\frac{\nu_{Km}}{\nu_{lm}}\right) \qquad (12b)$$

Combining (11), (12a) and (12b) yields the following estimating equation for labor's share in country i's revenues; we just focus on one factor labor and shift i from a factor to c country subscript:

$$S_{Li} = \gamma_0 + \gamma_1 \ln\left(\frac{L_i}{K_i}\right) + \frac{1}{2}\left(\frac{\emptyset_L \nu_L}{G(R)} - \frac{\emptyset_K \nu_K}{G(R)}\right) + \frac{f_K - f_L}{2} \qquad (13)$$

To get an estimating equation for wages, we divide both sides of equation (9) by the price level to obtain the following estimating equation for the real wage paid by firm i:

$$w_{Li} = \beta_0 + \beta_1 \frac{Y}{\nu_{L\,i}} + \beta_2 w_{Li}^* + \beta_3 f_K \frac{\nu_K}{\nu_{L\,i}} \quad \beta_4 w_K^* \frac{\nu_K}{\nu_{L\,i}} - \beta_5 f_{Li} \qquad (14)$$

This framework suggests that real wages and labor's share are positively related to labor's alternative return and capital's fixed costs of relocating, and negatively related to capital's alternative return elsewhere and labor's cost of relocating. The correlation between the labor-capital ratio $\frac{L}{K}$ and labor's share is ambiguous, since the derivative of labor share with respect to $\ln(\frac{L}{K})$ varies with the elasticity of substitution between labor and capital. In the Cobb–Douglas case, for example, the derivative of labor share with respect to $\ln(\frac{L}{K})$ is zero and factor shares should be unaffected by changes in endowments. However, the coefficient on $\ln(\frac{L}{K})$ could also be positive or negative, depending on whether the elasticity of substitution is high or low. Real wages are a positive function of labor productivity, captured by our G(R)/v. As long as the fixed costs for capital of relocating exceed capital's alternative return, real wages are positively related to capital intensity. However, if the fixed cost for capital is lower than its' alternative return, making it likely that capital will relocate, then real wages are a negative function of capital intensity.

In addition, the basic specification in (17) assumes only one output and no factor-biased technical change. If there were several outputs, then relative prices of labor versus-capital intensive goods would affect relative shares. Similarly, factor-biased technical change could also affect labor shares. A modified estimating equation which includes n relative prices P and factor-biased technical change θ is given by:

$$S_{Li} = \gamma_0 + \gamma_1 \frac{w_L^* v_L}{G(R)} - \gamma_2 \frac{f_L v_L}{G(R)} - \gamma_3 \frac{w_K^* v_K}{G(R)} + \gamma_4 \frac{f_K v_K}{G(R)}$$

$$+ \gamma_5 \ln\left(\frac{L_i}{K_i}\right) + \gamma_6 \ln\left(\frac{\theta_{Li}}{\theta_{Ki}}\right) + \sum_{q=1}^{n} \hat{\gamma}_g \ln\frac{P_{ni}}{P_{Li}} \qquad (15)$$

The estimating equation (15) embeds a number of potential explanations for labor's changing share in country-level value-added. Changes in labor's share could occur primarily due to factors unrelated to globalization, such as changes in endowments of L and K, or factor-biased technological change. Another possibility is that globalization affects factor shares through changes in final goods prices. This is the standard effect deriving from a Heckscher-Ohlin (HO) framework. In the HO framework, globalization affects final goods prices, which in turn affect returns to factors used intensively to produce those goods. This effect has been examined in some detail by

Harrigan and others (see, for example, Harrigan and Balaban (1997)) and is captured in our framework by the $\hat{\gamma}_i$s. To the extent that globalization affects factor shares by altering the bargaining power of labor relative to capital, then other factors should matter as well. These include alternative returns to capital and labor, as well as the fixed costs of relocating abroad[1], which allows us to rewrite (15) as:

$$S_{Li} = \gamma_0 + \gamma_1 \ln(L_i/K_i) + \gamma_2 \ln(\theta_{Li}/\theta_{Ki})$$
$$+ 1/2(\phi_L v_L/G\,(R) - \phi_K v_K/G\,(R)) + (f_K - f_L)/2 \qquad (16)$$

Clearly, we cannot distinguish between factor-augmenting and product-specific technical change, since these variables could affect the latter as well as the former. If, however, technological change is factor augmenting, then one testable implication is that γ_1 should equal γ_2. It is easy to show that the coefficient γ_1 (and consequently, γ_2) does not need to be positive. The derivative of labor share with respect to $\ln(L/K)$ is equal to:

$$\partial S_L/\partial \ln(L/K) = \gamma_1 = (1 + 1/\sigma) \,/\, \left[(S_L/S_K)\,(1 + S_K/S_L)^2 \right]$$

In the Cobb-Douglas case, the elasticity of substitution σ is equal to -1, so the derivative of labor share with respect to $\ln(L/K)$ is zero and factor shares should be unaffected by changes in endowments. However, the coefficient on L/K could also be positive or negative, depending on whether the elasticity of substitution is high or low.

Data: To estimate (15) or (16) requires data on labor shares, endowments, returns to factors in excess of the home competitive return if the factor relocates abroad, and measures of the fixed costs of relocating for labor and capital. The United Nations gathers detailed national accounts data across countries from 1950 onwards. Labor share is defined as total compensation to employees divided by either national income or Gross Domestic Product (GDP). The number of

---

[1]One issue that we have not discussed is openness per se, as measured either by policies such as tariffs or the outcomes of such policies, typically captured by trade shares. In our framework, barriers to trade affect factor shares through their impact on the prices of labor-intensive relative to capital-intensive goods. To the extent that our measure of relative prices fails to capture the importance of trade restrictions, an ideal variable would be a measure of relative tariffs on labor versus capital.

years available by country varies; some countries begin in 1950 while others begin in 1990. Compensation includes both wages to employees and other benefits (such as realization of stock options). Since national income also includes payments to unincorporated enterprises, which are typically included as part of operating surplus and classified as payments to capital, this definition of labor share is likely to represent a low estimate of labor's share. Krueger (1999) discusses in detail some of the pitfalls involved in using national accounts data to measure labor income. He argues that the reported labor income share is probably a ceiling. Gollin (2002) argues that at least part of payments to unincorporated enterprises, also known as self-employment income, should be included in labor's share. He argues that including self-employment restores the constancy of labor shares, using a smaller cross-section of the same data source as we do here. Consequently, I also estimate (16) including alternative measures of self-employment in my definition of labor share. However, fewer countries actually report self-employment income, and those countries that do report are primarily the upper income countries. Consequently, we are faced with a dilemma: As Gollin points out, at least part of self-employment income should be included in labor's share, however, if we only include those countries, then we exclude many countries.

Labor inputs can be captured by the nation's labor force, which is collected and reported by the World Bank. For capital stock I use the series constructed by Nehru *et al.* (1993), updated to include 1997 data. I assume that the fixed cost of relocating for labor is large (possibly infinite in the short run) and captured by the country and year specific effects. The fixed costs of relocating for capital can be captured by several measures. The nominal exchange rate captures the cost of purchasing new plant and equipment if relocation occurs. We would expect that a depreciated exchange rate would increase the costs of relocating for capital, raising labor's share. I measure the nominal exchange rate as the market rate, period average, as reported by the International Monetary Fund. Other fixed costs of relocating include capital account restrictions such as withholding taxes, which make it difficult for capital to relocate. These can be captured using variables from the International Monetary Fund's annual publication, Trade and Exchange Restrictions. We simply add up the different measures of capital controls (equal to 1 if there are controls; zero otherwise) to arrive at a composite measure. A country with no capital controls would have a value of zero; a country with all types of controls would have a maximum value of 5.

The independent variables ϕ_L and ϕ_K measure the return to labor and capital in the foreign country, relative to the home competitive return. Unfortunately, these are not directly observed. As a proxy for the return to labor if it relocates in a foreign country, I use the ratio of foreign GDP per worker to GDP per worker at home, lagged one period, as well as net remittances into and out of the country. We would expect that if alternative returns to labor are higher abroad, then inward remittances rise. In our model this would be associated with an increase in labor's share. As a proxy for the relative return to capital at home versus abroad, I use gross inflows and outflows of foreign direct investment. In future versions of this paper, alternative returns to both factors will also be calculated using the data on capital and labor payments, divided by measures of L and K. For each country, an alternative return to each factor can be calculated using the rest of the world data on factor payments and factor quantities.

The basic specification assumes only one output and no factor-biased technical change. If there were several outputs, then relative prices of labor versus-capital intensive goods would affect relative shares. Similarly, factor-biased technical change could also affect labor shares. A modified estimating equation which includes relative prices as well as factor-biased technical change and allows for time variation by adding subscript t is given by:

$$S_{Lit} = \gamma_0 + \gamma_1 \ln(L_i/K_i) + \gamma_2 \ln(\theta_{Lit}/\theta_{Kit}) + \gamma_3 \ln(P_{Lit}/P_{Kit})$$

$$+ 1/2(\phi_L v_L/G(R) - \phi_K v_K/G(R))_{it} + (f_{Kit} - f_{Lit})/2 \quad (17)$$

At the aggregate level, prices of labor-intensive and capital-intensive goods are not available. However, relative prices can be proxied in several different ways. Bourguigion and Morrisson (1990) argue that relative prices are a function of relative world supplies of factors. This suggests using world endowments of labor relative to capital as a proxy for relative prices. Another possibility, which is used in this paper, is to use the export and import price indices calculated by the World Bank. I define the price of labor-intensive goods as the average export price of the most labor-intensive countries, defined as those countries with labor to capital ratios in the top 5 percent of the distribution each year. Similarly, the price of capital-intensive goods is defined as the average export price of the most capital-intensive countries, defined as those countries with labor to capital ratios in the bottom 5 percent of the annual distribution. To allow these prices to have differential effects across countries, the relative price is multiplied by the country's labor to capital ratio.

The estimating equations (16) and (17) embed a number of potential explanations for labor's changing share in GDP. Changes in labor's share could occur primarily due to factors unrelated to globalization, such as changes in endowments of L and K, or factor-biased technological change. These effects are captured by coefficients γ_1 and γ_2. Another possibility is that globalization affects factor shares through changes in final goods prices. This is the standard effect deriving from a Heckscher-Ohlin (HO) framework. In the HO framework, globalization affects final goods prices, which in turn affect returns to factors used intensively to produce those goods. This effect has been examined in some detail by Harrigan and others (see, for example, Harrigan and Balaban (1997)) and which is captured in our framework by γ_3. To the extent that globalization affects factor shares by altering the bargaining power of labor relative to capital, then other factors should matter as well. These include alternative returns to capital and labor abroad, as well as the fixed costs of relocating.

One factor that we have not discussed is openness per se, as measured either by policies such as tariffs or the outcomes of such policies, typically captured by trade shares. In our framework, barriers to trade affect factor shares through their impact on the prices of labor-intensive relative to capital-intensive goods. To the extent that our measure of relative prices fails to capture the importance of trade restrictions, an ideal variable would be a measure of relative tariffs on labor versus capital. Unfortunately, relative tariffs are not available across countries and over time. Typically, the only available data are trade shares or average tariffs across all goods. However, to the extent that protection is typically imposed to protect labor interests, regardless of a country's comparative advantage, then aggregate measures could provide a useful indication of trends in the prices of labor-intensive goods. Evidence in countries such as the United States suggest that protection is typically focused on labor-intensive sectors. Even in developing countries, such as Mexico or Morocco, Currie and Harrison (1997) and Hanson and Harrison (1999) show that the pattern of protection is also skewed towards protecting labor-intensive goods. Consequently, the empirical analysis will include openness to trade as an independent variable, as an imperfect means of capturing the impact of trade policy on the relative prices of labor and capital intensive goods. To the extent that increases in trade reflect a fall in the protection of labor-intensive goods, we would expect increasing openness to be associated with a fall in labor shares.

IV. Empirical Results

Stylized Facts

The United Nations gathers detailed national accounts data across countries from 1950 onwards. As discussed above, labor shares are computed both as the share of wages and benefits in national income and as a fraction of GDP, following Gollin (2002). Table 1 summarizes changes in labor shares across income categories during the entire period, where labor share is defined as wages plus compensation divided by national income. We begin the analysis by focusing on changes in labor's share after 1993, since this has been a topic of recent concern. Countries are defined as rich if they are above the median GDP per capita in 1985. Raw means, reported in the first two rows and first two columns, indicate a slight decrease in labor's share in national income from the 1960s through 1993 to the 1993–1996 period. The means also show that labor's share in national income is almost the same in poor and rich countries.

Table 1. Changes in Labor Shares: Different Means by Income Category

	Poor	Rich	Bottom 20%	Bottom Middle 20%	Middle 20%	Upper Middle 20%	Top 20%
Mean labor share, prior to 1990	.447	.505	.323	.515	.430	.492	.528
Mean labor share, 1990–2000	.442	.488	.426	.453	.404	.467	.520
Mean within country change in labor share, prior to 1990	−.0001	.0005	−.004	−.001	−.0001	−.0008	.001
Mean within country change in labor share, 1990–2000	−.003	−.001	.001	−.010	−.003	−.002	.0002

These means, however, hide important within country changes in labor shares. Since the composition of the means may change as countries are added or leave the sample, the last three rows in Table 1 are more informative for indicating within country changes in labor's share. These means show that in poor countries, labor's share fell on average by .1 percentage points per year prior to 1993. The decline in labor's share was more rapid after 1993: labor's share fell on average by .3 percentage points per year. In the rich countries, labor's share grew by .2 percentage points prior to 1993 and fell by .4 percentage points per year after 1993. These means indicate a reversal in the trend for rich countries post- 1993, while they indicate a persistent decline in labor's share for poor countries during the entire period.

If we take means for all countries within each subperiod, then look at within country differences, we get a slightly different story. The last row in Table 1 shows again that poor countries on average exhibited a decline in labor share post-1993, if we take within country means before and after 1993 and then take the difference between the two. Using this approach, labor shares in rich countries increased slightly. Overall, the trends suggest a fall in labor shares in the poorer countries, and a slight increase in rich countries post 1993.

The next 5 columns of Table 1 report changes in labor shares by quintiles. The results are similar to those in the first two columns. In general, labor shares rise with income, although the progression is not perfect. Focusing on the last row of Table 1, the mean changes in labor income follow a clear pattern: labor share fell in the poorest countries, changed very little in the upper middle 20 percent of countries, and increased in the richest countries. The progression is quite clear: enormous declines in labor's share in the poorest 20 percent of countries, and significant increases in labor's share in the top 20 percent of all countries.

One question which naturally arises is how accurate are these data? Since this is the only comprehensive source of national accounts data, a systematic comparison with other data sources is not possible. However, UNIDO does collect manufacturing wages for a select number of countries. For six countries, calculated changes in labor shares relative to an index using the UNIDO data. For both data sources, we set 1977 equal to 100. Average manufacturing wages, weighted by employment in each subsector, were multiplied by the labor force and then divided by value-added. The movements in labor shares are denoted by lshgol1. Labor shares calculated using the UN data were then plotted on the same graphs, with UN data indicated by lshgol. What is remarkable about these two different data sources is that movements in labor shares are highly correlated, although the manufacturing wage data shows larger year to year fluctuations than the UN data. This is reasonable, since the manufacturing sectors of most countries only account for a small share in the labor force, and consequently we would expect less fluctuations in the UN data, which includes all sectors of the economy.

Figures 1 through 6 provide time series evidence on labor shares for individual countries in our sample. The first 4 figures show trends in labor shares, measured using labor compensation as a share in GDP. Graphs using labor compensation as a share of national income

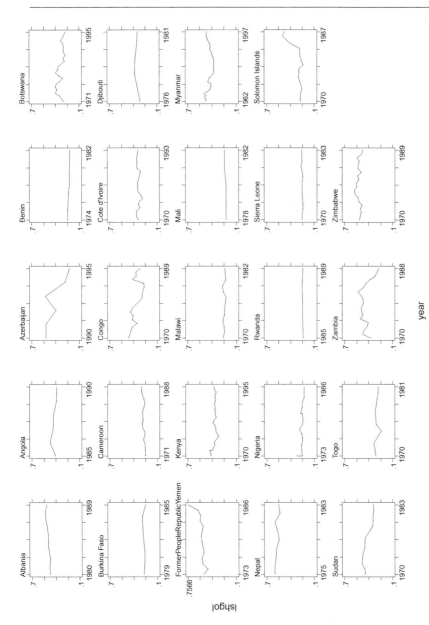

Figure 1: Trends in Labor Compensation/GDP (lshgol) Low Income Countries

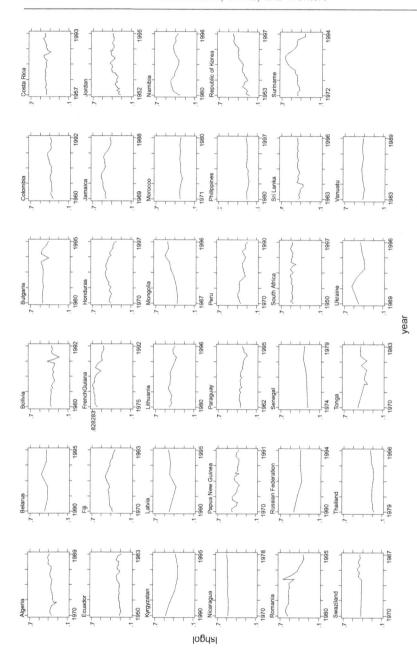

Figure 2: Trends in Labor Compensation/GDP (lshol): Lower Middle Income Countries

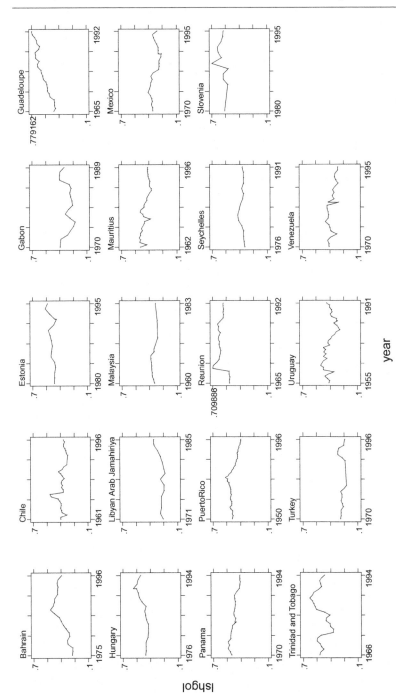

Figure 3: Trends in Labor Compensation/GDP (lshgol) Middle Income Countries

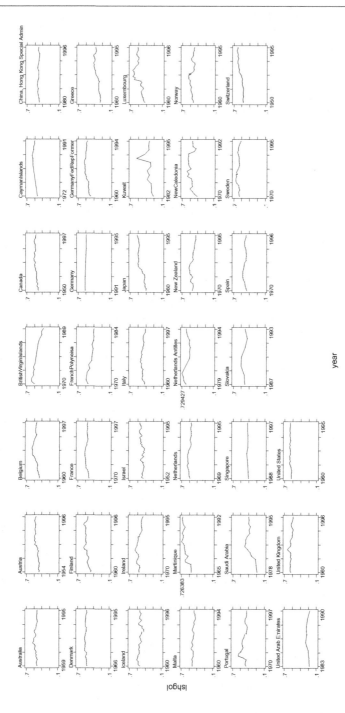

Figure 4: Trends in Labor Compensation/GDP (lshgol) Upper Income Countries

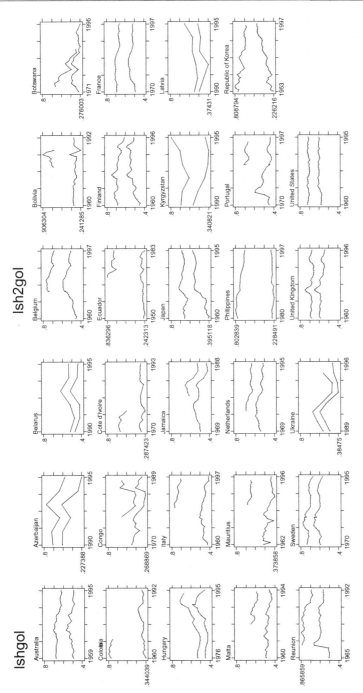

Figure 5: Trends in Labor Share: Labor Share defined as (Labor Compensation + Self-Employment Income)/GDP

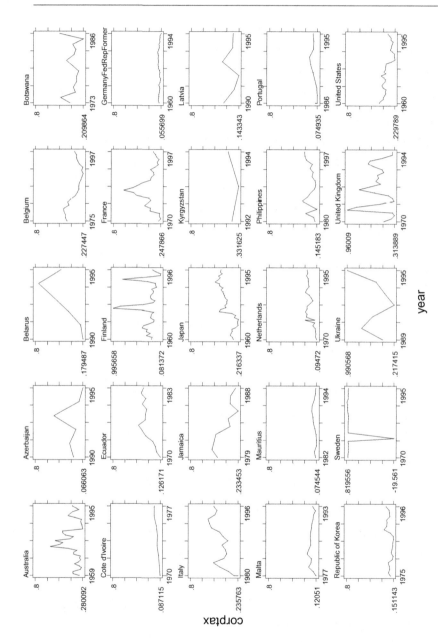

Figure 6: Trends in Corporate Tax Rates

are not included here, since the time series behavior of both is highly similar. The econometric results that follow also are very similar if we use labor compensation divided by national income or divided by GDP. A number of interesting facts emerge. First, among the high income countries (see Figure 4) the United States is almost the only country where labor's share in GDP has remained relatively stable. Since the late 1960s, labor's share in GDP in the United States has fluctuated by only a couple of percentage points of GDP. This contrasts sharply with many other countries, which have experienced both large increases as well as declines in labor shares. Among the high-income countries, Canada, Japan, and Switzerland steadily increased their labor shares over more than thirty years. However, a number of European countries have experienced declines in labor shares since the early 1970s. Those countries include Belgium, France, Ireland, Italy, the Netherlands, Norway, Portugal, Spain, Sweden, and the United Kingdom. Those declines explain the preoccupation by macro-economists such as Olivier Blanchard with falling labor shares in Europe. The results are consistent if we use national income as the denominator or GDP.

Figure 5 shows trends in labor shares if we include self-employment in the numerator with labor compensation. Including self-employment as part of labor's share significantly reduces the cross-country variation in labor's share, as pointed out very clearly in Gollin (2002). The reduction in dispersion is also evident from Figure 7. While Gollin (2002) made this point with a pure cross-section, his point is also correct if we extend his sample to include time series data, as we do in both Figures 5 and 7. However, it is important to note that the sample size is significantly reduced — to less than one third of the original sample. The sample is heavily weighted towards developed countries and a number of the eastern european countries. The second point is that even these measures of labor share do continue to vary over time, although clearly the variance is lower. Countries with large fluctuations in labor's share over time include Botswana, Congo, Finland, Hungary, Jamaica, the Netherlands, Korea, and Sweden. In these countries, labor's share

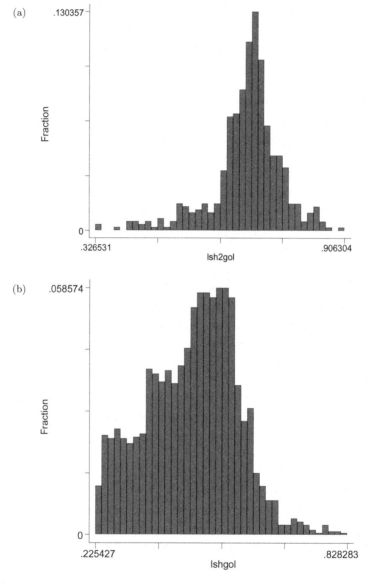

Figure 7: (a) The distribution of labor's share including self-employment, across all countries and years. (b) The distribution of labor's share excluding self-employment, across all countries and years

(even including self-employment) has fluctuated by more than 10 percentage points of GDP. Figure 5 also shows that there is a strong relationship between movements in the two measures of labor share over time for many countries. Simple correlations across the 35 countries with both measures shows that for 27 of the 35 countries, the correlation between labor share including and excluding self-employment is positive and significant and generally exceeds .7. Since self-employment has been declining in recent years (in part due to a reduction in agricultural income), this measure of labor's share shows a steady decline in many countries. Nevertheless, the range of change is smaller than if we measure labor's share using the more conventional measures. Again, the only stable country is the United States, where this modified measure of labor's share shows a variation of less than 3 percent of GDP over the last 37 years!

This paper focuses primarily on the impact of increasing globalization on labor shares. However, it is worth examining trends in one other measure that could be used to as indicators of the relative strength of capital versus labor: corporate tax rates. Rodrik (1997, p. 64) has argued that globalization has made it more difficult to tax capital and has increased labor's share of the tax burden. In theory, this is because it is easier for capital to relocate to low tax regions, while labor finds it more difficult to move.

Figure 6 reports corporate taxes paid by corporations for 25 countries with available data. There is no clear trend in corporate tax rates according to Figure 6. While it is certainly true that corporate tax rates in France, the United Kingdom, and the United States have fallen since the mid-1980s, corporate tax rates in Italy, Japan, the Philippines, the Netherlands, and Korea have increased. Nor, without further analysis, can we link these trends to globalization per se. In the remainder of this paper, we focus exclusively on explaining trends in labor shares.

Before turning to the estimation results, we report trends in labor shares using simple regressions with labor share regressed on time. The results are reported in Table 2 and Appendix Table 1. While Appendix Table A.1 reports the coefficients on time by country, Table 2 reports the results across all countries, as well as across

Table 2. Testing for a Time Trend in Labor Shares

	Coefficient on t (t-value in ())	R-Square	N	Number of Countries
Fixed effect estimation (all countries)				
Labor compensation/	.001	.001	3076	131
National income	(8.6)			
Labor	−.0001	.001	3626	152
compensation/GDP	(−0.8)			
Self-employed	−.003	.01	720	44
earnings (OSPUE)/GDP	(−12.2)			
Labor compensation +	−.002	.01	720	44
OSPUE/GDP	(−10.6)			
Labor compensation/National income				
Bottom 20%	−.002	.08	272	18
	(−4.6)			
Lower middle 20%	−.001	.01	380	18
	(−2.2)			
Middle 20%	0.000	.003	320	13
	(1.0)			
Upper middle 20%	.001	.02	388	15
	(2.6)			
Upper 20%	.002	.29	542	15
	(14.6)			
Labor compensation/GDP				
bottom 20%	−.002	.04	302	18
	(−3.4)			
Lower middle 20%	−.001	.07	447	20
	(−5.5)			
Middle 20%	−.001	.01	452	17
	(−4.2)			
Upper middle 20%	0.000	.01	452	17
	(1.5)			
Upper 20%	.002	.17	542	15
	(10.3)			

Notes: All specifications include country dummies. Percentiles based on median real GDP per capita over the period.

income quintiles based on 1985 GDP per capita. Defining labor shares as either labor compensation divided by national income or GDP, the trends are consistent with those reported in Table 1 and Chart 1. Labor share is rising across all countries, by .1 percentage point per year if labor share is defined as compensation/national income, and by .02 percentage points per year if labor share is defined as compensation/GDP. Across income categories, labor share is falling for the poor countries and rising for the rich countries. Using both definitions of national income, labor share is falling by .2 percentage points per year for countries in the bottom quintile, falling by .1 percentage points per year for the lower middle 20 percent, and falling slightly or rising for the middle and upper middle quintiles. Labor shares are rising for the top quintile, by .2 percentage points per year using either definition of labor share.

We also report results for self-employment. Across the 38 countries with available data, self-employment earnings as a share of GDP are falling, by an average of .3 percentage points per year. Consequently, if we define labor's share to include self-employment, we find that labor's share is falling across all countries with available data, by .2 percentage points per year. Clearly, our perceptions on the trends in labor's share are affected by the definition we use. However, it is also clear from the time trends reported in Tables 1 and 2 and the figures that labor share — however defined — is not constant over time.

Estimation Results

Results from estimating (17) using cross-country, annual time series data are reported in Table 3. In the remaining analysis, we chose to report results defining labor share as a percent of GDP, rather than national income. The results are similar if national income is used as the denominator, but the sample size is larger if we use GDP. A number of consistent results emerge across specifications, although with the addition of more independent variables the number of degrees of freedom falls significantly and standard errors become quite large. Across all specifications, the coefficient on relative endowments L/K is negative and significant. This suggests that one important factor driving labor shares is changes in endowments: increases in the labor force (or declines in the capital stock) lead to a fall in labor shares. This implies that the elasticity of substitution between labor and

Table 3. OLS Estimation

Independent Variables	(1)	(2)	(3)	(4)	(5)	(6)	(7) Below Median Per Capita GDP in 1985	(8) Above Median Per Capita GDP in 1985
Log (L/K)	−.077	−.097	−.085	−.105	−.098	−.088	−.066	−.122
	(−17.5)	(−10.6)	(−9.2)	(−8.0)	(−7.6)	(−6.4)	(−3.9)	(−7.5)
Capital	—	.001	.001	.002	.003	.002	.003	.003
controls		(0.9)	(0.6)	(1.6)	(2.4)	(2.1)	(1.4)	(2.0)
Relative GDP	—	−.227	−.119	−.178	−.050	−0.129	.119	−.375
per capita		(−2.2)	(−1.1)	(−1.8)	(−0.5)	(−1.4)	(1.4)	(−3.6)
Log (nominal	—	—	−.002	−.002	.0001	.001	−.003	.004
exchange rate)			(−1.9)	(−1.7)	(0.1)	(0.5)	(−2.1)	(2.7)
X+M/GDP	—	—	−.073	−.066	−.051	−.050	−.074	−.049
			(−7.2)	(−6.7)	(−5.1)	(−5.0)	(−6.0)	(−3.3)
Relative price	—	—	—	.004	.002	.001	.002	0.0
				(1.5)	(1.0)	(0.3)	(0.8)	(0.0)
Crisis	—	—	—	−.019	−.019	−.019	−.027	−.013
				(−4.5)	(−4.8)	(−4.8)	(−5.3)	(−1.9)
Inward DFI	—	—	—	—	−.153	−.192	.539	−.042
					(−0.9)	(−1.2)	(1.6)	(−0.3)
Outward DFI	—	—	—	—	0.072	0.022	13.996	−.119
					(0.6)	(0.2)	(2.7)	(−1.0)
Inward	—	—	—	—	2.094	1.471	−1.310	2.965
remittances					(0.9)	(0.6)	(−0.4)	(1.1)
Outward	—	—	—	—	−5.817	−5.740	37.833	−6.996
remittances					(−5.043)	(−5.1)	(3.5)	(−6.0)
Government	—	—	—	—	.401	.468	.515	.507
spending/GDP					(7.0)	(7.8)	(6.3)	(5.5)
GDP growth	—	—	—	—	—	−.068	−.034	−.105
						(−2.7)	(−1.3)	(−1.9)
Inflation	—	—	—	—	—	−.766	−.112	.349
						(−1.9)	(−0.3)	(3.9)
N	1608	1238	1229	1229	1227	1192	494	698
R-Square	.91	.93	.93	.93	.94	.94	.94	.91

Notes: T-statistics in (). Estimation allows for arbitrary heteroskedasticity. All estimates include time and country dummies. Dependent variable is labor share, defined as wages and compensation divided by GDP.

capital is relatively low. For example, a fall in the capital stock cannot be easily substituted with more labor, leading to a more than proportionate increase in return to capital relative to labor and resulting in a fall in labor's share. This is Poterba's explanation for the observed decline is US labor shares in the early 1990s. As indicated in columns (7) and (8), the results also suggest that capital and labor are less substitutable in rich countries than in poor countries: the coefficient on L/K is larger (and more negative) by a factor of 2 for rich countries relative to poor countries.

The coefficient on relative GDP per capita is generally negative, as predicted by the model. Higher income per person at home, relative to income abroad, weakens labor's bargaining position and leads to lower labor shares. Not surprisingly, however, this result is only true in "rich" countries. In columns (7) and (8), we distinguish between poor countries and rich countries by splitting the sample in two, based on the median GDP per capita in 1985. As the results indicate, the negative coefficient on GDP per capita in columns (2) through (6) are driven by the observations for rich countries.

Across a number of specifications, we find that capital controls are positive and statistically significant. These results are predicted by the model: higher fixed costs of relocating, as proxied by capital controls, weaken capital's bargaining position and lead to higher labor shares. The magnitude of the effect is large: For example, eliminating capital controls would raise labor's share in GDP between 1 and 2 percentage points. However, the significance on the capital control measure is not present in all specifications. In particular, capital controls are only significant if we introduce government spending as a share of GDP as an additional variable. We introduce government spending as an additional variable to investigate whether capital controls are a proxy for general government intervention in the economy. In fact the results suggest the opposite: the stronger effects of capital controls in the last four columns of Table 3 suggest that there is a negative relationship between capital controls and government spending in the data.

In column (3) we introduce the log of the nominal exchange rate. We had hypothesized that a more appreciated exchange rate would lower the fixed costs for capital of relocating abroad, resulting in a positive relationship between exchange rate depreciation and labor shares. Although our hypothesis is correct for rich countries, the coefficient is the opposite sign (negative) and significant for poor countries. One alternative interpretation is that the exchange rate captures the relative price of tradeables relative to non-tradeables. An exchange rate depreciation would indicate a fall in the price of non-tradeables, which could be linked with falling labor shares if non-tradeables are more labor-intensive. This is likely to be the case. In poor countries. Nevertheless, these results (and the results that follow) show a strong, significant correlation between exchange rate movements and labor shares for poor countries: an exchange rate depreciation is accompanied by a sharp fall in labor's share. This point is illustrated by Appendix Figure 1, which highlights the movements in labor's share in Mexico. Movements in labor share in Mexico have been driven almost entirely by movements in the exchange rate, which depreciated sharply in the early 1980s, appreciated in late 1980s and early 1990s, then depreciated sharply at the end of 1994.

In column (3) we also add the trade share in GDP, defined as exports plus imports divided by GDP. As we indicated earlier, the interpretation of the coefficient on this regressor is somewhat problematic. Nevertheless, the negative coefficient on trade shares is negative and significant, suggesting that an increase in trade shares is associated with a fall in labor shares. In column (4) we add our measure of relative price. As expected, the relative price of labor relative to capital intensive goods are positively correlated with labor's share, although the effect is not statistically significant.

In a recent paper, Diwan (1999) examines the relationship between labor shares and financial crises. Diwan defines financial crisis broadly, as a year where the nominal exchange rate depreciates by more than 25 percent between the beginning and the end of the calendar year. He finds a significant negative impact of financial crisis on labor shares. This leads him to conclude that labor is bearing disproportionately the burden (relative to capital) from financial crises associated with large swings in the exchange rate. To test whether our other measures, such as capital restrictions or trade shares, are proxying for such crises, we add Diwan's definition of financial crisis in column (4) of Table 3. Even after controlling for annual exchange rate changes, the crisis variable has a negative and statistically significant coefficient, supporting Diwan's finding that large swings in the exchange rate lead to a fall in labor's share. However, the addition of this variable leaves the other coefficients relatively unchanged. The results also suggest that an exchange rate crisis leads to a larger fall in labor's share in poor relative to rich countries, as indicated by the doubling of the coefficient on the crisis variable for poor relative to rich countries.

In columns (5) and (6) we add DFI inflows and outflows, inward and outward remittances, and government spending as additional regressors. We anticipated that DFI inflows would be a good measure of alternative returns to capital elsewhere. Consequently, we expected that an increase in inflows suggests low alternative returns to capital elsewhere, raising labor's share. Instead, the coefficient on DFI inflows is negative, while the coefficient on DFI outflows is positive, which is puzzling. One possibility is that inflows capture the ease with which investment is able to enter and leave the country. In this case, DFI flows are negative correlated with fixed costs of relocating capital, and the negative coefficient is consistent with the model. Although the coefficient on inward remittances is generally insignificant, there is a negative and significant relationship between labor's share and outward remittances. Countries where alternative returns to labor at home are higher than abroad, as proxied by the volume of outward remittances, have lower labor shares. This reflects either the lower bargaining power of labor at home or the impact of competition by immigrants on domestic wages, or both.

It is possible that the positive and significant impact of capital controls is proxying for general government intervention in an economy, which may increase labor shares through other means. For example, countries with capital controls may also intervene in labor markets, impose higher minimum wages, and take other measures to increase labor's share. To control for this possibility, we add government spending relative to GDP as an additional independent variable. This is a better direct measure of government intervention in the economy. The results suggest that government spending does have a significant redistributive impact. The coefficient on government spending is positive and significant, indicating that an increase in government spending is associated with an increase in labor's share. We add GDP growth and inflation in column (6), to test whether our results simply indicate that labor shares vary with the business cycle. Although the results indicate that labor shares are countercyclical (labor shares fall when GDP growth is higher), the addition of these variables do not affect the earlier results.

One potential problem with the estimates reported in Table 3 is that both labor shares and some of the independent variables are jointly determined. In Table 4 we redo the estimation using instrumental variables (IV). We instrument $\log(L/K)$, capital controls, DFI, government spending and trade shares with lags of all the right-hand side variables and the country's terms of trade. The results reported in Table 4 are robust to the use of IV techniques. Almost all of the point estimates in Table 4 remain very similar in magnitude, with no changes in statistical significance. The IV results continue to point to the following factors to explain a decline in labor's share: a rising labor to capital ratio, a fall in capital controls, increasing relative GDP per capita, and an exchange rate crisis. However, the negative impact of a large exchange rate depreciation on labor's share is restricted to poor countries. Trade shares are also negatively correlated with labor shares, but the results in the IV estimation suggest that in both magnitude and significance trade shares have a more important (negative) impact on labor shares in poor countries. Taken together, the results suggest that rising trade shares are associated with a decline in labor's share in poor countries, while inward DFI is associated with a decline in labor's share in rich countries. Government spending positively affects labor's share in all countries, as do capital controls.

Table 5 reports several extensions, focusing primarily on the definition of labor's share. In columns (1) through (4) of Table 5 we redefine labor's share to include self-employment. Unfortunately, many countries do not report self-employment income. The results are qualitatively the same, although there are some differences. The coefficient on $\log (L/K)$ remains negative, while the coefficient on

Table 4.   Instrumental Variable Estimation

Independent Variables	(1)	(2)	(3)	(4)	(5)	(6)	(7) Below Median Per Capita GDP in 1985	(8) Above Median Per Capita GDP in 1985
Log (L/K)	−.107	−.126	−.110	−.113	−.104	−.075	−.031	−.137
	(−10.7)	(−7.9)	(−6.8)	(−6.0)	(−6.4)	(−2.1)	(−0.8)	(−5.4)
Capital	—	.003	.002	.003	.004	.003	.002	.0003
controls		(1.8)	(1.5)	(1.8)	(2.7)	(1.4)	(0.4)	(0.2)
Relative GDP	—	−.129	.020	−.026	.094	−0.242	.016	−.640
per capita		(−1.2)	(0.2)	(−0.2)	(0.9)	(−1.1)	(0.1)	(−2.8)
Log (nominal	—	—	−.001	−.001	.0004	.003	−.006	.008
exchange rate)			(−1.0)	(−1.2)	(0.3)	(0.9)	(−2.2)	(4.4)
X+M/GDP	—	—	−.075	−.084	−.054	−.019	−.065	.034
			(−4.9)	(−5.5)	(−3.2)	(−0.6)	(−2.1)	(1.2)
Relative price	.004	.005	.005	.005	.004	−.004	.000	0.001
	(1.9)	(1.9)	(1.7)	(1.8)	(1.4)	(−0.4)	(0.0)	(0.4)
Crisis	—	—	—	−.017	−.018	−.030	−.041	−.028
				(−3.7)	(−4.2)	(−2.9)	(−4.0)	(−2.5)
Inward DFI	—	—	—	—	−.327	−.477	9.926	−.343
					(−1.2)	(−1.4)	(0.8)	(−1.1)
Outward DFI	—	—	—	—	0.078	−.165	41.248	−.340
					(0.5)	(−0.6)	(0.8)	(−2.3)
Inward	—	—	—	—	3.535	2.071	−.851	−1.417
remittances					(0.9)	(0.6)	(−0.1)	(−0.3)
Outward	—	—	—	—	−5.902	−6.052	45.403	−7.744
remittances					(−4.0)	(−3.9)	(1.4)	(−4.8)
Government	—	—	—	—	.360	.291	.418	.314
spending/GDP					(3.9)	(2.5)	(2.0)	(2.4)
GDP growth	—	—	—	—	—	−.468	−.405	−.568
						(−1.4)	(−2.2)	(−2.9)
Inflation	—	—	—	—	—	0.0	−.867	.000
						(0.0)	(0.0)	(0.0)
N	1375	1009	1009	1009	1008	977	392	585
R-Square	.92	.93	.93	.94	.94	.93	.92	.89

Notes: T-statistics in (). Estimation allows for arbitrary heteroskedasticity. All estimates include time and country dummies. Dependent variable is labor share, defined as wages and compensation divided by GDP. The relative price, the two exchange rate variables, and lagged relative GDP per capita are assumed to be exogenous; all other variables are instrumented with first and second lags, as well as with the country's terms of trade, defined as the export price divided by the average import price.

Table 5.   Extensions on the IV Estimation

Independent Variables	Labor Share Includes Self-Employment				Adding Interaction of Trade with log(L/K)
	(1) OLS	(2) OLS	(3) IV	(4) IV	(5) IV
Log (L/K)	−.063	−.065	−.054	−.060	−.104
	(−2.8)	(−3.0)	(−2.1)	(−2.2)	(−6.4)
Capital controls	.008	.007	.008	.006	.004
	(4.2)	(4.3)	(3.0)	(2.1)	(2.7)
Relative GDP	−.547	−.630	−.652	−.842	.095
per capita	(−2.0)	(−2.3)	(−2.2)	(−2.4)	(0.9)
Log (nominal	−.004	0.000	.002	.008	.0004
ex rate)	(0.9)	(0.0)	(0.3)	(1.3)	(0.3)
X+M/GDP	−.113	−.082	−.088	−.065	−.055
	(−6.4)	(−4.4)	(−3.0)	(−1.6)	(−0.7)
Relative price	.001	.001	−.004	−.003	.004
	(0.3)	(0.3)	(−0.9)	(−0.7)	(1.3)
Crisis	−.008	.000	.011	−.009	0.018
	(1.3)	(0.0)	(1.5)	(−0.7)	(−4.2)
Inward DFI	.752	0.719	1.004	.791	−.332
	(4.0)	(3.9)	(3.0)	(2.2)	(−1.2)
Outward DFI	−.187	−.167	−.010	−.281	.079
	(−1.5)	(−1.4)	(−0.1)	(−1.7)	(0.5)
Inward	8.367	9.764	7.546	11.093	3.492
remittances	(1.8)	(2.5)	(1.4)	(2.3)	(0.8)
Outward	−2.496	−2.364	−1.384	−2.805	−5.928
remittances	(−2.1)	(−2.1)	(−0.7)	(−1.5)	(−4.1)
Government	.270	.167	.063	.107	.359
spending/GDP	(2.2)	(1.4)	(0.4)	(0.9)	(3.9)
GDP growth	—	−.184	—	−.457	—
		(−3.5)		(−1.8)	
Inflation	—	.0001	—	.0001	—
		.0001		.0001	
Log(L/K)*	—	—	—	—	−.0001
(X+M/GDP)					(0.0)
N	358	356	323	320	1008
R-Square	.87	.89	.85	.87	.94

Notes: T-statistics in (). Estimation allows for arbitrary heteroskedasticity. All estimates include time and country dummies. Dependent variable is labor share, defined as wages and compensation divided by GDP. The only exception is column (2), where the dependent variable is labor compensation plus self-employment, divided by GDP. The relative price, the two exchange rate variables, and relative GDP per capita are assumed to be exogenous; all other variables are instrumented with first and second lags.

capital controls remains positive, and more than doubles in magnitude. The coefficient on relative GDP per capita is even larger in magnitude and remains negative. One difference is that the coefficient on both the nominal exchange rate and the crisis variable (reflecting large swings in the nominal exchange rate) is now close to zero, generally positive, and insignificant. This reflects the differences between rich and poor countries highlighted in Tables 3 and 4. As indicated earlier, this sample includes primarily rich countries, for whom exchange rate movements generally do not translate into a fall in labor shares.

The coefficient on trade shares is now larger in magnitude, negative, and statistically significant. The coefficient on inward DFI is positive and significant, suggesting that inward DFI is associated with an increase in labor's share. This is the major difference between this new labor share measure and the results reported in Tables 3 and 4. However, due to the small sample size, it is difficult to make generalizations about these results. In column (5) we explore the possibility that measures of globalization could affect labor shares by affecting the coefficient on L/K. The coefficient on the interaction of trade shares and L/K is generally insignificant, suggesting no effect of globalization through this particular channel. We also experimented with an interaction of effective tariffs and L/K, and obtained the same results.

Table 6 reports the results when the basic specification is redone using both five year averages and long differences. For the five year averages, all variables are averaged over five year intervals, and the OLS estimation is reported in the last four columns of Table 6. For the long differences, all variables are averaged in the first 10 years and the last 10 years of the sample, and then first-differenced. The results are reported in the first 3 columns of Table 6. What is remarkable about Table 6 is how little these transformations of the data change the basic results, particularly for the five year averages. The coefficient on the labor to capital ratio remains the same in magnitude and significance, with the same differences between rich and poor countries. Although the statistical significance of the coefficient

Table 6.   Five Year Averages and Long Differences: OLS Estimation

Independent Variables	Long Differences			Five-Year Averages			
	(1)	(2)	(3)	(4)	(5)	(6)	(7)
		Below Median Per Capita GDP in 1985	Above Median Per Capita GDP in 1985			Below Median Per Capita GDP in 1985	Above Median Per Capita GDP in 1985
Log (L/K)	−.075	−.044	−.075	−.114	−.123	−.107	−.128
	(−2.6)	(−0.7)	(−1.8)	(−3.9)	(−3.8)	(−2.6)	(−3.0)
Capital controls	.006	−.003	.009	.006	.004	.003	.002
	(0.8)	(−0.7)	(0.8)	(1.8)	(1.4)	(0.5)	(0.5)
Relative GDP	.559	−.240	−1.070	0.090	−.175	.341	−0.053
per capita	(−1.6)	(−0.8)	(−2.8)	(0.5)	(−0.9)	(1.0)	(−0.2)
Log (nominal	−.003	−.007	−.009	0.001	0.001	−.003	0.007
ex rate)	(−1.4)	(−5.8)	(−1.7)	(0.4)	(0.3)	(−1.7)	(2.2)
X+M/GDP	−.011	−.131	0.169	−.054	−.041	−.066	−.021
	(−0.2)	(−4.9)	(2.1)	(−2.0)	(−1.4)	(−1.7)	(−0.5)
Relative price	−.001	0.008	−.0001	.008	.008	.009	.007
	(−0.3)	(1.5)	(0.0)	(1.5)	(1.3)	(1.9)	(0.7)
Crisis	−.057	−.057	0.051	−.034	−.036	−.069	−.018
	(−1.8)	(−3.0)	(0.6)	(−2.6)	(−2.7)	(−4.5)	(−0.8)
Inward DFI	−5.312	108.141	−8.497	−.227	−.383	−3.547	−.154
	(−2.8)	(2.3)	(−2.8)	(−0.5)	(−0.7)	(−0.7)	(−0.3)
Outward DFI	−1.580	347.616	−4.927	−.195	−.066	16.136	−.348
	(−1.1)	(2.3)	(−1.9)	(−0.7)	(−0.2)	(1.3)	(−1.2)
Inward	−1.156	10.450	2.641	7.612	7.217	30.078	4.367
remittances	(−0.1)	(0.5)	(0.2)	(0.9)	(0.8)	(1.9)	(0.4)
Outward	−25.008	13.950	−30.910	−6.049	−.066	53.527	−7.237
remittances	(−4.7)	(0.1)	(−4.0)	(−2.6)	(−0.2)	(1.0)	(−2.9)
Government	.301	−.177	.498	.550	.434	.683	.536
spending/GDP	(1.3)	(−1.3)	(4.0)	(4.3)	(2.8)	(3.5)	(3.1)
GDP growth	—	—	—	—	−.184	—	—
					(−1.9)		
Inflation	—	—	—	—	.582	—	—
					(0.6)		
N	46	26	20	238	235	100	138
R-Square	.55	.77	.92	.96	.96	.97	.92

Notes: T-statistics in (). Estimation allows for arbitrary heteroskedasticity. Dependent variable is labor share, defined as wages and compensation divided by GDP.

on capital controls is affected by these transformations, the magnitude of the coefficient remains the same. We continue to find that trade shares are associated with a decline in labor shares. The effect

Table 7. Explaining Changes In Labor's Share, 1990–2004

Independent Variables	Change in Sample Mean, 1960–1989 to 1990–2004		Estimated Coefficient		Effect on Labor Share, Change from Earlier Period to Current Period	
	Poor	Rich	Poor	Rich	Poor	Rich
Log (L/K)	−.236	−.347	−.014	−.088	.005	.031
			(−1.5)	(−12.9)		
Capital controls (out of 1)	−.09	−.29	0.0	.009	0.0	−.002
			(0.0)	(2.8)		
Capital inflows (as % of GDP)	−.67	9.12	0.0	−.0003	0.0	−.003
			(0.0)	(−3.4)		
X + M/GDP (as % of GDP)	11.5	14.2	−.0001	−.0005	−.007	−.003
			(−0.7)	(−4.0)		
Crisis (out of 1)	.102	−.04	−.021	−.010	−.002	−.0004
			(−3.5)	(−2.2)		
Inflation			−.041	−.011		
			(−3.4)	(−1.0)		
Government spending/GDP	1.4	−1.9	.003	.002	.004	−.004
			(4.8)	(5.3)		

Notes: Poor defined as below median GDP per capita. Rich defined as above median GDP per capita. Change in sample mean calculated by first calculating within country means during 1960–1989 and 1990–2004, taking within country changes in means and then reporting the averages across rich and poor countries.

is large and statistically significant. Again, increasing government spending is associated with an increase in labor's share, exchange rate crises are associated with a fall in labor's share for poor countries, and inward DFI is associated with a decline in labor's share. Unfortunately, averaging the sample and taking long differences leads to much smaller sample sizes, and also affects the statistical significance of some coefficients.

Table 7 reports the actual changes in the independent variables between the earlier and later period, where "later" is defined as 1993 through 1996. Combined with the coefficient estimates reported in Table 4, this allows us to decompose the source of actual changes in labor's share. The results, reported in the last two columns, suggest that labor shares have increased in rich countries primarily because the capital stock has grown relative to the labor force. Another significant factor increasing labor's share in rich countries is the increase in government spending in GDP, which can account for a one percentage point increase in labor's share in national income post-1993 in the rich countries and a .4 percentage point decline in labor's share in the poor countries.

In the poor countries, although the increase in capital stock relative to the labor force has contributed to an increase in labor's share in national income, that increase has essentially been wiped out by the negative impact of reducing capital controls and depreciating exchange rates. So in the poorer countries, it does appear that globalization has had a detrimental impact on labor's share in national income. The poor countries have also been negatively affected by the larger increase in trade shares, and the fall in government spending.

Overall, the results suggest that quantitatively most important factor driving changes in labor shares are changes in relative endowments of capital relative to labor. However other factors related to liberalization of their economies have reduced labor's share in poor countries. These include reductions in capital controls and increases in trade shares, as well as a reduction in government spending and devaluations in poor countries. Large nominal exchange rate depreciations reduce the share of national income going to labor, while capital controls increase it. The magnitude of these effects is not small.

V.   Conclusion

During the 1990s, public attention increasingly focused on the potentially negative consequences of globalization. In particular, economists and other social scientists devoted extensive research efforts to understanding the links between trade liberalization and rising wage inequality. However, the focus on wage inequality eclipsed many other important research problems. This paper seeks to address these omissions by analyzing the impact of trade and capital flows on labor's share in GDP.

To test for the impact of different measures of globalization on labor shares, I combine detailed national accounts data from the United Nations with measures of trade openness, capital account restrictions, and capital flows. These data provide information on the share of labor compensation in national income or GDP across over 100 countries and over 40 years. Two interesting stylized facts emerge from the results. Contrary to received wisdom, the evidence suggests that labor shares are not constant over time. Between 1960 and the end of the 1990s, labor shares in poor countries fell, while shares in rich countries rose. Simply documenting these changes in labor's share is important; this is the first effort to show the significant fluctuations in labor's share over time. However, this paper seeks to go further, by testing whether different measures of globalization can explain these observed changes in labor shares.

Overall, the results suggest that changes in factor shares are primarily linked to changes in capital/labor ratios. However, measures of globalization (such as capital controls or direct investment flows) also play a role. Exchange rate crises in poor countries lead to declining labor shares, suggesting that labor pays disproportionately the price when there are large swings in exchange rates. Capital controls are associated with an increase in labor's share, suggesting that imposing such controls are beneficial to labor. In addition, increasing trade shares are associated with a fall in labor's share. This result is robust across specifications. Other factors, such as government spending, also matter. Increasing government spending is associated with an increase in labor shares, for both rich and poor countries. Finally, foreign investment inflows are associated with an increase in labor's share, if labor's share is measured including self-employment.

Acknowledgment

I would like to thank the Eugene Lang Foundation for financial support, Jim Harrigan and Ishac Diwan for useful discussions, Susan Collins for comments, and seminar participants at the Russell Sage Foundation, UC San Diego, Wharton, the World Bank and the IDB for comments. I would also like to thank Martin Rama for generously sharing his data on unionization and minimum wages, as well as Jason Scorse and Ravi Yatawara for superb research assistance.

Bibliography

Blanchard, Olivier, "The Medium Term", *Brookings Papers on Economic Activity*, 2:1997.

Borjas, George J. and Valerie A. Ramey, "Foreign Competition, Market Power, and Wage Inequality", *The Quarterly Journal of Economics*, November 1995.

F. Bourguignon and C. Morrisson, "Income Distribution, Development and Foreign Trade: A Cross-Sectional Analysis", *European Economic Review*, 34 (1990), 1113–1132.

Diwan, Ishac, "Labor Shares and Financial Crises", *Mimeo*, November 1999, The World Bank.

Avinash Dixit and Victor Norman, *Theory of International Trade*, Nisbet and Cambridge University Press, 1984.

Douglas Gollin, "Getting Income Shares Right", *Journal of Political Economy*, 110(2), April 2002.

Harrigan, James and Rita Balaban, "U.S. Wages in General Equilibrium: Estimating the Effects of Trade, Technology and Factor Supplies, 1963-1991", *Mimeo*, September 1997.

Krueger, Alan, "Measuring Labor's Share", NBER Working Paper Number 7006, March 1999.

Nehru, Vikram and Ashok Dhareshwar, "A New Database on Physical Capital Stocks: Sources, Methodology, and Results", *Mimeo*, World Bank, 1993.

Poterba, James, "Recent Developments in Corporate Profitability: Patterns and Explanations", *Mimeo*, March 1997.

Richardson, J. David and Elena B. Khripounova, "U.S. Labor Market Power and Linkages to International Trade: Identifying Suspects and Measures", Draft for U.S. Department of Labor, 1998.

Rodrik, Dani, Has Globalization Gone Too Far? Institute for International Economics, Washington, D.C., March 1997.

Slaughter, Matthew, "International Trade and Labor-Demand Elasticities", *Journal of International Economics*, June 2001.

Appendix

Table A.1. Trends in Labor Share (Reported Coefficient on Time)

Country	Labor Share Defined as Employee Compensation/GDP		Labor Share Defined as Employee Compensation Divided by Nat'l Income		Labor Share Defined as Employee Compensation Plus Self-Employed Income Divided by GDP	
	Coefficient	*t*-value	Coefficient	*t*-value	Coefficient	*t*-value
Albania	0.0066	6.36	*	*	*	*
Algeria	0.0033	3.02	0.0054	4.41	*	*
Angola	−0.0098	−1.18	−0.0017	−0.22	*	*
Australia	−0.0004	−1.31	0.0009	2.42	0.0018	−9.42
Austria	0.0023	13.53	0.0028	15.48	*	*
Azerbaijan	−0.0607	−9.05	−0.0705	−9.68	−0.0340	−4.51
Bahrain	0.0093	5.90	0.4312	8.61	*	*
Belarus	0.0005	0.08	*	*	0.0106	1.46
Belgium	0.0017	3.14	0.0020	3.25	−0.0034	−8.75
Belize	−0.0007	−1.80	−0.0337	−3.64	*	*
Benin	−0.0034	−5.63	−0.0042	−6.79	*	*
Bhutan	−0.0051	−14.74	−0.0138	−4.64	*	*
Bolivia	−0.0011	−2.00	−0.0015	−2.59	0.0097	1.07
Botswana	−0.0036	−3.06	−0.0054	−1.72	−0.0231	−17.59
Brit. Virgin Islands	−0.0107	−10.47	−0.0166	5.43	*	*
Bulgaria	−0.0033	−1.73	−0.0253	−1.39	0.0282	1.20
Burkina Faso	0.0063	4.05	0.0120	*	*	*
Burundi	−0.0120	−1.27	0.0049	4.01	−0.0094	−3.29
Cameroon	0.0021	3.90	0.0020	2.44	*	*
Canada	0.0013	7.34	0.0020	9.72	*	*
Cayman Islands	0.0031	1.49	−0.0032	−1.65	*	*
Chile	−0.0018	−3.42	0.0019	2.10	*	*
China/Hong Kong	−0.0004	−0.52	*	*	*	
Colombia	0.0012	3.31	0.0002	0.72	−0.0029	−1.83
Congo	−0.0070	−3.94	−0.0027	−0.74	0.0088	0.76
Costa Rica	0.0003	1.07	0.0007	3.17	*	*
Cote d'Ivoire	0.0005	1.00	0.0024	1.19	−0.0109	−2.24
Denmark	0.0002	0.55	0.0026	5.07	*	*
Djibouti	0.0059	0.75	0.0167	2.94	*	*
Ecuador	−0.0021	−3.51	−0.0078	−7.67	−0.0017	−1.20
Estonia	0.0041	2.63	−0.0014	−0.36	*	*
Fiji	−0.0015	−0.98	−0.0014	−0.82	*	*
Finland	0.0020	3.84	0.0042	6.52	−0.0020	−5.28
Former Federal Republic of Yemen	0.0104	2.61	0.0018	0.65	*	*

Table A.1. (*Continued*)

Country	Labor Share Defined as Employee Compensation/GDP		Labor Share Defined as Employee Compensation Divided by Nat'l Income		Labor Share Defined as Employee Compensation Plus Self-Employed Income Divided by GDP	
	Coefficient	*t*-value	Coefficient	*t*-value	Coefficient	*t*-value
France	0.0000	−0.08	0.0010	1.41	−0.0017	−6.37
French Guyana	−0.0109	−5.14	−0.0094	−6.69	*	*
French Polynesia	−0.0105	−10.44	*	*	*	*
Gabon	0.0027	0.86	0.0053	1.01	*	*
Germany	−0.0058	−4.10	0.0026	−1.64	*	
German Democratic Republic	0.0019	4.24	0.0029	5.63	*	*
Greece	0.0036	9.33	0.0048	10.03	*	*
Guadeloupe	0.0106	18.20			*	
Guyana	−0.0091	−3.43	0.0021	0.57	*	*
Honduras	−0.0012	−1.21	0.0009	0.07	*	*
Hungary	0.0059	3.95	*	*	0.0117	7.44
Iceland	−0.0015	−4.21	−0.0013	−3.82	*	
Indonesia	0.0007	0.23	−0.0034	−2.85	*	*
Ireland	−0.0032	−3.98	0.0013	1.23	*	*
Israel	0.0015	7.54	0.0037	11.03	*	*
Italy	−0.0008	−1.90	0.0002	0.32	−0.0041	−12.46
Jamaica	−0.0052	−3.25	−0.0033	−2.62	−0.0152	−5.29
Japan	0.0048	13.81	0.0058	15.15	0.0006	2.67
Jordan	0.0022	6.72	0.0037	14.82	*	*
Kazakhstan	−0.0013	−2.09	*	*	*	*
Kenya	*	*	−0.0011	−1.79	*	*
Kuwait	0.0149	5.33	0.0127	7.64	*	*
Kyrgyzstan	0.0339	−2.93	−0.0420	0.02	0.0211	1.40
Latvia	0.0071	0.75	0.0176	1.32	0.0212	2.06
Libyan Arab Jamahirya	0.0060	2.89	0.0039	1.43	*	*
Lithuania	−0.0044	−3.53	0.0064	2.40	*	*
Luxembourg	0.0037	6.30	−0.0002	−0.38	*	*
Malawi	−0.0031	−5.19	−0.0023	−1.85	*	*
Malaysia	−0.0022	−2.96	−0.0019	−2.37	*	*
Mali	0.0058	5.14	0.0140	*	*	*
Malta	−0.0015	−7.14	−0.0011	0.00	−0.0040	−5.62
Martinique	0.0064	7.42	*	*	*	*
Mauritius	−0.0031	7.05	−0.0027	−4.64	*	*
Mexico	−0.0034	−4.33	−0.0022	−3.04	*	*
Mongolia	0.0216	6.99	0.0161	2.47	*	*
Morocco	0.0000	−0.01	0.0008	0.65	*	*

(*Continued*)

Table A.1. (*Continued*)

Country	Labor Share Defined as Employee Compensation/GDP		Labor Share Defined as Employee Compensation Divided by Nat'l Income		Labor Share Defined as Employee Compensation Plus Self-Employed Income Divided by GDP	
	Coefficient	*t*-value	Coefficient	*t*-value	Coefficient	*t*-value
Mozambique	0.0177	4.51	0.0113	2.92	*	*
Myanmar	−0.0057	−0.86	0.0011	1.92	*	*
Namibia	−0.0020	−0.89	−0.0135	−3.46	*	*
Nepal	−0.0060	−3.42	−0.0020	−0.96	*	*
Netherlands	−0.0025	−5.27	−0.0016	−2.64	−0.0035	−7.81
Netherlands Antilles	−0.0063	−2.47	−0.0006	−0.24	*	*
New Zealand	−0.0034	−4.37	−0.0019	−2.20	*	*
New Caledonia	0.0010	0.50	*	*	*	*
Nicaragua	0.0026	3.10	0.0026	3.39	*	*
Niger	−0.0016	−0.51	0.0002	0.05	*	*
Nigeria	−0.0081	−7.10	−0.0072	−5.89	*	*
Norway	−0.0013	−3.11	−0.0002	−0.35	−0.0056	−0.57
Oman	−0.0012	−0.22	*	*	*	*
Pakistan	−0.0008	−2.73	0.0002	0.19	*	*
Panama	−0.0050	−10.81	−0.0026	−3.03	*	*
Papua New Guinea	−0.0034	−3.17	−0.0029	−2.37	*	*
Paraguay	−0.0026	−6.32	−0.0026	−5.67	*	*
Peru	−0.0069	−6.82	−0.0062	−7.67	*	*
Philippines	0.0010	1.75	0.0002	0.62	−0.0082	−11.19
Portugal	−0.0031	−2.87	−0.0017	−1.53	−0.0010	−0.66
Puerto Rico	−0.0022	−7.09	0.0049	12.57	*	*
Rep of Korea	0.0053	20.33	0.0067	24.37	−0.0033	−13.04
Reunion	0.0014	0.95	−0.0039	−5.13	−0.0056	−7.64
Romania	−0.0182	−6.71	−0.0425	−3.71	*	*
Russian Federation	−0.0259	−3.19	−0.0242	−1.38	*	*
Rwanda	0.0077	8.51	0.0093	9.06	*	*
Saudi Arabia	0.0135	8.54	0.0123	6.36	*	*
Senegal	0.0130	7.53	0.0124	6.01	*	*
Seychelles	0.0000	0.01	0.0012	1.15	*	*
Sierra Leone	−0.0063	−6.73	−0.0073	−6.43	*	*
Singapore	0.0015	1.79	−0.0012	−1.19	*	*
Slovakia	−0.0096	−1.54	*	*	*	*
Slovenia	0.0040	2.01	*	*	*	*
Solomon Islands	0.0112	3.84	0.0157	4.82	*	*
South Africa	0.0001	1.08	0.0007	3.18	*	*
Spain	−0.0010	−1.77	−0.0004	−0.69	*	*
Sri Lanka	0.0014	3.99	0.0018	2.31	*	*
St. Pierre	−0.0119	−5.98	*	*	*	*

Table A.1. (*Continued*)

Country	Labor Share Defined as Employee Compensation/GDP		Labor Share Defined as Employee Compensation Divided by Nat'l Income		Labor Share Defined as Employee Compensation Plus Self-Employed Income Divided by GDP	
	Coefficient	*t*-value	Coefficient	*t*-value	Coefficient	*t*-value
Suriname	0.0003	0.11	−0.0016	−0.56	*	*
Swaziland	0.0015	2.06	*	*	*	*
Sweden	−0.0009	−1.43	0.0018	2.28	−0.0021	−4.32
Switzerland	0.0032	20.98	0.0042	21.92	*	*
Thailand	0.0032	11.80	0.0043	12.92	*	*
Togo	−0.0028	−2.07	−0.0018	−1.13	*	*
Tonga	0.0003	0.06	−0.0013	−0.22	*	*
Trinidad and Tobago	0.0022	1.91	0.0027	1.77	*	*
Tunisia	−0.0043	−11.00	−0.0027	−7.76	*	*
Turkey	−0.0011	−1.40	−0.0009	−1.03	*	*
Ukraine	−0.0166	−2.21	−0.0193	−1.74	−0.0196	−1.57
United Arab Emirates	0.0063	4.02	0.0067	2.82	*	*
United Kingdom	−0.0015	−7.58	−0.0007	−2.53	−0.0004	−1.79
United Rep Tanzania	−0.0086	−11.10	−0.0086	−11.23	*	*
United States	0.0007	4.84	0.0015	8.34	0.0000	−0.02
Uruguay	−0.0028	−3.80	−0.0028	−3.93	*	*
Vanuatu	0.0012	0.54	−0.0012	−0.31	*	*
Venezuela	−0.0046	−4.45	−0.0053	−4.54	*	*
Yemen	−0.0032	−0.87	0.0212	3.34	*	*
Zaire	0.0198	5.53	0.0194	5.70	*	*
Zambia	−0.0057	−1.72	−0.0031	−0.91	*	*
Zimbabwe	0.0000	0.00	0.0007	0.60	*	*

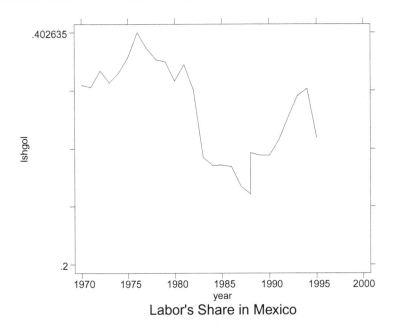

Labor's Share in Mexico

Figure A.1:

PART 2

Spillover Impacts of Foreign Direct Investment

Chapter 6

Do Domestic Firms Benefit from Direct Foreign Investment?
Evidence from Venezuela[†]

By BRIAN J. AITKEN AND ANN E. HARRISON*

Governments often promote inward foreign investment to encourage technology "spillovers" from foreign to domestic firms. Using panel data on Venezuelan plants, we find that foreign equity participation is positively correlated with plant productivity (the "own-plant" effect), but this relationship is only robust for small enterprises. We then test for spillovers from joint ventures to plants with no foreign investment. Foreign investment negatively affects the productivity of domestically owned plants. The net impact of foreign investment, taking into account these two offsetting effects, is quite small. The gains from foreign investment appear to be entirely captured by joint ventures. (JEL F2, O1, O3).

In the 1990's, direct foreign investment (DFI) became the largest single source of external finance for developing countries. In 1997, DFI accounted for about half of all private capital and 40 percent of total capital flows to developing countries. Following the virtual disappearance of commercial bank lending in the 1980's, policy makers in emerging markets eased restrictions on incoming foreign investment. Many countries even tilted the balance by offering special incentives to foreign enterprises—including lower income taxes or income tax holidays, import duty exemptions, and subsidies for infrastructure. The rationale for this special treatment often stems from the belief that foreign investment generates externalities in the form of technology transfer.

Can these subsidies be justified? Apart from the employment and capital inflows which ac-

company foreign investment, multinational activity may lead to technology transfer for domestic firms.[1] If foreign firms introduce new products or processes to the domestic market, domestic firms may benefit from the accelerated diffusion of new technology (David J. Teece, 1977). In some cases, domestic firms may increase productivity simply by observing nearby foreign firms. In other cases, diffusion may occur from labor turnover as domestic employees move from foreign to domestic firms. Several studies have shown that foreign firms initiate more on-the-job training programs than their domestic counterparts (Ralph B. Edfelt, 1975; Reinaldo Gonclaves, 1986). If these benefits from foreign investment are not completely internalized by the incoming firm, some type of subsidy could be justified.

Case studies present mixed evidence on the role of foreign investment in generating technology transfer to domestic firms. In Mauritius and Bangladesh, studies suggest that the entry of several foreign firms led to the creation of a booming, domestically owned export industry for textiles (Jong Wong Rhee and Therese Belot, 1989). Edwin Mansfield and Anthony Romeo (1980), however, found that only a few of the 15 multinationals in their survey helped

* Aitken: International Monetary Fund, 700 19th Street, NW, Washington, DC 20431; Harrison: Graduate School of Business, 615 Uris Hall, Columbia University, New York, NY 10027. The authors would like to thank three anonymous referees for very useful suggestions, as well as Susan Collins, John DiNardo, Rudi Dornbusch, Stan Fischer, David Genesove, Charles Himmelberg, Rob Porter, Ed Wolff, Mayra Zermeno, and seminar participants at Boston University, Brandeis University, Columbia University, Tufts University, MIT, Princeton University, and the NBER International and Productivity Lunches, and the NBER Summer Institute participants for useful comments and discussion. We would also like to thank Esther Jones for wonderful administrative assistance.

[1] See Richard E. Caves (1982) and Gerald K. Helleiner (1989) for surveys of technology transfer and foreign direct investment.

[†]This article originally appeared in *The American Economic Review*, **89** 605–618 © 1999 American Economic Association.

domestic firms acquire new technology. In a study of 65 subsidiaries in 12 developing countries, Dimitri Germidis (1977) found almost no evidence of technology transfer to local competitors. The lack of spillovers to domestic firms was attributed to a number of factors, including limited hiring of domestic employees in higher-level positions, very little labor mobility between domestic firms and foreign subsidiaries, limited subcontracting to local firms, no research and development by the subsidiaries, and few incentives by multinationals to diffuse their knowledge to local competitors.

Few researchers have attempted to go beyond qualitative case study evidence.[2] In this paper, we focus on two questions. First, to what extent do joint ventures or wholly owned foreign subsidiaries (hereafter referred to as "foreign" or "foreign-owned" firms) exhibit higher levels of productivity than their domestic counterparts? Second, is there any evidence of technology "spillovers" to domestically owned ("domestic") firms from these foreign entrants?

Using a richer data set, we are able to overcome important data restrictions faced by earlier researchers. In this paper, we use annual census data on over 4,000 Venezuelan firms, allowing us to measure the productivity effects of foreign ownership. Previous attempts to measure spillover effects from foreign investment faced a critical identification problem: if foreign invest-

ment gravitates towards more productive industries, then the observed correlation between the presence of foreign firms and the productivity of domestically owned firms will overstate the positive impact of foreign investment. As a result, one could find evidence of positive spillovers from foreign investment where no spillover occurs. Since we observe the behavior of each plant over time, we can control for fixed differences in productivity levels across industries which might affect the level of foreign investment. Our research confirms that these differences are in fact correlated with the pattern of foreign investment, biasing previous results.

We present two results. First, we find a positive relationship between increased foreign equity participation and plant performance, suggesting that individual plants do benefit from foreign investment. However, the positive own-plant effect is only robust for smaller plants, defined as plants with less than 50 employees. For large enterprises, the positive effects of foreign investment disappear when plant-specific differences are taken into account. This suggests that foreign investors are investing in the more productive plants. Second, productivity in domestically owned plants declines when foreign investment increases. This suggests a negative spillover from foreign to domestic enterprises, which we interpret as a market-stealing effect. If we add up the positive own-plant effect and the negative spillovers, on balance the impact of foreign investment on domestic plant productivity is quite small.

In Section I, we begin with a general discussion of the possible benefits as well as the costs of foreign investment. Section II discusses the Venezuelan data. Section III presents the estimation results and Section IV concludes the paper.

---

[2] There are several exceptions, however. In a pioneering paper, Caves (1974) tested for the impact of foreign presence on value added per worker in Australian domestically owned manufacturing sectors. Caves found that the positive disparity between foreign and domestic value added per worker disappears as foreign firms employed an increasing share of the labor in the sector, which is consistent with the spillover hypothesis. Steven Globerman (1979) replicated Caves (1974) using sectoral, cross-section data for Canadian manufacturing industries in 1972. The results are consistent with a weak spillover effect. Magnus Blomstrom and Hakan Persson (1983), Blomstrom (1986), and Blomstrom and Edward W. Wolff (1989) focus on Mexico where—as a developing country—the gap between domestic and foreign productivity and the scope for spillovers may be larger. They generally find that sectors with higher foreign ownership exhibited higher levels of productivity, faster productivity growth, and faster convergence of productivity levels to U.S. norms. Blomstrom (1989) provides a synthesis of his previous work on the impact of foreign investment in Mexico.

I. Foreign Investment, Competition, and Technology Spillovers: The Framework

The so-called "industrial organization" approach to foreign investment in manufacturing suggests that multinationals can compete locally with more informed domestic firms because multinationals possess nontangible productive assets, such as technological

VOL. 89 NO. 3   *AITKEN AND HARRISON: DIRECT FOREIGN INVESTMENT*   *607*

know-how, marketing and managing skills, export contacts, coordinated relationships with suppliers and customers, and reputation.[3] Since the assets are almost always gained through experience, they cannot be easily licensed to host country firms, but can be transferred at a reasonable cost to subsidiaries who locate in the host country (Teece, 1977). If multinationals do indeed possess such nontangible assets, then we would expect foreign ownership to increase a firm's productivity.

In addition, domestically owned firms might benefit from the presence of foreign firms. Workers employed by foreign firms or participating in joint ventures may accumulate knowledge which is valued outside the firm. As experienced workers leave the foreign firms, this human capital becomes available to domestic firms, raising their measured productivity. Likewise, some firm-specific knowledge of the foreign owners might "spill over" to domestic industry as domestic firms are exposed to new products, production and marketing techniques, or receive technical support from upstream or downstream foreign firms. Foreign firms may also act as a stable source of demand for inputs in an industry, which can benefit upstream domestic firms by allowing them to train and maintain relationships with experienced employees. In all these cases, foreign presence would raise the productivity of domestically owned firms.

But foreign presence can also *reduce* productivity of domestically owned firms, particularly in the short run. If imperfectly competitive firms face fixed costs of production, a foreign firm with lower marginal costs will have an incentive to increase production relative to its domestic competitor. In this environment, entering foreign firms producing for the local market can draw demand from domestic firms, causing them to cut production. The productivity of domestic firms would fall as they spread their fixed costs over a smaller market, forcing them back up their average cost curves. If the productivity decline from this demand effect is

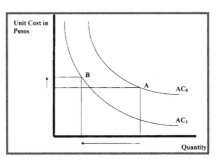

FIGURE 1. OUTPUT RESPONSE OF DOMESTIC FIRMS TO FOREIGN ENTRANTS

large enough, net domestic productivity can decline even if the multinational transfers technology or its firm-specific asset to domestic firms. These two offsetting effects were formally modelled by Aitken and Harrison (1997) and are depicted in Figure 1. Positive spillovers cause the domestic plant's average cost curve to fall from AC_0 to AC_1. However, the additional competition forces the plant to reduce output and move back up its new AC_1 curve. The net effect in Figure 1 is to increase overall costs of production.

In this paper, we estimate log-linear production functions at the plant level to answer two basic questions: (1) whether foreign equity participation is associated with an increase in the plant's productivity, and (2) whether foreign ownership in an industry affects the productivity of domestically owned firms in the same industry—i.e., whether there are positive or negative "spillovers" to domestic enterprises. Both hypotheses (1) and (2) can be nested in the same general specification:

$$(1) \quad Y_{ijt} = C + \beta_1 DFI\_Plant_{ijt}$$

$$+ \beta_2 DFI\_Sector_{jt}$$

$$+ \beta_3 DFI\_Plant_{ijt} * DFI\_Sector_{jt}$$

$$+ \beta_4 \mathbf{X}_{ijt} + \varepsilon_{ijt}.$$

Log output Y_{ijt} for plant i in sector j at time t is regressed on a vector of inputs $\mathbf{X}_{ijt}$ and two

---

[3] See Stephen Hymer (1960), Caves (1971) and, more recently, Elhanan Helpman (1984) and Ignatius J. Horstmann and James R. Markusen (1989). For surveys, see Joseph M. Grieco (1986); Alan M. Rugman (1986).

measures of foreign ownership. *DFI_Plant* is the share of foreign equity participation at the plant level, which varies between 0 and 100 percent. If foreign ownership in a plant increases that plant's productivity, we should observe a positive coefficient on *DFI_Plant*$_{ijt}$. *DFI_Sector*$_{jt}$ is a measure of the presence of foreign ownership in the industry, defined in more detail below. To the extent that the productivity advantages of foreign firms spill over to domestic firms, the coefficient on *DFI_Sector*$_{jt}$ should be positive. The coefficient on the interaction between plant-level and sector-level foreign investment (*DFI_Plant*$_{ijt}$ * *DFI_Sector*$_{jt}$) allows us to determine if the effects of foreign presence on other foreign firms differ from the effects on domestic firms. To the extent that plants with foreign investment benefit from the presence of other foreign plants, the coefficient should be positive. If joint ventures are negatively affected by the activities of other foreign plants, the coefficient should be negative.

II. Data Description

The data set employed in this paper was obtained directly from Venezuela's National Statistical Bureau, the Oficina Central de Estadistica e Informatica (OCEI). OCEI conducts an annual survey of industrial plants, known as the *Enquesta Industrial*. The years covered include 1976 through 1989, with the exception of 1980 (the industrial survey is not taken in census years). The industrial survey covers all plants in the formal sector with more than 50 workers, as well as a large sample of smaller plants. For the smaller plants, OCEI calculates the sample weights, permitting aggregation of output and other variables to estimate the importance of foreign investment in the local economy. The number of plants surveyed ranged from a low of 3,955 plants in 1982 to a high of 6,044 plants in 1978. The data set is not a balanced panel; the total number of plants varies across each year of the sample.

The original data set included 69,037 observations. To maintain confidentiality, the data set was released without plant identifiers. Consequently, we created a series of programs to relink the plants over time. In particular, we were able to use data collected on end-of-year

capital stock and beginning-of-year capital stock to link many plants. Details on the birth of the plant, its location, ownership, number of employees, and other information were available to ensure that the linking process was not spurious. Nevertheless, we were unable to link 15,569 observations, which were omitted from the sample. A number of other observations were deleted because there were too few plants in the sector, because the plant had zero sales, employment, material inputs or investment, or because the data failed to satisfy other basic error checks. All these deletions reduced the sample size to 43,010.

The data set contains information on foreign ownership, assets, output, employment, input costs, location, and product destination. *DFI_Plant* is defined as the percentage of subscribed capital (equity) owned by foreign investors. *DFI_Sector* is defined as foreign equity participation averaged over all plants in the sector, weighted by each plant's share in sectoral employment. In particular, foreign investment at the sectoral level is defined as:

$$(2) \qquad FS_{jt} = \frac{\sum\limits_{i} FS_{ijt} * Emp_{ijt}}{\sum\limits_{i} Employment_{ijt}}.$$

Since foreign firms tend to be more capital intensive than domestic firms, the share of foreign firms is significantly higher if weighted by physical capital. However, redoing the empirical analysis which follows using physical capital weights instead of employment weights leads to similar results.[4]

Output is defined as total output at the plant level, deflated by an annual producer price deflator which varies across four-digit industries. Skilled and unskilled labor is defined in terms of numbers of workers, rather than

---

[4] Foreign investment shares were computed using the original sample (prior to dropping any observations). In particular, OCEI's weights were used to reflate data which had been sampled, such as the smaller plants. This procedure was adopted in order to create a measure of foreign investment which corresponds as closely as possible to its overall sectoral share. Sector refers to the ISIC four-digit classification, which varies from 3111 to 3999.

worker hours, which were not available over the entire sample.

The importance of foreign equity participation during 1976 through 1988 varied significantly across sectors (see Appendix Table A1, available upon request from the authors). The share of foreign equity was particularly high in scientific equipment (35 percent in 1988), tobacco (32 percent in 1988), and confectionery (25 percent). In other sectors, foreign investment was very small or zero (petroleum refining, textiles and apparel, fish canning, wood-working machinery). Some sectors, such as petroleum refining, were closed to foreign investment during the sample period. In addition to the cross-section variation, there were also large changes in the share of foreign investment over the sample period. Reforms initiated in 1986 and extended in 1990 are likely to increase even further the importance of foreign investment in the domestic economy.[5]

[5] Venezuelan firms are classified by degree of foreign ownership into three types: national, with less than 20-percent foreign ownership; mixed with 20- to 49.9-percent foreign ownership; and foreign firms, with majority foreign control. Until 1989, the Superintendencia de Inversiones Extranjeras (SIEX) exercised substantial discretion in regulating the inflow of foreign investment. Profit remittances were limited to 20 percent (plus LIBOR) of the investment (based on book value). Since purchasing equity in existing firms was prohibited, foreign investment could only be in the form of direct investment registered with SIEX. Payments by a firm for its foreign partner's technology were prohibited, and contracts that called for royalty or patent payments needed SIEX approval.

During the period from 1975 to 1989, foreign firms were discriminated against in a number of ways. First, they faced higher tax rates on corporate income—50 percent versus 35 percent for domestic firms. They were also restricted from imposing confidentiality and exclusive use of trade secrets in joint ventures. Finally, foreign firms were obliged to buy bolivares at the official exchange rate rather than the free-market rate. In 1989, the restriction on profit repatriation was eliminated. Bureaucratic discretion was eliminated and SIEX was authorized to reject foreign investment applications only if they did not comply with the sectoral restrictions discussed above. When exchange rates were unified following reforms, the discrepancy between official and free-market exchange rates was eliminated. The restrictions on use of confidentiality and trade secret requirements are currently being negotiated as part of agreements on property rights, and the differential tax rates between foreign and domestic firms are addressed in pending tax legislation.

III. Effects of Foreign Investment on Productivity

A. Baseline Specification

Table 1 reports the results for equation (1). The dependent variable, the log of real output for plant i in sector j at time t, is regressed on its inputs and on foreign equity participation. Plant-level inputs (expressed in logarithms) include unskilled labor ($UNSKL_{it}$), skilled labor (SKL_{it}), materials (M_{it}), and capital (K_{it}).[6] In addition to a random component which varies across plants ε_{it}, we allow for a time-varying component D_t and control for productivity differences across industries by including four-digit level ISIC dummies. All reported estimates include corrections for heteroskedasticity. As reported in the first column of Table 1, the coefficient on foreign ownership within the plant (*Plant_DFI*) is positive and statistically significant, suggesting that there are large productivity gains associated with foreign equity participation. The point estimate, 0.105, suggests that output in plants which increased foreign equity participation from zero to 100 percent would be 10.5 percentage points higher than for comparable domestic plants. Since we already control for differences in inputs, this 10.5-percent increment is a pure total factor productivity gain.

[6] Output is calculated as the value of sales less the change in inventories, deflated by a four-digit level production (output) price deflator. Skilled and unskilled labor are measured as the number of skilled and unskilled employees. Although an ideal measure of labor input would be the number of hours worked, this information is only available for selected years. Material costs are adjusted for changes in inventories, then deflated by a production price deflator. Capital stock is the stock of capital reported by each firm at the beginning of the year, deflated by the GDP deflator. Due to space constraints, we do not report the coefficients on the inputs here. However, those are available from the authors upon request.

The producer price deflator that we use is an index for the using, not the supplying, industries. Ideally, we would want to calculate a material price deflator for each industry by using input-output tables to identify inputs, and take a weighted average of the price indices for those inputs. Unfortunately, no reliable input-output table for Venezuela was available. To the extent that output prices reflect underlying movements in the prices of material inputs, this approach is preferable to using an economywide price deflator.

610   THE AMERICAN ECONOMIC REVIEW   JUNE 1999

TABLE 1—IMPACT OF FOREIGN OWNERSHIP ON TOTAL FACTOR PRODUCTIVITY:
REGRESSING LOG OUTPUT AT THE PLANT LEVEL ON INPUTS AND THE SHARE OF FOREIGN OWNERSHIP
AT THE PLANT AND SECTOR LEVELS[a]

	Impact of direct foreign investment (DFI) on productivity		Impact of DFI on output		Impact of DFI on change in productivity			
	OLS with industry dummies[b]	OLS without industry dummies	Weighted least squares[c]	OLS with industry dummies and no factor inputs[d]	First differences[e] $(Y_t - Y_{t-1})$	Second differences[e] $(Y_t - Y_{t-2})$	Third differences[e] $(Y_t - Y_{t-3})$	Fourth differences[e] $(Y_t - Y_{t-4})$
	(1)	(2)	(3)	(4)	(5)	(6)	(7)	(8)
Foreign ownership in the plant	0.105	0.158	0.142	2.176	0.003	0.018	0.042	−0.011
(*Plant_DFI*)	(0.027)	(0.028)	(0.039)	(0.124)	(0.037)	(0.039)	(0.043)	(0.049)
Foreign ownership in the sector	−0.267	0.058	−0.206	−1.258	−0.238	−0.302	−0.248	−0.320
(*Sector_DFI*)	(0.061)	(0.030)	(0.155)	(0.232)	(0.067)	(0.065)	(0.071)	(0.083)
*Plant_DFI * Sector_DFI*	0.356	−0.212	0.314	5.003	0.262	0.420	0.384	0.658
	(0.181)	(0.189)	(0.226)	(0.810)	(0.223)	(0.246)	(0.252)	(0.288)
Number of plants	10,257	10,257	10,257	10,372	9,489	7,158	5,132	3,607
Number of observations	43,010	43,010	43,010	46,947	32,521	23,136	16,100	11,045
Hausman test[f]	38.4	—	82.9	—	—	—	—	—
R^2	0.96	0.95	0.96	0.32	0.53	0.60	0.64	0.65

[a] All specifications include annual time dummies. All standard errors (denoted in parentheses) are corrected for heteroske-dasticity. Unless otherwise specified, other independent variables (not reported here) include log materials, log skilled labor, log unskilled labor, and log capital stock. *Plant_DFI* is percentage of equity capital owned by foreigners. *Sector_DFI* is employment-weighted percentage of equity which is foreign owned at the four-digit ISIC level.
[b] Industry dummies defined at the four-digit ISIC level.
[c] Weights are the share of each plant in total annual industry output. Industry dummies are also included.
[d] Excludes the other independent variables described in note a above.
[e] Coefficients are estimated from a regression of changes in (log) output regressed on changes in (log) materials, skilled labor, unskilled labor, capital stock, changes in foreign investment at the plant and sector level, and annual time dummies.
[f] In column (2), tests for equality of coefficients between ordinary least squares (OLS) and OLS with industry dummies. In column (3), tests for equality of coefficients (excluding the time dummies) between specifications in columns (2) and (3). Bootstrapping routine used to calculate variance-covariance matrix difference for test of OLS versus weighted least squares (WLS). For details, see John Dinardo et al. (1996). In column (2), the critical 5-percent value for the $\chi^2(19) = 30.1$. In column (3), the critical 5-percent value for the $\chi^2(7) = 14.1$. A higher value indicates rejection of the test.

In contrast, we find that domestic plants in sectors with more foreign ownership are significantly less productive than those in sectors with a smaller foreign presence. The point estimate for *Sector_DFI* in the second row of Table 1 is large in magnitude, significant, and negative.[7]

[7] While expressing foreign presence as a *share* (of labor or of sales) facilitates comparisons between large and small industries, the share's behavior over time is influenced both by changes in foreign investment (the numerator) and changes in the size of the industry (the denominator). For example, if foreign plants do not adjust quickly to economic downturns, while domestic firms react immediately, this would lead us to observe a rising foreign share during periods of economic decline. If productivity is procyclical, we would wrongly infer that foreign investment has a negative impact on domestic productivity. Therefore, we also tried splitting foreign share into its numerator and denominator and including each as individual regressors. The results, reported in an earlier version of the paper, are consistent with the estimates presented in Tables 1 through

The results imply that an increase in the share of foreign investment from 0 to 10 percent leads to as much as a 2.67-percentage-point decline in domestic productivity.

The coefficient on the interaction term, *Plant_DFI * Sector_DFI,* is positive and statistically significant. The positive coefficient suggests that for plants with foreign equity participation, there are positive spillovers from foreign investment—in contrast to domestic firms. Joint ventures benefit from foreign investment in the plant as well as from foreign investment in other plants within the same sector.

Our finding of large, negative spillovers from foreign investment to domestic firms is in sharp

3. The coefficient on foreign investment—measured as the number of employees in foreign enterprises—is negative and significant.

contrast with previous econometric studies, which generally found positive spillovers. Previous researchers typically estimated some variant of equation (1) using a cross section of industries (rather than plants), where the coefficient on foreign share was interpreted as a measure of spillovers from foreign presence to domestic firms. Using data aggregated at the sectoral level, these studies were unable to control for differences in productivity across sectors which might be correlated with, but not caused by, foreign presence. If foreign investors gravitate towards more productive industries, then a specification which fails to control for differences across industries is likely to find a positive association between the share of DFI and the productivity of domestic plants even if no spillovers take place.

Evidence from Venezuela suggests this to be the case. We reestimate equation (1) without controlling for industry-specific productivity differences, a specification which is closest in spirit to earlier cross-section studies. The coefficient on *Sector_DFI* is now positive and statistically significant, which is consistent with the results of previous research (second column of Table 1). The point estimate suggests that the productivity of domestic firms is higher by 0.58 percent in industries with 10 percentage points more foreign share of employment. The coefficient on *Plant_DFI* is also larger in magnitude, rising to 0.158 from 0.105, while the interaction term is insignificant. A chi-square (Hausman) test for equality of coefficients across the two specifications in columns (1) and (2) is rejected, confirming that the differences are statistically significant.

The very different message suggested by the results in columns (1) and (2) provides an excellent example of the problems associated with cross-section estimation. If we fail to control for the fact that foreign investment is attracted to more productive sectors, we conclude that spillovers from foreign ownership are positive; once we introduce controls for industry-specific differences, however, we find evidence of negative spillovers on domestic productivity.

In column (3), we reestimate equation (1) using weighted least squares (WLS). The weights are given by each plant's share in employment. WLS allows us to attach greater importance to large plants in determining the overall impact of foreign investment. If we find significant differences between the coefficient estimates presented in columns (1) and (3), this would imply that foreign investment has different effects across small and large plants.

Under WLS, the results are qualitatively similar, with positive own-plant effects and negative spillovers. However, the positive impact of plant-level equity participation increases and the negative spillovers to domestically owned enterprises are smaller than reported in column (1). The results of the chi-square test suggest that these differences between OLS and WLS are statistically significant. In particular, it is likely that both the own-plant effect and the magnitude of negative spillovers vary systematically with plant size. We focus explicitly on the differences across small and large plants later in the paper.

Interpreted in the context of the framework discussed in Section II, the negative coefficient on *Sector_DFI* is consistent with a large detrimental impact of foreign investment on the scale of domestically owned production. We can test the implications of Figure 1 directly by observing whether the output of domestically owned firms contracts in response to a rise in foreign share. To do this, we simply reestimate equation (1), excluding plant-level inputs, which measures the relationship between domestic output levels and foreign presence. In the fourth column of Table 1, the coefficient on foreign share is large, negative, and statistically significant. The point estimate, -1.258, suggests that an increase in the share of foreign investment would lead to more than an equal and opposite decline in domestic output. If foreign investors increased their share of total sales in an industry by 10 percentage points, output produced by plants without foreign investment in that industry would decline by 12.58 percentage points. These results suggest that foreign investment reduces domestic plant productivity in the short run by forcing domestic firms to contract, thereby increasing their average costs.

As a further test for the robustness of the estimates, we reestimate equation (1) taking first-difference and long-difference transformations of the data (last four columns of Table 1). We begin with a first-difference transformation of the data and then move to a maximum of four-year differences.[8] Transforming the data into differences allows us to control for any fixed effects which could be present at the plant, instead of the industry, level. For example, the positive coefficient on *Plant_DFI* could arise from the fact that foreigners purchase shares in only the most productive domestic firms.

In the long-difference specifications, the coefficient on *Sector_DFI* remains negative and significant. It also increases in magnitude as we move from first to fourth differences, suggesting that the negative impact of foreign investment on domestic competitors does not quickly disappear but actually rises over time. The coefficient on *Plant_DFI* becomes small in sign and statistically insignificant, suggesting that the positive own-plant effects could arise from the fact that foreign investors are simply investing in the most productive firms. However, the coefficient on the interaction term remains positive and is significant at the 5-percent level. These results suggest that joint ventures do benefit from direct investment, but that the benefits are concentrated in sectors with a high share of foreign investment.

Overall, the evidence in Table 1 suggests that the positive impact of foreign investment on the productivity of domestically owned firms reported in some earlier studies is not robust when we control for differences in industry productivity. Foreign investors in Venezuela tend to locate in more productive industries, and increases in foreign investment lead to a decline in the productivity of domestic firms.

B. Could Spillovers Be "Local"?

One possible source of misspecification is that foreign investors generate positive technology spillovers, but only for plants located nearby. We might not observe these "local" benefits when we measure the impact of foreign investment for domestic firms in all regions if the benefits are too small to offset the overall negative impact across all regions. There are reasons to expect that any benefits

to domestic firms from foreign investment would be received first by their neighbors before they diffuse to other domestic firms. Whether trained workers leave the joint venture to work at nearby domestic firms, or whether the joint venture demonstrates a product, process, or market previously unknown to domestic owners, the benefits are likely to be captured first by neighboring domestic firms, and perhaps gradually spread to other, more distant domestic firms. If the positive benefits from foreign investment are received mainly by local firms, while the negative impact on market share is more widespread due to the importance of national instead of local markets, it should be possible to use the regional distribution of foreign investment to disentangle these offsetting effects.

To test for the possibility that technology is transferred at the local level, we broaden the analysis to include both regional and sectoral foreign share variables in the same regression. We measure regional foreign presence in the same way as national foreign presence; that is, we include in our estimation the share of employment in industry j in location s employed by foreign firms, denoted $Local\_Sector\_DFI_{jst}$.[9]

If foreign firms are attracted to regions which benefit from agglomeration economies or better infrastructure, then the coefficient on $Local\_Sector\_DFI$ could overestimate the positive impact of location-specific foreign investment on productivity. We address the possibility of an unobserved location fixed effect in two ways. First, we introduce proxy variables which reflect regional productivity differences. One such variable is the real wage of skilled workers, measured over all

---

[8] Since the panel is unbalanced, the number of observations declines as we take differences over a longer time horizon.

[9] We determine the location based on the Venezuelan Manufacturing Census. The census divides Venezuela into 23 regions, which in turn are subdivided into districts. Regions may have several or as many as 20 districts. In all, the total number of districts adds up to 220 separate locations, the level at which we conduct our estimation. In a country one-third larger than the state of Texas, this indicates that the average district size is 40 miles wide by 40 miles long (1,600 square miles). We calculated the average share of labor employed at foreign-owned firms for each industry and the standard deviation of this measure across districts. The size of the standard deviations indicates that foreign presence is quite unevenly distributed both across industries and across regions. In addition, most of the foreign investment is located in regions other than Caracas.

VOL. 89 NO. 3   AITKEN AND HARRISON: DIRECT FOREIGN INVESTMENT   613

TABLE 2—EFFECTS OF FOREIGN OWNERSHIP IN THE REGION ON TOTAL FACTOR PRODUCTIVITY:
REGRESSING LOG OUTPUT AT THE PLANT LEVEL ON INPUTS AND THE SHARE OF FOREIGN OWNERSHIP
AT THE PLANT LEVEL, THE SECTOR LEVEL, AND THE LOCAL LEVEL[a]

	OLS with industry dummies[b]		Within estimates[c]	
	(1) No regional controls	(2) With regional controls[d]	(3) No regional controls	(4) With regional controls[d]
Foreign ownership in the plant	0.161	0.154	0.063	0.067
(*Plant_DFI*)	(0.030)	(0.031)	(0.039)	(0.040)
Foreign ownership in the sector and region	0.068	0.015	0.035	0.040
(*Local_Sector_DFI*)	(0.023)	(0.024)	(0.032)	(0.034)
Plant_DFI * *Local_Sector_DFI*	−0.357	−0.271	−0.165	−0.189
	(0.066)	(0.068)	(0.077)	(0.080)
Foreign ownership in the sector over all regions	−0.290	−0.289	−0.317	−0.304
(*Sector_DFI*)	(0.062)	(0.063)	(0.055)	(0.057)
Plant_DFI * *Sector_DFI*	0.694	0.685	0.418	0.415
	(0.190)	(0.197)	(0.206)	(0.215)
Number of observations	43,010	41,333	43,010	41,333
Number of plants	10,257	10,190	10,257	10,190
R^2	0.96	0.96	0.98	0.98

[a] All specifications include annual time dummies. All standard errors (denoted in parentheses) are corrected for heteroskedasticity. Unless otherwise specified, other independent variables (not reported here) include log materials, log skilled labor, log unskilled labor, and log capital stock. *Plant_DFI* is percentage of equity owned by foreigners. *Sector_DFI* is employment-weighted percentage of equity which is foreign owned at the four-digit ISIC level.
[b] Industry dummies defined at the four-digit ISIC level.
[c] Estimated by subtracting from each variable its plant specific mean over all years.
[d] Regional controls include the real skilled wage and energy prices.

industries in the region. Variations in the real wage for skilled workers across regions could reflect locational advantages such as infrastructural differences, local agglomeration economies, or unobserved differences in the quality of labor. James E. Rauch (1991), for example, provides empirical evidence for the United States that variations in human capital accumulation across cities are reflected in higher wages for individuals. Since foreign investment in any one four-digit industry is unlikely to affect significantly the skilled wage for all industries in the region, the skilled wage across all industries should capture regional rather than industry-specific factors. Another factor which can be used to capture exogenous differences in productivity across regions in Venezuela is the price of energy. The Venezuelan government encouraged relocation to some regions by implementing uneven energy subsidies across regions, which could lead to apparent differences in productivity.

Second, we estimate plant-level "within" estimates by subtracting from each variable its

plant-specific mean over time. To the extent that those regional differences in productivity which might be correlated with foreign investment are relatively fixed over the sample period, this specification will produce unbiased estimates of the impact of regional foreign investment on productivity.

Using both estimation methods, we find little evidence for spillovers from local foreign investment (Table 2). The coefficients on countrywide foreign investment are negative and significant as before. If proxies for regional productivity are excluded, the coefficient on regional foreign investment is positive, albeit only marginally statistically significant [column (1)]. When wages for skilled workers and electricity prices are included, however, the coefficient on regional foreign investment becomes small in magnitude and insignificant [column (2)]. Individual firm productivity is consistently positively correlated with the real skilled wage and negatively correlated with electricity prices, as expected. This suggests that foreign investment is likely to locate in areas with highly productive skilled workers and lower energy prices, biasing the unadjusted estimates of the impact of regional foreign share upwards.

Despite the addition of regional foreign investment, the coefficients on *Sector_DFI* (country-wide, sectoral DFI) remain negative and significant in all specifications, with magnitudes similar to those reported in Table 1. The coefficient on *Plant_DFI* * *All_DFI* also remains positive and significant, indicating positive spillovers from sector-level DFI to plants with foreign equity. However, the interaction between *Plant_DFI* and *Local_Sector_DFI* is negative, suggesting that foreign plants do not benefit from foreign investors located nearby. Foreign plants benefit from a high overall level of DFI in the sector but may be hurt by foreign competitors in the same sector and geographic area.

The within estimates, reported in columns (3) and (4), yield similar results. There is no statistically significant impact of region-specific foreign investment on domestic firm productivity. The positive coefficient on foreign investment at the plant level (*Plant_DFI*) becomes small in magnitude and insignificant, which is consistent with the long-difference results in Table 1. As before, the positive coefficient on *Plant_DFI* * *All_DFI* indicates that the beneficial impact of DFI is restricted to foreign plants located in sectors with high levels of DFI.

The results in Tables 1 and 2 are robust over a variety of alternative specifications. In addition to experimenting with other measures which might reflect location-specific productivity differences, such as the number of firms in each location, we tested several variations on the definition of foreign share.[10] These alternative specifications yielded no significant differences. Alternatively, we explored the possibility

that technology transfer from foreign firms takes place slowly, and that the positive impact of foreign on domestic productivity is observed only after several years. To examine the impact of foreign investment on domestic firm productivity growth over a longer time horizon, we estimated the same specification in equation (1) but substituted lagged values for the shares of both national and regional foreign ownership. We allowed lags of up to eight years.[11] Our previous results remain unchanged. We continue to see a strong, negative impact of sectoral foreign share and a generally insignificant impact of local (regional) foreign share on productivity.

We conclude that there is no empirical support for the hypothesis that technology is transferred locally from joint ventures to domestically owned firms. Our empirical results confirm case study evidence for Venezuela, which claims few cases of technology transfer from multinationals to domestically owned firms (see, for example, Luis Matos, 1977).

C. Small versus Large Plants

The differences between the OLS and WLS results presented in Table 1 imply systematic differences across small and large plants. In Table 3, we report the coefficients from OLS and within estimation separately for small and large plants. Large plants are defined as plants with a mean of at least 50 employees over the entire sample period.

Although the results are consistent with those reported in Tables 1 and 2, some interesting differences appear. In particular, the positive own-plant effect is only robust for small plants. For small plants, the coefficient on *Plant_DFI* varies between 0.104 and 0.182, indicating that a 10-percentage-point increase in foreign equity participation would

---

[10] We reestimated equation (1) using two alternative definitions for foreign share. First, foreign share was redefined as the total number of employees in plants where at least 5 percent of assets are foreign owned, divided by the total number of employees in all plants in that sector. Second, foreign share was redefined as a zero-one variable, equal to one if there is any foreign investment at all in a region. The rationale for this specification is that the impact of foreign investment may be nonlinear, with one foreign plant in a sector potentially having as much impact on technology transfer as several foreign firms. These definitions, however, produce results similar to those in Tables 1 and 2.

[11] Similarly, we estimated the same specification as equation (1), but instead regressed the difference between current and lagged output as a function of the difference between each independent variable and its lag. We allowed differences of up to seven years. The results were similar to those we obtained by simply including lagged values of the foreign share variables.

TABLE 3—IMPACT OF FOREIGN OWNERSHIP BY PLANT SIZE:
REGRESSING LOG OUTPUT AT THE PLANT LEVEL ON INPUTS AND THE SHARE OF FOREIGN OWNERSHIP
AT THE PLANT LEVEL, THE SECTOR LEVEL, AND THE LOCAL LEVEL[a]

	Small plants (less than or equal to 49 employees)				Large plant (greater than 49 employees)			
	(1) OLS	(2) Within[b]	(3) OLS	(4) Within[b]	(5) OLS[c]	(6) Within[b,c]	(7) OLS[c]	(8) Within[b,c]
Foreign ownership in the plant	0.104	0.100	0.167	0.182	0.121	−0.018	0.174	−0.123
(*Plant_DFI*)	(0.052)	(0.055)	(0.065)	(0.084)	(0.031)	(0.049)	(0.036)	(0.073)
Foreign ownership in the sector and	—	—	0.061	0.072	—	—	−0.020	0.196
region			(0.035)	(0.058)			(0.032)	(0.218)
(*Local_Sector_DFI*)								
Plant_DFI * Local_Sector_DFI	—	—	−0.395	−0.359	—	—	−0.203	−0.285
			(0.138)	(0.170)			(0.080)	(0.247)
Foreign ownership in the sector over all	−0.349	−0.340	−0.366	−0.363	−0.127	−0.214	−0.128	−0.180
regions)	(0.074)	(0.074)	(0.076)	(0.093)	(0.105)	(0.111)	(0.113)	(0.173)
(*Sector_DFI*)								
Plant_DFI * Sector_DFI	1.184	0.046	1.475	0.559	0.351	0.411	0.590	1.033
	(0.595)	(0.564)	(0.584)	(0.837)	(0.205)	(0.279)	(0.225)	(0.372)
Number of observations	29,179	29,179	28,069	28,069	13,831	13,831	13,264	13,264
Number of plants	7,620	7,620	7,563	7,563	2,637	2,637	2,627	2,627
R^2	0.90	0.96	0.90	0.94	0.90	0.94	0.90	0.96

[a] Industry dummies included in all OLS specifications. All standard errors (denoted in parentheses) are corrected for heteroskedasticity. Unless otherwise specified, other independent variables (not reported here) include log materials, log skilled labor, log unskilled labor, and log capital stock. *Plant_DFI* is percentage of equity owned by foreigners. *Sector_DFI* is employment-weighted percentage of equity which is foreign owned at the four-digit ISIC level.
[b] Estimated by subtracting from each variable its plant-specific mean over all years.
[c] Regional controls include the real skilled wage and energy prices.

be associated with an increase in productivity of between 0.1 and 0.2 percentage points. For large plants, however, the coefficient on *Plant_DFI* is not robust across specifications, becoming insignificantly different from zero when we take into account plant-specific effects. The results suggest that the lack of robustness in the own-plant effect identified in Tables 1 and 2 are due entirely to large plants. Across these plants, foreign investors apparently target the more productive enterprises. For small plants, however, there appears to be a strong, independent positive effect of foreign equity participation on productivity levels.

The spillover effects of DFI, captured by *Sector_DFI,* also vary across plant size. The point estimates are negative for both small and large plants, but the magnitudes are double or triple in size for small plants, suggesting a much larger market-stealing effect. In addition, the coefficients are only significant for small plants, suggesting that (negative) spillovers are concentrated on smaller enterprises who cannot compete as effectively with foreign entrants as their larger domestic competitors.

D. *Overall Effects of Foreign Investment*

The results point to two quite different conclusions about the impact of foreign investment on productivity in Venezuela's manufacturing sector. On the one hand, plants with higher foreign participation exhibit positive productivity gains—although these results are only robust for smaller plants. On the other hand, plants which do not receive foreign investment exhibit productivity declines as a result of increasing foreign activity. We now measure the net impact of these two offsetting forces.

We use the following approach to determine the overall effect of foreign investment on the productivity of the manufacturing sector. Using the coefficient estimates reported in Tables 1 through 3 and the actual values of *Plant_DFI, Sector_DFI,* and *Local_Sector_DFI,* we get a net effect of DFI for each plant. We then sum this effect across all firms, weighted by the value of the firm's production, to derive the net effect on Venezuelan manufacturing for each year. In Table 4, we report the average effect over all years.

The net impact of DFI is small in magnitude and positive if we use WLS, but negative

TABLE 4—NET IMPACT OF FOREIGN OWNERSHIP ON TOTAL FACTOR PRODUCTIVITY IN THE ECONOMY:
WEIGHTED REGRESSION OF OUTPUT AT THE PLANT LEVEL ON INPUTS AND THE SHARE OF FOREIGN OWNERSHIP
AT THE PLANT AND SECTOR LEVELS[a]

	National effects only		National and regional effects		
	OLS[b] (1)	Weighted least squares[c] (2)	OLS[d] (3)	Within: Small plants[e] (4)	Within: Large plants[f] (5)
Foreign ownership in the plant (Plant_DFI)	0.105 (0.027)	0.142 (0.039)	0.154 (0.031)	0.182 (0.084)	−0.123 (0.073)
Foreign ownership in the sector and region (Local_Sector_DFI)	—	—	0.015 (0.024)	0.072 (0.058)	0.196 (0.218)
Plant_DFI * Local_Sector_DFI	—	—	−0.271 (0.068)	−0.359 (0.170)	−0.295 (0.247)
Foreign ownership in the sector over all regions (Sector_DFI)	−0.267 (0.061)	−0.206 (0.155)	−0.289 (0.063)	−0.363 (0.093)	−0.180 (0.173)
Plant_DFI * Sector_DFI	0.356 (0.181)	0.314 (0.226)	0.685 (0.197)	0.559 (0.837)	1.033 (0.372)
Net impact of DFI[g]	−0.0068	0.0004	−0.0072	−0.0100	−0.0043
Number of observations	43,010	43,010	41,333	28,069	13,264

[a] All specifications include annual time dummies. All standard errors (denoted in parentheses) are corrected for heteroskedasticity. Unless otherwise specified, other independent variables (not reported here) include log materials, log skilled labor, log unskilled labor, and log capital stock. *Plant_DFI* is percent of equity owned by foreigners. *Sector_DFI* is employment-weighted percent of equity which is foreign owned at the four-digit ISIC level.
[b] Coefficients are taken from the first column of Table 1.
[c] Coefficients are taken from the third column of Table 1. Weighted by the plant's share of total employment.
[d] Coefficients are taken from the second column of Table 2.
[e] Coefficients are taken from the fourth column of Table 3.
[f] Coefficients are taken from the eighth column of Table 3.
[g] The net impact of DFI is calculated by multiplying the coefficients in the first five rows by their actual values and then adding them together for each plant. We then sum this net effect across all plants, weighted by each plant's share of employment. The reported net effect is the average across all years.

overall using OLS or plant-level within estimates. The point estimates using unweighted
OLS suggest that the net impact of foreign
investment is to reduce total factor productivity levels by 0.7 percentage points annually.
The weighted estimates, however, suggest a
very small overall net gain: DFI raises plant
total factor productivity by 0.04 percentage
points a year. The within estimates, which
lead to negative own-plant effects for large
enterprises, suggest a negative overall impact
of DFI of 1 percentage point a year for small
plants and 0.4 percentage points a year for
large plants, adding up to a 1.4-percentage-
point decline annually. Even if we focus only
on the WLS estimates, which assign a greater
weight to large enterprises, the evidence suggests that the plant-level gains only slightly
outweigh the negative spillover effects.

IV. Conclusion

Using a panel of more than 4,000 Venezuelan plants between 1976 and 1989, we identify two effects of foreign direct investment
on domestic enterprises. First, we find that
increases in foreign equity participation are
correlated with increases in productivity for
recipient plants with less than 50 employees,
suggesting that these plants benefit from the
productive advantages of foreign owners.
Second, we find that increases in foreign ownership negatively affect the productivity of
wholly domestically owned firms in the same
industry. These negative effects are large and
robust to alternative model specifications. Although previous studies generally found positive effects, we show that these results can be
explained by the tendency for multinationals

to locate in more productive sectors and to invest in more productive plants.

On balance, our evidence suggests that the net effect of foreign ownership on the economy is quite small. Weighted least-squares estimates suggest that the positive effects for recipient firms slightly outweigh the negative effects on firms that remain domestically owned; other approaches yield a net negative impact of DFI. We conclude that there are benefits from foreign investment, but that such benefits appear to be internalized by joint ventures. We find no evidence supporting the existence of technology "spillovers" from foreign firms to domestically owned firms.

Our results raise several issues for further research. To what extent can the results for Venezuela be extended to other developing countries? The level of foreign investment in Venezuela might be too low, or the economy not sufficiently developed or diversified, to receive large benefits from foreign presence. The scope for spillovers might be greater in the export-oriented economies in East Asia.[12] We also ignore other potential gains from foreign investment, such as increased employment and inflows of capital. Finally, we may fail to capture the long-run effects of DFI. If positive effects are permanent, while the negative effects are transitory, then as unprofitable firms exit, the negative productivity effects could decline. The productive advantage of foreign ownership might increase the stock of human capital if domestic workers absorb this advantage through training and learning-by-doing. Over long periods of time, this advantage might eventually spill over through labor mobility. However, we found little evidence that such spillovers occur within our sample.

---

[12] However, results for Indonesia suggest this is not the case. Estimating production functions on data from a census of Indonesian manufacturing firms for 1975–1989, we find results similar to those for Venezuela: productivity is higher in plants which receive foreign investment, but there is a negative spillover effect for domestically owned plants in the same industry. An interesting difference is that the positive effect is much larger than that estimated for Venezuela, and the negative effect is much smaller. We also find that the positive plant-level effect of foreign investment is quite large, but becomes insignificant in a first-difference or within specification, as reported in Table 1 for Venezuela.

REFERENCES

Aitken, Brian J. and Harrison, Ann E. "Do Domestic Firms Benefit from Foreign Direct Investment? Evidence from Panel Data." Mimeo, Columbia University, 1997.

Blomstrom, Magnus. "Foreign Investment and Productive Efficiency: The Case of Mexico." *Journal of Industrial Economics*, September 1986, *35*(1), pp. 97–110.

_____ . *Foreign investment and spillovers.* London: Routledge, 1989.

Blomstrom, Magnus and Persson, Hakan. "Foreign Investment and Spillover Efficiency in an Underdeveloped Economy: Evidence from the Mexican Manufacturing Industry." *World Development*, June 1983, *11*(6), pp. 493–501.

Blomstrom, Magnus and Wolff, Edward W. "Multinational Corporations and Productivity Convergence in Mexico." Mimeo, New York University, 1989.

Caves, Richard E. "International Corporations: The Industrial Economics of Foreign Investment." *Economica*, February 1971, *38*(149), pp. 1–27.

_____ . "Multinational Firms, Competition, and Productivity in Host-Country Markets." *Economica*, May 1974, *41*(162), pp. 176–93.

_____ . *Multinational enterprise and economic analysis.* Cambridge: Cambridge University Press, 1982.

Dinardo, John; Johnston, Jack and Johnston, John. *Econometric methods.* New York: McGraw-Hill, October 1996.

Edfelt, Ralph B. "Direct Investment in a Developing Economy: Towards Evaluating the Human Resource Development Impact in Brazil." Ph.D. dissertation, University of California, Los Angeles, 1975.

Germidis, Dimitri. *Transfer of technology by multinational corporations.* Paris: Development Centre of the Organization for Economic Cooperation and Development, 1977.

Globerman, Steven. "Foreign Direct Investment and 'Spillover' Efficiency Benefits in Canadian Manufacturing Industries." *Canadian Journal of Economics*, February 1979, *12*(1), pp. 42–56.

Goncalves, Reinaldo. "Technological Spillovers and Manpower Training: A Comparative Analysis of Multinational and National Enterprises in Brazilian Manufacturing." *Jour-*

nal of Development Economics, July 1986, *11*(1), pp. 119–32.

Grieco, Joseph M. "Foreign Investment and Development: Theories and Evidence," in Thodore H. Moran, ed., *Investing in development: New roles for private capital.* New Brunswick, NJ: Transaction Books, 1986, pp. 35–60.

Helleiner, Gerald K. "Transnational Corporations and Direct Foreign Investment," in Hollis Chenery and T. N. Srinivasan, eds., *Handbook of development economics.* Amsterdam: North-Holland, 1989.

Helpman, Elhanan. "A Simple Theory of International Trade with Multinational Corporations." *Journal of Political Economy*, June 1984, *92*(3), pp. 451–71.

Horstmann, Ignatius J. and Markusen, James R. "Firm-Specific Assets and the Gains from Direct Foreign Investment." *Economica*, February 1989, *56*(221), pp. 41–48.

Hymer, Stephen. "The International Operations of National Firms: A Study of Direct Investment." Ph.D. dissertation, Massachusetts Institute of Technology, 1960.

Mansfied, Edwin and Romeo, Anthony. "Technology Transfer to Overseas Subsidiaries by U.S.-Based Firms." *Quarterly Journal of Economics*, December 1980, *95*(4), pp. 737–50.

Matos, Luis. "Multinational Corporations and Transfer of Technology: The Case of Venezuela," in Dimitri Germidis, ed., *Transfer of technology by multinational corporations.* Paris: Development Centre of the Organization for Economic Cooperation and Development, 1977.

Rauch, James E. "Productivity Gains From Geographic Concentration of Human Capital: Evidence from the Cities." Mimeo, University of California, San Diego, 1991.

Rhee, Jong Wong and Belot, Therese. "Export Catalysts in Low-Income Countries." Working paper, World Bank, 1989.

Rugman, Alan M. "New Theories of the Multinational Enterprise: An Assessment of Internalization Theory." *Bulletin of Economic Research*, May 1986, *38*(2), pp. 101–18.

Teece, David J. "Technology Transfer by Multinational Firms: The Resource Cost of Transferring Technological Know-how." *Economic Journal*, June 1977, *87*(346), pp. 242–61.

Chapter 7

Does direct foreign investment affect domestic credit constraints?[†]

Ann E. Harrison[a],[*], Margaret S. McMillan[b]

[a]*Department of Agricultural and Resource Economics, 329 Giannini Hall, University of California, Berkeley, Berkeley, CA 94720-3310, USA*
[b]*Department of Economics, 304 Braker Hall, Tufts University, Medford, MA 02155, USA*

Received 23 March 2001; received in revised form 18 January 2002; accepted 6 June 2002

Abstract

Firms in developing countries cite credit constraints as one of their primary obstacles to investment. Direct foreign investment may ease credit constraints by bringing in scarce capital. Alternatively, if foreign firms borrow heavily from domestic banks, they may crowd local firms out of domestic capital markets. Using firm data from the Ivory Coast, we test whether: (1) domestic firms are more credit constrained than foreign firms, and (2) whether borrowing by foreign firms exacerbates domestic firm credit constraints. Results provide support for both hypotheses. We also find that state-owned enterprises (SOEs) are less financially constrained than other domestic enterprises.
© 2002 Published by Elsevier B.V.

Keywords: Foreign Direct Investment; Credit Constraints

JEL classification: F23

"Not all direct foreign investment around the world represents net capital flows. Often such investments are financed in local markets."
Martin Feldstein (2000)

*Corresponding author.
E-mail addresses:* harrison@are.berkeley.edu (A.E. Harrison), Margaret.McMillan@tufts.edu (M.S. McMillan).

[†]This article originally appeared in *Journal of International Economics*, **61** 73–100

74   *A.E. Harrison, M.S. McMillan / Journal of International Economics 61 (2003) 73–100*

1. Introduction

   Firms in developing countries typically cite credit constraints as one of their primary obstacles to investment.[1] Direct foreign investment may ease credit constraints by bringing in scarce capital. For example, domestically owned businesses in poor countries are much more likely to face credit constraints than multinational firms.[2] This is one of the reasons policy makers in developing countries have eased restrictions on inward DFI and in many instances provide special incentives for DFI. Yet, if foreign firms borrow heavily from local banks, they may exacerbate domestic firm credit constraints by crowding them out of domestic capital markets.[3]
   Apart from anecdotal and survey evidence, there is little empirical evidence on capital market imperfections and firm level investment in developing countries[4]. One reason for the limited empirical evidence is the difficulty in obtaining detailed firm-level data for these countries. Most of the existing evidence is difficult to interpret because these surveys are typically administered by institutions in a position to make loans such as the World Bank. Hence, firms have an incentive to report that they are credit constrained. Leading theorists, however, recognize the important role that capital market imperfections play in developing countries.[5] There is also a large body of empirical evidence for developed countries that suggests that capital market imperfections play an important role in determining firm-level investment decisions.[6]
   In this paper, we analyze whether incoming foreign investment in developing countries plays an important role in alleviating domestic firms' credit constraints. We measure the impact of incoming direct foreign investment on domestic firms' credit constraints using firm-level data for the Ivory Coast. Specifically, we use an augmented Euler investment model to test the following hypotheses: (1) domestic

---

[1] In a recent survey of executives in 20 African countries, financing constraints were cited as a major obstacle to business expansion (Harvard Institute for International Development and World Economic Forum, 1998). In the Ivory Coast, financing constraints were ranked third out of 21; the first and second obstacles were taxation and political instability.

[2] In a recent survey on Kenya, the primary complaint of domestically owned businesses was credit constraints. Multinational enterprises in Kenya, however, did not cite credit constraints as a problem. Rather, they cited access to foreign exchange as their primary obstacle to doing business.

[3] For example, Stiglitz in an address to the Chicago Council on Foreign Relations (1998) argues that there is broad agreement about the fact that foreign direct investment brings additional capital. Feldstein (2000) argues that this is not necessarily the case.

[4] A recent exception is Love (2000), which shows that the sensitivity of investment to availability of internal funds (a proxy for financing constraints) is linked to overall financial development. Other exceptions are Tybout (1983), Harris et al. (1994), Jaramillo et al. (1996), Gelos and Werner (1999), Patillo (2000), and Bigsten et al. (2000).

[5] See for example, Aghion et al. (1999) and Banerjee and Newman (1994).

[6] For an excellent survey, see "Capital-Market Imperfections and Investment," by R. Glenn Hubbard (1998). See also Schiantarelli (1996) on methodological issues

A.E. Harrison, M.S. McMillan / Journal of International Economics 61 (2003) 73–100   75

firms face different credit constraints than foreign firms, and (2) borrowing by foreign firms affects the credit constraints of domestic firms. We modify the standard Euler investment model by introducing a borrowing constraint and then use as proxies for the shadow value of the constraint two measures of financial distress, the debt to asset and interest coverage ratios. In the absence of such constraints, these financial variables should not play a role in determining future investment. Using this framework, we also explore the differential impact of DFI on the credit constraints of state-owned enterprises (SOEs) and private domestic firms.

The results suggest that only domestic firms face credit constraints in the Ivory Coast. We also find evidence of crowding out. Specifically, we find that the share of foreign long-term borrowing at the sector level exacerbates domestic firms' credit constraints and has no effect on foreign firms' credit constraints. When we split domestic firms into public (government-owned) and private firms, we find that public firms' investment decisions are not sensitive to debt ratios or the cost of debt. Nor is there any evidence that public firms are affected by foreign borrowing in domestic credit markets. We interpret this as evidence in support of the notion of a soft budget constraint for public firms. In contrast, private domestic firms appear more credit constrained than foreign firms and are crowded out by foreign borrowing. Finally, we find little evidence that this crowding out takes place via product markets.

Why would borrowing by foreign firms crowd out domestic firms? One plausible mechanism by which this may happen is indirect. Foreign firms may simply be more profitable and/or have access to more collateral and thus be a better investment for lending institutions.[7] A World Bank country economic report for Cote d'Ivoire (1978) suggests that local banks found lending to local enterprises more costly because they were generally considered more risky. This problem was compounded by the fact that interest rates were fixed, thus creating excess demand for loans and the likelihood of credit rationing. Because of interest rate ceilings, banks could not compensate for the extra cost of lending to domestic firms and hence preferred to lend to foreign firms.[8]

To determine why domestic firms are more credit constrained than foreign firms, we compare the profitability of domestic and foreign firms using standard ratio analysis. Overall, foreign firms are somewhat more profitable than domestic firms. Thus, it may be that given the choice, lenders prefer to lend to foreign firms. However, when we interact relative profitability with debt ratios and interest coverage, we find little evidence that it is relative profitability that is driving our

---

[7]Alternatively, it may have been that foreign firms had better relationships with the bankers for any of a variety of reasons.

[8]This same study states that because of low domestic interest rates, foreign firms preferred to keep excess liquidity offshore. And, as a result, the government borrowed heavily abroad to capitalize local banks.

results. Instead, the share of foreign borrowing remains significant. We conclude that the relative profitability of foreign firms is not driving our results. This paper does not attempt to calculate the implications of our results for overall welfare in Cote d'Ivoire. To properly account for the total impact of DFI on the host country, we would need to take into account the impact of foreign investment on domestic wages, profits, and employment; the role of foreign investors in promoting technology transfer; and the contribution of foreign investors to tax revenues. This is beyond the scope of this paper. However, we do compute the net impact of DFI on the availability of capital, adding together the inflows from equity purchases and foreign borrowing and subtracting the local borrowing of these firms. Because the majority of DFI in Cote d'Ivoire was financed locally, DFI did not represent a large increase in net capital flows to the economy. In fact, borrowing on local credit markets by foreign firms significantly exceeded the sum of equity purchases and foreign borrowing by these firms. From that perspective, total capital available to purely domestic firms actually shrank.

Our contribution is twofold. First, we shed light on an important question in development economics: does DFI ease or exacerbate domestic firms' credit constraints? Second, this paper provides an additional test of the approaches used by Fazzari, Hubbard, and Peterson (1988), Whited (1992), and Bond and Meghir (1994) to identify credit constraints. This literature relies on an observed correlation between investment and measures of internal (cash flow) or external (debt) funds, after controlling for other factors, to identify credit constraints. If there were no capital market imperfections, then a firm's financial structure should have no impact on investment. Typically, as a test of the approach, this literature selects firms which are a priori likely to be credit constrained, such as small firms, firms with high debts, or firms paying out low dividends. Researchers then examine whether these firms exhibit higher correlations between either investment and cash flow (FHP), or between investment and debt to asset ratios and interest coverage (Whited, 1992). Kaplan and Zingales (1997) have criticized this approach, arguing that firms which are identified as credit constrained by FHP are in fact not constrained, based on company statements and balance sheet evidence.[9] Our research provides additional support for both FHP and Whited (1992) by adding a new selection criterion: foreign ownership. One advantage of this approach is that ownership seems to provide a more exogenous criterion for splitting the sample than firm size or dividend policy, which has been the focus of

---

[9]FHP respond to this critique with a number of counter-arguments. They argue that the sample used by Kaplan and Zingales is too homogeneous to provide reliable results. FHP point out that using measures like cash stock relative to fixed investment, unused lines of credit and leverage are not reliable as indicators of relative financing constraints. They also point out that asking managers how constrained they are is not informative; in particular, company reports (relied on by Kaplan and Zingales to prove that some low dividend payout firms were not really constrained) do not indicate whether applications for loans were actually denied. See Fazzari, Hubbard, and Peterson (2000).

A.E. Harrison, M.S. McMillan / Journal of International Economics 61 (2003) 73–100 77

previous studies on credit constraints. In developing countries, we would expect that firms with foreign equity participation (and hence preferential access to capital markets) should be less credit constrained, and consequently should exhibit no relationship between investment and the availability of (internal or external) funds.

The remainder of this paper is organized as follows. Section 2 outlines the general approach used for testing for credit constraints and crowding out. Section 3 discusses the Ivorian banking sector and describes the data. Section 4 presents results of estimation. Section 5 explores the underlying reasons for the differences between domestic and foreign firms borrowing capabilities and also presents extensions on the basic results. Section 6 discusses the implications and Section 7 concludes.

2. Testing for credit constraints and crowding out: the framework

A large body of literature is devoted to determining the impact of financing constraints on investment behavior. The central idea of these studies is that investment should not be determined by a firm's net worth or internal funds but only by the firm's expected future profitability. The primary means for testing this hypothesis has been to estimate investment equations including Tobin's Q (as a proxy for expected future profitability) and measures of net worth as explanatory variables. To the extent that measures of net worth predict investment behavior, researchers conclude that financing constraints are present.

We use a similar approach except that the firms in our sample are not publicly traded and hence we do not have a direct measure of Tobin's Q. Instead, we use an Euler equation approach augmented to include the possibility of borrowing constraints. This follows fairly closely the approach used by Whited (1992), Bond and Meghir (1994) and Love (2000). Using this framework, we focus on two basic questions: (1) are firms in the Ivory Coast credit constrained, and (2) does borrowing by foreign firms exacerbate the credit constraints of domestic firms. Both of these hypotheses can be nested in the same general specification. To test for the presence of credit constraints, we proxy for the shadow value of relaxing the borrowing constraint using two firm-level measures of financial distress, the debt to assets ratio (DAR) and the interest coverage ratio (COV).

The basic idea is that, in the context of the Euler equation, these indicators of financial distress should not have any impact on future investment in a world of perfect information. If, however, there are information asymmetries which restrict borrowing, then firms that are financially distressed today will be forced to substitute investment tomorrow for investment today. Hence, the model predicts a positive relationship between the shadow value of the constraint (proxied by DAR and COV) and future investment. To test for a differential impact of ownership, we include interaction terms equal to our proxies for credit constraints multiplied by ownership. Finally, to test for the possibility of crowding out, we include a

78   *A.E. Harrison, M.S. McMillan / Journal of International Economics 61 (2003) 73–100*

variable that measures the overall level of foreign borrowing by sector and a variable that measures the overall level of foreign sales by sector. The model is described below in more detail.

2.1. An Euler equation specification

We estimate a version of the Euler equation, combining insights from Whited (1992), Bond and Meghir (1994), Gilchrist and Himmelberg (1995) and Love (2000). This is a relation between investment rates in successive periods, derived from dynamic optimization in the presence of symmetric, quadratic costs of adjustment. Under these assumptions, and as long as we assume that expectations are formed accordingly, the Euler equation model has the advantage of controlling for all expectational influences on the investment decision. Thus, we are not as susceptible to the criticism that financial variables are merely picking up information about expected future profitability of the firm.

The theoretical framework is very similar to Bond and Meghir (1994), except that we explicitly introduce a borrowing constraint in the framework, along the same lines as Whited (1992) and Love (2000). One potential criticism of Bond and Meghir (1994) is that they interpret rejection of their model as an indicator of credit constraints. Although this interpretation is quite plausible, the advantage of explicitly including credit constraints in the initial formulation is that it is no longer necessary to reject the model in order to find evidence of credit constraints, nor is it necessary to assume that rejection of the model implies the presence of credit constraints. The other advantage of our approach is that since the coefficient on cash flow is no longer the critical variable of interest for identifying credit constraints, the possibility that cash flow proxies for unobserved profit opportunities no longer poses a critical estimation problem.

A firm i is assumed to maximize the present discounted value of current and future net cash flows. The firm borrows at time t an amount given by B_{it}, and pays interest on the debt given by i_{it}. Inflation is denoted by π_{it}. The credit constraint is modeled either as a non-negative dividend constraint or as a ceiling on borrowing, denoted by B_{it}^{*}. Letting L_{it} denote variable factor inputs, w_{it} the price of variable factors, p_{it}^{I} the price of the investment good, p_{it} the price of output, β_{t+j}^{t} the nominal discount factor between period t and period $t+j$, δ the rate of depreciation, $F(K_{it}, L_{it})$ the production function gross of adjustment costs, $G(I_{it}, K_{it})$ the adjustment cost function and $E_t(.)$ the expectations operator conditional on information available in period t, the firm solves

$$\max E_t \left[\sum_{j=0}^{\infty} \beta_{t+j}^{t} R(K_{i,t+j}, L_{i,t+j}, I_{i,t+j}) \right] \tag{1}$$

Subject to the following constraints:

$$K_{it} = (1 - \delta)K_{i,t-1} + I_{it} \tag{1.1}$$

$$B_{it} \leq B_{it}^{*} \tag{1.2}$$

$$B_{it} \geq 0 \tag{1.3}$$

$$R_{it} = p_{it}F(K_{it}, L_{it}) - p_{it}G(K_{it}, L_{it}) - w_{it}L_{it} - p_{it}^{I}I_{it} - i_{t-1}B_{it-1} + B_{it}$$
$$- (1 - \pi_{t-1})B_{i,t-1} \tag{1.4}$$

and

$$R_{it} \geq 0. \tag{1.5}$$

The first constraint, (1.1) is the capital stock accounting identity. Capital stock in this period is equal to capital stock in the last period, net of depreciation, plus this period's investment. The second constraint (1.2) restricts borrowing to be less than some maximum amount of outstanding debt for firm i at time t. The third constraint (1.3) imposes the constraint that debt must be greater than or equal to zero. The fourth constraint (1.4), defines the firm's dividends (equivalent to net revenue). Dividends are defined as cash inflows less cash outflows. Inflows include sales and net borrowing, while outflows include factor and interest payments and investment expenditures. The final constraint (1.5) restricts dividends (or net revenue) to be non-negative. This constraint has the same effect as a restriction on new share issues, and as in the case of a restriction on issuing debt, can be loosely interpreted as a premium on outside equity finance.

The Euler equation characterizing the optimal investment path relates marginal adjustment costs in adjacent periods. If η_{it} represents the shadow value of the constraint (e), γ_{it} represents the shadow value of the constraint (b), and ϕ_{it} represents the shadow value of the constraint (c) then we can write,

$$(1 - \delta)(1 - (\gamma_{it} - \phi_{it}))\beta_{t+1}^{t}E_{t}\left[\left(\frac{\partial R}{\partial I}\right)_{i,t+1}\left(\frac{1 + \eta_{i,t+1}}{1 + \eta_{it}}\right)\right] = \left(\frac{\partial R}{\partial I}\right)_{it}$$
$$+ \left(\frac{\partial R}{\partial K}\right)_{it} \tag{2}$$

Defining $\theta_{it} = (1 + \eta_{i,t+1}/1 + \eta_{it})$, the first order condition becomes:

$$(1 - \delta)(1 - (\gamma_{it} - \phi_{it}))\beta_{t+1}^{t}E_{t}\left[\theta_{it}\left(\frac{\partial R}{\partial I}\right)_{i,t+1}\right] = \left(\frac{\partial R}{\partial I}\right)_{it} + \left(\frac{\partial R}{\partial K}\right)_{it}$$

The right-hand side of Eq. (2) represents the marginal cost of investment today net of the marginal increase in output (because investment is assumed to be immediately productive). The left-hand side of Eq. (2) represents the present value of the marginal adjustment cost of investing tomorrow. Note that because investment is immediately productive, postponing the investment decision involves no future loss in output. The value $\gamma_{it} - \phi_{it}$ represents the (net) multiplier associated with the borrowing constraint. Compared to an unconstrained firm, the

80   A.E. Harrison, M.S. McMillan / Journal of International Economics 61 (2003) 73–100

firm facing a binding liquidity constraint has a higher value of $\gamma_{it} - \phi_{it}$ and thus incurs a higher marginal cost of investment today. Thus, the constrained firm behaves as if it has a higher discount rate and for a given level of adjustment costs today, will require a higher rate of return on investment today relative to investment tomorrow. Ceteris paribus, constrained firms will intertemporally substitute investment tomorrow for investment today.

The factor θ_{it} is the relative shadow cost of external finance in periods t and $t + 1$. If the shadow cost of external funds is higher in period t than it is expected to be in period $t + 1$ then $\theta_{it} < 1$ and it acts as an additional discount factor which makes current period funds more expensive to use than the next period funds and therefore induces the firm to postpone or reduce investment. In perfect capital markets, $\eta_{it} = \eta_{i,t+1} = 0$ for all t and hence $\theta_{it} = 1$, and $\gamma_{it} - \phi = 0$ and the firm is not constrained.

If we rewrite $\theta_{it} = 1 - \Lambda_{it}$, where $\Lambda_{it} = (1 - (1 + \eta_{i,t+1})/(1 + \eta_{it}))$, then our combined debt and dividend constraint is given by $(1 - (\gamma_{it} - \phi_{it}))(1 - \Lambda_{it})$. We now define,

$$\Omega_{it} = \gamma_{it}. - \Lambda_{it}\gamma_{it} + \theta_{it} - \Lambda_{it}\theta_{it}$$

So,

$$1 - \Omega_{it} = (1 - \Lambda_{it})(1 - (\gamma_{it} - \theta_{it})).$$

Substituting, (2) becomes:

$$(1 - \delta)\beta_{t+1}^{t} E_t\left[(1 - \Omega_{it})\left(\frac{\partial R}{\partial I}\right)_{i,t+1}\right] = \left(\frac{\partial R}{\partial I}\right)_{it} + \left(\frac{\partial R}{\partial K}\right)_{it} \qquad (2')$$

The major challenge is to find empirical proxies for the derivative of net revenue R with respect to I and K, as well as to find proxies for Ω_{it}. If we specify the adjustment cost function as $G(I_{it}, K_{it}) = (b/2)^*[(I/K)_{it} - c]^2 K_{it}$, which is linearly homogenous in investment and capital, Bond and Meghir (1994) show that the derivatives of net revenue with respect to I and K can be written as:

$$\left(\frac{\partial R}{\partial I}\right)_t = -b\alpha p_t\left(\frac{1}{K}\right)_t + bc\alpha p_t - p_t^t \qquad (3a)$$

$$\left(\frac{\partial R}{\partial K}\right)_t = \alpha p_t\left(\frac{Y}{K}\right)_t - \alpha p_t\left(\frac{\partial F}{\partial L}\frac{L}{K}\right)_t + b\alpha p_t\left(\frac{i}{K}\right)_t^2 - bc\alpha p_t\left(\frac{I}{K}\right)_t \qquad (3b)$$

where, $Y = F - G$ denotes net output and $\alpha = 1 - (1/\varepsilon) > 0$. We allow for imperfect competition but the price elasticity of demand ($\varepsilon > 0$) is assumed to be constant. Y is assumed to be linearly homogeneous in K and L.

If we begin by assuming that there are no credit constraints ($\Omega_{it} = 0$), then combining (3a) and (3b) above, and adding the subscript j to denote sector, yields the following estimating equation:

A.E. Harrison, M.S. McMillan / Journal of International Economics 61 (2003) 73–100   81

$$\left(\frac{I}{K}\right)_{ij,t+1} = \beta_t\left(\frac{I}{K}\right)_{ijt} - \beta_2\left(\frac{I}{K}\right)^2_{ijt} - \beta_3\left(\frac{C}{K}\right)_{ijt} + \beta_4 U_{ijt} + \beta_5\left(\frac{Y}{K}\right)_{ijt} + s_j$$
$$+ v_{ij,t+1}. \tag{4}$$

where

$$C_{ijt} = p_{ijt}\, F(K_{ijt}, L_{ijt}) - p_{ijt}\, G(I_{ijt}, K_{ijt}) - w_{ijt} L_{ijt}$$

is real cash flow and U_{ijt} is the real user cost of capital. Expected future investment (proxied by actual future investment) is positively related to current investment and negatively related to the square of current investment. Future investment is negatively related to current cash flow and positively related to the user cost of capital. Under imperfect competition, future investment is positively related to current (Y/K). We also include sector-specific effects.

The negative association between current cash flow and future investment is explained in the following way. A high level of current cash flow implies lower net marginal adjustment costs today. Because in equilibrium, marginal adjustment costs are equated across periods in expectation, this implies lower expected marginal adjustment costs and hence lower expected investment tomorrow.

2.2. Testing for credit constraints and crowding out using the Euler specification

We need to modify the basic specification in (4) to test for credit constraints. As is evident from the first order condition (2'), we need to find empirical proxies for Ω. If we linearize (using a Taylor expansion) the product of $(1 - \Omega)$ and next period's derivative of net revenue with respect to investment, then we can take Ω to the right-hand side of (4). We will empirically proxy for Ω with two firm-level measures of financial distress: the ratio of debt to fixed assets (DAR), and a measure of interest coverage (COV). In a world with no credit constraints, these measures should have no impact on investment since all that matters is the expected future profitability of investment. In a credit constrained world, these two measures will be positively related to future investment. Firms that are financially distressed are more likely to be up against their borrowing constraints and are hence more likely to postpone investment until tomorrow.

Following Whited (1992), DAR is the ratio of the market value of the firm's debt to the value of the firm's fixed assets. Thus, DAR can be interpreted both as a measure of a firm's lack of collateral and as a measure of a firm's current demand for borrowing relative to its capacity to borrow. The interest coverage ratio, COV, is defined as the ratio of the firm's interest expense to the sum of the firm's interest expense plus cash flow. A higher value of COV today means that a firm is exhausting relatively more resources on servicing its debt and is likely to be closer to its debt capacity.

To test whether foreign presence in sector j and year t alters domestic firms' credit constraints, we interact these firm-level variables with the share of foreign borrowing in sector j and year t. This yields the following empirical proxy for Ω:

$$
\begin{aligned}
\Omega = {} & \beta_5\, DAR_{ijt} + \beta_6\, COV_{ijt} \\
& + \beta_7\, DAR^{*}_{ijt} FDEBT\_Sector_{jt} + \beta_8\, COV^{*}_{ijt} FDEBT\_Sector_{jt} \\
& + \beta_9^{*} FDEBT\_Sector_{jt}
\end{aligned}
\tag{5}
$$

The coefficients on *DAR* and *COV* are expected to be positive and significant if the firm is credit constrained. The coefficients β_7 and β_8 are expected to be positive and significant if foreign borrowing ($FDEBT\_Sector_{jt}$) exacerbates credit constraints for firms in sector j at time t. This interaction term is meant to capture "credit rationing" by lenders. We interpret the coefficients on the interaction of our *DAR* and *COV* variables with foreign debt as an indicator of crowding out.

One potential area of concern is that foreign firms' share of the debt market is really capturing the negative impact of foreign entry on domestic market share, and consequently on the level of investment. To control for that possibility, we also test the following modified equation:

$$
\begin{aligned}
\Omega = {} & \beta_5 DAR_{ijt} + \beta_6 COV_{ijt} \\
& + \beta_7 DAR^{*}_{ijt} FDEBT\_Sector_{jt} + \beta_8 COV^{*}_{ijt} FDEBT\_Sector_{jt} \\
& + \beta_9^{*} FDEBT\_Sector_{jt} \\
& + \beta_{10} DAR^{*}_{ijt} FSALE\_Sector_{jt} + \beta_{11} COV^{*}_{ijt} FSALE\_Sector_{jt} \\
& + \beta_{12}^{*} FSALE\_Sector_{jt}
\end{aligned}
\tag{6}
$$

$FSALE\_Sector_{jt}$ is a measure of the level of foreign sales in sector j at time t. If the level of foreign sales in sector j makes domestic firms less profitable and therefore less able to borrow in sector j at time t, then the coefficients β_{10} and β_{11} should be positive. Eq. (6) consequently is a robustness check on our crowding out hypothesis via financial markets. If, instead, domestic firms are crowded out of local markets due to product market competition, then adding these additional terms should reduce or eliminate the significance of crowding out in the financial sector.

2.3. Estimation issues

A number of issues come up in estimation. First, the user cost of capital is typically unobservable. Like most researchers, including Bond and Meghir (1994), we proxy for the user cost of capital using firm dummies. Second, our model is restrictive in the sense that we would expect domestically owned and foreign owned enterprises to exhibit both different degrees of credit constraints as well as different sensitivities to foreign entry. To allow for a differential degree of constraints, we introduce the variable *DFI Firm*, which is the share of foreign

A.E. Harrison, M.S. McMillan / Journal of International Economics 61 (2003) 73–100   83

equity participation at the plant level, varying between 0 and 100 percent. What this means is that we will allow all the coefficients in Eqs. (4), (5) and (6) to vary with the degree of foreign ownership. We will also allow for an independent effect of foreign ownership in a plant on investment. If foreign ownership increases the overall level of investment, we should observe a positive coefficient on DFI_Firm_{ijt}. If foreign firms are less credit constrained (or not constrained at all) than domestic firms then the sign of the coefficient on the interactions between DAR and COV and DFI_Firm should be negative (or zero).

Our final estimating equation is thus:

$$
\frac{I_{ijt+1}}{K_{ijt}} = \sum_{O=d}^{f}
\left[
\begin{array}{l}
\beta_1^O\left(\dfrac{I}{K}\right)_{ijtO} - \beta_2^O\left(\dfrac{I}{K}\right)_{ijtO}^2 - \beta_3^O\left(\dfrac{C}{K}\right)_{ijtO} + \beta_4^O U_{iO} + \beta_5^O\left(\dfrac{Y}{K}\right)_{ijtO} + \beta_6^O DAR_{ijtO} \\[2mm]
+ \beta_7^O COV_{ijtO} + \beta_8^O DAR_{ijtO}^* FDEBT\_Sector_{jtO} + \beta_9^O COV_{ijtO}^* FDEBT\_Sector_{jtO} \\[2mm]
+ \beta_{10}^O FDEBT\_Sector_{jtO} + \beta_{11}^O DAR_{ijtO}^* FSALE\_Sector_{jtO} \\[2mm]
+ \beta_{12}^O COV^* FSALE\_Sector_{jtO} + \beta_{13}^O FSALE\_Sector_{jtO} + s_{jO} + d_{t+1,O} + \varepsilon_{ijtO}
\end{array}
\right]
\tag{7}
$$

Where O stands for ownership, d is domestic and f is foreign. Firms with more than an average of 49% foreign ownership over the sample period are considered foreign, otherwise, they are domestic. We also include sector dummies, s, and time dummies, d.

3. Background information

3.1. The banking sector

In the 1980s, a dominant features of the Ivorian financial system was the country's membership in the West African monetary union, which limited independent monetary policy and led to a policy of regulated interest rates. Credit demand significantly exceeded supply, leading to credit rationing and constraining the ability of firms to borrow locally to meet the investment needs. The system was dominated by commercial banks, who did little in terms of resource mobilization or term lending to productive sectors. The system was primarily designed to provide trade-related loans, with the small proportion of lending to productive activities going primarily to large and well-established concerns, many foreign owned. In part, banks were driven to these lending practices because of interest rate ceilings, which led to very small profit margins and consequently discouraged them from taking risks.

By 1984, there were 21 licensed banks in Cote d'Ivoire. The biggest four banks controlled over three-quarters of all non-government deposits. Another important characteristic of the top four banks was that all four were closely linked with French shareholder banks. For example, ownership of the largest bank, SGB-CI,

84   *A.E. Harrison, M.S. McMillan / Journal of International Economics 61 (2003) 73–100*

was divided between the French Bank Societe Generale (37%), other foreign banks (25%), private Ivorians (29%), and the Ivorian government (9%).

3.2. Data

The firm data are taken from the Banque de Donnees Financieres (BdDF), which is instructed to gather annual information on all industrial firms in the Ivory Coast. The panel is unbalanced, with the number of firms in individual years ranging from around 250 in the 1970s to nearly 500 in the mid-1980s. Although the coverage of the industrial sector is incomplete (informal enterprises are excluded and small formal firms are under-represented), the BdDF covers almost all large and medium-sized formal manufacturing enterprises. From this sample, we deleted a number of observations where firms reported zero or negative sales, employees, and/or material inputs. This left us with a sample of 399 firms over the period 1974–1987. Since the panel is unbalanced, not all firms are represented over all years.

We estimate Eq. (7) using our panel of 399 Ivorian firms during the period 1974–1987. These estimates require data on real output, capital stock, labor costs, material costs, investment, borrowing and ownership shares. We do not use reported profits; instead we compute operating cash flow as total sales less the cost of labor, material inputs and taxes. The value of the real capital stock was constructed using the perpetual inventory method. All variables were deflated by two-digit sectoral level price deflators to obtain real values. Table 1 reports summary statistics for the 399 firms in our sample.

Our measure of foreign borrowing at the sectoral level is defined as:

Table 1
Descriptive statistics of variables used in analyses

Variable	Number of observations	Mean	Standard deviation
Public ownership	2403	0.06	0.16
Private ownership	2403	0.19	0.31
Foreign ownership	2403	0.75	0.33
Investment/capital stock	2403	0.31	0.29
Log of real sales	2403	19.92	1.43
Operating cash flow/capital stock	2403	0.41	0.35
Share of foreign LT borrowing in sector j year t	2317	0.69	0.28
Share of foreign ST borrowing in sector (SC)	2317	0.74	0.22
Share of foreign ST borrowing in sector (BC)	2317	0.65	0.23
Share of foreign public borrowing in sector	2403	0.72	0.23
Share of total foreign borrowing	2317	0.69	0.25
Share of foreign sales	2403	0.72	0.24

Note: (1) SC stand for suppliers credits and BC bank credits. (2) The total variance of the share of foreign borrowing is 0.061 of which 52% is cross-sectoral variation and the remaining 48% is time-series variation. The total variance of the share of foreign sales is 0.056 of which 46% is cross-section variation and the remaining 56% is time-series variation.

A.E. Harrison, M.S. McMillan / Journal of International Economics 61 (2003) 73–100   85

$$FDEBT\_Sector_{jt} = \frac{\sum_i DEBT_{ijt}^* DFI\_Firm_{ijt}}{\sum_i DEBT_{ijt}} \tag{8}$$

Our measure of foreign sales at the sectoral level is defined as:

$$FSALE\_Sector_{ijt} = \frac{\sum_i REAL\ SALES_{ijt}^* DFI\_Firm_{ijt}}{\sum_i REAL\ SALES_{ijt}} \tag{9}$$

Our justification for using sector level variables derives from the fact that in order to mitigate portfolio risk, banks frequently diversify according to sector[10]. As an illustration, one 1995 publication which discusses bank risk management explains that "diversification means avoiding concentration in a single company, *industry group* or geographic area" [italics added for emphasis]. We also have evidence that in 1976 banks in the Ivory Coast were assigned sectoral limits by the Banque Centrale des Etats de L'Afrique de L'Ouest (World Bank, 1978)[11].

The importance of foreign equity participation during the period 1974 to 1987 is significant and variable by sector (see Table 2). The share of foreign equity was particularly high in the leather industry (93.12%) while in other sectors such as food it was less important (61.53%). Domestic participation is split between private and SOEs with private domestic firms taking the lead in all sectors but rubber and cement. In addition to cross-section variation, there were also substantial changes in the share of foreign ownership over the sample period.. Although variable, foreign participation in the Ivorian economy was significant. As a share of total reported sales in the economy foreign firms accounted for 83.15% in 1975 and 70.10% in 1987. The importance of borrowing by foreign firms is a slightly trickier issue since it is likely that foreign firms have access to funds overseas while domestic firms may not. As a share of total credit in the economy foreign firms accounted for 76.32% in 1975 and 60.89% in 1987. This probably overstates somewhat the extent to which foreign firms relied on local bank financing as opposed to other sources of financing. Nevertheless, data for 1985 (Table 2) indicate that on average only 12.8% of foreign firms' long-term funds came from overseas. Thus, a substantial portion of borrowing by foreign firms was done locally.

The number of firms in each sector and the distribution of ownership are provided in Table 2. For purposes of presentation, we aggregate up to the 2-digit SIC level (ten sectors): food processing, textiles & apparel, leather products, wood

[10]Chapter 10 in Active Bank Risk Management: enhancing investment & credit portfolio performance, The Globecom Group Ltd., 1995.
[11]The majority of manufacturing activity was located in Abidjan and thus it would have been impossible to diversify on a regional basis (World Bank, 1978).

86   *A.E. Harrison, M.S. McMillan / Journal of International Economics 61 (2003) 73–100*

Table 2
Ownership structure for 1975–1987 and origin of long term borrowing by foreign firms in 1985

Sector	Ownership structure by sector 1975–1987				Origin of long term borrowing by foreign firms in 1985 (millions of cfa francs)		
	Number of firms	Domestic public	Domestic private	Foreign	Total borrowing	Amount borrowed abroad[a]	Percent borrowed abroad
Food	85	8.05%	30.31%	61.53%	15,315	2031	13.26
Textiles & Clothing	38	11.15%	17.08%	71.60%	5610	596	10.62
Leather products	15	0%	6.89%	93.12%	559	52	9.30
Wood products	60	0.28%	25.89%	73.49%	7380	839	11.37
Chemicals	53	4.40%	13.61%	82.00%	6820	687	10.07
Rubber & Cement	6	20.42%	19.31%	60.27%	4610	167	3.62
Building materials	17	7.77%	24.03%	68.20%	1160	177	15.26
Transportation materials	35	0.69%	2.05%	99.14%	3690	1867	50.60
Tools	45	0.53%	2.33%	93.22	3870	262	6.93
Paper products	45	8.70%	24.16%	67.14%	3420	45	1.32
Total	399	5.14%	18.52%	75.97%	52,344	6,723	12.84

[a] The majority of borrowing from abroad was done in France. However some credit was sourced elsewhere but details of the origins of these loans are not available.

A.E. Harrison, M.S. McMillan / Journal of International Economics 61 (2003) 73–100   87

products, chemicals, rubber & cement, building materials, transportation materials, tools and paper products. Our analysis defines sectors at the four-digit level but is robust to defining sectors at the two and three digit level.

4. Investment equation estimates

The standard solution to measuring the user cost of capital is to assume that it can be captured by a firm fixed effect, which we already allow for in Eq. (7). Our approach to accounting for firm-fixed effects is to sweep out the fixed effects by taking deviations from firm means. However, this could induce bias in the lagged dependent variable which is one of the independent variables in Eq. (7). One solution to this problem is to account for the potential firm fixed effect by taking a within transformation, and then applying instrumental variables (IV) estimation or Generalized Method of Moments (GMM) estimation. Our approach is to sweep out the firm fixed effect by taking a Helmert transformation of Eq. (5), and then estimate the transformed equation using GMM.[12]

Table 3 reports the results from estimating Eq. (7). The basic specification is reported in column (1). We allow the coefficients to vary across foreign-owned and domestically-owned firms. As indicated earlier, a foreign firm is defined as one for which more than 49 percent of the equity is owned by foreigners. The basic specification does not include debt or interest coverage. The restrictions imposed by the model are generally accepted: the coefficient on lagged investment is positive, the coefficient on squared (lagged) investment is negative, the coefficient on Y/K is positive and the coefficient on cash flow is negative. Since we have more instruments than exogenous variables, we have a number of overidentifying restrictions in each regression. Hansen's J statistic, reported in Table 3, is distributed as a chi-square and indicates whether the overidentifying restrictions of the model are accepted.[13] In every case, the overidentifying restrictions are accepted.

---

[12]The Helmert transformation involves taking deviations from future means (see Arellano and Bover, 1991 for details). This procedure leaves the untransformed variables orthogonal to the transformed error term for period $t - 1$ and greater. Hence, we use as instruments, levels of the variables dated $t - 1$ and earlier.

[13]Because we are using GMM and because we have more instruments than exogenous variables (we have used levels of all variables in the regressions plus sector dummies as instruments), we have a number of overidentifying restrictions. Specifically, the number of overidentifying restrictions comes from fact that we have to assume that the error term is orthogonal to each of the instruments or at least close to orthogonal or that the expectation of the product of the error and the instrument is approximately equal to zero. Hansen's J is a statistic derived from the sample values of the error terms and the instruments. If the moment conditions were satisfied, HJ would be exactly equal to zero. We can say how statistically different from zero HJ is because it is distributed as a chi-square with degrees of freedom equal to the number of instruments minus the number of parameters we are estimating.

Table 3
GMM estimates of augmented Euler investment equation to test for credit constraints and crowding out

Dependent variable: Investment/fixed assets	(1) Basic model		(2) Test for credit constraints		Tests for "crowding out" or "credit rationing"				Comparison of private and state-owned enterprises			
					(3) Via financial sector		(4) Via product markets		(5) Test for credit constraints		(6) "Crowding out" via financial sector	
	D	F	D	F	D	F	D	F	SOE	Private	SOE	Private
Explanatory variables												
Lagged (investment/fixed assets)	0.592 (0.141)	0.342 (0.073)	0.563 (0.149)	0.357 (0.055)	0.539 (0.127)	0.358 (0.046)	0.589 (0.125)	0.353 (0.054)	0.358 (0.492)	0.539 (0.158)	0.738 (0.256)	0.431 (0.144)
Lagged (investment/fixed assets)^2	-0.331 (0.127)	-0.151 (0.043)	-0.293 (0.115)	-0.137 (0.058)	-0.282 (0.104)	-0.135 (0.047)	-0.317 (0.111)	-0.132 (0.032)	-0.094 (0.112)	-0.279 (0.111)	-0.397 (0.232)	-0.245 (0.090)
Lagged (sales/fixed assets)	0.017 (0.008)	0.011 (0.003)	0.031 (0.010)	0.012 (0.005)	0.039 (0.012)	0.013 (0.003)	0.039 (0.006)	0.012 (0.004)	0.059 (0.019)	0.009 (0.002)	0.039 (0.014)	0.037 (0.013)
Lagged cash flow (CF)	-0.041 (0.021)	-0.021 (0.005)	-0.086 (0.025)	-0.019 (0.007)	-0.096 (0.038)	-0.019 (0.005)	-0.101 (0.029)	-0.018 (0.007)	-0.122 (0.079)	-0.021 (0.003)	0.037 (0.122)	-0.024 (0.011)
Lagged debt to assets ratio (DAR)			0.103 (0.031)	0.004 (0.037)	0.051 (0.012)	0.128 (0.127)	0.081 (0.033)	0.014 (0.149)	-0.027 (0.128)	0.116 (0.039)	-0.027 (0.134)	0.061 (0.015)
Lagged interest coverage ratio (COV)			0.011 (0.002)	0.001 (0.001)	0.012 (0.003)	0.009 (0.016)	0.022 (0.003)	0.005 (0.008)	0.006 (0.015)	0.011 (0.001)	-0.006 (0.009)	0.014 (0.004)
Share foreign borrowing sector J year t					-0.061 (0.032)	0.189 (0.084)	-0.219 (0.161)	0.183 (0.089)			0.822 (0.577)	-0.216 (0.004)
DAR * Share foreign borrowing					0.356 (0.016)	-0.163 (0.146)	0.431 (0.152)	-0.213 (0.367)			0.422 (0.566)	0.361 (0.101)
COV * Share foreign borrowing					0.026 (0.009)	-0.012 (0.023)	0.031 (0.011)	-0.013 (0.004)			-0.026 (0.133)	0.017 (0.003)
Share foreign sales sector J year t							-0.407 (0.224)	-0.063 (0.151)			0.111 (0.151)	-0.330 (0.124)
DAR * Share foreign sales							0.157 (0.359)	0.102 (0.333)			0.202 (0.233)	0.227 (0.359)
COV * Share foreign sales							0.017 (0.005)	0.007 (0.023)			0.027 (0.023)	0.012 (0.008)
N	2068		1876		1937		1876			1937	1876	
Harsen J statistic	65.06		51.25		54.15		51.46			48.82	46.57	
P-value	0.51		0.88		0.81		0.87			0.92	0.95	

A.E. Harrison, M.S. McMillan / Journal of International Economics 61 (2003) 73–100   89

Column (2) introduces the two proxies for credit constraints, the ratio of lagged debt to assets (*DAR*), and the lagged interest coverage ratio (*COV*). The coefficients on *DAR* and *COV* are significant and positive for domestic firms, equal to 0.103 and 0.011 respectively. For foreign firms, however, those coefficients, at 0.004 (for *DEBT*) and 0.001 (for *COV*) are close to zero in magnitude and insignificant. This suggests that domestic firms are credit constrained, while foreign enterprises are not. The addition of *DEBT* and *COV* substantially improves the fit of the model, as indicated by the fall in the value of the Hansen J Statistic.

Column (3) tests for crowding out in the financial sector. As in column (2), we allow the coefficients on the independent variables to vary across foreign and domestic enterprises. The coefficient on the interaction of *DAR* and *COV* and the share of foreign borrowing at the sector level indicates the extent of crowding out. The results in column (3) indicate that foreign firms crowd out domestic firms. The coefficient on *DAR* and *COV* interacted with sectoral foreign share of total borrowing is positive and statistically significant. The coefficient on *DAR* alone is half the magnitude in column (1), confirming that a large part of the credit constraints identified in column (1) are due to foreign entry. The results in column (3) also indicate that there is no crowding out of foreign firms: *DAR* and *COV* interacted with sectoral foreign share of borrowing is not significant.

The focus of this paper is the coefficient on the share of foreign borrowing interacted with *DAR* and *COV*. The coefficients on *DAR* and *COV* are equal to 0.05 and 0.01 for domestic enterprises, which we interpret as the extent of credit constraints facing those firms when there is zero foreign borrowing. The distribution of the share of foreign borrowing has a mean of 0.69 and a standard deviation of 0.28 (Table 1). Therefore a one standard deviation increase in the share of foreign borrowing implies an increase of 0.09 for the coefficient on *DAR*, which is nearly a 300 percent increase, from 0.05 to 0.14. A one standard deviation increase in the share of foreign borrowing implies an increase in the coefficient on *COV* of 0.007, which implies nearly a doubling of the coefficient on *COV*. Another way to interpret the magnitudes is to ask how an increase in foreign borrowing from 60 to 70 percent of sectoral borrowing would affect the coefficients on *DAR* and *COV*. This would imply that the coefficient on *DAR* would increase from 0.05 to 0.09, nearly doubling its value, while the coefficient on *COV* would increase by 25 percent (from 0.012 to 0.015).

One possible explanation for the observed correlation between *DAR* (or *COV*) and foreign sector share of total borrowing and investment could be the following: domestic firms face greater domestic competition with foreign entry. Increased competition—which could be correlated with the foreign share in domestic borrowing—leads to both lower investment and a decline in profits, which are correlated with cash flow. We test for this possibility in column (4). We add two additional terms, *DAR**Share Foreign Sales and *COV**Share Foreign Sales to the basic specification. Share Foreign Sales is defined as the share of foreign-owned firms in total sales in a particular sector and year. If foreign borrowing is simply a

90   A.E. Harrison, M.S. McMillan / Journal of International Economics 61 (2003) 73–100

proxy for competition, then the crowding out variables should become statistically insignificant. The results in column (4) suggest that this is not the case. The coefficients on *DAR* and *COV* interacted with foreign borrowing remain the same in magnitude and are statistically significant. The coefficient on Share Foreign Sales is negative and significant for domestic firms and insignificant for domestic firms. However, Share Foreign Sales interacted with *DAR* and *COV* are generally insignificant. This suggests that while foreign competition has a direct negative impact on investment by domestic firms, it does not affect domestic firms credit constraints.

In a number of African countries, SOEs play a major role in all aspects of the economy, including manufacturing. Cote d'Ivoire is no exception. Table 2 shows that SOEs account for a large share of sales in a number of sectors, such as food products, rubber and cement. Yet, SOEs are likely to face a very different set of credit constraints than their private sector counterparts. Bertero and Rondi (2000) indicate that the cash flow-investment correlation could differ from private sector firms for a number of reasons. To the extent that SOEs benefit from a soft budget constraint, they may be less credit constrained than private enterprises. This would indicate a weaker link (or no link at all) between investment and cash flow. On the other hand, an argument could also be made that the link between cash flow and investment is likely to be stronger for public enterprises. Bertero and Rondi (2000) argue that agency problems are more severe in public enterprises. To the extent that managers of SOEs are more likely to pursue private objectives, they may wish to over invest relative to the optimum. This may lead us to find a stronger link between cash flow and investment for this set of firms.

The last two columns of Table 3 redo the specification reported in columns (2) and (4), but allow coefficients to vary across public and private enterprises. Although the coefficients on investment and lagged investment are significantly different in magnitudes, for both the private enterprises and the SOEs the signs are as expected. While the coefficients on *DAR* and *COV* remain significant and positive for domestically owned private enterprises, the coefficients on both measures of credit constraints are insignificant for SOEs. These results are consistent with the perception that SOEs, due to their access to soft loans or government support, are less likely to be credit constrained than private sector enterprises. The evidence also suggests that there is no crowding out; SOEs are unaffected by foreign investors. These results are robust to adding *DAR* and *COV* interacted with the share of foreign sales. We also tested for crowding out by public sector enterprises, but found that their borrowing had no impact on other enterprises. The results (not reported here) suggest that crowding out is restricted to foreign enterprises.

There appears to be fairly robust evidence of crowding out of domestic firms by foreign firms. The interaction between our debt and interest coverage measures with the level of foreign borrowing at the sector level is positive and significant across all specifications. Finally, the results suggest that crowding out only affects

A.E. Harrison, M.S. McMillan / Journal of International Economics 61 (2003) 73–100   91

domestically owned, private enterprises. Neither SOEs nor other foreign enterprises are crowded out by foreign entry in their sector.

5. Extensions

Results of our analysis suggest that only domestic firms are credit constrained and that foreign firms crowd out domestic firms in local capital markets. Both (1) as a test of the Euler equation approach and (2) to allow us to gain insights into why foreign firms are crowding out domestic firms, we report quantitative measures of operational and financial health in Table 4. If the Euler equation approach accurately measures the extent of credit constraints, then we would expect that foreign firms would appear to be less constrained using quantitative

Table 4
Why would domestic firms get crowded out? A comparison of firm characteristics by ownership

Variable	N	Mean domestic SOE	Mean domestic private	Mean foreign	t-statistic in for change mean
A. Investment, cash flow and sales growth					
I_t/K_{t-1}	2403	0.166	0.325	0.363	1.962
Cash flow$_t/K_{t-1}$	2403	0.254	0.421	0.417	0.454
Real sales growth$_t$	2403	0.089	0.039	0.042	0.547
Real capital stock (millions of CFA)	2403	1,579.0	148.0	249.1	4.195
B. Debt ratios and growth[2]					
Debt to assets ratio (DAR)$_t$	2403	0.427	0.269	0.271	0.736
Interest coverage ratio (COV)$_t$	2403	0.858	0.419	0.373	2.018
Real debt growth	2403	0.331	0.182	0.345	3.098
C. Profitability ratios[3]					
Profit margin	2251	0.099	0.044	0.047	0.886
Return on assets	2251	0.161	0.006	0.084	4.745
Asset turnover	2403	2.779	3.437	4.249	8.027
D. Firm size					
Sales (millions of CFA)	2403	3157	322	857	8.579
Number of employees	2403	501	68	149	7.423

(1) Results were obtained by regressing ratios on a dummy variable for ownership and a constant. *T*-statistic is for the difference in mean between private domestic and foreign firms. (2) Debt to assets ratio is the real value of outstanding debt divided by the real value of current assets and is meant to capture both a firm's demand for borrowing relative to its capacity to borrow and as a measure of collateral. The interest coverage ratio, *COV*, is defined as the ratio of the firm's interest expense to the sum of the firm's interest expense plus cash flow. A higher value of *COV* today means that a firm is exhausting relatively more resources on servicing its debt and is likely to be closer to its debt capacity. (3) Profit margin is defined as the ratio of real profits to real sales, return on assets is defined as the ratio of real profits to real assets and asset turnover is defined as the ratio of real sales to real assets.

92   *A.E. Harrison, M.S. McMillan / Journal of International Economics 61 (2003) 73–100*

ratios such as cash flow to investment and debt to capital. We also report different measures of profitability across the two sets of firms. Foreign firms may crowd out domestic firms on local credit markets simply because they are more profitable. We are particularly interested in identifying whether foreign firms crowd out domestic firms, after controlling for the same level of profitability, a possibility we will explore later in this section. Such a result would suggest that crowding out may not be an efficient outcome; there may be a "bias" in favor of allocating credit to foreigners.

5.1. Financial ratio analysis

5.1.1. Economic and debt ratios

The results in Panels A and B of Table 4 suggest that, using a wide range of indicators, domestic firms are more credit constrained. The means show that investment relative to capital is significantly lower for domestic relative to foreign firms. Although cash flow levels are similar for private domestic and foreign firms, sales growth is slightly lower. The next set of ratios in Table 4 are leverage ratios. Overall, the debt to assets ratio is about the same for private domestic and foreign firms, but significantly higher for SOEs. The interest coverage ratio (*COV*) is significantly higher for private firms relative to foreign enterprises, indicating that they face higher borrowing costs. Real debt growth is significantly lower for private domestic enterprises compared to SOEs and foreign enterprises. These results are consistent with the earlier regression results showing that domestic firms are more financially constrained than both foreign enterprises and SOEs.

5.1.2. Profitability ratios

The next set of ratios in Table 4 measure profitability. Using three different measures of profitability, there is some evidence that firms with foreign assets are more profitable than private domestic enterprises. However, the evidence is mixed. There is no statistically significant difference between profit margins for domestic private and foreign firms. Return on assets and asset turnover indicate how intensely the firm's assets are being put to use. The substantially higher ratios for foreign as compared to domestic firms may indicate that foreign firms are more profitable. However, the higher return on assets for foreign firms could be partly explained by their lower interest payments, as indicated by the lower interest coverage ratio.

5.1.3. Firm size

The last set of ratios in Table 4 measure firm size. One possible critique of our results is that they simply reflect the fact that foreign enterprises are larger than domestic enterprises, and therefore more profitable and less credit constrained. The means reflecting differences in firm size suggest that this may be the case. Using sales or employee measures of firm size, the results indicate that private domestic

A.E. Harrison, M.S. McMillan / Journal of International Economics 61 (2003) 73–100   93

enterprises are significantly smaller than foreign firms. Again, the means highlight the importance of separating SOEs from other domestic enterprises. SOEs are significantly larger than either foreign or private domestic enterprises, and also more profitable than their private sector counterparts.

5.2. Does firm size or higher profitability explain the impact of foreign investment?

If foreign firms are significantly larger than domestically owned enterprises, then domestic firms may be crowded out due to size rather than ownership issues. There is a vast literature documenting that smaller enterprises are discriminated against on credit markets relative to large firms. Table 5 lists the baseline specification from Table 3, then adds a number of different variables to check for the robustness of the crowding out variable. In column (2), we add the interaction of *DAR* and *COV* with measures of foreign relative to domestic firm size. The results indicate that relative firm size in not driving the results. The coefficients on *DAR* and *COV* interacted with the share of foreign borrowing remain significant and positive.

The profitability ratios in Table 4 highlight the possibility that foreign firms may crowd out domestic enterprises because they are simply more profitable. We test for whether crowding out occurs as a result of the superior profitability of foreign firms by adding the interaction of *DAR* and *COV* with the sector-level relative profitability of foreign enterprises. We measure the profitability of foreign firms relative to the profitability of domestic firms by taking the ratio of the measure of the profitability of foreign firms in sector *j* year *t* to the measure of profitability for the domestic firm. These results are robust to two separate measures of profitability, the relative return on assets or relative asset turnover, but since the results were unaffected only results using return on assets are reported in Table 5. We conclude that relative profitability may matter, but it is not driving our results on crowding out of domestic firms by foreign enterprises.

5.3. Alternative measures of risk groups

One potential criticism of our approach is that banks do not use four-digit level classifications in determining loan levels. Consequently, measuring the share of foreign borrowing at the four-digit level may not adequately capture the role played by foreign firms on local credit markets. Consequently, we explored three alternative approaches to analyzing the role played by foreign firms in local borrowing. First, instead of defining the sector at the four-digit level, we redefined sectors at the more aggregated two digit level. This allows for the possibility that banks allocate funds with sector targets defined at a more aggregated sector level than the four-digit level. Second, we classified firms into borrowing groups based on how correlated their profits were. This approach is similar to sorting firms

Table 5
GMM estimates of augmented Euler investment equation: Robustness checks of crowding out variable

Dependent variable:Investment/fixed assets	(1) Baseline specification		(2) Relative firm size		(3) Relative profitability		(4) Sector at two digit level		(5) Grouped by "Market Beta"		(6) Grouped by firm Size	
	D	F	D	F	D	F	D	F	D	F	D	F
Explanatory variables												
Lagged (investment/fixed assets)	0.589	0.353	0.658	0.341	0.416	0.424	0.489	0.333	0.548	0.345	0.558	0.374
	(0.125)	(0.054)	(0.199)	(0.075)	(0.189)	(0.056)	(0.235)	(0.114)	(0.143)	(0.057)	(0.283)	(0.145)
Lagged (investment/fixed assets)^2	−0.317	−0.132	−0.348	−0.134	−0.169	−0.178	−0.327	−0.142	−0.299	−0.131	−0.367	−0.155
	(0.111)	(0.032)	(0.008)	(0.043)	(0.011)	(0.049)	(0.111)	(0.034)	(0.108)	(0.062)	(0.124)	(0.067)
Lagged (sales/fixed assets)	0.039	0.012	0.014	0.010	0.027	0.011	0.039	0.012	0.027	0.010	0.048	0.037
	(0.006)	(0.004)	(0.006)	(0.004)	(0.013)	(0.003)	(0.007)	(0.003)	(0.012)	(0.003)	(0.016)	(0.014)
Lagged cash flow (CF)	−0.101	−0.018	−0.056	−0.011	−0.064	−0.014	−0.111	−0.018	−0.077	−0.014	−0.036	−0.027
	(0.029)	(0.007)	(0.008)	(0.004)	(0.022)	(0.008)	(0.031)	(0.009)	(0.031)	(0.005)	(0.012)	(0.013)
Lagged debt to assets ratio (DAR)	0.081	0.014	0.099	−0.436	0.096	−0.244	0.271	−0.222	0.331	−0.082	0.327	0.061
	(0.033)	(0.149)	(0.029)	(0.541)	(0.32)	(0.271)	(0.114)	(0.339)	(0.111)	(0.088)	(0.118)	(0.117)
Lagged interest coverage ratio (COV)	0.022	0.005	0.038	0.022	0.036	−0.043	0.022	−0.005	0.019	−0.016	0.026	−0.014
	(0.003)	(0.008)	(0.011)	(0.037)	(0.014)	(0.071)	(0.006)	(0.011)	(0.004)	(0.012)	(0.004)	(0.015)
Share foreign borrowing sector *J* year *t*	−0.219	0.183	−0.235	0.136	−0.215	0.119	−0.229	0.183	−0.133	0.116	−0.222	0.016
	(0.161)	(0.089)	(0.084)	(0.055)	(0.048)	(0.041)	(0.051)	(0.090)	(0.059)	(0.129)	(0.077)	(0.009)

A.E. Harrison, M.S. McMillan / Journal of International Economics 61 (2003) 73–100   95

D_{AR} * share foreign borrowing	0.431 (0.152)	-0.213 (0.367)	0.393 (0.163)	0.587 (0.553)	0.297 (0.338)	0.319 (0.440)	0.345 (0.161)	0.147 (0.267)	0.130 (0.051)	0.249 (0.222)	0.212 (0.009)	0.361 (0.221)
COV * Share foreign borrowing	0.031 (0.011)	-0.013 (0.004)	0.087 (0.029)	-0.033 (0.033)	0.049 (0.013)	0.044 (0.062)	0.031 (0.015)	-0.013 (0.004)	0.032 (0.015)	0.021 (0.911)	0.036 (0.011)	0.017 (0.077)
Share foreign sales sector J year t	-0.407 (0.224)	-0.063 (0.151)	-0.417 (0.213)	-0.053 (0.141)	-0.301 (0.124)	-0.073 (0.161)	-0.307 (0.164)	-0.073 (0.151)	-0.404 (0.214)	-0.053 (0.251)	-0.317 (0.144)	-0.063 (0.251)
D_{AR} * Share foreign sales	0.157 (0.359)	0.102 (0.333)	0.167 (0.359)	0.122 (0.224)	0.147 (0.259)	0.112 (0.222)	0.257 (0.459)	0.102 (0.333)	0.167 (0.459)	0.102 (0.333)	0.157 (0.359)	0.102 (0.333)
COV * Share foreign sales	0.017 (0.005)	0.007 (0.023)	0.011 (0.015)	0.007 (0.023)	0.011 (0.014)	0.008 (0.033)	0.026 (0.015)	0.007 (0.023)	0.016 (0.014)	0.007 (0.022)	0.018 (0.015)	0.007 (0.033)
Relative firm size sector J year t			0.010 (0.008)	0.002 (0.002)								
D_{AR} * Relative firm size			-0.031 (0.031)	0.001 (0.001)								
COV * Relative firm size			-0.021 (0.023)	0.001 (0.009)								
Relative profitability sector J year t					0.020 (0.019)	-0.027 (0.022)						
D_{AR} * Relative profitability					0.043 (0.033)	0.001 (0.011)						
COV * Relative profitability					-0.007 (0.006)	-0.014 (0.014)						
N	1876	1876	1876	1876	1876	1876	1915	1915	1906	1906	1876	1876
Hansen J statistic	51.46	42.89	42.89	37.09	37.09	37.09	43.30	43.30	10.44	10.44	46.57	46.57
P-value	0.87	0.93	0.93	0.98	0.98	0.98	0.70	0.70	0.40	0.40	0.95	0.95

Notes: (1) The Helmert transformation is used to eliminate firm-level fixed effects. Instruments used are levels of all variables in the regression and sector and/or risk category dummies. (2) Standard errors in parentheses are robust and corrected for correlation across observations within sectors. (3) In all specifications, domestic firms are those firms for which average foreign ownership over the life of the firm is less than or equal to 49%. (4) Results are robust to outliers using the dfbeta criterion prior to estimation by GMM. (5) Relative profitability and size are computed by sector year as the ratio of foreign firm profitability(size) to domestic firm profitability(size). (6) Market beta is estimated as correlation between firm level profit margin and industry-wide profit margin. Firm size is based on the real value of sales. Similar results are obtained using the number of workers.

according to their market beta in the finance literature. However, our approach is somewhat different than the standard methodology in finance, primarily because we do not have stock prices or any information on stock market activity. Instead of the usual approach to deriving a firm's beta, we regressed each firm's annual profit margin (defined as real profits over real sales) on the economy-wide profit margin. The resulting estimated coefficient is the firm's "market beta". We then sorted firms into ten approximately equal groups, according to the value of their "beta". This approach assumes that banks allocate funds across different risk groups based on how correlated their profits are with each other, and that banks diversify risk by limiting funds allocated within any high or low beta group. Finally, we also defined loan groups by classifying firms according to size. This assumes that banks allocate loans according to firm size.

The results of these alternative classifications for loan groups are reported in Table 5. All three alternative specifications yield the same results as before: (1) domestic enterprises are credit-constrained, foreign firms are not; and (2) foreign borrowing crowds domestic firms out of the local credit markets. This "crowding out" is observed regardless of whether the sector is defined at the 2 or 4 digit level. Crowding out is also significant if we assume that banks distribute credit on the basis of size or on the basis of market betas. These results suggest that our estimates are robust to different assumptions about how banks allocate credit across firms.

Although not the focus of this paper, it is also interesting to examine what the results in Table 5 imply about the impact of foreign borrowing on the level of domestic investment. While the focus of this paper is on credit constraints, it is also important to understand the determinants of domestic investment. We can measure the impact of foreign borrowing on domestic investment by taking the derivative of Eq. (7) with respect to *FDEBT_Sector*. The net impact of changes in the share of foreign borrowing on the level of domestic investment is given by the sum of $\beta_8^0 DAR + \beta_9^0 COV + \beta_{10}^0$. If we choose sample means for *DAR* and *COV*, the sum of these three components is always negative. This suggests that an increase in the foreign share of total borrowing is associated with a fall in the level of domestic investment. This result is consistent across all specifications in Table 5.

6. Policy implications

To properly account for the total impact of DFI on the host country, we would need to take into account the impact of foreign investment on domestic wages, profits, and employment; the role of foreign investors in promoting technology transfer; and the contribution of foreign investors to tax revenues. This is not addressed in this paper. However, we do compute the net impact of DFI on the

A.E. Harrison, M.S. McMillan / Journal of International Economics 61 (2003) 73–100   97

availability of capital, adding together the inflows from equity purchases and foreign borrowing and subtracting the local borrowing of these firms.

The fact that foreign firms borrowed locally does not necessarily mean that the net impact of DFI on capital flows was negative. We also must consider the fact that foreign firms brought in equity. Table 6 shows the total amount borrowed by foreign firms and the total amount of equity brought in by foreign firms. In all years, the amount borrowed domestically substantially exceeds the equity contribution of foreign firms. Note that these figures do not properly measure the impact of foreign investment on net capital flows, as they do not account for repatriated profits and workers remittances. Table 6 indicates that because the majority of DFI was financed locally, DFI did not represent a significant increase in net capital flows to the economy. In fact, borrowing on local credit markets by foreign firms significantly exceeded the sum of equity purchases and foreign borrowing by these firms. To the extent that joint ventures are not considered local firms, the results suggest that the total amount of funds available to purely domestically owned firms actually shrank with the increase in foreign investment.

These negatives must be balanced against potential positives in order to obtain a complete picture of the welfare implications of the DFI. Beneficial effects of DFI include technology transfer, employee training and higher wages, and tax revenues. Table 6 indicates that foreign firms did contribute a significant amount to total tax revenues. This is the focus of research elsewhere (Branstetter and Feenstra, 1999). Branstetter and Feenstra analyze the welfare gains from the

Table 6
Contribution of DFI to capital

Year	Foreign tax/ total tax	Foreign tax/ foreign sales	Total foreign borrowing (bn. cfa francs)	Total foreign equity (bn. cfa francs)	Foreign equity/foreign borrowing
75	79.03%	17.63%	44.00	26.70	60.68%
76	81.87%	19.14%	64.00	33.10	51.72%
77	78.27%	23.48%	79.70	33.20	41.66%
78	75.60%	26.01%	112.00	37.40	33.39%
79	75.10%	27.62%	136.00	42.60	31.32%
80	75.67%	30.00%	162.00	50.40	31.11%
81	74.72%	31.46%	169.00	52.80	31.24%
82	74.34%	33.97%	181.00	56.40	31.16%
83	72.00%	34.43%	208.00	59.40	28.56%
84	74.91%	40.93%	199.00	65.40	32.86%
85	74.52%	42.19%	195.00	61.10	31.33%
86	71.03%	42.74%	204.00	66.00	32.35%
87	65.63%	39.44%	185.00	63.70	34.43%

Notes: Total Foreign Borrowing does not reflect total foreign local borrowing as these numbers are only available for 1985. In 1985, foreign firms borrowed 12.84% of all monies borrowed abroad. Thus, in 1985, the amount borrowed locally was approximately 170 billion cfa francs. Foreign inflows in 1985 were 61 billion cfa francs and equity as a share of foreign borrowing was approximately 36%.

Globalization, Firms, and Workers

inflow of foreign investment into China, calculating the implied weights in the social welfare function. However, they do not address the possibility that foreign investors could affect local credit markets, possibly crowding out domestic firms.

This issue is an important one because one major reason cited in policy discussions for why foreign firms should be encouraged to relocate in one's home country is that these foreign firms bring in scarce capital. Our results suggest that policy makers should be more careful about assuming that direct foreign investment expands the availability of credit for domestic investors. The extreme case would be a foreign investor who sets up a foreign firm in the host country and finances 100 percent of his or her investment from local credit markets. To the extent that foreign investors may present more profitable investment opportunities, local banks may be applauded for awarding them a higher percentage of loans. Yet our results suggest that the crowding out of local firms by foreign investors largely cannot be explained by differences in profitability. In summary, our results suggest that the expected benefits from foreign investors in terms of jobs, technology transfer, and competition must be weighed against the potential cost of greater credit constraints on domestic firms.

7. Conclusion

In this paper, we attempt to answer a question, which has not been addressed elsewhere: does the entry of foreign enterprises in developing country credit markets hurt their domestic competitors? Although foreign investment conveys benefits by bringing in scarce capital, those benefits may be mitigated if foreign enterprises crowd out domestic enterprises in the local credit markets. Our results suggest a difference between the credit constraints faced by domestic and foreign firms. In addition, we find that one major reason why domestic enterprises are more credit constrained than their foreign counterparts in the same sector is due to crowding out by foreign entrants. Further, we find that one contributing factor is that foreign firms are more profitable and more liquid. Hence, foreign firms might be a better investment for local banks than domestic firms. Nevertheless, our results remain even after we control for the higher profitability of foreign enterprises. In other words, even after controlling for the profitability of foreign firms, domestic enterprises are still "crowded out" by their foreign competitors.

We also examine the performance of state-owned enterprises (SOEs) relative to their private sector counterparts. For SOEs, debt to asset measures and interest coverage do not significantly affect investment, indicating that SOEs are not credit constrained. Nor is there any evidence that they are affected by foreign borrowing on domestic credit markets. These results suggest that SOEs are not credit constrained, perhaps because during this period they could be characterized by being subject to a soft budget constraint. In addition, SOEs are not crowded out by

A.E. Harrison, M.S. McMillan / Journal of International Economics 61 (2003) 73–100   99

foreign enterprises of domestic credit markets, in contrast to their private sector counterparts.

We explore whether our results on crowding out could be due to unobserved factors, such as increased competition from foreign enterprises or differences in firms' size. Our results suggest that this is not the case. Although the Ivory Coast may be an unusual case, our empirical results suggest that policy makers should be cautious in assuming that foreign investors expand credit opportunities for domestic enterprises. In the Ivory Coast, foreign investors certainly eased credit constraints for firms with foreign investment, but firms which did not receive foreign investment became more credit constrained. These results are probably driven by a number of factors. First, interest rates were set below market rates, which led to credit rationing. This led foreign investors to borrow heavily on local credit markets, and at the same time encouraged banks to lend to less risky investors, since margins were low. Second, the banking sector was highly concentrated and dominated by firms with ties to French banks, which were probably biased towards lending to foreign firms.

Acknowledgements

Thanks to Eleanor Park for excellent research assistance. Thanks to Pierluigi Balduzzi and Fabio Schiantarelli for helpful conversations, and to Ray Fisman, Charlie Himmelberg, Glenn Hubbard, Ethan Ligon, Dan Richards, Dani Rodrik and Toni Whited for comments on an earlier draft. We would also like to thank seminar participants at Oxford University's Centre for the Study of African Economies, Tufts, UC Davis, UC Berkeley, and Columbia University for helpful comments.

References

Aghion, P., Caroli, E., Garcia-Penalosa, C., 1999. Inequality and economic growth: The perspective of the new growth theories. Journal of Economic Literature 37 (4), 1615–1660.

Banerjee, A.V., Newman, A.F., 1994. Poverty, incentives and development. American Economic Review 84 (2), 211–215.

Bertero, E., Rondi, L., Investment, 2000. Cash Flow and Managerial Discretion in State-Owned Firms, Evidence across soft and hard budget constraints, LSE Financial Markets Group Special Paper, n. 119.

Bigsten, A., Collier, P., Dercon, S., Fafchamps, M., Gauthier, B., Gunning, J.W., Soderbom, M., Oduro, A., Oostendorp, R., Patillo, C., Teal, F., Zeufack, A., 2000. Credit Constraints in Manufacturing Enterprises in Africa, Centre for the Study of African Economies Working Paper Series 2000.24.

Bond, S., Meghir, C., 1994. Dynamic investment models and the firms financial policy. Review of Economic Studies 61, 197–222.

Branstetter, L.G., Feenstra, R.C., 1999. Trade and Direct foreign investment in China:A Political Economy Approach, NBER Working Paper No. W7100.

100   *A.E. Harrison, M.S. McMillan / Journal of International Economics 61 (2003) 73–100*

Fazzari, S.M., Hubbard, R.G., Petersen, B.C., 1988. Financing constraints and corporate investment. Brookings Papers on Economic Activity 1, 141–149.

Fazzari, S.M., Hubbard, R.G., Petersen, B.C., 2000. Investment-cash flow sensitivities are useful: A comment on Kaplan and Zingales. Quarterly Journal of Economics 115 (2), 695–706.

Feldstein, M., 2000. Aspects of Global Economic Integration: Outlook for the Future, NBER Working Paper 7899.

Gelos, G.R., Werner, A.M., 1999. Financial Liberalization, Credit Constraints, and Collateral:Investment in the Mexican Manufacturing Sector, IMF Working Paper, WP/99/25.

Gilchrist, S., Himmelberg, C., 1995. Evidence on the role of cash flow for investment. Journal of Monetary Economics 36, 541–572.

The Globecom Group Ltd., 1995. Active Bank Risk Management: Enhancing Investment & Credit Portfolio Performance, Irwin Professional Publications, Burr Ridge.

Harris, J.R., Schiantarelli, F., Siregar, M., 1994. The effect of financial liberalization on the capital structure and investment decisions of Indonesian manufacturing establishments. World Bank Economic Review 8 (1), 17–47.

Harvard Institute for International Development and World Economic Forum, 1998, The Africa Competitiveness Report 1998, World Economic Forum, Geneva.

Hubbard, R.G., 1998. Capital-market imperfections and investment. Journal of Economic Literature XXXVI, 193–225.

Jaramillo, F., Schiantarelli, F., Weiss, A., 1996. Capital market imperfections before and after financial liberalization: An Euler equation approach to panel data for Ecuadorian firms. Journal of Development Economics 51 (2), 367–386.

Kaplan, S.N., Zingales, L., 1997. Do investment-cash flow sensitivities provide useful measures of financing constraints? Quarterly Journal of Economics CXII, 169–215.

Love, I., 2000. Financial Development and Financing Constraints: International Evidence from the Structural Investment Model, Ph.D. Dissertation, Columbia Business School.

Patillo, C., 2000. Risk, financial constraints and equipment investment in Ghana: a firm-level analysis. In: Collier, P., Patillo, C. (Eds.), Investment and Risk in Africa. St. Martin's Press, New York.

Schiantarelli, F., 1996. Financial constraints and investments: Methodological issues and international evidence. Oxford Review of Economic Policy 12, 70–89.

Tybout, J.R., 1983. Credit rationing and investment behavior in a developing country. Review of Economics and Statistics 65 (4), 598–607.

Whited, T., 1992. Liquidity constraints, and corporate investment: Evidence from panel data. The Journal of Finance 47 (4), 1425–1460.

World Bank, den Tuinder, B.A., 1978. Ivory Coast The Challenge of Success, A World Bank Country Economic Report. The Johns Hopkins University Press, Baltimore.

Chapter 8

Global capital flows and financing constraints[†]

Ann E. Harrison[a,b,*], Inessa Love[c,1], Margaret S. McMillan[d,2]

[a]*University of California, Berkeley, 329 Giannini Hall, UC Berkeley, Berkeley, CA 94720-3310, USA*
[b]*NBER, USA*
[c]*The World Bank, 1818 H St. NW MC3-300, Washington, DC 20433, USA*
[d]*Department of Economics, Tufts University, USA*

Received 1 April 2002; accepted 1 October 2003

Abstract

Firms often cite financing constraints as one of their primary obstacles to investment. Global capital flows, by bringing in scarce capital, may ease host-country firms' financing constraints. However, if incoming foreign investors borrow heavily from domestic banks, multinational firms may exacerbate financing constraints by crowding host-country firms out of domestic capital markets. Combining a unique cross-country firm-level panel with time-series data on restrictions on international transactions and capital flows, we find that different measures of global flows are associated with a reduction in firm-level financing constraints. First, we show that one type of capital inflow—direct foreign investment (DFI)—is associated with a reduction in financing constraints. Second, we show that restrictions on capital account transactions negatively affect firms' financing constraints. We also show that DFI inflows are associated with lower sensitivity of investment to cash flow for firms without foreign assets and for domestically owned enterprises. Finally, the results indicate that these effects are stronger for low-income than for high-income regions.
© 2004 Published by Elsevier B.V.

Keywords: Capital flows; Financing constraints; Direct foreign investment

Not all direct foreign investment around the world represents net capital flows. Often such investments are financed in local markets. Martin Feldstein (2000).

---

* Corresponding author. University of California, Berkeley, 329 Giannini Hall, UC Berkeley, Berkeley, CA 94720-3310, USA. Tel.: +1-510-643-9676.
E-mail addresses: harrison@are.berkeley.edu (A.E. Harrison), ilove@worldbank.org (I. Love), mmcmilla@tufts.edu (M.S. McMillan).
[1] Tel.: +1-202-458-0590.
[2] Tel.: +1-617-627-3137.

[†]This article originally appeared in *Journal of Development Economics*, **75** 269–301
© 2004 Elsevier Science Publishers B.V.

270 *A.E. Harrison et al. / Journal of Development Economics 75 (2004) 269–301*

There is now broad agreement about the value of direct foreign investment, which brings not just capital but also technology and training. Joseph Stiglitz (1998).

1. Introduction

Firms in developing countries typically cite financing constraints as one of their primary obstacles to investment. Some argue that countries should eliminate restrictions on international transactions and encourage incoming capital flows, especially direct foreign investment (DFI). DFI may ease these firms' financing constraints by bringing in scarce capital. This is one reason why policy makers in developing countries have eased restrictions on inward DFI and in many instances provide special incentives for multinational firms. Yet if foreign firms borrow heavily from local banks, they may exacerbate domestic firms' financing constraints by crowding them out of domestic capital markets. Foreign investors may borrow on domestic capital markets for a variety of reasons, including as a hedging device against exchange rate fluctuations or in response to artificially low domestic interest rates.[3] Yet most observers assume that joint venture activity and acquisitions by multinationals are accompanied by significant capital inflows.[4] Although we cannot measure the amount of local borrowing by multinationals, we can examine the impact of incoming DFI on firm investment behavior.[5]

There has been almost no previous research examining the impact of DFI on host-country firms' financing constraints. One reason for the limited empirical evidence is the difficulty in obtaining detailed firm-level data across countries. In this paper, we combine firm-level panel data from Worldscope with cross-country time-series data on restrictions on international transactions and capital flows to test whether different measures of global flows are associated with a reduction in the sensitivity of firm-level investment to cash flow, which is consistent with a reduction in firm-level financing constraints. First, we test whether different types of capital inflows are associated with a reduction in financing constraints. Our main focus is DFI, but we also test for the effect of portfolio inflows and

---

[3] In many developing countries, interest rates have historically been set at artificially low levels, leading to credit rationing in cases where the interest rate is set below the market clearing level.

[4] For example, Stiglitz (1998) in an address to the Chicago Council on Foreign Relations argues that there is broad agreement about the fact that direct foreign investment brings additional capital. Feldstein (2000) argues that this is not necessarily the case. Helleiner (1988) in a survey for the *Handbook of Development Economics* suggests that it is unlikely that much new equity capital will result from expanded DFI flows.

[5] More generally, there are different types of foreign direct investment. One type is a joint venture between a local company in need of capital and a foreign company. In this setup, the local company typically receives financing from the foreign company in the form of an equity injection. Clearly, this arrangement is expected to reduce the financing constraints of the local company. Another type of foreign direct investment is where a foreign company sets up a subsidiary. As the foreign company typically limits its loan exposure to the local subsidiary, the subsidiary will need to borrow to finance investments. The net effect on the financing constraints under this second type of foreign direct investment are therefore less clear. Our data on DFI inflows is aggregate, and thus, we cannot separate the two types of DFI. Therefore, our main results represent the "average" effect of DFI on the "average" firm in our sample. However, to get at the issue of which type of DFI is more prevalent, we do separate domestically owned firms from foreign-owned firms to test whether the "spillover" effects are positive or negative later in the paper.

A.E. Harrison et al. / Journal of Development Economics 75 (2004) 269–301   271

other flows such as commercial bank loans. We find that only DFI is associated with a reduction in financing constraints. Second, we test whether restrictions on capital movement affect firms' financing constraints. Our results suggest that one type of capital control—restrictions on capital account transactions—negatively affects firms' financing constraints. Finally, we show that DFI inflows are associated with less sensitivity of investment to cash flow for firms without foreign assets and for domestically owned enterprises. These results suggest that foreign inflows are associated with a reduction in firm-level credit constraints even for domestically owned enterprises. The results also indicate that these effects are stronger in low-income countries.[6]

Our work is related to the large body of literature on capital market imperfections and firm investment; an excellent survey of this literature is in Hubbard (1998). A number of papers have used the Euler equation methodology to estimate the effect of financing constraints on investment, with most studies concentrating on firms in developed countries. Surveys suggest that financing constraints are an even more important deterrent to investment in developing countries.[7] Theoretically, capital market imperfections are likely to be more severe in these countries, which will result in stronger financing constraints due to unavailability of external financing.[8]

Most empirical evidence of financing constraints in developing countries comes from studies on individual countries, which are difficult to generalize.[9] Research that links the level of financial development to financing constraints across countries includes Demirguc-Kunt and Maksimovic (1998), Rajan and Zingales (1998), and Love (2003). Demirguc-Kunt and Maksimovic (1998) finds that firms grow faster than they could have using only internally generated funds in more financially developed countries. Rajan and Zingales (1998) demonstrate that industries that require more external finance grow faster in more developed capital markets; and Love (2003) shows that firm's investment is less sensitive to the availability of internal funds in more financially developed countries. Recent evidence also links financial market liberalization to investment and financing constraints across countries. For example, Laeven (2003) finds that financial liberalization

---

[6] Our results are in contrast to Harrison and McMillan (2001), who found that financing constraints of firms in Cote d'Ivoire were exacerbated by the presence of foreign firms, which borrowed heavily on domestic credit markets and crowded out local firms. However, that paper is quite different in two respects. First, it examines the impact of multinational firm borrowing on domestic firms' behavior—this information is not available across countries. Second, it focuses on a very poor country with a variety of credit market imperfections, which drove foreign firms to borrow heavily from local banks. However, this current paper only includes two low-income countries, India and Pakistan, and it does not include any countries from Sub-Saharan Africa. This may be important because we would expect the domestic firms in the very poorest countries to be the most credit constrained, and at the same time, it is likely that governments in the poorest countries implement policies to help ease these constraints such as interest rate controls.

[7] For example, in a recent survey of executives in 20 African countries, financing constraints were cited as a major obstacle to business expansion, see Africa Competitiveness Report (Harvard Institute for International Development and World Economic Forum, 1998). However, these surveys could overestimate the degree of constraints because they are typically administered by institutions in a position to make loans, such as the World Bank.

[8] See, for example, Aghion et al. (1999) and Banerjee and Newman (1994).

[9] See, for example, Jaramillo et al. (1996) for Ecuador; Harris et al. (1994) for Indonesia; Gelos and Werner (1999) for Mexico; Patillo (2000) for Ghana; Harrison and McMillan (2001) for Cote d'Ivoire; and Bigsten et al. (2000) for several African countries.

reduces firms financing constraints, especially for small firms. Galindo et al. (2001) find that financial reform has led to an increase in the efficiency with which investment funds are allocated. Bekaert et al. (2001) and Henry (2000) find that the cost of equity capital decreases significantly after financial liberalizations. In addition, Bekaert et al. (2001) find that equity market liberalizations increase real economic growth by approximately 1% per year. Yet none of these studies examine the impact of restrictions on international transactions or capital flows on firm-level financing constraints. This paper seeks to fill this gap.

To test whether capital inflows affect firm-level financing constraints, we use augmented investment Euler equations. We modify the investment model by introducing a constraint on external financing, which generates a shadow cost of external funds. This provides a theoretical justification for our measure of financing constraints. In the absence of financing constraints, investment should respond only to investment growth opportunities, which we control for with a measure of the marginal product of capital. Therefore, the availability of internal funds should not affect current investment. We interpret the sensitivity of investment to the availability of internal funds (measured by the stock of liquid assets) as a proxy for the degree of financing constraints. We find that firms in countries with greater DFI inflows have less investment-cash sensitivity, after controlling for other factors.

We also test for the impact of restrictions on international transactions on firm-level financing constraints. Lewis (1997) explores the relationship between income and consumption growth, using aggregate data in a cross-country framework. Using an Euler equation for consumption, she argues that the relationship between domestic income and consumption should be weak if individuals are not credit constrained. In particular, she shows that individuals are more credit constrained in countries with restrictions on international transactions. Our framework tests for the impact of restrictions on international transactions on firms (as opposed to individuals). Our results for firms support her results for individuals. Firms are more financially constrained in countries that impose controls on capital account transactions. Unlike Lewis (1997), however, we find that other types of controls—such as import surcharges or surrender requirements for exporters—have no impact on individual firm's financing constraints.

An important question is which types of firms are most likely to benefit from capital inflows. Using data available both through Worldscope and from another database, Amadeus, we are able to identify two different types of firms in our data. First, we distinguish between domestically owned firms and firms with some foreign ownership. Second, we distinguish between firms with foreign assets abroad (which are more likely to be multinational firms) and enterprises with no foreign assets. We find domestically owned firms are more constrained, on average, than firms with either foreign ownership or foreign assets. We also find that incoming DFI has a significant impact on investment-cash flow sensitivities for domestically owned firms and firms with no foreign assets. These results are consistent with the hypothesis that foreign investment is associated with a greater reduction in the credit constraints of firms which are less likely to have access to international capital markets. We argue that this is plausible because incoming foreign investment provides an additional source of capital, freeing up scarce domestic credit which can then be redirected towards domestic enterprises.

A.E. Harrison et al. / Journal of Development Economics 75 (2004) 269–301   273

We also examine whether our results vary across income levels. We show that DFI is associated with a larger reduction in credit constraints and a larger increase in investment in lower income countries. This is not surprising as we expect DFI to have the largest effects in countries where credit market imperfections are most important.

The remainder of this paper is organized as follows. Section 2 outlines the general approach used for testing for financing constraints and the impact of DFI. Section 3 describes the data. Section 4 presents results of the estimation of the basic model, focusing on DFI inflows, and robustness checks. Section 5 examines the impact of restrictions on international transactions on credit constraints, Section 6 presents extensions and sample splits, and Section 7 concludes.

2. Testing for financing constraints and the impact of global flows: the framework

Numerous studies have used the Q theory of investment and Euler equations to study financing constraints.[10] Both the Q theory and Euler model of investment come from the same optimization problem (reproduced below). However, the assumptions required to estimate the Q model are stronger then those required to estimate the Euler equation model. Specifically, the Q model requires that stock market valuations be in line with the manager's valuation of the marginal return on capital. This assumption is questionable, especially in our cross-country study, as our countries are significantly different in their levels of financial development (and therefore, the degree of market imperfections). In addition, numerous recent papers highlight other problems with the Q methodology, such as severe measurement error and identification problems (see Kaplan and Zingales, 2000; Erikson and Whited, 2000; Bond and Cummins, 2001). Therefore, our preferred methodology is the Euler equation model of investment.

A series of recent papers have questioned the validity of using investment-cash flow sensitivities as a proxy for financing constraints. The debate, started by Kaplan and Zingales (1997), was continued by numerous studies, some of which support the use of investment-cash flow sensitivity as an indicator of credit constraints (Fazzari et al., 2000; Allayannis and Abon, 2004; Chirinko and von Kalckreuth, 2003) while others question it (Gomes, 2001; Moyen, 2002; Alti, 2003). Most papers which question this methodology relate more directly to the Q model of investment rather than an Euler equation model (although some criticisms apply to both models). In addition, none of the recent theoretical models that question this methodology were derived in a dynamic multi-period setting with investment adjustment costs (see Bond et al., 2003).

Since no theoretical consensus has been reached, the relationship between investment and cash flow sensitivities continues to be an important empirical question. In a recent paper, using the Euler equation methodology, Love (2003) finds that firms in less financially developed countries exhibit higher investment-cash flow sensitivities, especially the small firms. Independently, the survey evidence (see, for example, Beck et al.,

---

[10] See, for example, Whited (1992), Hubbard and Kashyap (1992), Hubbard et al. (1995), and Calomiris et al. (1995) for work on US firms, Bond and Meghir (1994) for the UK firms, and Bond et al. (1996) for comparison of four developed countries: Belgium, France, Germany, and the UK.

274 *A.E. Harrison et al. / Journal of Development Economics 75 (2004) 269–301*

2002) confirms that firms in countries with lower levels of financial development are more financially constrained, especially small firms. Taken together, these results support the intuition that investment-cash flow sensitivities are a reflection of a higher degree of financing constraints.

Recognizing the limitations of our approach, we test the sensitivity of our results to model specification by investigating two alternative investment models: a sales accelerator model and the Q model of investment.

2.1. The model

The model used to derive the Euler equation and Q model specifications is standard in the literature (see references in footnote 8) and follows closely the specification in Love (2003). The firm value is given by:

$$V_t(K_t, \xi_t) = \max_{\{I_{t+s}\}_{s=0}^\infty} D_t + E_t \left[\sum_{s=1}^\infty \beta_{t+s-1} D_{t+s} \right] \tag{1a}$$

where

$$D_t = \Pi(K_t, \xi_t) - C(I_t, K_t) - I_t \tag{1b}$$

$$K_{t+1} = (1 - \delta)K_t + I_t \tag{1c}$$

$$D_t \geq 0 \tag{1d}$$

Here, D_t is the dividend paid to shareholders and is given by the "sources equal uses" constraint (Eq. (1b)); β_{t+s-1} is a discount factor from the period $t+s$ to period t. In the capital accumulation constraint (Eq. (1c)), K_t is the beginning of the period capital stock; I_t is the investment expenditure, and δ is the depreciation rate.[11] The restricted profit function is denoted by $\Pi(K_t, \xi_t)$, where ξ_t is a productivity shock. The adjustment cost of investment is given by the function $C(I_t, K_t)$ and is assumed to result in a loss of a portion of investment. The financial frictions are introduced via a nonnegativity constraint on dividends (Eq. (1d)), and the multiplier on this constraint is denoted λ_t. This multiplier is interpreted as a shadow cost associated with raising new equity, which implies that external (equity) financing is costly.[12]

The Q model of investment is obtained as a first-order condition from the above model and is given by:

$$\left(\frac{\partial C}{\partial I} \right)_t = \text{const} + \beta_t E_t [q_{t+1}] \tag{2}$$

---

[11] We ignore the price of investment, which is replaced by fixed and time effects in the estimation. We also ignore tax considerations due to data constraints.

[12] This interpretation of the nonnegativity constraint on dividends is common in the literature (see, for example, Whited (1992). This does not imply that firms cannot raise any equity finance, but only that there is a premium associated with equity issuance.

A.E. Harrison et al. / Journal of Development Economics 75 (2004) 269–301   275

where $(\partial C/\partial I)$ is the marginal adjustment cost of investment and q_{t+1} is the "marginal q," i.e., it is the shadow value of capital equal to the increase in the value of the firm after a 1 unit increase in capital.

Combining this first-order condition with the envelope condition and rearranging, we obtain the Euler equation:

$$1 + \left(\frac{\partial C}{\partial I}\right)_t = \beta_t E_t \left[\Theta_t \left\{\left(\frac{\partial \Pi}{\partial K}\right)_{t+1} + (1 + \delta)\left(1 + \left(\frac{\partial C}{\partial I}\right)_{t+1}\right)\right\}\right] \tag{3}$$

where $\Theta_t = ((1 + \lambda_{t+1})/(1 + \lambda_t))$.

Here, $(\partial \Pi/\partial K)$ is the marginal profit of capital, i.e., the contribution of an extra unit of capital to the firm's profits, referred to below as MPK. The intuition behind this Euler equation is that the marginal cost of investing today on the left-hand side (given by the adjustment cost and the price of investment goods, normalized to one) is equal to the discounted marginal cost of postponing investment until tomorrow, on the right-hand side. The latter is equal to the sum of the foregone marginal benefit of an extra unit in capital, given by MPK, plus the adjustment cost and price of investment tomorrow (again normalized to one).

In the Euler equation, the factor Θ_t is the relative shadow cost of external finance in periods t and $t+1$, and it serves as a proxy for the degree of financing constraints. If the shadow cost of external funds is higher in period t than it is expected to be in period $t+1$, then $\Theta_t < 1$, and it acts as an additional discount factor which makes current period funds more expensive to use than the next period funds and therefore induces the firm to postpone or reduce its investment. In this case, we say that the firm is "financially constrained," and Θ_t is the (degree of) financing constraints. With perfect capital markets $\lambda_t = \lambda_t + 1 = 0$ for all t and hence $\Theta_t = 1$, and the firm is never constrained. With capital-market imperfections, λ_t depends on a vector of state variables, including the productivity shock ξ_t. Therefore, λ_t is time varying and can be identified with observable firm characteristics. In this paper, as a proxy for Θ_t, we use the stock of liquid assets, specifically the stock of cash and marketable securities scaled by fixed capital (hereafter referred to as cash stock). The cash stock has an intuitive interpretation as "cash on hand" that firms can use for investment if the opportunity presents itself (as in the Myers and Majluf, 1984 model). We also use the cash flow as an alternative measure of liquidity. The cash stock is our preferred measure because it is less likely to be associated with the future growth opportunities than the cash flow measure (see Love, 2003 for further discussion).

Unlike the Euler equation model in which financing variables enter as a parameterization of the discount factor Θ_t in the Q model, these financing factors are simply appended to the model. In this sense, the Euler equation has a more structural interpretation of the effect of financing constraints than the Q model.

2.2. Parameterizing the model

We closely follow Love (2003) in parameterizing the model and refer to that paper for a detailed discussion. We measure MPK using a sales-to-capital ratio (assuming a

Cobb–Douglas production function). The fixed effects help us to capture the firm-specific capital intensity and markups. We assume a quadratic adjustment cost function, which results in a linear marginal adjustment cost of investment:

$$\frac{\partial C}{\partial I_{it}} = \alpha \left(\frac{I}{K_{it}} - g \frac{I}{K_{it-1}} - v_i \right) \tag{4}$$

This adjustment cost function is slightly more general than the one used in the traditional models because it includes the lagged investment-to-capital ratio with an additional parameter g which is added to capture strong persistence in investment-to-capital ratios present in the data.[13]

To simplify the estimation and interpretation of the coefficients, we linearize the Euler equation using a first-order Taylor approximation around the means. In this sense, our model is a first-order approximation to the true model, which has a somewhat richer structure. This approximation improves the tractability of the model and allows us to focus on the most important effects. As a result, we ignore some second-order effects.[14]

Finally, we assume rational expectations, which allows us to replace expectations with realized values plus an expectation error e_{it}, which is orthogonal to any information available at the time when the investment decision is made.

2.3. Empirical model and estimation

As we discussed above, we measure financing constraints by the sensitivity of investment to cash stock (or cash flow). We argue that the larger this sensitivity, the more constrained the firm is because it has to rely on its internal funds to finance its investment. The primary goal of this paper is to determine whether capital inflows (in particular, DFI) or restrictions on international transactions have an impact on firm-level financing constraints. This will be reflected in the effect of capital inflows or capital controls on the investment-cash sensitivity which we capture using an interaction term of DFI with cash stock. We substitute our

---

[13] This extended functional form allows for the more common form with g=0, which could be tested empirically. The intuition for this added term is that it may be easier for the firm to continue investment at some fraction g of the previous period ratio, since, for example, it has hired workers or made some other arrangements which would be costly to cancel. Parameter v_i could be interpreted as some firm-specific level of investment at which adjustment costs are minimized.

[14] For example, we ignore the derivative of the adjustment costs with respect to capital which results in the addition of the squared investment-to-capital ratios to the model. We have tested the model with these terms, and our results are unchanged. A more subtle issue arises because of our generalized specification of the adjustment cost function. Allowing lagged investment to enter into this specification affects the derivation of the Euler equation as the value function would have to depend on two state variables (lagged investment and current capital stock). However, the result is the addition of the second-order terms to the model (more specifically, the squared product of two financial constraints factors and adjustment costs) which we ignore. However, our results are robust to adding $I/K(t+2)$ term to the model.

A.E. Harrison et al. / Journal of Development Economics 75 (2004) 269–301 277

parameterizations of the MPK and adjustment costs in a linearized version of Eq. (3) to obtain our empirical model:

$$\frac{I}{K_{it}} = \beta_1 \frac{I}{K_{it+1}} + \beta_2 \frac{I}{K_{it-1}} + \beta_3 \frac{S}{K_{it}} + \beta_4 \text{Cash}_{it-1} + \beta_5 \text{Cash}_{it-1} \text{DFI}_{ct} + \beta_6 \text{DFI}_{ct}$$
$$+ f_i + d_t + e_{it} \tag{5}$$

Here, f_i denotes firm fixed effects[15] and d_t denotes time dummies. We also test the alternative specifications, which present a variation on the above model. In the Q model, the first and the third terms are replaced by Tobin's Q, and in the accelerator model, they are replaced by current and lagged sales growth. In the Q model, Tobin's Q captures the expected marginal return on investment and in the accelerator model current and lagged sales growth proxy for expected future growth. Our specifications of the Q model and accelerator model also allow for slow adjustment of the capital stock to its desired level and hence include lagged investment and the firm-specific user cost of capital (captured by the fixed effects).

We focus on the coefficient β_5, the interaction of the level of cash stock (a firm-level variable) with the country-time level of DFI inflows. If DFI reduces firms' financing constraints, this coefficient should be negative, which implies that the total sensitivity of investment to the cash stock (given by the sum of $\beta_4 + \beta_5 \text{DFI}$) is reduced with DFI inflows. Alternatively, a positive coefficient on β_5 would suggest a crowding out effect. The coefficient β_4 measures the sensitivity of investment to the cash stock in an average country-year with zero DFI inflows. It is expected to be positive if some of the firms in our sample are credit constrained.

We use the same framework to test for the effect of restrictions on international transactions by replacing the DFI measure in Eq. (5) with measures of restrictions on international transactions. We also add additional interactions of the cash stock with the control variables of interest (such as financial development, GDP growth, private domestic credit, M2, inflation, and country risk) to the model in Eq. (5) to test if the DFI effect (on the cash coefficient) is robust to controlling for other potential effects on financing constraints.

To estimate the model, we first remove fixed effects using a forward mean-differencing transformation, which removes only the forward mean, i.e., the mean of all the future observations available for each firm year.[16] As discussed above, the expectation error e_{it} is orthogonal to the information available at the time when the investment decision is made. We assume that the investment decision for year t is made at the beginning of that year (which is equivalent to end of year $t - 1$). Therefore, the information available at the time of decision is dated $t - 1$ since year t information does not arrive until the end of year t. Therefore, we use the GMM procedure, with $t - 1$ and $t - 2$ lags of all of the regressors as instruments. Our instruments include only lagged DFI (i.e., time $t - 1$ and $t - 2$), which

---

[15] Fixed effects capture firm-specific parameters in the adjustment cost function and the MPK. They also capture the average firm-specific level of financing constraints and the price of investment goods.

[16] This transformation is otherwise known as "orthogonal deviations" or the Helmert transformation and is described in Arrellano and Bover (1995) and Bond and Meghir (1994). Unlike the first-differencing, the forward mean differencing preserves the error structure and therefore does not require any correction for the serial correlation in the error terms.

278 *A.E. Harrison et al. / Journal of Development Economics 75 (2004) 269–301*

allows for the endogeneity of current DFI. This is important if current flows and current investment are simultaneously determined. We test the validity of the instruments by reporting both a Sargan test of the over-identifying restrictions and direct tests of serial correlation in the residuals.[17]

3. Data

Firm-level data come from the Worldscope database, which contains data on large publicly traded firms in which there is an investor interest. The firm data are available for 38 countries and cover over 7000 firms for the years 1988–1998 (however, the years before 1991 and the year 1998 have fewer observations). Details are given in Appendix A. The coverage within countries varies widely from as little as 1% of all listed domestic firms included (for India) to as many as 82% (for Sweden), as calculated by La Porta et al. (1997). Table A1 gives the list of countries in the sample with the number of firms and observations per country. The number of firms in each country varies widely across the countries, and the less developed countries are underrepresented. This creates a problem with pooled cross-country estimation, as overrepresented countries may influence the coefficients in a nonsystematic way. To correct for this problem, we rerun all main results including only the 150 largest firms in each country.[18]

Unfortunately, our main data source, Worldscope, does not contain data on the nationality of the owners. This omitted information is potentially important because it would allow us to identify whether DFI inflows benefit only foreign firms and joint ventures or whether DFI also benefits wholly domestically owned firms. To obtain foreign ownership data, we used the Amadeus-Bureau Van Dijk database, which includes firm-level data on over 5 million private and publicly owned firms located in 34 European countries.[19] Only 14 countries (all relatively high-income countries) are present in both databases, and only 1006 firms (which represent about 20% of the total observations) from Worldscope match with the Amadeus data. Therefore, we run a separate set of tests using only the Amadeus data.[20] In addition to providing information on ownership, the Amadeus data covers a wider spectrum of firms since it includes both publicly traded and small privately held firms. We are able to split this sample on the basis of the level of development since it includes data for 8 eastern European countries and 14 western European countries and on the basis of ownership (see Table A1 for details). Finally, to obtain ownership information for the 15 low-income countries in our original sample, we use current and past issues of Dun and Bradstreet's (various issues) *Who Owns Whom*. Information for Latin America is only available beginning in 1996. Since we observe no changes in ownership over the period 1996–2001, we classify firms that are

---

[17] Our tests of serial correlation are based on a Gauss–Newton regression and described in Davidson and MacKinnon (1993, pp. 357–373). Following Arrellano and Bover (1995), reported standard errors are based on the first-step results.

[18] We rank companies by their relative size of PPENT (fixed capital) in each year for each country (using total assets in US dollars produces similar results).

[19] From this universe of firms, we select only those firms for which 5 consecutive years of fixed capital are available. This leaves us with 22 countries.

[20] Because the Amadeus data set is so large, we use a randomly selected sample of 1000 firms per country.

A.E. Harrison et al. / Journal of Development Economics 75 (2004) 269–301   279

foreign during this subperiod as foreign throughout our entire sample period (see Table A1 for details).[21]

The main firm-level variables are investment, sales, and cash stock, all scaled by the beginning of the period capital for consistency.[22] Variable definitions are given in Table A2. We supplement the firm-level data with country-level data on capital inflows, including portfolio investment, private capital flows, and direct foreign investment. The capital flow data are taken from the IMF publication *International Financial Statistics*, CD-ROM, (1988–1998). Our main capital flow variable is inflows of DFI, which we scale by aggregate gross domestic investment (GDI) and alternatively by GDP. In addition, we look at net DFI, defined as inflows minus outflows, portfolio investment (both inflows and net flows), and "other" flows. Other flows consist mainly of commercial bank loans but also include many other private flows which are neither portfolio investment nor DFI. Direct foreign investment occurs when foreigners purchase over 10% of the total equity of the firm. Investments of less than 10% are considered portfolio investment.

Other country-time varying control variables include growth rate in real GDP, the stock of liquid liabilities (M2) scaled by GDP, credit to private sector by deposit money banks and nonfinancial institutions, inflation rate (all come from the IMF's IFS database) and country risk (from the International Country Risk Guide, IRIS, [2001]). As an additional robustness check, we add a country-level measure of financial development, denoted FD, constructed using indicators developed by Demirguc-Kunt and Levine (1996).[23]

Table A3 reports means of the key variables over the sample period 1988–1998. The first three columns are capital flow variables scaled by gross domestic investment. Countries with the highest amount of DFI in our sample are Singapore, New Zealand, Chile, and Belgium. Countries with the lowest amount of DFI are Japan and South Korea. These countries have traditionally been closed to direct investment. More recent data would show an increase in direct investment in South Korea, but our data end in 1998. As a share of gross domestic investment, countries with the highest shares of portfolio investment are Belgium, the United Kingdom, and Venezuela.

Table A4 reports country-level means of the (time-varying) restrictions on international transactions obtained from the International Monetary Fund's annual report, Trade and Exchange Restrictions. The IMF assigns a value of 1 if the country has a control and zero otherwise. Historically, the IMF has collected information on five types of controls: (1)

---

[21] Using Dun and Bradstreet, we are able to identify roughly 62% of the firms in our sample. Of these firms, only 7.5% are foreign owned. Dun and Bradstreet includes only firms that are conglomerates and only identifies majority ownership. Published volumes do not provide the date that the information is recorded. Based on consultations with the publishers, we take the information to be valid two periods prior to the publication date.

[22] The model requires one to use the beginning of the period capital stock as a scaling factor for calculating adjustment costs and MPK. One alternative is to use lagged capital stock (i.e., period $t-1$ used as the beginning of the period t capital stock). However, this would not be appropriate if there are mergers, acquisitions, divestitures or other capital-changing events, which are hard to identify. We use the approximate value given by the ending period capital, minus investment and depreciation in that year, which is more robust to the capital-changing events.

[23] This measure combines five indicators of financial development: market capitalization over GDP (i.e., the size of the stock market), total value traded over GDP, total value traded over market capitalization, the ratio of liquid liabilities to GDP, and the credit going to the private sector over GDP. Each indicator is standardized to have mean zero and variance one, after which the indicators are averaged to produce a standardized index with mean zero and variance one.

restrictions on capital account transactions, (2) restrictions on current account transactions, (3) surcharges on imports, (4) requirements for advanced import deposits, and (5) export taxes, in the form of repatriation and/or surrender requirements for export revenues. The first control includes any kind of restriction on the capital account, while the second restriction includes restrictions on trade in goods and services. Interestingly, use of restrictions on international transactions is not confined to the poorest countries. Conversely, all of the countries that did not implement restrictions on international transactions (Canada, Hong Kong, the UK, the US, Singapore, the Netherlands, and New Zealand) are high-income countries. This suggests that the correlation between income and use of restrictions on international transactions is positive but not perfect. In aggregate, 31 out of 38 countries used some type of capital control during our sample period. The most common types of restrictions on international transactions are restrictions on capital transactions and repatriation and surrender requirements for exports.

Summing across all types of restrictions on international transactions, the evidence in Table A4 suggests that the most open countries are Canada, the Netherlands, New Zealand, Singapore, the US, and the UK. The most closed economies are Pakistan and South Africa, followed by Colombia and India. These rankings correspond with anecdotal evidence concerning the openness of the current and capital account across our sample countries.

Table A5 reports correlation coefficients, *p*-values and number of observations for the relationship between DFI and restrictions on international transactions, and the relationship between DFI and our macroeconomic indicators. As expected, the correlation between DFI and restrictions on international transactions is strongly negative and significant (− 0.32). The two controls most correlated with DFI are restrictions on capital transactions and repatriation and surrender requirements for exports. The latter is not surprising, as much of DFI goes to the export sector. The former directly affects DFI, and so we would expect this measure to be negatively correlated with DFI, since a restriction on capital transactions could be a direct restriction on incoming or outgoing DFI. One must be cautious in assigning causality. Although restrictions on international transactions do affect DFI inflows, it is equally plausible that restrictions on international transactions are (negatively) correlated with income level and that income levels determine (among other things) DFI flows. However, in the lower panel of Table A5, we see that DFI and our macroeconomic variables are not very strongly correlated. Although DFI is not correlated with GNP per capita or M2, it is strongly correlated with GDP growth. In addition, DFI is not significantly correlated with either a country's level of financial development (proxied by FD) or the magnitude of private credit.

4. Investment equation estimates

Table 1 reports the GMM results for Eq. (5). The basic specification is reported in column (1). The validity of the instruments, tested by the Sargan test and serial correlation tests, is easily accepted for most specifications. Thus, in our discussion of the results, we note only those cases in which the instruments are rejected. We report first-stage GMM estimates (which are likely to have better small-sample properties, see Arellano and Bond, 1991); however, our estimates from the second stage are qualitatively very similar. As an extra

A.E. Harrison et al. / Journal of Development Economics 75 (2004) 269–301 281

Table 1
Main results on FDI flows

Dependent variable: I/K_t	Scaled by gross domestic investment				Scaled by GDP			Manufacturing only	
	(1)	(2)	(3)	(4)	(5)	(6)	(7)	(8)	(9)
	All firms	Rank 150	0 < DFIN < 0.5	(3) and Rank 150	All firms	Rank 150	(6) and 0 < DFIN < 0.5	Scaled by GDI	Scaled by GDP
I/K_{t+1}	0.093	0.095	0.056	0.204	0.314	0.119	0.216	0.067	0.485
	(0.051)	(0.057)	(0.028)	(0.113)	(0.155)	(0.073)	(0.116)	(0.037)	(0.296)
I/K_{t-1}	0.231	0.241	0.229	0.227	0.224	0.237	0.223	0.252	0.206
	(0.024)	(0.032)	(0.021)	(0.018)	(0.019)	(0.03)	(0.024)	(0.014)	(0.024)
S/K_t	0.025	0.029	0.034	0.023	0.019	0.022	0.018	0.030	0.022
	(0.007)	(0.009)	(0.012)	(0.008)	(0.011)	(0.01)	(0.013)	(0.006)	(0.015)
$Cash_{t-1}$	0.061	0.067	0.064	0.084	0.044	0.072	0.063	0.042	0.032
	(0.012)	(0.008)	(0.014)	(0.02)	(0.013)	(0.024)	(0.02)	(0.008)	(0.015)
$DFI_t \times Cash_{t-1}$	− 0.458	− 0.636	− 0.409	− 0.566	− 2.212	− 2.729	− 2.183	− 0.377	− 2.518
	(0.148)	(0.309)	(0.128)	(0.274)	(0.654)	(1.311)	(1.042)	(0.172)	(1.251)
DFI_t	0.937	1.149	0.954	0.867	6.891	8.132	4.671	0.697	6.479
	(0.449)	(0.447)	(0.304)	(0.373)	(2.445)	(3.914)	(2.161)	(0.339)	(2.489)
Observations	22,504	13,221	20,867	12,756	23,796	13,964	13,609	13,043	13,924
Diagnostic tests (p-values)									
Sargan test	0.741	0.887	0.618	0.501	0.835	0.804	0.529	0.728	0.844
First-order serial correlation	0.515	0.481	0.512	0.463	0.601	0.627	0.642	0.522	0.325
Second-order serial correlation	0.834	0.723	0.826	0.714	0.472	0.519	0.531	0.816	0.546

Robust standard errors are in parentheses (clustered at the firm level). All specifications include time dummies. Estimated by GMM, instruments used are the first and second lags of all of the regressors. Variable definitions are given in Table A2.

precaution, we allow for "clustering" of errors on the firm level to correct for any possible nonindependence of errors on the firm level (although the direct tests of serial correlation are rejected).

In column (1) of Table 1, direct foreign investment (DFI) is scaled by gross domestic investment (GDI). This specification imposes no cutoffs on DFI and includes all firms with non-missing observations. The coefficient on lagged cash stock is positive and statistically significant, which indicates that, on average, investment is sensitive to the stock of cash, which is consistent with the existence of credit constraints. As expected, the coefficients on lagged and future investment and the sales-to-capital ratio are also positive and significant. The coefficient on DFI alone is positive and significant, indicating a positive correlation between country-level DFI and firm-level investment.

The focus of this section is the coefficient on DFI × Cash. The coefficient is negative and statistically significant. This indicates that inflows of DFI are associated with a reduction in the sensitivity of investment to the cash stock. The coefficient on cash stock is equal to 0.06, which we interpret as investment-cash sensitivity in an average country in a year with zero

DFI inflow. The distribution of DFI across country-years has mean of 0.09 and standard deviation of 0.08; therefore, a one standard deviation increase in DFI inflows implies a 0.04 decrease in the cash sensitivity; that is a change from 0.06 to 0.02, roughly a 60% decline in cash sensitivity. These numbers imply that DFI inflows have a large and economically significant influence on the investment-cash sensitivity, which we interpret as a reduction in the firm's financing constraints.

The remainder of this section is devoted to showing that this result is robust to a variety of alternative specifications. In column (2), we restrict the sample to the largest 150 firms in each country. Since most of the firms in the sample are from the largest countries, such as the United States, this restriction is introduced to see if data for the United States is driving the results. Restricting the sample to the largest 150 firms in each country has very little impact on the results. The interaction between DFI and cash stock remains large and statistically significant.

Column (3) restricts the sample to all observations where country-level inward DFI is greater than zero and less than 50% of gross domestic investment (GDI). This allows us to exclude extreme country observations where DFI may account for the major share of domestic investment. This only removes 12 enterprises from the sample and leaves the results virtually unchanged. Further restricting the sample to the largest 150 firms in each country has no significant impact (column (4)) on the results.

In columns (5)–(7), we scale DFI by gross domestic product (GDP) instead of gross domestic investment. Although the point estimates change due to the different scaling factor, the results are unaffected: firms in countries with high levels of DFI are less credit constrained. Column (6) further restricts the sample to observations where DFI values are not extreme, and columns (7) in addition restricts to the largest 150 firms in each country (similarly to column (4)). Finally, in columns (8) and (9), we restrict our sample to include only manufacturing firms (i.e., excluding agriculture, utilities, and trade), and again, the results are similar.

Table (2) checks the robustness of these results to different model specifications. We use two alternative empirical specifications: a sales accelerator model (column (1)) and the Q model of investment (columns (2) and (3)). Because our instruments are rejected in the simple Q model in column (2), we add lagged investment to the model in column (3). Columns (4) and (5) are replications of the Euler model used in Table 1, except that instead of using cash stock, we use two alternative measure of cash flow: the first measure is net income (before preferred dividends) plus depreciation, and the second measure is cash flow from operations (equal to the first measure plus changes in working capital). Column (6) is a replication of column (1) from Table 1 with the addition of a debt-to-assets ratio. For each of the investment models that we consider, investment is sensitive to the cash stock, but this sensitivity is significantly reduced by inflows of foreign direct investment. In addition, foreign direct investment has a direct positive effect on firm level investment. We conclude that these results are not driven by model choice. The possibility still remains that cash stock proxies for future investment opportunities and that the sensitivity of investment to cash stock does not reflect financing constraints. However, if cash stock does represent future growth opportunities, it is hard to think of a reason why DFI would lessen the sensitivity of investment to future growth opportunities. Our preferred interpretation is that the

A.E. Harrison et al. / Journal of Development Economics 75 (2004) 269–301   283

Table 2
Robustness to alternative specifications

Dependent variable: I/K_t	(1)	(2)	(3)	(4)	(5)	(6)
	Accelerator model	Q model	Q model	Euler model	Euler model	Euler model
I/K_{t+1}				0.469	0.267	0.056
				(0.222)	(0.109)	(0.029)
I/K_{t-1}	0.439		0.267	0.201	0.217	0.234
	(0.101)		(0.011)	(0.019)	(0.023)	(0.022)
S/K_t				0.014	0.022	0.034
				(0.012)	(0.014)	(0.011)
$(I/K_{t-1})^2$	− 0.203					
	(0.119)					
Sales growth$_t$	− 0.049					
	(0.032)					
Sales growth$_{t-1}$	0.042					
	(0.011)					
Q_{t-1}		0.023	0.019			
		(0.011)	(0.009)			
Debt/K_{t-1}						− 0.112
						(0.074)
Cash$_{t-1}$	0.054	0.039	0.063	0.088	0.063	0.039
(or cash flow)	(0.012)	(0.012)	(0.009)	(0.019)	(0.02)	(0.013)
DFI$_t$ × Cash$_{t-1}$	− 0.239	− 0.803	− 0.301	− 0.864	− 1.289	− 0.501
(or cash flow)	(0.088)	(0.159)	(0.094)	(0.40)	(0.511)	(0.16)
DFI$_t$	0.087	2.573	0.432	0.428	0.802	1.048
	(0.292)	(0.594)	(0.321)	(0.337)	(0.445)	(0.468)
Observations	22,690	25,348	25,348	22,800	22,802	21,842
Diagnostic tests (p-values)						
Sargan test	0.601	0.249	0.623	0.456	0.813	0.867
First-order serial correlation	0.239	.011	0.564	0.446	0.767	0.782
Second-order serial correlation	0.528	0.012	0.93	0.526	0.986	0.926

Robust standard errors are in parentheses (clustered at the firm level). All specifications include time dummies. Estimated by GMM, instruments used are the first and second lags of all of the regressors. Variable definitions are given in Table A2. Columns (4) and (5) report results using two alternative measures of liquidity; the first measure is defined as net income plus depreciation, and the second measure includes changes in the working capital, in addition. Column (6) is our column (1) from Table 1 with a measure of debt.

sensitivity of investment to cash stock is an indicator of financing constraints and that DFI reduces this sensitivity.

Direct foreign investment is likely to be correlated with a number of country-level measures of economic well-being, including GDP growth and the general level of financial development. Incoming foreign investment could also be driven by domestic policies which expand the availability of domestic credit. In both of these cases, the results could simply arise from omitted variable bias, where DFI proxies for the expansion of domestic credit or other measures economic well being. To test for this possibility, Table 3 redoes the specification reported in Table 1 (model 1), but includes a number of country-specific variables as robustness checks on DFI. In the first column, we add the interaction of cash stock and financial development (FD) to check whether DFI is essentially a proxy for

Table 3
Robustness to correlates of FDI

Dependent variable: I/K_t	(1) Financial development	(2) GDP growth	(3) M2	(4) Private credit	(5) Inflation	(6) Country risk	(7) Country-time dummies
I/K_{t+1}	0.245	0.172	0.229	0.267	0.689	0.878	0.255
	(0.139)	(0.109)	(0.141)	(0.156)	(0.267)	(0.312)	(0.093)
I/K_{t-1}	0.232	0.242	0.234	0.222	0.201	0.191	0.226
	(0.021)	(0.018)	(0.024)	(0.023)	(0.023)	(0.022)	(0.018)
S/K_t	0.019	0.029	0.028	0.021	0.011	0.007	0.023
	(0.011)	(0.011)	(0.014)	(0.012)	(0.012)	(0.014)	(0.007)
$Cash_{t-1}$	0.039	0.038	0.029	0.028	0.022	0.023	0.044
	(0.013)	(0.013)	(0.011)	(0.013)	(0.011)	(0.009)	(0.013)
$DFI_t \times Cash_{t-1}$	− 0.549	− 0.454	− 0.278	− 0.343	− 0.201	− 0.132	− 0.117
	(0.167)	(0.137)	(0.084)	(0.122)	(0.073)	(0.054)	(0.032)
DFI_t	1.127	0.876	0.392	0.666	0.165	− 0.044	
	(0.511)	(0.365)	(0.201)	(0.386)	(0.143)	(0.113)	
$Control_t \times Cash_{t-1}$	− 0.244	6.861	0.137	− 0.354	− 0.013	0.009	
	(0.113)	(5.262)	(0.101)	(0.122)	(0.010)	(0.013)	
$Control_t$		− 1.618	0.086	0.066	0.008	0.011	
		(1.313)	(0.065)	(0.065)	(0.014)	(0.012)	
Observations	22,293	22,484	22,023	22,022	17,078	17,306	22,601
Diagnostic tests (p-values)							
Sargan test	0.887	0.618	0.476	0.332	0.538	0.713	0.341
First-order serial correlation	0.919	0.582	0.132	0.719	0.578	0.509	0.223
Second-order serial correlation	0.867	0.434	0.721	0.483	0.944	0.567	0.546

Robust standard errors are in parentheses (clustered at the firm level). All specifications include time dummies (except model 7 that includes country-time dummies). Estimated by GMM, instruments used are the first and second lags of all of the regressors. Variable definitions are given in Table A2.

financial development. However, the inclusion of FD, which varies across countries but not over time, does not affect the coefficient on DFI × Cash. Consistent with Love (2003) in countries with more financially developed markets, firms appear to be less credit constrained.

Next, we test several country and time-varying indicators that could be associated with larger DFI inflows. In column (2), we add the interaction of cash stock and GDP growth. Since foreign investment is attracted to fast-growing countries, DFI may simply be capturing the fact that fast-growing countries experience a reduction in financing constraints. Inclusion of GDP growth interacted with cash stock has no impact on the DFI × Cash coefficient.

In columns (3) and (4), we test whether DFI proxies for changes in the availability of domestic credit. Domestic credit is defined alternatively as M2 relative to GDP and the ratio of private credit to GDP. Although we find that an expansion in domestic credit (only using the private credit measure) eases the financing constraints of firms, as expected, inclusion of this variable does not affect the significance of the coefficient on DFI × Cash, although its magnitude is reduced.

A.E. Harrison et al. / Journal of Development Economics 75 (2004) 269–301 285

In columns (5) and (6), we add two additional measures of economic well-being that vary by country and time: inflation and country risk. Again, the idea is that DFI may simply be a proxy for a country's overall performance and that in countries that perform better, firms may be less credit constrained. The interaction between DFI and cash remains significant after the inclusion of these two variables, although the magnitude is again much smaller. Also, the direct relationship between firm-level investment and DFI is weaker with the inclusion of these variables. Finally, in column (7), we add country-time dummies as a proxy for any macroeconomic factors that vary by country over time (and we exclude DFI in levels since now it is captured by country-time dummies). Our main results remain intact though the magnitudes become somewhat smaller. To summarize, the results in Table 3 suggest that the impact of direct foreign investment on domestic financing constraints is remarkably robust.

5. Testing for the impact of restrictions on international transactions

If direct foreign investment inflows affect firm financing constraints in host countries, then restrictions on international transactions (including capital controls which inhibit inflows of DFI) are likely to exacerbate financing constraints. Table 4 presents the results of testing for the impact of restrictions on international transactions on firm-level financing constraints. The first control includes any kind of restriction on the capital account, while the second restriction includes restrictions on trade in goods and services. Restrictions on incoming DFI are most likely to be associated with the first type of control (i.e., restrictions on capital account transactions), which covers direct restrictions on inflows or outflows of foreign investment. Other controls, however, could also have an indirect effect, by reducing the overall profitability of investment and thus discouraging foreign investment inflows.

Table 4 reports the impact of each type of control on financing constraints separately. We focus on the coefficient on the interaction of each different type of restriction and cash stock, Restriction × Cash. As indicated in the table, the only type of restriction which has a significant impact on financing constraints is the restriction on payments for capital transactions. The coefficient is highly significant and positive, indicating that country-years with restrictions on payments for capital transactions have more credit-constrained firms. In addition, the coefficient on the restriction alone is significant and negative. This suggests that restricting capital flows negatively affects firm-level investment.

The second to fifth columns of Table 4 test for the impact of other types of foreign exchange or trade restrictions on financing constraints. None of the other types of restrictions affect firm financing constraints. However, there is a negative and statistically significant relationship between import surcharges and firm-level investment. Countries with higher import surcharges have lower investment, after controlling for other determinants of investment. This result confirms the findings of Levine and Renelt (1992), who argue that trade restrictions operate through their impact on investment, rather than directly on technological change and growth. This suggests that openness to trade could be a critical factor in encouraging domestic investment. Columns (6) and (7) check the robustness of the results on the impact of capital account restrictions on financing constraints. Including either M2 or GDP growth has no impact on the result that countries with capital account restrictions

Table 4
Restrictions on the movement of capital

Dependent variable: I/K_t	Scaled by gross domestic investment				Scaled by GDP		
	(1)	(2)	(3)	(4)	(5)	(6)	(7)
	E2	E1	F2	F1	GS	E2 and M2	E2 and GDP growth
I/K_{t+1}	0.589	0.543	1.019	0.409	0.828	0.618	0.667
	(0.211)	(0.234)	(0.393)	(0.22)	(0.289)	(0.189)	(0.218)
I/K_{t-1}	0.278	0.278	0.212	0.289	0.222	0.277	0.278
	(0.022)	(0.031)	(0.03)	(0.028)	(0.034)	(0.032)	(0.024)
S/K_t	0.033	0.032	0.028	0.033	0.032	0.028	0.039
	(0.012)	(0.014)	(0.009)	(0.012)	(0.011)	(0.008)	(0.014)
$Cash_{t-1}$	0.078	0.109	−0.019	0.128	0.028	0.067	0.078
	(0.044)	(0.054)	(0.093)	(0.056)	(0.067)	(0.029)	(0.045)
$Restriction_t \times Cash_{t-1}$	0.201	0.063	−0.011	−0.143	−0.014	0.223	0.223
	(0.057)	(0.156)	(0.224)	(0.16)	(0.089)	(0.067)	(0.073)
$Restriction_t$	−0.024	−0.032	0.009	−0.078	−0.019	−0.021	−0.018
	(0.007)	(0.033)	(0.017)	(0.034)	(0.014)	(0.011)	(0.011)
$Control_t \times Cash_{t-1}$						0.013	−1.473
						(0.234)	(1.021)
$Control_{t-1}$						−0.012	−0.213
						(0.049)	(0.254)
Observations	21,910	21,190	21,190	21,190	21,190	21,650	21,851
Diagnostic tests (p-values)							
Sargan test	0.33	0.828	0.161	0.445	0.113	0.489	0.422
First-order serial correlation	0.94	0.211	0.118	0.132	0.139	0.956	0.212
Second-order serial correlation	0.44	0.743	0.323	0.928	0.245	0.973	0.143

Robust standard errors are in parentheses (clustered at the firm level). All specifications include time dummies. Estimated by GMM, instruments used are the first and second lags of all of the regressors. Variable definitions are given in Table A2. Each restriction is a country-year dummy variable defined as follows: E2–restrictions for payments for capital transactions, E1–restrictions for payments for current transactions, F2–advance deposit required for imports, F1–import surcharges, and GS–government surrender requirements or restrictions on the repatriation of capital.

have more credit-constrained firms. The results in Table 4 suggest that our results on capital account restrictions are not driven by a negative correlation between capital account restrictions and M2 or GDP growth.

6. Extensions

6.1. Impact of other types of flow

A natural question to ask is whether the impact of DFI on firm financing constraints in host countries is a unique characteristic of DFI or may be extended to the effects of other types of flows. In Table 5, we explore whether other types of flows have the same impact on financing constraints as incoming DFI. We test for the impact of net DFI (inflows less

A.E. Harrison et al. / Journal of Development Economics 75 (2004) 269–301   287

Table 5
Do other types of capital flows ease credit constraints?

Dependent variable: I/K_t	(1) FDI net	(2) Portfolio inflows	(3) Portfolio net	(4) Other inflows	(5) Other net
I/K_{t+1}	0.348	0.023	1.074	0.274	0.275
	(0.167)	(0.014)	(2.063)	(0.314)	(0.368)
I/K_{t-1}	0.239	0.238	0.219	0.239	0.238
	(0.032)	(0.022)	(0.063)	(0.022)	(0.027)
S/K_t	0.038	0.037	0.043	0.024	0.028
	(0.012)	(0.012)	(0.013)	(0.009)	(0.011)
$Cash_{t-1}$	0.078	0.018	0.017	0.021	0.055
	(0.022)	(0.013)	(0.067)	(0.012)	(0.019)
$Flow_t \times Cash_{t-1}$	− 0.945	− 0.912	7.153	− 0.598	− 2.62
	(0.256)	(1.254)	(17.443)	(0.442)	(2.128)
$Flow_t$	0.223	0.343	− 1.332	0.045	0.342
	(0.056)	(0.228)	(3.044)	(0.035)	(0.263)
Observations	21,372	22,473	20,648	22,526	21,626
Diagnostic tests (p-values)					
Sargan test	0.467	0.138	0.334	0.028	0.023
First-order serial correlation	0.512	0.078	0.312	0.067	0.075
Second-order serial correlation	0.373	0.222	0.956	0.112	0.244

Robust standard errors are in parentheses (clustered at the firm level). All specifications include time dummies. Estimated by GMM, instruments used are the first and second lags of all of the regressors. Variable definitions are given in Table A2. Net flows are inflows minus outflows.

outflows), portfolio investment, and other investment. Other investment typically includes commercial bank loans. The results in column (1) show that net DFI inflows are also significant, which is consistent with our earlier results on gross DFI inflows. The portfolio inflows do not have a significant effect on financing constraints. The coefficient on cash interacted with other inflows in columns (4) and (5) is negative, but not significant (plus the model is rejected with Sargan test *p*-values of 0.028 and 0.023). Thus, based on the evidence, it appears that DFI plays a unique role in easing financing constraints. In addition, direct foreign investment is the only type of flow which is positively and significantly associated with firm-level investment in our sample.

It is not that surprising that portfolio flows have no impact on firms' financing constraints. Portfolio flows tend to be short term in nature and more volatile than DFI (World Bank, 2001). In addition, while DFI implies a direct injection of funds into the firm, portfolio investment (which could be equivalent to purchasing stocks on the stock market) does not necessarily result in injections of liquidity. Our results are consistent with Collins and Bosworth (1999) who find that—in the aggregate—DFI has a highly beneficial effect on domestic investment, while portfolio flows have no discernible effect on investment. They also find that there is very little correlation between DFI, portfolio flows, and bank loans. One difference between our results and Collins and Bosworth is our finding that other inflows have no effect. This may be due to differences in samples—Collins and Bosworth have 58 developing countries in their sample and look at aggregate investment as opposed to firm-level investment.

6.2. Impact of DFI on financing constraints by income levels

In this section, we test whether the impact of foreign investment on host-country financing constraints varies with the level of development. It is likely that the impact of foreign investment would be smaller in countries where credit markets are well developed and constraints on credit are less pervasive. Column (1) of Table 6 tests this hypothesis by splitting the Worldscope sample into high-income and medium–low-income countries (using World Bank definitions of income categories). Column (2) performs the split between western and eastern Europe using our Amadeus sample. We first observe that the coefficient on cash stock in low-income countries is twice that in high-income countries, suggesting that firms in low-income countries are more constrained, on average. In addition, we find that the coefficient on the interaction between cash and DFI is between three and five times greater in low-income than in high-income countries. This suggests that DFI eases financing constraints more in low-income countries. These results are consistent with the work by Bond et al. (2003), suggesting that an important determinant of financing constraints is differences in financial systems. For example, they find that firms' investment is highly sensitive to financial variables in the United Kingdom and not sensitive to financial variables in Belgium. They argue that this finding is consistent with the suggestion that financial constraints on investment are more severe in the more market-oriented U.K.

6.3. Which firms benefit most from the DFI inflows?

We would like to be able to identify the mechanism through which foreign inflows affect domestic financing constraints. For example, are financing constraints eased because firms that were previously denied credit are able to substitute domestic credit with foreign equity inflows, or do foreign inflows provide a signal to foreign banks operating in the country, triggering them to lend more to domestic enterprises? Although we cannot answer these questions in any definitive way, we attempt to better understand these mechanisms by splitting our sample by firm type. In particular, we separately estimate the impact of DFI inflows on firms with or without foreign assets and on firms with and without foreign ownership. We expect that firms with foreign assets are more likely to have access to international capital markets and therefore be less affected by DFI. Similarly, we expect firms with foreign ownership to be less financially constrained than those without foreign ownership.

In Table 6, column (3), we redo the basic specification, but we separate firms with foreign assets from other firms. Only half the firms in Worldscope have information concerning foreign assets, and we define a firm with foreign assets as a firm with foreign assets greater than zero (we also used sample splits based on the 5% or 10% cutoffs of the foreign assets and obtained similar results). The results indicate that firms with and without foreign assets exhibit similar sensitivities of investment to the cash stock, the point estimate on cash stock is statistically indistinguishable for the two samples. In addition, DFI reduces the sensitivity of investment to the cash stock for both types of firms. The evidence suggests that the level of DFI in a particular economy affects not just firms with foreign assets, which are more likely to be multinational firms and have access to international capital markets, but also firms without such access.

Table 6
Does the impact of FDI vary according to sample?

Database	(1) Worldscope		(2) Amadeus		(3) Worldscope		(4) Amadeus		(5) Worldscope	
Dependent variable: I/K_t	High income	Low income	Western Europe	Eastern Europe	Without foreign assets	With foreign assets	Foreign owned	Not foreign owned	Foreign owned	Not foreign owned
I/K_{t+1}	0.209	0.789	0.087	0.067	−0.011	0.133	0.234	0.502	0.400	0.334
	(0.121)	(0.232)	(0.038)	(0.022)	(0.066)	(0.064)	(0.122)	(0.229)	(0.245)	(0.143)
I/K_{t-1}	0.247	0.142	0.096	0.077	0.078	0.173	0.010	0.147	0.233	0.234
	(0.018)	(0.054)	(0.033)	(0.039)	(0.013)	(0.021)	(0.033)	(0.041)	(0.033)	(0.036)
S/K_t	0.032	0.019	0.018	0.022	0.054	0.043	0.031	0.022	0.015	0.023
	(0.014)	(0.008)	(0.008)	(0.014)	(0.012)	(0.009)	(0.012)	(0.009)	(0.007)	(0.008)
$Cash_{t-1}$	0.033	0.059	0.033	0.057	0.063	0.059	0.042	0.038	0.042	0.034
	(0.011)	(0.018)	(0.015)	(0.019)	(0.014)	(0.012)	(0.018)	(0.009)	(0.011)	(0.009)
$DFI_t \times Cash_{t-1}$	−0.167	−0.519	−0.056	−0.271	−0.467	−0.292	−0.060	−0.032	−0.609	−0.189
	(0.059)	(0.167)	(0.022)	(0.088)	(0.063)	(0.043)	(0.017)	(0.013)	(0.133)	(0.061)
DFI_t	0.072	0.253	0.194	1.621	0.332	0.114	0.142	0.145	0.136	0.219
	(0.033)	(0.111)	(0.077)	(0.054)	(0.054)	(0.039)	(0.053)	(0.057)	(0.066)	(0.066)
Observations	18,669	3835	5686	1826	4977	3278	483	2250	192	2186
Diagnostic Tests (p-values)										
Sargan test	0.545	0.353	0.531	0.519	0.643	0.389	0.812	0.516	0.223	0.235
First-order serial correlation	0.423	0.223	0.422	0.355	0.348	0.369	0.771	0.333	0.199	0.233
Second-order serial correlation	0.532	0.352	0.768	0.645	0.567	0.519	0.534	0.377	0.278	0.301

In addition, we would like to understand whether foreign investment inflows make it easier for other firms—those without foreign assets or without foreign partners—to invest. The answer to this question is likely to depend on the nature of the foreign investment. One type of foreign investment is a joint venture between a local company in need of capital and a foreign company. In this setup, the local company typically receives financing from the foreign company in the form of an equity injection. Clearly, this arrangement is expected to reduce the financing constraints of the local company. Another type of foreign direct investment is where a foreign company sets up a subsidiary. As the foreign company typically limits its loan exposure to the local subsidiary, the subsidiary will need to borrow to finance investments. New subsidiaries of multinationals or greenfield investments may exacerbate the credit constraints of domestic firms to the extent that an increased number of firms are now competing for the same limited amount of resources. The net effect on financing constraints under this second type of foreign direct investment are therefore less clear.

Our measure of DFI is an aggregate measure that does not distinguish between joint ventures and new subsidiaries. Although we do not have separate DFI inflows for each type of investment, however, we can separate out the firms that never received DFI to determine whether "spillover" effects are positive or negative.[24] Although Worldscope data do not include information on foreign ownership, we were able to obtain ownership information from two additional sources, Amadeus and Dun and Bradstreet's (various issues) *Who Owns Whom*. The Amadeus sample includes most of the high-income countries in our original sample plus eight eastern European countries. Additionally, it includes a larger spectrum of firms since it is not restricted to publicly traded firms. Of the firms with foreign ownership, none has less than 25%. Therefore, we split our sample based on whether or not the firm has any foreign ownership. For the low-income countries in our Worldscope sample, we use Dun and Bradstreet's (various issues) *Who Owns Whom* to identify foreign-owned firms, and a firm is classified as foreign if foreigners hold a majority ownership.

Columns (4) and (5) of Table 6 report the results of our basic specification, separating firms with foreign ownership from domestically owned firms. For both sets of firms, investment exhibits sensitivity to changes in the cash stock. In addition, DFI reduces the sensitivity of investment to changes in the cash stock for both types of firms. However, the magnitude of the impact for foreign-owned firms is two times the magnitude of the impact for domestically owned firms. This is consistent with the notion that firms receiving DFI would benefit more from these inflows. These results are also consistent with the notion that DFI inflows affect investment-cash flow sensitivities for wholly domestically owned firms, i.e., firms that do not directly benefit from DFI.

We caution the reader on three counts. First, although our sample includes both high- and low-income countries, it does not include many of the very poorest countries. For example, South Africa is the only African country included in the sample. However, these are the countries where financing constraints are likely to be the most severe. Second, the

---

[24] Although we are unable to identify which firms receive DFI in which year, we are certain that firms that have no foreign ownership and no foreign assets have never received DFI. This allows us to see if DFI has any effect on financing constraints of firms that do not receive DFI.

A.E. Harrison et al. / Journal of Development Economics 75 (2004) 269–301   291

impact of DFI on financing constraints is also likely to depend on the policy environment.[25] Third, our measure of DFI is an aggregate measure that does not distinguish between types of DFI. Therefore, our results are biased in favor of the type of DFI that is more prevalent in our sample. This implies that one should be cautious about interpreting the results at the country level. In any case, it is clear that there is scope for much more work on this topic, particularly in low-income countries.

7. Conclusion

This paper tests whether different measures of globalization affect host-country financing constraints. Direct foreign investment, by bringing in scarce capital, may ease firm financing constraints. Alternatively, if foreign firms borrow heavily from domestic banks, they may exacerbate domestic firms' financing constraints by crowding them out of domestic capital markets. Combining a unique cross-country firm panel with country-level data on DFI flows, we test whether foreign investment affects firm-level financing constraints. The result suggest that DFI inflows are associated with a reduction in firm-level financing constraints. Our results are robust to a number of controls, including measures of GDP growth, other measures of credit changes, and a proxy for financial development.

We also test whether restrictions on international transactions affect domestic firm financing constraints. Our results suggest that only one type of restriction—those on capital account transactions—negatively affect firm financing constraints Other types of exchange controls—such as repatriation requirements for exporters or import surcharges—have no impact on firm financing constraints. We also find that capital account restrictions and import surcharges negatively affect firm-level investment, after controlling for other factors.

Finally, we examine whether the impact of DFI varies across the level of economic development. Our results show that direct foreign investment eases domestic financing constraints in both high- and low-income countries, although the magnitudes are larger in low-income countries. To understand better the mechanism through which DFI eases financing constraints, we split our sample based on whether or not the firm is a multinational and whether or not the firm has any foreign ownership. Our results confirm that DFI reduces the sensitivity of investment to cash for all types of enterprises. These results are consistent with a story in which DFI eases credit constraints even for purely domestic firms.

8. Uncited references

Bekaert and Campbell, 2000
Fazzari et al., 1988

---

[25] For example, Harrison and McMillan (2001) show that in the Ivory Coast, joint ventures receive all the benefits as far as relaxation of credit is concerned, and domestic firms which are not partially foreign owned are actually crowded out of domestic credit markets. Though Harrison and McMillan (2001) examines the effects of ownership rather than capital flows, to some extent, we expect the two to be correlated. In that paper, we argue that the policy environment in the Ivory Coast had much to do with the result that foreign ownership had a crowding out effect.

Gilchrist and Himmelberg, 1995
Gilchrist and Himmelberg, 1998
Hart, 1995
Hayashi, 1982
International Monetary Fund, various issues
International Monetary Fund, 2000
Jensen and Meckling, 1976
Kim et al., 1998
Opler et al., 1999
Ross et al., 1996
Tybout, 1983
Schiantarelli, 1996

Acknowledgements

Inessa Love acknowledges support from Social Science Research Council Program in Applied Economics with funds provided by the John D. and Catherine T. MacArthur Foundation.

Appendix A. Sample Selection

All countries in the Worldscope database (May 1999 Global Researcher CD) with at least 30 firms and at least 100 firm year observations are included in the sample (the exception is Venezuela [VE] which is included with 80 observations only); former socialist economies are excluded. This results in a sample of 38 countries. The sample does not include firms for which the primary industry is financial (one digit SIC code of 6).

In addition, we delete the following (see Table A2 for variable definitions):

−All firms with 3 or less years of coverage;
−All firm years with missing ikb, skb, cash, and FDI;
−Observations with zero PPENT (200 observations);
−Observations with negative KBEG (277 observations) or Cash/K (25 observations);
−Observations with IK>2.5 (1% of all observations);
−Observations with SK>20 (5% of all observations);[26]
−Observations with Cash/K>1.9 (1% of all observations);
−50% of all US firms with at least 4 years of data available was selected by random sample.[27]

---

[26] This rule excludes firms for which capital is not a big factor in production. Half of these were in the US and UK; Japan, France, and Denmark totaled 25%.

[27] The original sample for the US had over 25,700 observations (firm-years), while for all other countries, at most, there are 12,000 for the UK, 5000 for Japan, less then 1000 for most countries (see Table 1). Even after the sampling, the US has the most data available.

A.E. Harrison et al. / Journal of Development Economics 75 (2004) 269–301   293

The resulting data set has about 46,000 observations; the number of observations by country is given in Table A1.

Table A1
Sample coverage across countries[a]

Country	Worldscope			Amadeus		Dun and Bradstreet	
	Observations	Firms	Average firm years	Firms	Percent foreign	Firms	Percent foreign firms
Argentina	189	25	3.6			19	26.32
Austria	434	55	7.9				
Australia	1307	185	7.1				
Belgium	525	70	7.5	711	6.87		
Brazil	587	93	6.3			54	11.11
Canada	2933	368	8.0				
Switzerland	1016	132	7.7	347	28.45		
Chile	391	54	7.2			37	5.41
Colombia	128	20	6.4			10	10.00
Germany	2437	461	5.3				
Denmark	962	122	7.9	354	18.87		
Spain	859	113	7.6	990	8.45		
Finland	679	85	8.0	973	35.62		
France	3148	403	7.8	992	6.58		
United Kingdom	8911	1089	8.2	677	10.01		
Indonesia	493	83	5.9			50	8.01
Ireland	357	45	7.9	54	71.11		
Israel	145	29	5.0				
India	1377	266	5.2			183	2.19
Italy	1105	133	8.3	999	8.24		
Japan	3623	591	6.1				
South Korea	901	185	4.9				
Mexico	483	69	7.0			50	9.06
Malaysia	1292	202	6.4			153	1.96
Netherlands	1270	146	8.7	23	0.00		
Norway	627	84	7.5	879	2.37		
New Zealand	273	41	6.7				
Peru	103	17	5.5			11	18.18
Philippines	286	42	6.8			45	4.44
Pakistan	368	70	5.3			5	40.00
Portugal	231	42	5.5	1000	21.28		
Sweden	1063	135	7.9				
Singapore	744	118	6.3				
Thailand	949	177	5.4			48	8.33
Turkey	110	18	4.6			10	0.00
USA	8222	1168	7.0				
Venezuela	69	11	6.3			9	11.11
South Africa	1047	132	7.9			49	30.61
Greece				940	12.37		
Luxembourg				142	58.90		
Bulgaria				999	7.76		

(continued on next page)

Table A1 (*continued*)

Country	Worldscope			Amadeus		Dun and Bradstreet	
	Observations	Firms	Average firm years	Firms	Percent foreign	Firms	Percent foreign firms
Czech Republic				983	29.29		
Croatia				181	25.39		
Hungary				332	36.82		
Poland				677	40.97		
Romania				939	6.39		
Slovakia				330	69.23		
Slovenia				153	2.51		
Total	46,044	7079	6.7	13,675	15.09[b]	733	7.51[b]

[a] Outliers excluded and including only observations for which all of ikb, skb, cash, and FDI are non-missing. Average number of firms per country is 127 excluding the US and the UK.

[b] These numbers represent the average foreign ownership over all countries weighted by the number of firms per country.

Table A2
Variable definitions

Abbreviation	Description
Firm level variables (from Worldscope)	
PPENT	property plant and equipment, net of depreciation
CAPEX	capital expenditure
DA	depreciation and amortization expense
K	beginning period capital = PPENT − CAPEX + DA
IK, I/K	investment-to-capital ratio = CAPEX$/K$
SK, S/K	sales-to-capital ratio = Sales$/K$
Cash	cash plus equivalents scaled by K
CF	cash flow (net income + DA), scaled by K
Debt	total liabilities, scaled by K
Size	log of total assets in US dollars
Rank	ranking based on size of PPENT (first, ranked by year, then averaged over the years), largest firm in each country has rank equal to 1 (described in Section 5).
Weight	weight is a country-level variable equal to one over the number of valid observations per country (described in Section 5).
Country-level variables	
FDI	foreign direct investment in the recipient country (IMF balance of payments statistics) scaled by aggregate gross domestic investment (IFS)
Portfolio flows	portfolio investment in the recipient country (IMF Balance of Payments Statistics) scaled by aggregate gross domestic investment (IFS)
Other flows	composed primarily of bank loans to the recipient country (IMF Balance of Payments Statistics) scaled by aggregate gross domestic investment (IFS)
FD	financial development equals to the sum of (standardized indices) ratio of liquid liabilities to GDP, ratio of domestic credit to private sector to GDP, market capitalization to GDP, total value traded to GDP, and turnover (total value traded to market capitalization). All indices are from Demirguc-Kunt and Levine (1996).
GNP PC	log of GNP per capita in US dollars in 1994, World Development Report 1996.
M2	stock of liquid liabilities of the financial system scaled by GDP (IFS).

A.E. Harrison et al. / Journal of Development Economics 75 (2004) 269–301   295

Table A2 (*continued*)

Abbreviation	Description
Domestic credit	ratio of credit allocated to the private sector by depositary institutions, scaled by GDP (IFS)
GDP and grGDP	gross domestic product and annual real growth rate of GDP (IFS)
E1	restrictions on payments on current transactions (IMF)
E2	restrictions on payments on capital transactions (IMF)
F1	import surcharges (IMF)
F2	advance import deposits (IMF)
GS	repatriation and surrender requirements for export (IMF)
Inflation	annual % change in consumer prices (IFS)
Country risk	index of country risk; Source: IRIS (2001). Sum of following five variables, with the first three transformed into 10-point scales. Quality of the Bureaucracy: high scores indicate "autonomy from political pressure" and "strength and expertise to govern without drastic changes in policy or interruptions in government services;" also existence of an "established mechanism for recruiting and training." Scored 0–6. Corruption in government: lower scores indicate "high government officials are likely to demand special payment" and "illegal payments are generally expected throughout lower levels of government" in the form of "bribes connected with import and export licenses, exchange controls, tax assessment, policy protection, or loans." Scored 0–6. Rule of law: this variable "reflects the degree to which the citizens of a country are willing to accept the established institutions to make and implement laws and adjudicate disputes." Higher scores indicate "sound political institutions, a strong court system, and provisions for an orderly succession of power." Lower scores indicate "a tradition of depending on physical force or illegal means to settle claims." Upon changes in government in countries scoring low on this measure, new leaders "may be less likely to accept the obligations of the previous regime." Original variable name in ICRG is "law and order tradition." Scored 0–6. Expropriation risk: assessment of risk of "outright confiscation" or "forced nationalization." Scored 0–10, with lower scores for higher risks. Repudiation of contracts by government: indicates the "risk of a modification in a contract taking the form of a repudiation, postponement, or scaling down" due to "budget cutbacks, a change in government, or a change in government economic and social priorities." Scored 0–10, with lower scores for higher risks.

Table A3
Means of variables used in analysis

Country	DFI	Portfolio	Other	GNP per capita	GDP growth	M2	FD	Inflation	Country risk
Argentina	0.12	0.21	0.10	8110	0.030	0.145	− 1.38	6.76	6.72
Australia	0.09	0.16	0.08	18,000	0.032	0.588	0.42	3.45	9.47
Austria	0.03	0.15	0.08	24,600	0.024	0.867	− 0.27	2.66	9.62
Belgium	0.21	0.55	1.60	22,870	0.022	0.615	− 0.82	2.34	9.46
Brazil	0.04	0.13	− 0.06	2970	0.022	0.226	− 1.04	11.77	6.99
Canada	0.07	0.20	0.06	19,510	0.024	0.723	0.03	2.76	9.80
Chile	0.21	0.06	0.05	3520	0.077	0.372	− 0.75	7.18	7.18
Colombia	0.09	0.05	0.06	1670	0.040	0.272	− 1.6	23.66	5.95
Denmark	0.06	0.15	0.10	27,970	0.021	0.579	− 0.49	2.44	9.93
Finland	0.04	0.19	0.07	18,850	0.019	0.555	− 0.41	2.77	9.84
France	0.07	0.09	0.14	23,420	0.019	0.672	0.1	2.32	9.42

(continued on next page)

Table A3 (*continued*)

Country	DFI	Portfolio	Other	GNP per capita	GDP growth	M2	FD	Inflation	Country risk
Germany	0.01	0.17	0.16	25,580	0.024	0.654	1.68	2.58	9.74
India	0.02	0.03	0.08	320	0.059	0.441	− 0.7	9.52	6.93
Indonesia	0.06	0.03	0.06	880	0.067	0.401	− 1.17	8.45	6.75
Ireland	0.11	0.10	0.85	13,530	0.055	0.487	N/A	2.54	9.19
Israel	0.05	0.04	0.10	14,530	0.053	0.706	0.01	11.11	8.72
Italy	0.02	0.16	0.10	19,300	0.019	0.660	− 0.64	4.87	8.39
Japan	0.00	0.04	0.02	34,600	0.030	1.825	3.33	1.19	9.46
Malaysia	0.18	− 0.02	0.03	3480	0.086	1.002	1.19	3.74	7.29
Mexico	0.09	0.09	0.00	4180	0.023	0.228	− 0.85	18.59	6.42
Netherlands	0.15	0.12	0.31	22,000	0.027	0.816	0.66	2.29	9.93
New Zealand	0.24	0.05	− 0.01	13,350	0.018	0.620	− 0.53	3.38	9.89
Norway	0.05	0.07	0.06	26,390	0.029	0.565	− 0.15	2.94	9.74
Pakistan	0.05	0.03	0.22	430	0.046	0.404	− 1.28	10.99	5.75
Peru	0.13	0.03	− 0.09	2110	0.022	0.141	N/A	13.52	5.61
Philippines	0.09	0.07	0.20	950	0.037	0.416	− 1.15	8.94	5.70
Portugal	0.09	0.12	0.21	9320	0.027	0.699	− 0.67	6.09	8.54
Singapore	0.37	0.04	0.37	22,500	0.087	1.114	1.6	2.26	8.77
South Africa	0.02	0.08	− 0.01	3040	0.016	0.443	0.25	11.22	7.51
South Korea	0.01	0.05	0.02	10,874	0.077	0.592	0.84	5.48	8.29
Spain	0.09	0.08	0.09	13,440	0.029	0.724	− 0.14	4.92	8.44
Sweden	0.14	0.06	0.35	23,500	0.014	0.475	− 0.31	4.22	9.95
Switzerland	0.06	0.12	0.41	37,930	0.011	1.191	2.20	2.37	9.97
Thailand	0.06	0.05	0.16	2410	0.080	0.738	0.36	5.08	7.78
Turkey	0.02	0.05	0.06	2500	0.042	0.225	− 0.2	31.40	6.62
UK	0.12	0.25	0.72	18,340	0.025	0.765	1.68	4.34	9.39
US	0.05	0.13	0.11	25,880	0.030	0.624	1.35	3.33	9.48
Venezuela	0.12	0.30	− 0.22	2760	0.026	0.320	− 1.26	28.34	6.39

All capital flows are scaled by gross domestic investment. N/A indicates not vailable.

Table A4
Means of capital control variables

Country	Restrictions on payments on current transactions	Restrictions on payments on capital transactions	Import surcharges	Advance import deposits	Repatriation and surrender requirements for exports	Sum of five controls
Argentina	0.60	0.60	1.00	0.00	0.60	3.00
Australia	0.00	0.00	0.00	0.00	0.08	0.08
Austria	0.00	0.50	0.00	0.00	0.00	0.55
Belgium	0.00	0.00	0.00	0.00	0.36	0.40
Brazil	0.75	0.75	0.00	0.00	1.00	2.43
Canada	0.00	0.00	0.00	0.00	0.00	0.00
Chile	0.67	0.78	0.44	0.00	0.78	2.75
Colombia	0.80	0.80	0.60	0.60	1.00	3.89
Denmark	0.00	0.18	0.00	0.00	0.18	0.40
Finland	0.00	0.45	0.00	0.00	0.00	0.50
France	0.00	0.64	0.00	0.00	0.64	1.40
Germany	0.00	0.00	0.00	0.00	0.07	0.08

Table A4 (*continued*)

Country	Restrictions on payments on current transactions	Restrictions on payments on capital transactions	Import surcharges	Advance import deposits	Repatriation and surrender requirements for exports	Sum of five controls
India	0.78	0.78	1.00	0.00	1.00	3.50
Indonesia	0.00	0.00	1.00	0.00	0.00	1.00
Ireland	0.00	0.55	0.00	0.00	0.64	1.30
Israel	0.20	0.60	0.20	0.00	1.00	2.00
Italy	0.00	0.64	0.00	0.00	0.64	1.40
Japan	0.00	0.08	0.00	0.00	0.08	0.09
Malaysia	0.00	0.10	0.10	0.00	0.40	0.33
Mexico	0.29	0.86	0.14	0.00	0.71	2.08
Netherlands	0.00	0.00	0.00	0.00	0.00	0.00
New Zealand	0.00	0.00	0.00	0.00	0.00	0.00
Norway	0.00	0.73	0.00	0.00	0.64	1.50
Pakistan	0.78	0.78	1.00	0.56	1.00	4.13
Peru	0.38	0.50	1.00	0.00	0.38	2.43
Philippines	0.67	0.78	0.44	0.44	0.44	3.00
Portugal	0.11	0.56	0.00	0.00	0.56	1.38
Singapore	0.00	0.00	0.00	0.00	0.00	0.00
South Africa	0.67	0.83	0.75	0.58	1.00	4.00
South Korea	0.10	0.80	0.00	0.00	1.00	1.89
Spain	0.00	0.71	0.00	0.00	0.71	1.54
Sweden	0.00	0.64	0.00	0.00	0.00	0.70
Thailand	0.00	0.78	0.78	0.00	1.00	2.63
Turkey	0.22	0.78	0.56	1.00	1.00	3.63
UK	0.00	0.00	0.00	0.00	0.00	0.00
US	0.00	0.00	0.00	0.00	0.00	0.00
Venezuela	0.30	0.80	0.40	0.10	1.00	2.44

Note that these are means by country over all years in the sample; basically, it is a proportion of years that the control was in effect.

Table A5
Cross-country correlations of DFI with restrictions on international transactions and macro-variables

DFI and restrictions on international transactions

	DFI	Restrictions on payments on current transactions	Restrictions on payments on capital transactions	Import surcharges	Advance import deposits	Repatriation and surrender requirements for export
Sum of 5 controls	− 0.3242* 0.00 334					
Restrictions on Payments on Current Transactions	− 0.1690* 0.00 371	1.00 400				
Restrictions on Payments on Capital Transactions	− 0.3321* 0.00 371	0.5257* 0.00 400	1.00 400			

(continued on next page)

Table A5 *(continued)*

DFI and restrictions on international transactions

	DFI	Restrictions on payments on current transactions	Restrictions on payments on capital transactions	Import surcharges	Advance import deposits	Repatriation and surrender requirements for export
Import surcharges	− 0.1184*	0.5292*	0.2888*	1.00		
	0.02	0.00	0.00			
	371	400	400	400		
Advance import deposits	− 0.1820*	0.4751*	0.3023*	0.4253*	1.00	
	0.00	0.00	0.00	0.00		
	371	400	400	400	400	
Repatriation and surrender requirements for export	− 0.2960*	0.4858*	0.7004*	0.3600*	0.3310*	1
	0	0	0	0	0	
	371	400	400	400	400	400

DFI and macro-variables

	DFI (scaled by DFI I)	DFI (scaled by GDP)	FD	GNP per capita	GDP growth	M2	Private Credit
FDI scaled by GDP	0.9209*	1.00					
	0.00						
	452	468					
FD	− 0.01	0.06	1.00				
	0.76	0.22					
	429	444	450				
GNP PC	0.0	− 0.02	0.6530*	1.00			
GNP PC	0.98	0.64	0.00				
	441	456	438	473			
growth GDP	0.2610*	0.2739*	0.0262	− 0.1835*	1.00		
	0.00	0.00	0.5865	0.00			
	438	451	432	455	467		
M2	0.05	0.1593*	0.7789*	0.6023*	0.0690	1.00	
	0.28	0.00	0.00	0.00	0.1665		
	403	418	402	411	404	422	
Private credit	− 0.02	0.03	0.8007*	0.6408*	− 0.0257	0.7706*	1
	0.64	0.56	0.00	0.00	0.6075	0.00	
	402	417	400	410	403	420	421

Note: Star denotes significance at the 10% level. The first number reported is the correlation coefficient, the second is the *p*-value, and the third is the number of observations.

References

Aghion, P., Eve, C., Cecilia, G.-P., 1999. Inequality and economic growth: the perspective of the new growth theories. Journal of Economic Literature 37 (4) (December), 1615–1660.

Allayannis, Y., Abon, M., 2004. The investment-cash flow sensitivity puzzle: can negative cash flow observations explain it? Journal of Banking and Finance (in press).

Alti, A., 2003. How sensitive is investment to cash flow when financing is frictionless. Journal of Finance 58 (2), 707–722.

Arrellano, M., Bond, S.R., 1991. Some Tests of Specification for Panel Data: Monte Carlo Evidence and an Application to Employment Equations. Review of Economic Studies 58, 277–297.

Arrellano, M., Bover, O., 1995. Another look at the instrumental variable estimation of error component models. Journal of Econometrics 68, 29–51.

Banerjee, A.V., Newman, F.N., 1994. Poverty, incentives and development. American Economic Review 84 (2) (May), 211–215.

Beck, T., Asli, D.-K., Maksimovic, V., 2002. Financial and legal constraints to firm growth: does size matter? World Bank Working Paper, 2784.

Bekaert, G., Campbell, H., 2000. Foreign speculators and emerging equity markets. Journal of Finance 55 (2), 565–613.

Bekaert, G., Campbell, H., Lundblad, C., 2001. Does financial liberalization spur growth. NBER Working Paper W8245.

Bigsten, A., Collier, P., Dercon, S., Fafchamps, M., Gauthier, B., Gunning, J.W., Soderbom, M., Oduro, A., Oostendorp, R., Patillo, C., Teal, F., Zeufack, A., 2000. Financing constraints in manufacturing enterprises in Africa, Centre for the Study of African Economies Working Paper Series 2000. 24 September 2000.

Bond, S., Cummins, J., 2001. Noisy share prices and the Q model of investment. Oxford University Manuscript, Oxford University.

Bond, S., Meghir, C., 1994. Dynamic investment models and the firms financial policy. Review of Economic Studies 61, 197–222.

Bond, S., Elston, J.A., Mairesse, J., Mulkay, B., 2003. Financial Factors and Investment in Belgium, France, Germany, and the United Kingdom: a comparison using company panel data. The Review of Economics and Statistics 85 (1), 153–165 (February).

Calomiris, C., Himmelberg, C.P., Wachtel, P., 1995. Commercial paper, corporate finance, and the business cycle: a microeconomic perspective. Carnegie–Rochester Conference Series on Public Policy 42, 203–250.

Chirinko, R., von Kalckreuth, U., 2003. Further evidence on the relationship between firm investment and financial status, Emory University Working Paper 03-02 (January).

Collins, S., Bosworth, B., 1999. Capital flows to developing economies: implications for saving and investment, Brookings Institution Working Paper.

Davidson, R., MacKinnon, R., 1993. Estimation And Inference In Econometrics. Oxford Univ. Press, New York.

Demirguc-Kunt, A., Levine, R., 1996. Stock market development and financial intermediaries: stylized facts. World Bank Economic Review 10, 291–321.

Demirguc-Kunt, A., Maksimovic, V., 1998. Law, finance and firm growth. Journal of Finance 53 (6), 2107–2131.

Dun, Bradstreet, various issues. Who Owns Whom. Australasia, Asia, Middle East and Africa and North America and South America, High Wycombe, Bucks, UK. D & B Limited.

Erikson, T., Whited, T., 2000. Measurement error and the relationship between investment and Q. Journal of Political Economy 108, 1027–1057.

Fazzari, S.M., Hubbard, R.G., Petersen, B.C., 1988. Financing constraints and corporate investment. Brookings Papers on Economic Activity 1, 141–195.

Fazzari, S.M., Hubbard, R.G., Petersen, B.C., 2000. Investment-cash flow sensitivities are useful: a comment on Kaplan and Zingales. Quarterly Journal of Economics 115 (2), 695–706 (May).

Feldstein, M., 2000. Aspects of global economic integration: outlook for the future. NBER Working Paper 7899 (September).

Galindo, A., Schiantarelli, F., Weiss, A., 2001. Does financial liberalization improve the allocation of investment? Micro Evidence from Developing Countries, Mimeo. Boston College.

Gelos, G.R., Werner, A.M., 1999. Financial liberalization, financing constraints, and collateral: investment in the Mexican manufacturing sector. IMF Working Paper, WP/99/25.

Gilchrist, S., Himmelberg, C., 1995. Evidence on the role of cash flow for investment. Journal of Monetary Economics 36, 541–572.

Gilchrist, S., Himmelberg, C.P., 1998. Investment, fundamentals and finance. In: Bernanke, B.S., Julio, J.R. (Eds.), NBER Macro Annual 1998. The MIT Press, Cambridge, pp. 223–274.

Gomes, J.F., 2001. Financing investment. American Economic Review 91 (5), 1263–1285 (December).

Harris, J.R., Schiantarelli, F., Siregar, M., 1994 (January). The effect of financial liberalization on the capital structure and investment decisions of Indonesian manufacturing establishments. The World Bank Economic Review, 17–47.

Harrison, A.E., McMillan, M.S., 2003. Does direct foreign investment affect domestic firms credit constraints? Journal of International Economics 61(1), 73–100.

Hart, O., 1995. Firms, Contracts, and Financial Structure. Oxford Univ. Press, London.

Harvard Institute for International Development and World Economic Forum, 1998. The Africa Competitiveness Report. World Economic Forum, Geneva, Switzerland.

Hayashi, F., 1982. Tobin's marginal Q and average Q: a neoclassical interpretation. Econometrica 50 (1), 213–224 (January).

Helleiner, G.K., 1988. Transnational Corporations and Direct Foreign Investment. In: Chenery, Scrinivasan (Eds.), Handbook of Development Economics, Vol.1 North Holland, pp. 1441–1480.

Henry, P.B., 2000. Stock market liberalization, economic reform and emerging market equity prices. Journal of Finance 55 (2), 529–564.

Hubbard, R.G., 1998. Capital-market imperfections and investment. Journal of Economic Literature 36, 193–225 (March).

Hubbard, R.G., Kashyap, A., 1992. Internal net worth and the investment process: an application to U.S. agriculture. Journal of Political Economy 100 (3), 506–534.

Hubbard, R.G., Kashyap, A., Whited, T., 1995. Internal finance and firm investment. Journal of Money Credit and Banking 27 (4), 683–701.

International Monetary Fund, various issues. Annual Report on Exchange Arrangements and Exchange Restrictions, IMF, Washington, DC.

International Monetary Fund, 2000. International Financial Statistics, CD-ROM. IMF, Washington, DC.

International country risk guide, IRIS, 2001.

Jaramillo, F., Schiantarelli, F., Weiss, A., 1996. Capital market imperfections before and after financial liberalization: an Euler equation approach to panel data for Ecuadorian firms. Journal of Development Economics 51 (2) (December), 367–386.

Jensen, M., Meckling, W., 1976. Theory of the firm: managerial behaviour, agency costs, and ownership structure. Journal of Financial Economics 3 (4), 305–360.

Kaplan, S.N., Zingales, L., 1997. Do investment-cash flow sensitivities provde useful measures of financing constraints? Quarterly Journal of Economics, 169–215.

Kaplan, S.N., Zingales, L., 2000. Investment-cash flow sensitivities are not valid measures of financing constraints. Quarterly Journal of Economics 115 (2), 707–712 (May).

Kim, C.-S., Mauer, D., Sherman, A.E., 1998. The determinants of corporate liquidity: theory and evidence. Journal of Financial and Quantitative Analysis 33 (3), 335–359.

Laeven, L., 2003. Does financial liberalization reduce financing constraints. Financial Management. 32 (1), 5–34.

La Porta, R., Lopez-de-Silanes, F., Shleifer, A., Vishny, R., 1997. Legal determinants of external finance. Journal of Finance, 1131–1150.

Levine, R., Renelt, D., 1992. A sensitivity analysis of cross-country growth regressions. American Economic Review, 942–963 (September).

Lewis, K., 1997. Are countries with Official International Restrictions "Liquidity Constrained?" NBER Working Papers 5991. National Bereau of Economic Research, Inc.

Love, I., 2003. Financial development and financing constraints: international evidence from the structural investment model. Review of Financial Studies 16 (3), 135–161.

Moyen, N., 2002. Investment-Cash Flow Sensitivities: Constrained vs. Unconstrained Firms, Working Paper, University of Colorado.

Myers, S., Majluf, N., 1984. Corporate financing and investment decisions when firms have information that investors do not have. Journal of Financial Economics 13 (2), 187–221.

Opler, T., Pickowitz, L., Stultz, R., Williamson, R., 1999. The determinants and implications of corporate cash holdings. Journal of Financial Economics 52 (1), 3–46.

Patillo, C., 2000. Risk, financial constraints and equipment investment in Ghana. In: Collier, P., Patillo, C. (Eds.), A Firm-level Analysis Ch. 4 of Investment and Risk in Africa. St. Martin's Press, New York, 96–120.

Rajan, R., Zingales, L., 1998. Financial dependence and growth. American Economic Review 88 (3), 559–586.

Ross, S.A., Randolph, W., Westerfield, J., 1996. Corporate Finance, 4th ed. The Irwin Series in Finance, Chicago, IL.

Tybout, J.R., 1983. Credit rationing and investment behavior in a developing country. Review of Economics and Statistics 65 (4), 598–607 (November).

Schiantarelli, F., 1996. Financial constraints and investments: methodological issues and international evidence. Oxford Review of Economic Policy 12, 70–89.

Stiglitz, J., 1998. The role of international financial institutions in the current global economy. Address to the Chicago Council on Foreign Relations, Chicago, February 27.

Whited, T., 1992. Debt, liquidity constraints, and corporate investment: evidence from panel data. Journal of Finance 47 (4), 1425–1460.

World Bank, 2000. Global Development Finance, Washington, DC, 2000.

Chapter 9

FDI Spillovers and Industrial Policy: The Role of Tariffs and Tax Holidays[†]

LUOSHA DU [a], ANN HARRISON [b,c] and GARY JEFFERSON [d,*]

[a] China Development Bank, Beijing, China
[b] University of Pennsylvania, Philadelphia, USA
[c] NBER, Cambridge, USA
[d] Brandeis University, Waltham, USA

Summary. — This paper examines how industrial policy – specifically tariff liberalization and tax subsidies – affects the magnitude and direction of FDI spillovers. We examine these spillover effects across the diverse ownership structure of China's manufacturing sector for 1998 through 2007. We find that tariff reforms, particularly tariff reductions associated with China's WTO ascension, increased the productivity impacts of FDI's backward spillovers. Tax policy – both corporate income and VAT subsidies – has seemingly drawn FDI into strategic industries that spawn significant vertical spillovers. We conclude that liberalization measures during the critical 1998–2007 period on balance served to enhance productivity growth in Chinese industry.
© 2014 Published by Elsevier Ltd.

Key words — foreign direct investment, industrial policy, manufacturing productivity, China, spillovers

1. INTRODUCTION

The Chinese government intervenes extensively to promote industrialization, relying on a range of policy instruments. In this paper, we examine three such policies that affect the magnitude and direction of the spillovers from foreign direct investment (FDI). These policies are the ownership structure of the enterprise system, including direct state ownership and accommodations to FDI, and tariffs and tax subsidies, both of which serve the purpose of promoting foreign investment in key sectors. In this paper, we extend our understanding of how each of these policies – state and foreign ownership, tariffs and trade reform, and tax incentives – operates through intra- and/or inter-industry FDI spillovers to affect the performance of Chinese-based manufacturing firms.

Incorporating these policy instruments into the analysis of FDI spillovers addresses two objectives. The first is to assess the effectiveness of different forms of industrial policy, including their indirect effects. A second purpose is to control for possible bias associated with econometric estimates of FDI spillovers resulting from the omission of industrial policies that are systematically correlated with FDI clusters. These FDI clusters include both within- industry clusters spurring horizontal spillovers or between-industry FDI clusters leading to vertical upstream or downstream effects. Given the likely interactions of industrial policy and FDI, studies of FDI spillovers should attempt to control for the direct and indirect impacts of these policies.

The period during 1998–2007 witnessed many policy shifts as China altered and experimented with a range of industrial policies. Tens of thousands of state-owned enterprises changed ownership or were liquidated. At the end of 2001, China became a member of the World Trade Organization (WTO). Average tariffs on manufacturing in China, which stood at 43% in 1994, following China's accession to the WTO fell to 9.4% by 2004.[1] FDI inflows accelerated, and by the end of the period China was one of the top destinations for foreign investment. Over these 10 years, many foreign investors in China faced much lower corporate tax rates than domestic enterprises. Before 2008, foreign investors received a 15% corporate tax rate while domestic enterprises faced a regular 33% corporate tax rate.[2] This policy of promoting foreign invested firms and other favored firms was only discontinued in 2008. It is difficult to imagine that these substantial changes have not, both directly and through their impact on FDI, affected the productivity performance of Chinese manufacturing.

Other countries have received extensive FDI within the context of state- and foreign-ownership, tariff protection, and tax incentives. However, probably no country to the extent of China has sponsored such an active range of industrial policies in combination with as heterogeneous a group of enterprise types. China's enterprise system includes an extensive system of state-owned enterprises (SOEs), including those with a mix of state and foreign ownership; foreign-owned firms distinguish overseas investment from Hong Kong, Macao, and Taiwan versus that from other areas including the OECD countries. Patterns of tariff protection and liberalization, as well as the fabric of tax subsidies, are likely to be interconnected with patterns of enterprise ownership.

* The authors gratefully acknowledge suggestions by the editor and two anonymous referees, who have significantly improved this paper. We are also grateful to the conference organizers at Fudan University, including the contributions of Peter Petri. We would also like to thank Justin Lin, Max Auffhammer, and Jeremy Magruder for their valuable comments, as well as seminar participants at Yale University, the Wharton Management Department at the University of Pennsylvania, and the World Bank. This work is partially based on work supported by the National Science Foundation under Grant No. 0519902, and through a Grant from the Research Support Budget of the World Bank. Final revision accepted: June 4, 2014.

[†] This article originally appeared in *World Development*, **64** 366–383 © 2014 Elsevier Science Publishers B.V.

Our results suggest that the trade reforms and tax policies adopted by China during the 10 years of our sample period increased the gains from incoming FDI. Our first result is that both tariff reductions and China's entry into the WTO increased the gains from vertical FDI spillovers. By interacting measures of tariff reform and WTO entry with our foreign investment measures, we find significant increases in the benefits from FDI after trade reform, especially for backward linkages. Second, we find that foreign investors who received corporate tax breaks transmitted larger externalities to domestic enterprises. Third, the evidence suggests that pairing foreign firms with SOEs led to gains for SOE partners that generally exceeded gains for other domestic firms.

We suggest a set of reasons for the robustness of downstream FDI and backward spillovers; some of these are general, while some are specific to China. Recent analyses of vertical FDI spillovers for other countries (see the survey in Harrison and Rodriguez-Clare (2010)) have emphasized the importance of backward linkages from domestic suppliers to foreign buyers. Strong backward linkages were present in studies of Lithuania, Great Britain, and Indonesia, for example. Other conditions are specific to China: formal and informal "technology for markets" programs have emphasized the provision of knowledge in exchange for market access in a variety of sectors such as automobiles where the acquisition of knowledge by local suppliers is a key constraint.

While the focus of this paper is on the interaction between FDI spillovers and domestic policies, the stand-alone results for ownership and spillover effects are themselves of interest. Horizontal spillovers, which measure spillovers from foreign to domestic firms in the same sector, are robust only for firms with foreign partners and for SOEs. Forward linkages, which include positive spillovers from upstream foreign suppliers to downstream firms, are generally significant. Backward linkages, which measure linkages from domestic suppliers to foreign buyers, are largest in magnitude and significant once we control for trade policies and their interaction with FDI.

In addition to measuring the impact of formal tariff reductions on final goods and on inputs, we also explore the impact of China's entry into the WTO at the end of 2001. Tariff changes do not capture the important shift in access to foreign markets induced by China's WTO entry. Tariff changes also do not capture other changes associated with WTO membership, such as reductions in non-tariff barriers and domestic content laws. To capture this, we also explore the impact of a WTO dummy on firm performance. For all enterprises except the foreign-invested firms, WTO entry was associated with a very large and significant improvement in performance. The evidence suggests that market access to foreign markets was a more important driver of firm performance, as measured by TFP growth, than internal tariff reductions.

We also explore the differential impact of tax subsidies bestowed on foreign investors. If the Chinese government correctly targets, through tax concessions, those sectors and firms with greater potential for creating spillovers, we would expect stronger linkages associated with tax breaks. We do, in fact, find statistically significant evidence of stronger FDI productivity externalities associated with sectors and firms that received tax breaks.

We examine these connections in the five sections that follow. Section 2 reviews the existing literature and Section 3 lays out the analytical framework of the paper. Our data set, described in Section 4, consists of a comprehensive panel of firm-level data constructed from extensive annual firm surveys covering the period 1998–2007. We use these data to implement our econometric strategy described in Section 5. Section 5

also describes and analyzes the key results of the analysis, and Section 6 presents the concluding comments.

2. LITERATURE REVIEW

China's transition from a highly centralized, monopolistic trade regime with extensive import and export controls began at the end of 1978. Figure 1 shows that the share of trade (exports plus imports) in GDP for China was less than 10% in the 1970s, but increased rapidly as the regime liberalized. By the mid-1990s, the share of trade in GDP had reached over 40%. Naughton (1996) documents the transition to a more open trade and foreign investment regime from 1978 onward. [3] One important feature of the reforms was its dualistic nature, similar to other types of dual track reforms introduced in China the last several decades. The dualism was characterized by a rapidly expanding system of export processing operating alongside a fairly protected domestic economy.

In 1980 the government established the first four Special Economic Zones and extended these to 14 coastal cities in 1984 (Brandt, Van Biesebroeck, Wang, & Zhang, 2012). Foreign investment inflows were encouraged to bring in capital, and the government began a policy of sometimes explicit and other times implicit bargaining to grant domestic market access to foreign companies in exchange for technological know-how. Duty-free importation was also allowed outside special zones, particularly for targeted foreign firms.

As Figure 1 shows, beginning in the mid-1990s China's integration into the global economy accelerated, with trade growing to 70% of GDP right before the financial crisis in 2007. One factor that has facilitated the continued growth in trade is the spectacular rise in inward foreign investment, which is documented in Figure 2. Major reforms to encourage incoming foreign investment were introduced in 1986 and 1991. Inducements to foreign investors included duty drawbacks, tariff exemptions, subsidies, infrastructure provisions, and tax holidays.

Numerous papers have examined the existence and magnitude of FDI spillovers in China. Jefferson and Ouyang (2014) review much of the literature and try to explain the lack of consistency regarding the research findings concerning China's FDI spillovers. Their central finding, resulting from their review of 16 Chinese FDI spillover papers, is that the multiplicity of data sources and research methodologies render impossible an effective comparison of the results. These differences include the use of value-added versus gross output measures of factor productivity; some analyses are derived with the assumption of constant returns to scale; others are not. Moreover, while the earlier papers focused largely on horizontal, intra-industry spillovers, more recent papers have included vertical, forward and backward, as well as horizontal spillovers. Different papers invariably impose different controls. Some papers control, often in different ways, for China's extensive set of ownership types; some seek to identify the channels through which FDI might affect host firm productivity, such as labor market movement and trade; most do not. With respect to econometric strategy, some use industry, region or province, or firm-level fixed effects; others do not. These are but some of the differences that Jefferson and Ouyang identify which frustrate efforts to arrive at robust conclusions regarding research on Chinese FDI spillovers. [4] By introducing tariff and tax policy into the analysis, this paper extends the variety of research approaches. We are able to compare FDI spillover impacts on different ownership types with such attention given in other papers.

Trade (Exports+Imports) as % of GDP: China versus the World

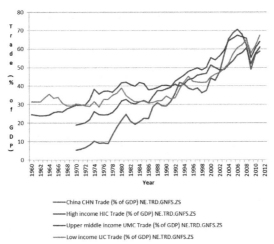

Figure 1. *Trade (exports + imports) as % of GDP: China versus the world.*

Net FDI Inflows into China, 1982-2012

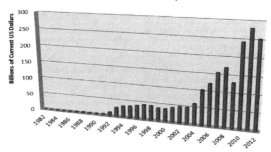

Figure 2. *Net FDI inflows into China: 1982–2012.*

None of the papers in the Jefferson review controls for tariffs or tax subsidies. However, outside of China, we do find an extensive literature that explores the role of trade liberalization and its impact on productivity for both developed and developing countries. While this literature is reviewed in detail in Harrison and Rodriguez-Clare (2010), we discuss some of the most relevant papers here. Recent papers on trade liberalization

include Trefler (2004) for Canada and Bustos (2011) for Argentina. Trefler (2004) explores the impact of tariff reductions on Canadian manufacturing after the passage of the North American Free Trade Agreement (NAFTA). Trefler finds that in the short run employment fell on average 5% and up to 12% in the most heavily affected sectors that had large tariff declines. He also finds large increases in Canadian labor productivity as a result of the tariff reductions, of 14–15%. Trefler concludes that parts of the labor force experienced significant short-term losses despite the longer term efficiency gains, and that this explains in part the public's disaffection with trade reform. Bustos (2011) uses a similar event: the reduction of tariffs under the MERCOSUR agreement, to explore the impact on Argentina's firms. She finds that firms facing tariff cuts increased their investments in both process and product upgrading.

One new area of research seeks to disentangle the effects of input and output tariffs. Illustrative of this research is Amiti and Konings (2007), who use Indonesian manufacturing census data to show that the effect of reducing input tariffs significantly increases productivity, and that this effect is much higher than that of reducing output tariffs. New research on India by Nataraj (2011) as well as Goldberg, Khandelwal, Pavcnik, and Topalova (2010a, 2010b), and Khandelwal and Topalova (2011) also shows that tariff reductions on both inputs and final goods are associated with productivity improvements. Khandelwal and Topalova (2011) estimate the impact on listed firms of the reductions in input and output tariffs on total factor productivity (TFP) in India. Like Amiti and Konings, they find that while reducing output tariffs raised TFP, reductions in input tariffs had an even bigger positive impact on measured TFP. Like this recent body of tariff literature, this paper distinguishes between the implications of input and final goods tariffs on FDI spillovers.

The interaction between trade policy and foreign investment flows have long been of research interest to scholars. The classic reference on the interaction between tariffs and FDI is Brecher and Diaz-Alejandro (1977), who formalize the argument proposed by Jagdish Bhagwati (1973) that incoming capital induced by high tariffs can lead to immiserizing growth and a fall in welfare. Foreign capital inflows exacerbate the production and consumption distortions created by tariffs, and by repatriating the profits abroad foreign firms further reduce domestic welfare. Further studies have suggested evidence of "tariff-jumping" FDI, suggesting that foreign firms are attracted to protected domestic markets. While these early studies do not directly speak to the effects of backward spillovers in the presence of tariff distortions, they do suggest that tariffs interact in a harmful way with foreign firms.

We are not aware of any studies which measure the differences in foreign investment spillovers across different levels of corporate tax rates. There are also very few published studies of the impact of trade reforms on firm productivity in China. One exception is Yu (in press) on the linkages between output tariffs, input tariffs, and processing trade in China. Yu merges the Chinese census data used in this paper with firm-specific measures of final goods and imported intermediate input trade to calculate firm-specific final goods and input tariffs. Yu finds that contrary to the results for Indonesia in Amiti and Konings (2007) and Khandelwal and Topalova (2011), reductions in final goods tariffs increased productivity more for processing firms than did reductions in intermediate input tariffs. Yu attributes this result in large part to the fact that firms under the processing trade regime were exempted from tariffs on intermediate inputs.

Existing research on the link between tax subsidies and FDI is largely focused on countries and regions apart from China. In their review, Morisset and Pirnia (1999) conclude "incentives will neither make up for serious deficiencies in the investment environment, nor generate the desired externalities." The authors find that, more important than tax preferences, investors are most attentive to "fundamental factors like economic conditions and political climate." Only when such factors are

"more or less equal" across locations that offer a similar range of fundamental factors, such as with the U.S. or within the E.U., tax policy may exert a significant impact. While the authors review no studies relating to China, they do find that firms operating in several similar country settings may exploit different tax regimes.

Solis (2011) reviews the literature on developing country subsidies for multinational corporations. He examines the link between subsidized FDI and six critical development factors: competitiveness, social development, democracy, governance, and entrepreneurship and finds no coherent or sustainable justification for FDI subsidies. While Solis does not include any empirical reference to China's experience with FDI, he does suggest that it may differ from that of Latin America with respect to the practice of the Chinese government in imposing greater conditionality on FDI and also having the ability to capture some of the rents from FDI.

Summarizing, we find that FDI may affect firms of different ownership types, depending upon the direction of the spillovers and the capacity of the recipient firms to absorb the impact of the spillovers, whether technology, competition, or some combination of the two. While much of the FDI spillover literature focuses on the impacts of FDI on different ownership types in China, we find no prior literature on ways in which tariffs and taxes in China have affected the nature of FDI spillovers in that country.

3. BASIC FRAMEWORK

To examine the impact of trade policy and foreign investment promotion, we employ a two-stage procedure. In the first stage we estimate a three-input gross-output production function by subsector for firm subsamples representing two ownership types: (1) all firms and (2) domestic firms with zero foreign investment that are not classified as SOEs. We use the estimated factor output elasticities for labor, capital, and materials to construct total measures of total factor productivity (TFP) for each firm and year. In the second stage, we regress the dependent variable, lnTFP, on the relevant FDI cluster, policy variables, and controls.

The first-stage production function is:

$$lnY_{ijt} = \alpha_0 + \alpha_L lnL_{ijt} + \alpha_K lnK_{ijt} + +\alpha_M lnM_{ijt} + \mu_{ijt}, \qquad (1)$$

where i is the firm in sector j and years t include 1998–2007.

For the purpose of estimating the first-stage production function, we employ the Olley–Pakes method to get unbiased estimates of the factor output elasticities. China's Input–Output table divides China's manufacturing industry into 71 sectors (as shown in Table 2). Our firm-level survey data include 4-digit level industry classifications. Hence, to construct the intra- and inter-industry spillover variables (as for constructing the input tariff variables), we need to aggregate the 4-digit classifications up to 71 sectors. [5]

When applying the Olley–Pakes estimation procedure, all output and input variables are deflated by their corresponding price indices. We deflate the output value by the 29 individual sector ex-factory price indices of industrial products. [6] Capital is deflated as the net value of fixed assets, which is deflated by a uniform fixed assets investment index, and labor is a physical measure of the total number of employees. Intermediate inputs purchased by firms for the purpose of producing gross output are deflated by the intermediate input price index. [7]

In the second-stage, we regress firm-level TFP on a series of firm-level and sector-level controls, as described in Eqn. (2):

WORLD DEVELOPMENT

Table 1. *Summary statistics for all years, 1998–2007*

	Levels			Growth rates		
	Number of observations	Mean	Std. Dev.	Number of observations	Mean	Std. Dev.
logY	1,545,626	10.015	1.343	1,086,616	0.135	0.563
logL	1,545,626	4.808	1.152	1,086,616	0.013	0.503
logK	1,545,626	8.468	1.719	1,086,616	0.107	0.753
lnTFP	1,545,626	1.828	0.367	1,086,616	0.056	0.308
Foreign share	1,545,626	0.089	0.267	1,086,616	0.012	0.377
(contributed by HK–Taiwan–Macau investors)						
Foreign share (contributed by other investors)	1,545,626	0.079	0.249	1,086,616	0.000	0.146
State share	1,545,626	0.089	0.272	1,086,616	−0.007	0.147
Horizontal FDI	1,545,626	0.254	0.142	1,086,616	0.004	0.046
Backward FDI	1,545,626	0.077	0.046	1,086,616	0.002	0.015
Forward FDI	1,545,626	0.103	0.173	1,086,616	0.004	0.066
Tariff on final goods	1,545,626	12.691	6.600	1,086,616	−0.869	2.295
Tariffs on inputs	1,545,626	9.185	4.064	1,086,616	−0.359	2.066

Notes: We define firm-level foreign share according to its different sources. Foreign share contributed by HK–Taiwan–Macau is defined as the share of firms' total equity owned by investors from HK–Taiwan–Macau. Foreign share contributed by other countries is defined as the share of firms' total equity owned by investors outside HK–Taiwan–Macau, principally from OECD countries. State share is defined as the proportion of the firm's state assets to its total equity. Horizontal captures the intra-industry FDI spillover while backward and forward represent inter-industry FDI spillovers. We define horizontal, backward, and forward in Eqns. (3)–(5), respectively. The unit for the tariff variable is percentage.

$lnTFP_{ijt} = \beta_0 + \beta_1 ForeignShareHKTM_{ijt}$
$\quad + \beta_2 ForeignShareFR_{ijt} + \beta_3 StateShare_{ijt}$
$\quad + \beta_4 Horizontal_{jt} + \beta_5 Backward_{jt} + \beta_6 Forward_{jt}$
$\quad + \beta_7 Output\_Tariff_{jt} + \beta_8 Input\_Tariff_{jt}$
$\quad + \beta_9 WTO + \sum_i \alpha_i + \sum_t \alpha_t + \varepsilon_{ijt}$ (2)

In Eqn. (2), $lnTFP \equiv lnY_{ijt} - [\alpha_L lnL_{ijt} + \alpha_K lnK_{ijt} + \alpha_M lnM_{ijt}]$, where α_L, α_K and α_M are obtained by the OP estimation. The α_i represent firm-level fixed effects and α_t represent annual time dummies. $ForeignShareHKTM_{ijt}$, $ForeignShareFR_{ijt}$, and $StateShare_{ijt}$ are defined as the share of the firm's total equity owned by Hong Kong–Taiwan–Macau investors, foreign investors, and the state, respectively. [8] By construction, these three firm-level controls are continuous variables that range from 0 to 1 in value. [9]

Following Javorcik (2004), we define three sector-level FDI variables. First, $Horizontal_{jt}$ captures the extent of foreign presence in sector j at time t and is defined as foreign equity participation averaged over all firms in the sector, weighted by each firm's share in sectoral output. In other words,

$$Horizontal_{jt} = \left[\sum_{i \text{ for all } i \in j} ForeignShare_{it} * Y_{it} \right] \Big/ \sum_{i \text{ for all } i \in j} Y_{it},$$ (3)

where $ForeignShare_{it}$ is the sum of $ForeignShareHKTM$ and $ForeignShareFR$.

Second, $Backward_{jt}$ captures the foreign presence in the sectors that are supplied by sector j. [10] Therefore, $Backward_{jt}$ is a measure for foreign participation in the downstream industries of sector j. It is defined as

$$Backward_{jt} = \sum_{k \text{ if } k \neq j} \alpha_{jk} Horizontal_{kt}$$ (4)

The value of α_{jk} is taken from the 2002 input–output table [11] representing the proportion of sector j's production supplied to downstream sector k.

Finally, $Forward_{jt}$ is defined as the weighted share of output in upstream industries of sector j produced by firms with

foreign capital participation. As Javorcik points out, since only intermediates sold in the domestic market are relevant to the study, goods produced by foreign affiliates for exports (X_{it}) should be excluded. Thus, the following formula is applied:

$$Forward_{jt} = \sum_{m \text{ if } m \neq j} \delta_{jm} \left[\left[\sum_{i \text{ for all } i \in m} ForeignShare_{it} * (Y_{it} - X_{it}) \right] \Big/ \left[\sum_{i \text{ for all } i \in m} (Y_{it} - X_{it}) \right] \right]$$ (5)

The value of δ_{jm} is also taken from 2002 input–output table. Since $Horizontal_{jt}$ already captures linkages between firms within a sector, inputs purchased within sector j are excluded from both $Backward_{jt}$ and $Forward_{jt}$.

To test for trade interactions with FDI and control for the effects of trade policies, we have created a time series of tariffs, obtained from the World Integrated Trading Solution (WITS), maintained by the World Bank. We first created a concordance between the tariff data and the Chinese census data at the most disaggregated level possible. [12] Then, we aggregate up tariffs to the same industry classification as sectoral FDI, giving us a total of 71 sectors (see Table 2). [13]

We also created a measure of input tariffs. To construct input tariffs, we use China's Input–Ouput table (2002) and follow the procedures suggested by Amiti and Konings (2007). The input tariffs are constructed as a weighted average of the output tariffs. [14] Finally, we construct a dummy variable, WTO, equal to one after China entered the World Trade Organization at the end of 2001. This is a time dummy equal to zero from 1998 through 2001 and equal to 1 from 2002 onward. The WTO dummy captures the impact of reforms not captured by tariff measures (such as reductions in non-tariff barriers). The WTO dummy also captures the aggregate increase in market access for Chinese firms to export destinations.

4. DATA AND BROAD TRENDS

The dataset employed in this paper was collected by the Chinese National Bureau of Statistics. The Statistical Bureau conducts an annual survey of industrial plants, which includes

Table 2. *Summary statistics on tariffs (by sector)*

Industry names	Final goods tariff		Input tariffs
	Mean	Change Between 1998 and 2007	Mean
1. Grain mill products	41.002	−18.290	19.799
2. Forage	13.501	−7.871	1.932
3. Vegetable oil refining	19.852	−21.772	8.796
4. Sugar manufacturing	37.101	10.710	14.656
5. Slaughtering and meat processing	18.949	−4.510	15.193
6. Fish and fish products	16.052	−12.419	10.698
7. All other food manufacturing	22.206	−13.238	12.642
8. Wines, spirits and liquors	27.569	−34.290	4.384
9. Soft drink and other beverages	28.916	−20.560	1.328
10. Tobacco products	49.584	−24.000	
11. Cotton textiles	14.963	−13.881	14.558
12. Woolen textiles	14.963	−13.881	11.505
13. Hemp textiles	14.961	−13.884	8.632
14. Textiles products	17.674	−15.005	12.958
15. Knitted and crocheted fabrics and articles	20.082	−17.936	13.452
16. Wearing apparel	21.997	−16.212	11.568
17. Leather, fur and related products	19.176	−8.271	3.691
18. Products of wood, bamboo, cane, palm, straw	8.849	−8.346	8.130
19. Furniture	11.701	−18.51	12.740
20. Paper and paper products	11.975	−12.734	13.265
21. Printing, reproduction of recording media	13.584	−14.950	15.092
22. Stationary and related products	18.112	−5.306	9.624
23. Toys, sporting and athletic and recreation products	12.120	−14.198	1.494
24. Petroleum and nuclear processing	6.499	−0.930	11.159
25. Coking	5.479	−0.080	7.447
26. Basic chemicals	6.848	−3.131	10.513
27. Chemical fertilizers	7.511	3.152	2.418
28. Chemical pesticides	8.974	−2.071	1.169
29. Paints, varnishes and similar coatings, printing ink	9.242	−3.710	10.096
30. Man-made chemical products	10.043	−6.108	11.981
31. Special chemical products	12.661	−5.804	10.784
32. Chemical products for daily use	16.088	−11.882	7.675
33. Medical and pharmaceutical products	6.535	−4.599	1.817
34. Chemical fibers	9.825	−12.423	11.829
35. Rubber products	16.167	−3.752	12.782
36. Plastic products	12.583	−8.299	12.860
37. Cement, lime and plaster	11.811	−2.741	9.913
38. Glass and glass products	15.457	−4.890	10.669
39. Pottery, china and earthenware	18.236	−12.031	6.928
40. Fireproof materials	9.777	−3.671	7.751
41. Other nonmetallic mineral products	10.030	−2.355	8.187
42. Iron-smelting	6.601	−3.760	7.720
43. Steel-smelting	6.601	−3.760	9.424
44. Steel pressing	6.601	−3.760	11.368
45. Alloy iron smelting	6.601	−3.760	6.282
46. Nonferrous metal smelting	6.189	−2.382	7.897
47. Nonferrous metal pressing	5.630	−2.331	11.921
48. Metal products	12.788	−4.814	12.599
49. Boiler, engines and turbine	10.081	−4.635	10.693
50. Metalworking machinery	10.978	−5.201	8.637
51. Other general industrial machinery	10.869	−6.203	11.131
52. Agriculture, forestry, animal husbandry and fishing machinery	8.253	−5.070	1.163
53. Other special industrial equipment	9.871	−5.426	9.798
54. Railroad transport equipment	4.082	−1.340	2.403
55. Motor vehicles	29.126	−26.921	7.771
56. Parts and accessories for motor vehicles and their engines	17.584	−18.570	13.769
57. Ship building	7.365	−1.151	2.488
58. Other transport equipment	25.944	−9.094	3.349
59. Generators	10.725	−6.465	9.195
60. Household electric appliances	18.441	−7.963	7.640
61. Other electric machinery and equipment	15.103	−5.202	12.144
62. Telecommunication equipment	10.992	−13.480	4.279

(continued on next page)

WORLD DEVELOPMENT

Table 2 *(continued)*

Industry names	Final goods tariff		Input tariffs
	Mean	Change Between 1998 and 2007	Mean
63. Electronic computer	8.422	−14.87	5.235
64. Other computer peripheral equipment	8.352	−14.828	7.261
65. Electronic devices	4.912	−7.010	10.988
66. Radio, television and communication equipment and apparatus	21.374	−13.97	5.635
67. Other electronic and communication equipment	9.528	−5.450	5.169
68. Instruments, meters, and other measuring equipment	10.097	−5.150	8.603
69. Cultural and office equipment	10.460	−9.548	4.231
70. Arts and crafts products	16.980	−7.374	6.483
71. Other manufacturing products	19.324	−5.036	9.855
Average (all sectors)	12.691	−8.862	9.185

manufacturing firms as well as firms that specialize in mining operations and those that produce and supply electricity, gas, and water. The data set is firm-level based, including all state-owned enterprises (SOEs), regardless of size, and non-state-owned firms (non-SOEs) with annual sales of more than 5 million Yuan. We use a ten-year unbalanced panel dataset, from 1998 to 2007. The number of firms per year varies from a low of 162,033 in 1999 to a high of 336,768 in 2007. The sampling strategy is the same throughout the period; the variation in numbers is driven by changes in ownership or sales volume relative to the threshold. [15]

The dataset contains information on output, fixed assets, total workforce, total wages, intermediate inputs, foreign investment, Hong Kong–Taiwan–Macau investment, sales revenue, and export sales. [16] We use the criterion of zero foreign ownership to distinguish domestic firms and foreign-owned firms, that is, domestic firms are those with zero foreign capital in their total assets. In the dataset, 1,197,597 observations or 77.5% of the observations meet the criterion of domestic firms; 22.5% are designated as foreign firms. [17]

Table 1 reports the summary statistics for the main variables used in the regressions. The summary statistics report the mean of the ratios, which is different than weighted means that would give more weight to larger firms. The first three columns report means for levels and the last three columns report means for growth rates of the key variables used in the analysis.

The statistical means highlight the remarkable growth rates exhibited by the manufacturing sector during this period, with average real output growing 13.5% a year, and the net capital stock growing 10.7% per year. Labor input grew significantly slower, with average annual increases of only 1.3% per year. Total factor productivity (TFP), which is calculated using the Olley–Pakes two-step approach described in more detail in the next section, grew on average 5.6% per year, implying a 40% contribution to overall growth. The means also document that, on average, foreign-invested assets have been almost evenly split between sources in Hong Kong, Taiwan, and Macau ("HKTM"), and foreign investment originating in other locations. The first three columns indicate that the state continues to play an important role in manufacturing, with a mean asset share of 8.9% during the sample period; over the sample period the total share of total foreign investment in manufacturing is significantly larger, at 16.8%. For the sample as a whole, the average state share during this period fell by approximately 0.7% per year.

The summary statistics for final goods and input tariffs appear in Tables 1 and 2. During the sample period, average tariffs fell for final goods and input tariffs by 87% and 36% respectively, significant declines for a 10-year period. While

the average level of tariffs during this period, which spans the years before and after WTO accession, was nearly 13%, as shown in Table 2, this average masks significant heterogeneity across sectors, with a high of 41% in grain mill products and a low of 4% in railroad equipment.

One issue which arises is the question of the endogeneity of the tariff changes in the data. Goldberg and Pavcnik (2007) argue that in the case of India's trade reforms that began in earnest in 1991, the largest tariff cuts were in those sectors where tariffs were initially high, in order to comply with WTO entry provisions. Thus, in the case of India, tariff reductions followed from initial tariff levels, a condition that helps to address the fear that tariff changes could be endogenous with respect to productivity changes at the firm level. We see a similar pattern of tariff reductions in the Chinese case. The scatter plot shown in Figure 4 demonstrates that tariff reductions were highest in those sectors where tariff levels were high at the beginning of the sample period. Thus the reductions were broadly rule-based rather than specific to industry characteristics. In addition, tariffs are defined at the 2-digit level; since tariff categories are quite broad (see Table 2), it is difficult to argue that they are set endogeneously with respect to disaggregated firm level behavior.

In Tables 3-1 and 3-2, we provide summary statistics for the FDI spillover variables in relation to the government's assignment of tax holidays. Table 3-1 reports annual figures for means of the output shares calculated separately for clusters of FDI that do and do not receive corporate income subsidies. In the left panel of Table 3-1, we define our sector-level foreign output shares for only those foreign firms that paid less than the statutory tax rate. In the right panel of Table 3-1, we include sector-level output shares for foreign-invested firms that paid the full rate. The trends show a steady increase in the share of subsidized foreign investment during 1998–2007. In 1998, at the beginning of the sample period, subsidized FDI accounted for less than to 8% of sectoral output, while foreign firms without any sort of tax holidays accounted for nearly 12% of sectoral output. By the end of the sample period, while the share of output represented by foreign-invested firms with no tax holidays remained virtually unchanged, the output share represented by foreign investors receiving some form of tax holiday had grown to nearly 14%.

Figure 3 shows the distribution of income taxes on profits paid by different types of enterprises for the year 2004. We calculated these effective tax rates using reported income taxes paid as a share of profits, as reported in our dataset. The top left-hand side quadrant shows that a large share of domestically-owned firms, both SOEs and non-SOEs, paid the 33% tax rate. In principle, foreign firms received a 15% tax subsidy.

As shown in Figure 3, only a small minority of foreign-invested firms paid the statutory rate of 33%, as indicated by the bottom right-hand side quadrant. In 2004, 7% of foreign-invested firms paid the statutory rate, compared to almost 40% for domestically-owned enterprises; a considerable proportion of the foreign-invested firms appear to have paid corporate tax rates of less than 20%.

Table 3-2 reports the percentage of firms that reported subsidies on their value-added taxes, which are reported separately from income taxes on profits. We were also able to calculate actual effective tax rates for value added, since firms separately reported value-added taxes paid as well as value-added. Relative to the proportion of firms receiving subsidies on their income taxes, fewer firms receive subsidies in the form of exemptions on value-added taxes. These exemptions increased until 2003, then declined. It is clear from these tables that income tax holidays were a more pervasive form of incentives until the 2008 tax reform.

5. ESTIMATION STRATEGY AND RESULTS

Below, we describe our estimation strategy, the baseline estimation results based on Eqn. (1), and several variations on that basic regression model for the purpose of examining various interaction effects among the industrial policies under study. Our estimation strategy also tests for the implications of firm heterogeneity within our sample. We also describe our robustness checks.

(a) Estimation strategy

We first compute estimates of total factor productivity (TFP) for each firm and each year observation. We divide the sample into two ownership sub-samples. These are (a) all firms and (b) domestic, private firms, which exclude foreign owned enterprises and SOEs. These subsamples and the relevant estimation results are shown in Table A.1.

The earlier literature on the estimation of production functions shows that the use of OLS may be inappropriate, since this method treats labor, capital, and other input variables as exogenous. As Griliches and Jacques (1995) argue, factor inputs should be considered endogenous, since their choice is affected by the firm's productivity. Firm-level fixed effects alone will not solve the problem, because time-varying productivity shocks can affect a firm's input decisions. Using OLS can therefore bias estimates of the relevant coefficients. To solve the simultaneity problem, we employ the procedure suggested by Olley and Pakes (1996) (henceforth OP), which uses investment as a proxy for unobserved productivity shocks.

Table A.1 reports comparisons of the coefficient estimates using the OP approach. As a robustness check, we also employ the procedure suggested by Levinsohn and Petrin (2003) (henceforth LP), which uses intermediate inputs as a proxy for unobserved productivity shocks. Applying these two-stage procedures, both OP (1996) and LP (2003), one would anticipate that the coefficient on labor and intermediate inputs should decrease relative to the OLS fixed effects estimator, while the coefficient on capital should increase. To save on space we only report the results using the OP, not the LP procedure or OLS with firm fixed effects. The results are qualitatively similar using both the OP and LP approaches, but LP suffers from the fact that the efficiency of material input use is ignored. The results are generally consistent with these predictions across ownership classes. Relative to OLS with firm fixed effects the coefficient on capital inputs is higher using OP across all specifications. We also generally find that the

coefficient on the labor shares and material shares are lower with OP compared to OLS.

One notable feature across all specifications is that the labor estimate is relatively small, compared to estimates for other countries, while the coefficient for material inputs is rather high. As a robustness check, we performed a test in which we use various variables within our sample to compute labor's factor income share. Although the estimation procedure shown in Table A.1 does not impose these restrictive conditions of perfect competition with constant returns to scale, the coefficients on the factor inputs in our estimating equations sum to 0.904, close to constant returns to scale. Hence, the factor income shares computed from the data in our data set should be similarly comparable to the factor output elasticities shown in Table A.1. Using the data for the full sample, we compute an average factor income share for 1998–2007 as equal to 0.105. While this is somewhat larger than 0.086, the OP estimate reported in Table A.1, the difference is small. Moreover, if our estimate of TFP deviates from the true TFP level by a constant time-invariant scalar, the fixed effects procedure that we use in the second stage should wash out the difference.[18]

(b) Baseline results

The baseline results are presented in Table 4. In all the results which follow, we separate firms into foreign-invested firms—those with some positive foreign ownership—and domestically-owned firms—defined as enterprises with zero foreign ownership. We first examine the impact of horizontal and vertical FDI spillovers.

(i) FDI spillover estimates

The results for "All firms" are shown in column (1) of Table 4; those for foreign-invested firms appear in column (2), and those for domestically-owned firms are shown in column (3). For the samples including all firms (column 1) and domestic firms only (column 3), the coefficients on the state's share in equity are negative and statistically significant, indicating that increases in state-invested shares are associated with lower productivity. We discuss the different effects of spillovers across more detailed ownership categories in Section 5c below. The results for the state share are consistent with the expectation of rising productivity for privatizing enterprises.

Table 4 shows a divergent pattern of results for horizontal and vertical FDI spillovers. Backward spillovers are largest in magnitude across all three samples. Seemingly, with higher proportions of FDI firms downstream, both foreign-invested and domestic upstream suppliers need to be more productive to prosper as suppliers. Our estimated coefficient on backward linkages implies that a one percentage point increase in backward FDI is associated with a 0.8–1.1 percentage point increase in TFP. These magnitudes are twice as large as those found by Blalock and Gertler (2008) for Indonesia but smaller than Javorcik's (2004) findings for Lithuania. The results are also somewhat smaller than the robust backward spillover estimates reported by Lin et al. (2009), although their paper does not break out the sample by foreign and domestic firms.

For horizontal, intra-industry spillovers, our results show robust results for foreign firms but not for domestic firms. Presumably domestic firms, at lower levels on the technology frontier, are less able to capture productivity-enhancing impacts from foreign firms within the same industry. By comparison, the forward spillovers show that domestic firms that are downstream from FDI suppliers appear to benefit more

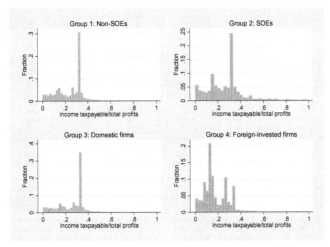

Figure 3. *Tax rate distribution with groups of firms (2004).*

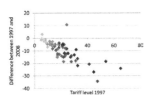

Figure 4. *Initial tariffs and subsequent tariff changes.*

than their foreign counterparts. This finding suggests that domestic-owned firms are more likely to purchase and benefit from upstream inputs supplied by foreign firms than other foreign firms.

(ii) *The impact of tariff protection/liberalization*

The coefficients on both the final goods tariffs and input tariffs in Table 4 are positive but not statistically significant. There are several reasons why the impact of input or final goods tariffs on productivity may be attenuated in China. A large fraction of firms, particularly exporters, are granted exemptions from paying tariffs; without additional information on which firms pay input tariffs, it is difficult to identify the effect of tariffs on inputs for individual firms. Second,

Table 3-1. *Summary statistics for subsidized and non-subsidized spillover variables (calculated based on income tax)*

Year	Number of observations	Subsidized						Non-subsidized					
		Horizontal		Backward		Forward		Horizontal		Backward		Forward	
		Mean	Std. Dev.	Mean	Std. Dev.	Mean	Std. Dev.	Mean	Std. Dev.	Mean	Std. Dev.	Mean	Std. Dev.
1998	95,879	0.076	0.060	0.022	0.015	0.024	0.047	0.112	0.068	0.033	0.018	0.038	0.050
1999	103,945	0.083	0.067	0.025	0.018	0.027	0.056	0.125	0.069	0.040	0.020	0.046	0.064
2000	102,465	0.096	0.072	0.029	0.020	0.033	0.070	0.130	0.070	0.041	0.021	0.049	0.068
2001	114,461	0.102	0.075	0.031	0.020	0.034	0.057	0.130	0.067	0.039	0.021	0.052	0.083
2002	122,218	0.107	0.080	0.031	0.023	0.041	0.091	0.128	0.066	0.037	0.018	0.047	0.059
2003	138,158	0.110	0.078	0.034	0.023	0.042	0.083	0.131	0.069	0.039	0.021	0.053	0.080
2004	202,551	0.132	0.090	0.041	0.027	0.054	0.110	0.129	0.063	0.038	0.020	0.051	0.070
2005	194,120	0.132	0.096	0.041	0.028	0.055	0.110	0.131	0.064	0.039	0.021	0.058	0.092
2006	216,924	0.138	0.094	0.043	0.028	0.057	0.101	0.126	0.061	0.039	0.020	0.057	0.097
2007	254,905	0.138	0.089	0.044	0.026	0.062	0.111	0.119	0.061	0.036	0.021	0.054	0.086

Notes: This table reports trends in subsidized and non-subsidized foreign investment. In the left panel of this table, we redefine our sector-level foreign share variables by restricting them to only those foreign firms who paid less than the statutory tax rate. In the right panel of this table, we redefine sector-level foreign share to restrict it to those firms who paid the full rate.

Table 3-2. *Summary statistics for subsidized and non-subsidized spillover variables (calculated based on value-added tax)*

Year	Number of observations	Subsidized						Non-Subsidized					
		Horizontal		Backward		Forward		Horizontal		Backward		Forward	
		Mean	Std. Dev.	Mean	Std. Dev.	Mean	Std. Dev.	Mean	Std. Dev.	Mean	Std. Dev.	Mean	Std. Dev.
1998	95,879	0.053	0.062	0.014	0.011	0.009	0.018	0.151	0.078	0.045	0.024	0.059	0.085
1999	103,945	0.049	0.056	0.013	0.012	0.007	0.012	0.169	0.089	0.052	0.027	0.069	0.107
2000	102,465	0.049	0.053	0.013	0.011	0.009	0.019	0.182	0.094	0.058	0.030	0.076	0.118
2001	114,461	0.049	0.050	0.013	0.011	0.008	0.017	0.187	0.095	0.057	0.029	0.080	0.123
2002	122,218	0.063	0.064	0.017	0.014	0.008	0.016	0.178	0.088	0.055	0.028	0.081	0.127
2003	138,158	0.070	0.075	0.018	0.018	0.013	0.038	0.177	0.083	0.056	0.027	0.085	0.130
2004	202,551	n.a.	n.a.	n.a.	n.a.	n.a.	n.a.	n.a.	n.a.	n.a.	n.a.	n.a.	n.a.
2005	194,120	0.061	0.058	0.017	0.015	0.014	0.035	0.207	0.102	0.064	0.034	0.101	0.162
2006	216,924	0.054	0.054	0.015	0.014	0.015	0.045	0.214	0.103	0.069	0.034	0.102	0.153
2007	254,905	0.047	0.056	0.013	0.015	0.012	0.038	0.214	0.097	0.068	0.032	0.105	0.159

Notes: In this table, we redo the exercise in Table 3-1 based on value-added tax information. The tax data are not available for 2004.

tariffs may be imposed for a number of reasons. If tariffs are successfully imposed in sectors where there are externalities in production, then the average effect of tariffs may reflect both (beneficial) targeting and (harmful) disincentives associated with x-inefficiency.

Third, to the extent that Melitz (2003) is correct, many of the productivity gains associated with trade reform may occur through reallocating production toward more efficient firms, rather than within-firm productivity increases associated with greater exposure to international competition. The framework for this paper explicitly measures only the within firm impact of productivity changes, rather than the cross-firm reallocation that could occur as the least efficient firms exit and the more efficient firms acquire greater market share. Nevertheless, recent estimates for both India and China suggest that during this sample period, as much as 95% of productivity increases in manufacturing were due to within firm productivity increases, not reallocation toward more productive firms (Aghion et al., 2014; Harrison, Martin, & Nataraj, 2013). This suggests that reallocation of production may not be the driving force behind productivity growth in China.

In contrast to the insignificant effects of tariff changes on within-firm productivity changes, the coefficient on the WTO dummy is positive and significant across all subsamples, but is much smaller for foreign-invested enterprises (FIEs). The positive and significant point estimates suggest that China's entry into the WTO at the end of 2001 was accompanied by a very large increase in within-firm productivity. These large and significant effects of WTO entry stand in contrast to the insignificant and positive tariff effects. Taken together, these results suggest that market access for Chinese exporters and overall changes in the post-WTO membership period led to enormous productivity gains, even if internal tariff reforms by themselves did not.

Table 4 and this section yield several robust findings. These are the pattern of backward FDI spillovers controlling for tariffs across ownership types, the differential impacts of horizontal spillovers appearing to benefit FIEs and SOEs only, and forward spillovers advantaging all enterprises. In addition, we find evidence that the tariffs on final goods and inputs had no significant impact, but that WTO entry led to a large and significant increase in performance across all firms. From this baseline, we now explore different policy and ownership interactions to enhance the gains from FDI spillovers.

(c) The role of ownership and FDI spillovers

In Table 4, we saw that the coefficient on the state's share in equity is generally negative and statistically significant,

indicating that higher levels of state-invested shares are associated with lower levels of productivity. The coefficient estimate, which was −0.017 in column (1) of Table 4, suggests that after controlling for other factors, moving from 100% SOE to 100% private would be associated with a productivity gain of nearly two percentage points. Now we will explore how other factors, including FDI spillovers and trade policy, vary by ownership type.

In Table 5, we divide the samples of foreign-invested and domestic firms into two groups, SOEs and non-SOEs, to test whether the formal ownership structure and the composition of asset ownership matter for FDI spillover policies and trade policies. As in Table 4, all of the regressions are estimated with firm-level fixed effects and year effects, and robust standard errors are clustered at the sector level. The results in columns (1) and (2) include all SOEs and all non-SOEs, with and without foreign-equity participation. Columns (3) and (4) show the results using the sample of foreign-invested firms, and columns (5) and (6) present the results using the sample of the domestically-owned firms with zero foreign equity participation.

The first two columns allow us to compare the impact of firm-level equity participation by foreign investors on the productivity of SOEs relative to non-SOEs. The coefficient on foreign participation from foreign investors outside of Greater China (HKMT) for SOEs is 0.007 and significant, compared to 0.05 and not significant for non-SOEs. This result suggests that foreign equity participation is associated with an improvement in productivity which is greater for SOEs. The larger and statistically significant coefficient associated with foreign equity participation in SOEs is consistent with the hypothesis that foreign firms have played an important role in improving SOE performance.

Comparing FDI spillover impacts on SOEs and non-SOEs, forward spillovers are significant and robust for all types of enterprises. As shown in the fourth column, SOEs with some foreign-investment appear to be most effective at capturing productivity benefits from both upstream and downstream FDI clusters. Some of this estimated benefit may result from flows of capital and technology from downstream FDI users to their upstream SOE suppliers and from upstream FDI suppliers to their downstream SOE buyers. This result suggests that foreign equity participation is associated with an improvement in productivity which is greater for SOEs.

With respect to horizontal spillovers, among the six estimates, we only see evidence of significant spillovers to other FIEs or to SOEs. Among the population of firms in our sample, this set of firms may best exhibit the combination of a significant technology gap and capacity to absorb the relevant technologies to narrow the gap. Private or non FIE-invested enterprises may not exhibit a substantial gap with foreign-invested firms or they may not have the absorptive capacity

Table 4. *Olley and Pakes regressions with contemporaneous spillover variables and tariff controls: all firms, foreign-invested, domestic firms with zero foreign investment*

	All firms	Foreign-invested firms	Domestic firms (0 foreign share)
Foreign share (by HK–Taiwan–Macau)	−0.00379	0.000847	
	(0.00312)	(0.00550)	
Foreignshare (by other countries)	0.00716**	0.0131**	
	(0.00342)	(0.00526)	
State share	−0.0170***	0.00545	0.000450
	(0.00346)	(0.00870)	(0.00351)
Horizontal	0.449**	0.403**	0.396
	(0.189)	(0.192)	(0.246)
Backward	0.989	1.152**	0.867
	(0.644)	(0.556)	(1.004)
Forward	0.427***	0.410***	0.744***
	(0.129)	(0.105)	(0.224)
lnTariff	0.0535	0.0800*	0.0562
	(0.0483)	(0.0411)	(0.0683)
lnTariff on inputs	0.0212	0.0354	0.0214
	(0.0139)	(0.0240)	(0.0147)
WTO Dummy	0.376***	0.0263***	0.315***
	(0.0393)	(0.00515)	(0.0288)
Constant	1.268***	1.299***	1.196***
	(0.151)	(0.141)	(0.173)
Observations	1,540,823	347,201	1,070,523
R-squared	0.165	0.180	0.161

Notes: Robust clustered standard errors, clustered at the sector level, are presented in parentheses. The dependent variable lnTFP. Each regression includes firm-fixed effects and year dummies. The dummy is defined as 1 if firm *i* has non-zero foreign share at period *t*, 0 otherwise. A * indicates significance at the 10% level, a ** indicates significance at the 5% level, and a *** indicates significance at the 1% level.

to effectively capture these proximate intra-industry technologies. This result is broadly consistent with the findings of the three papers reviewed in our literature review, which find negligible, or negative, intra-industry FDI spillover impacts.

Concerning the matter of tariffs and trade liberalization, Table 5 shows significantly different responses to tariffs across SOEs and non-SOEs. Relative to non-SOEs, in the face of higher final goods tariffs, SOEs exhibit significantly lower productivity, particularly in the foreign-invested sector. The point estimates on final goods tariffs, which are −0.076 for SOEs with foreign investment and −0.052 for those with no foreign assets, suggests that a 1% reduction in tariffs (ceteris paribus) would increase productivity by 0.076–0.052%, respectively. The relative responsiveness of productivity to tariff reduction in the state sector suggests that the persistence of tariff protection for SOEs may have created or sustained more inefficiency in the state enterprises. The coefficient on domestic, non-SOEs was 0.315, compared to 0.026 for FIEs without state ownership. This suggests that gains from WTO entry were 15 times larger for domestic relative to foreign enterprises.

The F-tests listed at the bottom of the Table 5 identify whether vertical and horizontal spillovers from FDI were significantly different across SOEs and non-SOEs. Across all subsets of enterprises, spillover differences from FDI exhibit a markedly different pattern for SOEs relative to private enterprises. Backward spillovers were three times as large for SOEs

with foreign partners relative to private firms with foreign partners. Forward spillovers were also significantly larger for SOEs with foreign partners relative to non-SOEs. However, for SOEs without foreign partners, spillovers were significantly smaller than for other domestic enterprises. The results suggest that the benefits to SOEs from foreign externalities were largest when those SOEs also had foreign partners. Due to these ownership differences, in the rest of the paper we further differentiate categories of ownership by reporting the separate effects of horizontal and vertical spillovers for SOEs, private, and joint venture enterprises.

(d) Trade policy changes and FDI spillovers

While there is a large literature which investigates the impact of FDI on productivity, as well as an even larger literature that explores the relationship between trade policies and productivity (for an overview of both these topics, see Harrison & Rodriguez-Clare, 2010), we are not aware of any study that examines how changing levels of protection affect the magnitude of FDI spillovers. In this section, we explore how FDI spillovers changed with a discrete change in trade policy: China's entry into the WTO.

Specifically, we explore changes in FDI spillover impacts before and after China's ascension to the WTO in 2001. We know that China's 2001 WTO ascension led to a substantial decline in tariffs. Table 2, for example, shows that for over 71 industry categories, during 1998–2007, China's average manufacturing final goods tariff was 12.7%. By 2007, the average final goods tariff in that year had declined by 8.9% to just 30% of the average for the sample period. Our question, therefore, is whether this across the board reduction in tariffs during 1998–2007 affected the magnitude or direction of China's FDI spillovers.

We explore how trade policy changes affected FDI spillovers through two different specifications. First, in Table 6A, we add an interaction term for WTO entry and FDI at the vertical and

Table 5. *Olley and Pakes regressions with contemporaneous spillover variables and tariff controls: non-SOEs vs. SOEs (with the sample of all firms, foreign-invested, and domestic firms with zero foreign share)*

	All firms		Foreign-invested firms		Domestic firms (zero foreign share)	
	Non-SOEs	SOEs	Non-SOEs	SOEs	Non-SOEs	SOEs
Foreign share (by HK–Taiwan–Macau)	−0.00392	0.0252	0.00113	−0.0691		
	(0.00310)	(0.0545)	(0.00555)	(0.0744)		
Foreign share (by other countries)	0.00698**	0.0553	0.0131**	0.0698		
	(0.00340)	(0.0427)	(0.00531)	(0.0708)		
State share	0.000622	−0.0233***	0.00483	−0.0112	0.000450	−0.0239***
	(0.00291)	(0.00397)	(0.00896)	(0.0351)	(0.00351)	(0.00399)
Horizontal	0.448**	0.435***	0.408**	−0.603	0.396	0.448***
	(0.197)	(0.129)	(0.193)	(0.491)	(0.246)	(0.128)
Backward	0.996	0.611	1.139**	3.592***	0.867	0.569
	(0.660)	(0.580)	(0.558)	(0.966)	(1.004)	(0.581)
Forward	0.441***	0.306**	0.410***	0.674***	0.744***	0.329**
	(0.133)	(0.116)	(0.105)	(0.236)	(0.224)	(0.125)
lnTariff	0.0676	−0.0525*	0.0815*	−0.0755**	0.0562	−0.0515
	(0.0511)	(0.0310)	(0.0414)	(0.0373)	(0.0683)	(0.0312)
ln Input tariff	0.0190	0.0411***	0.0353	0.0700**	0.0214	0.0406***
	(0.0145)	(0.0136)	(0.0240)	(0.0282)	(0.0147)	(0.0136)
WTO	0.144***	0.309***	0.0264***	0.203***	0.315***	0.310***
	(0.0327)	(0.0234)	(0.00518)	(0.0323)	(0.0288)	(0.0234)
Constant	1.242***	1.425***	1.295***	1.603***	1.196***	1.419***
	(0.161)	(0.0740)	(0.142)	(0.115)	(0.173)	(0.0745)
Observations	1,415,341	125,482	344,818	2,383	1,070,523	123,099
R-squared	0.170	0.098	0.180	0.239	0.161	0.097
Horizontal*ownership		−0.024		−0.369		−0.030
		(0.109)		(0.199)		(0.109)
F-stat (Horizontal*ownership = 0)		0.05		3.43		0.08
Prob > F		0.827		0.069		0.7825
Backward*ownership		−0.430		0.465		−0.408
		(0.280)		(0.380)		(0.274)
F-stat (Backward*ownership = 0)		2.36		1.50		2.23
Prob > F		0.130		0.226		0.141
Forward*ownership		−0.123		0.062		−0.140
		(0.065)		(0.103)		(0.066)
F-stat (Forward*ownership = 0)		3.66		0.36		4.57
Prob > F		0.061		0.549		0.037
F-stat (interaction terms jointly zero)		8.97		6.08		8.14
Prob > F		0.0001		0.011		0.0001

Notes: Robust clustered standard errors are presented in parentheses. The dependent variable for all regression is lnTFP. All regressions include firm fixed effects and year dummies. Ownership is a dummy variable, which equals one if a firm is a SOE and zero otherwise. A * indicates significance at the 10% level, A * indicates significance at the 10% level, a ** indicates significance at the 5% level, and a *** indicates significance at the 1% level.

horizontal level. This means that we add three interaction terms: Horizontal*WTO, Backward*WTO, and Forward*WTO. In Table 6B, we instead interact our FDI measures with tariffs. To the extent that trade policy affects the magnitude of FDI spillovers, we would expect the interactions to be significant. If greater trade liberalization positively affects spillovers, we would expect the interactions with the WTO dummy variable to be positive and the interactions with tariffs to be negative.

In Table 6A, we explore how vertical and horizontal linkages varied before and after China's WTO entry at the end of 2001. With China's entry into the WTO in the middle of the sample period, domestic content rules became illegal and tariffs were significantly reduced. The results in Table 6A indicate that vertical backward linkages were strengthened during the second half of the sample period, when tariffs were lowered and domestic content restrictions relaxed. Among the three

spillover directions, the most dramatic change is the set of backward spillover estimates for which the number of robust estimates *rises*. The interaction between Backward FDI and WTO is significant for all subsamples except for SOEs partnering with foreign enterprises. The coefficient estimates suggest that backward linkages shifted from negative to large, positive and significant post-WTO entry.

Table 6B confirms the findings from Table 6A, using actual tariff levels instead of the WTO dummy to measure the interaction with sectoral FDI linkages. Once we take into account the possible interaction with tariffs, we find large, significant, and positive effects of backward linkages across all types of enterprises. Horizontal linkages generally become small in magnitude and insignificant across all types of enterprises. Forward linkages remain significant for foreign-invested SOEs, but not for other types of firms. The interaction between tariffs and backward linkages is significant and negative, indicating that higher tariffs reduce backward spillovers, across all ownership types.

Hence, the most dramatic impact of China's WTO ascension on FDI spillover outcomes is evident in our backward linkage estimates. As shown in Tables 6A and B, the increase in backward spillover impacts is notable for each of the four distinct ownership types we explore: foreign-invested SOEs and non-SOEs and domestic-owned SOEs and non-SOEs. The across-the-board tariff reductions appear not to have affected the efficacy of horizontal and forward linkages. The increase in the robustness of backward linkages is likely to reflect the fact that liberalization of tariffs and domestic content restrictions required upstream suppliers to improve the efficiency and quality of the inputs they supplied to cost and quality-conscious downstream foreign-invested firms. With the reduction in barriers to trade, downstream foreign producers could choose to alternatively source from overseas foreign suppliers to substitute for established upstream producers that had benefited from pre-WTO trade barriers. The threat of alternative suppliers and the reduction in trade distortions together led to significant increases in backward linkages across all types of enterprises.

(e) The effects of tax incentives on FDI spillovers

In Tables 7 and 8 we explore the extent to which subsidized foreign investment exerts a differential impact on spillovers relative to unsubsidized foreign investment. While the standard income tax rates across all firms during the sample period 1998–2007 was 33%, a large share of foreign-owned firms was granted tax subsidies and faced tax rates that were significantly lower. We are able to calculate the extent of subsidies by calculating for each enterprise their effective tax rate, defined as taxes on corporate profits divided by net profits. The difference between the corporate tax rate and the actual tax rate paid is how we define the extent of the establishment-specific subsidy. Since the data separates out income taxes paid and value-added taxes paid by the enterprise, we are able to separately calculate tax holidays on both income tax and VAT obligations.

The summary statistics reported in Tables 3-1 and 3-2 suggest that the majority of foreign investment in China during the sample period benefited from income tax subsidies and a significant fraction benefited from subsidies on value-added taxes. To the extent that the Chinese government successfully targeted sectors and firms more likely to convey positive externalities, we would expect more robust spillovers effects emanating from the firms and sectors benefitting from subsidies. To test for the possibility of differential spillover effects, we split our sector-level foreign share variables into two groups: one is calculated based on foreign investment being subsidized (those paying less than the statutory tax rate)[19] and the other series is computed based on non-subsidized foreign investment.

The results, summarized in Table 7, once again show that much of the action centered on backward spillovers. For subsidized FDI in downstream industries, our estimated spillovers are both notably large and consistently robust at the 1% level across five out of six ownership types. For unsubsidized FDI, the backward spillovers become insignificant or even negative for all firms except SOEs with foreign investment. The F-tests at the bottom of Table 7 are only significant for subsidized FDI, suggesting that on average, tax holidays did indeed target sectors with greater externalities. By comparison, horizontal spillovers show no notable difference for intra-industry FDI that is subsidized or unsubsidized. The robust forward spillovers for foreign-invested firms, whether SOEs or not,

persist in about the same degree with and without subsidies to upstream industries.

The results in Table 7 suggest that subsidized downstream FDI generates more spillovers than unsubsidized FDI. While these results are consistent with smart tax policies, our results cannot at this point be interpreted as causal. What is evident, however, is that foreign-owned buyers of upstream domestic inputs were more likely to generate spillovers when they also received tax holidays. Downstream subsidized FDI may have attracted different kinds of downstream producers than unsubsidized investors. This issue deserves further research. What Table 7 does indicate is that tax holidays to downstream foreign firms were more likely to be associated with positive externalities than tax holidays to upstream foreign firms.

In Table 8, we test whether the results differ when we explore tax holidays on value-added taxes as a form of fiscal incentive rather than the income tax holidays examined above. In Table 8, we redefine subsidized firms on the basis of lower value-added taxes instead of lower corporate income taxes. We define firms as subsidized when they are exempted altogether from paying value-added taxes. Overall, the results in Table 8 are consistent with differences in the effects of foreign investment based on income tax incentives, i.e., the provision of subsidies is associated with larger, more robust spillovers. However, the composition of the spillover effects of VAT holidays differs somewhat from reductions in corporate income taxes. Here much of the action focuses on horizontal spillovers. The non-subsidized horizontal FDI seemingly creates fewer or no spillovers; by contrast, the horizontal spillovers associated with firms that enjoy VAT subsidies are consistently large and robust at the 1% level of significance.

The evidence presented in Tables 7 and 8 suggests that across both corporate taxes and VAT obligations, tax holidays were consistently associated with higher externalities from FDI. In the case of corporate tax holidays, most of the differences were in the magnitude of backward linkages. For VAT obligations, most of the differences were in intra-industry spillovers. While we cannot identify the causal linkages, the evidence is consistent with an industrial policy such as China's "technology for market" program, where foreign firms that agreed to make accessible aspects of their technology may have received, in return, corporate income tax holidays or VAT subsidies for their investment and production.

(f) Robustness tests

Since our dependent variable is firm-level productivity and the focus of the analysis is on how sector-level foreign investment affects domestic firm productivity, endogeneity is less likely to be an issue. To the extent that foreign investment might be attracted to sectors where suppliers or users are more productive, this condition is accounted for by the use of firm-level fixed effects. Furthermore, where foreign investment is drawn to sectors that exhibit either high or low tariffs (or possibly systematically high or low productivity levels), the inclusion of the tariff variable will control for this potential source of omitted variable endogeneity bias.

However, some might argue that foreign investors are drawn to sectors where they expect higher productivity growth in the future. To address this potential source of endogeneity, we also applied instrumental variables (IV) techniques which are available upon request from the authors. We used future tariffs (tariffs at time $t + 1$) as instruments. For backward linkages for domestic non-SOEs, the point estimates were magnified, confirming the importance of the linkages between domestic suppliers and foreign-owned buyers of their inputs. However, the

Table 6A. *Interaction between trade and FDI spillovers using WTO entry as measure of trade policy*

	All		Foreign-invested firms		Domestic firms	
	Non-SOEs	SOEs	Non-SOEs	SOEs	Non-SOEs	SOEs
Horizontal FDI	0.430**	0.379***	0.426**	−0.751	0.338	
	(0.181)	(0.112)	(0.198)	(0.532)	(0.208)	
Backward FDI	0.499	−0.259	0.486	2.977***	0.486	
	(0.734)	(0.551)	(0.682)	(1.070)	(1.035)	
Forward FDI	0.427**	0.272	0.325*	0.638**	0.848***	
	(0.197)	(0.183)	(0.164)	(0.262)	(0.272)	
Horizontal*WTO	0.0317	0.104	−0.00297	0.399*	0.0685	0.105
	(0.0671)	(0.0816)	(0.0653)	(0.231)	(0.0856)	(0.0824)
Backward*WTO	0.516***	0.812***	0.647***	0.00441	0.441*	0.824***
	(0.190)	(0.215)	(0.177)	(0.392)	(0.228)	(0.223)
Forward*WTO	0.00870	0.0164	0.0800	−0.101	−0.113	0.00580
	(0.0883)	(0.0993)	(0.0801)	(0.113)	(0.0875)	(0.100)
WTO	0.106***	0.233***	−0.0359	0.130***	0.279***	0.234***
	(0.0295)	(0.0260)	(0.0231)	(0.0299)	(0.0314)	(0.0263)
Observations	1,415,341	125,482	344,818	2,383	1,070,523	123,099
R-squared	0.171	0.101	0.182	0.250	0.161	0.100

Notes: All specifications include firm fixed effects and year dummies. Robust standard errors clustered at sector level. WTO is a dummy equal to 1 from 2002 onwards. Interaction terms are sectoral FDI measures interacted with the WTO dummy. Other controls also included from previous tables but not reported here (firm level FDI and SOE shares, input and final goods tariffs). A * indicates significance at the 10% level, a ** indicates significance at the 5% level, and a *** indicates significance at the 1% level.

Table 6B. *Interaction between trade and FDI spillovers using tariffs as measure of trade policy*

	All		Foreign-invested firms		Domestic firms	
	Non-SOEs	SOEs	Non-SOEs	SOEs	Non-SOEs	SOEs
Horizontal FDI	0.299	0.480	0.499	−0.418	−0.0708	0.524
	(0.408)	(0.361)	(0.401)	(0.536)	(0.483)	(0.368)
Backward FDI	1.843***	2.332***	1.434***	5.067***	3.162***	2.222***
	(0.588)	(0.725)	(0.632)	(0.966)	(0.685)	(0.745)
Forward FDI	0.381	0.562	0.562	0.945***	0.0878	0.499
	(0.599)	(0.560)	(0.485)	(0.362)	(0.783)	(0.581)
WTO	0.133***	0.308***	0.0262***	0.201***	0.313***	0.310***
	(0.0316)	(0.0236)	(0.00503)	(0.0327)	(0.0297)	(0.0236)
Tariff*Horizontal FDI	0.0700	−0.0163	−0.0342	−0.0830	0.211	−0.0296
	(0.128)	(0.138)	(0.132)	(0.122)	(0.156)	(0.140)
Tariff*Backward FDI	−0.423	−0.957**	−0.210	−1.023***	−1.068*	−0.916**
	(0.446)	(0.382)	(0.442)	(0.238)	(0.583)	(0.384)
Tariff*Forward FDI	0.0401	−0.139	−0.0820	−0.174	0.339	−0.101
	(0.303)	(0.254)	(0.238)	(0.130)	(0.405)	(0.262)
Constant	1.284***	1.399***	1.245***	1.509***	1.307***	1.390***
	(0.200)	(0.0840)	(0.187)	(0.128)	(0.208)	(0.0844)
Observations	1,415,341	125,482	344,818	2,383	1,070,523	123,099
R-squared	0.171	0.099	0.180	0.251	0.164	0.099

Notes: All specifications include firm fixed effects and year dummies. Robust standard errors clustered at sector level. WTO is a dummy equal to 1 from 2002 onwards. Interaction terms are sectoral FDI measures interacted with tariffs. Other controls also included from previous tables but not reported here (firm level FDI and SOE shares, input and final goods tariffs). A * indicates significance at the 10% level, a ** indicates significance at the 5% level, and a *** indicates significance at the 1% level.

coefficients on horizontal linkages became negative across all subsamples, but not statistically significant. The negative coefficient on the horizontal variable is consistent with our evidence suggesting lack of significant intra-industry spillovers to domestic non-SOEs as well as previous work by Aitken and Harrison (1999) and others suggesting that foreign firms take away market share from domestic competitors in the same industry.

6. CONCLUDING COMMENTS

In this paper, we investigate how tax and tariff policies affect FDI spillovers in Chinese industry. Is it possible to enhance the externalities from FDI through trade policies or tax holidays? We find that the answer is yes. We also explore how externalities from FDI, tariffs, and tax holidays vary across China's heterogeneous ownership structure. To our knowledge, this is the first study to examine whether targeted subsidies for FDI are associated with stronger linkages from FDI to domestically-owned and foreign-invested firms. To identify the interactions between FDI spillovers and trade policies, we examine the role of both tariff reductions and China's entry into the WTO.

By taking into account trade policy changes and interactions between trade and FDI, our results indicate significantly higher effects of backward linkages in China. In fact, prior

Table 7. *Olley and Pakes regressions for grouped data with contemporaneous subsidized and non-subsidized spillover variables and tariff controls: non-SOEs vs. SOEs (All firms, foreign-invested, and domestic firms with zero foreign investment*

	All		Foreign-invested firms		Domestic firms	
	Non-SOEs	SOEs	Non-SOEs	SOEs	Non-SOEs	SOEs
HorizontalS	0.347*	0.367**	0.268	−0.636	0.384	0.373**
	(0.206)	(0.164)	(0.195)	(0.543)	(0.247)	(0.164)
BackwardS	1.287*	2.193***	0.780	3.807***	1.838**	2.115***
	(0.701)	(0.707)	(0.564)	(0.905)	(0.908)	(0.727)
ForwardS	−0.0673	0.0322	0.0651	0.672**	−0.0875	0.0513
	(0.323)	(0.264)	(0.253)	(0.277)	(0.399)	(0.272)
HorizontalNS	0.520**	0.271*	0.547**	−0.545	0.336	0.290*
	(0.228)	(0.146)	(0.221)	(0.397)	(0.289)	(0.147)
BackwardNS	0.889	−0.991	1.931	2.949**	−0.0909	−0.941
	(1.358)	(0.864)	(1.205)	(1.327)	(1.687)	(0.864)
ForwardNS	1.030*	0.716*	0.803**	0.618***	1.694**	0.741*
	(0.543)	(0.385)	(0.391)	(0.218)	(0.790)	(0.394)
Observations	1,415,341	125,482	344,818	2,383	1,070,523	123,099
R-squared	0.172	0.098	0.182	0.239	0.164	0.098
F-stat (HS = HNS)	0.67	0.23	2.27	0.09	0.03	0.16
Prob > F	0.416	0.635	0.138	0.768	0.86	0.687
F-stat (BS = BNS)	0.06	8.36	0.64	0.57	1.17	7.42
Prob > F	0.81	0.005	0.427	0.454	0.284	0.008
F-stat (FS = FNS)	1.71	1.23	1.44	0.05	2.41	1.21
Prob > F	0.196	0.272	0.236	0.821	0.126	0.276
F-stat (three conditions jointly)	2.11	4.29	3.24	0.2	1.58	3.9
Prob > F	0.109	0.008	0.028	0.895	0.205	0.0131

Notes: Robust clustered standard errors at the sector level are presented in parentheses. The dependent variable for all regressions is lnTFP. Controls included but not reported in the Table include the log of Final Tariffs and the log of input tariffs, as well as a WTO dummy equal to 1 after China entered the WTO. All regressions include firm fixed effect and year dummy variables. HS = subsidized horizontal, and HNS = non-subsidized horizontal; BS = subsidized backward, and BNS = non-subsidized backward; FS = subsidized forward, and FNS = non-subsidized forward. A * indicates significance at the 10% level, a ** indicates significance at the 5% level, and a *** indicates significance at the 1% level.

Table 8. *Olley and Pakes regressions for grouped data with contemporaneous subsidized and non-subsidized spillover variables (calculated based on value-added tax) and tariff controls: non-SOEs vs. SOEs (all firms, foreign-invested, domestic firms)*

	All firms		Foreign-invested firms		Domestic firms	
	Non-SOEs	SOEs	Non-SOEs	SOEs	Non-SOEs	SOEs
HorizontalS	0.727**	0.856***	0.590**	−0.601	0.797**	0.892***
	(0.303)	(0.267)	(0.236)	(0.470)	(0.454)	(0.270)
BackwardS	−0.690	0.533	−0.377	3.234***	−0.866	0.440
	(1.145)	(0.961)	(0.854)	(1.069)	(1.815)	(0.991)
ForwardS	0.229	0.424*	0.499	0.669***	−0.0625	0.394*
	(0.425)	(0.235)	(0.349)	(0.216)	(0.490)	(0.228)
HorizontalNS	0.275	0.299***	0.267	−0.624	0.175	0.308***
	(0.167)	(0.112)	(0.183)	(0.530)	(0.191)	(0.112)
BackwardNS	1.813**	0.334	1.928**	3.195**	1.659	0.293
	(0.817)	(0.664)	(0.784)	(1.309)	(1.065)	(0.668)
ForwardNS	0.485**	0.258	0.385**	0.676**	0.929***	0.292
	(0.228)	(0.179)	(0.179)	(0.285)	(0.331)	(0.187)
Observations	1,222,322	116,138	298,385	2,308	923,937	113,830
R-squared	0.184	0.105	0.203	0.228	0.170	0.104
F-stat (HS = HNS)	3.44	4.71	4.1	0.01	2.54	4.9
Prob > F	0.069	0.0341	0.0473	0.93	0.116	0.031
F-stat (BS = BNS)	3.37	0.03	3.66	0	1.96	0.02
Prob > F	0.0714	0.854	0.061	0.98	0.167	0.896
F-stat (FS = FNS)	0.17	0.19	0.05	0	1.01	0.07
Prob > F	0.683	0.663	0.817	0.98	0.21	0.786
F-stat (three conditions jointly)	20.02	4.27	3.15	0	1.02	4
Prob > F	0.121	0.009	0.031	0.99	0.21	0.012

Notes: Robust clustered standard errors are presented in parentheses. The dependent variable for all regressions is lnTFP. All regressions include firm fixed effect and year dummy variables. Since the information on value added is missing for the year of 2004, we exclude the year of 2004 from regressions. HS = subsidized horizontal, and HNS = non-subsidized horizontal; BS = subsidized backward, and BNS = non-subsidized backward; FS = subsidized forward, and FNS = non-subsidized forward. A * indicates significance at the 10% level, a ** indicates significance at the 5% level, and a *** indicates significance at the 1% level.

to China's entry into the WTO backward linkages appear to be negative and the very large and significant backward externalities only emerge once we take into account the impact of trade reforms on FDI. The positive impact of backward linkages which emerges post-trade reform is consistent with the early literature on immiserizing FDI, which posited negative effects of FDI in highly protected economies.

Across a variety of specifications, we find that backward and forward linkages increased the productivity of Chinese and joint venture enterprises. Horizontal linkages, however, were generally restricted to FIEs and SOEs. In other words, positive externalities within the same sector were restricted to public enterprises or to other joint ventures. During our sample period, all of these spillover channels, particularly the vertical linkages, were affected by industrial policy associated with tariff reductions and the deployment of corporate income and VAT subsidies.

Exploiting the exogenous change in trade policies with China's entry into the WTO at the end of 2001, we investigate the impact of China's substantial tariff liberalization on the magnitude and direction of FDI productivity spillovers. We do this in two ways. First we interact tariff changes with our measures of sectoral FDI. Second, we interact WTO entry with sectoral FDI. Using both approaches shows that trade liberalization was accompanied by significant increases in FDI linkages, particularly for backward linkages. Since China's entry into the WTO created pressure to phase out domestic content rules (in order to comply with the WTO), we might have expected to find a reduction in backward linkage spillovers. Instead, backward linkages became stronger after WTO entry, possibly because the additional competition forced domestic suppliers to improve their efficiency and quality. The increase in vertical linkages from FDI following the reduction in trade distortions is consistent with an earlier academic literature that posited welfare losses from FDI attracted by tariff distortions.

Finally, we explore the spillover implications of tax subsidies that have been targeted to foreign investment within certain sectors and by certain firms. We find strong evidence that subsidized foreign investment generates greater productivity spillovers than unsubsidized investment. The estimates imply that a 1% increase in the share of foreign investment in downstream sectors raises the supplying firm's productivity by 2–3 percentage points. Across our sample spanning a ten-year period, vertical linkages accounted for an important source of productivity gains for all types of enterprises.

One advantage of incorporating different industrial policy instruments into a single framework is that it allows us to compare the effectiveness of these different approaches on firm productivity. If a central goal of China's industrial policy has been to raise firm productivity, we find that the use of different instruments has had notable positive effects but also some perverse impacts. High tariffs, particularly high final goods tariffs, were associated with depressed productivity for SOEs. FDI spillovers are moderate to robust, with vertical backward and forward spillovers particularly strong. China's entry into the WTO also substantially strengthened the impacts of vertical FDI spillovers. FDI subsidies through the use of tax corporate income subsidies were associated with significantly larger backward FDI linkages; VAT subsidies have most strengthened the positive impact of horizontal spillovers. During the period of our study, 1998–2007, China's industrial policy has generally served to enhance the impacts of these spillovers.

NOTES

1. Naughton (2007, chap. 16).

2. However, the government adjusted this preferential policy in 2008. Beginning Jan 1, 2008, the following corporate tax policy for foreign-invested firms came into effect: foreign-invested firms that previously received preferential corporate tax rates would return to the regular tax rate within five years. In 2008, the tax rate increased from 15% to 18%; in 2009, the rate further increased to 20%; in 2010, the corporate tax rate rose to 22% and finally reached 25% in 2012.

3. Elements of the trade and investment reforms included exchange rate devaluation, relaxing rules on currency convertibility, increasing the number of foreign trade corporations from twelve national monopolies to many thousands, reducing non-tariff barriers, and gradually reducing tariffs and freeing up import prices.

4. Two of the papers reviewed by Jefferson and Ouyang (2014) use the above size firm-level data set and incorporate both horizontal and vertical FDI spillover possibilities, both of which are used in this paper. These papers are Lin, Liu, and Zhang (2009) and Girma, Gong, Görg, and Lancheros (2014). The samples drawn from those papers both use shorter time horizons than we use in this paper. Lin *et al.* (2009) distinguish between spillover effects originating from investment from Hong Kong, Macao, and Taiwan (HMT) and foreign, non-HMT investment. In either case, they find strong and robust vertical spillover effects on both state-owned firms and non-state firms. Girma *et al.* (2014) examine the impact of FDI spillovers, both horizontal and vertical, on new product innovation rather than TFP. They conclude that FDI clusters have negative impacts on innovation in SOEs. However, for a subsample of the SOEs – those that export, invest in human capital or R&D, or have prior

innovation experience (i.e., the more technologically advanced SOEs) – Girma *et al.* find that FDI has positive impacts on their innovation activity. A third paper by Hu and Jefferson (2002) that looks only at horizontal spillovers finds that SOEs are more susceptible to negative spillover effects than non-SOEs. Thus, while there are no common core findings, stitching the various findings together, this slice of the literature concludes that the spillover impacts across different ownership types are varied, depending on the direction of the spillover. SOEs, particularly those that are more technologically sophisticated, are likely to benefit from vertical FDI spillovers. Less technologically advanced SOEs appear not to benefit from horizontal spillovers.

5. For example, the furniture industry (coded as 19 in Table 2) includes 5 four-digit sub-sectors. These are wood furniture manufacturing (2,110), bamboo furniture manufacturing (2,120), metal furniture manufacturing (2,130), plastic furniture manufacturing (2,140), and other furniture manufacturing (2,190).

6. Sector-specific ex-factory price indices for industrial products appear in *China Urban Life and Price Yearbook* (2008, Table 4-3-3). The price indices are published for 29 individual sectors, consequently we created a concordance between the 29 and the 71 sectors.

7. Price indices for fixed investment and industry-wide intermediate inputs are reported in the *China Statistical Yearbook* (2006) (obtained from the website of the National Bureau of Statistics of China).

8. The omitted share, the non-state domestically-owned share, is represented by the constant term.

9. In some specifications, we run regressions with domestic firms only. For these cases, we use the sample of domestic firms with zero foreign investment. At the individual establishment level, we control for two types of FDI: $ForeignShareHKTM_{ijt}$, and $ForeignShareFR_{ijt}$. This allows us to determine whether some types of foreign investment are more productive than others. It is generally assumed that OECD-based FDI is more technology-intensive than HKMT FDI. On the other hand, HKMT FDI may be more physically and organizationally integrated with domestic operations than OECD-based FDI. Anecdotal evidence suggests large quantities of so-called foreign investors in China are actually domestic investors who channel investment through Hong Kong in order to take advantage of special treatment for foreign firms (so-called "round tripping"). If this is the case, then we would expect that firms with HKMT ownership might be less productive than other types of FDI.

10. For instance, both the furniture and apparel industries use leather to produce leather sofas and leather jackets. Suppose the leather processing industry sells 1/3 of its output to furniture producers and 2/3 of its output to jacket producers. If no multinationals produce furniture but half of all jacket production comes from foreign affiliates, the *Backward* variable will be calculated as follows: 1/3*0 + 2/3*1/2 = 1/3.

11. Input-output tables of China (2002) Table 4.2, which divides manufacturing industry into 71 sectors.

12. This was a challenge given that the two series are not in the same nomenclature. For example, we have different categories for ship-building, electronic computers, tobacco products, motor vehicles, and parts and accessories for motor vehicles.

13. To aggregate the tariff line items to the level which would allow us to create a concordance with the census data, we used output for 2003 as weights.

14. The weights are based on input-output table. For instance, if a chocolate producer uses 60% sugar and 40% cocoa pounder, the input tariff for that chocolate industry is equal to 60% of the sugar tariff plus 40% of the cocoa tariff. Since China's input-out tables only allow us to calculate input tariffs at the three-digit level, we use the same level of 3-digit disaggregation for final goods tariffs as well.

15. The data show that the 5 million yuan threshold is not a strict rule. Among non-SOEs, about 6% of the firms report annual sales of less than 5 million yuan in 1998; this number rises to % by 1999 and falls after 2003. In 2007, only 1% of non-SOEs have annual sales below 5 million yuan.

16. The original dataset over the ten-year period includes 2,226,104 observations and contains identifiers that can be used to track firms over time. Since the study focuses on manufacturing firms, we eliminate non-manufacturing observations. The sample size is further reduced by deleting missing values, as well as observations with negative or zero values for output, number of employees, capital, and the inputs, leaving a sample size of 1,842,786. Due to incompleteness of information on official output price indices, which are reported annually in the official publication, three sectors are dropped from the sample. They are the following sectors: processing food from agricultural products; printing, reproduction of recording media; and general purpose machinery. Thus, our final regression sample size is 1,545,626.

17. Actually, the international criterion used to distinguish domestic and foreign-invested firms is 10%, that is, the share of subscribed capital owned by foreign investors is equal to or less than 10%. In an earlier version of the paper, we tested whether the results are sensitive to using zero, 10%, and 25% foreign ownership. Our results show that between the zero and 10% thresholds, the magnitude and the significance levels of the estimated coefficients remain close, which makes us comfortable using the more restrictive sample of domestic firms for which the foreign capital share is zero. The results based on the 25% criterion exhibit small differences, but the results are generally robust to the choice of definition for foreign *versus* domestic ownership.

18. Moreover, if our estimate of TFP deviates from the true TFP level by a constant time-invariant scalar, the fixed effects procedure that we use in the second stage should wash out the difference.

19. As discussed earlier, the statutory tax rate in China is 33%. However, foreign-invested firms receive a preferential tax break of 15%. In this paper, we use the cut-off of a 20% tax rate to distinguish whether a foreign-invested firm is being subsidized.

REFERENCES

Aitken, B. J., & Harrison, A. E. (1999). Do domestic firms benefit from direct foreign investment? Evidence from Venezuela. *American Economic Review*, 89(3), 605–618.

Aghion, P., Cai, J., Dewatripont, M., Du, L., Harrison, A., & Legros, P. (2014), "Industrial Policy and Competition", NBER Working Paper.

Amiti, M., & Konings, J. (2007). Trade liberalization, intermediate inputs and productivity. *American Economic Review*, 97(5), 1611–1638.

Bhagwati, J. N. (1973). The theory of immiserizing growth: Further applications.

Blalock, G., & Gertler, P. J. (2008). Welfare gains from foreign direct investment through technology transfer to local suppliers. *Journal of International Economics*, 74(2), 402–421.

Brandt, L., Van Biesebroeck, J., Wang, L. H., & Zhang, Y. F. (2012). *WTO accession and performance of Chinese manufacturing firms*. CEPR Discussion Paper No. 9166.

Brecher, R., & Dias Alejandro, C. (1977). Tariffs, foreign capital and immiserizing Growth. *Journal of International Economics*, 7, 317–322.

Bustos, P. (2011). Trade liberalization, exports, and technology upgrading: Evidence on the impact of MERCOSUR on Argentinian firms. *The American Economic Review*, 101(1), 304–340.

Girma, S., Gong, Y., Görg, H., & Lancheros, S. (2014). Drivers of technology upgrading: Do foreign acquisitions matter to Chinese firms? *International Business and Institutions After the Financial Crisis*, 251.

Goldberg, P. K., & Pavcnik, N. (2007). Distributional effects of globalization in developing countries. *Journal of Economic Literature*, 45(1), 39–82.

Goldberg, P. K., Khandelwal, A. K., Pavcnik, N., & Topalova, P. (2010a). Multiproduct firms and product turnover in the developing world: Evidence from India. *The Review of Economics and Statistics*, 92(4), 1042–1049.

Goldberg, P. K., Khandelwal, A. K., Pavcnik, N., & Topalova, P. (2010b). Imported intermediate inputs and domestic product growth: Evidence from India. *The Quarterly Journal of Economics*, 125(4), 1727–1767.

Griliches, Z., & Jacques, M. (1995). *Production functions: The search for identification*. National Bureau of Economic Research (Cambridge, MA) Working Paper No. 5067, March 1995.

Harrison, A., Martin, L., & Nataraj, S. (2013). Learning versus stealing: How important are market-share reallocations to India's productivity growth? *World Bank Economic Review*, 27(2), 202–229.

Harrison, A. E., & Rodriguez-Clare, A. (2010). Trade, foreign investment, and industrial policy for developing countries. In D. Rodrik, & M. Rosenzweig (Eds.), *Handbook of development economics, Vol. 5* (pp. 4039–4214).

Hu, A., & Jefferson, G. H. (2002). FDI impact and spillover: Evidence from China's electronic and textile industries. *World Economy, 25*(8), 1063–1076.

Javorcik, J. B. (2004). Does foreign direct investment increase the productivity of domestic firms? In search of spillovers through backward linkages. *American Economic Review, 94*(3), 605–627.

Jefferson, G. H., & Ouyang, M. (2014). FDI spillovers in China: Why do the research findings differ so much? *Journal of Chinese Economic and Business Studies, 12*(1), 1–27.

Khandelwal, A., & Topalova, P. (2011). Trade liberalization and firm productivity: The case of India. *The Review of Economics and Statistics, 93*(3), 995–1009.

Levinsohn, J., & Petrin, A. (2003). Estimating production functions using inputs to control for unobservables. *Review of Economic Studies, 70,* 317–341.

Lin, P., Liu, Z. M., & Zhang, Y. F. (2009). Do Chinese domestic firms benefit from FDI inflow? Evidence of horizontal and vertical spillovers. *China Economic Review, 20,* 677–691.

Melitz, M. J. (2003). The impact of trade on intra-industry reallocations and aggregate industry productivity. *Econometrica, 71*(6), 1695–1725.

Morisset, J., & Pirnia, N. (1999). *How tax policy and incentives affect foreign direct investment*. World Bank, Policy Research Working Paper, published November 1999.

Nataraj, S. (2011). The impact of trade liberalization on productivity: Evidence from India's formal and informal manufacturing sectors. *Journal of International Economics, 85,* 292–301.

Naughton, B. (1996). China's emergence and prospects as a trading nation. *Brookings Papers on Economic Activity, 27*(2), 273–304.

Naughton, B. (2007). *The Chinese economy: Transition and growth*. MIT Press.

Olley, G. Steven, & Pakes, Ariel (1996). The dynamics of productivity in the telecommunications equipment industry. *Econometrica, 64,* 6.

Solis, O. (2011). *Subsidizing multinational corporations: Is that a development policy?* Kellogg Institute, Working Paper #381, November 2011.

Trefler, D. (2004). The Long and short of the Canada-U.S. free trade agreement. *The American Economic Review, 94*(4), 870–895.

Yu, M. L. (in press). Processing trade, tariff reductions, and firm productivity: Evidence from Chinese Products. *Economic Journal.*

APPENDIX A

Table A.1. *Summary of estimated coefficients on input variables using the Olley–Pakes two stage procedure*

	All enterprises			Domestic, private establishments only		
	Labor	Materials	Capital	Labor	Materials	Capital
Foodstuffs	0.063648	0.795382	0.039528	0.046787	0.846505	0.037731
Manufacture of beverages	0.062011	0.797568	0.039427	0.060272	0.783996	0.038303
Manufacture of Tobacco	0.072545	0.793483	0.00697	0.108622	0.699906	0.006198
Manufacture of Textiles	0.057483	0.8192	0.041548	0.047518	0.834871	0.048671
Manufacture of textile wearing apparel, footwear	0.097813	0.706444	0.056324	0.073357	0.742437	0.060367
Manufacture of leather, fur, feather	0.082379	0.795421	0.043285	0.065043	0.844919	0.042856
Processing of timber, manufacture of wood, bamboo	0.056418	0.814447	0.041392	0.041642	0.859254	0.039784
Manufacture of furniture	0.110771	0.761009	0.050201	0.10054	0.774004	0.053424
Manufacture of paper and paper products	0.056664	0.808117	0.048015	0.048811	0.812315	0.055325
Manufacture of articles for culture, education and sports	0.109501	0.727006	0.033724	0.067636	0.79291	0.02737
Processing of petroleum, coking, nuclear fuel	0.10447	0.774527	0.0155	0.092348	0.784275	0.005467
Manufacture of raw chemical materials, chemical products	0.067949	0.790304	0.033636	0.065466	0.792625	0.036906
Manufacture of medicines	0.086851	0.762153	0.070223	0.0884	0.763997	0.079882
Manufacture of chemical fibers	0.053973	0.892586	0.035822	0.065075	0.906072	0.018944
Manufacture of Rubber	0.092509	0.718883	0.057499	0.077012	0.723723	0.06136
Manufacture of Plastics	0.126058	0.697807	0.038696	0.106281	0.696002	0.054243
Manufacture of non-metallic mineral products	0.050259	0.814683	0.03636	0.043229	0.821056	0.042961
Smelting and pressing of non-ferrous metals	0.041025	0.862236	0.029997	0.041844	0.863016	0.033199
Smelting and pressing of metals	0.10535	0.750012	0.013021	0.110405	0.73531	0.007556
Manufacture of metal products	0.115651	0.683249	0.051367	0.10836	0.6673	0.055312
Manufacture of special purpose machinery	0.075696	0.786973	0.046593	0.072163	0.806896	0.052035
Manufacture of transport equipment	0.09118	0.792991	0.066821	0.082191	0.814969	0.070575
Manufacture of electrical machinery and equipment	0.106034	0.774765	0.046943	0.086655	0.796434	0.051404
Manufacture of communication, computers and other electronic equipment	0.207143	0.70811	0.046657	0.159348	0.729829	0.042883
Manufacture of measuring instruments, machinery for cultural activity, office work	0.135264	0.726912	0.042837	0.089397	0.764966	0.052725
Manufacture of artwork and other manufacturing	0.072451	0.778526	0.034818	0.056781	0.804089	0.035706
Total: Across all sectors	0.085971	0.773345	0.043454	0.071651	0.789283	0.047174

PART 3
Foreign Direct Investment and Offshoring

Chapter 10

U.S. Multinational Activity Abroad and U.S. Jobs: Substitutes or Complements?[†]

ANN E. HARRISON, MARGARET S. MCMILLAN,
and CLAIR NULL*

Critics of globalization claim that firms are being driven by the prospects of cheaper labor and lower labor standards to shift employment abroad. Yet the evidence, beyond anecdotes, is slim. This paper reports stylized facts on the activities of U.S. multinationals at home and abroad for the years 1977 to 1999. We focus on firms in manufacturing and services, two sectors that have received extensive media attention for supposedly exporting jobs. Using firm-level data collected by the Bureau of Economic Analysis (BEA) in Washington, D.C., we report correlations between U.S. multinational employment at home and abroad. Preliminary evidence based on the operations of these multinationals suggests that the sign of the correlation depends on the crucial distinction between affiliates in high-income and low-income countries. For affiliates in high-income countries there is a positive correlation between jobs at home and abroad, suggesting that foreign employment of U.S. multinationals is complementary to domestic employment. For firms that operate in developing countries, employment has been cut in the United States, and affiliate employment has increased. To account for firm size, substitution across firms and entry and exit, we aggregate our data to the industry level. This exercise reveals that the observed "complementarity" between U.S. and foreign jobs has been driven largely by a contraction across all manufacturing sectors. It also reveals that foreign employment in developing countries has substituted for U.S. employment

* The authors' affiliations are, respectively, University of California, Berkeley, California; Department of Economics, Tufts University, Medford Massachusetts; NBER, University of California, Berkeley, California. E-mails: *harrison@are.berkeley.edu*; *mmcmilla@tufts.edu*; *claire@are.berkeley.edu*. For assistance with data, the authors would like to thank Raymond Mataloni, Joan Hamory, Fritz Foley, and Stanley Watt. For helpful comments, we wish to thank David Card and the fellows at the Radcliffe Institute for Advanced Study, especially Larry Katz. For financial assistance, the authors gratefully acknowledge the National Science Foundation. McMillan acknowledges the Radcliffe Institute for Advanced Study for both financial support and time to devote to this project. Views expressed in this paper are those of the authors and do not necessarily reflect those of the Bureau of Economic Analysis. The statistical analysis of firm-level data on U.S. multinational companies was conducted at the International Investment Division, Bureau of Economic Analysis, and the U.S. Department of Commerce under arrangements that maintain legal confidentiality requirements. The views expressed in this paper are those of the authors and do not reflect official positions of the U.S. Department of Commerce.

347

[†]This article originally appeared in *Industrial Relations*, **46** 347–365 © 2007 John Wiley & Sons, Inc. Publishers.

348 / Ann E. Harrison, Margaret S. McMillan, and Clair Null

in several highly visible industries, including computers, electronics, and transportation. The fact that there were U.S. jobs lost to foreign affiliates in key sectors, despite broad complementarity in hiring and firing decisions between U.S. parents and their affiliates, helps explain why economists view the impact of globalization on U.S. jobs as benign despite negative news coverage for declining industries.

Introduction

Critics of globalization claim that U.S. firms are shutting down factories at home and shifting employment abroad to countries with cheaper labor and lower labor standards. Yet the evidence, beyond anecdotes, is slim. Are U.S. employers really shifting employment abroad, expanding affiliate employment at the cost to U.S. manufacturing employment? The limited evidence on this question is inconclusive. Working papers by Brainard and Riker (1997) and by Riker and Brainard (1997) found that jobs abroad do substitute for jobs at home but the effect is small. They also found that employment in developing countries by U.S. firms is very sensitive to the cost of labor. A more recent working paper by Desai, Foley, and Hines (2005) found the opposite—an increase in the number of jobs abroad is associated with an increase in the number of jobs at home. Amiti and Wei (2005) also found evidence to support the notion that U.S. multinationals treat U.S. and foreign labor as complementary: When a U.S. multinational firm expands employment abroad, employment at home also increases. In a now infamous press release for the Economic Report of the President (2004), Greg Mankiw pointed out that U.S. outsourcing is good for the U.S. economy.

Despite the rosy expectations of most of these academic economists, union leaders and journalists are less optimistic. The newspapers are filled with anecdotes of plants closing operations in the United States to relocate operations abroad. While most of these stories emphasized the manufacturing sector in the past, interest has recently shifted to services. Stories about textile and garment factories closing in Texas and elsewhere have been replaced by fears of U.S. programming jobs being lost to highly skilled Indians in Bangalore. In France, fears of lost jobs were one factor that recently motivated voters to reject a proposal for the European constitution.

There is no question that the share of jobs and investment by U.S.-based multinationals is increasingly located overseas (see Tables 1 and 2). Anecdotal evidence also suggests that the relocation of jobs overseas is not just confined to low-skill labor. For example, in a recent survey of firms in the computer industry, researchers found that the second most important

TABLE 1

TRENDS OF U.S. MULTINATIONALS IN MANUFACTURING 1977–1999

Variable	1977	1982	1989	1994	1999	% change 1977–1999	% change 1982–1999
Number of parents	1746	1154	1211	1199	878	−98.86	−31.44
Number of countries in which parents have affiliates	21.19	20.61	20.35	21.54	19.78	−7.14	−4.17
Developed countries	12.25	12.54	13.47	13.41	11.33	−8.13	−10.70
Developing countries	8.80	7.98	6.81	8.09	8.45	−4.11	5.63
Affiliate share of jobs (%)	28.33	26.57	31.43	33.91	35.62	20.46	25.40
Developed country affiliate share of jobs (%)	20.09	18.43	21.59	22.78	20.98	4.24	12.14
Developing country affiliate share of jobs (%)	8.22	8.11	9.84	11.08	14.64	43.88	44.62
Affiliate share of compensation (%)	18.97	17.56	22.96	25.61	24.17	21.52	27.36
Developed country affiliate share of compensation (%)	16.35	14.44	20.15	21.95	19.27	15.16	25.09
Developing country affiliate share of compensation (%)	2.59	3.09	2.80	3.63	4.89	47.05	36.80
Affiliate share of total investment (%)	25.99	23.29	25.14	29.08	29.10	10.66	19.96
Developed country affiliate share of investment (%)	20.12	17.29	20.95	23.72	20.88	3.63	17.21
Developing country affiliate share of investment (%)	5.67	5.80	4.17	5.33	8.22	30.97	29.36
Parents							
Total employment	11,017	9771	9137	6893	7181	−53.42	−36.07
Real total compensation (per worker)	31.34	31.82	33.25	36.67	37.87	17.24	15.97
Labor's share	0.96	0.91	0.84	0.86	0.79	−21.54	−15.03
Developed country affiliates: all							
Total employment	3089	2753	2876	2376	2531	−22.05	−8.78
Real total compensation (per worker)	21	21	27	31	27	20.32	20.05
Labor's share	0.61	0.59	0.57	0.57	0.30	−101.76	−95.15
Developing country affiliates: all							
Total employment	1263	1079	1311	1156	1766	28.48	38.91
Real total compensation (per worker)	11	10	9	9	8	−38.25	−19.93
Labor's share (%)	1.09	1.18	0.61	0.60	0.67	−62.86	−76.96

NOTE: Data are for manufacturing parents and their manufacturing affiliates with nonmissing observations for labor's share of income, positive employment, and nonzero production employment. Multiple affiliates in one country are treated as one affiliate. Weighted by employment shares, where applicable. Real wages, real benefits, and real total compensation are in '000 of 1982–1984 U.S. dollars; real net income and real total assets are in '000,000 of 1982–1984 U.S. dollars. Employment figures are in '000. Return on capital is net income over total assets. Variability in countries of affiliates is defined as the total number of countries in which the parent added or dropped an affiliate between the previous benchmark survey and the present one.
SOURCE: BEA.

350 / ANN E. HARRISON, MARGARET S. MCMILLAN, AND CLAIR NULL

TABLE 2

TRENDS OF U.S. MULTINATIONALS IN SERVICES 1977–1999

Variable	1977	1982	1989	1994	1999	% change 1977–1999	% change 1982–1999
Number of parents	58	76	112	133	242	317.24	218.42
Number of countries in which parents have affiliates	6.74	4.12	4.92	6.97	11.62	72.31	182.10
Developed countries	5.19	3.10	4.27	5.64	7.61	46.66	145.72
Developing countries	1.56	1.02	0.65	1.33	3.94	153.04	284.93
Affiliate share of jobs (%)	15.43	9.21	16.93	19.13	25.09	62.59	172.39
Developed country affiliate share of jobs (%)	11.67	7.09	15.36	16.22	19.41	66.30	173.65
Developing country affiliate share of jobs (%)	3.76	2.12	1.57	2.91	5.67	50.86	167.86
Affiliate share of compensation (%)	13.41	7.25	14.99	17.30	21.75	62.20	200.04
Developed country affiliate share of compensation (%)	11.20	6.06	14.45	16.38	19.29	72.23	218.23
Developing country affiliate share of compensation (%)	2.21	1.19	0.54	0.92	2.46	11.26	107.00
Affiliate share of total investment (%)	13.97	6.76	17.65	21.60	23.17	65.93	242.99
Developed country affiliate share of investment (%)	11.88	5.79	17.06	20.15	19.47	63.86	236.02
Developing country affiliate share of investment (%)	2.09	0.96	0.59	1.45	3.70	77.35	284.04
Parents							
Total employment	532	867	1377	1658	4795	801.93	453.30
Real wages (per worker)	16.79	15.94	17.71	17.03	20.78	23.74	30.36
Labor's share (%)	91.46	88.00	85.70	90.68	81.24	−11.17	−7.68
Developed country affiliates: all							
Total employment	73	68	255	333	1243	1593.31	1734.97
Real wages (per worker)	13.28	15.05	13.88	14.45	13.86	4.37	−7.91
Labor's share (%)	75.93	45.66	82.20	72.93	75.48	−0.60	65.30
Developing country affiliates: all							
Total employment	24	20	26	60	363	1436.03	1696.20
Real wages (per worker)	7.43	9.03	5.38	4.69	4.45	−40.11	−50.72
Labor's share (%)	88.58	94.40	84.72	90.09	84.79	−4.28	−10.17

NOTE: Data are for parents and affiliates with nonmissing observations for labor's share of income and positive employment. Multiple affiliates in one country are treated as one affiliate. Excluding firms in the top and bottom 1 percent on the basis of labor shares and return to capital. Weighted by employment shares, where applicable. Real wages are in '000 of 1982–1984 U.S. dollars. Employment figures are in '000.
SOURCE: BEA.

determinant of an overseas production site was the availability and cost of skilled labor.[1] In July, 2003, the *New York Times* reported that IBM is thinking of accelerating the relocation of white-collar, high-paying jobs to China, India, the Philippines, Russia, and other countries.[2] In January 2004, the *Wall*

---

[1] See McMillan, Pandolfi, and Salinger (1999).

U.S. Multinationals and U.S. Jobs / 351

Street Journal reported that IBM expects to save $168 million dollars annually by shifting several thousand high-paying programming jobs overseas.[3]

In this paper, we use simple stylized facts to show that the degree of "complementarity" between U.S. and foreign labor depends on (1) the location of foreign affiliates and (2) the level of aggregation of the data. By doing this, we are able to reconcile the arguments for "complementarity" between economic activity at home and abroad with anecdotal evidence in the popular press of factory closings and downward pressure on wages. Our data are firm-level data collected by the Bureau of Economic Analysis (BEA) in Washington, D.C. on employment, wages, net income and investment. These firms accounted for approximately 60 percent of U.S. sales and employment in manufacturing, 70 percent of exports, and 80 percent of private R&D in manufacturing during the 1980s and 1990s (Mataloni and Fahim-Nader 1996). We focus primarily on trends in employment at home and abroad, separating employment in low-income countries and employment in other industrialized countries.

We begin by describing the data and documenting the trends in key variables for U.S. multinationals in both manufacturing and services. Between 1977 and 1999, multinational manufacturing firms shed more than three million jobs in the United States. Affiliates in high-income countries shed around half a million jobs while the number of jobs in affiliates in low-income countries expanded by between half (1977–1999) and three quarters of a million (1982–1999). Real wages increased in U.S.-based multinationals and in high-income country affiliates while they fell in low-income affiliates. In all three locations, labor's share of income fell, suggesting that wage increases failed to compensate for aggregate job losses (see Table 1).

We then report correlations between employment at home and abroad at the firm level. At the firm level, employment expansions and contractions in U.S. multinational parents and their affiliates on average move in the same direction. This positive correlation between jobs at home and abroad suggests that foreign employment for U.S. multinationals is complementary to domestic employment. However, these averages mask significant heterogeneity across different kinds of enterprises. For parents that hire workers in developing countries—roughly half the sample—the story is different. For these firms, there is substitution between employment at home and employment abroad. This evidence highlights the importance of differentiating between jobs in low-income countries and jobs in other industrialized

---

[2] Steven Greenhouse, "IBM Explores Shift of Some Jobs Overseas," Business/Financial Desk, Section C, Page 1. *New York Times*, 7/23/03.

[3] *Wall Street Journal*, 1/19/04.

352 / ANN E. HARRISON, MARGARET S. MCMILLAN, AND CLAIR NULL

countries. It is consistent with the notion that some firms do relocate activity abroad to reduce their total wage bill. Our evidence also suggests that while some jobs have been "exported abroad," this is only part of the explanation for the sharp contraction in parent employment. While three million jobs were lost in the United States, the net increase in jobs in developing countries was at most three quarters of a million, suggesting a general trend in all parts of the globe toward substituting capital for labor.

We then examine broad correlations between employment at home and abroad by aggregating the firm-level data to the industry level. This exercise is important because U.S. firms could respond to global opportunities in ways other than through substituting employment in the United States for affiliate employment elsewhere. If U.S. firms simply close down operations, then employment at home could be replaced by employment abroad through substitution across firms. In other words, substitution can occur both *within* the same firm and *between* firms as some firms exit and their activity is taken over by affiliates of other U.S. firms. This second kind of substitution is likely to be overlooked if researchers focus purely on within firm effects. Both Brainard and Riker (1997), Riker and Brainard (1997), and Desai, Foley and Hines (2005) restricted their analysis to within firm changes, which misses this possible reallocation of employment—from the United States to foreign affiliates—across firms within a sector. This kind of substitution can—at least partially—be captured by studying employment patterns at the industry level. Studying employment patterns at the industry level has the additional advantages of capturing patterns in the data as a result of entry and exit or heterogeneity due to firm size.

Our preliminary analysis suggests that some substitution did occur at the industry level. Some parents reduced employment in the United States, while other U.S. parents in the same sector increased employment abroad through the establishment and expansion of their affiliates.[4] While there is broad complementarity between U.S. and foreign jobs for many sectors, foreign employment in developing countries has replaced U.S. employment in several highly visible industries, including computers, electronics, and transportation. Moreover, the "complementarity" that does exist has, in most cases, been driven by a contraction in manufacturing employment both in the United States and abroad. The fact that there were U.S. jobs lost to foreign affiliates in key sectors, while at the same time there was broad complementarity in hiring (and firing) across parents and affiliates,

---

[4] At this stage, we have only looked at these relationships within the broad headings of manufacturing and services. This leaves open the possibility that when we aggregate the two, we find broad complementarity.

helps explain why economists are painting a rosy picture of globalization's impact on U.S. labor and at the same time there is negative news coverage for declining industries.

This research is part of a larger research agenda among international and labor economists that aims to identify how globalization is affecting the jobs and lives of American workers. Many researchers who examine the links between globalization and labor markets conclude that much of the increase in inequality and falling unskilled worker wages is due to skill-biased technical change. It is frequently difficult to disentangle technical change from the effects of globalization. Related work includes research by Slaughter (2000, 2001), Rodrik (1997), and Richardson and Khripounova (1998). These authors argued that globalization is affecting labor by increasing the elasticity of labor demand. However, Slaughter's (2001) study shows that the rising elasticity of demand for unskilled labor cannot be easily linked to different measures of globalization. Budd and Slaughter (2000) showed that union wage determination in Canada is affected by changing profits in both Canada and in the United States. Their work suggests that globalization does affect union wages, although they do not test for the impact on labor shares or for the impact on non-unionized workers. Rob Feenstra and Gordon Hanson have done a number of studies analyzing the effect of outsourcing on labor market outcomes; their work is reviewed in Feenstra and Hanson (2003).

We begin by outlining broad trends in employment and wages for U.S. parent companies and their affiliates in developed and developing countries. We report these trends separately for manufacturing and services. The results document the large fall in manufacturing employment at home, and increasing affiliate employment in developing countries. The results also point to large increases in activities of U.S. multinationals in services, with expanding employment both at home and abroad. In "Employment at Home and Abroad," we report the correlations between hiring and firing at home and abroad for U.S. multinationals. We then turn to the industry-level patterns, showing the relationship between employment at home and abroad for both manufacturing and services. The concluding comments point to directions for further research.

Broad Trends in U.S. Multinational Activity: The BEA Data

We analyzed the firm-level surveys on U.S. direct investment abroad, collected each year by BEA of the U.S. Department of Commerce. BEA collects confidential data on the activities of U.S.-based multinationals

354 /   Ann E. Harrison, Margaret S. McMillan, and Clair Null

defined as the combination of a single U.S. entity that has made the direct investment, called the parent, and at least one foreign business enterprise called the foreign affiliate. We use the data collected on majority-owned nonbank foreign affiliates and nonbank U.S. parents for the benchmark years between 1977 and 1999. The benchmark years are 1977, 1982, 1989, 1994, and 1999 and include more comprehensive information than the annual surveys. To our knowledge, very little work has been done with the firm-level data using the entire length of the time series from 1977 through 1999.

Creating a panel using the benchmark years of the BEA survey data is a nontrivial task. First, not all firms are required to report to the BEA, and reporting requirements vary across years. Second, because we are interested in understanding what is happening at the industry level, we must consider the implications of the changes to the Standard Industrial Classification (SIC) codes in 1972 and 1987 and the switch from SIC codes to the North American Industrial Classification System (NAICS) codes in 1997. Third, because the BEA parent identification codes changed between 1977 and 1982, we had to create a bridge linking the 1977 parents to the 1982 parents.[5] and finally, the fact that parents are allowed to consolidate information for several affiliates in one country on a single form calls for special care in the aggregation and interpretation of affiliate level data.

All foreign affiliates with sales, assets, or net income in excess of a certain amount in absolute value must report to the BEA. This amount was $.5 million dollars in 1977, $3 million dollars in 1982, 1989, and 1994, and jumped to $7 million dollars in 1999. In addition, a new reporting requirement was imposed on parents in 1999. Parents whose sales, assets, or net income exceeded $100 million (in absolute value) were required to provide more extensive information than parents whose sales, assets, or net income fell below $100 million.[6] To determine whether the changes in reporting requirements biased our sample toward small firms in the early years, we imposed a double filter on the data using the uniform cutoff for affiliates of $5.59 million 1982 U.S. dollars and $79.87 1982 U.S. dollars for parents. As it turns out, the reporting requirements were large enough that imposing the filter on the data makes little difference. Therefore, we used all of the available data.

To document what has happened within industries in manufacturing over time, we created a concordance that allows us to assign SIC codes to the

---

[5] Prior to our arrival, a bridge had been created but it was incomplete, linking only around 25 percent of the parents from 1977 to parents in 1982. With our bridge based on employee identification numbers, we were able to link more than 50 percent of the parents from 1977 to parents in 1982.

[6] Parents who do not meet this cutoff but who have affiliates that meet the $7 million cutoff are still required to provide extensive information for affiliates.

North American Industry Classification System (NAICS) codes. This was necessary because in 1999, the BEA collected data on NAICS codes and not SIC codes. We chose to convert SIC codes to NAICS codes on the grounds that the NAICS codes more accurately describe production processes. The 1977 and 1982 benchmark years are based on the 1972 SIC codes. The 1989 and 1994 benchmark years are based on the 1987 SIC codes. The 1999 benchmark data are based on the 1997 NAICS codes. In addition to the fact that the industry codes are not directly comparable across all benchmark years, the BEA industry codes have been slightly modified to reflect that fact the these are enterprise data and are called respectively SIC-ISI and NAICS-ISI. Working with these codes, we created a program (available upon request) that assigns the SIC-ISI codes for the years 1977–1994 to NAICS-ISI codes.

Linking parents from 1977 to the remaining benchmark years proved relatively straightforward. This is because in addition to a parent identification code created by the BEA (which changed between 1977 and 1982), each parent has an employee identification number (EIN) assigned to it by the Internal Revenue Service, which did not change during the period 1977–1999. Using the EIN number plus the country in which the affiliate operates, we are also able to track parent/affiliate pairs over time.

While the number of U.S. parents included in the BEA sample may appear small (see Table 1), these enterprises accounted for the majority of economic activity in U.S. manufacturing during the entire sample period. Between 1982 and 1999, sales by these enterprises accounted for approximately 60 percent of total manufacturing sales in the United States.[7] In 1994, these enterprises accounted for 66 percent of all exports of goods, and nearly 60 percent of employment in manufacturing. These enterprises also account for most of U.S. research and development expenditures: in 1994, the U.S. parents included in the BEA sample accounted for 82 percent of total U.S. research and development expenditures.

The variables we use are reported to the BEA on the basis of the fiscal year. General trends in employment weighted averages are reported in Table 1 for manufacturing and in Table 2 for services. The numbers in Table 2 include all firms classified in services under the SIC classification prior to 1997 and under the NAICS system post-1997. Because the NAICS system classifies some industries as services that were not previously classified as services, the employment numbers are slightly exaggerated. However, when we restrict our analysis of services to only those subcategories that can be exactly matched across years, we get nearly identical trends.

---

[7] See Mataloni and Fahim-Nader. (1996), pgs 11–32 and my own calculations.

356 / Ann E. Harrison, Margaret S. McMillan, and Clair Null

Table 1 shows that between 1977 and 1999, multinational manufacturing firms shed more than three million jobs in the United States.[8,9] In addition, Table 1 also documents that labor's share of income in the United States has fallen from 90 percent to 75 percent. The loss of jobs in the United States has been mirrored by job reductions in affiliates in developed countries. In developed country affiliates, employment fell by roughly half a million. Labor's share and wages in the developed countries follow the U.S. labor share and wages, although in the developed country affiliates, labor's share is substantially lower as are real wages. These job losses have been only partially offset by an increase in the number of jobs in developing countries, where the number of jobs increased by half a million between 1977 and 1999 and by three quarters of a million between 1982 and 1999. In developing countries, labor's share also fell. Unlike in the developed countries, real wages paid by U.S.-based multinationals to employees in their developing country affiliates has actually fallen. The evidence for the U.S. parents is in line with the aggregate trends in the U.S. manufacturing sector. According to the NBER Manufacturing Productivity Database, labor's share in value-added declined from 0.53 to 0.31—roughly 50 percent—over the period 1958 to 1996. Over the period of time for which the two data sets overlap, real wages, employment, and labor's share in income all move in the same direction—down.

There has been a substantial shift in activity from developed to developing country affiliates. Affiliate employment as a share of total employment globally for U.S. multinationals increased from 28 percent in 1977 to 35 percent in 1999. The increase was almost entirely driven by a doubling of affiliate employment shares in developing countries, from 8 percent to 15 percent. Affiliate employment in developed countries, as a share of total worldwide employment, remained roughly constant over the entire period at around 20 percent. Total affiliate share of employment, employee compensation, and investment in the firms' total has increased by 26, 27, and 12 percent, respectively. This increase in overseas activity has been largely reserved for developing countries where the respective increases are 78, 89, and 45 percent, respectively.

The increase in developing country activity has been accompanied by a reduction in labor's share at the parent level of 18 percent. Labor's share

---

[8] Our sample consists of all parents that were ever classified in manufacturing and their manufacturing affiliates.

[9] Our numbers differ from numbers published by the BEA for several reasons. Our data do not include estimated data, our variables are weighted by parent employment when applicable and our sample takes into account the fact that some manufacturing firms have been reclassified under wholesale trade.

has also fallen overseas by around 27 percent in developed country affiliates and 39 percent in developing country affiliates. Although part of the reduction in labor's share in the parent and in developed country affiliates is driven by reductions in employment, the reduction in labor's share in developing countries is not: employment in developing country affiliates increased by 46 percent. Though not shown in the table, our data indicate that there was a 120 percent increase in the number of nonproduction workers hired in developing countries.

The contraction in domestic jobs in the manufacturing sector has been more than offset by job creation in the services sector. Table 2 shows that between 1977 and 1999, employment by U.S. parents increased by more than four million or 802 percent. Expansion at home has been more than matched by expansion abroad. In developed country affiliates, employment increased from 73,000 in 1977 to 1.2 million in 1999 and in developing country affiliates, employment went from 24,000 in 1977 to 363,000 in 1999. While the share of affiliate activity still counts for less than the share of affiliate activity in manufacturing, it has grown much more rapidly in services than in manufacturing. Affiliate share of employment, employee compensation, and investment in the firms' total has risen by 63, 62, and 66 percent, respectively. Except for affiliate share of compensation, this increase in overseas activity has been fairly evenly spread between developed and developing country affiliates. This increase in developing country activity has been accompanied by a reduction in labor's share at the parent level of 11 percent. Unlike in manufacturing, labor's share overseas has remained relatively constant.

Tables 1 and 2 suggest that job losses in the manufacturing sector may have been offset by employment increases in the service sector. However, it is important to keep in mind that throughout the period 1977–1999, real compensation per worker in the service sector amounts to little more than half of real compensation per worker in the manufacturing sector. This may be partly a reflection of the change in the mix of workers in the U.S. manufacturing sector—if unskilled U.S. workers have been replaced by unskilled foreign workers, then the average wage in the U.S. manufacturing sector reflects the wages of skilled workers. However, the fact that this differential existed even in 1977 before the big contraction in U.S. manufacturing suggests that this is not the only reason for the difference. Since data on the composition of employment for U.S. parents is less detailed than the information on the skill mix of foreign affiliates, it is difficult to reach any strong conclusions on this point. What Tables 1 and 2 do show is that employment in manufacturing has shifted to services, and that average compensation in services was well below compensation in manufacturing even at the start of the sample period.

358 / Ann E. Harrison, Margaret S. McMillan, and Clair Null

FIGURE 1

All Affiliates

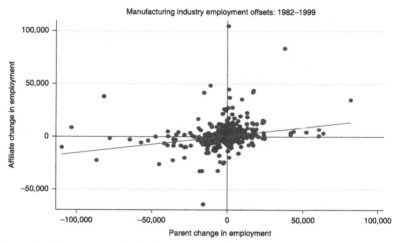

SOURCE: Author's calculations based on BEA's outward FDI data.

Employment at Home and Abroad

This section discusses broad trends in the pattern of employment changes in U.S. parents and their affiliates. We restrict our analysis to the period 1982 to 1999 for comparability with the work by Brainard and Riker (1997); Riker and Brainard (1997); and Desai, Foley, and Hines (2005) who used these same data beginning in 1982.[10] We begin by reporting activities within the same enterprise over time. To test whether U.S. parents are substituting U.S. employment with affiliate employment, we created a series of employment offsets at the firm level. Figures 1 through 3 track the same parent and its affiliates over time, documenting the extent of hiring and firing within the same parent and its affiliates.[11] We begin with all affiliates and all parents for the entire period 1982 through 1999 and then separate the sample

---

[10] If we extend the period to 1977 and redo the results for 1977 to 1999, the results look very similar.

[11] We need to be somewhat careful about calling these changes in employment hires and fires as some of the activity might simply reflect acquisitions and spin-offs. However, at least in the aggregate, since most sales of U.S. multinationals are to other U.S. multinationals, the firms would still remain in our database even if they were acquired by another firm. Therefore, it is reasonable to assume that the overall "contraction" in the manufacturing sector represents a loss of U.S. jobs.

to examine employment changes in high- and low-income countries. In all three figures, the horizontal axis represents changes in parent employment between 1982 and 1999 while the vertical axis represents changes in affiliate employment over this same period. Points in the upper right-hand side quadrant and lower left-hand side quadrant represent complementarity: firms expanding (contracting) at home are also expanding (contracting) abroad. Critics of globalization have focused on the upper left-hand side quadrant where a contraction at home corresponds with an expansion abroad.

Figure 1 shows that for all affiliates, employment abroad and employment at home are complementary. Most of the firm activity is on the diagonal quadrants in Figure 1—this is confirmed by the positively sloped regression line. The cluster of points around zero suggests that for the majority of firms, employment changes both at home and abroad have been small.

Figure 2 plots the relationship between employment at home and employment in high-income affiliates. The story is similar to that found in Figure 1 with the complementarity slightly more pronounced. The employment offsets for the U.S. parent and its developing country affiliates shown in Figure 3 are somewhat different, however. In this case, the majority of firms lie in the off-diagonal quadrants as confirmed by the downward sloping regression line. However, the fact that the line is practically flat (albeit downward sloping) suggests that the relationship between employment in developing countries and employment at home may not be that important.

Figures 1 to 3 report trends in employment *within* the same enterprise. However, it is possible that much of the substitution away from U.S. employment toward employment abroad has occurred between enterprises. Some firms may have contracted U.S. employment while other firms expanded affiliate employment. These possibilities cannot be captured by tracking the same enterprise over time. By tracking *within* firm changes in employment, we also miss entry and exit. This is potentially very important because we miss large firms that may have shut down altogether. To the extent that this happens in conjunction with small increases in employment at home and abroad in other firms we would see complementarity in the firm level results and substitution at the industry level.

Finally, the data in Figures 1 through 3 suggest that it is important to distinguish between "small" and "large" firms. The positive correlations between employment at home and abroad could be driven by the small changes that are relatively symmetrically distributed around zero. Since our focus is employment, we would like to give extra weight to the firms that hire relatively more workers. An informal way of doing this is aggregating up to the industry level. The small changes around zero will disappear and we will be left with the net effect of employment changes in the large firms that

360 / Ann E. Harrison, Margaret S. McMillan, and Clair Null

FIGURE 2

High-Income Affiliates

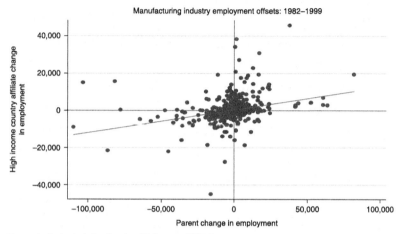

SOURCE: Author's calculations based on BEA's outward FDI data.

FIGURE 3

Middle-/Low-Income Affiliates

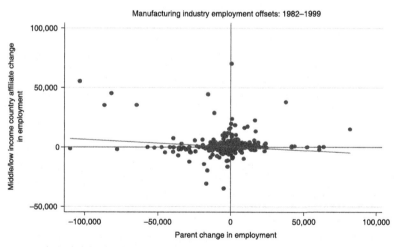

SOURCE: Author's calculations based on BEA's outward FDI data.

FIGURE 4

ALL AFFILIATES

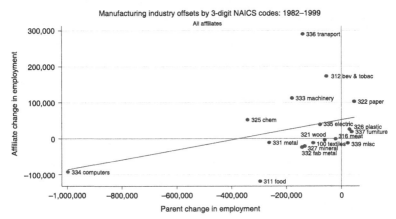

Manufacturing industry offsets by 3-digit NAICS codes: 1982–1999

SOURCE: Author's calculations based on BEA's outward FDI data.

are not so symmetrically distributed around zero. To address all of these possibilities, we turn now to trends in employment at the aggregate industry level.

Figure 4 reports employment offsets at the 3-digit level for the manufacturing sector. Changes in parent (U.S.) total employment are indicated by the horizontal axis and changes in affiliate total employment are indicated by the vertical axis. A point in the upper right-hand quadrant indicates expansion both at home and abroad. A point in the lower left-hand side quadrant indicates contraction at home and abroad. Substitution occurs if data points are either in the upper left-hand quadrant (indicating contraction at home and expansion in affiliate employment) or in the lower right-hand quadrant (indicating expansion at home and contraction abroad). Most U.S. critics of globalization center on supposed activity in the upper left-hand quadrant, which would indicate expansion of affiliate employment and contraction of employment in the United States: the so-called substitution of foreign for U.S. jobs. As Figure 4 shows, most of the activity of U.S. manufacturing multinational enterprises has taken place in the lower left-hand quadrant, indicating employment contraction both at home and abroad.

Figures 5 and 6 separate changes in employment from 1982 to 1999 based on the location of the parent's affiliates. Figure 5 reports employment offsets at the three-digit level for developed country affiliates and parents; Figure 6 reports the same trends for developing country affiliates. The

362 / ANN E. HARRISON, MARGARET S. MCMILLAN, AND CLAIR NULL

FIGURE 5

HIGH-INCOME AFFILIATES

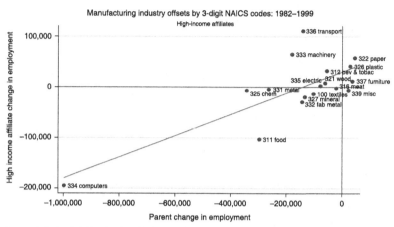

Manufacturing industry offsets by 3-digit NAICS codes: 1982–1999

SOURCE: Author's calculations based on BEA's outward FDI data.

trends are similar across Figures 4 and 5—employment in high-income affiliates and parent employment are complementary but that relationship is driven by the contraction in manufacturing. However, Figure 6 reveals that employment in low-income affiliates substitutes for employment in the United States. Moreover, the downward sloping regression line appears to be driven by contraction in two key sectors: computers and electronics.

Why are the firm and industry offsets so different? We mentioned three possibilities that deserve further elaboration: entry and exit, firm size, and across-firm substitution. Roughly one quarter of the job losses in our sample are due to firm "deaths" and not a sale or acquisition. Entrants account for a relatively small number of jobs. We do not pick these firms up when we do the within-firm analysis. Additionally, small firms (with less than fifteen thousand employees) account for 75 percent of the firms in our sample but only 24 percent of total employment. Small firms tend to have affiliates only in high-income countries while large firms tend to have affiliates in both high- and low-income countries. Since small firms are more numerous, they cloud somewhat the story in the within-firm offsets.

While the stylized facts reported in this paper are useful for explaining why opinions on the outsourcing of U.S. jobs are so different, these facts don't tell us enough about the underlying mechanisms at work. The fact that substitution occurs only between U.S. jobs and jobs in low-wage

U.S. Multinationals and U.S. Jobs / 363

FIGURE 6

MEDIUM-/LOW-INCOME AFFILIATES

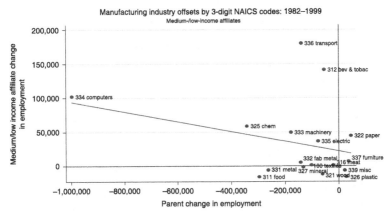

Manufacturing industry offsets by 3-digit NAICS codes: 1982–1999

Medium-/low-income affiliates

SOURCE: Author's calculations based on BEA's outward FDI data.

countries suggests that labor costs are important. An alternative explanation could be based on differential demand shocks. Individuals in countries at the low end of the income distribution may exhibit different preferences than those in high-income countries and/or U.S. multinationals may be better at marketing their products abroad than at home. Yet the explanation for substitution of U.S. jobs most popular in the U.S. press is a story about labor costs: labor is relatively cheaper in developing countries, therefore profit-seeking U.S. multinationals fire expensive U.S. workers and hire workers in low-income countries. To properly identify the causal mechanisms at work, we are developing a conceptual framework that incorporates both of these possibilities.

Finally, we wish to emphasize the aggregate employment shift toward services. We saw in Tables 1 and 2 that the contraction in manufacturing employment by U.S. parents was largely offset by increasing service sector employment. One recent concern is that the kind of employment substitution we observe between some developing country affiliates and the U.S. parent is now occurring in the service sector as well. Though not reported here, our data indicate that—at least for the period 1977 to 1999—this was not the case. Unlike the employment offsets for manufacturing, where nearly all the data points are in the lower left-hand side quadrant (indicating contraction at home and abroad), the offsets indicate that in services,[12]

364 / Ann E. Harrison, Margaret S. McMillan, and Clair Null

all the activity is in the upper right-hand side quadrant. Although the recent concerns regarding offshoring or outsourcing of service sector employment may be valid, the aggregate trends for the period between 1977 and 1999 in the BEA services data do not support such claims.

Concluding Comments

This paper outlines broad trends in U.S. multinational employment at home and abroad. Over the period 1977 to 1999, multinational manufacturing firms have shed more than three million jobs in the United States. During this period, labor's share of income has fallen and real wages have increased. The loss of jobs in the United States has been partially offset by an increase in the number of jobs in developing countries. Even overseas, as the number of jobs has increased, real wages and labor's share of income have declined. These labor market outcomes have been accompanied by a substantial shift in the operations of U.S. multinationals abroad.

We then examine the relationship between employment changes at home and abroad for U.S. multinational firms, presenting evidence on trends in both manufacturing and services. We also report broad trends in employment patterns both at the U.S. parent and at its affiliates. We document that whether employment changes in the U.S. parent and its affiliates tend to move in the same direction depends on whether the jobs abroad are in low-income or high-income countries. Jobs in low-income affiliates are substitutes for U.S. jobs while jobs in high-income affiliates are complementary with U.S. jobs. Thus, the sharp contraction in U.S. manufacturing jobs between 1977 (1982) and 1999 was accompanied by a contraction in jobs in high-income affiliates. While we focused primarily on the manufacturing sector in this paper, we do find evidence that in the service sector there has been job expansion both for the U.S. parents and its foreign affiliates in high- and low-income countries.

The substitution of jobs in low-income countries for jobs in the United States is even stronger at the industry level. One reason is because many of the U.S. enterprises that previously manufactured in the United States are no longer active, indicating that it is necessary to analyze behavior between, rather than within, enterprises. Another reason is because much of the job relocation to developing countries has occurred within large enterprises, and industry-level results give more weight to large enterprises. At the

---

[12] These are not all of the data used in Table 2 but only the data (including business services) that could be exactly matched between SIC and NAICS across years.

industry level, there has been significant job relocation in a number of key areas: computers, electronics, and transportation. At the industry level, employment offsets for the U.S. parent and its developing country affiliates indicate that employment is not complementary: Expansion abroad is accompanied by contraction in the United States.

The kinds of employment shifts documented in this paper are natural in light of the differences in labor costs in the United States and in its developing country affiliates. In addition, the tables and graphs also make clear that employment in manufacturing has been contracting almost everywhere, presumably due to technological change that makes it possible to substitute capital for labor. Our ultimate goal—which is beyond the scope of this paper—is to estimate the extent to which technological change versus global cost pressures can explain aggregate employment contraction and rising capital intensity. It is also important to remember that substitution of foreign jobs for U.S. jobs may have saved some U.S. jobs; some firms were able to stay in business because they were able to substitute foreign for U.S. labor.

REFERENCES

Amiti, Mary, and Shang-Jin Wei. 2005. "International Service Outsourcing, Productivity and Employment: Evidence from the U.S." IMF Working Paper No. WP/05/238.

Brainard, Lael S., and David A. Riker. 1997. "Are U.S. Multinationals Exporting U.S. Jobs?" NBER Working Paper No. 5958.

Budd, John W., and Matthew J. Slaughter. 2000. "Are Profits Shared Across Borders? Evidence on International Rent Sharing." NBER Working Paper No. 8014.

Desai, Mihir A., C. Fritz Foley, and James R. Hines. 2005. "Foreign Direct Investment and Domestic Economic Activity." NBER Working Paper No. 11717.

Economic Report of the President. 2004. Council of Economic Advisors. Washington: United States Printing Office.

Feenstra, Robert C., and Gordon Hanson. 2003. "Global Production Sharing and Rising Inequality: a Survey of Trade and Wages." In *Handbook of International Trade*, Vol. II, Part I, edited by E. Kwan Choi and James Hartigan. Boston, MA: Blackwell Publishing.

Mataloni, Raymond J. Jr., and Mahnaz Fahim-Nader. 1996. "Operations of U.S. Multinational Companies: Preliminary Results from the 1994 Benchmark Survey." *Survey of Current Business, Bureaus of Economic Analysis* 6(12):11–37.

McMillan, Margaret, Selina, Pandolfi, and Lynn Salinger. 1999. "Promoting Labor Intensive Exports in Developing Countries: Evidence from the Textile and Electronics Industries." HIID, LAER Working Paper No. 22.

Richardson, J. David, and Elena B. Khripounova. 1998. "U.S. Labor Market Power and Linkages to International Trade: Identifying Suspects and Measures." Draft for U.S. Department of Labor.

Rodrik, Dani. 1997. "Has Globalization Gone Too Far?" Washington, D.C.: Institute for International Economics.

Riker, David A., and Lael S. Brainard. 1997. "U.S. Multinationals and Competition from Low-Wage Countries." NBER Working Paper No. 5959.

Slaughter, Matthew. 2000. "Production Transfer within Multinational Enterprises and American Wages." *Journal of International Economics* 50(April):449–72.

———. 2001. "International Trade and Labor–Demand Elasticities." *Journal of International Economics* 54(June):27–56.

Chapter 11

OFFSHORING JOBS? MULTINATIONALS AND U.S. MANUFACTURING EMPLOYMENT[†]

Ann Harrison and Margaret McMillan*

Abstract—Using firm-level data collected by the U.S. Bureau of Economic Analysis, we estimate the impact on U.S. manufacturing employment of changes in foreign affiliate wages. We show that the motive for offshoring and, consequently, the location of offshore activity, significantly affects the impact of offshoring on parent employment. In general, offshoring to low-wage countries substitutes for domestic employment. However, for firms that do significantly different tasks at home and abroad, foreign and domestic employment are complements. These offsetting effects may be combined to show that offshoring by U.S.-based multinationals is associated with a quantitatively small decline in manufacturing employment.

I. Introduction

DURING the past three decades, domestic manufacturing employment of U.S.-based multinationals has fallen steadily (table 1). Between 1982 and 1999, affiliate foreign employment as a share of total employment by U.S. multinationals increased, climbing from 30% to nearly 44% of their labor force. These parallel developments have led critics of globalization to conclude that U.S. firms are cutting employment at home and shifting employment abroad. Concerns about offshoring have intensified as newly released data indicate a further decline in manufacturing employment by both U.S.-based multinationals and for the U.S. economy as a whole.

Why are the employment consequences of offshoring so important? After all, most trade models predict that the factor reallocations resulting from globalization are associated with net gains in aggregate welfare. First, there are likely to be short-run costs of adjustment as workers may not quickly leave one type of employment for another. These types of costs have been formalized in trade models where factors are specific to the production of certain types of goods. To the extent that unskilled workers are more likely to suffer transitional losses, these are important distributional consequences and need to be carefully identified and understood.

Received for publication September 23, 2008. Revision accepted for publication January 28, 2010.
* Harrison: University of California, UC Berkeley, and NBER; McMillan: Tufts University and NBER.
For assistance with data, we thank Raymond Mataloni, Fritz Foley, and Stanley Watt. For helpful comments, we thank David Card, the fellows at the Radcliffe Institute for Advanced Study, Larry Katz, Francis Kramarz, seminar participants at the BEA, Columbia University, the University of Michigan, Stanford, UC Berkeley, Yale University, the IMF, the Paris School of Economics, the University of Maryland, Pierluigi Balduzzi, and two anonymous referees. For financial assistance, we gratefully acknowledge the National Science Foundation. M.M. acknowledges the Radcliffe Institute for Advanced Study for both financial support and time to devote to this project. The statistical analysis of firm-level data on U.S. multinational companies was conducted at the International Investment Division, Bureau of Economic Analysis of the U.S. Department of Commerce under arrangements that maintain legal confidentiality requirements. The views expressed in this paper are our own and do not reflect official positions of the U.S. Department of Commerce. We gratefully acknowledge research assistance from Joan Hamory, Clair Null, and Andrew Waxman.

Second, these short-run costs could lead to an erosion of support for free trade, as discussed by the chair of the Federal Reserve (Bernanke, 2006). And finally, understanding the magnitude of these changes is important for the design of social safety nets. For example, on October 22, 2004, the U.S. Congress passed the American Jobs Creation Act of 2004. The act contains a provision to encourage profit repatriation back to the United States by multinationals—explicitly for the purpose of job creation at home. Yet the evidence linking offshore activities to falling domestic labor demand is in fact unclear. Bernanke (2006) emphasizes the need to identify losers and compensate them for the costs of increasing competition as a way to ensure that support for free trade continues.

In this paper, we use a standard labor demand equation to identify the effect of offshoring on home employment. We allow different degrees of substitution (or complementarity) depending on the motive for offshoring and whether offshoring takes place in high- or low-income affiliate locations. We differentiate between the motives for offshoring using the following measures of vertical integration between parents and their affiliates: imports from foreign affiliates, exports for further processing, exports for resale, and export platform offshoring. At the same time, we control for other confounding changes, such as other factor price changes, demand shocks, and technological change. To address the possibility that methodological differences might be driving the conflicting results described above, we also estimate wage elasticities using a translog specification and a constant elasticity of substitution specification.

We find that the insights derived from trade theory go a long way toward explaining the apparently contradictory evidence on the relationship between offshoring and domestic manufacturing employment. Before controlling for the degree of vertical integration, we find that affiliate employment in low-income countries substitutes for domestic employment: a 10 percentage point reduction in wages in low-income countries is associated with a 1% reduction in U.S. parent employment. However, for parents that export significant amounts of goods to low-income countries for further processing, foreign wage reductions are associated with an increase in domestic employment. Conversely, for parents that export significant amounts of goods to high-income countries for further processing, foreign wage reductions are associated with decreases in parent employment. Using data on affiliate employment composition in the computers and electronics sector, the sector with the highest share of exports for further processing, we show that the results differ across high- and low-income affiliate locations, in part because the tasks performed in these locations are very different. Tasks performed by affiliates in

---

[†]This article originally appeared in *The Review of Economics and Statistics*, **93** 857–875 © 2011 Massachusetts Institute of Technology Press.

256

Globalization, Firms, and Workers

858 THE REVIEW OF ECONOMICS AND STATISTICS

TABLE 1.—EMPLOYMENT BY U.S. MULTINATIONALS, 1982–1999

	1982	1989	1994	1999
Parent employment				
BEA manufacturing[a]	11,758	10,706	9,622	7,954
Our sample[b]	10,689	9,668	9,104	7,564
Affiliates				
Employment in high-income countries	2,595	3,171	3,048	2,903
Employment share of total in high-income countries	18%	22%	22%	24%
Employment in low-income countries	1,064	1,405	1,584	1,868
Employment share in low income countries	7%	10%	12%	15%
Total affiliate employment	3,659	4,576	4,632	4,772
Employment share of all affiliates	26%	32%	34%	39%

[a]Mataloni (1995) and Mataloni and Yorgason (2006). Employment is industry of parent and includes petroleum extraction.
[b]Our totals differ and/or R&D

high-income locations are similar to those performed in the United States, while tasks performed in low-income locations are significantly different or complementary to those performed in the United States.

We also find that imports from foreign affiliates do not affect the relationship between domestic employment and affiliate wages. This is true regardless of whether the imports come from high- or low- income countries. This is possibly due to data limitations, which we discuss in the text. We find some evidence that exports for resale are complementary with domestic employment. Finally, we show that export platform offshoring is a prominent feature of almost all industries and firms. Thus, we are unable to separately detect a significant effect of export platform offshoring on domestic employment.

By combining our point estimates with changes in variable means, we show that offshoring is not the primary driver of declining domestic employment of U.S. manufacturing multinationals between 1977 and 1999. Declining domestic employment of U.S. multinationals is primarily due to falling prices of investment goods such as computers, which substitute for labor. Other contributing factors include rising domestic wages and increasing import competition. Our research highlights both the importance of heterogeneous firm responses to opportunities for direct investment abroad and the need to account for other avenues through which international competition affects U.S. labor demand.

Our results are consistent with the literature that focuses on the impact of international trade on U.S. jobs. Revenga (1992) finds a negative impact of changes in import prices on U.S. employment growth. Katz and Murphy (1992) also find that increased import competition negatively affected relative labor demand in the United States, particularly in the 1980s with the increase in the U.S. trade deficit. Borjas, Freeman, and Katz (1997) find that increased trade with developing countries depresses wages at the bottom of the income distribution. Bernard, Jensen, and Schott (2006) examine the impact of U.S. imports on both the survival and employment of U.S. manufacturing firms. They find that imports harm U.S. manufacturing employment only when those imports are from low-wage countries.

This paper also helps to clarify the reasons for the discrepancies in results across previous papers on this topic. First, previous studies have asked different questions. For example, Brainard and Riker (2001) use a factor demand approach to show that labor employed by affiliates overseas substitutes at the margins for labor employed by parents at home, but they emphasize that the results differ depending on geographic location. In particular, they emphasize strong substitution between workers at affiliates in developing countries, with workers in countries like Mexico and China competing for jobs with each other. Borga (2005) and Desai Foley, and Hines (2009) ask a different set of questions. Borga (2005) examines simple correlations between measures of offshoring and parent employment and makes no attempt to disentangle the relative importance of offshoring compared to other factors that determine domestic employment. Desai et al. (2009) focus on the correlation between expansion in activity at home and abroad. They show a positive association between growth in domestic investment, assets, employment, and total compensation for multinational parents and their foreign affiliates.

Second, previous studies have used a variety of different methods. While Desai et al. (2009) adopt an instrumental variable approach to estimate the association between growth in employment at home and abroad for U.S. multinationals, Muendler and Becker (2009) and Brainard and Riker (1997) estimate translog factor share equations. Using German multinational data, Muendler and Becker (2009) also explore the importance of selection into affiliate locations for the consistency of their estimates.

Third, previous empirical studies on employment and offshoring have not distinguished the differing motivations for foreign investment. Theoretical models of trade and foreign investment imply that different types of foreign investments will be associated with different kinds of effects on domestic labor demand. There is currently no agreement in the theoretical literature on whether horizontally integrated foreign investment (H-FDI) or vertically integrated foreign investment (V-FDI) is more likely to lead to domestic job losses.

An early version of the V-FDI model is presented in Helpman (1984). In the Helpman framework, there is an equilibrium where the parent (the headquarters) imports low-wage goods and exports headquarters services. In such a world, domestic demand for labor to produce the homogeneous good in the headquarters country would fall, and wages would continue to decline until factor price equalization is eventually achieved. Such a framework implies that under some initial relative endowments, V-FDI can be associated with intrafirm imports of low-wage goods, largely invisible exports from headquarters of intangibles such as management skills and knowledge arising from product-specific R&D conducted at home, falling domestic demand for unskilled labor, and falling domestic wages.

Markusen (1989) presents an alternative model in which V-FDI is associated with rising labor demand at home. In Markusen, domestic and foreign specialized inputs are complements by design, and trade generates welfare gains by increasing the number of specialized inputs (which are produced under increasing returns to scale technology) available. There are also models that focus on the implications for labor demand of V-FDI versus H-FDI. Markusen and Maskus (2001) show how different incentives for foreign investment lead to different organizational structures, which should produce different degrees of substitution between employment at home and abroad. Horizontal multinationals, defined as firms that produce the same products in different locations, are primarily motivated by trade costs to locate abroad.[1] For H-FDI, investment abroad substitutes for parent exports, and foreign affiliate employment should substitute for home employment. In their framework, V-FDI leads to complementarity between trade and foreign investment. Vertically integrated enterprises are motivated by factor endowment differences (and, consequently, factor price differences in a world where there is no factor price equalization) to locate different components of production in different locations. As Brainard and Riker (1997) pointed out, one implication of this type of modeling approach is complementarity between parent and affiliate employment.

The remainder of this paper is organized as follows. In section II, we describe the Bureau of Economic Analysis data on outward direct investment and our choice of sample. Section III describes the empirical framework and discusses econometric issues. Section IV presents the results, and section V concludes.

II. The BEA Data

We analyze firm-level surveys on U.S. direct investment abroad, collected each year by the Bureau of Economic Analysis (BEA) of the U.S. Department of Commerce. The BEA collects confidential data on the activities of U.S.-based multinationals, defined as the combination of a single U.S. entity that has made the direct investment, called the parent, and at least one foreign business enterprise, called the foreign affiliate. We use the data collected on majority-owned, nonbank foreign affiliates and nonbank U.S. parents for the benchmark years from 1982 and 1999. These bench-

mark years (1982, 1989, 1994, and 1999) include more comprehensive information than the annual surveys do.[2]

Creating a panel using the benchmark years of the BEA survey data is a nontrivial task for several reasons. First, not all firms are required to report to the BEA, and reporting requirements vary across years. Second, we must consider the implications of the changes to the Standard Industrial Classification (SIC) codes in 1972 and 1987 and the switch from SIC codes to the North American Industrial Classification System (NAICS) codes in 1997. The fact that parents are allowed to consolidate information for several affiliates in one country on a single form calls for special care in the aggregation and interpretation of affiliate-level data.

All foreign affiliates with sales, assets, or net income in excess of a certain amount in absolute value must report their data to the BEA. This amount was $3 million in 1982, 1989, and 1994 and rose to $7 million in 1999. In addition, a new reporting requirement was imposed on parents in 1999. Parents whose sales, assets, or net income exceeded $100 million (in absolute value) were required to provide more extensive information than parents whose sales, assets, or net income fell below that level.[3] To determine whether the changes in reporting requirements made small firms overrepresented in our sample in the early years, we imposed a double filter on the data using the uniform cutoff for affiliates (based on the strictest reporting requirement of $100 million in 1999) of $5.59 million in 1982 U.S. dollars and $79.87 in 1982 U.S. dollars for parents. As it turns out, the reporting requirements were large enough that imposing the filter on the data makes little difference on our initial results. Therefore, we use all of the available data.

Finally, we face selection issues with our sample of manufacturing firms.[4] We keep those parents whose primary

[1] For simplicity, we will occasionally refer to horizontally integrated firms as horizontal firms and vertically integrated firms as vertical.

[2] While the BEA collects annual data on U.S. direct investment abroad, these data do not include all the variables we need and can find in the benchmark years.

[3] Parents that do not meet this cutoff but have affiliates that meet the $7 million cutoff are still required to provide extensive information for affiliates.

[4] To document what has happened within industries in manufacturing over time, we created a concordance that allows us to assign SIC codes to NAICS codes. This was necessary because in 1999, the BEA collected data on NAICS codes and not SIC codes. We chose to convert SIC codes to NAICS codes since all future information will be collected on the basis of NAICS codes. For example, data for the benchmark year 2004 will be available shortly and firms report based on NAICS codes. The 1977 and 1982 benchmark years are based on the 1972 SIC codes. The 1989 and 1994 benchmark years are based on the 1987 SIC codes. The 1999 benchmark data are based on the 1997 NAICS codes. In addition to the fact that the industry codes are not directly comparable across all benchmark years, the BEA industry codes have been slightly modified to reflect the fact that these are enterprise data and are called, respectively, SIC-ISI and NAICS-ISI. Working with these codes, we created a program (available on request) that assigns the SIC-ISI codes for the years 1977 to 1994 to NAICS-ISI codes. Both parents and affiliates are classified into their primary industry of sales using the following algorithm, which tracks the algorithm used by the BEA: the top five industries by parent or affiliate sales are used to assign to each parent or affiliate one of the 22 aggregates. Sales are collapsed into the top five industries of sales, and then the maximum sale by industry is identified. A parent or affiliate is classified as being in manufacturing if its maximum sales across the top five industries of sales is in manufacturing.

industry of sales is manufacturing, since our goal is to determine whether manufacturing jobs at home are being replaced by manufacturing jobs abroad. However, some parents were reclassified from manufacturing to wholesale trade and services. To account for this, we keep all parents that were ever classified in manufacturing and their affiliates.[5]

Table 1 reports the number of manufacturing employees of U.S. manufacturing parents in both the United States and foreign affiliate locations. U.S. employment of manufacturing parents declined from nearly 12 million in 1982 to slightly below 8 million in 1999. The second row of table 1 shows the employment coverage of our sample after we performed the cleaning procedures described above. The sample size remains almost the same, particularly in the later years. Almost all of the increase in foreign affiliate employment occurred in low-income affiliate locations.

The share of U.S. multinational employment concentrated in affiliates increased from 26% in 1982 to 39% in 1999. Although total affiliate employment increased by more than 1 million employees, the foreign employment gains did not fully offset the domestic losses. This suggests other important determinants of falling domestic employment for U.S. multinationals. Alternative explanations, which we incorporate into our empirical framework, include changing prices of capital, labor-saving technical change, and increased import competition.

Manufacturing multinationals reporting to the BEA accounted for the majority of economic activity in U.S. manufacturing during the sample period. Table A1 reports the coverage of the BEA data for benchmark years 1982 through 1999. In 1982, gross product by these enterprises accounted for over 80% of total manufacturing and 77% of manufactured exports in the United States. By 1999, the BEA's coverage had declined slightly: these enterprises accounted for 63% of U.S. exports and about half of manufacturing employment. These firms also accounted for more than 80% of total private U.S. research and development expenditures throughout the sample period (Mataloni & Fahim-Nader, 1996). Table A1 also shows that the proportion of services that firms accounted for by the BEA sample is extremely small. During the sample period, the BEA sample accounted for only between 6% and 8% of total gross product in services. Consequently, we restrict our analysis to manufacturing, which we believe provides a more representative sample.

How reliable are these data? These are the only data officially collected by a U.S. government agency on affiliate activity abroad. We have initiated a number of data checks to analyze the reliability of the coverage.[6] We were able to cross-check the employment numbers for U.S. affiliate activity reported by the BEA with data on inward foreign investment reported by the official statistical agencies in Germany and Sweden. These checks are reported in Table A2. We report total employment in both countries as indicated by the BEA database and show that it is quite close to the numbers collected by the national statistical agencies. Although there are some discrepancies between BEA and German and Swedish data, this may be at least partially accounted for by variation in reporting based on fiscal year versus calendar year. The BEA classifies a firm in 1999 if its fiscal year ends in 1999—this could be for any month in 1999. Although most firms have their fiscal year ending in December, enough have earlier end dates that some of the 1999 BEA employment figures correspond to a mix of the 1998 and 1999 employment figures reported by the statistical bureaus for Sweden and Germany.

III. Empirical Framework

Previous work has used very different econometric models to specify the impact of foreign affiliate activity on labor demand at home, making it difficult to identify whether the conflicting results stem from different approaches or different data sets and time periods. Brainard and Riker (1997) estimate labor demand as a function of wages in different locations, Desai et al. (2009) estimate a reduced-form equation with growth in log labor at home as a function of log labor abroad, and Brainard and Riker (2001), Hanson, Slaughter, and Mataloni (2001), and Muendler and Becker (2009) use a short-run translog cost function approach to derive factor shares as a function of wages in different locations. Katz and Murphy (1992) and Card (2001), focusing on the effects of immigration and trade, both use a CES functional form to derive an equilibrium relationship between the ratio of employment at home to employment abroad and the ratio of wages at home to wages abroad.

We chose to derive labor demand from a generalized cost function as our primary specification. Our preferred approach is attractive for several reasons. It puts minimal restrictions on the nature of the production function, unlike the CES specification, which imposes a constant elasticity of substitution across different factor inputs. Our approach is also more flexible than previous approaches in the

---

[5] A number of parents have been reclassified from manufacturing to wholesale trade and services. For example, several firms were in manufacturing but are now classified in wholesale trade because almost all of their manufacturing is done overseas, not in the United States. To account for this, we chose our sample in two different ways. First, we included parents that were either classified in manufacturing or had previously been classified in manufacturing and their affiliates. Next, we included only parents that were currently in manufacturing in any given year and their affiliates. Since the results are not sensitive to this distinction, we use the larger of the two samples, keeping all parents that were ever classified in manufacturing and all of their affiliates.

[6] We are particularly grateful to Marc Muendler and Karolina Eckholm for helping us do this cross-checking. They provided the data on the activities of U.S. multinational affiliates in Germany and Sweden. We also contacted Statistics Canada to check whether they record information on affiliates of U.S. multinationals in Canada, which would allow us to cross-check U.S. data on foreign affiliates there with Canadian data on inward foreign investment. Statistics Canada informed us that they do not gather data on affiliates because it is too difficult to define a foreign affiliate and referred us to the BEA.

Offshoring Jobs? Multinationals and U.S. Manufacturing Employment   259

OFFSHORING JOBS?   861

offshoring literature that have imposed a short-run cost function and kept capital inputs fixed. In the translog approach, we worry that identifying elasticities of substitution or complementarity and calculating standard errors is a less transparent process (depending, among other things, on the choice of factor shares) than estimating a labor demand equation. However, for completeness, we also derive estimating equations using a generalized translog and CES function approach. We shall see that the implied elasticities of complementarity (or substitution) are remarkably robust across these different specifications.

Modifying Hamermesh (1993), let us consider a firm using N domestic factors and N^* foreign factors of production $X_1, \ldots, X_N, X_{1^*}, \ldots, X_{N^*}$. We begin by assuming there are only two locations (domestic and foreign) but will generalize to j locations in the empirical specification that follows. Let the production function for a U.S. multinational firm i producing total aggregate worldwide output Y_i and using N domestic and N^* foreign inputs X_i and X_{i^*} be

$$Y_i = f(X_{1i}, \cdots, X_{Ni}, X_{1^*}, \cdots, X_{Ni^*}). \quad (1)$$

Output Y can include production at home and abroad, and production could be exported or sold on domestic markets. Then the associated cost function, based on the demands for X_1 through X_N and X_{1^*} through X_{N^*} is given by

$$C_i = g(w_{1i}, \cdots, w_{Ni}, w_{1^*}, \cdots, w_{Ni^*}, Y_i), \quad (2)$$

where the w_i's and w_{i^*}'s are the N and N^* input prices at home and in the foreign affiliate location. One can use Shepard's lemma to derive the factor demand for the nth input for U.S. multinational firm i:

$$X_{ni} = X_{ni}^d(w_{1i}, \cdots, w_{Ni}, w_{1^*}, \cdots, w_{Ni^*}, Y_i),$$
$$n = 1, \ldots, N, n^* = 1, \ldots, N^*. \quad (3)$$

Our first approach will be to estimate a log-linear version of equation (3), focusing on U.S. labor demand and extending this equation to allow three locations. With three locations, there are three types of labor inputs: home labor, foreign labor in low-income affiliates, and foreign labor in high-income affiliates. This framework is flexible enough to allow a range of production technologies, including Brainard and Riker's (1997) assumption that production is vertically decomposed across high-wage and low-wage regions. We also allow two other types of inputs, making the total number of inputs N in each location equal to three: labor, physical capital, and research and development inputs. As with wages, we allow physical capital and research and development inputs to be separately identified depending on location.

One estimation issue that arises is that global output Y for firm i is jointly determined with domestic U.S. employment. If we were to estimate equation (3) directly, we

would have a significant simultaneity problem. We solve this by assuming that aggregate worldwide output Y for firm i is a function of domestic and foreign prices:

$$Y_i = Y(P, P^*).$$

Substituting this into equation (3) yields

$$X_{ni} = X_{ni}^d(w_{1i}, \cdots, w_{Ni}, w_{1^*}, \cdots, w_{Ni^*}, P, P^*),$$
$$n = 1, \ldots, N, n^* = 1, \ldots, N^*. \quad (4)$$

Our first set of estimating equations is based on log-linearization of equation (4), generalizing to j locations, and takes the following form:

$$\ln L_{iht} = \beta_0 + \sum_j \alpha_j \ln P_{jt} + \sum_j \eta_j w_{ijt} + \sum_j \omega_j r_{ijt} + \sum_j \chi_j l_{ijt} + d_t + f_i + \varepsilon_{ijt}. \quad (5)$$

The dependent variable $\ln L$ is the natural logarithm of net annual employment by the U.S. parent in the United States, the P's are final goods prices, w is the wage in location j and time t, r is the price of capital in location j and time t, and t is the price of research and development goods. We allow for time effects d and a firm-specific (common to the parent and its affiliate) fixed effect f_i, which takes into account both firm-specific productivity differences and other nonvarying firm characteristics, while j indexes location and t indexes time.

A. Identifying the Motives for Offshoring

Markusen and Maskus (2001), in their comprehensive survey of general equilibrium approaches to the multinational firm, define horizontal multinationals as "firms that produce the same product in multiple plants, serving local markets by local production." This definition of horizontal integration implies that intrafirm trade will be low, since foreign investment substitutes for U.S. exports. Vertical firms are defined as "firms that fragment the production process into stages based on factor intensities and locate activities according to international differences in factor prices." An important finding of Markusen and Maskus is that foreign investment replaces trade in the case of horizontal multinationals but is positively correlated with trade in the case of vertical foreign investment. Although we cannot directly test the motivation for foreign investment with our data, our data set is rich enough that we can construct credible proxies to help us distinguish between different motives for offshoring.

Conceptually, there is a clear distinction between horizontal FDI (H-FDI) and vertical FDI (V-FDI). In practice though, firms often do both simultaneously. And within the class of V-FDI, there is a range of activities, including resales FDI and export platform FDI. To get at these nuances empirically, we compute a variety of measures of

TABLE 2.—Defining Horizontal and Vertical Foreign Direct Investment

Measures of Vertical Integration as Share of Parent Sales: Coefficient Estimates from Regression of Measure of Vertical Integration on Industry Dummies

Industry (97 NAICS code)	Imports from Foreign Affiliates	Exports for Further Processing	Exports for Resale	Share Affiliate Production Exported
Textiles and Apparel	0.007**	−0.006	−0.019	0.321**
Food	0.005	−0.006	−0.021	0.044
Beverages and Tobacco	0.018**	−0.011**	−0.021	0.195**
Leather Products	0.002	−0.014**	0.001	0.152
Wood Products	0.041**	0.005	−0.019	0.149**
Paper	−0.004	−0.006	−0.021	0.144**
Chemicals	0.009**	0.029**	−0.005	0.071**
Plastics and Rubber	0.001	0.012**	−0.017	0.066*
Nonmetallic Minerals	0.009**	−0.000	−0.021	0.198**
Primary Metals	0.009**	0.004	−0.018	0.134**
Fabricated Metals	0.005	0.009**	0.007	0.061*
Machinery	0.015**	0.035**	0.000	0.111**
Computer and Electronics	0.034**	0.097**	0.027	0.131**
Electrical Equipment	0.013**	0.017**	−0.007	0.031
Transportation Equipment	0.019**	0.011**	−0.016	0.122**
Toys, Dolls & Miscellaneous	0.015**	0.042**	0.001	0.076**
Constant	0.009**	0.022**	0.019**	0.265**
Number of observations	4,338	4,338	4,338	4,338
R^2	0.049	0.189	0.025	0.027

The constant term is the mean for Petroleum and Coal since it is the omitted industry. **Indicates that the within-industry mean is statistically significantly different from the constant term at the 1% level. For a detailed description of which industries are included in Miscellaneous, see http://www.census.gov/eped/naics/NAICS33C.HTM#N339.

vertical integration at the firm level and interact these firm-level measures of vertical integration with our wage variables in our estimating equations. The firm-specific measures of vertical integration are calculated as the mean of the measure of vertical integration over the entire sample period so as to avoid the endogeneity problem associated with including measures of intrafirm trade as explanatory variables. The alternatives to defining vertical integration at the firm level are to define vertical integration as the beginning-of-period level or to define it at the industry level. Both of these approaches have significant drawbacks. The first ignores changes over time in vertical integration, and the second masks significant within-sector firm heterogeneity. Thus, our preferred measure is the firm-level measure of vertical integration.

To get a sense for what determines the various types of vertical integration, we regress each of our measures of vertical integration on a set of industry dummies clustering the standard errors at the industry level. Table 2 presents the coefficient estimates from this regression. Petroleum and Coal Products is the omitted industry so that the constant term is the mean of the dependent variable for firms in the Petroleum and Coal Products industry. All of the other coefficients should be interpreted relative to the constant term. For example, over the entire sample period, the mean of imports from foreign affiliates as a share of parent sales in Textiles and Apparel is 0.009 plus 0.007 or 0.016 and is significantly greater than the mean for Petroleum and Coal Products at the 99% level. Each column represents a different measure of vertical integration: the dependent variable in column 1 is total imports from foreign affiliates, the dependent variable in column 2 is exports to foreign affiliates for further processing, the dependent variable in column 3 is exports to affiliates for resale, and the dependent variable in column 4 is the share of affiliate production that is exported.

Only one industry stands out as notable for the share of affiliate production exported: textiles and apparel. In textiles and apparel, the mean share of affiliate production exported is 58.6%. This is reassuring in that it is consistent with what we know about the textile and apparel industry. We omit the results for total exports to foreign affiliates because they closely resemble the results in column 2, indicating that the cross-industry variation in exports to foreign affiliates is driven by the variation in exports for further processing. Exports for resale vary little across industries.

Like Hanson, Mataloni, and Slaughter (2005), our preferred measure of the type of vertical integration characterized by a fragmentation of the production process across various locations in response to factor cost differences is exports for further processing. Unfortunately, the BEA does not record information on whether imports from foreign affiliates are final goods imports or imports of intermediate goods, making it difficult to interpret these numbers. Nevertheless, we report both sets of statistics for the sake of completeness. Grossman and Rossi-Hansberg (2007) also use intrafirm trade to quantify the increase in vertical activities of multinationals, pointing out that intrafirm trade "mostly reflects the international division of labor within multinational enterprises." By this measure of vertical integration, the computer and electronics industry clearly stands out as the most vertically integrated industry with exports to affiliates for further processing at roughly 12% of sales.

Finally, much horizontal FDI is motivated by trade barriers (such as tariffs or quotas). Textiles and apparel and beverages and tobacco are typically the most protected sectors in both industrial and developing countries. Evidence to support this for developing countries can be found in Harrison and Hanson (1999). Tariffs in the United States are currently at very low levels. However, prior to trade liberalization (1979, for example), trade frictions for the United States followed the same pattern. They were highest for textiles and apparel, beverages and tobacco, leather, and nonmetallic minerals (cement). These patterns imply that firms in highly protected sectors (textiles and apparel) or in sectors with high costs of transportation (cement) must frequently engage in horizontal investments in order to access domestic foreign markets.

B. Data and Estimation Issues

To estimate equation (5), we need data on U.S. employment, capital prices, wages, final goods prices, and research and development prices. We also need factor prices and output prices for each of the j locations in which the multinational firm has operations. We measure U.S. employment as the (log) number of individuals employed by the parent in the United States, since hours or even employment broken down by skill levels are not collected for U.S. parents. Domestic prices of investment are defined at the disaggregated industry level and are taken from the NBER's manufacturing database. Domestic U.S. wages are computed at the industry level using both the BEA and UNIDO data sets (see the discussion below). And finally, domestic final goods prices are captured by the log of industry sales deflated by the producer price index.

While in principle there could be as many factor and final goods prices as there are countries in the BEA database, in practice the number of j locations is limited by data availability and the need for parsimony in estimation. We restrict our j locations to three: domestic (U.S.) activity, high-income locations, and low-income locations. One problem is that many firms, especially small enterprises, do not have any operations in low-income countries. To permit us to include these firms in the estimation, we set wages for these firms equal to 0 and add a dummy variable indicating whether the firm has a missing observation for low-income affiliates.

Our proxy for final goods prices abroad is the log of affiliate sales deflated by the foreign price index. Our measure of foreign investment prices comes from the Penn World Tables. While in principle all foreign factor prices should be broken down into low-income foreign and high-income foreign affiliate locations, collinearity in investment and consumption prices has led us to aggregate these prices across foreign affiliate locations. Because both capital and goods are significantly more mobile than individuals, the factor price differentials across high- and low-income affiliate locations are much larger for labor inputs.

To control for exposure to international competition, we use data on import penetration made available at the four-digit ISIC level by Bernard et al. (2006). We also include a measure of import penetration from low-wage countries, also computed by these authors. These measures of import competition include imports of final goods as well as imported intermediate inputs. To the best of our knowledge, no time-series data are available for the period 1982 to 1999 that separately identify final goods imports from imported intermediate inputs. However, even if there were, existing evidence suggests that it would be very difficult to disentangle the two effects. This is because the aggregate trends over time in the two series are highly correlated both over time and across industries. (See figures 4 and 5 of Ebenstein, et al., 2009, for the time-series correlation.) Our own calculations show that for the period 1997 to 2005, the correlation in the two measures across industries is 0.85.

We do not have adequate measures of prices for research and development goods. However, we believe that these are important inputs into production and could account for a significant impact on manufacturing employment, particularly if research and development inputs are associated with labor-saving technical change. Consequently, we proxy for prices of research and development goods with research and development spending as a share of parent sales. Though there are other ways to measure R&D (for example, R&D spending per R&D employee by country), none are well suited to our analysis because they severely limit sample size.

Since wages are calculated at the country level using BEA aggregates of the firm-level measures, we assume that wages are exogenously determined. However, we also test for the validity of this assumption by using wages collected by UNIDO. Following Hanson et al. (2005), wages are employment-weighted averages of wages in high- and low-income affiliates, where the weights are given by the competitor's share of employment within countries belonging to each high- and low-income category. We use competitor's wages to avoid the endogeneity problems associated with using the parent's own employment choices. Affiliate country locations are defined as either high or low income based on the World Bank's country classifications (see table A8).

IV. Results

We report sample means in table 3. Consistent with the trends in table 1, parent employment fell over the sample period by 20%. Real wages in the sample went up in the United States by 11.6% and in high-income affiliate locations by 22.9% but fell by 21.5% in low-income affiliate locations. Table A8 shows that the annual average changes in wages and employment in the manufacturing sector reported by UNIDO are similar to what we find using the BEA data. Apart from East Asia, the numbers in table A4 show real wage declines in low-income countries of between 1% and 2% per year and employment gains of

TABLE 3.—SUMMARY STATISTICS

Variable	No. of Observations	Mean	Standard Deviation	Change in Mean, 1982–1999
Log U.S. Employment	3,946	7.558	1.673	−0.204
Log U.S. Manufacturing Wages, BEA	3,946	3.331	0.398	0.116
Log High-Income Affiliate Wages	3,946	3.158	0.487	0.229
Log Low-Income Affiliate Wages	3,946	2.044	0.794	−0.215
Log U.S. Price of Investment, NBER Manufacturing Database	3,946	0.698	0.067	−0.276
Log Foreign Price of Investment, Penn World Tables (PWT)	3,946	0.629	0.318	−0.099
U.S R&D Expenditure (% Sales)	3,946	0.037	0.052	0.011
High-Income Affiliate R&D Expenditure (% Sales)	3,946	0.006	0.018	0.004
Low-Income Affiliate R&D Expenditure (% Sales)	3,946	0.001	0.004	0.000
Import Penetration, Bernard et al. (2006)	3,946	0.174	0.118	0.121
Import Penetration from Low-Income Countries, Bernard et al. (2006)	3,946	0.059	0.065	0.059
Log Parent Sales by Industry	3,946	12.286	0.923	0.109
Log Affiliate Sales by Industry	3,946	9.363	0.557	0.314
Imports from Foreign Affiliates (% Sales)	3,946	0.027	0.069	0.021
Exports for Foreign Affiliates (% Sales)	3,946	0.051	0.158	0.023
Exports for Further Processing (% Sales)	3,946	0.031	0.111	0.022
Exports for Resale (% Sales)	3,946	0.021	0.105	0.006
Share of Affiliate Production Exported	3,946	0.366	0.331	−0.005

between 2% and 9% per year over the sample period. Similar to the BEA numbers, the UNIDO statistics for high-income countries show average real wage increases of .41% per year and average employment declines of .68% per year.

Research and development expenditure as a share of parent sales averaged 3.7% for U.S. parents, .6% for affiliates in high-income countries, and .1% for affiliates in low-income countries. R&D spending as a share of sales rose significantly in the United States and in high-income affiliate locations but changed very little in low-income affiliate locations.

Average import penetration in the four-digit SIC sector over the period was 17.4% and increased by 12.1 percentage points over the sample period. Average import penetration from low-wage countries increased by 5.9 percentage points over the sample period. The real price of investment fell by 27.9 percentage points over the period in the United States and 9.9 percentage points abroad. These price declines reflect in part the importance of falling computer-related costs for these firms. Industry sales in the United State increased by 10.9% in the United States and by 31.4% abroad, reflecting the growing importance of overseas markets for U.S. multinationals.

A. Fixed Effect Results for Labor Demand

We report the results of estimating equation (5) in table 4. The log of U.S. employment is our dependent variable, and we use a within transformation of the data to eliminate firm fixed effects. All specifications include time dummies to control for year-specific shocks. Column 1 of table 4 reports coefficient estimates without controlling for the motives for offshoring. In each of columns 2 through 5, we interact different measures of vertical integration with our wage variables to test whether the motive for offshoring

affects the impact of offshoring on domestic employment. Our measures of vertical integration between parents and affiliates are imports from foreign affiliates (column 2), exports to affiliates for further processing (column 3a), exports to foreign affiliates for further processing by destination (column 3b), exports to foreign affiliates for resale (column 4) and affiliate exports as a share of affiliate sales (column 5).

The results in column 1 indicate that employees in low-income affiliates are substitutes for U.S. employees. The point estimate of 0.097 on low-income affiliate wages indicates that a 1% fall in foreign wages would lead to a 0.097% fall in U.S. parent employment. The point estimate on high-income affiliate wages suggests the opposite: a 1% fall in high-income affiliate wages would be associated with a 0.006% increase in parent employment. However, the point estimate on wages in high-income countries is statistically insignificant. In columns 2 through 5, we allow the slope coefficients on our foreign wage variables to vary according to degrees of vertical integration as defined in table 2.

The coefficients on the interaction terms differ substantially depending on the definition of vertical integration. In columns 2, 4, and 5, the coefficients on the interaction terms are not significant. Thus, differentiating parents on the basis of total imports from foreign affiliates, exports for resale as a share of sales or the share of affiliate production exported provides no additional information regarding the degree of substitutability between domestic and foreign labor. By contrast, the results in columns 3a and 3b indicate that exports for further processing play an important role in determining margins of multinational labor substitution. The point estimate on low-income affiliate wages interacted with exports for further processing equals −3.127 and jumps to −3.915 when low-income affiliate wages are interacted with exports for further processing to low-income

TABLE 4.—WITHIN ESTIMATES OF LABOR DEMAND: U.S. PARENTS

	(1)	(2)	(3a)	(3b)	(4)	(5)
	Pooled	Imports from Affiliates	Exports for Processing	Exports for Processing	Exports for Resale	Export Platform FDI
Log U.S. Industrial Wages	−0.359	−0.332	−0.401	−0.350	−0.386	−0.466
	[0.042]**	[0.045]**	[0.047]**	[0.041]**	[0.045]**	[0.114]**
Log Industrial Wages High-Income Countries	−0.006	−0.015	−0.036	−0.048	0.026	0.051
	[0.035]	[0.038]	[0.041]	[0.049]	[0.038]	[0.086]
Log Industrial Wages Low-Income Countries	0.097	0.097	0.126	0.104	0.098	0.057
	[0.016]**	[0.018]**	[0.019]**	[0.017]**	[0.018]**	[0.046]
Log Industrial Wages High-Income Countries × Vertical		0.316	1.185	1.741	−1.803	−0.098
		[0.544]	[0.788]	[0.876]**	[0.806]**	[0.128]
Log Industrial Wages Low Income Countries × Vertical		−0.004	−3.127	−3.915	−0.043	0.064
		[0.392]	[0.945]**	[0.744]**	[0.272]	[0.069]
Log of the U.S. Price of Capital	0.403	0.393	0.389	0.589	0.330	0.398
	[0.175]**	[0.175]**	[0.175]**	[0.195]**	[0.184]**	[0.175]**
Log of the Foreign Price of Capital	0.187	0.190	0.172	0.162	0.185	0.193
	[0.071]**	[0.071]**	[0.071]*	[0.071]*	[0.071]**	[0.071]**
Import Penetration	−0.232	−0.232	−0.232	−0.192	−0.237	−0.232
	[0.096]**	[0.096]**	[0.095]**	[0.077]**	[0.096]**	[0.096]**
Import Penetration from Low-Wage Countries	0.081	0.094	0.112	0.181	0.053	0.076
	[0.338]	[0.339]	[0.337]	[0.488]	[0.339]	[0.339]
R&D (% Sales)	0.834	0.846	0.896	0.737	0.791	0.843
	[0.447]*	[0.447]*	[0.447]*	[0.311]*	[0.448]*	[0.448]*
R&D (% Sales) in High-Income Countries	1.516	1.529	1.453	1.449	1.488	1.558
	[0.695]*	[0.695]*	[0.693]*	[0.599]*	[0.694]*	[0.695]*
R&D (% Sales) in Low-Income Countries	4.985	5.046	4.795	4.949	4.957	4.956
	[2.413]*	[2.418]*	[2.406]*	[2.427]*	[2.413]*	[2.414]*
Log of Industry Sales	0.153	0.154	0.152	0.142	0.153	0.153
	[0.029]**	[0.029]**	[0.029]**	[0.029]**	[0.029]**	[0.029]**
Log Affiliate Sales by Industry	−0.051	−0.049	−0.053	−0.033	−0.050	−0.049
	[0.041]	[0.041]	[0.041]	[0.041]	[0.041]	[0.041]
Time dummy 1989	−0.028	−0.029	−0.034	−0.055	−0.033	−0.028
	[0.043]	[0.043]	[0.043]	[0.044]	[0.043]	[0.043]
Time dummy 1994	−0.024	−0.026	−0.032	0.009	−0.034	−0.024
	[0.060]	[0.060]	[0.060]	[0.061]	[0.060]	[0.060]
Time dummy 1999	0.080	0.075	0.068	0.115	0.064	0.079
	[0.078]	[0.078]	[0.078]	[0.079]	[0.079]	[0.078]
Observations	3,946	3,946	3,946	3,946	3,946	3,946
R^2	0.09	0.09	0.09	0.09	0.09	0.09

Standard errors corrected for arbitrary heteroskedasticity are in brackets. *Significant at 5%, **Significant at 1%. Each of columns 2–5 includes an interaction term between the wage measures and vertical integration defined at the firm level as the mean of the variable in the column heading over the entire sample period. In column 3b, exports for further processing are broken down by location: exports to high-income countries are interacted with wages in high-income countries, and exports to low-income countries are interacted with low-income country wages.

countries. These point estimates imply that for parents that export significant amounts of goods to low-income countries for further processing, domestic and foreign labor are complements. The point estimate on high-income affiliate wages interacted with exports for further processing is 1.185 but statistically insignificant in column 3a, but increases to 1.741 and becomes significant when interacted with exports for further processing to high-income countries. The implication of this last result is that workers in high-income affiliates substitute for U.S. workers in companies that export significant amounts of goods to high-income countries for further processing.

The own-wage elasticity, which varies between −0.33 and −0.47 across columns 1 through 5, suggests that a 1% increase in the domestic U.S. manufacturing wage reduces labor demand by 0.33% to 0.47%. The magnitude is in line with the dozens of studies cited in Hamermesh (1993), who reports that most studies find that the own-wage elasticity for labor lies between 0.3 and 0.7. The coefficient on the

industry-specific home price of investment is positive across all specifications, indicating that reductions in the price of domestic investment goods reduce domestic labor demand. The coefficient on investment abroad is similarly positive. These coefficient estimates imply that capital and labor are generally substitutes. This is consistent with a story in which less skilled workers are being replaced by capital (computers) and consistent with previous labor demand studies on capital-labor substitution cited in Hamermesh (1993).

Negative employment effects are also associated with increases in import penetration (arm's-length trade). The point estimates range from −0.192 to −0.237 across specifications, indicating that a 1 percentage point increase in import penetration during the sample period would imply a decline in U.S. manufacturing employment of 0.192 to 0.237 percentage points.

Positive employment effects are associated with our proxies for the prices of technology inputs, the share of research and development expenditure in parent sales. The results indicate that a 1 percentage point increase in the parent research and development expenditure shares would be associated with employment increases between 0.737 and 0.896 percentage points. For affiliates in high-income locations, a 1 percentage point increase in the affiliate research and development share is associated with employment increases between 1.449 and 1.558 percentage points. For affiliates in low-income locations, a 1 percentage point increase in the affiliate research and development share is associated with employment increases between 4.795 and 5.046 percentage points. In spite of the very large point estimates on affiliate research and development expenditure shares, the changes in means in table 4 make it clear that R&D activities in affiliates have not had an economically significant impact on U.S. parent employment.

Positive employment effects are also associated with our proxies for final goods prices in the United States, the log of the real value of industry sales. The results indicate that a 1 percentage point increase in final goods prices would be associated with employment increases between 0.142 and 0.152 percentage points. Negative but statistically and economically insignificant employment effects are associated with increases in final goods prices abroad: a 1 percentage point increase in our proxy for final goods prices abroad is associated with employment declines of between −0.033 and −0.053 percentage points.

The net effect of vertical integration as measured by exports for further processing is equal to the coefficient on low- (high-) income affiliate wages plus the coefficient on the interaction between low- (high-) income affiliate wages multiplied by the value of vertical integration at different points in the distribution. The net effect of offshoring to low-wage countries is nonmonotonic and turns positive only for the last two quartiles of the distribution. Thus, the employment effects of offshoring to low-wage countries are positive only for firms that export significant amounts of goods to low-wage countries for further processing. Column 2 of table 2 shows that, on average, these firms are most likely to be in the computers and electronics industry.

The opposite signs on the interaction between wages and exports for further processing imply that employees of affiliates in high- and low-income countries must be performing different tasks. To check this, we use information on employee type for the four countries that received more than 80% of the share of exports for further processing in 1999: Canada, Mexico, China, and Brazil. Unlike parent employment, affiliate employment is recorded for the following categories: production workers, nonproduction workers, and research and development employees. Using this information, we computed for each country the share of production employees, nonproduction employees and research and development employees. The results in table 5 show that roughly two-thirds of all employees in the developing countries are production employees. By contrast, only around a

TABLE 5.—COMPOSITION OF EMPLOYMENT IN THE COMPUTER INDUSTRY, BY COUNTRY, 1999

	Canada	Mexico	China	Brazil
Production employees	39.10%	65.70%	62.60%	66.66%
Nonproduction employees	57.20	33.60	36.50	33.05
R&D employees	3.70	0.70	0.90	0.29
Total	100.00%	100.00%	100.00%	100.00%

third of the workforce in Canada is made up of production employees. Though we do not have the data to prove it directly, these results strongly suggest that employees in the computer and electronics industry in Canada perform tasks that are more similar to those of U.S. employees, while employees in Mexico, Brazil, and China perform tasks that are significantly different from the tasks that U.S. workers perform.

The critical parameters of interest in table 4 are the coefficients on affiliate wages and affiliate wages interacted with our measures of vertical integration, which indicate whether affiliate employment substitutes for or is complementary with home employment. In column 2 of table 6, we report results using an alternative definition of affiliate wages. Instead of constructing country-level wages from the BEA sample, we use country wages reported by UNIDO. Wages are calculated based on surveys administered by UNIDO, supplemented with secondary sources (such as national statistical agencies) gathered by UNIDO as well. Wages are calculated as compensation divided by number of employees, collected at the three-digit ISIC level (Revision 2). All values are converted to U.S. dollars using the IMF exchange rate series RF. As in table 4, we weight country-level wages using the parent's initial distribution of employment across affiliate locations when the parent first appears in the sample.

The results in table 6 are consistent with our earlier results, suggesting that the source for country-level wages does not affect our coefficient estimates. The coefficients on high- and low-income affiliate wages are the same sign and close in magnitude to the previous results. As before, the results indicate that offshoring to low-wage countries generally depresses home employment except for parents that export a significant amount of goods for further processing to low-wage countries. Negative employment effects are associated with offshoring to high-wage countries, and the magnitude of the effect is a function of the share of exports sent to high-wage countries for further processing.

B. Attrition Bias

We face potentially important selection problems. Between each benchmark year, roughly 20% of the parents drop out of our sample and do not reappear. If some of these firms relocate all operations abroad and close down their U.S. operations, then our estimates of the employment

TABLE 6.—IMPLIED ELASTICITY OF LABOR DEMAND ACROSS ALTERNATIVE SPECIFICATIONS

	(1)	(2)	(3)	(4)
Implied Elasticity of Labor Demand η_{ij} (% Change in Li in Response to % Change in wj)	Basic Specification (table 5)	Replacing BEA Wages with UNIDO wages	CES Specification	Translog Cost Function
Coefficient estimates without controls for degree of vertical integration				
Parent wages	−0.359	−0.287	–	−0.225
High-income affiliate wages	−0.006	−0.001	−0.007	−0.003
Low-income affiliate wages	0.097	0.102	0.081	0.112
Coefficient estimates controlling for degree of vertical integration (exports for further processing)				
Parent wages	−0.351	−0.299	–	−0.313
High-income affiliate wages	−0.048	−0.003	−0.007	−0.004
Low-income affiliate wages	0.104	0.122	0.091	0.132
High-income Affiliate Wages × Vertical	1.741	1.666	1.765	1.701
Low-income Affiliate Wages × Vertical	−3.915	−4.103	−3.221	−4.245

Coefficients taken from column 3b of table 4 and unreported coefficients for robustness checks including replacing BEA wages with UNIDO wages and using estimating equations based on CES and translog functional forms. Factor shares used to compute elasticities taken from sample means. All coefficients are significant at the 95% level, and standard errors for CES and translog coefficient estimates are bootstrapped.

costs of multinational activity could be downward biased. Following Wooldridge (2002), we test for survivorship bias by including a lead of the selection indicator $s_{i,t+1}$ in our estimating equations, where $s_{i,t+1}$ is equal to 0 for firms that do not exit the sample and switches from 0 to 1 in the period just before attrition. The coefficient on the lead of the selection indicator was negative and significant for both vertically and horizontally integrated firms. The significant and negative sign on the selection variable is a possible indicator that firms that exit the sample are those most likely to contract employment. To address this potential criticism, we correct for selection bias using two approaches: a Heckman-type selection correction and inverse probability weighting.

Following Wooldridge (2002) our first approach, a Heckman-type correction, models this selection problem as follows. If our equation of interest is given by

$$y_{it} = x_{it}\beta + u_{it}, t = 2, \ldots, T,$$

then conditional on the parent reporting in the previous period, $s_{i,t-1} = 1$, we can write a reduced-form selection equation for $t \geq 2$ as

$$s_{it} = 1[w_{it}\delta_t + v_{it} > 0],$$
$$\text{where,} \quad v_{it} | \{x_{it}, w_{it}, s_{i,t-1} = 1\} \sim Normal(0, 1).$$

In the context of panel data with an unobserved firm fixed effect and attrition, Wooldridge (2002) proposes as a solution a variant of a two-stage Heckman correction. In each period, Wooldridge proposes estimating a selection equation using a probit approach and calculating lambda, the inverse Mills ratio, for each parent i. Once a series of lambdas has been estimated for each year and parent, the estimating equations are augmented by these lambdas.

This approach is successful only if we can identify determinants of the binary selection variable s_{it} before the firm exits the sample (in period $t - 1$) that do not belong in the estimating equation. We identified candidate variables

using the insights derived from a class of models indicating that heterogeneity in productivity is a significant determinant of whether firms enter into international trade or foreign investment (see Melitz, 2003). These models suggest that only the most profitable firms are likely to engage in trade or foreign investment. Since we already control for output and factor price shocks using a variety of input and output prices, parent profitability in the previous period does not belong in the estimating equations (indeed, auxiliary regressions show that lagged profits from the benchmark surveys five years earlier do not predict current period employment). Consequently, we use as the excluded determinant of survival the parent's profitability in the previous period.

Table A5 reports the second-stage estimates using this two-step approach. The sample size decreases significantly, since implementing the selection correction eliminates the first time-series observation for each parent. The coefficients on the inverse Mills ratios are statistically insignificant across all specifications, indicating that selection is not biasing our results. Additionally, adding the inverse Mills ratio to control for selection does not change the sign and barely changes the point estimates on the coefficients of interest. The coefficients on affiliate wages in low-income countries remain positive and statistically significant across all specifications. The coefficient on the interaction between high-income affiliate wages and exports for further processing to high income countries is positive and significant, while the coefficient on the interaction between low-income affiliate wages and exports for further processing to low-wage countries changes sign depending on the degree of vertical integration.

We also explored using inverse probability weighting as outlined in Wooldridge (2002) to correct for selection bias. This approach consists of the following two-step procedure. In each time period, we estimate a binary response model for the probability of survival for the group in the sample at time $t - 1$. Using the fitted probabilities from the first step, we obtain the following weights:

TABLE 7.—CALCULATING THE IMPACT OF DIFFERENT ASPECTS OF GLOBALIZATION ON PARENT LABOR DEMAND

Factors Affecting U.S. Labor Demand	Impact of 1% Increase in Factor	Actual Increase in Sample	Percentage Change in Labor Demand	Keeping Only Significant Coefficients
	(1)	(2)	(3)	(4)
Log U.S. Industrial Wages	−0.351	0.116	−4.072	−4.072
Log Industrial Wages in High-Income Countries	−0.048	0.229	−1.099	
Log Industrial Wages in Low-Income Countries	0.104	−0.229	−2.382	−2.382
Log of U.S. Price of Capital	0.439	−0.276	−12.116	−12.116
Log of Foreign Price of Capital	0.162	−0.099	−1.604	−1.604
Import Penetration	−0.192	0.121	−2.323	−2.323
Import Penetration from Low-Wage Countries	0.181	0.059	1.068	
R&D Spending (% Sales)	0.737	0.011	0.811	0.811
R&D Spending in High-Income Countries (% Sales)	1.449	0.004	0.580	0.580
R&D Spending in Low-Income Countries (% Sales)	4.949	0.0001	0.049	0.049
Log of Industry Sales	0.142	0.109	1.548	1.548
Log of Affiliate Sales by Industry	−0.033	0.314	−1.036	
Log Industrial Wages in Low-Income Countries × Exports for Further Processing	−3.127	−0.008	2.502	2.502
Log Industrial Wages in High-Income Countries × Exports for Further Processing	1.741	0.005	0.871	0.871
Net Impact of All Above Variables			−17.204	−16.137

Coefficients in columns 1 are taken from column (3b) of table 4. Numbers in column 2 are taken from means table 4. Numbers in column 3 are calculated by multiplying by 100 × column 1 × column 2. Column 4 is calculated the same way as column 3, but only the coefficients that were significant in table 4 are reported. The final row net impact sums up all the previous effects.

$$\hat{p}_{it} = \hat{\pi}_{it} * \hat{\pi}_{i,t-1*} \dots \hat{\pi}_{l,1},$$

where hats denote fitted probabilities. This methodology allowed us to choose covariates in the probits that are essentially everything we can observe for units in the sample at time $t - 1$ that might affect attrition. In our case, we included all of the regressors in our original model plus firm size, firm profitability, and the firm's share of employment in low-income countries. Using this approach also did not affect our estimates, and consequently we do not report them here.

In both cases, the first-stage results indicate that expansion into low-wage countries is positively correlated with the probability of firm survival. Thus, we find some evidence that the jobs lost as a result of offshoring might have been lost anyway. However, controlling for this possibility does not change the sign or magnitude of our wage elasticities in table 4.

C. Extensive and Intensive Margin

All of the results we presented examine activity at the intensive margin. As Muendler and Becker (2009) noted, expansion (contraction) of employment at existing affiliates—the intensive margin—may have different employment effects from opening (closing) new operations—the extensive margin. In what follows, we show that the vast majority of affiliate employment expansions and contractions take place at the extensive margin. Even in China where most of the employment expansion took place between 1994 and 1999, the activity took place at the intensive margin. Although there was significant entry into

China between 1982 and 1989, these affiliates had very few employees (11,000 in total) when they were established. Thus, this activity at the extensive margin in China between 1982 and 1989 could not have had much of an impact on parent employment between 1982 and 1989.

Before proceeding, we note an important data limitation. Parents can report affiliate activity on an aggregated basis or file separate reports for each affiliate. Because there is no way to distinguish this in the data, the only certain information is whether a parent is present in a particular country in a given time period. Therefore, the BEA statistics on affiliate activity could mask some underlying opening and closing of specific plants by the same parent.[7]

Table A6 shows entry and exit to and from low-wage countries where activity at the extensive margin is most likely to be an issue because of extensive deregulation in these countries over the sample period. The numbers represent counts of parents with affiliates in low-income countries, and the percentages indicate the percentage of affiliate employment in low-income countries accounted for by those affiliates. Each of the three panels shows activity between two consecutive years: 1982–1989, 1989–1994, and 1994–1999. For example, the top panel shows that between 1982 and 1989, thirty parents entered developing country markets for the first time. These thirty parents accounted for only 4.39% of the total employment expansion in low income affiliates. Table A7 shows that affiliate employment in low-income countries increased by around 353,978 between 1982 and 1989. Of this expansion, only

---

[7] We take care of this in the data analysis by aggregating information for affiliates of parents in the same country year, thus making all of the affiliate data comparable.

Offshoring Jobs? Multinationals and U.S. Manufacturing Employment   267

OFFSHORING JOBS?   869

15,539 jobs were a result of activity at the extensive margin. The magnitudes of activity at the extensive margin are even smaller for the periods 1989 to 1994 and 1994 to 1999.

Since Mexico accounts for more than a third of all affiliate employment in low-income countries, we repeat this exercise for Mexico in Table A6. Once again, the magnitudes of employment expansion and contraction at the extensive margin are small. Between 1982 and 1989, affiliate employment in Mexico increased by 288,012. Of this increase, only 10% or 28,012 jobs, were created at the extensive margin. Between 1994 and 1999, when the effects of NAFTA would be prominent, 87% of affiliate activity took place at the intensive margin, while only 6% of affiliate activity (or 9,180 jobs) took place at the extensive margin.

D. Alternative Specifications: Translog and CES Specifications

We also test for the robustness of our results to two alternatives: a framework based on a translog cost function and a framework based on CES production functions. The translog approach has been adopted by Brainard and Riker (2001), Hanson et al. (2001), and Muendler and Becker (2009). This alternative approach has the advantage that the translog cost function approximates many well-behaved cost functions. The translog total variable cost (TC) function (omitting time and parent subscripts) for wages W, investment prices r, research and development input prices t and output Y is given by

$$
\begin{aligned}
\ln TC = {}& \alpha_0 + \sum_j \varpi j \ln Y + \sum_j \alpha_{jw} \ln W + \sum_j \nu_j \ln r \\
& + \sum_j \alpha_{jA} \ln t + \frac{1}{2}\sum_j \sum_k \alpha_{jY}(\ln Y)^2 \\
& + \frac{1}{2}\sum_j \sum_k \xi_{jk}(\ln W)^2 + \frac{1}{2}\sum_j \sum_k \beta_{jk}(\ln t)^2 \\
& + \frac{1}{2}\sum_j \sum_k \omega_{jk}(\ln r)^2 + \sum_j \sum_k \vartheta_{jk} \ln W \ln r \\
& + \sum_j \sum_k \tau_{jk} \ln Y \ln t + \sum_j \sum_k \rho_{jk} \ln Y \ln W \\
& + \sum_j \sum_k \chi_{jk} \ln r \ln t + \sum_j \sum_k \varphi_{jk} \ln r \ln Y \\
& + \sum_j \sum_k \kappa_{jk} \ln t \ln W + \varepsilon.
\end{aligned}
$$

(5)

Differentiating ln TC with respect to ln Wj according to Shepard's lemma and allowing for a firm fixed effect yields labor's share in total costs in location j for parent i at time t:

$$
\begin{aligned}
LSHARE_{ijt} = {}& \beta_0 + \sum_j \rho_j \ln Y_{ijt} + \sum_j \kappa_j \ln t_{ijt} \\
& + \sum_j \xi_j \ln w_{ijt} + \sum_j \vartheta_j \ln r_{ijt} + f_i + \varepsilon_{ijt},
\end{aligned}
$$

(6)

where $LSHARE$ is defined as the cost share of labor expenditures in location j for parent i in time t, relative to expenditures on labor and capital across all locations. We impose the restrictions implied by the framework; in particular, it must be the case that the coefficients on factor prices sum to 0.

For completeness, we also consider aggregating capital and labor across locations using a CES function (Katz & Murphy, 1992, and Card, 2001, use this approach). Thus, we define L as

$$
L_i = \left[\sum_j (e_{ij} N_{ij})^{\frac{\sigma-1}{\sigma}} \right]^{\frac{\sigma}{\sigma-1}},
$$

(7)

where e represents productivity shocks, L_i is the total quantity of labor used, and σ is the Allen elasticity of substitution between labor in location i and j and is defined below.[8] Manipulation of the first-order conditions for profit maximization yields the following estimating equations:

$$
\begin{aligned}
\ln(L_h/L_{hif}) &= \sigma \ln \frac{p_h}{p_{hif}} + (\sigma - 1)\ln \frac{e_h}{e_{hif}} \\
&\quad - \sigma \ln \frac{w_h}{w_{hif}},
\end{aligned}
$$

(8a)

$$
\begin{aligned}
\ln(L_h/L_{lif}) &= \sigma \ln \frac{p_h}{p_{lif}} + (\sigma - 1)\ln \frac{e_h}{e_{lif}} \\
&\quad - \sigma \ln \frac{w_h}{w_{lif}}.
\end{aligned}
$$

(8b)

Equations (8a) and (8b) underscore the fact that as long as there is some substitution (or complementarity) between domestic and foreign labor, the cost of labor abroad plays an important role in determining the demand for U.S. labor. In addition, one of the restrictions of the CES specification is that the Allen elasticity of substitution between parent and low-income affiliates should be the same as the elasticity of substitution between parent and high-income affiliates.

E. Comparing Elasticities of Labor Demand across Specifications

All three approaches yield coefficient estimates that can be used to derive elasticities of factor demand η and Allen

---

[8] If sigma is equal to 0, we have the case of perfect complements (that is, left shoes and right shoes, The leontief function that looks like $L = \min(L_h, L_f)$. This is obviously extreme but might be applicable to some kinds of natural resource extraction. The polar opposite is σ tending to infinity (labor at home and labor abroad are perfect substitutes so $L = L_h + L_f$). This is also extreme, but some version of this might be realistic for production workers.

elasticities of substitution σ. In equation (5), the key parameters are the elasticities of factor demand η. Typically inputs i and j are referred to as p-complements if η_{ij} is less than 0 and p-substitutes if η_{ij} is greater than 0. The key parameters in equation (6) are the ξ_j's. To convert these into Allen partial elasticities of substitution between locations, we can calculate the following based on observed labor shares s_j:

$$\sigma_{jk} = (\xi_{jk} + s_j s_k)/s_j s_k \; and \; \sigma_{jj} = (\xi_{jj} + s_j s_j - s_j)/s_j s_j.$$
$$(9)$$

The Allen partial elasticity of substitution σ_{jk} gives us the percentage change in the ratio of L_j to L_k with respect to the percentage change in the ratio of w_k to w_j. The Allen partial elasticity of substitution is directly estimated as the coefficient on relative wages using the CES approach—equations (8a) and (8b). To convert the Allen partial elasticity of substitution into an elasticity of factor demand, we multiply by the factor share:

$$\eta_{ij} = s_j \sigma_{ij} = \partial \ln L_i / \partial \ln w_j.$$
$$(10)$$

We report elasticities of substitution for each of the three estimation strategies in table 6. Factor shares are computed by taking the sample means of the data. For the translog approach, we report the implied elasticities from estimating equation (6). The coefficients on affiliate wages imply that foreign labor in horizontal multinationals substitutes for home labor in both high- and low-income affiliate locations. For vertical multinationals, the results are the opposite: workers in low-income locations are complementary to domestic employees. As expected, the own-price elasticity is negative. The results are generally consistent with the results of our labor demand specification reported in columns 1 and 2.

The point estimates are consistently positive for low-income affiliate wages but not precisely estimated for high-income affiliate wages. These results imply that across all specifications, low-income affiliate employment substitutes for domestic employment. However, when multinationals are differentiated on the basis of how much they export for further processing, the results change. Employees in high-income affiliates substitute for domestic employment, while employees in low-income affiliates complement domestic employment.

We summarize the effects of factor price changes, trade, and technical change on U.S. manufacturing employment in table 7. We combine the coefficient estimates presented in table 4 with the actual mean changes in wages, investment prices, trade, research and development employment, and goods prices taken from table 3. We see that the major determinants of contraction in U.S. manufacturing parent employment are (a) falling prices of investment goods (which incorporate the falling prices of computers) (b) rising real wages in the United States, (c) falling real wages in

low-income affiliate locations, and (d) increasing import competition. While much of the debate on offshoring focuses on falling real wages in low-income affiliate locations, the impact of relative wage changes on U.S. parent labor demand is only one factor that explains contraction in parent employment. The combined effects of higher domestic wages and falling foreign wages account for only a 6.4% decline in U.S. employment. In comparison, falling investment prices account for a 13.7% decline and increasing import competition from low-wage countries accounts for a 2.3% decline in home employment. Moreover, for multinationals that export significant amounts of goods to developing countries for further processing, falling real wages in low-income affiliates boosted employment.

V. Conclusion

Over the period 1982 to 1999, domestic employment of U.S. multinationals contracted by nearly 4 million jobs, possibly foreshadowing the overall reduction in U.S. manufacturing employment that accelerated from 1999 onwards. During this period, the number of workers hired by affiliates in developing countries increased, while real wages paid to these workers declined. These facts are consistent with the hypothesis that U.S. parents are exporting low-wage jobs to low-income countries. In this paper, we show that this hypothesis is only partly supported by the evidence.

Using data on U.S.-based multinationals from the BEA, we measure the impact on U.S. manufacturing employment of changes in foreign affiliate wages, controlling for changing demand conditions, import competition, and technological change. We find that the evidence on the links between offshoring and domestic employment is mixed and that the effect depends on both the type and the location of foreign investment. We conclude that the heterogeneity in effects is one reason that previous research on this topic has yielded such apparently contradictory results.

For firms most likely to perform the same tasks in foreign affiliates and at home, foreign and domestic employees are substitutes. For these firms, lower wages in affiliate locations are associated with lower employment in the United States: A 1 percentage point fall in affiliate wages is associated with reductions in parent employment of between 0.009% and 0.598%. However, for firms that do significantly different tasks at home and abroad, foreign and domestic employment are complements: A 1 percentage point decline in low-income affiliate wages is associated with increases in parent employment of between 0.089% and 0.761%. The complementarity between domestic and foreign employment for firms where affiliates perform significantly different tasks is consistent with the theoretical models developed and discussed by Markusen (1989) and Markusen and Maskus (2001).

Finally, we show that other factors, including falling investment goods prices and import competition, are quantitatively more important determinants of falling US manufac-

Offshoring Jobs? Multinationals and U.S. Manufacturing Employment   269

OFFSHORING JOBS?   871

turing employment. Together these other factors account for 16.02% of the decline in manufacturing employment.

REFERENCES

Bernanke, Ben S., "Global Economic Integration: What's New and What's Not?" remarks prepared at the Federal Reserve Bank of Kansas City's Thirtieth Annual Economic Symposium, Jackson Hole, WY, (August 25, 2006). Available at http://www.federalreserve.gov/boarddocs/speeches/2006/20060828.

Bernard, Andrew, J. Bradford Jensen, and Peter Schott, "Survival of the Best Fit: Exposure to Low-wage Countries and the (Uneven) Growth of U.S. Manufacturing," *Journal of International Economics* 68 (2006), 219–237.

Borga, Maria, "Trends in Employment at US Multinational Companies: Evidence from Firm Level Data" (pp. 135–164), in Lael Brainard and Susan Collins (Eds.), *Brookings Trade Forum* (Washington, DC: Brookings Institution, 2005).

Borjas, George J., Richard Freeman, and Lawrence F. Katz, "How Much Do Immigration and Trade Affect Labor Market Outcomes?" (pp. 1–90), in *Brookings Papers on Economic Activity* (Washington, DC: Brookings, 1997).

Brainard, Lael, and David Riker, "US Multinationals and Competition from Low Wage Countries," NBER working paper no. 5959 (1997).

——— "Are US Multinationals Exporting US Jobs?" (pp. 410–426), in D. Greenaway and D. R. Nelson (Eds.), *Globalization and Labour Markets* (Northampton, MA: Edward Elgar Publishing, 2001).

Card, David, "Immigrant Inflows, Native Outflows, and the Local Market Impacts of Higher Immigration," *Journal of Labor Economics* 19:1 (2001), 22–64.

Desai, Mihir, Fritz Foley, and James Hines, "Foreign Direct Investment and Domestic Economic Activity," Harvard Business School working paper no. 11717 (2009).

Ebenstein, Avraham, Ann Harrison, Margaret McMillan, and Shannon Phillips, "Estimating the Impact of Trade and Offshoring on American Workers Using the Current Population Surveys," NBER working paper no. 15107 (2009).

Economic Report of the President (Washington, DC: U.S. Government Printing Office, February 21, 2007). Available at http://www.gpoaccess.gov/eop/2007/2007_erp.pdf

Grossman, Gene, and Esteban Rossi-Hansberg, "The Rise of Offshoring: It's Not Wine for Cloth Anymore," in Federal Reserve Bank of Kansas City, *The New Economic Geography: Effects and Policy Implications* (2007).

Hamermesh, Daniel S., *Labor Demand* (Princeton, NJ: Princeton University Press, 1993).

Hanson, Gordon, Raymond Mataloni, and Matthew Slaughter, "Vertical Production Networks in Multinational Firms," this REVIEW 87 (2005), 664–678.

Hanson, Gordon, Matthew Slaughter, and Raymond Mataloni, "Expansion Abroad and the Domestic Operations of US Multinational Firms" (pp. 245–294), in Susan Collins and Dani Rodrik (Eds.), *Brookings Trade Forum* (Washington, DC: Brookings Institution, 2001).

Harrison, Ann, and Gordon Hanson, "Who Gains From Trade Reform? Some Remaining Puzzles," *Journal of Development Economics* 59 (1999), 125–154.

Helpman, E., "A Simple Theory of International Trade and Multinational Corporations," *Journal of Political Theory* 92 (1984), 451–471.

Katz, Lawrence F., and Kevin M. Murphy, "Changes in Relative Wages, 1963–1987: Supply and Demand Factors," *Quarterly Journal of Economics* 107 (February 1992), 22–64.

Markusen, James R., "Trade in Producer Services and in Other Specialized Intermediate Inputs," *American Economic Review* 79 (1989), 85–95.

Markusen, James R., and Keith Maskus, "General-Equilibrium Approaches to the Multinational Firm: A Review of Theory and Evidence," NBER working paper no. 8334 (2001).

Mataloni, Raymond, "A Guide to BEA Statistics on U.S. Multinational Companies," *Survey of Current Business* 75 (1995), 38–55.

Mataloni, Raymond J. Jr., and Mahnaz Fahim-Nader, "Operations of US Multinational Companies: Preliminary Results from the 1994 Benchmark Survey," *Survey of Current Business* 76 (December 1996), 11–37.

Mataloni, Raymond J. Jr., and Daniel R. Yorgason, "Operations of US Multinational Companies: Preliminary Results from the 2004 Benchmark Survey," *Survey of Current Business* 86 (2006), 37–68.

Melitz, Marc, "The Impact of Trade on Intra-Industry Reallocations and Aggregate Industry Productivity," *Econometrica* 71 (2003), 1695–1725.

Muendler, Marc-Andreas, and Sascha O. Becker, "Margins of Multinational Labor Substitution," UCSD working paper no. 14776 (2009).

Revenga, Ana L., "Exporting Jobs? The Impact of Import Competition on Employment and Wages in US Manufacturing," *Quarterly Journal of Economics* 107 (1992), 255–284.

Wooldridge, Jeffrey M., *Econometric Analysis of Cross-Section and Panel Data* (Cambridge, MA: MIT Press, 2002).

APPENDIX

Tables

TABLE A1.—COVERAGE OF THE BEA SAMPLE

Year and Variable	Coverage of BEA Sample in Manufacturing	Coverage of BEA Sample in Services	Coverage of BEA Sample in Total U.S. Economic Activity (Includes Manufacturing, Services, Other, Wholesale Trade)
1982			
Total number of employees in BEA sample (thousands)	11,758.1	993.8	18,704.6
Gross product in the BEA sample (U.S. millions of dollars)	421,050	25,997	796,017
Coverage of the BEA sample (in %) relative to gross product for all firms operating in the United States	80%	6%	33%
Value of dollar export sales by firms in the BEA sample (millions)	163,383	NA	NA
Coverage of the BEA sample (in %) relative to exports of all firms operating in the United States	77%	NA	NA
1989			
Total number of employees in BEA sample (thousands)	10,706.8	1,700	18,785.4
Gross product in the BEA sample (U.S. millions of dollars)	586,568	57,090	1,044,884
Coverage of the BEA sample (in %) relative to gross product for all firms operating in the United States	67%	6%	25%
Value of dollar export sales by firms in the BEA sample (millions)	236,371	NA	NA
Coverage of the BEA sample (in %) relative to exports of all firms operating in the United States	65%	NA	NA
1994			
Total number of employees in BEA sample (thousands)	9,622.5	2,653.4	18,947.4
Gross product in the BEA sample (U.S. millions of dollars)	690,466	102,520	1,325,945
Coverage of the BEA sample (in %) relative to gross product for all firms operating in the United States	59%	8%	26%
Value of dollar export sales by firms in the BEA sample (millions)	337,036	NA	NA
Coverage of the BEA sample (in %) relative to exports of all firms operating in the United States	59%	NA	NA
1999			
Total number of employees in BEA sample (thousands)	7,954.9	2,220,174	23,006.8
Value of dollar export sales by firms in the BEA sample (millions)	441,587	NA	NA
Coverage of the BEA sample (in %) relative to exports of all Firms operating in the United States	62.5%	NA	NA

Based on Mataloni and Fahim-Nader (1996) and Mataloni and Yorgason (2006).

TABLE A2.—CROSS CHECKING THE ACCURACY OF THE BEA DATABASE

	Imposing a Cut-Off (reporting requirement of a balance sheet total of at least 7 million euros for Germany; U.S. reporting requirements vary over time; no reporting requirement for Sweden)	Imposing No Cut-Off on Germany Affiliate Reporting
BEA data		
Employees of U.S. affiliates in 1999 in Germany	458,744	NA
Employees of U.S. affiliates in 1999 in Sweden	67,044	NA
German government data (direct U.S. ownership only)		
Employees of U.S. affiliates in 1998	466,941	488,866
Employees of U.S. affiliates in 1999	509,537	532,594
Employees of U.S. affiliates in 2000	488,157	509,176
Swedish government data		
Employees of U.S. affiliates in 1997 (majority owned only)	51,138	NA
Employees of U.S. affiliates in 1998 (majority owned only)	61,089	NA
Employees of U.S. affiliates in 1999 (majority owned only)	78,621	NA

TABLE A3.—DESCRIPTION OF VARIABLES AND DATA SOURCES

Variable Name	Source	Description
Log Wage (Industry Level)	U.S. Bureau of Economic Analysis	Wages and salaries of employees and employer expenditures for all employee benefit plans in parents computed separately for parents, high-income affiliates, and other affiliates and averaged across industries.
Log Wage (Industry Level)	UNIDO	Wages calculated based on surveys administered by UNIDO, supplemented with secondary sources (such as national statistical agencies). Wages calculated as compensation divided by number of employees at the 3-digit ISIC level Revision 2. All values converted to U.S. dollars using the IMF exchange rate series rf. Data taken from INDSTAT3, published in 2006 by UNIDO.
Log Employment	U.S. Bureau of Economic Analysis	Log of the number of full-time and part-time employees on the payroll at the end of the fiscal year in all affiliates. However, a count taken during the year was accepted if it was a reasonable proxy for the end-of-year number. Computed separately for parents, high-income affiliates, and other affiliates.
R&D Share R&D Share (High-Income Affiliates) R&D Share (Low-Income Affiliates)	U.S. Bureau of Economic Analysis	Number of employees in research and development as a percentage of total employment. Computed separately for U.S. parents, affiliates in high-income locations, and affiliates in low-income locations.
U.S. Investment Price	NBER Manufacturing Database	This is the variable PIINV in the NBER's manufacturing productivity database. It is set to 1 in 1987. It combines separate deflators for structures and equipment, based on the distribution of each type of asset in the industry. This is a deflator for new investment flows, not the existing capital stock. See www.nber.org.
Foreign Investment Price	Penn World Tables	PPP price of domestic investment calculated from the PWT 6.1. See appendix for PWT 6.1 for more details or http:// pwt.econ.upenn.edu.
Foreign Consumer Goods Price	Penn World Tables	PPP price of consumption goods calculated from the PWT 6.1. See appendix for PWT 6.1 for more details or http:// pwt.econ.upenn.edu.
U.S. Import Penetration	Bernard et al. (2006)	Imports into the United States divided by imports into the United States plus total production in the United States less exports from the United States by year by four-digit SIC 1987 revision code industrial classification.
U.S. Import Penetration from Low-Income Countries	Bernard et al. (2006)	Share of products in an industry sourced from at least one country with less than 5% of U.S. per capita GDP

TABLE A4.—ANNUAL CHANGES IN REAL WAGES AND EMPLOYMENT BY REGION AND INCOME

Region	Average Annual Percentage Change in Real Wages (per employee)	Average Annual Percentage Change in Employment
Developed economies	1.48	−0.62
East Asia and Pacific[a]	0.28	4.00
Europe and Central Asia	8.31	−4.29
Latin America and Caribbean	−1.40	1.02
Middle East and North Africa	−1.88	3.21
South Asia	−0.78	3.77
Sub-Saharan Africa[b]	−4.54	1.83
World	**0.21**	**1.27**
Income Group		
High income: OECD	1.07	−0.94
High income: non-OECD	1.88	−0.29
Low income	−3.34	1.61
Lower middle income[c]	1.39	1.36
Upper middle income[d]	−0.34	0.20

Madagascar was excluded from the sample due to data inconsistencies. Source: Authors' calculations based on UNIDO INDSTAT2 data. Time period covered is 1980–2007.
[a]The numbers are 0.78% and 4.05%, respectively, if China is excluded from the sample;
[b]The numbers are −4.81% and 2.01%, respectively, if South Africa is excluded from the sample
[c]The numbers are 1.53% and 1.25%, respectively, if China is excluded from the sample
[d]The numbers are −0.28% and 0.23%, respectively, if South Africa is excluded from the sample.

TABLE A5.—TESTING FOR THE IMPACT OF SELECTION INTO EXIT: HECKMAN CORRECTION

	(1)	(2)	(3)	(4)	(5)	(6)
	Pooled	Imports from	Exports to Affiliates	Exports for Processing	Exports for Resale	Platform FDI
Log U.S. Industrial Wages	−0.329	−0.310	−0.415	−0.381	−0.372	−0.380
	[0.040]**	[0.044]**	[0.045]**	[0.045]**	[0.042]**	[0.102]**
Log Industrial Wages High-Income Countries	−0.020	−0.031	−0.066	−0.039	−0.049	−0.012
	[0.035]	[0.039]	[0.043]	[0.041]	[0.038]	[0.087]
Log Industrial Wages Low-Income Countries	0.057	0.062	0.080	0.084	0.062	0.079
	[0.017]**	[0.019]**	[0.020]**	[0.019]**	[0.019]**	[0.045]
Log of the U.S. Price of Capital	0.172	0.163	0.150	0.128	0.197	0.157
	[0.040]**	[0.040]**	[0.039]**	[0.039]**	[0.039]**	[0.040]**
Log of the Foreign Price of Capital	0.076	0.082	0.061	0.066	0.071	0.077
	[0.074]	[0.075]	[0.074]	[0.074]	[0.074]	[0.075]
Import Penetration	−0.406	−0.411	−0.414	−0.407	−0.409	0.404
	[0.202]*	[0.202]*	[0.200]*	[0.201]*	[0.201]*	[0.202]*
Import Penetration from Low-Wage Countries	−0.054	−0.056	−0.010	−0.040	−0.024	−0.050
	[0.358]	[0.359]	[0.356]	[0.357]	[0.356]	[0.359]
R&D (% Sales)	0.747	0.753	0.713	0.872	0.581	0.774
	[0.451]	[0.451]	[0.450]	[0.451]	[0.451]	[0.452]
R&D (% Sales) in High-Income Countries	0.534	0.538	0.377	0.448	0.466	0.537
	[0.697]	[0.697]	[0.692]	[0.694]	[0.694]	[0.697]
R&D (% Sales) in Low-Income Countries	3.642	3.788	3.626	3.599	3.607	3.670
	[2.276]	[2.282]	[2.259]	[2.267]	[2.263]	[2.278]
Log of Industry Sales	0.086	0.087	0.078	0.084	0.081	0.086
	[0.032]**	[0.032]**	[0.032]*	[0.032]**	[0.032]**	[0.032]**
Log Affiliate Sales by Industry	−0.088	−0.087	−0.092	−0.089	−0.092	−0.085
	[0.043]*	[0.043]*	[0.042]*	[0.043]*	[0.042]*	[0.043]*
Log U.S. Industrial Wages × Vertical		−0.553	2.265	2.172	3.045	0.083
		[0.534]	[1.560]	[1.902]	[0.245]	[0.154]
Log Industrial Wages High-Income Countries × Vertical		0.377	1.114	0.772	1.946	−0.051
		[0.515]	[0.531]*	[0.754]	[0.931]*	[0.129]
Log Industrial Wages Low-Income Countries × Vertical		−0.217	−0.463	−3.923	−0.329	−0.035
		[0.371]	[0.166]**	[1.299]**	[0.245]	[0.067]
Lambda for 1994	−0.031	−0.031	−0.039	−0.036	−0.034	−0.032
	[0.039]	[0.039]	[0.039]	[0.039]	[0.039]	[0.039]
Lambda for 1999	0.080	0.078	0.070	0.070	0.081	0.077
	[0.068]	[0.069]	[0.068]	[0.068]	[0.068]	[0.069]
Observations	3,177	3,177	3,177	3,177	3,177	3,177
R^2	0.08	0.08	0.09	0.08	0.09	0.08

Standard errors corrected for arbitrary heteriskedasticity are in brackets. *Significant at 5%. **Significant at 1%. Each of columns 2–6 includes an interaction term between the wage measures and vertical integration defined at the firm level as the mean of the variable in the column heading over the entire sample period. All specifications include time dummies.

TABLE A6.—ACTIVITY AT THE INTENSIVE AND EXTENSIVE MARGINS

A: Entry or Exit to and from Low-Wage Countries				B: Entry and Exit to and from Mexico			
Activity 1982–1989	In	Out	Total	Activity 1982–1989	In	Out	Total
In	586	67	653	In	313	72	415
	85.8%	9.81%	95.61%		78.67%	11.51%	89.18%
Out	30	0	30	Out	51	0	21
	4.39%		4.39%		10.82%		10.82%
Total	616	67	683	Total	364	72	436
	90.19%	9.81%	100%		89.49%	11.51%	100%
Activity 1989–1994				Activity 1989–1994			
In	542	74	616	In	331	33	364
	85.33%	8.55%	93.88%		89.21%	5.27%	94.48%
Out	53	0	53	Out	29	0	29
	6.12%		6.12%		5.51%		5.51%
Total	595	74	669	Total	360	33	393
	91.45%	8.55%	100%		94.72%	5.27%	100%
Activity 1994–1999				Activity 1994–1999			
In	516	79	595	In	340	20	360
	86.69%	9.14%	95.83%		89.18%	7.15%	96.33%
Out	36	0	36	Out	26	0	26
	4.17%		4.17%		3.67%		3.67%
Total	552	79	631	Total	366	20	386
	90.86%	9.14%	100%		92.85%	7.15%	100%

The number entries are the counts of parents belonging in each cell. The percentages below these numbers are the shares of affiliate employment accounted for by the row column entries.

OFFSHORING JOBS?   875

TABLE A7.—LOW-INCOME AFFILIATE EMPLOYMENT AND EMPLOYMENT SHARES
BY COUNTRY OVER TIME

	1982	1989	1994	1999
Low-income affiliate employment by country				
Mexico	208,860	496,872	501,066	654,076
Brazil	332,370	462,105	468,184	384,854
China	77	11,131	33,560	133,371
Malaysia	55,583	50,055	73,073	85,365
Thailand	14,804	18,375	25,460	81,054
South Africa	76,728	32,024	30,432	53,288
India	27,798	37,032	21,193	48,124
Argentina	63,130	35,956	53,580	41,007
Philippines	73,651	63,430	68,278	40,980
Total	853,001	1,206,979	1,274,824	1,522,118
Low-income affiliate share of employment by country				
Mexico	19.63%	35.36%	31.63%	37.69%
Brazil	31.24	32.89	29.56	15.25
China	0.01	0.79	2.12	9.82
Malaysia	5.22	3.56	4.61	4.57
Thailand	1.39	1.31	1.61	4.34
South Africa	7.21	2.28	1.92	2.85
India	2.61	2.64	1.34	2.58
Argentina	5.93	2.56	3.38	2.20
Philippines	6.92	4.51	4.31	2.19
Total	80.17	85.91	80.48	81.48

TABLE A8.—CLASSIFICATION OF COUNTRIES INTO LOW-VERSUS HIGH-INCOME CATEGORIES

Countries classified as low income by the World Bank	Countries classified as high income by the World Bank
Estonia (1,470), Guyana (1,504), China (1,579), Malawi (1,689), Romania (1,866), Sri Lanka (1,898), Ukraine (2,151), India (2,325). Dominican Republic (2,763), Tanzania (3,057), Zimbabwe (3,109), Uzbekistan (3,136), Zambia (3,152), Vietnam (3,326), Indonesia (3,401), Botswana (3,517), Pakistan (3,631), Nigeria (3,940), Honduras (4,111), Thailand (4,168), Costa Rica (4,236), Yemen. Rep. (4,248), Senegal (4,318), Philippines (4,427), Slovak R. (4,531), Colombia (4,603), El Salvador (4,622), Egypt, Arab Rep. (4,756), Fiji (4,824), Kenya (5,098), Malaysia (5,334), Hungary (5,426), Ghana (5,475), Poland (5,540), Jamaica (5,557), Ecuador (5,596), Panama (6,453), Mexico (6,465), Guatemala (6,786), Trinidad and Tobago (6,994), Venezuala, RB (7,393), Swaziland (7,500), Russian Federation (7,527), Uruguay (7,997), Turkey (8,370), Morocco (8,422), Tunisia (9,058), Nicaragua (9,206), Malta (9,211), Chile (9,485), South Africa (10,257), Barbados (10,480), Peru (11,065), Brazil (11,227)	Singapore (11,885), Portugal (14,236), Bahamas (14,288), Taiwan (14,699), Saudi Arabia (14,912), Korea, Rep. (15,549), Bahrain (16,047), Netherlands Antilles (16,596), Hong Kong, China (17,478), New Zealand (17,736), Argentina (18,003), Israel (19,572), Greece (22,855), Australia (23,313), Ireland (23,392), Spain (25,848), United Kingdom (26,487), Sweden (27,380), Italy (30,574), Austria (31,209), Finland (32,049), Denmark (32,934), Norway (33,022), United Arab Emirates (33,603), France (33,628), Aruba (34,745), Canada (35,268), Netherlands (35,973), Belgium (40,134), Luxembourg (43,614), Germany (44,146), Switzerland (44,248), Japan (57,126)

Nominal manufacturing wages in 1994 U.S. dollars in parentheses.

Chapter 12

ESTIMATING THE IMPACT OF TRADE AND OFFSHORING ON AMERICAN WORKERS USING THE CURRENT POPULATION SURVEYS[†]

Avraham Ebenstein, Ann Harrison, Margaret McMillan, and Shannon Phillips*

Abstract—We link industry-level data on trade and offshoring with individual-level worker data from the Current Population Surveys from 1984 to 2002. We find that occupational exposure to globalization is associated with significant wage effects, while industry exposure has no significant impact. We present evidence that globalization has put downward pressure on worker wages through the reallocation of workers away from higher-wage manufacturing jobs into other sectors and other occupations. Using a panel of workers, we find that occupation switching due to trade led to real wage losses of 12 to 17 percentage points.

I. Introduction

BETWEEN 1983 and 2002, the U.S. economy experienced a boom in offshoring and a doubling of imports of manufactured goods from low-income countries. Over this same period, roughly 6 million jobs were lost in manufacturing, and income inequality increased sharply. These parallel developments led some critics of globalization to conclude that "good" manufacturing jobs had been shipped overseas, putting downward pressure on wages of middle-class American workers. Concern over these developments motivated the U.S. Congress to pass the American Jobs Creation Act of 2004. Yet the degree to which changes in the U.S. labor market are related to growth in international trade and offshoring is still the subject of heated debate.

The standard approach to identifying effects of import competition on wages is to use variation in the prices (or quantities) of imported goods across industries over time as an exogenous shock and examine the impact on industry-specific labor market outcomes. This approach has been used to measure the impact of globalization on industry wage differentials and the effects of sector-specific import competition on wages and employment. For example, Feenstra and Hanson (1999) use a two-step procedure, first iden-

tifying the impact of outsourcing and high-technology investments on productivity and prices and then tracing through the impact of induced productivity and price changes on relative wages among production and nonproduction workers. Using data for the U.S. manufacturing sector between 1979 and 1990, they find that the real wages of production workers were probably unaffected by offshoring activities, while the real wages of nonproduction workers increased by 1 to 2 percentage points. Bernard, Jensen, and Schott (2006), in the first paper to distinguish between imports from high-income versus low-income countries, find that only low-income imports negatively affected firm exit, survival, and employment growth.

A key limitation of the previous literature on the labor market effects of globalization is that it typically focuses on changes within manufacturing. In this paper, we focus on potential wage impacts across occupations, both within manufacturing and across the broader economy. In a typical occupation, some workers are in tradable sectors (e.g., manufacturing), and others are in nontradable sectors (e.g., fast food services). To expand our analysis of wage outcomes due to globalization beyond manufacturing, we begin by defining the concept of occupational exposure to international trade or offshoring activities.[1] Inasmuch as the demand for a particular worker's skill is affected by trade, those who are working in either the tradable or nontradable goods (or services) sector could be hurt by foreign competition. Also, if occupational tenure and experience is a more important determinant of wages than industry experience, then focusing on exposure at the industry level may understate the costs of globalization.

In order to examine this empirically, we link industry-level data on trade and offshoring with individual-level worker data from the Current Population Surveys (CPS). We find a significant divergence between the impact of occupational exposure and industry exposure to globalization on wage outcomes. In particular, we find no significant negative effects of either international trade or offshoring on wages of all types of workers if we measure globalization at the industry level. When we focus on occupational exposure and include workers in both manufacturing and services, however, we find large and significant effects. Our

Received for publication May 23, 2011. Revision accepted for publication April 8, 2013. Editor: Gordon Hanson.

* Ebenstein: Hebrew University of Jerusalem; Harrison: University of Pennsylvania and NBER; McMillan: Tufts University and NBER; Phillips: Boston College.

We thank the editor, two anonymous referees, Rajeev Dehejia, Gene Grossman, James Harrigan, and John MaLaren for helpful comments on earlier versions of the manuscript. We also thank seminar participants at the University of Maryland, the University of Virginia, and Yale University for helpful comments. Special thanks to David Autor, Robert Feenstra, Wayne Gray, and Lawrence Edwards for providing data critical to our analysis. Excellent research assistance was provided by Catherine Almirall, Revital Bar, Joan Fang, and Michael Freedman.

A supplemental appendix is available online at http://www.mitpressjournals.org/doi/suppl/10.1162/REST_a_00400.

[1] We are greatly indebted to Gordon Hanson for suggesting this idea.

[†]This article originally appeared in *The Review of Economics and Statistics*, **96** 581–595 © 2014 Massachusetts Institute of Technology Press.

analysis indicates that workers in routine occupations, such as those employed in blue-collar production occupations, have suffered the greatest losses from globalization. These results are consistent with recent empirical work demonstrating the importance of occupational tenure and downplaying the importance of tenure within a particular industry for a worker's wages (Kambourov & Manovskii, 2009a, 2009b).[2]

We also explore how the impact of globalization has changed over time. A number of scholars have suggested that wage pressure from developing countries is likely to have increased during the 1990s. Feenstra (2008) singles out expanded competition from China as having exerted pressure on U.S. wages, and he is not alone in this view (see also Freeman, 1995, and Krugman, 2008). Empirical evidence for this conjecture is limited, however.[3] We find that while the impact of trade and offshoring on U.S. wages through the mid-1990s was small in magnitude and insignificant, the effects became much larger in the second half of the 1990s. By the end of our sample period in 2002, we find significant and economically important effects of globalization on wages using our occupational exposure measure. Based on our study, it is likely that the impact of globalization on U.S. wages in since 2002 has increased further as more firms have engaged in offshoring to low-wage destinations.[4]

We examine the impact of globalization on U.S. workers by focusing attention on how they are affected by imports, exports, and offshoring to low- and high-income countries. Our results indicate that a 10% increase in occupational exposure to import competition is associated with nearly a 3.0% decline in real wages for workers who perform routine tasks among workers in our 1984 to 2002 sample and a 4.4% decline for workers taken from 1997 to 2002.[5] We also find substantial wage effects of offshoring to low-wage countries: a 10 percentage point increase in occupation-specific exposure to overseas employment in low-wage countries is associated with a 0.7% decline in real wages for workers performing routine tasks for our entire sample and a 2.0% decline for 1997 to 2002. For routine occupations with sig-

nificant export activity, wages are positively linked to export growth. For these workers, a 10 percentage point increase in export share at the occupation level is associated with a 6.7 percentage point increase in wages over the sample period. For the end of the period (1997–2002), every percentage point increase in export shares for routine workers is associated with a percentage point increase in wages.

We also find that globalization has put downward pressure on worker wages through the reallocation of workers away from higher-paid manufacturing sectors toward other sectors and a shift of workers out of trade-vulnerable occupations. First, we find that domestic employment has declined in industries with expansion in low-income-country employment, consistent with evidence that multinational firms have shifted production overseas.[6] Then, using a subset of the CPS data where we are able to match the same worker over time, we estimate a first-stage equation with the exposure of an occupation to trade as an instrument for whether a worker switched occupations. In the second stage, we find that occupation switching due to trade led to real wage losses of 12 to 17 percentage points between 1984 and 2002.[7] Any analysis of the wage effects of globalization that is restricted to manufacturing workers would miss the downward pressure on wages resulting from workers leaving manufacturing and entering the service sector. The associated distributional implications are potentially important, given historically large wage premiums paid to manufacturing (relative to service) workers in the United States (see figure 1 for a graphical exposition) and significant empirical evidence that industries compensate workers differently.[8] It is also worth noting that our results are unlikely to be explained by the fact that weaker workers are more likely to switch occupations (Trefler & Lui, 2011). When we control for unobserved differences in worker quality among those who switch occupations, we continue to find suggestive results that the wage declines associated with globalization are due to worker's switching occupations.

An important limitation of our study (and other papers in this literature) is that we are unable to fully separate the

---

[2] Kambourov and Manovskii (2009a) find that "returns to occupational tenure are substantial." They also indicate that "when occupational experience is taken into account, tenure with an industry or employer has relatively little importance in accounting for the wage one receives." This finding is consistent with human capital being occupation specific. Their results imply that switching occupations will have a much greater impact on worker wages than switching industries.

[3] One important exception is Autor, Dorn, and Hanson (2012), who exploit differences in U.S. regional exposure to import competition from China to show significant effects on employment, unemployment, and wages from 1990 to 2007.

[4] Since the CPS changed its occupational coding scheme in 2003, we do not attempt analysis beyond 2002 in this paper. Our analysis of Bureau of Economic Analysis data indicates that offshoring to low-wage countries has increased markedly since 2002, with employment in low-income countries (e.g., China) exceeding that of high-wage countries.

[5] This finding is consistent with recent work highlighting the differential impact of offshoring by worker skill type. Hummels et al. (2011) use matched worker and firm data from Denmark and find that offshoring raises skilled worker wages but lowers unskilled worker wages, while exporting raises the wages of all types of workers.

[6] Our results corroborate results on employment declines within manufacturing by Harrison and McMillan (2011), who use firm-level data on multinational manufacturing firms, but they stand in contrast to Desai, Foley, and Hines (2009), who do not distinguish between high-wage and low-wage affiliate employment and find that offshoring is unambiguously positive for U.S. employment.

[7] Other scholarship has documented the cost of trade-induced shifts in employment. Menezes-Filho and Muendler (2011) use a Brazilian trade reform to document significant short-run costs to workers and sticky intersectoral labor reallocation. Artuc, Chaudhuri, and McLaren (2010) develop a theoretical model showing that adjustment costs for workers are likely to be significant and can explain why there is likely to be sluggish reallocation and short-term negative wage effects on workers under trade liberalization. Cosar (2011) also explores sluggish labor market adjustments by developing a two-sector small, open economy, overlapping-generations model that is calibrated to Brazilian data. The paper finds that human capital is a much bigger barrier to labor mobility than search frictions.

[8] See, for example, Katz and Summers (1989) and Krueger and Summers (1988).

IMPACT OF TRADE AND OFFSHORING ON AMERICAN WORKERS   583

FIGURE 1.—TRENDS IN EMPLOYMENT AND WAGES IN THE MANUFACTURING AND SERVICE SECTORS

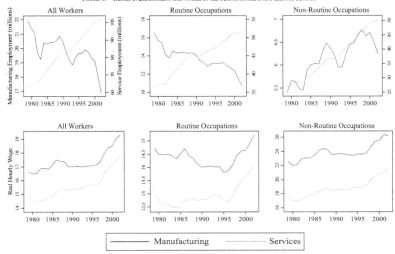

Employment and wage calculations are based on the Current Population Survey Merged Outgoing Rotation Groups (MORG). Sample includes all part-time and full-time workers. Wages are in 2005 dollars. The definition of routine workers is based on occupational task content. Details are available in the data appendix.

impact of trade and offshoring from other changes in the labor market. Two primary identification challenges exist. First, it may be that trade and offshoring are the result of changes in the domestic labor market. For example, if firms choose to move operations offshore in response to changes in the domestic labor market (e.g., unions), this reverse causality would invalidate the causal interpretation of our results. Second, it may be that technological change is correlated with trade in a manner preventing causal interpretation of our coefficient estimates. For example, if more routine tasks are more easily performed overseas or automated, we will be unable to accurately characterize the counterfactual of how wages would have evolved in the absence of globalization. Insofar as some workers face competitive pressure from low-wage workers in foreign countries and automation, it will be difficult to separately identify the impact of either exposure. We attempt to address these concerns in several ways. First, by combining industry-level trade or offshoring data with individual-level information on wages and worker characteristics, we hope to sidestep the issue of reverse causality since it is difficult for one worker to affect aggregate trade outcomes. Second, we pay considerable attention to capturing technological change across industries that could influence both worker wages and globalization outcomes. We include annual measures of total factor productivity, capital accumulation, price of investment goods by industry, and computer use

rates by industry and occupation, which represents our best attempt to account for technical change that could potentially affect workers directly. Third, we explore the robustness of our results to instrumental variable estimation, where we exploit factors that should affect the tradability of certain goods, or the desirability of certain offshore locations (results available in online appendixes). These instruments may themselves be endogenous, however. Consequently, we focus our attention mainly on results that rely on fixed effects by industry and occupation and the available control variables to measure the impact of globalization on workers. The focus of this paper is on the importance of occupation versus industry-level measures of exposure to globalization, and that focus is important regardless of identification issues, which will continue to remain a challenge. In the absence of a "clean" natural experiment or a fully compelling instrument for the tradability of certain occupations, our results must be interpreted with appropriate caution.[9]

_____
[9] In a recent paper, Jensen and Kletzer (2005) attempt to measure the tradability of service sector goods using an approach that considers the spatial concentration of service industries and occupations. They posit that more spatially concentrated industries or occupations are more tradable and find evidence consistent with this hypothesis in U.S. data. We chose not to pursue this strategy, as geographical concentration may reflect other factors, such as state-specific regulations that lead to clustering of certain industries or occupations.

584   THE REVIEW OF ECONOMICS AND STATISTICS

The paper is organized as follows. Section II describes our data; documents broad trends in trade, offshoring, wages, and employment; and presents the empirical specification. Section III presents our main empirical findings regarding the impact of offshoring and trade on domestic wages and employment at the occupation versus the industry level. Section IV concludes.

II. Data Description, Empirical Strategy, and Trends

A. Data Description

Our sample of U.S. workers is taken from the Current Population Survey Merged Outgoing Rotation Groups for 1983 to 2002, which provides data for over 3.4 million workers who are assigned a consistent classification for their industry and occupation during the period.[10] Offshore activity in each industry is measured by the total employment of foreign affiliates among multinational U.S. firms, separated into high- and low-income affiliate locations, as collected by the Bureau of Economic Analysis (BEA).[11] Our data on import penetration and export shares are taken from Bernard at al. (2006), which we recalculated and updated through 2002. Since relative price series for imports and exports are incomplete, we substitute for prices by using the share of exports in production and import penetration at the four-digit SIC level.[12] We control for productivity changes that could also affect labor demand as well as wages using the NBER's calculations of total factor productivity provided by Wayne Gray. This data source also provides us with measures of the prices of investment goods, capital-to-labor ratios, and the real price of shipments by industry and year.[13] These are included in our main specifications to control for technological change that could also affect wage rates. Finally, we match our workers to information on computer use rates by industry and occupation from CPS computer supplements conducted during our sample period (1984, 1989, 1993, 1997, 2000). Using

the available surveys, we interpolate and extrapolate computer use rates for the entire window.[14] Summary statistics for the individual worker sample matched to our offshoring, trade, technology, and price data are available in table A1.

We use Autor et al.'s (2003) distinction between routine and nonroutine tasks to allow us to separately identify the impact of different measures of globalization across different types of workers. To the extent that routine tasks are more easily offshored or replaced with imports, we would expect globalization to have a larger impact on workers performing these types of tasks. Autor et al. (2003) describe routine jobs as "tasks that can be expressed using procedural or 'rules-based' logic, that is, codified in a fully specified sequence of logical programming commands ('If-Then-Do' statements) that designate unambiguously what actions the will perform and in what sequence at each contingency to achieve the desired result." While they use routineness to designate which jobs can be easily performed by computers, we would argue that routine jobs are also more readily codified, communicated, and consequently transferred overseas. Examples of these jobs include attaching hands to faces of watches, sewing fasteners and decorative trimming to articles, and services tasks that we think of as offshorable, such as answering telephones.

Following Autor et al. (2003), we aggregate five measures of the routineness of tasks into a single index for each occupation k. Two indicators, Routine Manual and Routine Cognitive, measure the routineness of tasks by occupation in each of these dimensions. These range from 1 for tasks that are not routine to 10 for tasks that are fully routine. The three other measures are (1) Direction, Control, and Planning of Activities (DCP), which measures non routine cognitive tasks; (2) Eye, Foot, and Hand coordination (EFH) activities, which require nonroutine manual task completion; and (3) the Math indicator, which measures the quantitative or analytical reasoning skills required. The index of routineness by worker education level, industry, and year is given by:

$$Routine_k$$
$$= \frac{Routine\,Cognitive_k + Routine\,Manual_k}{Routine\,Cognitive_k + Routine\,Manual_k + DCP_k + EFH_k + Math_k}.$$

The index ranges from 0 to 1.[15] The last three terms, *DCP*, *EFH*, and *Math*, refer to cognitive tasks that are higher order in their complexity and presumably are asso-

---

[10] We express our gratitude to David Autor for providing us with concordances that provided a consistent coding scheme of industries and occupations for the period. The CPS occupation and industry codes were reclassified in 2003 to correspond to the North American Industrial Classification System, which made it difficult to compare data before and after the change. We begin with 1984 because our equation codes for the 1979–1981 period are not consistent with the classification for later years, and we use lags in our empirical specification that lead us to drop 1983.

[11] The BEA sample of multinational firms accounted for 80% of total output in manufacturing in 1980, suggesting that the coverage is fairly extensive. However, using these data, we are unable to distinguish between imports from affiliates (arm's-length trade between firms) and imports from nonaffiliates.

[12] Results using prices instead of quantities are available in the online appendix. The results are qualitatively similar to our main results using quantities.

[13] These data were aggregated from the four-digit to three-digit SIC level using the employment distribution in 1979. The three-digit SIC level was converted to our industry classification scheme using a concordance provided by David Autor that was a census-based scheme that consistently defined industries for our sample period. A similar method was used to match CPS workers to the trade data.

[14] These data were also provided by David Autor and are used in Autor et al. (1998).

[15] See Autor et al. (2003) for a thorough description of these variables. Our calculation of routine is the sum of routine manual tasks (Finger Dexterity) and routine nonmanual (Set Limits, Tolerances, or Standards), as a share of those tasks and nonroutine manual (Eye, Hand, Foot), nonroutine analytic (General Educational Development, Mathematics), and nonroutine interactive (Direction, Control, and Planning) tasks. More details on this classification scheme are available in the online appendix.

ciated with larger costs of performing outside a firm's central location.

B. Empirical Strategy

Our empirical strategy is to regress log wages of worker i in industry j in period t (W_{ijt}) on lagged measures of exposure to offshoring and international trade (G_{ijt-1}) using annual data from 1983 to 2002, first at the industry level and subsequently at the occupation level, which we will define below. This paper examines the impact of globalization (i.e., offshoring and trade) on wages and the domestic labor market response to offshoring and trade in the short run. After controlling for all observables such as education, age, race, ethnicity, and experience, workers in a frictionless world could costlessly move from one industry or occupation to another. We test this hypothesis and find that barriers exist at the occupation but not at the industry level.

We use lagged measures of exposure to offshoring and trade for two reasons. First, since offshoring requires time to implement, and wage adjustment is not instantaneous, it is unlikely that the causal effect of offshoring on wages will play out within a single calendar year. Second, within a given year, offshoring, trade exposure, and wages are likely to be affected by simultaneous shocks. We use four measures of exposure to offshoring and international trade: offshoring to low-income affiliate locations, offshoring to high-income affiliate locations, export shares, and import penetration. To allow for the possibility that offshoring to low-income locations might have different effects from offshoring to high-income locations, we include as separate regressors the log of employment in sector j by U.S.-based multinationals in low- and high-income countries.

There are three additional challenges to identifying the causal effect of globalization on wages. First, the industries that are most likely to globalize may also be those with lower wages or greater volatility. We address this concern by including industry fixed effects (I_j) in our specification. Second, globalization and wages may be jointly affected by common time-varying shocks, such as the business cycle and exchange rate fluctuations. We control for these by including time fixed effects (d_t). Third, we control for time-varying shocks at the industry level that could be confounded with changes in globalization by adding a number of controls. TFP_{jt-1} captures changes in productivity by industry and year that could affect demand for labor.[16] We also attempt to capture productivity changes including two (arguably) exogenous measures, the price of investment goods and computer use rates. The price of investment goods $PINV_{jt-1}$ captures in part the role of falling computer prices and the potential impact of labor-saving technology on labor market outcomes. We also control for industry factor intensity (lagged capital to labor ratio $KLRATIO_{jt-1}$)

and computer use rates by industry and year ($COMP_{jt}$) to account for contemporaneous changes in an industry's wage rate based on the ability to substitute labor with computers.[17] Finally, we control for individual characteristics including age, sex, race, experience, education, and location (Z_{ijt}):

$$W_{ijt} = \beta_0 Z_{ijt} + \beta_1 G_{jt-1} + \beta_2 TFP_{jt-1} + \beta_3 PINV_{jt-1} \\ + \beta_4 KLRATIO_{jt-1} + \beta_5 COMP_{jt} \\ + \beta_6 d_t + \beta_7 I_j + \varepsilon_{ijt}. \quad (1a)$$

To examine the relationship between wages and globalization at the occupation level, we retain the same setup as in equation (1a) but modify the G vector to create a measure of occupational exposure to offshoring or trade. Each variable in the G vector was created from a merged data set of BEA offshore employment data, trade data, and CPS monthly outgoing rotation group individual-level data, by industry and year. We calculate for each occupation its exposure to trade using the distribution of workers employed in this occupation across industries in 1983. For each occupation k and industry j, we have $\alpha_{kj83} = \frac{L_{kj83}}{L_{k83}}$, where L_{kj83} is the total number of workers in occupation k and industry j in 1983 and L_{k83} is the total number of workers across all industries in occupation k. We then calculate occupation-specific import penetration in year t for occupation k as

$$\sum_{j=1}^{J} \alpha_{kj83} IMP_{jt},$$

where IMP_{jt} is the measure of import penetration for goods in industry j in year t. We continue to control for technological changes by industry and set these technological changes equal to unity for workers outside manufacturing.[18]

This leads to a specification of the form:

$$W_{ijkt} = \beta_0 Z_{ijkt} + \beta_1 G_{kt-1} + \beta_2 TFP_{jt-1} + \beta_3 PINV_{jt-1} \\ + \beta_4 KLRATIO_{jt-1} + \beta_5 COMP_{jt} + \beta_6 d_t \\ + \beta_7 I_j + \beta_8 Occupation_k + \varepsilon_{ijkt}, \quad (1b)$$

where k indexes the worker's occupation, and workers within the same k occupation may be in different j industries.[19] Our G vector is now an occupation-specific measure for each worker, and we have added occupation fixed

---

[16] Since total factor productivity is a function of wages, we estimate our equations with and without total factor productivity. The results are similar with and without controlling for TFP.

[17] Our results are similar if we control for computer use rates in the previous year.

[18] An alternative approach would be to create occupation-specific measures of each of our control variables. In the online appendix, we estimate models with occupational-specific measures of TFP, the price of investment goods, and the capital-to-labor ratio. The results are qualitatively similar to the results presented in the main text. These are presented in table A9.

[19] For workers outside manufacturing, the control variables for TFP, PIINV, and REALSHIP are not available and are therefore assumed constant in our main specifications.

effects to absorb variation specific to time-invariant features of occupations. Note that we also control for variation in computer use rates by occupation and year, which is meant to account for wage changes driven by the ability of some occupations to benefit from computer technology (Autor et al., 1998). We will estimate this specification for all occupations separately by the degree of how routine the tasks are within a given occupation and for samples of workers who switch occupations. One important implicit assumption in our approach is that barriers to changing occupations are similar across routine and nonroutine occupations. Kambourov and Manovskii (2008) show this to be the case. They also decompose occupation switching across routine and nonroutine occupations and show that between 1968 and 1997, workers were not able to escape routine occupations by switching into nonroutine ones.

C. Trends in Offshoring, Trade, Employment, and Wages

In this section, we outline broad trends in the data for employment, wages, and the relationship between wages and measures of globalization. In figure 1, we compare the trends in employment and wages in the manufacturing sector alongside the same trends in the service sector between 1979 and 2002. We present these trends separately for workers performing routine and nonroutine tasks. Total manufacturing employment (using the CPS employment numbers) fell from 22 to 17 million from 1979 to 2002, with rapid declines at the beginning of the early 1980s and in the late 1990s. Within manufacturing, the labor force has become increasingly high skilled, with a large decline of roughly 6 million in the number of workers in routine occupations and a modest increase of roughly 1 million in the number of workers performing nonroutine occupations.

In contrast, demand for both types of workers continued to grow in the service sector, and many of the displaced routine manufacturing workers may have found employment in the service sector. These trends have important implications for the U.S. wage distribution. As shown at the bottom of figure 1, where we report the real hourly wage among CPS workers, manufacturing workers enjoyed a large wage premium during the entire period among both routine and nonroutine workers. Insofar as manufacturing provided an opportunity to earn high relative wages, even for low-skill workers, its decline might also have played a role in increasing U.S. income inequality during the period.[20]

[20] See Autor, Katz, and Kearney (2008) for a review of these trends. It is worth noting that while the trends in figure 1 are informative, they do not control for other factors that affect income, such as sex, age, and experience. We redid the trends in wages by educational attainment using wage residuals. These wage residuals were computed using Lemieux's (2006) approach for each educational category separately. We also added industry dummies to control for interindustry wage differentials. The wage residuals show similar trends, with falling wage premiums for less educated workers and rising wage premium for more educated workers. Similar results are observed for wage premiums when workers are stratified by the routineness of occupation. Results are available from the authors on request.

FIGURE 2.—TRENDS IN DOMESTIC AND AFFILIATE EMPLOYMENT AMONG MULTINATIONAL FIRMS

Authors' calculations based on the most comprehensive available data, and based on firm-level surveys on U.S. direct investment abroad, collected each year by the Bureau of Economic Analysis of the U.S. Department of Commerce. Using these data, we compute the number of employees hired abroad by country and year and then aggregate employment by low (high) income country according to World Bank income classifications.

The three panels displaying wage trends exhibit significant differences during the sample period. Real wages grew in the 1980s, fell or stagnated in the 1990s, and then begin increasing around 1995 to 1996. Over the entire period, the gap between manufacturing and service wages narrowed, particularly from the mid-1990s onward. These different trends are one factor that leads us to break our samples into different time periods. We turn now to an examination of how offshoring and trade may be related to these employment and wage trends within manufacturing and in the overall economy.

As shown in figure 2, foreign affiliate employment in low-income countries by U.S.-based multinationals nearly doubled over the entire sample period, while affiliate employment in high-income countries remained roughly constant. The increase in developing country activity has been accompanied by a reduction in the U.S. workforce for these parents from almost 12 million workers in 1982 to 7 million workers in 2002.

In figure 3, we report changes in the distribution of occupation wage residuals across the 476 occupations in the CPS. Each point in the figure represents the occupation-specific wage premium in 1983 and 2002. The wage premium was calculated by taking the residual in a regression of real log wages on education category dummies; experience category dummies; an interaction of education and experience; and controls for sex, race, year, and state.[21] These premiums were then collapsed into one term for each occupation and year. In order to compare the occupational wage residual changes by their potential exposure to offshoring, we stratify occupations by whether they are above the median occupation in terms of routine task content. As

[21] The data sets are made available online for replication at the Dataverse Network Project.

FIGURE 3.—OCCUPATIONAL WAGE PREMIUMS IN 1983 AND 2002 AMONG ROUTINE AND NONROUTINE OCCUPATIONS

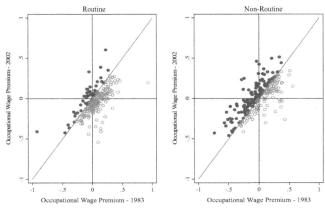

Wage premiums are calculated by a standard Mincerian regression of the log wage on education, experience, age, sex, race, year fixed effects, and state fixed effects among all workers in the CPS MORG between in 1983 and 2002. Each point on the plot is a separate occupation identified in the CPS (*N* = 464). The occupations are considered routine if the share of tasks that is routine is greater than the median occupation. Occupations with higher wage premiums in 1983 are shaded.

TABLE 1.—OLS ESTIMATES OF CHANGE IN OFFSHORING AND IMPORT PENETRATION GIVEN INDUSTRY SKILL COMPOSITION IN 1983

	Dependent Variable: Log Difference in Employment Offshored (1983–2002)				Dependent Variable: Import Penetration Difference (1983–2002)	
	Low-Income Countries		High-Income Countries			
	(1)	(2)	(3)	(4)	(5)	(6)
Industry share of routine jobs, 1983	5.132**	5.501**	−0.980	−0.053	1.217***	1.237***
	(2.40)	(2.59)	(2.03)	(2.26)	(0.34)	(0.33)
Difference in log of price of investment between 1983 and 2002		−0.262		0.234		−0.079
		(0.45)		(0.40)		(0.06)
Difference in total factor productivity level between 1983 and 2002		0.084		−0.056		0.0242**
		(0.07)		(0.06)		(0.01)
Difference in capital to labor ratio between 1983 and 2002		−0.230		−1.218		−0.249
		(1.21)		(1.06)		(0.16)
Difference in computer use rates between 1983 and 2002		0.441		−0.391		0.028
		(0.68)		(0.59)		(0.09)
Number of observations	66	59	66	59	66	61
R^2	0.07	0.12	0.00	0.07	0.17	0.35

Affiliate (or offshore) employment data are taken from the BEA annual survey of U.S. firms with multinational affiliates for 1983–2002. Low-income countries are defined according to the World Bank income categories. Employment data are taken from all workers in the Current Population Surveys Merged Outgoing Rotation Groups for the same period. Import penetration and export share are taken from Bernard et al. (2006). Investment good prices, total factor productivity measures, and the capital-to-labor ratio by industry and year are taken from the NBER productivity database. Computer use rates are taken from October CPS supplements during the sample period. Details for each of the data sources are available in the data appendix. Robust standard errors are reported in parentheses below the coefficient estimates. Significant at *10%, **5%, ***1%.

shown in figure 3, over the sample period, routine occupations were more likely to experience declines in wage premiums, possibly because these tasks can be performed overseas at lower cost. Of 240 routine occupations, 187 experienced wage premium declines and only 53 had increases in their wage premium. In contrast, among 236 nonroutine occupations, 134 experienced increases and only 102 experienced declines.

Before estimating equations 1a and 1b, in table 1 we provide a descriptive regression that is consistent with the results presented in figure 3. In particular, table 1 shows that an industry's share of routine jobs in 1983 is a good indica-

tor of subsequent offshoring to low-income locations and increasing import penetration. The dependent variables are the log difference between 1983 and 2002 in employment offshored to low-income countries (in columns 1 and 2) or high-income countries (in columns 3 and 4) and the change in import penetration (in columns 5 and 6). As shown in column 1, an industry's share of routine jobs in 1983 is a significant predictor of the subsequent increase in employment offshored to low-income countries, explaining roughly 7% of the variation across industries as a single regressor. We estimate that industries with 1 percentage point more routine jobs in 1983 experienced a 5.1% increase in offshore

TABLE 2.—OLS Estimates of Wage Determinants Using Occupational versus Industry Exposure to Offshoring and Trade, 1984–2002
Dependent Variable: Log Wage

Variable	Offshoring and Trade Measured by Industry-Specific Exposure, Manufacturing Only				Offshoring and Trade Measured by Occupation-Specific Exposure, All Sectors			
	All Occupations	Most Routine	Intermediate Routine	Least Routine	All Occupations	Most Routine	Intermediate Routine	Least Routine
Lagged log of low-income-affiliate employment	0.001	0.002	0.000	0.002	−0.0401**	−0.0702***	0.018	0.072
	(0.002)	(0.002)	(0.003)	(0.003)	(0.016)	(0.016)	(0.029)	(0.056)
Lagged log of high-income-affiliate employment	0.0143***	0.00793*	0.011	0.0239***	0.0339**	0.0508***	−0.003	−0.045
	(0.005)	(0.005)	(0.007)	(0.008)	(0.015)	(0.014)	(0.026)	(0.048)
Lagged export share	0.022	−0.021	0.002	0.047	0.255**	0.667***	0.232	−0.815*
	(0.043)	(0.058)	(0.048)	(0.045)	(0.121)	(0.157)	(0.184)	(0.420)
Lagged import penetration	0.077	0.090	0.042	−0.050	−0.290***	−0.296***	−0.761	1.083
	(0.050)	(0.061)	(0.057)	(0.074)	(0.091)	(0.099)	(0.466)	(0.750)
Number of observations	551,528	316,048	150,319	85,161	3,068,095	1,109,835	1,156,208	802,052
R^2	0.46	0.39	0.41	0.38	0.50	0.42	0.54	0.40

See table 1 for sources. Robust standard errors are reported in parentheses below the coefficient estimates. The workers are taken from CPS samples from 1984 to 2002, with their lagged values of the independent variables taken from 1983 to 2001. The standard errors are clustered by industry and five-year period in columns 1–4 and by occupation and five-year period in columns 5–8. The classification of occupations into routine categories is determined by the proportion of tasks that are routine in each occupation, with low being occupations with more than two-thirds, intermediate being occupations with one-third and two-thirds, and high being occupations with less than one-third of tasks designated routine. We also control for the lagged log price of investment, lagged total factor productivity, and lagged capital to labor ratio among manufacturing workers. Among nonmanufacturing workers, these controls are set equal to unity. Wage specifications control for a worker's gender, age, race, experience, whether in a union, and include industry, year, education, and state fixed effects. The occupation-specific exposure regressions also include two-digit occupation fixed effects. Controls for computer use rates are imputed by the worker's industry (columns 1–4) and by occupation (columns 5–8). Significant at *10%, **5%, ***1%.

employment to low-income countries by 2002, and this result is statistically significant at the 5% level. However, in column 3, there is no significant relationship with offshoring to high-income countries. The significant relationship between an industry's share of routine jobs in 1983 and subsequent offshoring to low-income countries, which stands in contrast to high-income-country offshoring, is one reason to maintain the distinction between offshoring to high- and low-income countries in the subsequent analysis.

Column 5 shows that the industry share of routine jobs in 1983 is also a significant predictor of future increases in import penetration. We find a 1.2 percentage point increase in our import penetration measure among industries with 1 percentage point more routine jobs, suggesting that industries with more routine jobs have also faced greater import competition. In columns 2, 4, and 6, we include a range of additional predictors and continue to find similar effects for the industry share of routine jobs. Our control variables, which include industry averages of the price of investment goods, total factor productivity, capital-to-labor ratios, and computer use rates, do not qualitatively affect the results.

In the remainder of the paper, we continue to make a distinction between high- and low-income offshore locations and to differentiate workers by the routine content of their jobs. The patterns in the figures and table 1 indicate rising trade and offshoring to low-income countries in industries with workers whose jobs are characterized by a high routine content.

III. Offshoring, Trade, and the Impact on Domestic Workers

A. Wage Impacts of Offshoring and Trade at the Industry versus Occupation Level

In table 2, we present our main results showing how the impact of offshoring and trade are quite different when

using industry versus occupation measures of exposure. In the first four columns, we present our estimates for equation (1a), which defines exposure to trade or offshoring at the industry level. In the last four columns, we redo the analysis using our occupation exposure measure, as outlined in equation (1b). We also present the main results where we stratify the workers based on the routine content of the worker's occupation, since we anticipate that routine tasks are more easily monitored offshore than more complex tasks, and so domestic workers performing these tasks may be more affected by offshoring and trade (Grossman & Rossi-Hansberg 2008). Note that the standard errors are clustered by industry and five-year period in columns 1 through 4 and by occupation and five-year period in the last four columns. Industry regressions include industry fixed effects, and occupation regressions include occupation as well as industry fixed effects.

Columns 1 through 4 of table 2 identify the impact on wages of workers in industries that were more exposed to international trade or offshoring during the 1984–2002 period.[22] In these four columns, only workers within the manufacturing sector are included in the estimation. The results suggest a very limited role for offshoring or trade in explaining log wages. There is no statistically significant relationship between low-income-affiliate employment, lagged export share, or lagged import penetration and industry-level wages; indeed, the point estimates are close to 0. There is a positive and statistically significant relationship between high-income-affiliate employment and domestic wages, although the magnitude is not large: the point estimate suggests that a 1% increase in affiliate employment in high-

[22] Note that we exclude 1983 for consistency with our occupation results, which can only be estimated from 1984 to 2002, since occupation was coded consistently only from 1983 and on, and we are using lagged measures of our independent variables.

IMPACT OF TRADE AND OFFSHORING ON AMERICAN WORKERS   589

TABLE 3.—OLS ESTIMATES OF WAGE DETERMINANTS USING OCCUPATIONAL EXPOSURE TO OFFSHORING AND TRADE AMONG SUBSAMPLES OF CPS WORKERS, 1984–2002
Dependent Variable: Log Wage

Specification	Lagged Log of Low-Income Affiliate	Lagged Log of High-Income Affiliate	Lagged Export Share	Lagged Import Penetration	Observations	R^2
1984–1991	0.003	−0.005	0.06	−0.215***	1,390,331	0.52
	(0.012)	(0.01)	(0.109)	(0.067)		
1992–2002	−0.0558***	0.0449***	0.490***	−0.321***	1,677,763	0.49
	(0.013)	(0.011)	(0.081)	(0.062)		
1984–1996	−0.015	0.0102	0.181**	−0.261***	2,181,111	0.51
	(0.009)	(0.008)	(0.076)	(0.057)		
1997–2002	−0.107***	0.0946***	0.478***	−0.306***	886,983	0.48
	(0.026)	(0.024)	(0.118)	(0.093)		
Female	−0.0477***	0.0434***	0.376***	−0.178***	1,491,461	0.49
	(0.013)	(0.012)	(0.093)	(0.038)		
Union	0.004	−0.011	−0.104	−0.075	549,055	0.37
	(0.01)	(0.009)	(0.077)	(0.073)		
High school or less	−0.0407***	0.0319***	0.227***	−0.209***	1,475,119	0.44
	(0.009)	(0.008)	(0.081)	(0.049)		
College or more	−0.0250**	0.0228**	0.12	−0.116	1,592,975	0.44
	(0.011)	(0.01)	(0.073)	(0.111)		
Over age 40	−0.0560***	0.0482***	0.11	−0.202***	1,262,929	0.48
	(0.01)	(0.009)	(0.071)	(0.053)		
Over age 50	−0.0552***	0.0487***	0.11	−0.287***	550,041	0.48
	(0.013)	(0.012)	(0.088)	(0.064)		

See table 1 for sources.
Each row represents a separate regression. The independent variables are listed in the column headings, and the subsample of interest is listed in the row heading. Robust standard errors are clustered by occupation and five-year period and are reported in parentheses below the coefficient estimates. Wage specifications control for a worker's gender, age, race, experience, whether in a union, and imputed computer use rate by occupation and include year, education, state, industry, and two-digit occupation fixed effects. Significant at *10%, **5%, ***1%.

income countries is associated with a 0.01% increase in wages, and this is found even for workers in the most routine occupations. In these first four columns, which rely on differences in exposure to trade or offshoring across industries, the evidence suggests that trade has no substantial negative effect on worker wages.

In columns 5 through 8 of table 2, we present results from specification (1b) where we measure exposure to trade or offshoring at the occupation level. The effects of both offshoring and trade are larger in sign and generally significant at the 5% level, in contrast to the industry-level results reported in the first four columns. In the first row of column 5, the coefficient on low-income affiliate employment suggests that a 10% increase in employment offshored within an occupation is associated with a 0.4% wage reduction for US workers. For workers in the most routine occupations, we find that a 10% increase in low-income affiliate employment abroad is associated with a 0.7% decline in domestic wages, whereas workers in less routine occupations were largely unaffected by offshoring. Although the magnitude of the effect is small, the results are consistent with an interpretation that workers in low-income locations perform the same tasks that low-skilled workers perform in the United States and are therefore substitutes for workers in the United States.

We also find a positive effect of lagged high-income-affiliate employment on wages. Workers in high-income locations appear to perform tasks that are complementary to workers in the United States, and so expansion of employment in high-income countries can benefit domestic workers. These results are robust to a range of specification choices, including whether we use prices of imported and exported

goods instead of quantities, and our chosen set of control variables, such as controlling for the real price of shipments by sector to account for variation in product demand.[23] The results are qualitatively similar to the results presented here, and are available in the online appendix.

Our results indicate that a 10% increase in occupational exposure to import competition is associated with nearly a 3% decline in real wages for workers who perform routine tasks. While some occupations have experienced no increase in import competition (such as teachers), import competition in other occupations (such as shoe manufacturing) has increased by as much as 40 percentage points.[24] For occupations with significant export activity, wages are positively linked to export growth. For these workers, a 10 percentage point increase in export share at the occupation level is associated with a 6.6 percentage point increase in wages over the sample period.

Krugman (2008) and Feenstra (2008) both hypothesize that the effects of international trade and offshoring may have increased recently relative to earlier decades. In table 3, we split the sample into earlier and later time periods. In par-

---

[23] The results indicate that workers with price decreases in their product market have suffered the largest wage declines, with this pattern most pronounced in routine occupations. Similar to our core results, however, this effect is observed only using occupational exposure measures of import price changes. Special thanks to Lawrence Edwards for generous use of his price series data on imports. Other specifications we have tested include removing measures of TFP and controlling for price changes in the service sector using a CPI/PPI index, both of which provide results similar to those presented in table 2. Likewise, the results including the real price of shipments are similar to the results in table 2.

[24] See the online appendix for further information on import exposure by occupation.

590   THE REVIEW OF ECONOMICS AND STATISTICS

TABLE 4.—OLS ESTIMATES OF WAGE DETERMINANTS USING OCCUPATIONAL VERSUS INDUSTRY EXPOSURE TO OFFSHORING AND TRADE, 1997–2002
Dependent Variable: Log Wage

Variable	Offshoring and Trade Measured by Industry-Specific Exposure, Manufacturing Only				Offshoring and Trade Measured by Occupation-Specific Exposure, All Sectors			
	All Occupations	Most Routine	Intermediate Routine	Least Rotine	All Occupations	Most Routine	Intermediate Routine	Least Rotine
Lagged log of low-income-affiliate employment	−0.009	−0.005	−0.0221***	0.002	−0.107***	−.198***	0.147***	0.330*
	(0.006)	(0.008)	(0.008)	(0.013)	(0.040)	(0.038)	(0.050)	(0.165)
Lagged log of high-income-affiliate employment	−0.002	−0.014	0.004	0.016	0.0947**	0.169***	−0.140***	−0.299**
	(0.009)	(0.010)	(0.013)	(0.022)	(0.037)	(0.035)	(0.042)	(0.143)
Lagged export share	−0.021	−0.111	0.039	0.049	0.478***	0.999***	0.292	−0.808
	(0.072)	(0.078)	(0.092)	(0.075)	(0.178)	(0.240)	(0.271)	(0.948)
Lagged import penetration	0.119	0.196**	−0.067	−0.094	−0.306**	−0.437**	−0.035	1.668
	(0.073)	(0.094)	(0.150)	(0.176)	(0.146)	(0.160)	(0.587)	(1.419)
Number of observations	132,104	71,985	36,982	23,137	886,984	291,894	337,057	258,033
R^2	0.44	0.35	0.40	0.34	0.48	0.39	0.51	0.37

See table 1 for sources. Robust standard errors are reported in parentheses below the coefficient estimates. The workers are taken from CPS samples from 1997 to 2002, with their lagged values of the independent variables taken from 1996 to 2001. The standard errors are clustered by industry and five-year period in columns 1–4, and by occupation and five-year period in columns 5–8. The classification of occupations into routine categories is determined by the proportion of tasks that are routine in each occupation, with low being occupations with more than two-thirds, intermediate being between one-third and two-thirds, and high being occupations with less than one-third of tasks designated routine. We also control for the lagged log price of investment, lagged total factor productivity, and lagged capital-to-labor ratio among manufacturing workers. Among nonmanufacturing workers, these controls are set equal to unity. Wage specifications control for a worker's gender, age, race, experience, whether in a union, and include industry, year, education, and state fixed effects. The occupation-specific exposure regressions also include two-digit occupation fixed effects. Controls for computer use rates are imputed by the worker's industry (columns 1–4) and by occupation (columns 5–8). Significant at *10%, **5%, ***1%.

ticular, we allow the impact of globalization to vary between 1984 and 1991, and 1992 through 2002, when our sample ends. We also explore whether the impact of globalization varied for female workers, unionized workers, across education levels, and for different age groups. The results in table 3 suggest that there is no significant association between log wages and employment in offshore locations in the early years of our sample (1984–1991, 1984–1996). However, in the later periods (1992–2002, 1997–2002), worker wages are negatively and significantly associated with increased offshore employment in low-income-affiliate locations. In the years 1997 to 2002, the coefficient estimates in the fourth row of table 3 indicate that a 10% increase in low-incomeaffiliate employment is associated with a 1% decrease in domestic wages. These negative coefficients contrast with the positive coefficients on high-income-affiliate employment. For 1997 through 2002, a 10% increase in highincome-affiliate employment is associated with nearly a 1% increase in domestic wages.

Table 3 also reports the coefficient on lagged imports and exports, measured at the occupation level. The point estimates for occupation-specific import penetration are statistically significant across all time periods, with the coefficients ranging from −0.21 to −0.32. These coefficients indicate that a 10 percentage point increase in import penetration is associated with a wage decline in the exposed occupation of 2% to 3%. The coefficients become larger and more negative in magnitude in the later time periods. The evidence also points to a positive and significant association between export share and domestic wages, but the point estimates are positive and significant for export share only in the later part of the sample period.

In table 3, we also explore heterogeneity in our results across different demographic groups. Anecdotes in the popular press and elsewhere suggest that women, union workers, and older workers may have been disproportionately affected by international competition. If we restrict the sample to either women or union workers, there is no evidence that their wages were more negatively affected than the rest of the sample. In fact, the wages of unionized workers appear to have been relatively unaffected by export activity or import competition. However, the wages of workers without higher education and older workers do appear to have been disproportionately affected by offshoring activities, as the point estimates are larger for these groups of workers. The estimates in table 3 indicate that all of the negative and significant effects of offshore employment and import penetration were concentrated on workers with a high school education or less.

Since the results point to much stronger effects of offshore activities on domestic wages in the later part of the sample period, we reproduce table 2 for the 1997 through 2002 period in table 4. The results confirm that for the last five years of our sample, offshoring and international trade exerted much larger effects on occupation-specific wages than the earlier years. The results also confirm that over the most recent sample period, industry-level wage effects are negligible. In columns 1 through 4, all but two of the point estimates are statistically insignificant and the magnitudes are close to 0, indicating that offshoring or trade does not significantly affect industry-level wage premiums.

Columns 5 through 8 suggest that occupation-specific changes in offshoring and trade are associated with significant wage effects, particularly for workers in the most routine occupations. For these workers, a 10% increase in offshoring to low-income countries is associated with a 2% decrease in wages. For most workers, however, a 10 percentage point increase in high-income-affiliate employment is associated with a 1.7% increase in wages. One explanation is that workers in high-income locations perform tasks that are complementary to routine workers in the United States.

TABLE 5.—FALSIFICATION EXERCISE USING EXPOSURE TO OFFSHORING AND TRADE IN 2002 AND WAGE IMPACT BY PERIOD
Dependent Variable: Log Wage

Variable	Offshoring and Trade Measured by Occupation-Specific Exposure in 2002	
	1984–1989	1997–2002
Log of low-income-	0.015	−0.0862**
affiliate employment in 2002	(0.055)	(0.042)
Log of high-income-	−0.014	0.0769**
affiliate employment in 2002	(0.050)	(0.038)
Export share in 2002	−0.079	0.445***
	(0.248)	(0.157)
Import penetration in 2002	−0.118	−0.358***
	(0.150)	(0.124)
Number of observations	1,036,302	886,958
R^2	0.53	0.48

See table 1 for sources. Robust standard errors are clustered at the occupation level and reported in parentheses below the coefficient estimates. The independent variables reported for the globalization exposure are taken from the worker's occupational exposure in 2002. The sample in each column includes workers in all sectors for the listed period. The regressions include the same controls that are included in the regressions using occupational exposure in table 2. Significant at *10%, **5%, ***1%.

A 1% increase in export shares is associated with a 1% increase in wages, while a 1% increase in import penetration is associated with a −0.44% decline in wages. The effects of these globalization measures are generally small in magnitude and insignificant for individuals who work in the occupations with the least routine content.

While we control for a number of observables, there are other shocks that might be difficult to control for and could affect workers in routine occupations. To verify that our results are not driven by secular trends in which wage changes, globalization, and technological change are all moving together over time, we present a falsification exercise in table 5. In particular, we regress current period wage changes for 1984 through 1989 on future globalization shocks for 2002. Our future globalization shocks are the logs of low- and high-income-affiliate employment in 2002, as well as export shares and import penetration in 2002. If the analysis is driven by spurious trends, the coefficient on 2002 measures of globalization should be significant in explaining wages for the 1984 through 1989 period. Table 5 shows that 2002 measures of globalization do not significantly affect wages in the earlier period. In contrast, 2002 measures of globalization do significantly affect wages from 1997 through 2002. For example, our offshoring measure to low-income countries is significantly negatively correlated with wage changes among workers during this later period. This is new evidence that our results are not being driven simply by a spurious correlation between offshoring and domestic wage changes.[25]

[25] It is worth discussing alternative possibilities that could undermine our interpretations of our findings. For example, it may be that even if the United States engaged in autarky in this later period, domestic workers would have been replaced by machines, thereby implicating offshoring when the workers' decline was inevitable. This possibility naturally cannot be evaluated in our data. Also, if our technology control variables are measured with error, it may be that the wage declines we observe are a by-product of the substitutability between these workers and capital. However, we would argue that the strong correlation between the timing of increased offshore employment and declining domestic wages seems unlikely to be fully explained by stories of this nature.

B. Offshoring, Trade, and the Reallocation of Labor across Sectors

In this section, we try to identify mechanisms for the differences between industry-level and occupation-level exposure to offshoring and trade. We begin by analyzing the relationship between offshoring and domestic manufacturing employment. We then examine the wage consequences of switching industries, sectors, and occupations using a panel of CPS workers who are followed for more than one period.

In table 6, we present an analysis of employment trends in manufacturing in response to offshoring. Our unit of analysis is each Education × Industry × Year cell. There are 5 education categories for workers, 67 manufacturing industries, and 19 years of data (1984–2002). In column 1, we present pooled results for all industries, and in the remaining columns we split industries by the fraction of an industry's workforce performing routine tasks. When we pool across all task types, the results in column 1 indicate that the impact of offshoring depends on whether affiliate employment is located in high- or low-income countries. A 1% increase in employment in low-income countries reduces domestic employment by 0.02%, while a 1% increase in employment in high-income countries increases domestic employment by 0.07%. Breaking the results down according to how routine the workforce is, we see that the negative effects of offshoring to low-income countries are largest for workers in the most routine industries. The point estimate in column 2, at −0.041, suggests that a 1% increase in affiliate employment in low-income locations is associated with a 0.041% reduction in employment of workers in the most routine occupations.

In contrast, greater offshoring to high-income countries is associated with a significant increase in employment in the United States. Across all workers, the evidence suggests that a 1% increase in affiliate employment in high-income locations is associated with a .074% increase in employment at home. For routine workers, the impact is more positive, with a 1 percentage point increase in offshore employment in high-income countries associated with a .15% to .19% increase in U.S. employment. This evidence suggests that offshore employment in high-income locations is complementary with employment at home. The evidence presented in table 6 is consistent with Harrison and McMillan (2011), who use firm-level BEA data to show that domestic employment of U.S. multinationals is complementary with their employment in high-income locations but that increasing employment of U.S. firms in low-income locations substitutes for employment in the United States.[26]

[26] Our online appendix includes a rich set of robustness checks for these results. Among these are a set of results based on instrumental variables estimation where we instrument for trade and offshoring using the variables that capture changes over time in the cost of trade and offshoring. The instruments are Internet access, telephone connections including cell phone use, and the industry share of routine jobs. The results confirm the negative relationship between offshoring to low-income countries, import penetration, and manufacturing employment.

TABLE 6.—OLS ESTIMATES OF EMPLOYMENT DETERMINANTS IN MANUFACTURING, 1984–2002
Dependent Variable: Log U.S. Manufacturing Sector Employment

Variable	All	Most Routine	Intermediate Routine	Least Routine
Lagged log of low-income-affiliate employment	−0.0202*	−0.0413**	0.007	−0.046
	(0.011)	(0.02)	(0.021)	(0.044)
Lagged log of high-income-affiliate employment	0.0736**	0.148**	0.192***	0.013
	(0.031)	(0.064)	(0.05)	(0.132)
Lagged log of price of investment	0.124	0.489***	0.197	−0.094
	(0.093)	(0.16)	(0.209)	(0.52)
Lagged total factor productivity level	0.000	0.0680**	−0.0612***	0.602
	(0.017)	(0.033)	(0.023)	(0.632)
Lagged export share	−0.393	−0.555	0.112	−0.216
	(0.258)	(0.666)	(0.321)	(1.326)
Lagged import penetration	−0.614*	−0.313	−0.084	0.133
	(0.356)	(0.682)	(0.338)	(1.547)
Lagged capital to labor ratio	−0.867**	−0.983	−1.108**	−0.338
	(0.373)	(1.043)	(0.436)	(1.504)
Lagged computer use rates by industry	−0.036	0.049	−0.122	−0.700
	(0.147)	(0.269)	(0.207)	(0.482)
Number of observations	6,399	1,662	4,248	489
R^2	0.86	0.78	0.55	0.65

See table 1 for sources. Robust standard errors are reported in parentheses below the coefficient estimates and are clustered by industry. All models include year and industry fixed effects. Low-income-affiliate employment is defined according to the World Bank income categories. The sample size corresponds to five education groupings × 19 years × 67 industries, less missing values. The results shown in columns 2–4 are (for column 2) industry and year combinations where more than two-thirds of the tasks are routine, (for column 3) cells where between one-third and two-thirds of tasks are routine, and (for column 4) cells where than a one-third of the tasks are routine. Significant at *10%, **5%, ***1%.

The coefficients on offshoring in table 6 are significant but small in magnitude and suggest both substitution (in low-income countries) and complementarity (in high-income locations). In contrast, the coefficients are large and negative but imprecisely estimated for both import penetration and export activity. For the pooled sample, a 1 percentage point increase in import penetration reduces U.S. manufacturing employment by 0.61%. While it is not surprising that the coefficient on import competition is negative, the negative coefficient on sectoral export shares is less intuitive and deserves explanation. The negative coefficients may indicate that export growth was labor saving for workers with less than a college degree, which is sensible if a significant degree of offshoring takes place through exports for further processing. Likewise, the negative and significant coefficient on total factor productivity suggests that productivity growth has been labor saving for most educational categories.[27] Productivity growth in manufacturing has been achieved in conjunction with falling employment.

The results in table 6 suggest that productivity growth, export growth, and import competition have been associated with (sometimes significant) declines in domestic manufacturing employment and that the effects of offshoring have been smaller in magnitude and mixed in sign. These results are important insofar as they suggest a fluid labor market where changes in other factor prices and global competition lead to employment reallocation. Furthermore, these results provide an explanation for our finding in table 2 that the within-industry wage effects of trade and offshoring are smaller than the within-occupation effects. If trade and offshoring lead some workers to shift sectors (in

particular, to exit high-wage jobs in manufacturing), then it is possible that the wages of those who retain their jobs or find new jobs in the same industry are not significantly affected by offshoring, whereas those who shift sectors or occupations are more negatively affected.[28] We examine this conjecture in table 7.

To explore the impact of switching out of manufacturing on wage outcomes, we construct a sample of manufacturing workers observed in CPS samples in consecutive years between 1983 and 2002. We regress the change in log wages between period t and $t + 1$ for a given worker on an indicator for switching occupation, including a rich set of controls for the worker's age, sex, education, race, union status in the first period, and industry in the first period. If switching occupation is costly, it may explain why the negative impact on wages is so large in our main results. As shown in table 7, the data indicate that trade-induced occupation switching does indeed have serious negative wage consequences for workers. Using our matched sample of CPS ORG workers who are observed in consecutive years, we compare the wage difference in period t and $t + 1$ for workers who switch occupations versus those who do not. In panel A, we examine workers who switch across three-digit occupational categories. In column 1, we examine the wage impact of all occupations switched and find that the impact is negligible; an occupation change is associated with a 0.54% increase in wages. One possible explanation for this result is that some

[27] The results in table 6 are robust to excluding total factor productivity as a control variable.

[28] In results available in the online appendix, we directly assess the wage consequences among those who switch industries within manufacturing. We find that (1) switching within manufacturing has mild wage consequences, (2) but leaving manufacturing has a more negative impact, and (3) leaving manufacturing is particularly costly for workers who switch occupations. These were not included in the main text due to space considerations.

TABLE 7.— WAGE IMPACT OF SWITCHING OCCUPATIONS USING CPS WORKERS IN REPEATED SAMPLES, 1984–2002

	OLS	First Stage	Two-Stage Least Squares
	Log Wage Difference	Switched Occupation	Log Wage Difference
	(1)	(2)	(3)
A: Defining an occupation switch by switching three-digit occupation			
Switched Occupations between T and $T + 1$	0.0054		−0.121**
	(0.005)		(0.051)
Interoccupation Wage Differential Gap Term[a]	0.281		0.190
	(0.223)		(0.252)
Tradable Occupation (1 = yes)		0.0942***	
		(0.022)	
Number of observations	851,467	851,467	851,467
F-test of Instrument		18.91	
B: Defining an occupation switch by switching one-digit occupation			
Switched occupations Between T and $T + 1$	−0.00153		−0.172***
	(0.001)		(0.059)
Interoccupation wage Differential gap term	−0.0506		−0.0594
	(0.076)		(0.131)
Tradable occupation (1 = yes)		0.0693***	
		(0.020)	
Number of observations	851,467	851,467	851,467
F-test of instrument		11.66	

Sample is composed of CPS MORG workers observed in two consecutive samples. Robust standard errors reported in parentheses below coefficient estimates. Standard errors are clustered by three-digit occupation. All models include year, state, and education level fixed effects. Other demographic controls are age, sex, nonwhite, and union status in the first period. An occupation is defined as tradable if the occupational exposure from low-income countries (as described in table 2) is above the median level among manufacturing workers in the sample. This is used to generate a binary variable for all workers in the sample and is the instrument for occupational switches. In panel A, we define an occupation switch by the worker reporting a different three-digit occupation. In panel B, an occupation switch is defined by a worker reporting a different one-digit occupation.
[a]The Interoccupation Wage Differential Gap term is calculated by regressing the workers' log wage on observable characteristics and a set of occupation dummies among all workers and among workers who switch occupations between periods. The difference in means of these terms is included in our regressions to control for potential selection on unobservables of those who switch occupations. Significant at *10%, **5%, ***1%.

switches are upward (as measured by average occupational wages), and others are downward, leaving a mixed result for all switches. This hypothesis is put forward in Trefler and Liu (2011), who find evidence that switches of both types are common in response to trade.

In order to examine the impact of trade-induced occupational switching on wage outcomes, we consider a system of equations for estimation. In our first stage, we examine the impact of occupational exposure on the probability of switching occupations between periods. We create a dichotomous measure of our instrument. All workers who are employed in occupations above the median level of offshore exposure from low-income countries are considered "tradable." The results, presented in column 2, indicate that being in a tradable occupation is associated with a 9.4 percentage point increase on the probability of switching occupations between periods. In our second stage, we examine the relationship between switching occupations and wage declines when this switch is induced by trade. We find that trade-induced occupation switches are associated with a 12.1% decline in wages between periods. This result is consistent with our earlier results highlighting negative consequences of globalization on wages of workers who perform tasks that can be performed in low-income countries. In panel B, we perform a similar analysis but use a broader classification of occupation. If a narrower definition of occupation implies that a worker is more likely to be performing a similar task, these switches will presumably have less important wage consequences. Consistent with this hypothesis, the results in panel 2 indicate that trade is less likely to induce a switch to a new two-digit occupation (6.9 percentage points), but upon switching, the negative wage

consequences are even more severe: a trade-induced occupational switch across two-digit categories is associated with a 17.2% decline in wages. These results suggest that switching occupations is very costly to workers and provides support for our main results, suggesting that occupational exposure to competition from trade or offshoring has more significant consequences than industry exposure.

One possibility is that workers who switch occupations in a downward manner are less productive in unobserved dimensions of worker quality. Weaker workers may sort into less demanding occupations, and this may not be captured by the human capital measures available in the CPS (e.g., education). While we are unable to observe variation in the quality of workers on unobserved dimensions, we attempt to address this possibility by adding a control to the wage equation, which is the difference between the interoccupation wage differential for all workers in a sector and the interoccupation wage differential for workers who leave that sector in the following period. If workers who remain and those who leave a sector are similar, then this difference should be close to 0, and adding it as an additional control should have no impact on our estimate. The negative impact of switching occupations on wages is unaffected by the inclusion of the interoccupation wage differential term (see also Trefler & Liu, 2011, for an application to services). Our results are suggestive that in manufacturing, worker heterogeneity does not explain the significant decline in wages of workers who leave their occupation due to trade or offshoring pressures.

Our results are consistent with work by Kambourov and Manovskii (2008, 2009a, 2009b), who find large wage declines among workers who switch occupations; this evidence suggests an important role for occupation-specific human capital in a worker's wage profile. Kambourov and Manovskii (2008, 2009a, 2009b) also argue that occupation switching may be an important cause of the increase in U.S. wage inequality, as younger workers are missing out on the benefits to occupational tenure enjoyed by workers in previous decades. Insofar as this is partly driven by competition from overseas, this highlights another mechanism by which offshoring may be responsible for declining U.S. wages and increasing wage inequality.

IV. Conclusion

This paper reexamines the impact of trade and offshoring, two primary measures of globalization, on U.S. workers. Using CPS data, which we merge with data on exports, imports, and BEA data on offshoring, we make three main contributions. First, we draw a distinction between the impact of globalization on industrial wage differentials and on occupation wage differentials. Globalization has had small or insignificant effects on industry wage differentials but significant effects on occupation wage differentials. These results are consistent with recent empirical work demonstrating the importance of occupational tenure and downplaying the importance of tenure within a particular industry in determining a worker's wage.

Second, we extend previous analyses that focused exclusively on manufacturing sector workers to explore the impact of trade and offshoring on all workers. Third, we use a two-stage approach to show that one important avenue through which globalization affects wages is by pushing workers out of the manufacturing sector to take lower-paying jobs elsewhere. Using a CPS panel of workers and the exposure of an occupation to trade as an instrument for whether a worker switched occupations, we find that occupation switching due to trade led to real wage losses of 12 to 17 percentage points between 1983 and 2002. The results are robust to the inclusion of a term from Trefler and Lui (2011) that captures the possibility that the least able workers are most likely to switch into lower-paying occupations.

Our results provide new evidence that the negative consequences of trade on workers are mediated through a reallocation of labor across sectors and into different occupations. While older models of trade posited that workers could move in a costless manner to new jobs in the face of pressure from foreign labor, we identify large and significant wage declines among workers who leave manufacturing; the wage decline is particularly pronounced for those who switch occupations. These results are consistent with new trade models that introduce frictions into the labor reallocation process, such as Cosar (2010) and Artuc et al. (2010). Our evidence is consistent with greater frictions in moving across occupations rather than across industries.

We also explored how the impact of globalization on wages has changed over time. Our different measures of globalization have no significant impact on wages during the first half of our sample. While our sample extends from 1984

to 2002, both offshoring and trade exert significant effects on wages only in the second half of this period. The effects of these globalization measures are confined to individuals who work in routine occupations, indicating that much of the brunt of globalization is borne by individuals who perform tasks that are easily copied by workers elsewhere.

REFERENCES

Artuç, Erhan, Shubham Chaudhuri, and John McLaren, "Trade Shocks and Labor Adjustment: A Structural Empirical Approach," *American Economic Review* 100 (2010), 1008–1045.

Autor, David H., Lawrence F. Katz, and Melissa S. Kearney, "Trends in US Wage Inequality: Revising the Revisionists," this REVIEW 90 (2008), 300–323.

Autor, David H., Lawrence F. Katz, and Alan B. Krueger, "Computing Inequality: Have Computers Changed the Labor Market?" *Quarterly Journal of Economics* 113 (1998), 1169–1213.

Autor, David H., Frank Levy, and Richard Murnane, "The Skill Content of Recent Technological Change: An Empirical Exploration," *Quarterly Journal of Economics* 118 (2003), 1279–1334.

Autor, David, David Dorn, and Gordon H. Hanson, "The China Syndrome: Local Labor Market Impacts of Import Competition in the United States," University of California, San Diego, unpublished manuscript (2012).

Bernard, Andrew, J. Bradford Jensen, and Peter Schott, "Survival of the Best Fit: Exposure to Low-Wage Countries and the (Uneven) Growth of US Manufacturing," *Journal of International Economics* 68 (2006), 219–237.

Cosar, A. Kerem, "Adjusting to Trade Liberalization: Reallocation and Labor Market Policies," University of Chicago, Booth School of Business, unpublished manuscript (2010).

Desai, Mihir, C. Fritz Foley, and James R. Hines, "Domestic Effects of the Foreign Activities of US Multinationals," *American Economic Journal: Economic Policy* 1 (2009), 181–203.

Freeman, Richard, "Are Your Wages Set in Beijing?" *Journal of Economic Perspectives* 9 (1995), 15–32.

Feenstra, Robert C., "Offshoring in the Global Economy," Ohlin Lecture at the Stockholm School of Economics, September 17–18, 2008.

Feenstra, Robert C., and Gordon H. Hanson, "The Impact of Outsourcing and High-Technology Capital on Wages: Estimates for the US, 1972–1990," *Quarterly Journal of Economics* 114 (1992), 907–940.

Grossman, Gene M., and Esteban Rossi-Hansberg, "Trading Tasks: A Simple Theory of Offshoring," *American Economic Review* 98 (2008), 1978–1997.

Harrison, Ann, and Margaret McMillan, "Offshoring Jobs? Multinationals and U.S. Manufacturing Emploment," this REVIEW 93(3), 857–875.

Hummels, David, Rasmus Jørgensen, Jakob R. Munch, and Chong Xiang, "The Wage Effects of Offshoring: Evidence from Danish Matched Worker-Firm Data," NBER working paper 17496 (2011).

Jensen, J. Bradford, and Lori G. Kletzer, "Tradable Services: Understanding the Scope and Impact of Services Offshoring," Institute for International Economics working paper WP 05-9 (2005).

Kambourov, Gueorgui, and Iourii Manovskii, "Rising Occupational and Industry Mobility in the United States: 1968–97," *International Economic Review* 49 (2008), 41–79.

——— "Occupational Specificity of Human Capital," *International Economic Review* 50 (2009a), 63–115.

——— "Occupational Mobility and Wage Inequality," *Review of Economic Studies* 76 (2009b), 731–759.

Katz, Lawrence F., and Lawrence H. Summers, "Industry Rents: Evidence and Implications," *Brookings Papers on Economic Activity, Microeconomics* 1989, 209–290.

Krueger, Alan B., and Lawrence H. Summers, "Efficiency Wages and the Inter-Industry Wage Structure," *Econometrica* 56 (1988), 259–293.

Krugman, Paul, "Trade and Wages, Reconsidered," *Brookings Papers on Economic Activity*, Spring (2008), 103–154.

Lemieux, T, "Increasing Residual Wage Inequality: Composition Effects, Noisy Data, or Rising Demand for Skill?" *American Economic Review* 96 (3) (2006), 461–498.

Menezes-Filho, Naércio, and Marc-Andreas Muendler, "Labor Reallocation in Response to Trade Reform," NBER working paper 17372 (2011).

Trefler, Daniel, and Runjuan Liu, "A Sorted Tale of Globalization: White Collar Jobs and the Rise of Service Offshoring," NBER working paper 17559 (2011).

Chapter 13

Multinationals and Anti-Sweatshop Activism[†]

By ANN HARRISON AND JASON SCORSE*

During the 1990s, anti-sweatshop activists campaigned to improve conditions for workers in developing countries. This paper analyzes the impact of anti-sweatshop campaigns in Indonesia on wages and employment. Identification is based on comparing the wage growth of workers in foreign-owned and exporting firms in targeted regions or sectors before and after the initiation of anti-sweatshop campaigns. We find the campaigns led to large real wage increases for targeted enterprises. There were some costs in terms of reduced investment, falling profits, and increased probability of closure for smaller plants, but we fail to find significant effects on employment. (JEL F23, J31, J81, L67, O14, O15)

Anti-sweatshop campaigns increased dramatically in the 1990s. These campaigns took different forms: direct pressure to change legislation in developing countries, pressure on firms, newspaper campaigns, and grassroots organizing. Activists targeted multinational firms in the textiles, footwear, and apparel sectors and helped spread consumer boycotts throughout college campuses. Yet there has been almost no academic research that analyzes precisely how these anti-sweatshop campaigns affected the workers they were designed to assist.

This paper examines the impact of anti-sweatshop activism on labor market outcomes in Indonesia. Indonesia makes an ideal case study because it was the focus of campaigns introduced in the 1990s to improve conditions for workers. The pressure took several forms. The United States threatened to withdraw special tariff privileges for Indonesian exports if Indonesia failed to address human rights issues. The Indonesian government responded by making minimum wage increases a central component of its labor market policies in the 1990s.[1] The nominal minimum wage quadrupled and its real value more than doubled between 1989 and 1996.[2] Indonesia was also the target of consumer awareness campaigns waged against such companies as Nike, Adidas, and Reebok. As a result of activist pressure, these firms were induced to sign codes of conduct pledging to raise wages and improve working conditions in factories producing their products.

We identify the impact of anti-sweatshop campaigns on wages through two approaches. First, we compare wage growth in textile, footwear, and apparel (TFA) plants relative to wage growth in the rest of manufacturing. We restrict the treatment group to foreign-owned or exporting TFA

* Harrison: Development Research Group, World Bank and Department of Agricultural and Resource Economics, University of California, Berkeley, 329 Giannini Hall, Berkeley, CA 94720 (e-mail: ann.harrison@berkeley.edu); Scorse: Graduate School of International Policy Studies, Monterey Institute of International Studies, 460 Pierce St., Monterey, CA 93940 (e-mail: jason.scorse@miis.edu). The authors would like to thank Garrick Blalock for generously sharing his data and expertise on Indonesia. The authors would also like to thank Jeff Ballinger, Teri Caraway, David Card, Kimberly Elliott, David Lee, Sylvie Lambert, Margaret McMillan, Dara O'Rourke, Sandra Spolaski, seminar participants at DELTA, Georgetown University, UC-Davis, INSEAD, PPIC, the World Bank, UC-Berkeley, and Yale University, and especially the editor and two anonymous referees for very useful suggestions. Ann Harrison also thanks the National Science Foundation and University of California Berkeley for research support.

[1] For a discussion of the role of minimum wages in Indonesia, see SMERU Research Institute (2001) or Martin Rama (1996).

[2] See Appendix Table A1 for trends in the minimum wage.

[†]This article originally appeared in *The American Economic Review*, **100** 247–273 © 2010 American Economic Association.

factories. Second, we exploit geographic variation in the anti-sweatshop movement *within* the TFA sector in Indonesia. The anti-sweatshop campaign targeted contractors for Nike, Reebok, and Adidas. Consequently, we compare the real wage growth of TFA plants in districts with contractors working for these firms relative to TFA plants in other districts. The advantage of this second approach to identification is that it controls for any changes that affected the TFA sector as a whole.

To measure the impact of the anti-sweatshop movement, we use a difference-in-difference methodology, comparing wages before and after the advent of the campaigns. Both approaches indicate that targeted plants increased real wages in response to activist pressure. Compared to non-TFA plants, foreign-owned and exporting TFA firms increased real wages 10 to 20 percent across all of Indonesia. Comparing wage growth in districts targeted by activists relative to other districts, the effects are even larger. Real wages increased as much as 30 percent in large foreign-owned and exporting TFA plants relative to other TFA plants. Most of these wage increases are due to higher compliance with minimum wages on the part of targeted plants.

One question that arises is whether such large real wage increases led to higher unemployment. Our estimates suggest that there were large, negative effects of the minimum wage increases on aggregate manufacturing employment. The coefficient on the minimum wage indicates that a 10 percent increase in the real minimum wage reduces production worker employment by 1.2 percent. However, we fail to find significant negative employment effects of the additional wage increases at targeted TFA plants. Employment growth in the TFA sector exceeded growth in other sectors during the sample time period. Although TFA plants increased wages in large part by increasing compliance with minimum wages, greater compliance was not associated with significant employment losses relative to non-TFA plants.

One explanation for why the short-run employment costs of the anti-sweatshop campaigns are difficult to identify is that TFA plants had the flexibility to adjust to higher wages along other dimensions. Some plants exited the sector; small exporters in regions targeted by activists were more likely to close. Across all TFA plants, profits fell relative to other sectors. Profit declines were largest in the districts targeted by anti-sweatshop activities. It appears that the anti-sweatshop movement resulted in a type of forced profit sharing, where higher wages for TFA workers were financed largely through lower returns to capital.

Our results are robust to a range of alternative specifications. We include controls for confounding factors that are likely to be correlated with wage growth, including changes in plant size, the educational attainment of the workforce, region-specific variation in minimum wage changes, foreign-ownership, export status, investments in technology, productivity growth, different initial wage levels, differences in output growth, and changes in profitability.[3] We also contrast the changes in wages for unskilled (production) workers with those for skilled (nonproduction) workers, whose wages generally exceeded the statutory minimum. Finally, we show that wages in foreign-owned and exporting firms in our treatment districts, but outside of the TFA sectors, were not affected.

The remainder of the paper is organized as follows. In Section I, we outline the development of anti-sweatshop campaigns, discuss the identification strategy, and set up a framework for estimation. We present results on wages in Section II. Section III examines the impact of anti-sweatshop activism on employment, profits, investment, plant entry and exit, and explores the extent to which the results reflect different degrees of compliance with minimum wage laws. Section IV concludes.

---

[3] Some robustness tests, such as those controlling for initial wages or adding profit margins, are reported only in the working paper version of this article, available on the AER Web site (http://www.aeaweb.org/articles.php?doi=10.1257/aer.100.1.247).

VOL. 100 NO. 1   HARRISON AND SCORSE: MULTINATIONALS AND ANTI-SWEATSHOP ACTIVISM   249

I. Background, Identification Strategy, and Framework for Estimation

A. Background

The roots of the anti-sweatshop campaign in Indonesia can be traced to a 1989 study commissioned by the United States Agency for International Development(USAID). The study, carried out by the Asian American Free Labor Institute–Indonesia under the direction of Jeff Ballinger, discovered that of all the factories that produced goods for the export sector, plants that manufactured for Nike paid the lowest wages.[4] Organizations such as Global Exchange, Press for Change (founded by Ballinger), and the National Labor Committee used the momentum generated from the increasing mainstream media attention on poor factory conditions in Nike plants to create an international campaign against sweatshop conditions in factories contracting for Nike, and to a lesser extent, Adidas and Reebok.[5]

The campaign against Nike's contractors in the early 1990s focused almost exclusively on Indonesia. One major reason is that much of the research documenting poor working conditions and low minimum wage compliance was completed by Jeff Ballinger while working for the AFL-CIO in Indonesia; no comparable work was carried out in China (currently the site of the largest number of Nike contractors). In addition, significant anger was directed against the foreign (primarily East-Asian) owners of these subcontracting factories within Indonesia. The relatively more open political atmosphere also contributed to the ability of US groups to work with local NGOs in Indonesia.

Nike established its own codes of conduct in 1992 in order to comply with labor standards and establish living wages, but these practices were not fully implemented until 1995–1996.[6] During this period, nongovernmental organizations (NGOs) conducted persistent and steady appraisals of working conditions in and around Nike vendor factories in order to hold the company to account for the treatment of its workers.

The campaign against Nike, Adidas, and Reebok in Indonesia was essentially a media campaign, which operated (and continues to operate) through contacts with newspaper columnists, magazine writers, TV shows, and other outlets. One way to gauge the extent of negative media exposure brought about by the anti-sweatshop campaigns is to count the dramatic increase in the number of articles about sweatshops and child labor that appeared in major international newspapers in the 1990s.[7] There was a 300 percent increase in the number of articles regarding child labor and a 400 percent increase in the number of articles focusing on sweatshop activities.

If we restrict the analysis to articles about sweatshops in Indonesia alone, the trends are very similar. The ratio of the number of articles on sweatshops or child labor relative to articles on

---

[4] In 1992 Ballinger's work appeared in *Harper's Magazine* in a short piece entitled, "The New Free-Trade Hell: Nike's profits jump on the backs of Asian workers," and in 1993 CBS featured Ballinger in a report about poor working conditions in Asian factories.

[5] Coupled with media strategies, including ads that satirized Nike symbols and slogans (e.g., the "swooshtika" in place of the Nike "swoosh" symbol), the anti-sweatshop activists waged a public relations war against Nike and other big clothing retailers. The movement in the United States and Europe was assisted by electronic forums where young activists shared information and planned their campaigns.

[6] See David F. Murphy and David Matthew (2001).

[7] The trends in number of articles published about child labor and the anti-sweatshop campaigns discussed in this and the following paragraph are described in more detail in the working paper version of this article. We graph both the number and the proportion of articles devoted to the anti-sweatshop movement. Our list of "Major US and World Publications" is available on the Web site for Lexis-Nexis (http://wiki.lexisnexis.com/academic/index. php?title=Academic_URLs_for_News_Sources). Examples include the *New York Times, Business Week, Economist, Newsweek, Boston Globe, Times* (London), *Christian Science Monitor, Herald* (Glasgow), *Washington Post, Hong Kong Standard*, etc. We also analyzed the trends for US newspapers alone, available from the authors upon request. The trends are very similar whether we restrict the analysis to US newspapers or use all major international sources.

250   *THE AMERICAN ECONOMIC REVIEW*   *MARCH 2010*

general economic issues on Indonesia in major world newspapers increased from zero to a high of 10 percent of all articles at the peak in 1996. In 1997 there was an increasing shift in focus toward the financial crisis, which erupted at the end of 1997. Interest in child labor and sweatshop labor fell in the late 1990s—at least relative to other issues of economic interest—but has been increasing again in the last several years.[8]

While previous studies do not directly address the impact of anti-sweatshop activism on wages, an excellent overview of foreign ownership and wages can be found in Drusilla K. Brown, Alan V. Deardorff, and Robert M. Stern (2004).[9] A discussion of the links between trade and labor standards is provided by Brown (2001). Other related work includes Eric V. Edmonds and Nina Pavcnik (2001), who explore how rice prices affected the use of child labor in Vietnam.[10] Previous work has also examined the rationale for labor standards, as well as the determinants of ratification of International Labour Organization (ILO) conventions. [11]

B. *Identification and Framework for Estimation*

Our identification strategy is twofold. First, anti-sweatshop activism in Indonesia was uniquely focused on firms in the TFA sectors. Consequently, we begin by comparing real wage growth in those sectors versus other sectors, paying particular attention to the foreign-owned and exporting firms most likely to act as suppliers or contractors.[12] Real wages are calculated by deflating the nominal wage by the consumer price index (CPI), where the CPI is equal to 100 in 1996.

Our second treatment exploits the fact that anti-sweatshop activists in Indonesia concentrated on contractors for the three most highly visible retailers: Nike, Adidas, and Reebok. While Nike, Adidas, and Reebok did not take equity positions in their contractors, they did source heavily from foreign-owned and exporting firms whose owners came from other parts of Asia, including Korea, Taiwan, and Japan. Nike's primary mode of operation was (and continues to be) through arm's-length contracts. Unfortunately, confidentiality restrictions do not permit us to identify the *actual* contractors in the census data (since firm names are withheld in the Indonesian census data made available to researchers). Instead, we have identified likely contractors using census

---

[8] Why did interest in these issues increase so rapidly in the mid-1990s? In 1996–1997, there were a series of high-profile exposes on Nike, Gap, Wal-Mart, Disney, and others. For instance, in the second quarter of 1996 the Kathie Lee Gifford sweatshop scandal was highlighted in the news. These exposes were picked up by student movements on campuses. Student groups staged protests and sit-ins and subsequently kept these issues in the news, and contributed to the creation of groups designed to respond to sweatshop problems. The convergence of high-profile exposes, student activism, and the creation of new groups designed to address anti-sweatshop concerns fueled the increase in newspaper coverage. Post-1996, the shift in focus toward the Asian financial crisis contributed to a decline in interest in these issues. The student movement also weakened and moved on to other issues. This section has benefited greatly from discussions with Kimberly Elliott, Dara O'Rourke, and Sandra Spolaski.

[9] For an early paper showing that foreign-owned enterprises in developing countries are more likely to pay higher wages than comparable domestically owned enterprises, see Brian Aitken, Ann Harrison, and Robert Lipsey (1996)

[10] Edmonds and Pavcnik find that in rural areas, where most people are both rice producers and consumers, the income effect of higher rice prices has greatly outweighed the higher opportunity costs of not employing children in the workforce, and therefore child labor has declined significantly. However, in urban areas, where families are only rice consumers, the effects of the rice exports on price has led to increases in child labor since urban incomes have declined. Since Vietnam is predominantly rural, the overall effect has been a decline in child labor.

[11] Nancy H. Chau and Ravi Kanbur (2001) postulate that if ratification of these conventions were costless, or if the benefits greatly outweighed the costs, one would expect complete compliance across countries. Given that this is not the case, Chau and Kanbur investigate the determinants of signing. They find little evidence that variables predicted by standard economic theory—such as per capita gross domestic product (GDP), degree of openness to trade, or average education—are determining factors, but rather that countries with higher domestic standards have a higher probability of adoption. Keith Maskus (1996) refutes the argument that a lack of international standards has led to significant erosion of low-skilled wages in developed countries, or is a significant determinant of trade performance and foreign direct investment throughout the developing world.

[12] Our analysis is focused on real wages; we refer to nominal wages only to contrast the two since inflation was high during the 1990s.

VOL. 100 NO. 1   HARRISON AND SCORSE: MULTINATIONALS AND ANTI-SWEATSHOP ACTIVISM   251

data on foreign ownership, export status, and district of operation. Using information released by all three companies regarding the locations of their contractors in Indonesia, we have identified the districts in which companies targeted by activists operated in the 1990s. Consequently, our second approach compares the changes in wages and employment in TFA plants in regions with Nike, Adidas, and Reebok contractors, relative to other regions.

One important limitation is that our list of vendors for Nike, Adidas, and Reebok (available from the authors upon request) is from 2004. Since the vendor list is more recent than our census data, there could be a selection bias in our identification of treatment districts. It is difficult to sign the direction of the bias, since it is equally likely that only the pro-worker or anti-worker vendors have survived. However, by matching the names of enterprises described in newspaper accounts of sweatshops in Indonesia with names that appeared in the 2004 list of Nike vendors, we have been able to verify that many of the companies initially accused of the worst exploitation are still operating in Indonesia.

A proper framework for evaluating a firm's decision to raise wages in the context of anti-sweatshop activism would take into account both the costs and benefits of setting wages above the market-clearing level. In a competitive market with no external pressures, a worker's wages are set equal to the value of their marginal product. This implies that if log real wages are given by w, the log product price is p, the marginal product of labor is given by the partial derivative of output (Y) relative to labor input (L), and worker- or region-specific characteristics are captured by the vector $\mathbf{Z}$, then a standard log-linear reduced-form wage equation for an establishment i in region r at time t is given by

$$(1) \qquad \log w_{irt} = a_1 + a_2 \log p_{irt} + a_3 \log (\delta Y/\delta L)_{irt} + \alpha_4 \mathbf{Z}_{irt} + r_{rt} + f_i + e_{it}.$$

Since there are likely to be a number of establishment-specific effects (f_i) as well as time-varying regional effects (r_{rt}) that are unobserved, we will estimate (1) in differences, thus eliminating the establishment-level fixed effects but not the regional effects, which are allowed to vary over time. We model the costs and benefits of setting wages above the market-clearing level as a function of $G(u,F)_{it}$, where G represents a markup over competitive wages and is a positive function of the probability of exposure by activists (w) and any official sanctions F associated with violating labor market regulations. G could, for example, measure the costs in terms of foregone sales or lost contracts due to negative publicity if the firm failed to adhere to minimum wages. This yields the following equation:

$$(2) \qquad d \log w_{irt} = a_2 d \log p_{irt} + a_3 d \log(\delta Y/\delta L)_{irt} + \alpha_4 \mathbf{dZ}_{irt} + G(u,F)_{it} + r'_{rt} + e'_{it}.$$

Clearly, not all firms face the same probability of detection or the same penalties associated with operating sweatshop factories; only those with high probability of detection u or costly penalties associated with detection F are likely to change their wage-setting behavior.

As human rights activism and anti-sweatshop organizations proliferated, the probability of detection and the penalty for paying low wages or failing to adhere to the minimum wage increased, particularly for firms with high visibility, such as large multinationals or well-established exporters. We allow the treatment to vary with both export status and foreign-ownership, defined prior to treatment at the beginning of the sample period. We define export status *EXP* and foreign-ownership *FOR* as dummy variables equal to one if the establishment exported 10 percent or more of its output or had 10 percent or more foreign-ownership in 1990 and continued to do so over the entire sample period.

We explore two alternative treatments. We alternatively define *TREATMENT* as equal to one if one of the following is true: the plant was in a TFA sector at the beginning of the period: or the plant operated in a district that had contractors for Nike, Reebok, or Adidas.

Allowing the impact of activism to vary depending on whether the contractor is a foreign-owned or exporting enterprise leads to the following specification for $G(F, u)$:

$$G(F, u) = b_1 EXP_{it0} + b_2 FOR_{it0} + b_3 TREATMENT_{it0} + b_4(EXP \times TREATMENT)_{it0}$$
$$+ b_5(FOR \times TREATMENT)_{it0}.$$

Consequently, introducing deviations from competitive wage setting due to activism leads to

$$(3) d\log w_{irt} = a_2 d\log p_{irt} + a_3 d\log(\delta Y/\delta L)_{irt} + \alpha_4 \mathbf{dZ}_{irt} + b_1 EXP_{it0} + b_2 FOR_{it0} + b_3 TREATMENT_{it0}$$
$$+ b_4(EXP \times TREATMENT)_{it0} + b_5(FOR \times TREATMENT_{it0}) + r_{rt} + e'_{it}.$$

Equation (3) is essentially a difference-in-difference approach to estimating the impact of anti-sweatshop campaigns on wage outcomes. We regress log change in real wages (with 1996 as the base year) between 1990 and 1996 on a number of determinants, and then test whether there is any difference for our two treatment groups. Since firms that subcontracted for the major TFA multinationals were typically either foreign owned or export oriented or both, we focus primarily on the interaction terms b_4 and b_5.

We include controls for a number of potentially confounding determinants of the observed wage changes. We control for price changes using changes in log output and profitability at the level of the individual establishment. Factors that affect the marginal product of labor are also included in the estimation, including changes in capital stock, changes in material inputs, technology expenditures, total factor productivity growth, and changes in firm size, defined as the change in the total number of employees. Other components of the vector $\mathbf{dZ}$ include changes in worker characteristics (specifically education levels) and changes in the statutory minimum wage.

To give the reader an idea of the importance of TFA enterprises for manufacturing employment in Indonesia in the 1990s, Figure 1 shows the share of TFA employees in total production worker employment. Employment in the TFA sector as a share of total production worker employment increased from 25 percent to 35 percent during the period. The percentage of production workers in foreign-owned TFA plants rose from 2 percent to over 5 percent, while the percentage of production workers in TFA exporting plants increased from 5 to nearly 20 percent. Figure 1 shows that TFA plants employed a major share of production workers in the manufacturing sector in Indonesia.

II. Wages and Anti-Sweatshop Activism in Indonesia

A. *Data Summary*

The data for this analysis come from the annual manufacturing survey of Indonesia collected and compiled by the Indonesian government's statistical agency BPS (Badan Pusat Statistik). The completion of this survey is mandatory under Indonesian law for firms with more than 20 employees. The number of observations ranges from approximately 13,000 in 1990 to over 18,000 in 1999. Over the ten-year period there is an average of 4.5 observations per establishment, reflecting either plant closings or changing reporting requirements.

VOL. 100 NO. 1   HARRISON AND SCORSE: MULTINATIONALS AND ANTI-SWEATSHOP ACTIVISM   253

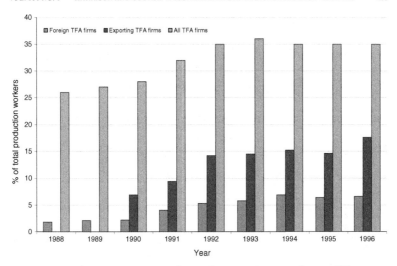

FIGURE 1. SHARE OF TOTAL PRODUCTION WORKERS EMPLOYED IN FOREIGN AND EXPORTING TFA
IN INDONESIA 1988–1996

In the first two rows of Table 1A, we report mean real wages (in thousands of 1996 rupiahs) for the manufacturing sector in 1990 and 1996. We focus on this seven-year period because information on export orientation was not collected before 1990, and the financial crisis that erupted in 1997 makes any evaluations post-1996 problematic.[13] We define the plant's average wage for both production and nonproduction workers as basic compensation (salary) by type of worker, divided by the number of workers in that skill category. For the remainder of the analysis, we focus almost exclusively on production worker wages, which we use as our measure of unskilled wages.

Based on an exchange rate of about 2,000 rupiahs to the dollar, real annual wages for TFA and non-TFA domestic plants at the onset of the sample period averaged approximately US$550. If we compare columns 1 and 4, we see that wages in nonexporting, domestically owned plants were remarkably similar for TFA and non-TFA plants at the onset of the sample period. Between 1990 and 1996, average annual production worker wages in both TFA and non-TFA domestic enterprises increased by about $200.

At the onset of the sample period, however, both foreign-owned and exporting TFA enterprises paid their unskilled workers significantly less than other enterprises. A comparison of columns 2 and 5 shows that, in 1990, workers in foreign-owned TFA plants were paid half as much as workers at other foreign-owned plants. In the first row, comparing columns 3 and 6 indicates that exporters in TFA plants paid their workers 30 percent less than in other exporting plants. These large differences were one factor that contributed to the focus of anti-sweatshop activists on workers in the TFA sector.

---

[13] Nevertheless, we have experimented with adding 1997 and show that the main results presented in Tables 2 and 3 are robust to extending the sample. These results are available from the authors upon request.

TABLE 1A—MEAN PRODUCTION WORKER WAGES IN 1990 AND 1996
(*Contrasting textiles, footwear, and apparel (TFA) versus other sectors*)

	Textiles, footwear, and apparel			Other establishments			Difference		
	Domestic[a]	Always foreign[b]	Always exporting[c]	Domestic[a]	Always foreign[b]	Always exporting[c]	(1)–(4)	(2)–(5)	(3)–(6)
	(1)	(2)	(3)	(4)	(5)	(6)	(7)	(8)	(9)
1. Mean wage in 1990, all observations	1,078.2 (15.5)	1,775.1 (112.1)	1,462.4 (122.8)	1,134.2 (13.2)	3,560.8 (182.1)	1,934.6 (102.7)	56.0 (27.9)	−1,805.6 (419.1)	−472.2 (205.2)
2. Mean wage in 1996, all observations	1,441.2 (19.6)	2,268.8 (79.2)	2,079.2 (100.0)	1,552.4 (14.4)	3,798.6 (137.8)	2,125.2 (54.6)	−111.1 (32.1)	−1,529.7 (280.0)	−46.0 (115.6)
3. Change in mean wage, 1990-1996	363.0 (25.7)	513.7 (151.2)	616.8 (187.1)	418.1 (20.2)	237.8 (241.1)	190.6 (111.2)	−54.9 (36.7)	275.9 (497.6)	426.2 (188.5)
4. Change in mean wage, balanced sample[d]	349.4 (33.4)	740.1 (196.3)	474.2 (170.0)	374.7 (26.6)	814.9 (318.8)	259.4 (135.2)	−25.3 (47.4)	−74.8 (497.6)	214.8 (188.5)
5. Mean change in log wage, 1990–1996	0.30 (0.03)	0.29 (0.09)	0.40 (0.05)	0.37 (0.01)	0.08 (0.05)	0.13 (0.04)	−0.07 (0.02)	0.21 (0.11)	0.27 (0.07)
6. Mean change in log wage, balanced sample	0.30 (0.03)	0.36 (0.10)	0.35 (0.06)	0.30 (0.02)	0.22 (0.07)	0.16 (0.05)	0.00 (0.02)	0.14 (0.10)	0.19 (0.10)

Note: Standard errors in parentheses.
[a] A plant that is neither foreign-owned nor exports the entire period.
[b] Includes at least 10 percent foreign equity over the entire period.
[c] Exports at least 10 percent of output over the entire period.
[d] Defined as establishments present in both 1990 and 1996.

One question that naturally arises is why these workers were paid so little. While one explanation could be their low level of skill, the regressions in the remainder of the paper control for the observed skill composition of workers in each establishment, and firm-level fixed effects control for unobserved skill differences that remain constant over time. An important consideration in explaining the wage differences is the high concentration of female production workers in these sectors. Three of the five most female-intensive sectors (with female production workers accounting for 50 percent or more of total production workers) in Indonesian manufacturing in 1995 were textiles, footwear, and apparel.[14] Joeseph G. Altonji and Rebecca M. Blank (1999) review the existing evidence and report that female-dominated occupations pay significantly less, after accounting for all observable worker characteristics, even in the United States.

By 1996, the wage gap between exporting and foreign-owned TFA and exporting and foreign-owned non-TFA plants had narrowed considerably. In 1996, the difference in wages between exporting TFA and exporting non-TFA plants amounted to only 46,000 rupiahs ($23) per employee per year. The difference—computed in the last column of Table 1A—is not statistically significant. The gap between wages in foreign-owned TFA enterprises and foreign-owned non-TFA firms also narrowed, but by less: foreign-owned non-TFA establishments continued to pay 1,529 thousand rupiahs, or $750 dollars, more per worker in total salary in 1996 (second row, column 8) than foreign-owned TFA firms. The trends in Table 1A suggest that the wage benefits from anti-sweatshop activism were limited to workers in export-oriented or foreign-owned plants.

[14] In Indonesia, the share of female workers in the census is highly inversely correlated with wages. These results are available from the authors upon request.

VOL. 100 NO. 1   HARRISON AND SCORSE: MULTINATIONALS AND ANTI-SWEATSHOP ACTIVISM   255

TABLE 1B—COMPARISON OF TREATMENT GROUPS RELATIVE TO CONTROLS PRIOR TO TREATMENT (1988–1990)

Results of *t*-test difference in means for the control relative to treatment for the following variables:	Foreign-owned enterprises			Exporters		
	Treatment	Control	*t*-test of difference	Treatment	Control	*t*-test of difference
Average production worker wages ('000s of real rupiahs per worker)	2,029 (124.9)	3,847 (127.8)	5.76**	1,656 (92.49)	2,618 (66.64)	6.51**
Size (total number of employees)	975.7 (80.33)	374.1 (20.39)	−10.1**	616.5 (38.11)	442.3 (15.67)	−4.61**
Profits (value added less payments to workers as a share of value added)	0.343 (0.019)	0.349 (0.009)	0.26	0.364 (0.011)	0.348 (0.005)	−1.22
Log change in production worker wages	0.061 (0.076)	−0.004 (0.026)	−0.88	0.079 (0.035)	0.033 (0.016)	−1.16
Log change in number of production workers	0.065 (0.023)	0.072 (0.018)	0.15	0.136 (0.023)	0.117 (0.013)	−0.63
Log change in material inputs	0.080 (0.069)	0.141 (0.035)	0.65	0.212 (0.061)	0.144 (0.025)	−1.09
Log change in capital stock	0.255 (0.205)	0.245 (0.071)	−0.05	0.142 (0.097)	0.272 (0.044)	1.24
Total factor productivity growth	0.038 (0.056)	0.063 (0.025)	0.36	0.005 (0.040)	0.052 (0.015)	1.25
Output growth	0.097 (0.061)	0.123 (0.026)	0.36	0.229 (0.049)	0.146 (0.021)	−1.65

Notes: Treatment is textiles, footwear, and apparel (TFA) exporting or foreign enterprises relative to other sectors. Standard errors in parentheses. Values calculated for the 1988 through 1990 period, except for total factor productivity growth (TFPG) and capital stock where we use 1988 and 1989 only. All values in real rupiahs are deflated by the CPI, based in 1996. Productivity growth is defined as the log change in output less the weighted changes in inputs, where inputs include production and nonproduction workers, materials, and capital stock. The weights are equal to an average of the shares of each of the inputs in total costs in the current and last period, except capital which is equal to one less other input shares.

** Indicates significance at the 1 percent level.
* Indicates significance at the 5 percent level.

Rows 3 and 4 of Table 1A report wage growth from 1990 to 1996 in levels; rows 5 and 6 report the wage growth in logs. The difference-in-difference—the difference in wage growth across TFA and non-TFA plants—is reported in the last three columns of the table. The results show that wage increases for TFA workers were significantly higher in exporting and foreign-owned establishments. Again, the only exception is for workers in domestically owned plants selling only locally: in these plants, wages for TFA workers increased by 7 percentage points less than for unskilled workers in other sectors. The difference-in-difference between foreign or exporter wage growth in the TFA and non-TFA sectors is reported in the last two rows and last two columns of Table 1A. Across all plants, exporting and foreign TFA plants increased real wages by 21 to 27 percent more than other plants. For the balanced panel, the wage increase for foreign or exporting plants relative to non-TFA plants is between 14 and 19 percent.

To summarize, the trends presented in Table 1A indicate very different patterns of wage growth for TFA plants in the 1990s. While production workers in most exporting and foreign-owned plants generally received smaller wage increases than the rest of the manufacturing labor force in the 1990s, *the opposite was true for workers in TFA factories.* In foreign-owned and exporting TFA plants, unskilled wages grew 30 to 40 percent in real terms between 1990 and 1996.

256   *THE AMERICAN ECONOMIC REVIEW*   *MARCH 2010*

TABLE 1C—COMPARISON OF TREATMENT GROUPS RELATIVE TO CONTROLS PRIOR TO TREATMENT (1988–1990)

Results of *t*-test difference in means for the control relative to treatment for the following variables:	Foreign-owned enterprises			Exporters		
	Treatment	Control	*t*-test of difference	Treatment	Control	*t*-test of difference
Average production worker wages	1,577	2,381	3.35**	1,371	1,813	2.30*
('000s of real rupiahs per worker)	(106.6)	(194.9)		(62.9)	(137.9)	
Size (total number of employees)	810.9	1,104.2	−1.83	683.9	579.6	−1.31
	(128.4)	(99.9)		(67.6)	(45.8)	
Profits (value added less payments to	0.345	0.342	−0.07	0.338	0.378	−0.07
workers as a share of value added)	(0.035)	(0.020)		(0.014)	(0.014)	
Log change in production worker wages	−0.024	0.108	0.83	0.080	0.078	−0.02
	(0.073)	(0.112)		(0.051)	(0.046)	
Log change in number of production workers	0.105	0.042	−1.32	0.109	0.148	0.77
	(0.056)	(0.018)		(0.040)	(0.029)	
Log change in material inputs	0.145	0.043	−0.709	0.231	0.203	−0.211
	(0.115)	(0.086)		(0.088)	(0.079)	
Log change in capital stock	−0.015	0.373	0.867	−0.065	0.223	1.344
	(0.579)	(0.164)		(0.203)	(0.108)	
Total factor productivity growth	0.084	0.018	−0.52	0.012	0.003	−0.10
	(0.072)	(0.076)		(0.032)	(0.055)	
Output growth	0.215	0.032	−1.46	0.279	0.207	−0.68
	(0.106)	(0.072)		(0.073)	(0.063)	

Notes: Treatment is TFA enterprises in treatment regions versus other TFA enterprises. Standard errors in parentheses. Values calculated for the 1988 through 1990 period, except for TFPG and capital stock where we use 1988 and 1989 only. All values in real rupiahs are deflated by the CPI, based in 1996. Productivity growth is defined as the log change in output less the weighted changes in inputs, where inputs include production and nonproduction workers, materials, and capital stock. The weights are equal to an average of the shares of each of the inputs in total costs in the current and last period, except capital which is equal to one less other input shares.
   ** Indicates significance at the 1 percent level.
   * Indicates significance at the 5 percent level.

Tables 1B and 1C examine differences in the two treatment groups and the control groups prior to the onset of the anti-sweatshop movement. We test the difference in means for 1988 through 1990 for wages, size, profits, and growth in wages, productivity, and output. The pretreatment period is short due to data limitations prior to 1988; nevertheless, the same tests on wages, size, and output for 1984 through 1989 yielded similar results. Size is defined as total number of employees. Profitability is defined as value added less wages as a share of value added. Total factor productivity growth is defined as the log change in output less the weighted changes in inputs, where inputs include production and nonproduction workers, materials, and capital stock. The weights are equal to an average of the shares of each of the inputs in total costs in the current and last period. The capital share is the residual, computed after subtracting the other factor shares and assuming constant returns to scale.

Table 1B provides *t*-tests of differences between the TFA sector and other non-TFA manufacturing sectors of both foreign-owned and exporting firms. The results show that TFA establishments paid lower wages and were larger than establishments in other sectors, but that initial profits were not significantly different. Variables measured in changes—including log changes in wages, production workers, material inputs, capital stock, and total factor productivity growth (defined below) were not significantly different. There are no significant differences between the control and treatment groups when wages, output, inputs (including production workers), and productivity are measured in changes. Since the difference-in-difference methodology used in

VOL. 100 NO. 1   HARRISON AND SCORSE: MULTINATIONALS AND ANTI-SWEATSHOP ACTIVISM   257

the paper to identify treatment effects relies on changes rather than levels, the fact that there are no statistically significant differences between the treatment and control groups when examining growth rates between 1988 and 1990 is reassuring.

Table 1C reports the results of *t*-tests when the treatment is TFA enterprises in districts with Nike, Reebok, and Adidas contract establishments (our second treatment group) versus TFA enterprises in other districts (our second control group), again examining both foreign-owned and exporting firms separately. As expected, differences between the treatment and control groups are even smaller when we compare different sets of firms within the same manufacturing subsector. Although treatment firms paid significantly lower wages prior to the onset of the anti-sweatshop movement than the control group, they were similar in size and earned almost identical profits prior to treatment. In changes, the differences between treatment and control groups are never statistically significant, whether we examine wage growth, output growth, production worker growth, material inputs, capital stock, or productivity growth.

B. *Main Results*

None of the tests of mean differences in Table 1A controls for differences in plant characteristics. We address this shortcoming in Tables 2 and 3, which present the main results of the paper. Table 2 presents the results of estimating equation (3), with *TREATMENT* defined as belonging to the TFA sector. The dependent variable is the change in the log wage between 1990 and 1996. The first column of Table 2 reports coefficient estimates when we include only ownership dummies for foreign ownership, export orientation, participation in the treatment group, the minimum wage, and interactions between *TREATMENT*, foreign ownership, and export orientation. The minimum wage is defined as the log of the minimum wage in the district where the plant operated in 1996 less the log of the minimum wage in 1990. If that difference is negative, indicating that the minimum wage was not binding in 1990, then the minimum wage is set at zero. This definition of minimum wage changes allows the impact of increases in the minimum wage to be nonlinear, with zero impact on the firm's wage if the minimum wage is not binding and an expected log-linear impact if the minimum wage is binding.[15]

The results are consistent with the difference-in-difference presented in Table 1A; while wages in most foreign-owned or exporting plants did not increase faster than in other plants, TFA establishments were the exception. The coefficient on *TREATMENT* for foreign ownership or exporting enterprises is very similar: 0.106 for foreign and 0.119 for exporting. Controlling for the impact of minimum wage changes, the results suggest that production worker wages in foreign-owned or exporting TFA plants grew 10.6 to 11.9 percent faster than in other plants.

Column 2 in Table 2 adds a number of controls to the basic specification. Plant controls include log changes between 1990 and 1996 in real material inputs and capital stock, plant size, region controls, total factor productivity growth, technology expenditures, and output growth. The results in column 2 also include details on educational attainment for employees at the individual plant (reported in the years 1995 through 1997 and averaged in our estimation across all three years). For production workers, the annual survey reports number of both male and female workers who have had no school, some primary school, junior high school, senior high school, and college. The addition of plant characteristics and educational attainment of the workers does not change the magnitude or significance of the coefficients on Foreign × *TREATMENT*

---

[15] In the dataset, 73 percent of plants had average wage levels below the 1996 regional minimum wage in 1990; for these plants, the real minimum wage increased by 70 percent. For the remaining 27 percent of plants with initial wages above the 1996 minimum, the change in the minimum wage was set to zero. Across all plants, the average increase in the (real) minimum wage was 50 percentage points.

258 *THE AMERICAN ECONOMIC REVIEW* *MARCH 2010*

TABLE 2—OLS LONG DIFFERENCE-IN-DIFFERENCES ESTIMATION: REGRESSING PRODUCTION WORKER WAGE DIFFERENCES FOR 1990–1996 ON THE MINIMUM WAGE GAP, PLANT CHARACTERISTICS, AND OTHER CONTROLS

	Ownership dummies only (1)	Adding plant, worker, and region controls (2)	Combining foreign and exporting enterprises (3)	Same as (3) but excluding textiles as treatment (4)	Excluding minimum wage as a control and excluding textiles (5)	Dependent variable is nonwage benefits for production workers (6)	Dependent variable is wages plus nonwage benefits, all controls (7)	Dependent variable is log wages for non-production workers (8)
Foreign[a]	0.094	0.061	—	—	—	—	—	—
	(1.87)	(0.97)						
Exporter[b]	−0.057	−0.052	—	—	—	—	—	—
	(1.35)	(0.98)						
Foreign or exporter (FOREXP)	—	—	−0.001	0.010	−0.097	−0.006	0.010	−0.036
			(0.03)	(0.32)	(3.85)**	(0.43)	(0.33)	(0.97)
TREATMENT[c]	−0.059	−0.039	−0.037	−0.049	−0.031	0.002	−0.049	0.045
	(1.57)	(1.99)	(1.76)	(2.12)*	(0.98)	(0.29)	(2.19)*	(1.72)
Foreign × TREATMENT	0.106	0.124	—	—	—	—	—	—
	(2.25)*	(3.18)**						
Exporting × TREATMENT	0.119	0.110	—	—	—	—	—	—
	(2.30)*	(2.21)*						
FOREXP × TREATMENT	—	—	0.102	0.097	0.202	−0.034	0.096	−0.057
			(2.92)**	(2.43)*	(5.67)**	(0.77)	(2.41)*	(1.13)
Minimum wage[d]	0.554	0.675	0.669	0.667	—	−0.023	0.667	0.150
	(9.79)**	(7.53)**	(7.30)**	(7.41)**		(1.11)	(7.42)**	(3.42)**
Observations	6,165	5,920	5,920	5,920	5,920	5,335	5,920	5,099
R^2	0.12	0.23	0.23	0.23	0.13	0.03	0.23	0.07

Notes: Treatment is establishments in textiles, footwear, and apparel sectors. Dependent variable: log plant unskilled wage in 1996–log plant unskilled wage in 1990. Robust *t* statistics in parentheses. Constant term included in all specifications but not reported here.

[a] Includes some foreign equity over the entire period.

[b] Exports some share of output over the entire period.

[c] *TREATMENT* is defined as an establishment in the TFA sector.

[d] Defined as the log of the minimum wage in 1996 less the log of the minimum wage in 1990, unless the plant pays above the 1996 minimum wage in 1990, in which case the minimum wage change is set equal to zero.

** Indicates significance at 1 percent level.

* Indicating significance at 5 percent level.

and exporting × *TREATMENT*, which are now 0.124 and 0.110, respectively. These additional controls allow us to reject alternative explanations for the increase in wages for foreign-owned enterprises, such as the fact that foreign owners may have invested in plants with higher productivity growth, higher output growth, or better trained workers.

Since the point estimates for foreign × *TREATMENT* and exporting × *TREATMENT* are very close, in column 3 we combine foreign ownership and exporting status into one variable, *FOREXP*. Most foreign-owned enterprises in Indonesia exported a majority of their output, so it is difficult to separately identify the impact of foreign ownership and export status on wage growth. The remaining specifications in Table 2 combine foreign ownership and export status, although the results are not dependent on doing so. Column 4 tests whether the results are sensitive to excluding plants whose primary product is textiles and retaining only plants producing apparel and footwear. The point estimate on *FOREXP* in column 4 is now 0.097, which suggests that wages for unskilled workers in this sector increased by 9.7 percentage points more than in other sectors, after controlling for worker and plant characteristics.

In columns 1 through 4 of Table 2, we include the minimum wage as a control. However, both the decision to comply with the minimum wage and its actual level could be considered endogenous. Later in the paper we explore the determinants of compliance with the minimum wage as a function of anti-sweatshop activism. In Appendix Table A2, we show that minimum wage levels in Indonesia during the sample period were highly correlated with the CPI, lagged wages in the previous period, and low export shares. Appendix Table A2 also shows that minimum wages were set at a higher level in treatment districts with Nike, Reebok, and Adidas contractors. To address this possible endogeneity, we eliminate the minimum wage as a control in column 5 of Table 2. Now the coefficient on *TREATMENT* interacted with *FOREXP* is equal to 0.202, suggesting that the net effect of *FOREXP* and higher compliance with the minimum wage was to increase real wages by 20.2 percent relative to other sectors.

Columns 6 and 7 test whether firms cut nonwage benefits to offset the higher wages induced by minimum wage changes and activist pressure. The results show that treatment firms did not. When the dependent variable is nonwage benefits (column 6), the coefficient on *FOREXP* × *TREATMENT* is close to zero and not significant. Column 7 reports the results when wages and nonwage benefits are added together. Since wages account for most of the income for unskilled workers, the results are very similar in magnitude to those reported in the first six columns. The coefficient estimate, equal to 0.096, suggests that real wages and nonwage benefits increased by 9.6 percentage points more for TFA firms than for other firms.

To demonstrate that the anti-sweatshop movement was primarily focused on unskilled workers, in column 8 we use log wages for nonproduction workers as our dependent variable instead of production wages. As indicated earlier, nonproduction workers are typically associated with skilled workers. Since the anti-sweatshop movement focused on poorly paid workers, we would expect the impact on skilled workers to be small; this specification also allows us to test whether we are picking up spurious effects of positive unobserved demand shocks. The results suggest that there was no significant impact of *FOREXP* × *TREATMENT* on nonproduction worker wage growth. The coefficient estimate is −0.057 and not statistically significant.

The coefficient on the minimum wage is also reported in Table 2. It is equal to 0.675 when all controls are added, which suggests that a 1 percent increase in the real value of the minimum wage was associated with a 0.675 percent increase in the real unskilled wage. The coefficient is robust to the addition of plant, worker, and region controls. We note that it is possible to add region controls because the minimum wage is set at the more disaggregated district level. Given a 50 percentage point increase in the constructed minimum wage facing the sample firms (see footnote 15), the coefficient implies that minimum wage increases were associated with a 34 percent increase in real wages.

In Table 3, the sample includes only TFA plants, and *TREATMENT* is defined as being located in districts with Nike, Adidas, or Reebok contractors. This smaller sample allows us to compare the evolution of wages within the TFA sector across treatment and control districts—between those that were the target of anti-sweatshop campaigns and those that were not. The coefficient on *FOREXP* alone is generally negative and significant for large firms (those defined as having 100 or more employees), indicating that on average foreign-owned or exporting enterprises had lower wage growth than other firms. In addition, the coefficient on *TREATMENT* alone is also negative and significant for large firms, indicating lower than average wage growth in the treatment districts. However, foreign-owned or exporting enterprises in treatment districts—those enterprises targeted by the activists—exhibited significantly higher wage growth. Large foreign-owned or exporting TFA firms in these districts exhibited wage growth *between 22 and 52 percent higher* in real terms than other enterprises, after controlling for worker and plant characteristics. While the coefficient on *FOREXP* × *TREATMENT* is positive and significant in columns 1, 2, 4, and 6, it is negative for small enterprises.

Globalization, Firms, and Workers

260   THE AMERICAN ECONOMIC REVIEW   MARCH 2010

TABLE 3—OLS Long Difference-in-Difference Estimation: Regressing Production Worker Wage Differences
for 1990–1996 on the Minimum Wage Gap, Plant Characteristics, and Other Controls
(Textiles, Footwear and Apparel Only)

Dependent variable: Log plant unskilled wage in 1996–log plant unskilled wage in 1990	All firms (1)	Large firms (at least 100 employees) (2)	Small firms (less than 100 employees) (3)	Large firms (apparel and footwear only) (4)	Small firms (apparel and footwear only) (5)	Large firms (apparel and footwear including minimum wages) (6)	Small firms (apparel and footwear including minimum wages) (7)
Foreign or exporter (FOREXP)[a]	−0.071 (1.04)	−0.152 (2.30)*	0.098 (1.25)	−0.346 (2.10)	0.091 (0.99)	−0.282 (−2.04)	0.071 (0.65)
TREATMENT[b]	0.024 (0.36)	−0.014 (0.16)	0.051 (1.64)	−0.218 (3.37)*	0.088 (1.24)	−0.182 (2.86)*	0.061 (1.00)
FOREXP × TREATMENT	0.216 (1.78)	0.295 (2.36)*	−0.209 (2.65)*	0.518 (2.49)*	−0.070 (0.64)	0.434 (2.68)*	−0.165 (1.33)
Minimum wage[c]	—	—	—	—	—	1.001 (7.31)**	0.686 (3.01)*
Observations	1,123	535	588	214	286	214	286
R^2	0.20	0.17	0.32	0.20	0.31	0.36	0.39

Notes: Treatment is establishments in districts with Nike, Reebok, and Adidas contractors. Robust *t*-statistics in parentheses. Constant term included in all specifications but not reported here.
[a] Includes some foreign equity over the entire period or exports some share of output over the entire period.
[b] An establishment in the TFA sector in a district where Nike/Reebok/Adidas contractors operate.
[c] The minimum wage is defined as the log of the minimum wage in 1996 less the log of the minimum wage in 1990, unless the plant pays above the 1996 minimum wage in 1990, in which case the minimum wage change is set equal to zero.
** Indicates significance at the 1 percent level.
* Indicates significance at the 5 percent level.

C. Robustness

We perform a test of robustness using nonlinear matching techniques. Additional robustness tests are reported elsewhere.[16] To test whether there is something "special" about the treatment districts that could lead to spurious results within a chosen sector, we redo our estimation using as *TREATMENT* the affected districts (those with Nike, Reebok, or Adidas vendors) for each manufacturing sector separately. While a number of approaches are possible for estimating treatment effects using nonlinear matching techniques, we adopt a procedure using nearest neighbor matching as outlined by Alberto Abadie et al. (2004).

This approach allows us to estimate sample average treatment effects of anti-sweatshop activism on wage growth, using as controls those firms that match most closely firms that have been treated. To identify the most appropriate control group (the "nearest neighbor"), one must specify a list of covariates. For the treatment effects reported in Table 4, we include as our set of

---

[16] These additional tests are reported in Tables 4 and 5 of the working paper version of this article, available on the AER Web site. In additional robustness tests, we do the following: (i) add the long of production workers as an additional control variable; (ii) control for low initial wages by adding a dummy variable equal to one if the firm paid below the 1996 minimum wage in 1990; (iii) add profit margins as a control, to address the possibility that differences in product types or export opportunities could account for wage growth differentials; and (iv) perform a series of "nonsense" regressions by replacing the dummy variable for TFA plants with a dummy variable for other sectors. None of the additional tests alters the main results in Tables 2 and 3

TABLE 4—AN ADDITIONAL TEST OF ROBUSTNESS: A MATCHING ESTIMATOR BY SECTOR
(Dependent variable: Log plant unskilled wage in 1996–log plant unskilled age in 1990)

Industry (ISIC classification)	Estimating sample average treatment effect using matching estimation treatment defined as foreign or exporting enterprises located in districts with Nike, Reebok, or Adidas contractors Coefficient on *TREATMENT*	
	Large enterprises (at least 100 workers)	All enterprises
Textiles, footwear, and apparel only	0.212 (2.30)*	0.224 (2.68)**
Food, beverages, and tobacco	0.169 (0.55)	0.121 (0.40)
Wood and furniture	−0.162 (0.73)	−0.086 (0.50)
Paper products	−0.072 (0.24)	−0.085 (0.28)
Chemicals and petroleum products	−0.014 (0.11)	−0.122 (0.92)
Nonmetallic mineral products	0.057 (0.19)	0.173 (0.44)
Basic metal industries	−0.094 (0.25)	0.011 (0.03)
Fabricated metal products and machinery	−0.110 (0.87)	0.024 (0.18)
Other manufacturing	−0.618 (2.96)**	−0.365 (1.35)

Notes: Z-statistics in parentheses. We use nearest neighbor matching as outlined by Abadie et al. (2004). Enterprises matched to the treatment group on the basis of export and foreign status, location, size, output growth, growth in capital stock, growth in material inputs, educational attainment of the workforce, TFPG, and investments in technology. *TREATMENT* defined as a foreign-owned or exporting enterprise located in treatment districts.
   ** Indicates significance at the 1 percent level.
   * Indicates significance at the 5 percent level.

covariates all the controls discussed earlier except the minimum wage (which is not included because of our concern about possible endogeneity and which is highly collinear with location). Enterprises in the control group are matched to the treatment group on the basis of foreign ownership and export status, location, size, output growth, growth in capital stock, growth in material inputs, educational attainment of the workforce, TFPG, and investments in technology.

It is not possible, in the context of our matching estimation, to allow for multiple treatment effects simultaneously. Consequently, in Table 4 *TREATMENT* is simply defined as being a foreign-owned *or* exporting enterprise (*FOREXP*) located in districts with anti-sweatshop activism. The impact of activism on wages estimated using nonlinear matching is remarkably similar to the OLS results reported in the first two columns of Table 3. In the first row of Table 4, anti-sweatshop activism is associated with real wage increases of between 21 and 22 percent. In the remaining rows of Table 4, we substitute for TFA with all other manufacturing sectors for treatment and show that the effects are significant and positive only for TFA enterprises.

The results in Table 1 through Table 4 suggest that wages increased systematically more for large exporting and foreign-owned TFA plants in treatment districts relative to other plants with similar characteristics. Below, we explore whether these wage gains had potentially adverse effects, such as employment losses and falling investment, or caused plants to shut down operations in Indonesia.

III. Other Outcomes

A. *Employment*

The classic approach to minimum wages suggests that an increase in mandated wages should lead to a fall in employment, as employers are driven up their labor demand curve. Prior to the 1990s, standard textbook treatments of minimum wages reported that imposing a wage floor would lead to adverse consequences for employment. However, David D. Card and Alan B. Krueger (1994, 1997) argue that the imposition of a minimum wage need not have negative employment consequences if there are imperfections in the labor market. These imperfections include the following possibilities: (i) the existence of monopsony employers; (ii) search costs for employers; and (iii) efficiency wages. If any of these three imperfections characterizes the local labor market, an increase in the minimum wage (or an increase in compliance with the existing minimum wage) could lead to an increase or no change in employment.

This unorthodox finding, which has caused an enormous debate among labor economists, has interesting implications for labor market policies in developing countries. If policymakers can raise wages by increasing the statutory minimum or encouraging compliance with the existing minimum without increasing unemployment, then minimum wage policies could become a powerful tool for combating poverty. This was precisely the thinking behind a 1995 World Bank report that strongly recommended the introduction of a national minimum wage to reduce poverty in Trinidad and Tobago.

A number of papers test the impact of minimum wages on employment in developing countries (see, for example, Eric Strobl and Frank Walsh 2000; Linda A. Bell 1997; William F. Maloney and Jairo A. Nuñez 2001; Martin Rama 1996; SMERU Research Institute 2001). All these studies suggest there is a widespread lack of compliance with the legislated minimum wage.

In Table 5, we repeat the type of analysis presented in Tables 1A–C and use the same type of difference-in-difference approach adopted by Card and Krueger (1994) to examine the impact of minimum wages and anti-sweatshop activism on employment in Indonesia. The first row reports the number of production workers in 1990, and the second row reports the number of production workers in 1996. The third row reports the difference for all plants, while the fourth row reports the difference in employment between 1990 and 1996 only for plants with data on employment in both years. Columns 1 through 3 report employment for TFA establishments, columns 4 through 6 for other establishments, and the last three columns compare the two groups.

Across domestic TFA enterprises, the mean number of employees fell slightly, from an average of 95 employees per plant to an average of 90 employees per plant. Columns 2 and 3 show that TFA employment growth was concentrated in foreign-owned and exporting enterprises. Between 1990 and 1996, foreign-owned and exporting plants added nearly 400 production workers, on average. In contrast, establishments in other sectors grew very little. Columns 7 through 9 report the difference-in-difference, which is the difference in the change in employment across TFA and non-TFA firms between 1990 and 1996. Focusing on rows 3 and 4 and columns 8 and 9, we see that exporting and foreign-owned TFA plants increased employment by 300 to 400 workers more than other plants. The results in Table 5 suggest that anti-sweatshop activism vis-à-vis TFA enterprises did not appear to hurt their employment, at least relative to growth in employment of other types of enterprises.

Tables 6A and 6B repeat the analysis in a regression context. We replace the log of production worker wages with the log of production worker employment as the dependent variable. The

Table 5—Average Production Worker Employment per Establishment in 1990 and 1996

	Textiles, footwear, and apparel establishments			Other establishments			Difference		
	Domestic[a] (1)	Always foreign[b] (2)	Always exporting[c] (3)	Domestic[a] (4)	Always foreign[b] (5)	Always exporting[c] (6)	(1)–(4) (7)	(2)–(5) (8)	(3)–(6) (9)
1. Mean employment in 1990, all available observations	94.82 (5.53)	737.75 (97.87)	403.64 (45.99)	62.39 (1.60)	288.67 (24.43)	399.60 (24.71)	32.42 (4.24)	449.08 (70.26)	4.04 (52.75)
2. Mean employment in 1996, all available observations	90.00 (4.74)	1,126.97 (109.79)	765.97 (66.37)	61.60 (1.60)	353.50 (19.73)	297.14 (12.73)	28.40 (4.08)	773.47 (67.44)	468.82 (42.65)
3. Change in mean employment, 1990-1996	−4.82 (7.3)	389.22 (197.70)	362.33 (118.17)	−0.79 (2.31)	64.83 (33.99)	−102.46 (26.18)	−4.03 (4.23)	324.39 (70.5)	464.79 (52.9)
4. Change in mean employment balanced sample[d]	14.69 (15.51)	561.99 (237.76)	432.67 (143.82)	12.17 (4.09)	119.68 (54.88)	117.98 (49.59)	2.48 (5.3)	442.3 (91.5)	314.69 (60.0)
5. Change in mean log employment, all observations	0.03 (0.03)	0.23 (0.20)	0.22 (0.10)	−0.02 (0.01)	0.19 (0.08)	−0.37 (0.06)	0.05 (0.02)	0.04 (0.11)	0.59 (0.07)
6. Change in mean log employment, balanced sample	0.08 (0.05)	0.54 (0.17)	0.45 (0.19)	0.09 (0.02)	0.30 (0.11)	0.18 (0.09)	−0.01 (0.02)	0.24 (0.16)	0.12 (0.12)

Note: Standard errors in parentheses.
[a] A plant that is neither foreign-owned nor exports the entire period.
[b] Includes some foreign equity over the entire period.
[c] Exports some share of output over the entire period.
[d] Defined as establishments present in both 1990 and 1996.

coefficients on *FOR × TREATMENT* and *EXP × TREATMENT* are positive and sometimes significant. With or without controls, the results are consistent across specifications. There is no evidence that either treatment is associated with employment declines. In fact, employment growth was generally higher for TFA exporters and foreign-owned enterprises, including those operating in districts where anti-sweatshop activists targeted Nike, Reebok, and Adidas.

However, the results in Tables 6A and 6B show a robust and negative impact of the minimum wage increase on employment growth. In column 3, the coefficient on the minimum wage increase is −0.123, which suggests that a 100 percentage point increase in the minimum wage would be accompanied by a 12.3 percentage point decline in employment. In our sample, the mean increase in the minimum wage measure was 50 percent, indicating an employment loss of 6 percent. The different specifications presented in columns 3 and 4 of Table 6A and columns 1 through 5 of Table 6B suggest that a 100 percentage point increase in the real minimum wage would be accompanied by employment declines of 12 to 36 percent. The significant negative impact on employment needs to be seriously considered in any campaign to increase the mandated minimum wage or to increase compliance with the minimum wage.[17]

[17] Indonesia, however, is an unusual case: most countries do not experience 100 percent real increases in the value of the minimum wage over a five-year period.

TABLE 6A—OLS LONG DIFFERENCE-IN-DIFFERENCE ESTIMATION: REGRESSING PRODUCTION WORKER EMPLOYMENT
DIFFERENCES FOR 1990–1996 ON THE MINIMUM WAGE GAP, PLANT CHARACTERISTICS, AND OTHER CONTROLS
(*Dependent variable: Log production worker employment in 1996–log production worker employment in 1990*)

	Ownership dummies only (1)	Ownership dummies only (2)	All controls (3)	Treatment excludes textiles (4)
Foreign [a]	0.196 (3.50)**	—	—	—
Exporter [b]	0.067 (2.19)*	—	—	—
Foreign or Exporter (FOREXP)	—	0.121 (4.37)**	0.019 (0.79)	0.024 (1.08)
TREATMENT [c]	−0.016 (0.51)	−0.015 (0.46)	0.002 (0.13)	0.032 (1.14)
Foreign × TREATMENT	0.104 (1.07)	—	—	—
Exporting × TREATMENT	0.106 (0.70)	—	—	—
FOREXP × TREATMENT	—	0.104 (0.92)	0.098 (1.88)	0.104 (1.35)
Minimum wage [d]	0.009 (0.19)	0.004 (0.10)	−0.123 (8.77)**	−0.125 (8.86)**
Observations	6,165	6,165	5,920	5,920
R^2	0.01	0.01	0.32	0.32

Notes: Treatment defined as belonging to TFA sector. Robust *t*-statistics in parentheses. Constant term included but not reported here.

[a] Includes some foreign equity over the entire period.

[b] Exports some share of output over the entire period.

[c] Treatment is defined as an establishment in the TFA sector.

[d] Defined as the log of the minimum wage in 1996 less the log of the minimum wage in 1990, unless the plant pays above the 1996 minimum wage in 1990, in which case the minimum wage change is set equal to zero.

** Indicates significance at 1 percent level.

* Indicating significance at 5 percent level.

B. *Other Outcomes: Output Growth, Investment, Productivity, Profits, and Exit*

The evidence in Tables 1 through 6 points to strong positive effects of anti-sweatshop campaigns on wage growth for production workers and insignificant effects on employment. We might, however, expect other adverse outcomes to be adversely affected. Table 7 reports the impact of treatment on output growth, investment, productivity, and profits. Consistent with the insignificant effects on employment, the first two columns of Table 7 show that output growth for the two treatment groups was not significantly different than for other enterprises. However, profits were significantly and negatively affected. Growth in profitability for foreign-owned TFA firms in the treatment districts was significantly lower than for similar plants. Lower growth in profits appeared to be linked to lower growth in capital stock and lower productivity growth, at least for foreign-owned TFA plants in treatment districts.

In Tables 8A and 8B we explore whether the pressures imposed by anti-sweatshop activists induced more firms to shut down operations. We estimate the probability of exit in period $t + 1$ as a function of plant and worker characteristics in period t, using annual data. If the pressures imposed by anti-sweatshop activities led to higher exit or relocation abroad, then the benefits of

VOL. 100 NO. 1   HARRISON AND SCORSE: MULTINATIONALS AND ANTI-SWEATSHOP ACTIVISM   265

TABLE 6B—OLS LONG DIFFERENCE-IN-DIFFERENCE ESTIMATION: REGRESSING PRODUCTION WORKER EMPLOYMENT DIFFERENCES FOR 1990–1996 ON THE MINIMUM WAGE GAP, PLANT CHARACTERISTICS, AND OTHER CONTROLS
(*Dependent variable: Log production worker employment in 1996–log production worker employment in 1990*)

	All TFA firms (1)	No minimum wage as a control (2)	Large firms only (3)	Footwear and apparel firms only (4)	FA enterprises, large firms only (5)	FA enterprises, large firms only (6)
Foreign or exporter [a] (FOREXP)	0.044 (1.69)	0.074 (2.39)*	−0.012 (0.60)	0.077 (1.52)	0.086 (1.22)	0.113 (1.76)
TREATMENT [b]	0.006 (0.16)	0.011 (0.35)	−0.031 (0.94)	0.083 (3.07)*	0.044 (0.91)	0.059 (1.21)
FOREXP × TREATMENT	0.156 (2.87)**	0.125 (2.55)*	0.162 (3.21)**	0.091 (1.13)	0.056 (0.56)	0.028 (0.34)
Minimum wage[c]	−0.179 (3.99)**	—	−0.116 (6.09)**	−0.345 (5.32)**	−0.357 (3.58)**	—
Observations	1,123	1,123	535	500	214	214
R^2	0.47	0.46	0.54	0.60	0.66	0.65

Notes: Treatment defined as operating in treatment districts, TFA enterprises only. Robust *t*-statistics in parentheses. Constant term included but not reported here.
  [a] Includes some foreign equity over the entire period, or exports some share of output over the entire period.
  [b] Treatment is defined as locating in a district where Nike, Adidas, or Reebok contractors operate.
  [c] Defined as the log of the minimum wage in 1996 less the log of the minimum wage in 1990, unless the plant pays above the 1996 minimum wage in 1990, in which case the minimum wage change is set equal to zero.
  ** Indicates significance at 1 percent level.
  * Indicating significance at 5 percent level.

higher wages could be offset by a higher probability of job loss. We begin with the whole sample, with results from a probit estimation of the likelihood of exit reported in column 1 of Table 8A. If the treatment is defined as belonging to the TFA sector, there is no evidence that exporters or foreign-owned firms are more likely to shut down. In fact, foreign-owned plants in general are less likely to exit, as indicated by the significant and negative coefficient of −0.01 in the first row and column of Table 8A.

Andrew B. Bernard and Frederic Sjoholm (2004) point out that not taking into account the size of a plant is misleading, because small plants are much more likely to exit than large plants. In particular, they point out that in the Indonesian data, plants with fewer than 20 workers were eliminated from the sample after 1989, changing the composition of the sample in favor of larger plants, which are less likely to exit. One possibility is that exporters and foreign-owned plants in the TFA sector are less likely to exit because they are significantly larger than other plants. To address this possibility, in column 2 we include only those plants with at least 100 workers. The coefficients are unaffected; foreign-owned enterprises in the treatment group were significantly less likely to exit during the sample period. Minimum wages have about the same impact as before, raising exit probabilities significantly.

In columns 3, 4, and 5, we restrict the analysis to TFA plants and define *TREATMENT* as operating in districts with Nike, Reebok, and Adidas contractors. Columns 3 and 4 show that foreign-owned plants located in the treatment districts are also less likely to exit—2 percent less likely than other plants. These lower probabilities of exit for foreign-owned enterprises are consistent with the unconditional exit probabilities depicted in Figure 2. However, higher minimum wages did increase the probability of exit, with a 10 percent increase in the real minimum wage leading to a higher probability of plant exit by 0.6 to 1.1 percent.

TABLE 7—THE IMPACT OF TREATMENT ON OTHER OUTCOMES:
OUTPUT GROWTH, CHANGE IN CAPITAL STOCK, TFPG, AND PROFITS
(*Dependent variable is indicated in columns below*)

	Output growth (1)	Output growth (textiles, footwear and apparel only) (2)	Growth in capital stock (3)	Growth in capital stock (textiles, footwear, and apparel only) (4)	TFPG (5)	TFPG (textiles, footwear, and apparel only) (6)	Change in profits (7)	Change in profits (textiles, footwear, and apparel only) (8)
Foreign [a]	0.038	0.156	0.266	0.022	−0.044	0.140	0.034	−0.008
	(0.92)	(2.75)**	(4.09)**	(0.18)	(1.32)	(3.31)**	(2.77)**	(0.54)
Exporter [b]	−0.010	0.066	−0.111	0.174	−0.020	−0.018	−0.014	0.033
	(0.39)	(0.62)	(2.36)*	(1.56)	(1.38)	(0.26)	(1.58)	(1.21)
TREATMENT [c]	−0.011	0.075	0.005	0.174	−0.015	0.044	0.006	0.035
	(0.67)	(1.90)	(0.15)	(4.98)**	(1.99)	(2.03)	(0.83)	(9.67)**
Foreign × TREATMENT	0.100	−0.082	−0.244	−0.077	0.095	−0.172	−0.062	−0.05
	(2.62)**	(1.02)	(2.67)**	(0.63)	(3.77)**	(3.84)**	(3.80)**	(2.13)*
Exporting × TREATMENT	0.023	−0.092	0.133	−0.248	−0.007	−0.019	0.018	−0.039
	(0.57)	(0.88)	(1.90)	(1.67)	(0.19)	(0.25)	(0.85)	(1.88)
Observations	6,165	1,173	6,165	1,173	5,920	1,123	5,915	1,135
R^2	0.71	0.79	0.24	0.31	0.05	0.10	0.20	0.28

Notes: Robust *t*-statistics in parentheses. Constant term included but not reported here. Definitions for TFPG and profits given in Tables 1B and 1C.

[a] Includes some foreign equity over the entire period.

[b] Exports some share of output over the entire period.

[c] In columns 1, 3, 5, and 7, treatment is defined as an establishment in the TFA sector. In columns 2, 4, 6, and 8, treatment is defined as locating in a district where Nike, Adidas, or Reebok contractors operate.

** Indicates significance at 1 percent level.

* Indicating significance at 5 percent level.

In column 5 we turn to an analysis of plants with fewer than 100 employees. Small TFA exporters in treatment districts are 4.5 percentage points more likely to exit than other small TFA exporters. These results are statistically significant and suggest that *TREATMENT* is associated with a higher probability of plant shutdown for small exporters. Table 8B excludes controls for worker characteristics and minimum wages. Since worker characteristics are recorded for only three years in the 1990s, including worker characteristics restricts the sample to surviving plants or plants exiting after 1995, when worker characteristics were first recorded. In this larger sample, the evidence is consistent with a lower probability of exit for foreign-owned enterprises, including both TFA and non-TFA foreign plants.[18]

However, the evidence is consistent with higher exit probabilities for small TFA exporters in the treatment group, as indicated in the last columns of both Tables 8A and Table 8B. While exporters in general were less likely to exit, small TFA exporters operating in the treatment districts were significantly more likely to exit than other small TFA exporters, with a 15.5 percent

---

[18] Our results are somewhat different from those of Bernard and Sjoholm (2004), who find that foreign-owned plants in Indonesia are more footloose than other plants. Our results suggest that foreign-owned plants are *less* footloose. This could be because the number of foreign-owned enterprises in Indonesia in the 1980s—Bernard and Sjoholm examine data that end in 1989—was small and consequently a few plants could lead to large rates of entry and exit. Our data focus on the 1990s, when there were many more foreign-owned plants in Indonesia.

TABLE 8A—DETERMINANTS OF EXIT: PROBIT ESTIMATES 1988–1996
(*Coefficients are derivatives*)

	All firms (1)	Large firms with at least 100 employees (2)	TFA firms only (3)	Large TFA firms (4)	Small TFA firms (5)
Foreign [a]	−0.010 (2.18)*	−0.002 (0.68)	−0.006 (1.47)	0.001 (0.16)	−0.019 (0.52)
Exporter [b]	0.006 (0.81)	−0.000 (0.11)	0.001 (0.13)	0.000 (0.07)	0.020 (1.34)
TREATMENT [c]	0.009 (4.48)**	0.010 (3.01)**	−0.005 (0.77)	−0.000 (0.00)	−0.015 (1.47)
Foreign × TREATMENT	−0.007 (0.84)	−0.007 (1.30)	−0.021 (2.00)*	−0.015 (2.68)**	—
Exporting × TREATMENT	−0.005 (0.98)	−0.002 (0.59)	0.005 (0.33)	0.001 (0.08)	0.045 (3.48)**
Change in minimum wage	0.075 (2.61)*	0.059 (3.37)**	0.087 (2.36)*	0.056 (2.98)**	0.108 (1.96)*
Observations	81,840	28,438	15,847	7,004	8,748

Notes: Includes controls for educational attainment of employees. Dependent variable is a dummy variable equal to one if the plant exits and equal to zero if the plant survives in period $t + 1$. All independent variables are from period t. Observations are annual data taken from the full unbalanced panel for 1990 through 1996. Robust z statistics in parentheses. Reported coefficients are the change in the probability of exit, evaluated at the sample mean. All specifications include the full set of controls from the previous tables.
[a] Includes some foreign equity over the entire period.
[b] Exports some share of output over the entire period.
[c] In columns 1 and 2 treatment is defined as an establishment in TFA sector. In the other columns treatment is defined as locating in a district where Nike, Adidas, and Reebok operate.
** Indicates significance at 1 percent level.
* Indicating significance at 5 percent level.

higher probability of exiting compared to other enterprises. This significantly higher probability of exit is consistent with the unconditional exit probabilities depicted in Figure 2.

One possibility is that TFA exporters are simply more volatile, exhibiting higher rates of entry as well. However, we find that this is not the case. Unreported results show that during the 1990s, not only were TFA plants more likely to exit, but entry rates dropped as well. Higher rates of entry by TFA plants relative to other sectors were followed by a fall in entry rates, which by the end of the 1990s were comparable to non-TFA plants. Additional unreported probit regressions confirm that there was less entry into the TFA sector, particularly among exporters.

If entry fell and exit rates rose for exporting TFA plants, how can we account for the fact that total employment in TFA plants did not fall? In other words, how can we explain that TFA production worker employment as a percentage of total manufacturing employment increased at the same time that exit became proportionately higher? The reason, as shown in Table 5, is that remaining TFA plants—particularly exporters and foreign-owned plants—increased production worker employment by as much as 50 percent. Employment increases within surviving plants compensated for higher exit by some TFA enterprises.

C. *Does Better Compliance with Minimum Wage Laws Explain the Observed Wage Gains?*

An important question remains: were the wage increases in treatment firms simply a result of better compliance with the rising minimum wage? We address this question in Table 9. The

TABLE 8B—DETERMINANTS OF EXIT: PROBIT ESTIMATES 1988–1996
(Coefficients are derivatives)

	All firms (1)	Large firms with at least 100 employees (2)	Small firms with fewer than 100 employees (3)	TFA firms only (4)	Large TFA firms (5)	Small TFA firms (6)
Foreign [a]	−0.043 (6.78)**	−0.019 (3.47)**	−0.049 (4.86)**	−0.060 (8.50)**	−0.034 (4.62)**	−0.079 (0.98)
Exporter [b]	−0.032 (2.47)**	−0.024 (2.15)*	0.017 (1.14)	−0.027 (1.31)	−0.009 (1.05)	−0.020 (0.42)
TREATMENT [c]	0.018 (3.92)**	0.017 (2.75)**	0.025 (5.16)**	−0.018 (0.92)	0.002 (0.18)	−0.032 (1.56)
Foreign × TREATMENT	−0.024 (2.85)**	−0.023 (2.69)**	−0.019 (0.36)	−0.013 (0.64)	−0.028 (1.96)*	0.020 (0.16)
Exporting × TREATMENT	0.016 (0.99)	0.021 (1.71)	−0.019 (0.50)	0.032 (1.29)	0.002 (0.19)	0.155 (2.20)*
Change in minimum wage	—	—	—	—	—	—
Observations	93,757	30,988	62,719	18,367	7,657	10,666

Notes: Excludes controls for average wages, minimum wage changes, and educational attainment of employees. Dependent variable is a dummy variable equal to one if the plant exits and equal to zero if the plant survives in period $t + 1$. All independent variables are from period t. Observations are annual data taken from the full unbalanced panel for 1990 through 1996. Robust z statistics in parentheses. Reported coefficients are the change in the probability of exit, evaluated at the sample mean. All specifications include the full set of controls from the previous tables.

[a] Includes some foreign equity over the entire period.

[b] Exports some share of output over the entire period.

[c] In columns 1, 2, and 3, treatment is defined as an establishment in the TFA sector. In the other columns, treatment is defined as locating in a district where Nike, Adidas, or Reebok contractors operate.

** Indicates significance at 1 percent level.

* Indicating significance at 5 percent level.

first three columns report the change in compliance with the statutory minimum wage as a function of treatment, controlling for plant and worker characteristics. The dependent variable is the change in compliance between 1990 and 1996, where compliance is a dummy variable equal to one if the firm's average production worker wage exceeded the statutory minimum wage in that district. The results in column 1 show that if *TREATMENT* is defined as the TFA sector, then foreign or exporting treatment firms increased compliance with the minimum wage by 15.1 percentage points relative to the control (firms in other sectors). If *TREATMENT* is defined as operating in districts targeted by anti-sweatshop activism, then the results in columns 2 and 3 indicate that *TREATMENT* led to increased compliance by 12.4 to 37.1 percent relative to other TFA firms. The first three columns of Table 9 suggest that the anti-sweatshop movement was associated with a large and significant increase in compliance with the minimum wage.

The next four columns of Table 9 measure the contribution of higher minimum wage compliance to the wage increases associated with *TREATMENT*. To do this, we add a triple interaction term between foreign-ownership or export status *FOREXP*, *TREATMENT*, and the minimum wage gap. If activism led to higher wages by increasing compliance with the minimum wage, then this interaction term should capture that effect and the coefficient on *FOREXP × TREATMENT* should become small in magnitude and insignificant. The results presented in columns 4 through 7 show that this is indeed the case.

The coefficient on *FOREXP × TREATMENT* becomes insignificant and close to zero, while the coefficient on the triple interaction is large in magnitude and significant. These results suggest

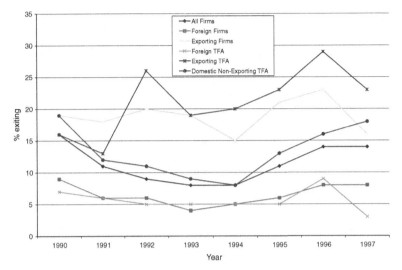

FIGURE 2. PERCENTAGE OF FIRMS EXITING IN YEARS 1990–1997

that anti-sweatshop activism led to higher wages primarily by increasing compliance with the minimum wage. In columns 8 and 9, we add the triple interaction to the employment regressions from Tables 8A and 8B. The inclusion of the additional term does not affect the results, suggesting that, while anti-sweatshop activism was associated with additional wage growth, it was not associated with greater employment declines, or with falling employment stemming from more vigilant compliance with the minimum wage. While, on average, the large minimum wage increases were associated with falling employment, the increasing compliance of establishments targeted by anti-sweatshop activism was not. Combining the results presented in Tables 6 through 9 suggests that plants targeted by the campaigns either raised wages, cut profits, and maintained employment, or simply exited the industry.

IV. Conclusion

During the 1990s, anti-sweatshop activists campaigned to improve working conditions and raise wages for workers in developing countries. Indonesia, which had more Nike contractors than any other country apart from China during this period, was a primary target for these activists. The Indonesian government also greatly increased the minimum wage throughout the 1990s. This paper analyzes the impact of these twin interventions on labor market outcomes in Indonesian manufacturing. The results suggest that on top of the large wage increases induced by minimum wage changes, real production worker wages rose an additional 10 to 20 percent for TFA relative to non-TFA establishments. Within the TFA sector, plants targeted by anti-sweatshop activists experienced even larger real wage increases. Large TFA establishments in treatment districts increased production worker wages by as much as 30 percent relative to other

270   *THE AMERICAN ECONOMIC REVIEW*   *MARCH 2010*

TABLE 9—IMPACT OF COMPLIANCE WITH MINIMUM WAGES ON WAGE AND EMPLOYMENT OUTCOMES

	Dependent variable is change in compliance with minimum wage			Dependent variable is change in the log of production wages				Dependent variable is change in the log of production workers	
	All enterprises and all controls	Textiles, footwear, and apparel only	Footwear and apparel only	All enterprises and all controls	All enterprises with at least 100 employees	Textiles, footwear, and apparel only	Footwear and apparel only	All enterprises	Textiles, footwear, and apparel only
Foreign or Exporter (FOREXP)[a]	0.027 (1.43)	0.082 (0.97)	−0.113 (1.07)	−0.002 (0.08)	−0.068 (1.65)	0.044 (1.13)	−0.130 (1.18)	0.019 (0.80)	0.041 (1.55)
TREATMENT[b]	−0.105 (7.14)**	0.106 (7.43)**	0.009 (0.48)	−0.049 (1.60)	0.020 (0.37)	0.194 (2.62)*	0.239 (4.06)**	0.030 (0.97)	−0.026 (0.27)
FOREXP × TREATMENT	0.151 (2.90)*	0.124 (1.47)	0.371 (3.44)**	0.007 (0.08)	−0.047 (0.43)	−0.021 (0.31)	0.111 (1.14)	0.003 (0.04)	0.159 (1.10)
Minimum wage[c]	−0.082 (1.10)	−0.142 (1.23)	0.027 (0.12)	0.659 (6.95)**	0.678 (5.75)**	0.696 (9.46)**	0.999 (5.45)**	−0.121 (8.00)**	−0.197 (3.54)**
TREATMENT × minimum wage	—	—	—	0.020 (0.47)	−0.077 (0.72)	−0.223 (3.57)**	−0.375 (3.38)**	−0.044 (1.58)	0.046 (0.55)
TREATMENT × FOREXP × min wage	—	—	—	0.177 (1.61)	0.287 (2.07)*	0.165 (6.49)**	0.271 (2.67)*	0.164 (2.61)*	−0.002 (0.01)
Observations	5,875	1,114	494	5,920	2,431	1,123	500	5,920	1,123
R^2	0.10	0.13	0.16	0.23	0.23	0.29	0.34	0.32	0.47

Notes: Robust *t* statistics in parentheses. Constant term included but not reported here. Compliance is a zero-one dummy variable equal to one if the establishment's average production worker wage is above the district statutory minimum wage.

[a] Includes some foreign equity or exports over the entire period.

[b] In columns 1, 4, 5, and 8 treatment is defined as an establishment in the textiles, footwear, and apparel (TFA) sector. In the remaining columns, treatment is defined as locating in a district where Nike, Adidas or Reebok contractors operate.

[c] Defined as the log of the minimum wage in 1996 less the log of the minimum wage in 1990, unless the plant pays above the 1996 minimum wage in 1990, in which case the minimum wage change is set equal to zero.

** Indicates significance at 1 percent level.

* Indicating significance at 5 percent level

plants. As we show in the paper, much of the wage increases within targeted plants reflected higher compliance with the minimum wage relative to non-TFA or nontreatment plants after the onset of the anti-sweatshop campaigns.

One question that naturally arises is how such large real wage increases could be sustained without adverse consequences for employment.[19] We examine whether these higher wages led firms to cut employment or shut down operations. Our results suggest that the minimum wage increases led to employment losses for production workers across all sectors in manufacturing. While anti-sweatshop activism did not have additional adverse effects on employment within the TFA sector, it did lead to falling profits, reduced productivity growth, and plant closures for smaller exporters.

---

[19] It is important to keep in mind that for a well-known brand name such as Nike, labor costs from developing country factories in 1998 accounted for only about 4 percent of the total cost of a $90 shoe (see http://cbae.nmsu.edu/~dboje/NIKfaqcompensation.html). This interview with Nike is from 1998, but is no longer part of Nike's "official" Web site.

VOL. 100 NO. 1   HARRISON AND SCORSE: MULTINATIONALS AND ANTI-SWEATSHOP ACTIVISM   271

It is important to note that the wage gains documented in this paper could be temporary. In the late 1980s and early 1990s, the TFA sector in Indonesia was booming, as suppliers from higher-cost East-Asian locations shifted operations to lower-cost locations nearby. Yet in the last ten years, footwear and apparel companies such as Nike have shifted to vendors in other low-wage countries, including China, Vietnam, and Cambodia. Vietnam has now replaced Indonesia as the second largest vendor location (after China), as measured by the number of workers employed in Nike supplier factories. While Nike continues to use Indonesian contract factories to source 20 percent of its footwear operations, this share will continue to fall if factories in Vietnam produce lower-cost and higher-quality goods.

Many research and policy questions remain unanswered. Designing anti-sweatshop campaigns in such a way as to make wage gains and better factory conditions sustainable, without endangering employment or leading plants to relocate elsewhere, is challenging. The new anti-sweatshop activism emphasizes the introduction of "living wages," which are significantly harder to define and consequently to implement, compared to codes of conduct focused on compliance with minimum wages. Extending the type of analysis presented in this paper to other countries would also be informative.

APPENDIX

TABLE A1—MINIMUM WAGES IN DATASET IN INDONESIA, 1988–1999

Year	Consumer price index with 1996 = 100	Minimum wage in nominal values (hundreds of rupiahs)	Minimum wage in 1996 values (hundreds of rupiahs)	Minimum wage in US dollars	Exchange rate in rupiahs per dollar
1988	0.527	351	667	388	1,717
1989	0.561	355	634	355	1,787
1990	0.604	503	833	443	1,882
1991	0.661	633	957	484	1,982
1992	0.711	717	1,008	492	2,051
1993	0.780	832	1,066	509	2,095
1994	0.846	1,193	1,409	652	2,160
1995	0.926	1,418	1,531	684	2,239
1996	1.000	1,560	1,560	644	2,348
1997	1.067	1,699	1,592	539	2,953
1998	1.680	1,963	1,167	118	9,875
1999	2.027	2,308	1,138	146	7,809

272 THE AMERICAN ECONOMIC REVIEW MARCH 2010

TABLE A2—FIRM-SPECIFIC AND DISTRICT-SPECIFIC DETERMINANTS OF THE MINIMUM WAGE FOR 1990–1996
(*Dependent variable: Log of the minimum wage*)

	(1)	(2)	(3)	(4)	(5)
Dummy for location in treatment district	0.074 (1.70)	0.138 (4.25)**	0.073 (1.70)	—	0.103 (2.20)*
TFA sector dummy	−0.006 (0.29)	−0.0004 (0.02)	—	−0.006 (0.27)	−0.034 (1.15)
Output growth	0.003 (1.58)	0.002 (1.38)	0.003 (1.58)	0.003 (1.58)	0.005 (1.45)
Total factor productivity growth	−0.009 (1.81)	−0.005 (1.05)	−0.009 (1.81)	−0.009 (1.82)	−0.018 (2.15)*
Lag log production wages	0.007 (2.37)*	0.010 (3.40)**	0.007 (2.37)*	0.007 (2.37)*	0.009 (1.45)
Wholesale price index	−0.070 (1.69)	−0.073 (1.72)	−0.070 (1.69)	−0.071 (1.68)	−0.150 (2.59)*
Consumer price index	0.659 (14.15)**	0.800 (16.08)**	0.658 (14.17)**	0.659 (14.05)**	0.687 (11.80)**
Foreign-ownership	0.000 (0.51)	0.000 (0.81)	0.000 (0.51)	0.000 (0.51)	0.000 (0.11)
Export share of sales (0 to 100)	−0.0001 (2.80)**	—	−0.0001 (2.80)**	−0.0001 (2.78)**	−0.0002 (2.44)*
Tariffs	—	—	—	—	0.0001 (0.48)
Observations	84,204	89,247	84,204	84,204	42,047
R^2	0.62	0.67	0.62	0.81	0.63

Notes: t-statistics in parentheses. All regressions estimated taking into account fixed effects at the level of the individual establishment, with errors clustered at the district level and robust standard errors. Year dummies included in all specifications. Establishment-specific determinants of the log minimum wage include output growth, TFPG as defined in Tables 1B and 1C, TFA sector dummy, production wages, foreign ownership, and the export share of sales. In column 5 the number of observations is cut in half due to the fact that tariff information is available for only half the observations.

REFERENCES

Abadie, Alberto, David Drukker, Jane L. Herr, and Guido W. Imbens. 2004. "Implementing Matching Estimators for Average Treatment Effects in Stata." *The Stata Journal*, 4(3): 290–311.

Aitken, Brian, Ann Harrison, and Robert E. Lipsey. 1996. "Wages and Foreign Ownership: A Comparative Study of Mexico, Venezuela, and the United States." *Journal of International Economics*, 40(3-4): 345–71.

Altonji, Joseph G., and Rebecca M. Blank. 1999. "Race and Gender in the Labor Market." In *Handbook of Labor Economics Volume 3c*, ed. Orley Ashenfelter and David Card, 3143–3259. Amsterdam: Elsevier Science, North-Holland.

Bell, Linda A. 1997. "The Impact of Minimum Wages in Mexico and Colombia." *Journal of Labor Economics*, 15(3): S102–35.

Bernard, Andrew B., and Fredrik Sjoholm. 2004. "Foreign Owners and Plant Survival." National Bureau of Economic Research Working Paper 10039.

Brown, Drusilla K. 2001. "Labor Standards: Where Do They Belong on the International Trade Agenda?" *Journal of Economic Perspectives*, 15(3): 89–112.

Brown, Drusilla K., Alan V. Deardorff, and Robert M. Stern. 2004. "The Effects of Multinational Production on Wages and Working Conditions in Developing Countries." In *Challenges to Globalization: Analyzing the Economics*, ed. Robert E. Baldwin and L. Alan Winters, 279–326. Chicago: University of Chicago Press.

Card, David, and Alan B. Krueger. 1994. "Minimum Wages and Employment: A Case Study of the Fast-Food Industry in New Jersey and Pennsylvania." *American Economic Review*, 84(4): 772–93.

Card, David D., and Alan Krueger. 1997. *Myth and Measurement: The New Economics of the Minimum Wage.* Princeton: Princeton University Press.

Chau, Nancy H., and Ravi Kanbur. 2001. "The Adoption of International Labor Standard Conventions: Who, When, and Why?" In *Brookings Trade Forum 2001,* ed. Dani Rodrik and Susan M. Collins, 113–56. Washington DC: The Brookings Institution.

Edmonds, Eric V., and Nina Pavcnik. 2001. "Does Globalization Increase Child Labor? Evidence from Vietnam." National Bureau of Economic Research Working Paper 8760.

Maloney, William F., and Jairo A. Nuñez. 2001. "Measuring the Impact of Minimum Wages: Evidence from Latin America." World Bank Policy Research Working Paper 2597.

Maskus, Keith. 1996. "Should Core Labor Standards be Imposed Through International Trade Policy?" World Bank Policy Research Working Paper 1817.

Murphy, David F., and David Matthew. 2001. "Nike and Global Labour Practices." Case study prepared for the New Academy of Business Innovation Network for Socially Responsible Business, Bristol, UK.

Rama, Martin. 1996. "The Consequences of Doubling the Minimum Wage: The Case of Indonesia." World Bank Policy Research Working Paper 1643.

SMERU Research Institute. 2001. "Wage and Employment Effects of Minimum Wage Policy in the Indonesian Urban Labor Market." Research Report. SMERU Research Institute: Jakarta, Indonesia.

Strobl, Eric, and Frank Walsh. 2000. "Minimum Wages and Compliance: The Case of Trinidad and Tobago." Center for Research in Economic Development and International Trade Working Paper 01/12.

PART 4

Industrial Transformation in Developing Countries

Chapter 14

Learning versus Stealing: How Important Are Market-Share Reallocations to India's Productivity Growth?[†,*]

Ann E. Harrison, Leslie A. Martin, and Shanthi Nataraj[†]

Recent trade theory emphasizes the role of market-share reallocations across firms ("stealing") in driving productivity growth, whereas previous literature focused on average productivity improvements ("learning"). We use comprehensive, firm-level data from India's organized manufacturing sector to show that market-share reallocations were briefly relevant to explain aggregate productivity gains following the beginning of India's trade reforms in 1991. However, aggregate productivity gains during the period from 1985 to 2004 were largely driven by improvements in average productivity. We show that India's trade, FDI, and licensing reforms are not associated with productivity gains stemming from market share reallocations. Instead, we find that most of the productivity improvements in Indian manufacturing occurred through "learning" and that this learning was linked to the reforms. In the Indian case, the evidence rejects the notion that market share reallocations are the mechanism through which trade reform increases aggregate productivity. Although a plausible response would be that India's labor laws do not easily permit market share reallocations, we show that restrictions on labor mobility cannot explain our results. JEL codes: F13, F14, F16, O24, O25.

Over the last two centuries, economists have frequently returned to the question of how nations gain from trade. Early studies focused primarily on aggregate productivity gains driven by interindustry specialization according to

†. Ann E. Harrison is a professor at the Wharton School of the University of Pennsylvania and a Research Associate at the National Bureau of Economic Research; her email address is annh@wharton.upenn.edu. Leslie A. Martin is a lecturer (assistant professor) in the Department of Economics at the University of Melbourne; her email address is Leslie.Martin@unimelb.edu.au. Shanthi Nataraj (corresponding author) is an Associate Economist at RAND Corporation; her email address is snataraj@rand.org. This material is based upon work supported by the National Science Foundation under Grant No. SES-0922332. We thank Mr. M.L. Philip, Mr. P.C. Nirala, Dr. Praveen Shukla, and Mr. M.M. Hasija at the Ministry of Statistics and Programme Implementation for their assistance in elucidating the Annual Survey of Industries data collection process; Rana Hasan, Karl Jandoc, and Steve O'Connell for discussions regarding the firm-level data; Pauline Grosjean and Ben Crost for providing us with their district-level concordances, which formed the basis for ours; and three anonymous referees as well as seminar participants at the IMF, the World Bank, and Georgetown University for their valuable comments. A supplementary appendix to this article is available at http://wber.oxfordjournals.org/.

202

*This article originally appeared in *The World Bank Economic Review*, **27** 202–228

comparative advantage. In the 1980s, the importance of learning by doing and the role of trade in facilitating the exploitation of economies of scale were emphasized by Paul Krugman and others. Recently, productivity gains associated with the entry of more productive firms and the exit of less productive ones have generated significant interest. A related question is whether trade reforms lead to the redistribution of market share between incumbents with different productivity levels.

This most recent wave of trade theory stresses the importance of market-share reallocations in increasing aggregate productivity following trade liberalization (Bernard, Eaton, Jensen, and Kortum 2003; Melitz 2003). The "new new" trade theory emphasizes gains from trade in the presence of "heterogeneous firms." In heterogeneous firm models, firms of different productivities, sizes, and profit levels coexist. A trade reform that exposes firms to greater competition or enables more firms to sell in export markets will lead less productive firms to exit or to lose market share. In a Melitz (2003) world, the primary sources of productivity gains associated with trade reform are the exit of less productive firms and the expansion of more productive firms.

Although early heterogeneous firm models, such as the model by Melitz (2003), assumed that firms had exogenous, fixed productivity levels, recent research allows for changing productivity within the firm.[1] This may occur when some product lines are discontinued and other product lines are developed. Consequently, trade reforms can lead to changes in within-firm productivity as firms shift their focus to high-productivity products. These theories recall earlier literature that emphasized that trade could improve average productivity within surviving firms.[2]

The policy implications that arise from these explanations for the gains from trade differ significantly. In a world where market share reallocation away from less productive firms matters more than learning or product shifting within the same firm, it is crucial to facilitate firm entry, exit, and downsizing. In a world where there is learning or shifting of product types within a firm, it is also crucial to work within the enterprise to facilitate the learning that accompanies trade reform. However, few empirical studies quantify the relative importance of average productivity gains and gains from market-share reallocations in the wake of major trade liberalization.

In this paper, we use a comprehensive, firm-level dataset to examine the role of market-share reallocations in driving aggregate productivity growth in India's organized manufacturing sector from 1985 to 2004. The organized manufacturing sector in India consists of firms that are registered under sections 2m(i) and 2m(ii) of the Factories Act. All firms with 20 or more employees (10 if a power source is used) are required to register. In 1991, India

---

1. See Arkolakis and Muendler 2010; Bernard, Redding, and Schott 2010; Bernard, VanBeveren, and Vandenbussche 2010; Bernard, Redding, and Schott 2011; Eckel and Neary 2010; Feenstra and Ma 2007; Mayer, Melitz, and Ottaviano 2011; Nocke and Yeaple 2008.
2. See Corden 1974; Grossman and Helpman 1991; Helpman and Krugman 1985.

embarked on a series of reforms, including the liberalization of trade, licensing, and foreign direct investment (FDI) regulations. As part of the trade liberalization, nontariff barriers were removed from a number of product lines, and tariff levels were gradually reduced from extraordinarily high levels. The licensing regime, which required that firms seek permission from the "License Raj" to enter an industry and to change or expand production, was gradually dismantled. FDI restrictions that prohibited foreign firms from entering some sectors and restricted their participation in others were relaxed.

We begin by measuring aggregate productivity growth in the manufacturing sector and show that there were three distinct phases from 1985 to 2004. During this 20-year period, aggregate productivity (defined as output-weighted, mean firm productivity) grew by nearly 20 percent. From 1985 to 1990, the growth in aggregate productivity was driven by "learning," an increase in unweighted, average firm productivity. This measure of learning captures the change in productivity for the average firm and includes not only changes in productivity among surviving firms but also changes in average productivity that can be attributed to firm entry and exit. In the period immediately following the beginning of the reforms (1991–1994), the "stealing" of market share (the reallocation of market share from less productive to more productive firms) became more important than learning for driving aggregate productivity growth. In the longer run (1998–2004), learning again became more important for aggregate productivity growth, with a minor contribution from stealing (reallocation).

Overall, we find that for the organized manufacturing sector as a whole, market-share reallocations were an important source of productivity growth in the years immediately following the beginning of the 1991 reforms, but not during other periods. In other words, in the Indian case, the contribution of the reallocation of market shares is concentrated at a given point in time. One implication is that trade reforms lead to short-term, one-off market share reallocations. Our results suggest that in the longer term, opening up trade in India had more important effects on average productivity.

Our main results rely on the widely used decomposition suggested by Olley and Pakes (1996). This method identifies changes in average productivity and reallocation but does not disentangle the contributions of survivors, entrants, and exiters. Although firm identifiers are not available for the organized sector data during most of the period that we study, we construct a panel dataset by matching individual firms from one year of the survey to the next. We match firms using beginning- and end-of-period information on capital and other types of stocks, supplemented with other identifying information. This panel allows us to test how our main results change when we employ an alternative decomposition method, suggested by Melitz and Polanec (2010). We find that our results are robust to these different approaches when decomposing the sources of productivity change during the period.

We then use the Olley-Pakes decomposition to examine the extent to which individual policy reforms are associated with industry-level productivity gains.

In particular, we exploit variations in tariff cuts, FDI liberalization, and industrial licensing reforms across industries to examine the contribution of each reform to changes in industry-level total factor productivity (TFP). We find that the average decline in final goods tariffs during the study period implies a 3 percent increase in aggregate productivity, whereas the average decline in input tariffs implies a 22 percent increase in aggregate and average productivity. Moreover, FDI liberalization accounts for a 4.7 percent increase in average productivity. Consequently, the reduction in input tariffs and opening up to foreign investment are the most important policy changes associated with improved firm performance in our sample. The industrial licensing reforms, which promoted internal competition, are associated with productivity gains among large firms and in states and industries that were relatively less exposed to external competition prior to the reforms. We use our constructed panel to show that the trade and FDI liberalizations are associated with increased productivity within firms, even when controlling for unobservable firm heterogeneity. Our results also suggest that, overall, the reforms are associated with average productivity improvements rather than market share reallocation across firms.

Finally, we explore whether our results can be explained by regulatory barriers that prevented market share reallocations, such as restrictive labor laws. Our results suggest that labor laws and a legal framework that prevented firm adjustment cannot explain our findings. We also explore the extent to which the reforms had differential effects in states and industries that were previously exposed to trade and among firms of different initial sizes. We find that delicensing and FDI reforms had larger effects on productivity among firms that were relatively less exposed to trade. These results suggest some substitutability between external and internal competition: where states or industries are not already exposed to trade through proximity to ports or international trade, industrial reforms that promote competition have larger effects.

Our study was motivated by the emphasis of contemporary trade theory on the importance of market-share reallocation in increasing aggregate productivity. Although a number of papers have tested implications of this literature, few of these studies directly examine the impact of trade liberalization on market-share reallocation.[3] Existing evidence on the importance of reallocation in promoting productivity growth is mixed.[4]

Our study also contributes to the substantial body of work examining India's 1991 reforms. Topalova and Khandelwal (2011) establish that reductions in final goods and input tariffs increased productivity among approximately 4,000 large, publicly listed manufacturing firms. Sivadasan (2009) uses a pooled, cross-sectional dataset, but not a panel, for the early years of the

---

3. See, for example, Arkolakis 2010; Bernard et al. 2003; Bernard, Jensen, and Schott 2006; Berthou and Fontagne forthcoming; Eaton, Kortum, and Kramarz 2011; Helpman, Melitz, and Yeaple 2004; Manova and Zhang 2012.

4. See, for example, Tybout and Westbrook 1995; Pavcnik 2002; Trefler 2004; Fernandes 2007; Menezes-Filho and Muendler 2011.

reforms (1986–1994) and finds that the reduction in final goods tariffs and FDI liberalization increased productivity. He also documents that these reforms were associated with average productivity increases, but not reallocation, in the early 1990s. Nataraj (2011) compares the reactions of the organized and unorganized manufacturing sectors to trade liberalization and finds that although the reduction in final goods tariffs increased productivity significantly in the unorganized sector, the reduction in input tariffs was more important for productivity growth in the organized sector. Aghion, Burgess, Redding, and Zilibotti (2008) find that following the removal of licensing requirements, the number of factories and output in the organized sector increased, particularly in states with relatively less restrictive labor regulations.

Our study contributes to these two strands of the literature in several ways. First, we document that although market-share reallocations were important to overall productivity growth immediately following the implementation of the 1991 reforms, most of the productivity improvements in manufacturing during the period from 1985 to 2004 occurred because average productivity increased. Market-share reallocations, the focus of most of the heterogeneous trade literature, were not as important. One implication is that in the Indian case, theories that emphasize within-firm changes in response to trade policy changes are more relevant.

Second, we tie these different sources of productivity growth to the various reforms. Our constructed panel is the largest, most representative panel of Indian manufacturing firms that covers the period of the reforms, allowing us to isolate within-firm productivity improvements. In contrast to the earlier literature on gains from trade with heterogeneous firms, which assumed exogenous productivity draws at the firm level and emphasized the role of market-share reallocations, we cannot explain the increases in productivity with market-share reallocations using our policy measures. Instead, our constructed panel suggests that trade and FDI reforms raised average, within-firm productivity. One plausible mechanism is that trade reforms led to productivity improvements because firms focused on their most productive goods. However, evidence on this type of effect in the Indian case is mixed: Goldberg, Khandelwal, Pavcnik, and Topalova (2010a) find that lower input tariffs accounted for approximately one-third of the increase in new products created by Indian firms, but the same authors (2010b) test for evidence of product rationalization in the Indian case and reject this possibility.

The rest of this paper is organized as follows. Section I provides a brief background on the Indian reforms; section II describes the data and outlines the construction of the panel of firms; section III discusses the empirical framework and presents results; and section IV concludes.

I. THE 1991 REFORMS

Prior to 1991, India imposed high tariffs and nontariff barriers on most goods. FDI (foreign ownership) was capped at 40 percent for most industries, and large manufacturing firms were required to obtain operating licenses. During the 1980s, India removed licensing requirements from approximately one-third of industries but retained its trade and FDI restrictions.

A combination of economic and political shocks created a balance of payments crisis in 1991, and the IMF agreed to assist the Indian government under certain conditions (Hasan, Mitra, and Ramaswamy 2007; Topalova and Khandelwal 2011). Major policy changes, including FDI and tariff liberalization, exchange rate liberalization, and the removal of the requirement for operating licenses in most industries, were announced in July 1991, and many of these policy changes were formalized in India's Eighth Five-Year Plan (1992–97).

The average final goods tariff rate on manufactured products fell from 95 to 35 percent between 1991 and 1997, and tariffs were harmonized across industries (industries with the highest prereform tariffs received the largest tariff cuts). India continued to lower its tariffs after the Eighth Five-Year Plan ended in 1997, although the reductions were no longer as uniform. Input tariffs also fell significantly during this period. The supplementary appendix (available at http://wber.oxfordjournals.org/) illustrates the tariff changes in more detail (figure S1.1).

In addition, India dismantled its "License Raj" during this period. Under the licensing regime, every firm with more than 50 employees (100 employees where a power source is not used) and a certain amount of assets was required to obtain an operating license. The license specified the amount of output a firm could produce, the types of goods it could make, and a number of other conditions. Approximately one-third of industries were delicensed (the requirement for a license was dropped) in 1985, and most remaining industries were delicensed as part of the 1991 reforms (Aghion et al. 2008). Several additional industries were delicensed during the following decade.

Beginning in 1991, majority FDI shares were also allowed in a number of industries with "automatic" approval (Sivadasan 2009). Approximately one-third of industries were opened to FDI in 1991. A few additional industries were liberalized by 1997, and in 2000, the government indicated that all industries would be eligible for automatic FDI approval, except those requiring an industrial license or meeting several other conditions (figure 1).

The occurrence of most of these policy changes as part of an externally required reform package reduced the likelihood that industries were selected into the reforms on the basis of political factors. Furthermore, to the extent that industries with certain characteristics may have been more likely to be liberalized, we use a fixed-effects estimation strategy that should address any time-invariant characteristics that may have affected selection. However, if the reforms are correlated with prereform trends in industry characteristics, our results may be biased. To evaluate the potential extent of this bias, we examine the correlations between changes during the reforms (1990–2004) and prereform trends for a number of industry characteristics (1985–1989). In the supplementary appendix (table S1.1), we show that there are no statistically significant correlations between prereform trends in industry characteristics and future reforms.

FIGURE 1. Trade, FDI, and Licensing Reforms

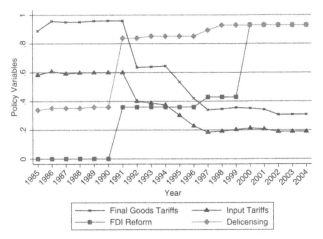

Mean values of policy variables from 1985 to 2004. Final goods and input tariff variables are fractions, with one representing an ad valorem tariff of 100 percent. FDI Reform is a dummy variable equal to one if any products within the industry are liberalized and zero otherwise. Delicensing is a dummy variable equal to one if any products within the industry are delicensed and zero otherwise. *Source*: Authors' calculations based on various publications of the Government of India, including the Customs Tariff Working Schedules, the Trade Analysis and Information System database, and Aghion et al. (2008).

Moreover, the supplementary appendix (table S1.9) shows that our results are robust to limiting our analysis to the period ending in 1997. Because the initial reforms were developed in the wake of the 1991 crisis, they are even less likely to be subject to potential selection issues than are reforms in later years.

II. DATA

Our primary dataset consists of firm-level surveys from the Annual Survey of Industries (ASI).[5] We obtained data for all available years between 1985 and 2004. Data were not available for 1995. Furthermore, the way in which input data were collected and made available for 1996 and 1997 made it impossible to construct certain key variables for those two years that were consistent with the other years. Therefore, we restrict our analysis to firm-level data for the

5. The ASI covers accounting years that ended on any day during the fiscal year. The 1985–86 survey (which we refer to as the 1985 survey) indicates the factory's accounting year that ended on any day between April 1, 1985, and March 31, 1986.

remaining 17 years between 1985 and 2004 (1985 through 1994 and 1998 through 2004).

The sampling universe for the ASI is all firms that are registered under sections 2m(i) and 2m(ii) of the Factories Act as well as firms registered under the Bidi & Cigar Workers Act and a number of utility and service providers. These firms constitute the "organized" sector; they account for approximately 80 percent of output but only 20 percent of employment in Indian manufacturing. We only include manufacturing firms in our analysis.[6] Large firms are considered part of the "census" sector and are surveyed every year. Smaller firms are considered part of the "sample" sector and are sampled every few years.[7] In the population-level analysis (but not the panel analysis), we apply the multiplier weights provided by the ASI. Each unit surveyed is generally a factory (plant); however, if an owner has two factories in the same state, sector (census versus sample) and industry, a joint return can be furnished. In the population of firms, fewer than 2 percent of the observations report having more than one factory. We will use the term "firm" to mean one observation in our dataset.

The key variables we construct from the ASI data are output, material input, labor, and capital.[8] We drop closed firms, and we only include firms with positive values of the key variables. To address a few extreme outliers, we also trim the top 0.5 percent of the output and material input values. We deflate output using industry-specific wholesale price indices (WPI) from the Government of India's Handbook of Industrial Statistics. Similarly, we construct material input deflators using the WPI along with India's 1993–94 Input-Output Transactions Table. Labor is measured as the total number of individuals employed by the firm, and capital is measured by deflating the book value of capital by the WPI for machinery. Summary statistics for the population are presented in table 1.[9]

---

6. Our sample is therefore representative of all manufacturing firms that have registered with each state's Chief Inspector of Factories. All firms that have 20 or more employees (10 or more employees if a power source is used) are required to register. In practice, a significant fraction of ASI firms report fewer than 10 employees. These firms may be registered for various reasons, including the possibility that they formerly had more than 10 employees but shrank, that they plan to grow in the future, and that registering may be a signal to creditors or other business partners.

7. The division between the two sectors depends on firm size. It changed several times from 1985 to 2004.

8. Output includes the ex-factory value of products, the increase in the stock of semifinished goods, and the value of own construction. Material input includes materials and fuel.

9. Sampling weights are applied to the summary statistics in the first column of table 1; hence, the results are representative of the overall organized sector. The second column shows results for the firms that were sampled without applying sampling weights. Because larger firms are surveyed more frequently than smaller firms, the mean and median values of output, capital, material inputs, and labor are much larger in the sampled population than in the estimated population. The term "firm-years" indicates the total number of firm-level observations over all of the years in our dataset, whereas "census-firm-years" indicates the total number of observations of "census" sector firms over all years.

TABLE 1. Summary Statistics for the Firm-Level Data

	Estimated population	Sampled Firms	Panel
Firm-years, no. obs.	1,410,725	580,941	414,074
Firms per year, mean	82,983	34,173	24,357
Census firm-years, no. obs.	277,178	277,178	247,777
Census firms per year, mean	16,304	16,304	14,575
Unique firm series			147,695
Output, mean (million Rs.)	18.7	32.0	41.8
Output, median (million Rs.)	2.6	3.6	5.3
Capital, mean (million Rs.)	6.9	12.8	17.0
Capital, median (million Rs.)	0.4	0.5	0.8
Materials, mean (million Rs.)	12.5	21.1	27.3
Materials, median (million Rs.)	1.9	2.6	3.9
Labor, mean (no. employees)	74.1	133.4	171.9
Labor, median (no. employees)	21	31	43
In panel, as fraction of total in sampled population:			
Output			0.93
Capital			0.95
Labor			0.92
Firm-years > 100 employees			0.94
Firm-years > 200 employees			0.96
Firm-years			0.71
Census firm-years			0.89

Source: Authors' calculations based on ASI data.

Summary statistics for the estimated population (using sampling weights), for the sampled population (not using sampling weights), and for firms that appear for two or more years in the panel. Only open firms with positive values of key variables are included. The term "firm-years" indicates the total number of observations, whereas "census firm-years" indicates the number of observations in the census sector. Mean and median values are averages across all years used in the analysis (1985–1994 and 1998–2004). Output, material inputs, and capital have been deflated to 1985 values and are expressed in millions of rupees. Fractions of output, capital, and so forth that appear in the panel are reported relative to the sampled (rather than the estimated) population.

Creating a Panel

The ASI data provide unique firm identifiers beginning in 1998. It has not previously been possible to track firms prior to 1998 and to follow them during the most significant reform period. We overcame this challenge by matching individual firms from one year of the survey to the next between 1985 and 1998. To construct our panel, we searched for firms that had matching open and close values between one year and the next (e.g., we searched for a match between the close value in 1985 and the open value in 1986) for one of several variables. To link firms for 1995, a year for which firm-level data have not been released, and for other years in which individual firms may not have been sampled, we matched firms on the basis of a number of static characteristics as well as growth projections. We then combined this constructed panel with the actual panel provided by the ASI from 1998 to 2004. Details on panel construction are provided in the supplementary appendix.

Because we observe each firm's age, we are confident that we can correctly identify survivors and entrants in our panel. However, given the substantial fraction of firms that are not surveyed every year, we are more reserved about our ability to identify exiting firms. The rates of exit that we observe in our panel are significantly higher than the rates that we extrapolate on the basis of the observed distributions of firm age. Therefore, when estimating productivity, we avoid methods that rely on accurately identifying firm exit and instead employ an index number method that is robust to potentially spurious exit.

Summary statistics for the panel (to which we do not apply sampling multipliers) are presented in the final column of table 1. Observations of firms in the "census" sector (indicated by the number of census-firm years) account for 60 percent of total firm-year observations in the panel, 48 percent of firm-year observations in the full sample of firms, and only 20 percent of firm-year observations in the estimated population. The panel should not be considered representative of the population; rather, it is a selection of relatively large firms. Nonetheless, 71 percent of firm-year observations appearing in the sample, representing 93 percent of total deflated output over the entire period and 92 percent of the labor force, are captured for at least two years in the panel (table 1, bottom rows).

A key contribution of our panel is that we are confident in the firms that we are able to match over time. This contribution allows us to examine the impacts of the reforms on within-firm learning. These impacts have not previously been examined for such a large subsample of the organized manufacturing sector.

Policy Variables

We matched applied tariff data from the Government of India's Customs Tariff Working Schedules and the Trade Analysis and Information System database with India's three-digit National Industrial Classification (NIC-87) codes using the concordance developed by Debroy and Santhanam (1993). We then calculated average final goods tariff rates within each of approximately 140 NIC codes. We also calculated input tariffs using India's Input-Output Transactions Table, following the method suggested by Amiti and Konings (2007).[10]

To capture the effects of the delicensing and FDI reforms, we used data from Aghion et al. (2008), supplemented by information from Press Notes from the Ministry of Commerce and Industry. Both the delicensing and FDI reform variables are equal to one if any products in a three-digit industry have been liberalized and are equal to zero otherwise. Figure 1 shows changes in these policy variables over time.

10. For example, if the footwear industry derives 80 percent of its inputs from the leather industry and 20 percent from the textile industry, the input tariff for the footwear industry is 0.8 times the final goods tariff for the leather industry plus 0.2 times the final goods tariff for the textile industry. In our baseline measure of input tariffs, we use both traded and nontraded inputs, assigning tariff rates of zero to nontraded inputs.

III. Empirical Framework and Results

We measure TFP for firm i in industry j at time t using a chain-linked, index number method. This measure is well suited for our data because approaches such as semiparametric methods (Olley and Pakes 1996, for example), which rely on panel data, cannot be used for the population of firms. Although we explore the robustness of our results to using a panel with linked firms over time below, in much of the analysis, we need an approach that allows us to exploit the population of firms. Another problem with the Olley-Pakes methodology and other semiparametric approaches is that they require an accurate identification of exit. Therefore, we employ the method suggested by Aw, Chen, and Roberts (2001):

$$TFP_{ijt} = \left(q_{ijt} - \overline{q_{jt}}\right) + \sum_{r=2}^{t}(\overline{q_{jr}} - \overline{q_{jr-1}}) - \left[\sum_{z=1}^{Z}\frac{1}{2}\left(\zeta_{ijt}^{z} + \overline{\zeta_{jt}^{z}}\right)\left(z_{ijt} - \overline{z_{jt}}\right)\right.$$
$$\left. + \sum_{r=2}^{t}\sum_{z=1}^{Z}\frac{1}{2}\left(\overline{\zeta_{jr}^{z}} + \overline{\zeta_{jr-1}^{z}}\right)\left(\overline{z_{jr}} - \overline{z_{jr-1}}\right)\right] \tag{1}$$

where q_{ijt} is the log of output, ζ_{ijt}^{z} is the revenue share of input z, and z_{ijt} is the log of input z. A firm's TFP is the deviation of its output from average output in that year and the difference in the average output in that year from the base year, minus the deviation of the firm's inputs from average inputs in that year, along with the difference in average inputs in that year from the base year. Inputs include labor, capital, and material inputs, which are measured and deflated as discussed in section II. Bars over variables indicate average values within a particular industry and year. Revenue shares for labor and material inputs are calculated as the share of each input in total revenue. Capital's revenue share is assumed to be one minus the sum of the other two shares.

Decomposing All-India TFP Growth

We begin by examining productivity changes for the population of firms from 1985 to 2004. To do so, we first calculate aggregate TFP in year t, Φ_t^{AGG}, as the sum of each firm's productivity, ϕ_{it}, weighted by its market share, ψ_{it}. Olley and Pakes (1996) show that this measure of aggregate TFP can be decomposed into two components:

$$\Phi_t^{AGG} = \sum_i \psi_{it}\phi_{it} = \overline{\phi_t} + \sum_i [\psi_{it} - \overline{\psi_t}][\phi_{it} - \overline{\phi_t}] = \Phi_t^{U} + R_t \tag{2}$$

where $\overline{\phi_t}$ and $\overline{\psi_t}$ are unweighted average productivity and market share, respectively. The first component, Φ_t^{U}, is unweighted average productivity. The second component, R_t, measures the covariance between firm productivity and market share. Changes in this measure represent a reallocation of market share between firms with different productivity levels.

We first construct these measures at the all-India level. To make the results representative of the population of firms and consistent over time, we premultiply each observation by the sampling weight provided by the ASI. Furthermore, to make the results more comparable with our later regression results, we only consider firms in state-industry groups (collections of firms in a particular state and three-digit industry) that exist over the entire period.

Following Pavcnik (2002), we normalize productivity values to zero in 1985. Hence, changes in productivity levels can be interpreted as growth since 1985. Between 1985 and 2004, aggregate productivity grew by 18 percent (figure 2). This increase in productivity implies an annual increase of slightly less than 1 percent per year, within the range found in previous studies.[11]

When we consider the time period as a whole, nearly all of this increase can be attributed to growth in average productivity, rather than reallocation. However, figure 2 suggests that there are three distinct phases between 1985 and 2004. First, from 1985 to 1990, average productivity rose by over 8 percent, while the reallocation component fell by more than 6 percent, indicating that more productive firms lost market share relative to less productive firms. Beginning in 1991, this trend was reversed: average productivity fell, whereas reallocation productivity rose sharply. By 1998, however, average productivity improvements were once again the more important driver of aggregate productivity growth. Reallocation productivity remained at approximately the level it reached between 1992 and 1993, but it did not increase further.

Our results suggest that market-share reallocations played an important role in aggregate productivity growth, but only during the few years immediately following the implementation of the 1991 reforms. Over the longer time horizon, average productivity improvements remained more important for explaining the increase in aggregate TFP.

Industry-Level TFP Changes and Policy Reforms

To what extent can the increase in productivity be attributed to trade and other policy reforms that occurred during the 1990s? To answer this question, we exploit variation in policies across industries to examine whether changes in the individual components of productivity are systematically related to specific reforms.

To use policy variation across industries, we recreate our aggregate, average, and reallocation TFP measures at the state-industry level (recall that a state-industry group is the collection of firms in a particular state and three-digit

---

11. There has been an extensive debate about TFP growth in the organized Indian manufacturing sector, particularly during the 1980s. Goldar (December 7, 2002) provides a summary of a number of TFP growth estimates and discusses many of the measurement issues involved. Our TFP estimates are based on a gross output (rather than value added) production function. Value-added TFP growth rates tend to be much higher than gross output growth rates.

FIGURE 2.   All-India Total Factor Productivity

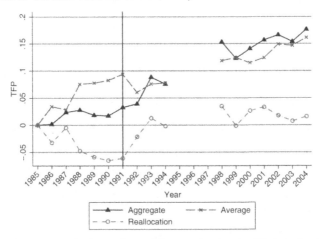

TFP decompositions for the population of firms, conducted at the all-India level, using the Olley and Pakes method. "Aggregate" indicates market-share-weighted mean productivity, "Average" indicates unweighted mean productivity, and "Reallocation" indicates the covariance between market share and productivity. *Source*: Authors' calculations based on ASI data.

industry). We use the state-industry level because this level of disaggregation allows us to consider variations in policies and other characteristics across both industries and states and because the ASI survey is designed to be representative at this level. We weight each group by the total number of firms that appear in that group across all years. This method ensures that the results are comparable to the all-India results because larger state-industry groups are given more weight.[12] We exploit the fact that the trade, licensing, and FDI reforms occurred differentially across industries to isolate the impacts of each policy on each productivity measure. Consider the relationship between our outcomes of interest and the

12. This weighting scheme ensures that average productivity is nearly the same at the state-industry and all-India levels. The reallocation component at the state-industry level follows the same general pattern as that observed in figure 2, but it is lower across most years. The reason is that at this level, we can only measure reallocation *within* state-industry groups. For example, suppose that the steel industry in Maharashtra is more productive than the chemical industry in Gujarat, and all firms in the former state-industry group increase output by 10 percent, whereas all firms in the latter state-industry group reduce output by 10 percent. The all-India reallocation measure will increase, but the state-industry reallocation measure will not. It would be ideal to capture market-share reallocations between and within state-industry groups, but our identification strategy relies on the variation in reforms across industries and over time and thus does not allow us to use an all-India measure of productivity. The supplementary appendix shows that our results are robust to performing the baseline regression analysis without including weights (table S1.12).

reforms:

$$\widehat{Y}_{jst} = \beta_1 \tau_{j,t-1} + \beta_2 \tau^I_{j,t-1} + \beta_3 Delic_{j,t-1} + \beta_4 FDI_{j,t-1} + \alpha_{js} + \alpha_t + \varepsilon_{jst} \qquad (3)$$

where $\widehat{Y}_{jst}$ is the estimated aggregate TFP ($\widehat{\Phi}^{AGG}_{jst}$), average TFP ($\widehat{\Phi}^U_{jst}$), or realloca-tion ($\widehat{R}_{jst}$) for industry j and state s at time t; $\tau_{j,t-1}$ and $\tau^I_{j,t-1}$ are final goods tariffs and input tariffs; $Delic_{j,t-1}$ is a dummy variable equal to one if any products in an industry are delicensed and zero otherwise; $FDI_{j,t-1}$ is a dummy variable equal to one if any products in an industry are FDI liberalized and zero otherwise; and α_{js} and α_t are state-industry and year dummy variables, respectively. Because our firm data are annual and policy changes occurred throughout the year, we lag all policy variables by one year. We employ a fixed-effects estimator to estimate equa-tion 3[13] and cluster all standard errors at the state-industry level.[14] We use a balanced panel of state-industries to avoid confounding within-group effects with the entry and exit of certain industries in particular states, and we weight all observations using the total number of firms in each state-industry group over all years.

Table 2 presents baseline results for 1986 to 2004.[15] Column (1) suggests that a 10-percentage-point reduction in final goods tariffs yields a 0.51 percent increase in aggregate productivity, whereas a 10-percentage-point reduction in input tariffs yields a 5.7 percent increase in aggregate productivity. Columns (2) and (3) present results for the average and reallocation components of pro-ductivity, respectively. Column (2) indicates that 10-percentage-point declines in final goods and input tariffs raise average productivity by 0.44 and 5.5 percent, respectively, although the coefficient on final goods tariffs is not statis-tically significant at the 10 percent level. FDI liberalization increases average productivity by 5 percent. The results are similar in magnitude for the impact of the reforms on both aggregate and average productivity. This similarity largely results because the reforms primarily affected average productivity, which we refer to in this paper as "learning."

In contrast, column (3) shows that input tariffs, final goods tariffs, and deli-censing changes do not significantly affect productivity gains through realloca-tion of market share. The only statistically significant result, for FDI reform, indicates that liberalization lowers rather than raises reallocation productivity. One potential reason for this puzzling result is that prior to the FDI reform, foreign investors only invested in the most productive Indian firms. By intro-ducing an "automatic" approval for majority FDI ownership, the reform de-creased the fixed cost of foreign investment and may therefore have encouraged

---

13. This is similar to including a full set of state-industry interactions.

14. The supplementary appendix (table S1.14) shows that our results are robust to clustering standard errors at the industry-year level.

15. We exclude 1985 because we do not have lagged policy variables for this year.

TABLE 2. Productivity Decompositions and Policy Changes: Baseline Results

	Aggregate (1)	Average (2)	Reallocation (3)
Final Goods Tariff	−.051	−.044	−.007
	(.026)**	(.030)	(.015)
Input Tariff	−.567	−.546	−.021
	(.104)***	(.116)***	(.061)
FDI Reform	.021	.050	−.030
	(.013)	(.014)***	(.010)***
Delicensed	−.006	.005	−.011
	(.017)	(.017)	(.011)
Obs.	17106	17106	17106
R^2	.082	.077	.014

Source: Authors' analysis based on data sources discussed in the text.

Each observation is a state-industry. Dependent variable names are given at the top of each column. "Aggregate" indicates market-share-weighted mean productivity, "Average" indicates unweighted mean productivity, and "Reallocation" indicates the covariance between market share and productivity. All specifications are fixed-effects analyses at the state-industry level and include year dummies. Each observation is weighted by the total number of firms in the state-industry across all years, and standard errors are clustered at the state-industry level.

investment in less productive firms, allowing them to increase their market shares.

In table 3, we estimate the extent to which policy reforms can explain overall productivity growth by multiplying the coefficients from table 2 by the average policy changes. The results suggest that trade liberalization, particularly the decline in input tariffs, is largely responsible for aggregate and average productivity growth. A 60-percentage-point decline in final goods tariffs implies an aggregate productivity increase of 3 percent and an average productivity increase of 2.6 percent (although the related regression coefficient is not statistically significant), and a 40-percentage-point decline in input tariffs implies aggregate and average productivity increases of approximately 22 percent. FDI liberalization also plays a role, implying a 4.7 percent increase in average productivity.[16] The variation in policies across industries cannot explain the gains in reallocation productivity that were observed in the initial years following the reforms. However, the policies explain the gains in average productivity, which was the more important driver of aggregate productivity growth during this period.

Firm-Level Regressions

Our results using the population of enterprises aggregated to the state-industry level suggest that average productivity ("learning") played a more important role in explaining aggregate productivity increases in India during the sample

16. In fact, the average policy changes can explain somewhat more than the total increase in productivity during this time period. In the regression framework, the coefficients on several year dummies are negative, implying that in the absence of policy reforms, productivity would have fallen.

TABLE 3. Productivity Increases Implied by Policy Changes

	Final Goods Tariffs	Input Tariffs	FDI Liberalization	Delicensing
Aggregate (%)	**3.0**	**22.1**	2.1	−0.4
Average (%)	2.6	**21.3**	**4.7**	0.3
Reallocation (%)	0.4	0.8	**−2.8**	−0.6

Source: Authors' analysis based on data sources discussed in the text.

Implied increases in aggregate, average, and reallocation productivity. Results are based on regression coefficients and average policy changes. Bold font indicates that the underlying regression results are statistically significant at the 10 percent level.

period than did reallocation of market share ("stealing"). In this section, we use firm-level data to confirm that learning was a key component of productivity change. If learning is important, we would expect our policy variables to explain productivity within the larger firm-level population and for the smaller constructed panel.

We now use the constructed panel to examine the average productivity results in more detail. We estimate the following equation at the firm level:

$$\widehat{\phi}_{ijst} = \beta_1 \tau_{j,t-1} + \beta_2 \tau^I_{j,t-1} + \beta_3 Delic_{j,t-1} + \beta_4 FDI_{j,t-1} + \alpha_i + \alpha_t + \varepsilon_{ijst}. \quad (4)$$

As discussed in section II, our constructed panel makes it difficult to accurately identify firm exit. However, we are confident in the firms that we are able to match. Hence, the fixed-effects estimator shown in equation 4 should allow us to identify within-firm changes in productivity.

Table 4 presents the results. In column (1), we include all firms that were used in the state-industry level analysis (the estimated population). This specification includes industry and year dummy variables. As we expect, the coefficients on the policy variables are similar to the average productivity results at the state-industry level.

Column (2) presents results for firms that appear in the panel for at least two years, without sampling multipliers. This specification includes industry and year dummy variables but not firm fixed effects, and it shows that the results for firms in the panel are similar to the overall results. The coefficients on input tariffs and FDI reforms remain the largest and most significant, indicating that reductions in input tariffs and the FDI reform made the largest contributions to increased productivity during the sample period.

Column (3) controls for a number of firm characteristics and shows that public firms and young firms (less than three years old) are relatively unproductive, whereas firms furnishing joint returns for multiple factories ("multiplant" firms) are relatively more productive.[17] The poor productivity performance of

---

17. The multiplant dummy should be cautiously interpreted because true multiplant firms may not be able or may not choose to submit joint returns (see section II)

TABLE 4. Firm-Level Productivity

	Population (1)	Panel Firms (2)	Panel Firms (3)	Firm FE (4)	OP (5)	Large Firms FE (6)
Final Goods Tariff	-.046	-.038	-.037	-.042	-.050	-.054
	(.027)*	(.019)**	(.019)*	(.008)***	(.007)***	(.011)***
Input Tariff	-.486	-.532	-.519	-.141	-.085	-.156
	(.108)***	(.088)***	(.087)***	(.034)***	(.029)***	(.053)***
FDI Reform	.045	.055	.053	.031	.027	.014
	(.015)***	(.012)***	(.011)***	(.004)***	(.004)***	(.005)***
Delicensed	-.005	-.002	-.002	-.002	.005	.027
	(.016)	(.013)	(.013)	(.005)	(.005)	(.007)***
Public			-.167			
			(.014)***			
Multiplant			.039			
			(.011)***			
Young			-.092			
			(.005)***			
Small			-.073			
			(.010)***			
Midsize			-.016			
			(.009)*			
Obs.	1322803	388430	388430	388430	384003	63062
R^2	.065	.057	.064	.002	.004	.046
Year FE	Yes	Yes	Yes	Yes	Yes	Yes
Industry FE	Yes	Yes	Yes	No	No	No
Firm FE	No	No	No	Yes	Yes	Yes

Source: Authors' analysis based on data sources discussed in the text.

Each observation is a firm. The dependent variable is TFP, calculated following Aw et al. (2001) in all columns except (5), in which TFP is calculated following Olley and Pakes (1996). Column (1) includes all firms that were part of the state-industry level analysis; columns (2)–(5) only include firms that appear in the panel for at least two years. Column (6) only includes the largest firms in each year. Columns (1)–(3) include industry and time dummies, and standard errors are clustered at the state-industry level. Columns (4)–(6) include year dummies and firm fixed effects, and standard errors are clustered at the firm level. "FE" indicates fixed effects.

public sector enterprises is consistent with the evidence for other countries, including China (Du, Harrison, and Jefferson 2011) and Indonesia (Bartel and Harrison 2005). We also created dummy variables for firms in three size categories: less than 20 employees (small), 20 to 99 employees (medium), and more than 100 employees (large, the omitted category). The results indicate a positive correlation between size and productivity.

In column (4), we present results with firm fixed effects, thus isolating within-firm changes in productivity. The coefficient on final goods tariffs remains similar. Although the coefficients on input tariffs and FDI reform are attenuated, they remain statistically significant at the 1 percent level. These results confirm that trade and FDI liberalizations are associated with substantial increases in productivity within individual firms. However, the results also indicate that the changing composition of firms and unobserved, firm-level characteristics may play important roles in the observed average productivity gains for the population of firms.

As discussed above, our baseline productivity measure does not depend on accurately identifying exit; the difficulty in identifying exit is a limitation of our panel. Nevertheless, in column (5), we assume that our assignment of exit is accurate, and we use the Olley and Pakes method to estimate productivity. The coefficients are similar to those in column (4), although the coefficient on final goods tariffs is slightly larger in magnitude, whereas the coefficients on input tariffs and FDI are slightly smaller.

To our knowledge, our constructed panel is the largest and most representative of the organized sector to date, consisting of approximately 25,000 firms per year. Our study complements the work of Topalova and Khandelwal (2011), who examine the impacts of India's trade liberalization on approximately 4,000 large firms. Although we cannot replicate their analysis, in column (6), we restrict our analysis to the largest 4,000 firms that appear in the panel in any given year. The results for the largest firms and for the whole panel are similar. The coefficient on delicensing, which was insignificant across all firms, becomes positive and statistically significant for the largest firms. These results suggest that delicensing was particularly important for spurring productivity increases among the largest firms. Additionally, our study extends Sivadasan (2009) in several important ways. First, we create a panel of firms that allows us to confirm that the impacts of the trade and FDI liberalization are important even after controlling for firm fixed effects and to directly show that "learning" is an important mechanism for understanding productivity increases over this 20-year period. Second, we examine long-run impacts on productivity by extending our analysis through 2004. Third, we distinguish between the effects of final goods and input tariffs and demonstrate that input tariffs play a larger role in boosting productivity.

State, Industry, and Firm Characteristics

We now explore whether the effects of the reforms vary across states or industries with different prereform characteristics and among firms of different sizes using the population of firms.

First, we consider whether the impact of liberalization on firm productivity is influenced by exposure to trade. We use three measures to proxy for trade exposure. First, we construct a dummy variable that is equal to one if a state-industry group is located in a state with a port and that is equal to zero otherwise. Second, we calculate each industry's share of imports in output in 1990 using data from the COMTRADE database, and we create a dummy variable for import exposure that is equal to one if the industry has an import share above the median and that is equal to zero otherwise. Third, we construct a similar measure for export share.

The delicensing and FDI reforms have larger effects on productivity among firms that are relatively less exposed to trade (table 5). In states without ports and in nonimporting industries, delicensing is associated with a 4 to 5 percent increase in average productivity. FDI reform is associated with a 7.7 percent increase in average productivity among nonexporting industries. The effect of the FDI reform on average productivity is attenuated in exporting industries, whereas the effect of the delicensing reforms is actually reversed in importing industries and in states with ports. These results suggest some degree of substitutability between external competition and internal competition: where states or industries are not already exposed to trade through proximity to ports, import competition, or exposure to foreign markets, industrial reforms that encourage competition have larger effects.

Next, we consider the role of labor regulations using two state-level measures: (1) the measure developed by Besley and Burgess (2004), which is based on state amendments to the Industrial Disputes Act, and (2) data from the Ministry of Labor on how often firm requests to close down or lay off workers are granted. We interact each measure with our reform variables and show (tables S1.2 and S1.3 in the supplementary appendix) that the effects of the policy reforms are largely similar across states, regardless of labor regulations. However, FDI reform is associated with a 7.4 percent increase in average productivity in states where it is difficult to lay off workers but only a 2.6 percent increase in average productivity in states where it is easy to lay off workers. This difference suggests that in states where it is difficult for firms to achieve an optimal input mix by laying off workers, they may be able to increase their productivity through other means, such as attracting FDI. In other words, FDI reform matters more when existing rigidities make it difficult for firms to optimize their production.

Finally, we consider whether productivity changes may differ across firms of different sizes. Using the population data but harnessing information from the panel, we classify firms into three categories, small (<20 employees), medium

TABLE 5. Productivity Decompositions and Policy Changes: Trade Exposure

	Aggregate (1)	Aggregate (2)	Aggregate (3)	Average (4)	Average (5)	Average (6)	Reallocation (7)	Reallocation (8)	Reallocation (9)
Final Goods Tariff	-.036 (.035)	-.027 (.019)	.013 (.025)	-.065 (.045)	.018 (.032)	.033 (.030)	.029 (.026)	-.045 (.026)*	-.021 (.023)
Input Tariff	-.600 (.113)***	-.538 (.109)***	-.622 (.102)***	-.502 (.123)***	-.616 (.111)***	-.587 (.115)***	-.098 (.069)	.078 (.065)	-.035 (.072)
FDI Reform	.026 (.017)	.028 (.017)*	.044 (.019)**	.053 (.020)***	.054 (.019)***	.077 (.018)***	-.027 (.012)**	-.026 (.013)**	-.033 (.013)**
Delicensed	.007 (.019)	.042 (.018)**	-.013 (.025)	.043 (.021)**	.046 (.019)**	.010 (.024)	-.036 (.015)**	-.004 (.014)	-.023 (.014)*
Port in State X Final Goods Tariff	-.0002 (.0005)			.0003 (.0006)			-.0005 (.0003)		
Port in State X Input Tariff	.0006 (.0009)			-.0005 (.001)			.001 (.0006)*		
Port in State X FDI Reform	-.007 (.017)			-.004 (.020)			-.004 (.015)		
Port in State X Delicensed	-.020 (.027)			-.058 (.027)**			.038 (.019)**		
Importing Industry X Final Goods Tariff		-.0003 (.0005)			-.001 (.0005)**			.0008 (.0003)**	
Importing Industry X Input Tariff		-.001			.0007			-.002	

(Continued)

TABLE 5. Continued

	Aggregate (1)	Aggregate (2)	Aggregate (3)	Average (4)	Average (5)	Average (6)	Reallocation (7)	Reallocation (8)	Reallocation (9)
		(.0009)			(.001)			(.0006)***	
Importing Industry X FDI Reform		−.013			−.004			−.009	
		(.016)			(.019)			(.015)	
Importing Industry X Delicensed		−.160			−.125			−.035	
		(.044)***			(.039)***			(.025)	
Exporting Industry X Final Goods Tariff			−.001			−.001			.0002
			(.0004)**			(.0005)**			(.0003)
Exporting Industry X Input Tariff			.001			.001			.00007
			(.0008)			(.001)			(.0007)
Exporting Industry X FDI Reform			−.038			−.048			.009
			(.017)**			(.018)***			(.014)
Exporting Industry X Delicensed			.011			−.013			.024
			(.031)			(.030)			(.020)
Obs.	17106	17106	17106	17106	17106	17106	17106	17106	17106
R^2	.083	.091	.085	.078	.083	.081	.015	.016	.014

Source: Authors' analysis based on data sources discussed in the text.

Each observation is a state-industry. Dependent variable names are given at the top of each column. "Aggregate" indicates market-share-weighted mean productivity, "Average" indicates unweighted mean productivity, and "Reallocation" indicates the covariance between market share and productivity. All specifications are fixed-effects analyses at the state-industry level and include year dummies. Each observation is weighted by the total number of firms in the state-industry across all years, and standard errors are clustered at the state-industry level. "Port in state" is a dummy variable equal to one if the state-industry group is located in a state with a port and zero otherwise. "Importing" ("Exporting") is a dummy variable equal to one if the industry's prereform share of imports (exports) in total output was greater than the median and zero otherwise.

(20–99 employees), and large (>100 employees), on the basis of the size of
the firm when we first observed it. In the supplementary appendix (table S1.4),
we show that across all types of firms, policy changes continue to drive average
productivity, but not reallocation of market share across firms. However, the
effects of the reforms vary by firm size. For example, FDI liberalization is most
important for large firms; the reform is associated with a 7.5 percent (9.1
percent) increase in aggregate (average) productivity for firms with 100 or
more employees, approximately twice the magnitude of the average effect.
Although the delicensing reforms are not associated with overall productivity
increases, they are associated with a 4.6 percent increase in aggregate productivity among large firms and a 3.9 percent increase in average productivity
among mid-sized firms. This heterogeneity is consistent with the fact that only
firms with 50 or more employees and a certain amount of assets were required
to obtain operating licenses prior to reform.

Robustness Tests

We test the robustness of our baseline results in a number of ways. The results
are presented in the supplementary appendix (tables S1.5 through S1.14). First,
we examine whether our results are robust to constructing TFP in different
ways: (1) winsorizing our baseline measure, (2) using a variation of our baseline measure that employs cost shares instead of revenue shares, and (3) using
ordinary least squares. Next, we examine several other modifications of the
baseline specification: using an alternative measure of capital; restricting the
analysis to the initial years of the reforms, during which policy changes were
less likely to be influenced by political considerations; using an alternative
measure of input tariffs; removing outlier values in tariff changes; weighting all
state-industry groups equally; including state-by-year dummy variables; and
clustering standard errors at the industry-year level. The appendix shows that
although there is some variation in the magnitude and significance of results,
they are robust to each of these tests.

Finally, to test the robustness of our productivity decomposition, we use an
alternative method suggested by Melitz and Polanec (2010). We divide the
panel of firms in any two consecutive periods, $t-1$ and t, into firms present in
both periods (*survivors*), firms that exit after period $t-1$ (*exiters*), and firms
that enter in period t (*entrants*). In period $t-1$, only exiters and survivors are
present; $S_{X,t-1}$ denotes the market share associated with exiters. In period t,
only entrants and survivors are present; $S_{E,t}$ denotes the market share associated with entrants. Melitz and Polanec show that the change in aggregate productivity from period $t-1$ to t can be decomposed as follows:

$$\Phi_t^{AGG} - \Phi_{t-1}^{AGG} = \left[\Phi_{S,t}^U - \Phi_{S,t-1}^U\right] + \left[R_{S,t} - R_{S,t-1}\right] + S_{E,t}\left[\Phi_{E,t}^{AGG} - \Phi_{S,t}^{AGG}\right]$$
$$+ S_{X,t-1}\left[\Phi_{S,t-1}^{AGG} - \Phi_{X,t-1}^{AGG}\right]. \tag{5}$$

The first and second terms on the right-hand side represent changes in within-firm productivity and the covariance between productivity and market share of firms that survive from $t - 1$ to t. The third term represents the contribution of firms that enter in period t, weighted by the market share of entrants, $S_{E,t}$. Similarly, the last term represents the contribution of firms that exit in period $t - 1$, weighted by the market share of exiters, $S_{x,t-1}$. Using this approach, we calculate the change in TFP between period $t - 1$ and period t and then add the change in TFP to the existing level of TFP in period $t - 1$. TFP is normalized to zero in 1985. In this analysis, we do not use the sampling multipliers.

To use this method, we must assign every firm in our panel to the category of survivor, entrant, or exiter in every year. Given the nature of our panel data, this method requires two relatively strong assumptions. First, to address the fact that we do not directly calculate TFP for 1995–1997, we impute missing values for TFP and output for each series that bridges these years using linear interpolation. We perform a similar linear interpolation of TFP and output for individual firms for which we have bridged over another year.[18]

Second, we must make some assumptions regarding firm exit. When we observe a potential exiter, it is unclear whether the firm actually exited, whether it still existed but was not surveyed in the following year, or whether it was surveyed but we failed to match it.[19] We address this challenge by estimating the "true" rate of exit for each cohort of firms (e.g., firms established between 1974 and 1976) on the basis of the number of surviving firms that we observe. In each year, we consider the potential pool of exiting firms (i.e., firms we do not observe in any subsequent year), and we assign exit status to the number of firms that we estimate to have exited from each cohort.[20] The remaining firms are assigned to the group of survivors.

The baseline results are robust to this alternative decomposition method (table 6).[21] A 10-percentage-point decline in input tariffs is associated with a 4.1 percent increase in aggregate productivity and a 4.8 percent increase in average productivity. FDI liberalization also increases aggregate productivity by

18. For example, if a firm was surveyed in 1992 and 1994 and we are able to link that firm across those years, we use a linear interpolation to estimate TFP and output for that firm in 1993.

19. In the actual panel from 1998 to 2004, the third case is not a concern, although we are still unable to distinguish between the first two cases in many instances.

20. To determine an appropriate method for assigning exit, we examined the distribution of TFP for potential exiters compared to that of survivors for two years (1999 and 2000) in which the observed exit rates are relatively close to estimated exit rates, indicating that the pool of potential exiters is likely to be representative of "true" exiters. We also examined TFP distributions in two years (1995 and 2004) when the observed exit rate is significantly higher than the estimated true exit rate, indicating that many true survivors are classified as exiters. In both cases, the distributions of potential exiters are slightly left-shifted, indicating that exiters are, on average, less productive than survivors. However, the two distributions of potential exiters are similarly left-shifted relative to the distributions of survivors, suggesting that the pool of potential exiters is fairly representative of the actual exiters. Therefore, we assign exit by selecting a random sample of firms from the pool of potential exiters.

21. In this case, the number of state-industry observations is larger because of the imputation of TFP in the panel.

TABLE 6. Robustness Test: Alternative Decomposition

	Aggregate (1)	AvgSurv (2)	ReallocSurv (3)	Entrants (4)	Exiters (5)
Final Goods Tariff	−.022	−.023	−.007	.002	.006
	(.022)	(.026)	(.019)	(.006)	(.008)
Input Tariff	−.408	−.476	.093	−.008	−.016
	(.096)***	(.106)***	(.082)	(.022)	(.033)
FDI Reform	.039	.044	−.011	−.0006	.006
	(.013)***	(.014)***	(.012)	(.002)	(.004)
Delicensed	−.010	.008	−.014	−.001	−.003
	(.015)	(.017)	(.015)	(.004)	(.005)
Obs.	19328	19328	19328	19328	19328
R^2	.059	.068	.035	.07	.003

Source: Authors' analysis based on data sources discussed in the text.

The decomposition is performed using the method suggested by Melitz and Polanec (2010), with false exit addressed as discussed in the text. Each observation is a state-industry. Dependent variable names are given at the top of each column. "Aggregate" indicates market-share-weighted mean productivity, "AvgSurv" and "ReallocSurv" indicate unweighted mean productivity and the covariance between market share and productivity for surviving firms, respectively, and "Entrants" and "Exiters" indicate the contributions of entering and exiting firms. All specifications are fixed-effects analyses at the state-industry level and include year dummies. Each observation is weighted by the total number of firms in the state-industry across all years, and standard errors are clustered at the state-industry level.

3.9 percent and average productivity by 4.4 percent. The policy reforms are not associated with reallocation among survivors, entrants, or exiters.

IV. CONCLUSION

In the Indian case, we show that market share reallocations were important drivers of productivity growth only at the beginning of the trade reforms in 1991. Over the longer 20-year period from 1985 to 2004, average productivity improvements played a larger role in determining aggregate productivity growth.

In contrast to the earlier trade literature on heterogeneous firms, such as Melitz (2003), we do not find a link between India's tariff liberalization and market-share reallocations. Instead, we find that both the trade and FDI reforms increase average firm productivity. Our constructed panel allows us to verify that even after controlling for unobservable, firm-specific characteristics, the trade and FDI reforms are associated with increased within-firm productivity. Although the delicensing reforms do not affect productivity in the organized manufacturing sector as a whole, they are linked to productivity gains among large firms and among firms not previously exposed to trade. One potential reason that we do not find a link between trade reform and reallocations could be that India's rigid labor laws prevent reallocation among firms. However, we find that the reforms have similar effects in states with different degrees of labor market rigidities.

Our findings, which suggest that "learning" is more important than "stealing" over the 1985 through 2004 period, are consistent with the most recent literature on heterogeneous firms (see, for example, Bernard, Redding, and Schott 2011), which suggests that firms exposed to increased competition from trade may focus on higher productivity product lines. This finding implies that much of the productivity increase associated with trade reform is likely to manifest as within-firm increases rather than productivity gains associated with shifting market shares toward more efficient enterprises. Unfortunately, given the nature of our data during the years in which the major reforms occurred, we are unable to confirm that product shifting occurred, and the existing evidence from a sample of large firms is mixed (Goldberg, Khandelwal, Pavcnik, and Topalova 2010a, 2010b). Exploring the specific channels through which individual firms increase their productivity in India remains an important avenue for future research.

REFERENCES

Aghion, P., R. Burgess, S. Redding, and F. Zilibotti. 2008. "The Unequal Effects of Liberalization: Evidence from Dismantling the License Raj in India." *The American Economic Review* 98 (4): 1397–1412.

Amiti, M., and J. Konings. 2007. "Trade Liberalization, Intermediate Inputs, and Productivity: Evidence from Indonesia." *The American Economic Review* 97 (5): 1611–1638.

Arkolakis, C. 2010. "Market Penetration Costs and the New Consumers Margin in International Trade." *Journal of Political Economy* 118 (6): 1151–1199.

Arkolakis, C., and M.-A. Muendler. 2010. "The Extensive Margin of Exporting Products: A Firm-level Analysis." NBER Working Paper 16641. National Bureau of Economic Research, Cambridge, MA.

Aw, B. Y., X. Chen, and M. J. Roberts. 2001. "Firm-level Evidence on Productivity Differentials and Turnover in Taiwanese Manufacturing." *Journal of Development Economics* 66 (1): 51–86.

Bartel, A. P., and A. E. Harrison. 2005. "Ownership versus Environment: Disentangling the Sources of Public-Sector Inefficiency." *The Review of Economics and Statistics* 87 (1): 135–147.

Bernard, A. B., J. B. Jensen, and P. K. Schott. 2006. "Trade Costs, Firms and Productivity." *Journal of Monetary Economics* 53: 917–937.

Bernard, A. B., J. Eaton, J. B. Jensen, and S. Kortum. 2003. "Plants and Productivity in International Trade." *The American Economic Review* 93 (4): 1268–1290.

Bernard, A. B., I. Van Beveren, and H. Vandenbussche. 2010. "Multi-Product Exporters, Carry-Along Trade and the Margins of Trade." National Bank of Belgium Working Paper Research Series No. 203. National Bank of Belgium, Brussels, Belgium.

Bernard, A. B., S. J. Redding, and P. K. Schott. 2010. "Multiple-Product Firms and Product Switching." *American Economic Review* 100 (1): 70–97.

———. 2011. "Multiproduct Firms and Trade Liberalization." *The Quarterly Journal of Economics* 126: 1271–1318.

Berthou, A., and L. Fontagne. Forthcoming. "How do Multi-Product Exporters React to a Change in Trade Costs?" *Scandinavian Journal of Economics*.

Besley, T., and R. Burgess. 2004. "Can Labor Regulation Hinder Economic Performance? Evidence from India." *The Quarterly Journal of Economics* 119 (1): 91–134.

Corden, W. M. 1974. *Trade Policy and Economic Welfare.* Oxford: Clarendon Press.

Debroy, B., and A. T. Santhanam. 1993. "Matching Trade Codes with Industrial Codes." *Foreign Trade Bulletin* 24 (1): 5–27.

Du, L., A. Harrison, and G. Jefferson. 2011. "Do Institutions Matter for FDI Spillovers? The Implications of China's 'Special Characteristics'." NBER Working Paper 16767. National Bureau of Economic Research, Cambridge, MA.

Eaton, J., S. Kortum, and F. Kramarz. 2011. "An Anatomy of International Trade: Evidence from French Firms." *Econometrica* 79 (5): 1453–1498.

Eckel, C., and J. P. Neary. 2010. "Multi-Product Firms and Flexible Manufacturing in the Global Economy." *The Review of Economic Studies* 77: 188–217.

Feenstra, R., and H. Ma. 2007. "Optimal Choice of Product Scope for Multiproduct Firms under Monopolistic Competition." NBER Working Paper 13703. National Bureau of Economic Research, Cambridge, MA.

Fernandes, A. M. 2007. "Trade Policy, Trade Volumes and Plant-Level Productivity in Colombian Manufacturing Industries." *Journal of International Economics* 71 (1): 52–71.

Goldar, B. 2002. "TFP Growth in Indian Manufacturing in 1980s." *Economic and Political Weekly* December 7: 4966–4968.

Goldberg, P. K., A. Khandelwal, N. Pavcnik, and P. Topalova. 2010a. "Imported Intermediate Inputs and Domestic Product Growth: Evidence from India." *The Quarterly Journal of Economics* 125 (4): 1727–1767.

———. 2010b. "Multiproduct Firms and Product Turnover in the Developing World: Evidence from India." *The Review of Economics and Statistics* 92 (4): 1042–1049.

Grossman, G., and E. Helpman. 1991. *Innovation and Growth in the Global Economy.* Cambridge, MA: MIT Press.

Hasan, R., D. Mitra, and K. V. Ramaswamy. 2007. "Trade Reforms, Labor Regulations, and Labor Demand Elasticities: Empirical Evidence from India." *The Review of Economics and Statistics* 89 (3): 466–481.

Helpman, E., and P. R. Krugman. 1985. *Market Structure and Foreign Trade: Increasing Returns, Imperfect Competition, and the International Economy.* Cambridge, MA: MIT Press.

Helpman, E., M. J. Melitz, and S. R. Yeaple. 2004. "Export Versus FDI with Heterogeneous Firms." *The American Economic Review* 94 (1): 300–316.

Manova, K., and Z. Zhang. 2012. "Export Prices across Firms and Destinations." *The Quarterly Journal of Economics* 127 (1): 379–436.

Mayer, T., M. J. Melitz, and G. I. P. Ottaviano. 2011. "Market Size, Competition, and the Product Mix of Exporters." NBER Working Paper 16959. National Bureau of Economic Research, Cambridge, MA.

Melitz, M. J. 2003. "The Impact of Trade on Intra-Industry Reallocations and Aggregate Industry Productivity." *Econometrica* 71 (6): 1695–1725.

Melitz, M. J., and S. Polanec. 2010. "Dynamic Olley-Pakes Decomposition with Entry and Exit." INNODRIVE Working Paper No. 11. INNODRIVE, Vaasa, Finland.

Menezes-Filho, N. A., and M.-A. Muendler. 2011. "Labor Reallocation in Response to Trade Reform." NBER Working Paper No. 17372. National Bureau of Economic Research, Cambridge, MA.

Nataraj, S. 2011. "The Impact of Trade Liberalization on Productivity: Evidence from India's Formal and Informal Manufacturing Sectors." *Journal of International Economics* 85: 292–301.

Nocke, V., and S. Yeaple. 2008. "Globalization and the Size Distribution of Multiproduct Firms." Centre for Economic Policy Research Discussion Paper DP6948. Centre for Economic Policy Research, London, UK.

Olley, G. S., and A. Pakes. 1996. "The Dynamics of Producticity in the Telecommunications Equipment Industry." *Econometrica* 64 (6): 1263–1297.

Pavcnik, N. 2002. "Trade Liberalization, Exit, and Productivity Improvements: Evidence from Chilean Plants." *Review of Economic Studies* 69 (1): 245–276.

Sivadasan, J. 2009. "Barriers to Competition and Productivity: Evidence from India." *The B.E. Journal of Economic Analysis & Policy, 2009* 9 (1): 42.

Topalova, P., and A. Khandelwal. 2011. "Trade Liberalization and Firm Productivity: The Case of India." *The Review of Economics and Statistics* 93 (3): 995–1009.

Trefler, D. 2004. "The Long and Short of the Canada-U.S. Free Trade Agreement." *The American Economic Review* 94 (4): 870–895.

Tybout, J. R., and M. D. Westbrook. 1995. "Trade Liberalization and the Dimensions of Efficiency Change in Mexican Manufacturing Industries." *Journal of International Economics* 39: 53–78.

Chapter 15

Industrial Policy and Competition[†,‡]

By Philippe Aghion, Jing Cai, Mathias Dewatripont, Luosha Du, Ann Harrison, and Patrick Legros*

Using a comprehensive dataset of all medium and large enterprises in China between 1998 and 2007, we show that industrial policies allocated to competitive sectors or that foster competition in a sector increase productivity growth. We measure competition using the Lerner Index and include as industrial policies subsidies tax holidays, loans, and tariffs. Measures to foster competition include policies that are more dispersed across firms in a sector or measures that encourage younger and more productive enterprises. (JEL L11, L25, L52, O14, O25, O47, P31)

In the aftermath of World War II, several developing countries opted for "industrial policies" aimed at promoting new infant industries or at protecting local traditional activities from competition by products from more advanced countries. However, these policies came into disrepute in the 1980s mainly on the grounds that industrial policy *prevents competition* and allows governments to pick winners (and, more rarely, to name losers) in a discretionary fashion, thereby increasing the scope for capture of governments by vested interests.

In this paper, we argue that properly governed sectoral policies, in particular sectoral policies that are *competition-friendly*, may enhance productivity and productivity growth. Without industrial policy, innovative firms may choose to operate in different sectors in order to face lower competition on the product market, leading to high sectoral concentration and low incentives to innovate because of a "monopoly replacement effect." In such a case, industrial policies that encourage firms to be active in the same sector, such as through tax holidays or other tax subsidy schemes, will decrease concentration in the targeted sector and enhance incentives for firms to innovate. Therefore there can be *complementarity* between competition and suitably designed industrial policies in inducing innovation and productivity growth.

*Aghion: Department of Economics, Harvard University, Littauer Center 22, 1805 Cambridge Street, Cambridge, MA 02138, and National Bureau of Economic Research (NBER) (e-mail: paghion@harvard.edu); Jing Cai: Department of Economics, University of Michigan, 611 Tappan Street, 365A Lorch Hall, Ann Arbor, MI 48109 (e-mail: caijing@umich.edu); Dewatripont: Banque National de Belgique and Université libre de Bruxelles (ECARES), 50 avenue F.D. Roosevelt, C.P. 114-04, 1050 Bruxelles, Belgique (e-mail: mdewat@ulb.ac.be); Du: China Development Bank, 18 fuxingmen neidajie, xichengqu, Beijing, China 100031 (e-mail: Duluosha@cdb. cn); Harrison: The Wharton School, University of Pennsylvania, 2016 Steinberg Hall-Dietrich Hall, Philadelphia, Pennsylvania 19104, and NBER (e-mail: annh@wharton.upenn.edu); Legros: Université libre de Bruxelles (ECARES), 50 avenue F.D. Roosevelt, C.P. 114-04, 1050 Bruxelles, Belgium (e-mail: plegros@ulb.ac.be). We thank the Editor, three anonymous referees, Jean Imbs, Amit Khandelwal, and conference participants at The World Bank, the Wharton International Lunch, Pennsylvania State University, Duke University, George Washington University, and the Asian Development Bank for very helpful comments.
†Go to http://dx.doi.org/10.1257/mac.20120103 to visit the article page for additional materials and author disclosure statement(s) or to comment in the online discussion forum.

1

‡This article originally appeared in *American Economic Journal: Macroeconomics*, **7** 1–32 © 2015 American Economic Association.

2   *AMERICAN ECONOMIC JOURNAL: MACROECONOMICS*   *OCTOBER 2015*

To document the potential complementarity between competition and industrial policy, we use a comprehensive dataset of all medium and large enterprises in China between 1998 and 2007 and consider the effect of industrial policies on firm-level productivity growth. Our main finding is that when sectoral policies are targeted toward competitive sectors or allocated in such a way as to preserve or increase competition, then these policies increase productivity growth. We measure competition using the Lerner Index and include as industrial policies subsidies, tax holidays, loans, and tariffs. Competition-friendly policies are defined as targeting that is more dispersed across firms in a sector or measures that encourage younger and more productive enterprises.

Our paper relates to a whole literature on the costs and benefits of industrial policy. First are the infant-industry models advocating government support to sectors with potential economy-wide knowledge externalities, but with high initial production costs that decrease only progressively over time as a result of learning-by-doing: the idea is that these sectors need to be protected against foreign competition in the short run until they become fully competitive (see, for example, Greenwald and Stiglitz 2006).[1] The infant industry argument has been challenged, both theoretically (the "pick-winners" argument) and empirically. For example, Krueger and Tuncer (1984) analyzed the effects of industrial policy in Turkey in the 1960s, and "showed" that firms or industries not protected by tariff measures were characterized by higher productivity in growth rates than protected industries.[2] However, none of these papers look at the design or at the governance of industrial policy.

Most closely related to our analysis is the paper by Nunn and Trefler (2010). Using cross-country, industry-level panel data, they analyze whether, as suggested by "infant industry" arguments, the growth of productivity in a country is positively affected by tariff protection biased in favor of activities and sectors that are "skill-intensive," that is to say, use more intensely skilled workers. They find a significant positive correlation between productivity growth and the "skill bias" due to tariff protection. As the authors point out though, such a correlation does not necessarily mean there is causality between skill bias due to protection and productivity growth: the two variables may themselves be the result of a third factor, such as the quality of institutions in countries considered. However, Nunn and Trefler (2010) show that at least 25 percent of the correlation corresponds to a causal effect. Overall, their analysis suggests that adequately designed (here, skill-intensive) targeting may actually enhance growth, not only in the sector that is being subsidized, but in other sectors as well. The issue remains whether industrial policy comes at the

---

[1] For an overview of infant industry models and empirical evidence, see Harrison and Rodríguez-Clare (2009). The infant industry argument could be summarized as follows. Consider a local economy that includes both a traditional sector (especially agriculture) and an industry in its infancy. Production costs in industry are initially high, but "learning by doing" decrease these costs over time, even faster as the volume of activity in this area is high. In addition, increased productivity, which is a consequence of this learning by doing phase, has positive spillovers on the rest of the economy, i.e., it increases the potential rate of growth also in the traditional sector. In this case, a total and instantaneous liberalization of international trade can be detrimental to the growth of the local economy, as it might inhibit the activity of the local industry whose production costs are initially high: what will happen in this case is that the local demand for industrial products will turn to foreign importers. It means that learning by doing in the local industry will be slowed itself, which will reduce the externalities of growth from this sector towards the traditional sector.

[2] However, see Harrison (1994) who shows that their results are not robust to rigorous statistical analysis.

cost of a lowering of competition, e.g., between high and low skill-intensive sectors or within a high-skill sector. As we show in this paper, industrial policy in the form of targeting may in fact take the form of enhancing competition in a sector, and serves the dual role of increasing consumer surplus and growth.

The paper is organized as follows. In Section I we sketch a simple model to guide our empirical analysis.[3] In Section II we present some brief historical background for industrial policy in China, as well as the data and measurement and some raw correlations between competition, industrial policies, and firm level performance. We describe in Section III the estimation methodology and presents the main empirical results. We conclude in Section IV.

I. The Theoretical Argument

In this section, we sketch our theoretical argument for why properly designed sectoral policy may enhance rather than harm competition. The argument can be summarized as follows: consider an economy where two firms can either differentiate horizontally or innovate to improve their productivity. Under laissez-faire the two firms will typically choose to diversify, i.e., to produce in different sectors in order to escape competition between them. Forcing (or encouraging) these firms to operate in the same sector and on an equal footing will induce them to resort to vertical innovation (i.e., to productivity-improving innovation) in order to escape competition with each other. This in turn will foster productivity growth.

Note that this argument is quite distinct from the infant-industry argument and is also novel in the literature on the effects of industrial policy. In particular it does not rely on learning-by-doing externalities or on knowledge externalities between an industrial (tradable good) sector and a traditional (non-tradable good) sector. Instead, it relies on standard growth externalities and on an escape-competition effect (see, for instance, Aghion et al. 2005). Thus, while (foreign) competition is damaging for domestic growth in the infant-industry model, here competition is always growth-enhancing.

A. *Basic Setup*

We consider a two-period model of an economy producing two goods, denoted by A and B. Denote the quantity consumed on each good by x^A and x^B. The representative consumer has income equal to $2E$ and utility $\log(x^A) + \log(x^B)$ when consuming x^A and x^B. This means that if the price of good i is p^i, demand for good i will be $x^i = E/p^i$. To simplify the writing, we assume that $E = 1$ throughout this paper.[4]

Production can be done by one of two "big" firms 1, 2, or by "fringe firms." Fringe firms act competitively and have a constant marginal cost of production of c_f, whereas firms $j = 1, 2$ have an initial marginal cost of c, where $1 > c_f \geq c$.

---

[3] The details of the model as well as the proofs are developed in Appendix B.

[4] As soon will be apparent, the rate of innovation is linear in E, and except for this size effect, what matters for the analysis are the ratios E/c and E/c_f.

The assumption $c_f \geq c$ reflects the cost advantage of firms 1, 2 with respect to the fringe, and the assumption $1 > c$ ensures that equilibrium quantities can be greater than 1. Marginal costs are firm-specific and are independent of the sector in which production is undertaken.

Firms can improve productivity through quality-improving innovation. For simplicity, we assume that only firms 1, 2 can innovate. Innovation reduces production costs, but the size of the cost reduction is different between the two sectors A and B. Without loss of generality, we assume that in sector A, innovations reduce production costs from c to $c/\gamma_A = c/(\gamma + \delta)$, whereas in sector B they reduce costs from c to $c/\gamma_B = c/(\gamma - \delta)$, where $\gamma - \delta > 1$ or $\delta < \gamma - 1$.[5]

We also make the simple assumption that, with equal probability, each firm can be chosen to be the potential innovator. To innovate with probability q this firm must incur effort cost $q^2/2$. This is like saying that each firm has an exogenous probability of getting a patentable idea, which then has to be turned into cost reduction thanks to effort exerted by the firm.

Finally, we assume Bertrand competition within each sector unless the two leading firms choose the same sector and collude within that sector. Let φ be the probability of the two leading firms colluding in the same sector when they have the same cost, and let us assume that when colluding the two firms behave as a joint monopoly taking the fringe cost c_f as given. In this case, the expected profit of each leading firm with cost $c < c_f$ is $\varphi \frac{1}{2} \frac{c_f - c}{c_f}$ since, when collusion fails, firms compete Bertrand.

B. *The Effects of Targeted Tax/Subsidies*

Firms can choose to be active in different sectors or in the same sector: we refer to the first situation as one of diversity, and the second as one of focus. Under focus, both firms choose the better technology A. Under diversity, one firm (call it firm 1) chooses A and the other (call it firm 2) chooses B (this is a coordination game and which firm ends up with technology A is random). Diversity is stable if the firm ending up with technology B does not want to switch to technology A; otherwise the equilibrium is focus. Conditional on this choice firms then decide to invest in order to innovate.

We look at how firms' choices whether to produce in the same sector or in different sectors, and their resulting innovation intensities, depend upon industrial policy. For industrial policy we will focus on interventions based on taxes or subsidies that are proportional to profit levels, that is, on tax levels t_A, t_B per profit level in sectors A, B, respectively, where $t_k < 0$ is a subsidy and $t_k > 0$ is a tax.[6] We restrict

---

[5] Even if $\delta = 0$, that is, if the two sectors are similar, industrial policy is beneficial. In previous versions of the paper we considered imperfect information about the identity of the high growth sector, and our results were qualitatively similar. This suggests that a regulator does not need necessarily to identify the "high growth" sector in order to implement the type of industrial policy we are considering.

[6] We assume without loss of generality an initial level of taxation equal to zero in each sector.

attention to the case where there is perfect information about γ_i and where the profit is net of the cost of innovation.[7]

We first derive the equilibrium choices under arbitrary tax/subsidy schemes $t_A \leq t_B$ ("laissez-faire" corresponds to the case $t_A = t_B = 0$), and show the interaction between our measure of competition φ and the growth rate that can be achieved via such a tax system. We then identify the growth-maximizing tax/subsidy scheme when the planner is subject to a budget constraint.

Considering the laissez-faire situation with $t_A = t_B = 0$, firms will choose focus only if the equilibrium profit is greater than the lowest profit obtained under diversity. This will be the case only if the degree of competition is not too high; hence, the stronger competition as measured by $(1 - \varphi)$, the higher the range of δs for which firms will choose diversity.

PROPOSITION 1: *There exists a cutoff value $\delta^F(\varphi)$, a decreasing function of φ, such that focus is the industry equilibrium if and only if $\delta \geq \delta^F(\varphi)$.*

Now, let us introduce a system of tax/subsidies, and let us use as a measure of targeting the ratio

$$(1) \qquad\qquad \tau \equiv \frac{1 - t_A}{1 - t_B}.$$

The larger τ is, the higher are the "tax holidays" in sector A with respect to sector B. It should be clear that τ is sufficient to characterize the incentives of firms to choose between diversity or focus. Alternatively, τ is a measure of the asymmetry in tax holidays between the two sectors. The effect of the tax ratio on industry equilibrium is summarized in the following result.

COROLLARY 1: *Consider a system of tax/subsidies with a targeting ratio $\tau = \frac{1 - t_A}{1 - t_B}$. When $\tau > 1$, there exists a cutoff $\Delta(\varphi, \tau) < \delta^F(\varphi)$, such that the firms choose focus in equilibrium whenever $\delta > \Delta(\varphi, \tau)$. Moreover this cutoff is decreasing in τ and in φ.*

Hence, a larger target ratio τ increases the range of values of δ for which there will be focus. Alternatively, if $\delta < \delta^F(\varphi)$, there exists a targeting tax τ, such that $\delta = \Delta(\varphi, \tau)$; because $\Delta(\varphi, \tau)$ is a decreasing function of τ, the lower the value of δ, the higher this value of τ should be.

Now solving for the optimal innovation investments, respectively under focus and under diversity, we obtain the complementarity between the degree of competition in a sector and the effectiveness of a tax/subsidy scheme.

---

[7] If the tax/subsidy is on the profit gross of the cost of innovation, then it will also affect the rate at which firms innovate. A reduction in the tax rate on gross profits has a similar effect as a subsidy to the marginal cost of innovation.

6   AMERICAN ECONOMIC JOURNAL: MACROECONOMICS   OCTOBER 2015

PROPOSITION 2: *An effective τ-industrial policy has a bigger effect on per capita GDP and on innovation intensity in more competitive industries.*

C. Predictions

The following predictions from the above theoretical discussion will guide our empirical analysis in the next sections:

- A tax policy that is more targeted toward sector A has a bigger impact on output and innovation: a higher value of τ (that is a lower t_A with respect to t_B) makes it more likely that focus will be the industry equilibrium. By Proposition 2, it follows that higher values of τ have a larger effect on innovation and on the level of per capita GDP, independently of φ.
- Since a policy that gives a tax holiday to only one firm will not modify the industry equilibrium, tax holidays that are common to the two firms have a bigger impact on innovation and the level of per capita GDP than a policy that would apply to a unique firm.
- There is complementarity between industrial policy through tax holidays and the degree of competition.

II. Background, Data, and Measurement

A. Background

The Chinese government has long been actively involved in promoting industrialization in China. Industrial policy relies on a whole range of instruments, including tariff protection, low interest loans, tax holidays, and subsidies for the purpose of promoting investment in key sectors. We begin by documenting the range of industrial policies and their changes over the sample period. Readers interested in more detailed descriptions of China's changing industrial policies over the sample period are referred to Du, Harrison, and Jefferson (2014) or Harrison (2014).

The first row of Table 1 reports the percentage of firms that received positive subsidies from the government. In 1998, 9.4 percent of all reporting firms received subsidies. That number climbed steadily during the sample period, reaching a high of 15.1 percent of all manufacturing firms in 2004, before falling to 12.4 percent in 2007. The number was even higher for state-owned enterprises (SOEs) and foreign firms (many of which formed joint ventures with SOEs), but lower for domestic firms with no public or foreign participation. For private domestic enterprises ("Domestic Private Only" in Table 1), the share of firms receiving subsidies was slightly lower, increasing from 8 percent of all firms in 1998 to a high of 13.8 percent in 2004, before falling to 11.6 percent in 2007.

The second row of Table 1 indicates the percentage of firms receiving tax holidays over the sample period. We define a firm as receiving a tax holiday if either the firm paid less than the statutory corporate income tax rate in that year or if the firm paid less than the statutory value-added tax rate. A large share of manufacturing

TABLE 1—SUMMARY STATISTICS

	1998	2000	2001	2002	2003	2004	2005	2007
All companies								
Percent of firms with subsidies	0.0937	0.110	0.115	0.129	0.138	0.151	0.137	0.124
Percent of firms with tax holidays	0.416	0.453	0.441	0.443	0.456	0.419	0.454	0.497
Ratio of interest payments to current liabilities	0.0557	0.0413	0.0366	0.0340	0.0319	0.0268	0.0313	0.0330
Average tariff on imports	19.48	18.68	13.84	13.58	12.23	10.91	10.17	10.12
SOEs only								
Percent of firms with subsidies	0.139	0.162	0.171	0.181	0.197	0.197	0.224	0.253
Percent of firms with tax holidays	0.306	0.355	0.334	0.343	0.365	0.337	0.367	0.455
Ratio of interest payments to current liabilities	0.0416	0.0288	0.0255	0.0238	0.0222	0.0184	0.0183	0.0200
Average tariff on imports	19.81	19.11	13.76	13.48	12.05	11.01	10.24	10.24
Foreign firms only								
Percent of firms with subsidies	0.0678	0.0839	0.103	0.133	0.154	0.181	0.146	0.142
Percent of firms with tax holidays	0.540	0.591	0.572	0.585	0.593	0.577	0.598	0.608
Ratio of interest payments to current liabilities	0.0408	0.0282	0.0249	0.0219	0.0198	0.0164	0.0185	0.0198
Average tariff on imports	21.29	19.83	14.65	14.41	12.99	11.45	10.68	10.45
Domestic private firms only								
Percent of firms with subsidies	0.0835	0.105	0.107	0.119	0.126	0.138	0.131	0.116
Percent of firms with tax holidays	0.418	0.431	0.417	0.412	0.421	0.374	0.413	0.467
Ratio of interest payments to current liabilities	0.0668	0.0491	0.0424	0.0391	0.0365	0.0304	0.0356	0.0368
Average tariff on imports	18.65	18.14	13.58	13.33	12.00	10.74	10.00	10.02

firms paid less than the full statutory rate during the sample period. The share of enterprises with tax holidays varies from 41.6 percent in 1998 to nearly 50 percent in 2007. Comparing the incidence of tax holidays across different types of enterprises, Table 1 shows that the incidence was lowest for SOEs and highest for firms with foreign equity participation. Up to 59 percent of foreign firms received some type of tax holiday in 2003, compared to only 36.5 percent for SOEs.

While low interest loans have been an important form of industrial policy in China, we do not have data on directed credit provided through state banks or local governments. However, firms do report total interest and current liabilities, so we can calculate an effective interest rate on loan obligations. We report those averages in the third row of Table 1. The average ratio of interest paid to current liabilities across all firms with nonzero interest or liabilities was 5.57 percent in 1998. The interest ratio steadily declined during the sample period, to a low of 2.7 percent in 2004, and then increased to 3.3 percent in 2007. Across different ownership categories, there was significant variation, with domestic private enterprises facing an effective interest rate that was almost double that faced by SOEs.

In the last row of Table 1 we report the average tariff on imports by year for 1998 through 2007. Since tariffs are set nationally by sector, there is not significant variation in tariffs across enterprise types. During the sample period, average tariffs came down dramatically, from an average of 20 percentage points in 1998 to an average of 10 percentage points in 2007. By contrast, average tariffs in the United States over the last several decades have been less than 5 percent. The largest drop in tariffs occurred in 2001, the year China joined the WTO.

8 AMERICAN ECONOMIC JOURNAL: MACROECONOMICS OCTOBER 2015

TABLE 2—INDUSTRIAL POLICIES BY SECTOR

Sector	Interest rate	Tariff	Subsidies	Tax holidays
Foodstuff	0.0424	21.67	0.109	0.476
Manufacture of beverages	0.0441	27.48	0.106	0.451
Manufacture of tobacco	0.0336	52.28	0.229	0.320
Manufacture of textiles	0.0357	14.39	0.120	0.444
Manufacture of textile wearing apparel, footwear	0.0256	20.32	0.101	0.492
Manufacture of leather, fur	0.0308	18.17	0.0959	0.486
Processing of timber, manufacture of wood, bamboo	0.0578	7.557	0.114	0.548
Manufacture of furniture	0.0397	8.776	0.0923	0.501
Manufacture of paper and paper products	0.0438	10.60	0.105	0.454
Manufacture of articles for culture, education, and sport activity	0.0230	11.99	0.126	0.474
Processing of petroleum, coking, processing of nuclear fuel	0.0391	6.046	0.106	0.388
Manufacture of raw chemical materials and chemical products	0.0391	9.513	0.145	0.452
Manufacture of medicines	0.0391	6.148	0.166	0.468
Manufacture of chemical fibers	0.0381	8.743	0.166	0.426
Manufacture of rubber	0.0376	15.66	0.116	0.455
Manufacture of plastics	0.0323	11.45	0.107	0.451
Manufacture of nonmetallic mineral products	0.0462	12.38	0.139	0.445
Smelting and pressing of nonferrous metals	0.0367	6.193	0.109	0.413
Smelting and pressing of metals	0.0397	5.602	0.160	0.433
Manufacture of metal products	0.0293	12.15	0.107	0.432
Manufacture of special purpose machinery	0.0288	9.112	0.138	0.419
Manufacture of transport equipment	0.0289	17.57	0.150	0.413
Manufacture of electrical machinery and equipment	0.0266	11.67	0.144	0.423
Manufacture of communication equipment, computers, and other electronic equipment	0.0182	7.081	0.155	0.538
Manufacture of measuring instruments and machinery for cultural activity and office work	0.0205	9.442	0.170	0.470
Manufacture of artwork and other manufacturing	0.0344	17.03	0.102	0.485

Table 2 reports average industrial policies across two-digit manufacturing sectors between 1998 and 2007. There was significant variation in the intensity of industrial policy across different subsectors. For example, the ratio of interest payments to current liabilities, our proxy for the (subsidized) interest rate facing the enterprise, was very low for the computer and telecommunications sector, averaging 1.8 percent, but significantly higher for nonmetallic minerals (4.6 percent), beverages (4.4 percent), and paper products (4.4 percent). Tariffs also show significant dispersion, with the highest tariffs on goods such as tobacco products (over 52 percent) and transport equipment (17 percent) and the lowest tariffs on wood products (7.6 percent) and fuels (6 percent). The percentage of firms receiving subsidies and tax holidays also varied across sectors, as reported in the last two columns of Table 2.

B. *Data and Measurement*

We measure industrial policy using four types of policy instruments: subsidies, interest paid as a share of current liabilities, tax holidays, and tariffs. Subsidies, interest payments, and tax holidays are allocated at the firm level, while tariffs are set at the national level. Our data for tariffs are available at the two or three digit level. Tariffs are set nationally and are exogenous with respect to a particular region or a particular firm. However, since tariffs do not vary across firms, we cannot use measures of policy dispersion within a sector to test whether tariffs are set in a way that preserves competition. For tariffs, all we can do is test whether the imposition of tariffs in more competitive sectors is more likely to result in higher firm performance.

To measure competition, we will compute a Lerner Index at both the county and sector level. The Lerner Index measures the importance of markups (the difference between prices and marginal costs) relative to the firm's total value-added. To calculate it, we first aggregate operating profits, capital costs, and sales at the industry, county, and year level. The Lerner Index is defined as the ratio of operating profits less capital costs to sales. Under perfect competition, there should be no excess profits above capital costs, so the Lerner Index should equal zero. Since the Lerner Index is an inverse measure of competition, we redefine competition as 1–Lerner, so under perfect competition it should equal 1. A value of 1 indicates perfect competition, while values below 1 suggest some degree of market power. We address the potential endogeneity of competition using initial period Lerners in all the estimating equations below.

The standard approach to measuring firm-level performance is to identify total factor productivity (TFP) levels or growth. Since TFP is an overall efficiency parameter, it is best understood as measuring process innovation—the cost reduction associated with improving the efficiency in producing an existing product. Another measure of innovation is product innovation—associated with the introduction of new products or higher quality goods. Our primary focus is on process innovation, since product innovation is not reliably measured and was also less pervasive for firms in the sample during this period.

The dataset, collected by the Chinese National Bureau of Statistics, is described in greater detail in Du, Harrison, and Jefferson (2012). We retain only the manufacturing enterprises and eliminate establishments with missing values or negative or zero values for key variables such as output, employees, capital, and inputs. The years covered include 1998 through 2007. This is a true panel, following the same firms over time. We dropped three sectors with incomplete information on prices from the sample.[8] The final sample size is 1,545,626 observations.

The dataset contains information on real and nominal output, assets, number of workers, renumeration, inputs, public ownership, foreign investment, sales revenue, and exports. Because domestically owned, foreign, and publicly owned enterprises behave quite differently, in all the regression results presented below we will restrict the sample to firms that have zero foreign ownership and have only minority state ownership. In the dataset, 1,069,563 observations meet the criterion.[9]

To control for the effects of trade policies, we have created a time series of tariffs, obtained from the World Integrated Trading Solution (WITS), maintained by the World Bank. We aggregated tariffs to the same level of aggregation as the foreign

---

[8] They are the following sectors: processing food from agricultural products; printing, reproduction of recording media; and general purpose machinery.

[9] Typically we distinguish domestic and foreign-invested firms based on whether the share of subscribed capital owned by foreign investors is equal to or less than 10 percent. The results are generally robust to the choice of definition for foreign versus domestic ownership.

10   AMERICAN ECONOMIC JOURNAL: MACROECONOMICS   OCTOBER 2015

investment data, using output for 2003 as weights. During the sample period, average tariffs fell by nearly 9 percentage points, which is a significant change over a short time period. While the average level of tariffs across all years was nearly 13 percent, this average masks significant heterogeneity across sectors, with a high of 41 percent in grain mill products and a low of 4 percent in railroad equipment.

Before adopting a more formal approach to analyzing the relationship between industrial policy, competition, and firm-level outcomes in the next section, we first report some raw correlations in Table 3. The remainder of the paper will focus only on domestically owned firms, but for the correlation results we include all enterprises in order to highlight the significant differences across ownership types. All the reported correlations are statistically significant at the 5 percent level. In particular these correlations indicate: (i) that firms receiving subsidies exhibited higher total factor productivity levels; (ii) that subsidies were significantly associated with new product introductions; (iii) that while subsidies and tax holidays are significantly and positively correlated with firm-level innovation, final goods tariffs are not; and (iv) that higher levels of TFP are positively correlated with firm-level subsidies and tax holidays; however, the two other industrial policy measures are negatively correlated with firm-level performance as defined by levels of TFP: final goods tariffs and low interest payments.

The raw correlations also confirm that SOEs and foreign firms behave quite differently from other enterprises. Industrial policies were also allocated differently for these enterprises, consistent with the evidence presented in Tables 1 and 2. Public sector enterprises were more likely to receive subsidies and tariff protection, but less likely to receive tax holidays. Public ownership was negatively associated with TFP, with a correlation coefficient of -0.19. These correlations are consistent with the perception of SOEs as less competitive and less efficient than other enterprises. Firms with foreign ownership (column 7) were systematically more likely to receive all types of industrial support. In contrast to SOEs, foreign ownership is positive and significantly correlated with TFP. The very different performance outcomes and industrial policy targeting for SOEs and foreign firms justify our decision to focus on domestically owned enterprises with only minority public ownership in the remainder of this paper.

Overall, these correlations suggest that some forms of industrial policy, such as subsidies and tax holidays, were associated with significant firm-level innovation, while others, such as tariffs, which typically discourage competition, were not. Our empirical analysis in the next section will confirm these conjectures.

III. Empirical Analysis and Results

In this section, we analyze the complementarity between industrial policy and competition using two approaches. First, we test the hypothesis that introducing industrial policies in more competitive sectors is more likely to lead to improved outcomes. This is a somewhat different approach from "picking winners:" instead, this approach suggests picking sectors where firms *already* compete intensively. The intuition would be that to make government support effective, it needs to be allocated where there is competition, and not collusion. Second, for given sectoral

TABLE 3

	Index_subsidy	Index_tax	Index_interest	Final tariff	TFP_OP	Public	Foreign	New product share in sales
Index_subsidy	1							
Index_tax	−0.0047	1						
Index_interest	−0.0248	−0.0087	1					
Final goods tariff	−0.0373	−0.0113	−0.016	1				
TFP_OP	0.0275	0.108	−0.0106	−0.118	1			
Public	0.0418	−0.0679	0.0344	0.142	−0.19	1		
Foreign	0.0116	0.146	0.0821	0.0529	0.152	−0.16	1	
New product share in sales	0.109	−0.0021	−0.0523	−0.037	0.0489	0.0728	−0.0034	1

Notes: Index_subsidy, index_tax, and index_interest are dummy variables that equal one if a firm receives subsidies, tax breaks, or a below-median borrowing interest rate, respectively. TFP is estimated with the Olley-Pakes method. For the OP estimation of TFP, we use a two-stage procedure. In the first stage, we use the OP regression method to obtain estimates for the input coefficients and then calculate TFP (the residual from the production function). In the second stage, we regress TFP on the remaining controls. Ownership variables public and foreign vary from 0 to 100 percent publicly or foreign owned.

choice, we investigate what would be the best strategy for allocating support across firms within a sector. In a nutshell, the first approach explores differences *across* sectors, whereas the second approach explores how best to allocate industrial policy support *within* a sector.

A. Estimation Methods

To implement our first approach, which tests Corollary 1, we measure the correlation of subsidies with competition and then see whether a stronger correlation coefficient at the city-year level raises firm performance. To measure whether subsidies are biased toward more competitive sectors in city r in year t, we calculate the correlation between the industry-city level initial degree of competition and current (period t) subsidies in sector j and city r:

$$(2) \qquad \Omega_{rt,\,subsidy} = \text{Corr}(SUBSIDY_{rjt}, COMPETITION_{rj0}).$$

Since all industrial policies vary over time, we thus obtain a time-varying change in the correlation between initial levels of competition in year zero and the patterns of interventions across different parts of China. We then explore whether higher correlations between current period subsidies and initial competition, as measured by $\Omega_{rt,\,subsidy}$, are associated with better performance. As an illustration, if in Shanghai the largest amount of subsidies are allocated to sectors with low markups, and small or zero subsidies are given to sectors with high markups in the year 2003, then, for Shanghai in 2003, this correlation coefficient will be close to unity.

Similarly, we introduce the variables $\Omega_{rt,\,interest}$ and $\Omega_{rt,\,tax}$, where

$$(3) \qquad \Omega_{rt,\,interest} = \text{Corr}(INTEREST_{rjt}, COMPETITION_{rj0})$$

$$(4) \qquad \Omega_{rt,\,tax} = \text{Corr}(TAX_{rjt}, COMPETITION_{rj0}).$$

12   *AMERICAN ECONOMIC JOURNAL: MACROECONOMICS*   *OCTOBER 2015*

The only type of industrial policy that does not vary across regions is tariffs, but the Ω variable for tariff policies will still vary by location and year because the composition of industrial sectors is different, and the degree of competition varies across regions. Consequently, we can compute a separate Ω variable by replacing subsidies with tariffs and replacing the correlation between initial competition and subsidies with the correlation between initial competition and current period tariffs. At the city level, the correlation between that city's degree of competition at the beginning of the sample period and current period tariffs should be strictly exogenous, as the level of competition is predetermined and tariffs are set at the national, not the city, level. Our last correlation measure is now defined as

$$(5) \qquad \Omega_{rt, \, tariffs} \; = \; \mathrm{Corr}(TARIFF_{jt}, COMPETITION_{rj0}).$$

Consequently we have four different correlation coefficients that vary only across locations and over time. These Ω variables measure a city's scope to target more competitive sectors where competition is predetermined using beginning of period Lerner indices.[10] To calculate our measure of competition, we first aggregate operating profits, capital costs, and sales at the industry level. Under perfect competition, there should be no excess profits above capital costs, so the Lerner Index should equal zero and the competition measure should equal one. A value of one indicates perfect competition, while values below one suggest some degree of market power.

Our second goal is to identify which approaches to allocating industrial support within a given sector are most effective. Our main empirical challenge is to capture the notion of firm-specific industrial support being allocated in a way that preserves or increases competition. We first consider the sectoral dispersion of industrial support as a measure of the degree of competitiveness. As an (inverse) measure of sectoral dispersion, we use the Herfindahl index constructed using the share of support each firm in a given sector receives relative to the total support awarded to the sector. We thus derive a measure of concentration, such as *Herf_subsidy*, which for subsidies is given by

$$(6) \qquad Herf\_subsidy_{ijrt} \; = \; \sum_{h \in j, \, h \neq i} \left(\frac{Subsidy_{ijrt}}{Sum\_subsidy_{jrt}} \right)^2.$$

We then do the same thing for tax holidays, and obtain a measure of concentration, *Herf_tax*, where

$$(7) \qquad Herf\_tax_{ijrt} \; = \; \sum_{h \in j, \, h \neq i} \left(\frac{TaxHoliday_{ijrt}}{Sum\_TaxHoliday_{jrt}} \right)^2.$$

The amount of tax holiday granted to any firm i is simply the quantity of tax revenues that the firm saves by qualifying for the tax holiday. During the time period of our analysis, corporate tax rates varied from 15 to 33 percent. Consequently, the amount of the tax holiday is equal to profits times the tax rate less actual taxes paid, plus any savings from exemptions to the value-added tax (which was set to 17

---

[10] Recall that the Lerner index is defined as the ratio of operating profits less capital costs to sales. It is an inverse measure of product market competition.

percent of value-added). If the statutory tax rate facing an enterprise was 20 percent, then we calculate the tax holidays as the difference between profits multiplied by 20 percent and actual taxes paid. The results are robust to choice of statutory tax rate (i.e., the top 33 percent rate versus a lower rate).

As with standard Herfindahl indices, a smaller number indicates a higher degree of dispersion of subsidies or tax holidays, or a more equitable (and competition-preserving) allocation of those across firms in the sector. We then take the 1 − these Herfindahl indexes to capture the degree of sectoral dispersion of the tax holidays or subsidies. The 1 − *Herf_subsidy* term, we call *CompHerf_subsidy*. The 1 − *Herf_tax* term, we call *CompHerf_tax*. To the extent that greater dispersion of subsidies within a sector induces greater focus by encouraging more firms to innovate within a specific sector, we would expect the coefficient on that variable in the productivity regression to be positive.

We also compute an analogous measure for loans. Since it is difficult to know what portion of loans are low interest, we identify by sector and year the mean interest rate paid. We compute industrial support as the difference between mean interest rates paid in a sector and actual interest paid by firms for those enterprises paying lower rates. To the extent that firms in a particular sector and region are unable to access capital, we would expect a more concentrated distribution of subsidized interest payments.

If we were to regress firm-level measures of total factor productivity (TFP) on these sectoral dispersion measures, such an approach could raise potential endogeneity issues. For example, if governments favor large and more successful firms in the allocation process, then a firm that accounts for a large share of total tax holidays or subsidies within a sector might also exhibit higher TFP. These would lead our estimation procedure to reflect spurious relationships between state support and performance. A similar possibility exists if the government tends to support weaker enterprises, which could bias the coefficient in the opposite direction.

To address the potential endogeneity of our policy instruments, we calculate them separately for each firm and exclude the firm's own industrial support (subsidies, tax holidays, interest payments) in estimating our Herfindahl measures. This means that in calculating 1 − *Herf_subsidy*, we exclude firm *i*'s subsidy in both the numerator and the denominator. For the inverse of the *Herf_tax* or the *Herf_ interest*, we do the same exclusion. Consequently, this sector-level measure is exogenous with respect to firm *i*'s performance.

Combining our Ωs, which measure the links between sectoral targeting and initial competition at the local level, and our Herfindahl indices, which measure the dispersion of industrial policy, the basic estimating equation can then be written as follows, where *m* indicates an industrial policy type:

$$(8) \quad \ln TFP_{ijrt} = \theta_1 Z_{ijt} + \theta_2 S_{jt} + \beta_m CompHerf_{imjrt} + \alpha_m \Omega_{mrt} + \ell_i + d_t + \epsilon_{ijt}.$$

where *Z* is a vector of firm-level controls including state ownership at the firm level. Although we are excluding 100 percent state-owned enterprises from the analysis, many so-called private firms retain some degree of state participation. The variable *S* includes sector-level controls, such as tariffs or the degree of (initial) competition

14   AMERICAN ECONOMIC JOURNAL: MACROECONOMICS   OCTOBER 2015

in the sector, or the degree of foreign penetration in the sector, as well as upstream and downstream foreign investment.[11]

CompHerf$_{imjrt}$ is a vector of industrial policies that measures the extent of sectoral dispersion in subsidies, tax holidays, and interest payments. The specification includes firm fixed effects ℓ_i as well as time fixed effects d_t. Our conjecture is that $\alpha_m > 0$, i.e., that industrial policies targeted toward sectors with higher competition as measured by the Lerner Index in the initial year of the sample are more TFP enhancing. We also conjecture that β_m is likely to be positive if the distribution of industrial policies targets innovators or promotes more competition. We explore different possible targeting schemes in our analysis below.

B. *Baseline Results*

We begin with the baseline estimates from (8). The critical parameters are the coefficients on the vector of industrial policies α_m and β_m. Table 4 reports the coefficient estimates. The dependent variable is the log of TFP, using both the Olley-Pakes (OP) method and OLS with firm-level fixed effects to compute input shares in the first stage as a comparison. Our OP approach follows Olley and Pakes (1996) in calculating sector-specific input coefficients in the first stage and is described in more detail in an online Appendix. As indicated earlier, all specifications include both time and firm fixed effects. We also include as controls different sector-level measures of foreign presence, but do not report them in Table 4.

More Dispersed Intervention Is More TFP-Enhancing.—To the extent that greater dispersion of subsidies within a sector induces greater focus by encouraging more firms to innovate within a specific sector, we would expect the coefficient on *CompHerf* to be positive. This is precisely what we obtain in the first row of Table 4, which shows positive and significant coefficients on *CompHerf* for subsidies. The coefficient estimates in column 1 indicate that a perfectly dispersed set of subsidies, leading to a Herfindahl for subsidies of 0 and consequently the complement of that at 1, would increase TFP by 3.9 percentage points.

The coefficient on $\Omega_{rt,\,subsidies}$ indicates the extent to which targeting at the city level via subsidies is more efficient in more competitive industries, as measured by the initial degree of competition at the beginning of the sample period. The coefficient estimates are reported in the second row of Table 4. While the coefficient is positive across all specifications, it is not significantly different from zero.

Together, the first two rows of Table 4 indicate that while allocating subsidies to initially more competitive sectors did not significantly affect productivity, a greater dispersion of subsidies was associated with improved firm performance. Later we will explore how moving beyond equitable allocations of subsidies to targeting innovative firms could further increase the positive impact of firm subsidies on performance.

---

[11] For more discussion of the measures of foreign presence, which include measures for horizontal ("horizontal") and vertical ("backward" and "forward") foreign exposure, see Du, Harrison, and Jefferson (2012).

TABLE 4—COMPETITIVENESS OF INDUSTRIAL POLICIES AND FIRM PRODUCTIVITY

Variables	TFP_OLSFE				TFP_OP			
	(1)	(2)	(3)	(4)	(5)	(6)	(7)	(8)
CompHerf_subsidy	0.0388***			0.0305***	0.0407***			0.0319***
	(0.00976)			(0.00824)	(0.0110)			(0.00918)
Cor_subsidy_lerner	0.00225			0.000959	0.00115			0.00009
	(0.00348)			(0.00397)	(0.00338)			(0.00394)
CompHerf_tax		0.0999***		0.0859***		0.103***		0.0861***
		(0.0207)		(0.0230)		(0.0229)		(0.0249)
Cor_tax_lerner		−0.0143***		−0.0151***		−0.0152***		−0.0161***
		(0.00396)		(0.00421)		(0.00417)		(0.00458)
CompHerf_interest			0.0766***	0.0568***			0.0845***	0.0669***
			(0.0169)	(0.0164)			(0.0195)	(0.0190)
Cor_interest_lerner			0.0133***	0.0124***			0.0126***	0.0122***
			(0.00399)	(0.00450)			(0.00389)	(0.00445)
Cor_tariff_lerner	−0.0411***	−0.0208**	−0.0330***	−0.0305**	−0.0312**	−0.0163	−0.0281***	−0.0199
	(0.0143)	(0.00975)	(0.00995)	(0.0147)	(0.0145)	(0.0101)	(0.0104)	(0.0149)
Lerner	10.63**	9.349***	9.404***	10.26**	12.98**	9.099**	9.396**	12.05*
	(4.712)	(3.449)	(3.417)	(4.535)	(6.320)	(3.677)	(3.677)	(6.102)
Lernersquare	−6.141**	−5.362***	−5.413***	−5.953**	−6.963**	−4.927**	−5.108**	−6.464*
	(2.591)	(1.898)	(1.886)	(2.493)	(3.458)	(2.060)	(2.066)	(3.344)
Exportshare_sector	0.328**	0.370***	0.346**	0.343**	0.632***	0.683***	0.651***	0.660***
	(0.141)	(0.139)	(0.139)	(0.141)	(0.178)	(0.175)	(0.175)	(0.178)
Stateshare	0.00293	5.35e-05	−0.000432	0.00301	0.00310	−0.000412	−0.000588	0.00315
	(0.00470)	(0.00428)	(0.00399)	(0.00504)	(0.00481)	(0.00425)	(0.00397)	(0.00514)
Index_subsidy	0.0116***	0.0110***	0.0116***	0.0105***	0.00805***	0.00759***	0.00833***	0.00674***
	(0.00181)	(0.00170)	(0.00168)	(0.00190)	(0.00193)	(0.00187)	(0.00185)	(0.00199)
Index_tax	0.0220***	0.0201***	0.0218***	0.0205***	0.0214***	0.0197***	0.0213***	0.0200***
	(0.00104)	(0.000951)	(0.000906)	(0.00108)	(0.00103)	(0.000897)	(0.000873)	(0.00103)
Index_interest	−0.0129***	−0.0142***	−0.0157***	−0.0120***	−0.0109***	−0.0124***	−0.0139***	−0.0101***
	(0.00163)	(0.00144)	(0.00148)	(0.00169)	(0.00187)	(0.00164)	(0.00167)	(0.00192)
lnTariff	0.0716	0.0619	0.0626	0.0690	0.0527	0.0416	0.0449	0.0476
	(0.0579)	(0.0556)	(0.0556)	(0.0576)	(0.0570)	(0.0551)	(0.0549)	(0.0565)
Constant	−2.876	−2.378	−2.398	−2.776	−4.500	−2.655	−2.794	−4.154
	(2.196)	(1.627)	(1.607)	(2.133)	(2.945)	(1.696)	(1.690)	(2.858)
Observations	810,740	903,455	962,076	746,304	810,740	903,455	962,076	746,304
R^2	0.205	0.205	0.205	0.208	0.181	0.183	0.182	0.184

Notes: Robust clustered standard errors are presented in parentheses. The dependent variable is TFP (estimated by OLS with fixed effects in columns 1, 2, 3, 4; estimated by Olley-Pakes method in columns 5, 6, 7, 8). For the OP estimation of TFP, it's indeed a two-stage estimation. In the first stage, we use the OP regression method to obtain estimates for the input coefficients and then calculate TFP (the residual from the production function). In the second stage, we regress TFP on the remaining controls. Each regression includes firm fixed effects and year dummies. CompHerf_subsidy, CompHerf_tax, and CompHerf_interest are Herfindhal indices of subsidy, tax, and interest rate policies, measured on the city-industry-year level. Corr_subsidy_lerner, corr_tax_lerner, and corr_tarriff_lerner are constructed by the correlation between the industry-city level initial degree of competition (represented by lerner index) and the current period of subsidies, taxes, and interest rates; all the correlations are on the city-year level. Each regression includes industry fixed effect and year dummies. Export share is calculated by export procurement divided by industrial sales. State share is defined as the proportion of the firm's state assets to its total equity. Those two shares are aggregated at the sector-year level. Index_subsidy, index_tax, and index_interest are dummy variables that are equal to one if a firm receives subsidies, tax breaks, or a below-median borrowing interest rate, respectively. Sector-level FDI and other (input) tariffs are also included as controls but not reported.

***Significant at the 1 percent level.
**Significant at the 5 percent level.
*Significant at the 10 percent level.

The next row of Table 4 looks at the correlation between firm-level TFP and our measure for the dispersion of tax holidays *CompHerf_tax*. The coefficient is statistically significant and positive, indicating that greater dispersion of tax holidays increases productivity. The coefficient estimate, which varies from 0.086 to 0.103, indicates driving the Herfindahl for the dispersion of tax holidays on income taxes

16   *AMERICAN ECONOMIC JOURNAL: MACROECONOMICS*   *OCTOBER 2015*

and value-added taxes to 0 would lead to an increase in TFP of 8.6 to 10.3 percentage points.

The coefficient estimate on the correlation between taxes and initial competition $\Omega_{rt,\,tax}$ at the city level in column 1, equal to -0.0143, indicates that if the correlation between tax holidays and competition at the city level was perfect (100 percent), then productivity would be 1.43 percent higher. Based on the sample means, a 1 standard deviation increase in the city-industry correlation would increase TFP by 0.3 percentage points for firms in that city and industry.

The fifth row of Table 4 reports the impact of wider dispersion of interest payments for loans on productivity outcomes. The coefficient on the Herfindahl for interest payments is positive and significant across all specifications, indicating that a wider dispersion of subsidized interest payments is consistent with higher productivity at the firm level. The coefficient estimate varies from 0.057 to 0.085, indicating that a perfectly disperse set of interest payments would be associated with higher productivity by 5.7 to 8.5 percentage points. A 1 standard deviation increase in the variable would be associated with a 1.2 to 1.6 percentage point increase in TFP.[12]

While the first three columns of Table 4 report the effects of different industrial policies separately, column 4 combines all of them in one specification. The coefficient estimates are unaffected. The results in column 4 indicate that a more equitable dispersion of subsidies, tax holidays, and interest payments across firms within a sector are unequivocally associated with higher productivity growth at the firm level. While a higher level of subsidies or tax holidays are associated with higher productivity in initially competitive sectors, the results are mixed or negative for loans and tariffs. We shall see below that the positive effects at the city level of subsidies and tax holidays, and the mixed role of tariffs and low interest loans, are consistent with their individual effects at the firm level.

Robustness.—The coefficient estimates when using OP to estimate TFP are reported in the last four columns of Table 4. Consistent with reviews of the productivity literature, the results are not very different when using OP estimates of TFP versus OLS with firm fixed effects. One difference is that the coefficient on the correlation of tariffs and initial competition becomes insignificant, but remains negative with an attenuated coefficient.

The remaining part of Table 4 reports the coefficients on the sector- and firm-level controls. At the sector level, competition measured using $1 - Lerner$ is positively and significantly associated with increased TFP. We also include a squared term, and the coefficient is negative. This nonlinear relationship between competition and productivity, which is increasing at lower levels and falling at higher levels, is consistent with the inverted U-shape found in particular by Aghion et al. (2005). If,

---

[12] While the first five rows of Table 4 suggest potentially significant positive effects of industrial policies, these are not uniform. In particular, the correlation between interest payments and competition is positive, suggesting improved TFP when effective interest rates are *higher* in more initially competitive sectors. Similarly, the correlation between tariffs and competition in the sector is negative, indicating that tariff interventions in more competitive sectors have been associated with lower TFP. The coefficient estimate, which ranges from -0.0199 to -0.0411, suggests that if higher tariffs were perfectly correlated with higher initial competition, then TFP would be from 2 to 4 percentage points lower.

instead, we measure competition using sectoral export shares, we also find a significant and positive association with TFP. This strong, positive, independent impact of competition, measured using either the sector-level Lerner Index or export shares, is consistent with an important role for competition in enhancing firm performance.

One question that might arise is the potential endogeneity of the Lerner Index and its square, which are included as controls. We address the potential endogeneity of the correlation and Herfindahl measures by explicitly excluding the own firm in the calculations, and using initial period Lerners to construct the correlations. For the Lerner control measures, endogeneity is also unlikely to be a problem as we use the initial period Lerner measure in that location and sector. Using Lerner measures as controls that were calculated at the beginning of the sample period mitigates possible reverse causality between firm behavior, sectoral productivity distributions, and market structure.

We also include controls for subsidies, tax holidays, tariffs, and low interest loans at the individual enterprise level. We include a zero-one control variable, *index_subsidy*, which is equal to one if the enterprise received nonzero and positive subsidy amounts in that year. We also include a zero-one control indicating whether the firm received tax holidays, *index_tax*. The tax break is defined as a zero-one variable indicating whether the firm paid either taxes at a lower rate than the statutory corporate tax rate or value-added taxes at a lower rate than the statutory rate. The coefficients on the subsidy and tax holiday dummies are positive and significant. We also include a control for loans, which is equal to one if the firm's interest payments to current liabilities (an effective interest rate) are below the average for that sector and year. The coefficient on the *index_interest* term is negative and significant. Firms that receive lower interest rates do not perform better when performance is measured using TFP. These results for loans as an industrial policy measure are consistent with the coefficients on the industry-city correlations, indicating better performance at the city level when interest payments are higher.[13]

Summarizing.—Overall, the results in Table 4 suggest that preserving competition through a more equitable targeting policy is associated with superior performance, as measured by productivity. We addressed the potential endogeneity of targeting by excluding a firm's own subsidies or tax holidays when estimating the impact of sectoral dispersion of subsidies or tax holidays on that firm's TFP. Overall, the evidence suggests that instruments such as tax holidays and subsidies have systemically been associated with improved productivity performance when combined with high initial levels of competition, as measured by the Lerner Index.

One interesting question to ask is how much actual tariff and subsidy levels at the city-industry level were in fact correlated with actual competition levels. The summary statistics in Table A1 in the Appendix suggest that in fact the Chinese

---

[13] The impact of tariffs depends on where they are allocated. While final tariffs facing a sector are positively associated with TFP, the effect is not statistically significant. Higher tariffs in input or using sectors have negative effects on firm TFP. These insignificant or negative effects of tariff protection on firm-level TFP are consistent with our results showing that even if tariffs are targeted at more competitive sectors they fail to yield improved performance. Tariffs discourage competition and are generally second-best incentive devices, so it is not surprising that using tariffs as a tool of industrial policy is not effective in the Chinese context.

18   AMERICAN ECONOMIC JOURNAL: MACROECONOMICS   OCTOBER 2015

government did not set tariff or subsidy levels higher in cities or industries where competition was more intense. The average correlation coefficient between tariffs and the Lerner measure is -0.02, suggesting almost 0 correlation between tariffs and competition. The correlation with subsidies is positive but close to 0, at 0.03. The only instrument where there is significant targeting is taxes, where the correlation with competition is equal to -0.1. The coefficient of -0.1 is suggestive of a strong negative association between more initial competition and lower taxes. While the evidence in Table 4 is consistent with higher performance as measured by TFP when policy instruments are introduced in conjunction with greater competition, the actual pattern of policies does not suggest that this is what the Chinese actually did. One interpretation is that there is enormous scope for improved performance outcomes associated with industrial policy if it is introduced in a way that preserves competition in the future.

C. *Targeting Innovative Enterprises*

Should some firms receive more support than others? This is the question we address in Table 5. If industrial policies are more effective when they induce greater competition between innovating firms, as we are hypothesizing, then it should in principle be possible to improve on a purely equitable distribution by targeting firms most likely to engage in innovation. The new heterogeneous firm literature pioneered by Hopenhayn (1992) and Melitz (2003) predicts that the most productive firms are also likely to be the largest firms. These firms are also likely, in the heterogeneous firm literature, to be the lowest cost and most competitive producers. Consequently, one possibility is to redo the analysis with Herfindahls but give greater weight to larger enterprises. We report the unweighted results in columns 1 and 2, and the results weighting by firm size using number of employees in column 3.

Another way to induce greater competition is to promote new entry and encourage younger firms to enter. To capture the importance of entry, we redo the Herfindahls and weight the individual subsidy, interest, and tax holiday allocations by the inverse of a firm's age. Effectively, this means giving the greatest weight to the youngest firms. These results are reported in column 4 of Table 5.

The results in Table 5 suggest that in the Chinese case, targeting younger but not bigger firms significantly increases the positive impact of industrial policies on total factor productivity.[14] For subsidies, the coefficient on the Herfindahl increases by a factor of 3. The coefficient estimate, at 0.10, indicates that a 1 standard deviation increase in the Herfindahl would increase a firm's TFP by 3 percentage points. One reason why targeting younger firms may be more beneficial is that younger firms generally have higher TFP (measured either using the OP procedure or OLS with firm fixed effects).

One potential pitfall of measuring process innovation using total factor productivity is when output is calculated using sector deflators with firm-level revenue. This revenue-based TFP is potentially misleading because it could reflect changes

---

[14] This is consistent with the analysis in Acemoglu et al. (2013).

VOL. 7 NO. 4   AGHION ET AL.: INDUSTRIAL POLICY AND COMPETITION   19

TABLE 5—THE IMPACT OF THE COMPETITIVENESS OF INDUSTRIAL POLICIES ON FIRM TFP:
WEIGHTED HERFINDHAL

Variables	TFP_OLSFE (1)	TFP_OP (2)	TFP_OP (3)	TFP_OP (4)
CompHerf_subsidy	0.0305***	0.0319***		
	(0.00824)	(0.00918)		
CompHerf_tax	0.0859***	0.0861***		
	(0.0230)	(0.0249)		
CompHerf_interest	0.0568***	0.0669***		
	(0.0164)	(0.0190)		
Comp_Herfsubsidy_weightsize			0.0255***	
			(0.00909)	
Comp_Herftax_weightsize			0.0555***	
			(0.0124)	
Comp_Herfinterest_weightsize			0.0616***	
			(0.00983)	
Comp_Herfsubsidy_weightage				0.102***
				(0.0313)
Comp_Herftax_weightage				0.0781***
				(0.0255)
Comp_Herfinterest_weightage				0.0541**
				(0.0253)
Lerner	10.26**	12.05*	12.72**	12.62**
	(4.535)	(6.102)	(6.253)	(6.262)
Lernersquare	−5.953**	−6.464*	−6.813*	−6.760*
	(2.493)	(3.344)	(3.420)	(3.424)
Index_subsidy	0.0105***	0.00674***	0.00781***	0.00786***
	(0.00190)	(0.00199)	(0.00198)	(0.00196)
Index_tax	0.0205***	0.0200***	0.0201***	0.0200***
	(0.00108)	(0.00103)	(0.00104)	(0.00105)
Index_interest	−0.0120***	−0.0101***	−0.0100***	−0.0100***
	(0.00169)	(0.00192)	(0.00191)	(0.00192)
Exportshare_sector	0.343**	0.660***	0.672***	0.673***
	(0.141)	(0.178)	(0.179)	(0.179)
Stateshare	0.00301	0.00315	0.00273	0.00289
	(0.00504)	(0.00514)	(0.00516)	(0.00511)
Constant	−2.776	−4.154	−4.474	−4.521
	(2.133)	(2.858)	(2.936)	(2.944)
Observations	746,304	746,304	747,158	746,740
R^2	0.208	0.184	0.182	0.182

Notes: Robust clustered standard errors are presented in parentheses. For column 1, the dependent variable is TFP (estimated by OLS with fixed effects); in columns 2, 3, and 4, TFP is estimated by OP as described in the text. Each regression includes firm fixed effects and year dummies. CompHerf_subsidy, CompHerf_tax, and CompHerf_interest are Herfindhal indices of subsidy, tax, and interest rate policies, measured on the city-industry-year level. Columns 1 and 2 use an unweighted Herfindhal index, column 3 computes a Herfindhal index weighted by firm size (number of employees), and column 4 weights the Herfindhal index using 1/age (year since establishment). Export share is calculated by export procurement divided by industrial sales. State share is defined as the proportion of the firm's state assets to its total equity. Those two shares are aggregated at the sector-year level. Index_subsidy, index_tax, and index_interest are dummy variables which equal to one if a firm receives subsidies, tax breaks, or a below-median borrowing interest rate, respectively. Sector FDI and tariff measures are included but not reported.

*** Significant at the 1 percent level.
** Significant at the 5 percent level.
* Significant at the 10 percent level.

20   AMERICAN ECONOMIC JOURNAL: MACROECONOMICS   OCTOBER 2015

in firm-specific quality or markups. One solution exists when firm-specific price deflators are available, which account for price heterogeneity (due to market power differences or quality differences) across firms. For the Chinese industrial census data, such firm-specific deflators are available for the years 1998 through 2003. Consequently, we redo the results presented in Table 5 with this shorter time series, using the firm-specific price deflators to calculate first output and then TFP. The results using firm-specific price deflators to calculate TFP are reported in Table 6.

The sample size using the earlier years is considerably smaller, at only a quarter of the full sample. However, the results are quite robust. The coefficient on the subsidy Herfindahl, calculated using the OP procedure, increases from 0.03 in Table 5 to 0.06, a doubling of magnitudes. The coefficients for the dispersion of tax holidays and low interest loans also increase significantly. The evidence suggests that using a much smaller sample and implementing firm-specific prices magnifies the effects significantly.

Another potential concern is the possible mismeasurement of TFP using OP when policies are omitted in the first stage. Recent developments in the productivity literature suggest that excluding policies in the first stage could lead to biased estimates in the first stage of OP, which estimates input share coefficients. To test for this possibility, we redid the analysis adding all the key policies in the first stage, and report the results in the last two columns of Table 6. The coefficients on the herfindahl terms remain significant and even more important in magnitude than the original specification reported in Table 4. The evidence in Table 6 suggests that our results emphasizing the positive impact of dispersion on productivity are robust to many different specifications and subsamples.

D. *Within-Firm versus Across-Firm Reallocation Effects of Industrial Policy*

In recent years, applied productivity researchers have shifted their focus away from the determinants of changes in behavior within the same firm to address market share reallocation across firms and the consequences for aggregate productivity. This shift in focus can be traced to the work of Olley and Pakes (1996), who propose a simple approach to disentangling within versus between components. The interest in *within* versus *between* firm reallocation also increased with the work of Hopenhayn (1992), Melitz (2003), and others, who assume that firms have a predetermined exogenous productivity draw, and that consequently much of industry productivity growth is not through learning within a firm but through reallocation of market shares across firms.[15]

Tables 4 through 6 explored the extent to which within-firm productivity gains were affected by how different types of industrial policies were allocated across firms. In Table 7, we explore reallocation toward more productive enterprises. This

[15] The empirical work in this area has somewhat lagged behind the theoretical contributions. One of the first to apply the Olley and Pakes (1996) decomposition was Pavcnik (2003), who found that reallocation accounted for up to two-thirds of productivity growth at the industry level and within-firm learning accounted for one-third. For India, the results are the opposite: Harrison, Martin, and Nataraj (2013) find that most of industry productivity growth is due to within-firm effects and almost none is due to market share reallocations. This result for India is corroborated by work by Sivadasan (2010).

TABLE 6—COMPETITIVENESS OF INDUSTRIAL POLICIES AND FIRM PRODUCTIVITY:
ROBUSTNESS CHECK WITH TFP CALCULATED BY FIRM-LEVEL PRICE DEFLATOR AND TFP
MODIFIED TO INCLUDE POLICIES IN FIRST-STAGE OP ESTIMATION

| | Using firm-level prices | | Adding policies in first-stage OP | |
Variables	TFP_OLSFE (1)	TFP_OP (2)	TFP_OLSFE (3)	TFP_OP (4)
CompHerf_subsidy	0.0325**	0.0560**	0.0306***	0.0427***
	(0.0150)	(0.0228)	(0.00857)	(0.0109)
CompHerf_tax	0.0497	0.126**	0.0857***	0.111***
	(0.0387)	(0.0568)	(0.0234)	(0.0285)
CompHerf_interest	0.0341	0.0920**	0.0573***	0.0876***
	(0.0299)	(0.0437)	(0.0172)	(0.0230)
Lerner	17.42***	21.61**	10.19**	10.09**
	(5.885)	(8.681)	(4.554)	(4.179)
Lernersquare	−9.200***	−11.22**	−5.902**	−5.474**
	(3.283)	(4.793)	(2.499)	(2.317)
Exportshare_sector	0.506	0.354	0.350**	0.606***
	(0.423)	(0.610)	(0.146)	(0.205)
Stateshare	0.0119	0.0147	0.00319	0.00107
	(0.00929)	(0.0108)	(0.00503)	(0.00411)
Index_subsidy	0.0110***	0.0101**	0.0104***	0.0107***
	(0.00325)	(0.00383)	(0.00191)	(0.00184)
Index_tax	0.0143***	0.0143***	0.0204***	0.0219***
	(0.00206)	(0.00218)	(0.00108)	(0.000902)
Index_interest	−0.0109***	−0.0162***	−0.0120***	−0.0161***
	(0.00248)	(0.00322)	(0.00173)	(0.00185)
Observations	182,248	182,248	746,304	962,076
R^2	0.082	0.129	0.207	0.191

Notes: Robust clustered standard errors are presented in parentheses. Regressions in the first
two columns are based on a subsample of firms existed for all years between 1998 and 2003.
We use this subsample in order to calculate the TFP using firm-level price-deflator, which is
calculated by current value of output divided by constant value of output. The dependent variable is TFP (estimated by OLS with fixed effects in columns 1 and 3; estimated by Olley-Pakes
method in columns 2 and 4). Each regression includes firm fixed effects and year dummies.
CompHerf_subsidy, CompHerf_tax, and CompHerf_interest are Herfindhal indices of subsidy,
tax, and interest rate policies, measured on the city-industry-year level. Export share is calculated by export procurement divided by industrial sales. State share is defined as the proportion
of the firm's state assets to its total equity. Those two shares are aggregated at the sector-year
level. Index_subsidy, index_tax, and index_interest are dummy variables that equal to one if
a firm receives subsidies, tax breaks, or a below-median borrowing interest rate, respectively.
Other controls include horizontal and vertical FDI shares and input and output tariffs, but the
coefficients are not reported in this table. Columns 3 and 4 include policy variables above in the
first stage of the OP estimation, which estimates factor share coefficients.

*** Significant at the 1 percent level.
** Significant at the 5 percent level.
* Significant at the 10 percent level.

in turn requires a measure of TFP at the sector level. We recalculate our measure of
TFP at the city-sector-year level, and execute the same specification as in Table 4
using these more aggregate reallocation terms. The results are reported in Table 7.
Now, instead of focusing on whether industrial policies encourage the same firm
over time to innovate more, we focus on whether industrial policies encourage reallocation of market shares toward the more productive enterprises. One can think of

TABLE 7—COMPETITIVENESS OF INDUSTRIAL POLICIES AND REALLOCATION

Variables	TFP_OLSFE (1)	TFP_OP (2)	TFP_OLSFE (3)	TFP_OP (4)	TFP_OLSFE (5)	TFP_OP (6)
CompHerf_subsidy	−0.0116*** (0.00207)	−0.0108*** (0.00194)				
CompHerf_tax	0.0283*** (0.00576)	0.0173*** (0.00494)				
CompHerf_interest	0.0528*** (0.00431)	0.0496*** (0.00426)				
Comp_Herfsubsidy_ weightsize			−0.00199 (0.00598)	0.00223 (0.00571)		
CompHerf_tax_weightsize			0.0175** (0.00806)	0.00853 (0.00764)		
CompHerf_interest_ weightsize			0.0667*** (0.00712)	0.0617*** (0.00659)		
CompHerf_subsidy_ weightage					0.0668*** (0.00776)	0.0536*** (0.00728)
CompHerf_tax_weightage					0.0892*** (0.00590)	0.0743*** (0.00648)
CompHerf_interest_ weightage					0.100*** (0.00573)	0.0880*** (0.00665)
Lerner	1.202*** (0.305)	1.082*** (0.273)	1.226*** (0.319)	1.095*** (0.282)	1.121*** (0.310)	1.008*** (0.275)
Lernersquare	−0.807*** (0.187)	−0.720*** (0.167)	−0.819*** (0.195)	−0.725*** (0.171)	−0.759*** (0.189)	−0.676*** (0.167)
Exportshare_sector	0.0156 (0.113)	0.00170 (0.106)	0.0127 (0.115)	0.00173 (0.106)	0.0195 (0.112)	0.00620 (0.104)
Stateshare	−0.0775 (0.0962)	0.0168 (0.0956)	−0.0596 (0.0991)	0.0317 (0.0977)	−0.0792 (0.0993)	0.0157 (0.0980)
Index_subsidy	0.000158 (0.00387)	−0.00416 (0.00353)	0.00754* (0.00410)	0.00432 (0.00378)	0.0286*** (0.00507)	0.0202*** (0.00469)
Index_tax	−0.00263 (0.00234)	−0.00148 (0.00203)	−0.00264 (0.00242)	−0.00201 (0.00215)	−0.00355 (0.00234)	−0.00279 (0.00207)
Index_interest	0.00671** (0.00288)	0.00637** (0.00279)	0.0125*** (0.00296)	0.0118*** (0.00284)	0.0157*** (0.00297)	0.0145*** (0.00288)
Constant	−2.539*** (0.199)	−2.417*** (0.231)	−2.622*** (0.198)	−2.494*** (0.230)	−2.696*** (0.200)	−2.553*** (0.234)
Observations	64,455	64,455	64,455	64,455	64,455	64,455
R^2	0.080	0.068	0.069	0.060	0.093	0.079

Notes: Robust clustered standard errors are presented in parentheses. The dependent variable is a measure of between-firm reallocation of TFP (estimated by OLS with fixed effects in columns 1, 3, and 5; estimated by Olley-Pakes method in columns 2, 4, and 6). CompHerf_subsidy, CompHerf_tax, and CompHerf_interest are Herfindhal indices of subsidy, tax, and interest rate policies, measured on the city-industry-year level. Columns 1–2 use unweighted Herfindhal indices, columns 3–4 are based on Herfindhal indices weighted by firm size (number of employees), and columns 5–6 calculate Herfindahl indices weighted by $1/age$ (year since establishment). Each regression includes industry fixed effects and year dummies. Export share is calculated by export procurement divided by industrial sales. State share is defined as the proportion of the firm's state assets to its total equity. Those two shares are aggregated at the sector-year level. Index_subsidy, Index_tax, and Index_interest are defined as the share of firms within each city-industry-year receiving subsidies, tax breaks, or below-median interest rates, respectively. All specifications include sector-level FDI controls.

*** Significant at the 1 percent level.
** Significant at the 5 percent level.
* Significant at the 10 percent level.

this as exploring the extensive margin of productivity growth rather than the intensive margin, which focuses on improvements in firm performance within the same firm over time.

The first two columns of Table 7 report the relationship between the reallocation component of industry-city-level production and our policy measures. Column 1 reports the measures when TFP is calculated using OLS with firm fixed effects, and column 2 reports the OP estimates. The results indicate that while a broader distribution of low interest loans and tax holidays are significantly and positively associated with greater productivity improvements due to reallocation toward more productive firms, the unweighted results for subsidies are negative. Taken together with our earlier results, we can conclude that while low interest policies were not effective in contributing to within-firm improvements in innovation, they did encourage reallocation of market share toward more innovative firms. Low interest policies and a broader dispersion of tax holidays contributed to the extensive margin of productivity growth. The same is not true for subsidies, which appear to have operated more at the intensive margin, inducing within firm productivity improvements.

The next four columns of Table 7 report the outcomes when we weight industrial policy by firm size or the inverse of age. The results indicate that the impact of subsidies switch from negative to positive, suggesting that they can play a positive role in encouraging the reallocation component of TFP growth if they are directed at younger or larger enterprises.[16] As with the earlier results, the largest impact on TFP occurs when industrial policies are oriented toward younger enterprises. The last two columns of Table 7 show significant TFP gains from reallocation of market share when subsidies, tax holidays, and low interest loans are focused on younger enterprises.

IV. Conclusion

In this paper, we have argued that sectoral state aid can foster productivity growth to a larger extent when it targets more competitive sectors and especially when it is not concentrated on one or a small number of firms within the sector.

Thus, using a comprehensive dataset of all medium and large enterprises in China between 1998 and 2007, we show that industrial policies (subsidies or tax holidays) that are allocated to competitive sectors (as measured by the Lerner Index) or allocated in such a way as to preserve or increase competition (e.g., by inducing entry or encouraging younger enterprises), have a more positive and significant impact on productivity or productivity growth.

If we focus on the intensive margin of within-firm behavior, spreading these instruments across more firms is associated with positive productivity increases at

---

[16]One question which arises is to what extent TFP growth in China reflects primarily increases in average firm productivity versus reallocation of market shares. In the Chinese case, only 5 percent of industry level TFP reflects the reallocation component, as reported in Appendix Table A2 The small role of market share reallocation underscores the importance of focusing on individual firm-level productivity changes, which has been the focus of most of our analysis. While market share reallocation has increased during the sample period, it is significantly smaller than in countries like the United States. The predominance of firm level productivity as accounting for industry level performance for China was also highlighted by Loren Brandt and his coauthors.

the firm level. Even greater benefits, leading to a doubling or tripling of the effects, is associated with allocating more benefits to more competitive (i.e., typically younger) firms.

We also find evidence of improved firm performance when industrial policies are targeted toward sectors with initially more competition. This is true for subsidies and tax breaks as instruments of industrial policy, but not for loans or tariffs. [17]

This in turn suggests that the issue should be on *how* to design and govern sectoral policies in order to make them more competition-friendly and therefore more growth-enhancing. Our analysis suggests that proper selection criteria together with good guidelines for governing sectoral support can make a significant difference in terms of growth and innovation performance.

Yet the issue remains: how to minimize the scope for influence activities by sectoral interests when a sectoral state aid policy is to be implemented? One answer is that the less concentrated and more competition-friendly the allocation of state aid to a sector, the less firms in that sector will lobby for that aid as they will anticipate lower profits from it. In other words, political economy considerations should reinforce the interaction between competition and the efficiency of sectoral state aid. A comprehensive analysis of the optimal governance of sectoral policies still awaits further research.

One question that might arise is how this approach can work when there are significant economies of scale. We tested the framework in the context of the Chinese domestic market, which is large enough to allow producers to exploit scale economies in most industrial sectors. In a smaller economy, the question of how to encourage more focus and rivalry while allowing firms to reap the cost gains from exploiting scale economies would have more relevance. In that context, competition could be preserved by exposing firms to international rivalry. It is not surprising that smaller economies like South Korea were able to exploit the benefits of competition by forcing firms that received targeted support to compete on global markets. Further research exploring the implementation of industrial policy under increasing returns remains an avenue for future research.

---

[17] In China, low interest loans and tariffs were associated on net with lower productivity performance of targeted manufacturing firms. Not surprisingly, thus allocating higher tariffs or more low interest loans towards more competitive sectors as a result was not associated with improved productivity performance. A main implication from our analysis is that the debate on industrial policy should no longer be for or against the wisdom of such a policy.

APPENDIX A

TABLE A1—MEANS AND STANDARD DEVIATIONS FOR VARIABLES

Variable	Mean	Standard deviation	Min.	Max.
CompHerf_subsidy	0.570	0.337	0	1
CompHerf_tax	0.871	0.196	0	1
CompHerf_interest	0.846	0.204	0	1
Corr_subsidy_lerner	0.0292	0.172	−1	1
Corr_tax_lerner	−0.100	0.216	−1	1
Corr_interest_lerner	0.0477	0.198	−1	1
Corr_tariff_lerner	−0.0164	0.165	−1	1
Lerner	0.988	0.0257	0.0275	1
Lerner_squared	0.976	0.0476	0.000756	1
Index_subsidy	0.114	0.318	0	1
Index_tax	0.423	0.494	0	1
Index_interest	0.690	0.462	0	1
Export_share	0.175	0.152	0.00634	0.685
Stateshare	0.0215	0.127	0	1
Horizontal_FDI	0.240	0.128	0.000722	0.939
Backward_FDI	0.0741	0.0401	0.00984	0.498
Forward_FDI	0.0987	0.148	0	1.264
lnTariff	2.389	0.472	0.861	4.174
ln_Indirect_tariff	1.971	0.413	0.902	3.230
ln_Input_tariff	2.074	0.638	−1.376	3.099
log of TFP (OLS with firm fixed effects)	2.016	0.448	−0.229	11.49
log of TFP (Olley Pakes)	1.853	0.464	−0.512	11.17

TABLE A2—PERCENTAGE OF TFP INCREASE DUE TO REALLOCATION OF MARKET SHARE
VERSUS AVERAGE FIRM PRODUCTIVITY INCREASES

Variable	Observations	Mean	Standard deviation
1999			
Reallocation share (OLS with fixed effects)	7,714	0.0359349	0.0509876
Average firm productivity (OLS with fixed effects)	7,714	0.9640651	0.0509876
Reallocation share (OP)	7,714	0.0351037	0.0535686
Average firm productivity (OP)	7,714	0.9648963	0.0535686
2000			
Reallocation share (OLS with fixed effects)	7,649	0.0389031	0.0538936
Average firm productivity (OLS with fixed effects)	7,649	0.9610969	0.0538936
Reallocation share (OP)	7,649	0.0377865	0.0579714
Average firm productivity (OP)	7,649	0.9622135	0.0579714
2001			
Reallocation share (OLS with fixed effects)	7,872	0.0403249	0.0520197
Average firm productivity (OLS with fixed effects)	7,872	0.9596751	0.0520197
Reallocation share (OP)	7,872	0.0389779	0.0533513
Average firm productivity (OP)	7,872	0.9610221	0.0533513
2004			
Reallocation share (OLS with fixed effects)	8,382	0.0485715	0.0558423
Average firm productivity (OLS with fixed effects)	8,382	0.9514285	0.0558423
Reallocation share (OP)	8,382	0.0456245	0.0563391
Average firm productivity (OP)	8,382	0.9543755	0.0563391
2007			
Reallocation share (OLS with fixed effects)	8,697	0.0552214	0.0572704
Average firm productivity (OLS with fixed effects)	8,697	0.9447786	0.0572704
Reallocation share (OP)	8,697	0.0523665	0.0581827
Average firm productivity (OP)	8,697	0.9476335	0.0581827

26   AMERICAN ECONOMIC JOURNAL: MACROECONOMICS   OCTOBER 2015

APPENDIX B

A. *Basic Setup*

Preferences and Production.—We consider a two-period model of an economy producing two goods, denoted by A and B. Denote the quantity consumed on each good by x^A and x^B. The representative consumer has income equal to $2E$ and utility $\log(x^A) + \log(x^B)$ when consuming x^A and x^B. This means that, if the price of good i is p^i, demand for good i will be $x^i = E/p^i$. To simplify the writing, we assume that $E = 1$ throughout this paper.[18]

The production can be done by one of two "big" firms $1, 2$, or by "fringe firms." Fringe firms act competitively and have a constant marginal cost of production of c_f whereas firms $j = 1, 2$ have an initial marginal cost of c, where $1 > c_f \geq c$. The assumption $c_f \geq c$ reflects the cost advantage of firms $1, 2$ with respect to the fringe and the assumption $1 > c$ insures that equilibrium quantities can be greater than 1. Marginal costs are firm-specific and are independent of the sector in which production is undertaken.

Innovation.—For simplicity, we assume that only firms $1, 2$ can innovate. Innovation reduces production costs, but the size of the cost reduction is different between the two sectors A and B. Without loss of generality, we assume that in sector A, innovations reduce production costs from c to $c/\gamma_A = c/(\gamma + \delta)$, whereas in sector B they reduce costs from c to $c/\gamma_B = c/(\gamma - \delta)$, where $\gamma - \delta > 1$ or $\delta < \gamma - 1$.

We also make the simple assumption that, with equal probability, each firm can be chosen to be the potential innovator. To innovate with probability q this firm must incur effort cost $q^2/2$. This is like saying that each firm has an exogenous probability of getting a patentable idea, which then has to be turned into cost reduction thanks to effort exerted by the firm.

Competition.—We assume Bertrand competition within each sector unless the two leading firms choose the same sector and collude within that sector. Let φ be the probability of the two leading firms colluding in the same sector when they have the same cost, and let us assume that when colluding the two firms behave as a joint monopoly taking the fringe cost c_f as given. In this case, the expected profit of each leading firm with cost $c < c_f$ is $\varphi \frac{1}{2} \frac{c_f - c}{c_f}$ since when collusion fails firms compete Bertrand.

Industrial Policy via Tax/Subsidies.—Laissez-faire can lead to *diversification* (different sector choices by the two firms) or *focus* (same choice, be it A or B). For industrial policy we will focus on interventions based on taxes or subsidies that are proportional to profit levels, that is on tax levels t_A, t_B per profit level in sectors A, B,

---

[18] As will be soon apparent, the rate of innovation is linear in E, and except for this size effect, what matters for the analysis are the ratios E/c and E/c_f.

respectively, where $t_k < 0$ is a subvention and $t_k > 0$ is a tax.[19] We restrict attention to the case where there is perfect information about γ_i and where the profit is net of the cost of innovation.[20]

Firms can choose to be active in different sectors or in the same sector: we refer to the first situation as one of diversity, and the second as one of focus. Under focus, both firms choose the better technology A. Under diversity, one firm (call it firm 1) chooses A and the other (call it firm 2) chooses B (this is a coordination game and which firm ends up with technology A is random). Diversity is stable if the firm ending up with technology B does not want to switch to technology A; otherwise the equilibrium is focus. Conditional on this choice firms then decide to invest in order to innovate.

Tax/subsidies affect the sectorial choice of activity of firms, for instance, they may choose focus rather than diversity. Because the tax applies to total profits, net of the cost of investing in order to innovate, the investment level is unaffected by the tax rate put in place. Growth, the expected probability of innovation is therefore influenced by the *variance* of taxes across sectors.

We first derive the equilibrium choices under arbitrary tax/subsidy schemes $t_A \leq t_B$ ("laissez-faire" being the case $t_A = t_B = 0$) and show the interaction between our measure of competition φ and the growth rate that can be achieved via such a tax system. We then identify the growth-maximizing tax/subsidy scheme when the planner is subject to a budget constraint.

B. *Equilibrium Profits and Innovation Intensities*

Diversity.—Under diversity, firm 1 is in sector A and firm 2 is in sector B, and both firms enjoy a cost advantage over their competitors. Let e denote the representative consumer's expense on sector A, p_1 the price charged by firm 1, and c_f the limit price imposed by the competitive fringe.

The representative consumer purchases x_1^A, x_f^A in order to maximize $\log(x_1^A + x_f^A)$ subject to $p_1 x_1^A + c_f x_f^A \leq e$. The solution leads to $x_1^A > 0$ only if $p_1 \leq c_f$. The consumer spends e and since firm 1's profit is $e - c_1 x_1^A$, firm 1 indeed chooses the highest price (hence the lowest quantity x_1^A) consistent with $p_1 \leq c_f$, that is $p_1 = c_f$. It follows that $x^A = x_1^A$ and therefore $x^A = e/c_f$.

The problem is symmetric in the other sector and since the representative consumer has total income 2, she will spend 1 on each sector, yielding $x^A = x^B = 1/c_f$.

Suppose first that there is no tax/subsidy in this sector. If the firm is not a potential innovator (which happens with probability $1/2$), its profit is equal to

$$\pi^{DN} = \frac{c_f - c}{c_f}.$$

---

[19] We assume without loss of generality an initial level of taxation equal to zero in each sector.

[20] If the tax/subsidy is on the profit gross of the cost of innovation, then it will also affect the rate at which firms innovate. A reduction in the tax rate on gross profits has a similar effect to a subsidy to the marginal cost of innovation.

28   AMERICAN ECONOMIC JOURNAL: MACROECONOMICS   OCTOBER 2015

If the firm in sector i is chosen to be a potential innovator, it will get a profit margin of $c_f - \frac{c}{\gamma_i}$ if it innovates and a profit margin of $c_f - c$ if it does not. Hence, the ex ante expected payoff of the firm conditional on being chosen to be a potential innovator, and upon choosing innovation intensity q, is equal to

$$\pi_i^{DI} = \max_q q\left(c_f - \frac{c}{\gamma_i}\right)x^i + (1 - q)(c_f - c)x^i - \frac{1}{2}q^2$$

or

$$\pi_i^{DI} \equiv \max_q q\frac{\gamma_i - 1}{\gamma_i}cx^i + (c_f - c)x^i - \frac{1}{2}q^2.$$

Using $x^i = 1/c_f$, the optimal probability of innovation under diversity q_i^D, and the corresponding ex ante equilibrium profit $\pi_i^{D_1}$ when chosen to be a potential innovator, are respectively given by

(B1)
$$q_i^D \equiv \frac{\gamma_i - 1}{\gamma_i}\frac{c}{c_f}$$

and

$$\pi_i^{DI} = \frac{\left(q_i^D\right)^2}{2} + \frac{c_f - c}{c_f}.$$

For further use, we shall denote

$$q_A^D = q^D(\delta) \equiv \frac{\gamma + \delta - 1}{\gamma + \delta}\frac{c}{c_f},$$

$$q_B^D = q^D(-\delta) \equiv \frac{\gamma - \delta - 1}{\gamma - \delta}\frac{c}{c_f}.$$

Overall, the ex ante expected payoff from diversifying on sector i is

$$\pi_i^D = \frac{1}{2}(\pi^{DI} + \pi_i^{DN}),$$

that is,

$$\pi_i^D = \frac{1}{4}\left(q_i^D\right)^2 + \frac{c_f - c}{c_f}.$$

With a tax rate t on profits in sector i, the investment in cost reduction is still equal to q_i^D, but the expected profit of the leading firm in sector i is

$$\pi_i^D(t) \equiv (1 - t)\pi_i^D.$$

Focus.—Consider first the case with full Bertrand competition within each sector (A or B). If both leading firms decide to locate in the same sector, it is optimal for them to choose the sector with higher growth potential, i.e., sector A. Under focus, the next best competitor for firm 1 is firm 2 rather than the fringe, so the equilibrium price is always equal to c, which is lower than c_f by assumption. Hence, in this case, $x^A = 1/c$ while $x^B = 1/c_f$, since the consumer buys from the fringe in sector B.

Suppose first that there is no tax/subsidy in sector A. If firm 1 is chosen to be a potential innovator, it will get a profit margin of $c - \frac{c}{\gamma + \delta}$ when it innovates, since it will then compete in Bertrand with the other firm and gets the full market share $1/c$. If it does not innovate, it will collude with probability φ in order to set a price c_f and split the demand $1/c_f$ with a profit margin $c_f - c$; if collusion fails, the firms make zero profit. Hence, the firm that is called to innovate solves

$$\pi^{FI} \equiv \max_q q \frac{\gamma + \delta - 1}{\gamma + \delta} + (1 - q)\varphi \frac{1}{2} \frac{c_f - c}{c_f} - \frac{q^2}{2}.$$

The optimal choice of q is then

(B2) $$q^F \equiv \frac{\gamma + \delta - 1}{\gamma + \delta} - \frac{\varphi}{2} \frac{c_f - c}{c_f}$$

and therefore

$$\pi^{FI} = \frac{(q^F)^2}{2} + \frac{\varphi}{2} \frac{c_f - c}{c_f}.$$

If the firm is not chosen to be the innovator, it will get positive profits only if the other firm fails and if collusion succeeds, that is, the expected profit is

$$\pi^{FN} = (1 - q^F) \frac{\varphi}{2} \frac{c_f - c}{c_f}.$$

Hence, the expected profit of each firm under focus in sector A is

$$\pi^F = \frac{1}{2} \pi^{FI} + \frac{1}{2} \pi^{FN}$$

$$= \frac{1}{4}(q^F)^2 + (2 - q^F) \frac{\varphi}{4} \frac{c_f - c}{c_f}.$$

Note that since the objective functions defining π^{FI} and π^{FN} are increasing in φ, the value functions are increasing in φ. Now, q^F is an increasing function of δ but is a decreasing function of φ, and has zero cross-partial variation with respect to δ, φ. It follows that

(B3) $$\frac{\partial^2 \pi^F}{\partial \delta \partial \varphi} = \frac{1}{2} \frac{\partial q^F}{\partial \delta} \frac{\partial q^F}{\partial \varphi} - \frac{\partial q^F}{\partial \delta} \frac{1}{4} \frac{c_f - c}{c_f},$$

$$< 0,$$

implying that the cross partial between δ and $1 - \varphi$ is positive.

30   AMERICAN ECONOMIC JOURNAL: MACROECONOMICS   OCTOBER 2015

If we introduce a tax rate of t in sector A, the probability of innovation of a firm is still q^F, while its expected profit is

$$\text{(B4)} \qquad \pi^F(t) \equiv (1 - t)\pi^F.$$

Industry Equilibrium and the Role of Taxation.—Consider the laissez-faire situation with $t_A = t_B = 0$. Focus will be the industry equilibrium if no firm prefers to be active in sector B, the lowest profit sector, that is, when $\pi^F \geq \pi_B^D$. This establishes Proposition 1, which shows that there exists a cutoff value $\delta^F(\varphi)$, a decreasing function of φ, such that focus is the industry equilibrium if and only if $\delta \geq \delta^F(\varphi)$.

Hence, the stronger competition as measured by $(1 - \varphi)$, the higher the range of δs for which firms will choose diversity.

Putting in place a system of tax/subsidies will modify the industry equilibrium since diversity arises in equilibrium only if $(1 - t_B)\pi_B^D > (1 - t_A)\pi^F$, which is more difficult to achieve the larger t_B with respect to t_A. We will use as a measure of targeting the ratio

$$\text{(B5)} \qquad \tau \equiv \frac{1 - t_A}{1 - t_B},$$

the larger τ is, the higher the "tax holidays" in sector A with respect to sector B. It should be clear that τ is sufficient to characterize the incentives of firms to choose between diversity or focus. Alternatively, τ is a measure of the asymmetry in tax holidays between the two sectors. Note that tax systems with $\tau = 1$ are neutral in the sense that they do not modify the industry equilibrium since $\Delta(\varphi, 1) = \delta^F(\varphi)$.

Tax policies that are targeted toward sector A, that is, have a higher value of τ will increase the likelihood of focus to be an industry equilibrium. Indeed, the industry equilibrium is focus whenever $\tau\pi^F > \pi_B^D$; the value $\Delta(\varphi, \tau)$ for which there is an equality is decreasing in τ since π^F is increasing in δ. It follows that targeting makes focus more likely, and establishes Corollary 1.

Hence, a larger target ratio τ increases the range of values of δ for which there will be focus. Alternatively, if $\delta < \delta^F(\varphi)$, there exists a targeting tax τ such that $\delta = \Delta(\varphi, \tau)$; because $\Delta(\varphi, \tau)$ is a decreasing function of τ, the lower the value of δ, the higher this value of τ should be.

Industrial Policy, Innovation, and the Level of Per Capita GDP.—Consider first the innovation rate under diversity versus focus, and the implication of this comparison for the effect of industrial policy. Focus maximizes the innovation rate if and only if it implies a higher innovation rate, namely whenever

$$2q^F(\varphi) > q^D(\delta) + q^D(-\delta)$$

$$= \left(\frac{\gamma + \delta - 1}{\gamma + \delta} + \frac{\gamma - \delta - 1}{\gamma - \delta} \right) \frac{c}{c_f}.$$

This condition is more likely to be satisfied the lower φ, i.e., the more intense the degree of within-sector competition, and it always holds for φ sufficiently small.

Whenever this condition is satisfied, but $\delta < \delta^F(\varphi)$, one can increase long-run growth through a tax/subsidy policy such that $\delta > \Delta(\varphi, t)$.

Now consider the effects of industrial policy on the level of output (i.e., the level of per capita GDP). If there is diversity, independently of the degree of innovation in this sector, the price is c_f, since in each sector the leading firm competes with the fringe only: innovation decreases the cost of production but does not affect directly the price. Therefore, output under diversity is equal to

(B6)
$$Y^D = \frac{2}{c_f}.$$

By contrast, under focus, innovation affects output directly. If there is no innovation, there is a probability φ that the firms collude and set a price c_f, but if they fail, the price will be equal to c since the two leaders compete in this case. If one firm innovates, the price will be equal to c. Hence, the level of output under focus is

$$Y^F = \frac{q^F}{c} + (1 - q^F)\left(\frac{\varphi}{c_f} + \frac{1 - \varphi}{c}\right)$$

$$= \frac{1}{c} - \varphi(1 - q^F)\left(\frac{1}{c} - \frac{1}{c_f}\right).$$

Therefore moving from diversity to focus increases output (i.e., the level of per capita GDP) by

$$\Delta Y = Y^F - Y^D$$

$$\propto \frac{c_f}{c} - \frac{\varphi}{2}(1 - q^F)\left(\frac{c_f}{c} - 1\right) - 1,$$

which is larger the smaller the product $\varphi(1 - q^F)$. Note that this difference is positive when $\varphi = 0$.

Overall, by Corollary 1, an industrial policy taking the form of a taxation on profits targeted toward sector A, that is, $\tau > 1$, will have an effect on innovation and the level of per capita GDP, if and only if there would be diversity without targeting and τ is large enough to induce the firms to choose focus. In this case we call the τ-industrial policy *effective*.

From (B2), q^F is decreasing in φ, and therefore $\varphi(1 - q^F)$ is increasing in φ. It follows that industrial policy has a bigger impact on growth and output, the lower φ: competition and industrial policy, are complements. This discussion proves Proposition 2 in the text; an effective τ-industrial policy has a bigger effect on per capita GDP and on innovation in more competitive industries.

32 *AMERICAN ECONOMIC JOURNAL: MACROECONOMICS* OCTOBER 2015

REFERENCES

Acemoglu, Daron, Ufuk Akcigit, Nicholas Bloom, and William R. Kerr. 2013. "Innovation, Reallocation, and Growth." Center for Economic Performance (CEP) Discussion Paper 1216.

Aghion, Philippe, Nicholas Bloom, Richard Blundell, Rachel Griffith, and Peter Howitt. 2005. "Competition and Innovation: An Inverted-U Relationship." *Quarterly Journal of Economics* 120 (2): 701–28.

Aghion, Philippe, Jing Cai, Mathias Dewatripont, Luosha Du, Ann Harrison, and Patrick Legros. 2015. "Industrial Policy and Competition: Dataset." *American Economic Journal: Macroeconomics.* http://dx.doi.org/10.1257/mac20120103.

Du, Luosha, Ann Harrison, and Gary H. Jefferson. 2012. "Testing for Horizontal and Vertical Foreign Investment Spillovers in China, 1998–2007." *Journal of Asian Economics* 23 (3): 234–43.

Du, Luosha, Ann Harrison, and Gary H. Jefferson. 2014. "FDI Spillovers and Industrial Policy: The Role of Tariffs and Tax Holidays." *World Development* 64: 366–83.

Greenwald, Bruce, and Joseph E. Stiglitz. 2006. "Helping Infant Economies Grow: Foundations of Trade Policies for Developing Countries." *American Economic Review* 96 (2): 141–46.

Harrison, Ann E. 1994. "An Empirical Test of the Infant Industry Argument: Comment." *American Economic Review* 84 (4): 1090–95.

Harrison, Ann. 2014. "Trade and Industrial Policy: China in the 1990s to Today." In *The Oxford Companion to the Economics of China,* edited by Shenggen Fan, Ravi Kanbur, Shang-Jin Wei, and Xiaobo Zhang, 161–70. Oxford: Oxford University Press.

Harrison, Ann, Leslie Martin, and Shanthi Nataraj. 2013. "Learning versus Stealing: How Important are Market-Share Reallocations to India's Productivity Growth?" *World Bank Economic Review* 27 (2): 202–28.

Harrison, Ann, and Andrés Rodríguez-Clare. 2009. "Trade, Foreign Investment, and Industrial Policy for Developing Countries." National Bureau of Economic Research (NBER) Working Paper 15261.

Hopenhayn, Hugo A. 1992. "Entry, Exit, and Firm Dynamics in Long Run Equilibrium." *Econometrica* 60 (5): 1127–50.

Krueger, Anne O., and Baran Tuncer. 1984. "An Empirical Test of the Infant Industry Argument." *American Economic Review* 72 (5): 1142–52.

Melitz, Marc J. 2003. "The Impact of Trade on Intra-Industry Reallocations and Aggregate Industry Productivity." *Econometrica* 71 (6): 1695–1725.

Nunn, Nathan, and Daniel Trefler. 2010. "The Structure of Tariffs and Long-Term Growth." *American Economic Journal: Macroeconomics* 2 (4): 158–94.

Olley, G. Stephen, and Ariel Pakes. 1996. "The Dynamics of Productivity in the Telecommunications Equipment Industry." *Econometrica* 64 (6): 1263–97.

Pavcnik, Nina. 2002. "Trade Liberalization, Exit, and Productivity Improvements: Evidence from Chilean Plants." *Review of Economic Studies* 69 (1): 245–76.

Sivadasan, Jagadeesh. 2009. "Barriers to Competition and Productivity: Evidence from India." *B. E. Journal of Economic Analysis and Policy* 9 (1): 1–66.

Printed in the United States
by Baker & Taylor Publisher Services